Laboratory Experiments for | Foundations of Chemistry

Ernest R. Toon   George L. Ellis

Consultant: Russel C. Bovie, Science Department Chairman,
Arcadia High School, Arcadia, California

Holt, Rinehart and Winston, Inc.
New York Toronto London Sydney

Ernest R. Toon *Associate Professor of Chemistry,*
Los Angeles Valley College,
Van Nuys, California

George L. Ellis *Los Angeles City Schools,*
formerly Chemistry Instructor at
North Hollywood High School,
North Hollywood, California

Acknowledgment of source appears with each photograph.

Cover: Growth trigons on natural diamond magnified 125 times. The crystal was photo-graphed through a Nikon Françon-Yamamoto interference microscope by the distinguished photomicrographer Julius Weber of Mamaroneck, New York.

CONTENTS

PREFACE

The laboratory activities provided in this manual represent the heart of the FOUNDATIONS OF CHEMISTRY course. These activities give a vital, dynamic quality to the course and provide the students with a common background of chemical knowledge around which meaningful lecture discussions may be centered. Each chapter in the text is closely integrated with at least one laboratory activity in the manual. The manual contains a wide assortment of both original and conventional experiments which have been used for a number of years in classes taught by the authors and their colleagues. Students find the experiments interesting, challenging, and instructive.

Emphasis is placed on experiments which yield data that, when analyzed and interpreted, reveal important relationships, trends, and regularities which can be used as a basis for developing unifying principles and concepts. In some instances, the students are directed to pool their data so they can draw valid tentative conclusions. Where this procedure is not practical, the student is told to draw tentative conclusions by assuming that his data are typical of that which would be obtained from a large number of observations.

Many of the experiments are designed so they can precede the class discussion of the concept being investigated. This arrangement has the advantage of allowing the student to make what are, for him, new discoveries. In the process of discovering regularities, trends, and principles the student also learns many of the facts of descriptive chemistry which serve as important chemical background and help to give more meaning to class discussions.

A wide selection of quantitative experiments is provided to emphasize the importance of careful observation and accurate measurement. These experiments provide the student with an opportunity to evaluate his laboratory technique when he compares his experimental result with the correct value.

Each experiment is characterized by these features:

(1) a brief *General Discussion* section which supplies background information and sets the stage for the experiment,

(2) concisely stated *Objectives* which help the student focus on his reasons for being in the laboratory,

(3) explicit *Procedures* which help guide the student efficiently and help him achieve his objectives,

(4) clear illustrations of the apparatus and physical setup,

(5) a list of the *Materials* required for the experiment which can be prepared and set out in advance of the laboratory period,

(6) well-organized data tables listing in logical sequence the data to be recorded and calculations to be made,

(7) a *Follow-up Discussion* section designed to help the student interpret the results of the experiment and to develop further or to illustrate an application of a concept.

(8) a *Follow-up Questions* section containing directions and questions designed to help the student evaluate his understanding of the experimental work by using the concepts and applying the principles associated with the experiment to new situations.

Many of the experiments contain a *Further Experimentation* section. In this section, suggestions are given for extending an open-ended type experiment or performing one related in principle to the original. A minimum of direction is given for these supplementary experiments so that the interested student has ample opportunity to use his imagination and ingenuity in developing procedures and data tables.

A number of the experiments contain two or more parts. Each part can be performed in a

50-minute period. Some parts require less time. More experiments are included than can be done by any class in a year. The individual experiments vary greatly in depth so that the manual may be used for any group of chemistry students. The number, range, and depth of the experiments in this manual allow the instructor great latitude in selecting experiments for his particular class.

The sequence of experiments in the second edition of this manual has been revised to agree with the sequence of chapters in the second edition of *Foundations of Chemistry*. The approach to a number of the experiments has been changed so that the student cannot anticipate or look up the solution to the laboratory problem. For example, in Experiment 15-1 the student is given a series of unidentified but coded Brønsted acids and bases and asked to rank them in order of their relative strengths on the basis of the reactions they undergo.

Whenever possible the discussion sections are used to link in a logical fashion several experiments. For example, in Experiment 2-2 Avogadro's principle is used to determine the molecular mass of an unknown gas. This is followed by two experiments in which the student obtains a value for Avogadro's number and then uses the number in required calculations. To avoid wasting an expensive material, the student analyzes in Experiments 3-6 and 3-7 the silver produced in Experiment 3-4.

Several of the longer experiments that appeared in the first edition have been modified and divided into two separate experiments. For example, Experiment 14-1 on Chemical Equilibrium in the first edition has been separated into two experiments in the second edition: 13-1 (Chemical Equilibrium) and 16-2 (Formation and Dissolution of Precipitates).

The concepts of equivalent mass, normality, and colloids do not appear in the second edition of the text. For those who feel that these concepts should be retained in an elementary course, two experiments are provided which serve to introduce them. These are Experiments 15-7 and 16-4. Modifications designed to improve results have been made in a large number of the original experiments. In addition, 17 new experiments have been added. These are listed below.

Experiment 2-1	Separation, Purification, and Identification of the Components of a Mixture
Experiment 2-3	Estimation of Avogadro's Number
Experiment 3-3	Precipitation Reactions— Net Ionic Equations and General Solubility Rules
Experiment 4-2	Effect of Temperature Change on the Volume of a Gas—Determination of Absolute Zero
Experiment 5-1	The Charge on an Electron
Experiment 7-1	Periodicity of Physical, Chemical, and Atomic Properties
Experiment 8-1	Shapes of Molecules and Polyatomic Ions
Experiment 10-1	Molar Heat of Fusion of Ice
Experiment 11-1	Thermochemistry: Enthalpy of Formation of $NH_4Cl(s)$
Experiment 14-1	Solutes, Solvents, and Solutions
Experiment 14-4	Molecular Mass of Sulfur by Freezing-Point Depression Method
Experiment 15-1	Relative Strengths of Brønsted Acids and Bases
Experiment 15-5c	Analysis of Antacids
Experiment 15-7	Equivalent Mass and Normality—Determination of the Equivalent Mass of an Unknown Acid
Experiment 16-3	Progressive Precipitation: The Formation and Dissolution of Slightly Soluble Silver Compounds
Experiment 16-4	Analysis of an Unknown Chloride Using an Adsorption Indicator
Experiment 19-2	Total Hardness in Water: Compleximetric Titration

The authors wish to express their sincere appreciation to Mr. Russell Bovie of Arcadia, California, High School who prepared a detailed critique of the first edition and who suggested, devised, and tested procedures for a number of experiments which appear in the second edition and are new to the *Foundations of Chemistry* program. We also gratefully acknowledge the many helpful suggestions we received from Dr. Evamaria Chookolingo, professor of chemistry at Los Angeles Valley College, Mr. William Knaack, professor of chemistry at Los Angeles Valley College, Dr. William Harris, Chairman of the Chemistry Department, Los Angeles Valley College, and our editor, Elbert C. Weaver, formerly chairman of chemistry at Phillips Academy, Andover, Massachusetts.

STUDENT APPARATUS

A list of recommended materials for each laboratory station:

Pyrex test tubes (six 6″, six 3″, and one 8″)
50-, 150-, and 250-ml beakers
125- and 250-ml erlenmeyer flasks
500-ml florence flask
watch glass
4–6 glass plates
stirring rods
25- and 100-ml graduated cylinders
funnel
4–6 wide-mouth bottles
evaporating dish
porcelain crucible and lid
ring and ring stand (usually on table top or in cupboard)
wire screen with asbestos center
test-tube clamp
test-tube rack
test-tube brush
clay triangle
burner and wing top
crucible tongs
medicine dropper
funnel (thistle) tube
forceps
matches
litmus paper (blue and red)
funnel support
buret clamp (single)

Introducing the Laboratory Program

Experimentation and observation are the primary sources of chemical knowledge. In the laboratory, facts and principles are discovered, and concepts and theories are investigated and tested. The experiments in this manual are designed to illustrate, to make real, and to extend your understanding of the concepts and principles discussed in your text and by your instructor. Some of the experiments are designed to give you the opportunity to discover some facts and principles before you encounter them in your textbook. All of the experiments require careful observation. Many of them are quantitative and require careful measurement under controlled conditions.

Laboratory activities are an essential part of your chemistry course. Experimental investigations provide data which can be used to verify, modify, or develop chemical theories. Laboratory activities will serve many functions in this course. They will be used to (a) provide *data* which will serve as a basis for *the development* and *discussion of* theoretical principles, (b) *answer questions* and *solve problems* raised in discussion sessions, (c) *verify statements and laws* discussed in class, (d) familiarize and acquaint you with *laboratory apparatus, experimental techniques,* and *properties of chemical substances,* and (e) *summarize and give meaning to concepts.*

Regardless of their function, the value and success of your laboratory experiences will depend, to a large extent, upon your ability to *make accurate measurements, make careful observations, and carefully control the conditions of an experiment.*

Although the laboratory procedures are quite explicitly stated, you will have ample opportunity to apply your ingenuity and imagination when you try to interpret your observations and results.

In addition, some of you may wish to design experiments to investigate other problems and ideas which occur to you or those suggested in the manual for further experimentation. For this experimentation you should prepare an outline and present it to your instructor who will check it and offer you advice.

You will find that laboratory work is both interesting and instructive. The value which you obtain from it depends largely upon your attitude. Observation of the GENERAL SUGGESTIONS which follow will help to insure that you obtain maximum benefit from your laboratory experiences.

GENERAL SUGGESTIONS

1. Prior to each laboratory activity, read and study the experiment which you are to perform. If there is any question regarding the objectives or procedure, consult your instructor. Note carefully which materials you will require. Because of time limitations, plan and organize your work so that you operate at maximum efficiency.

2. Prepare your laboratory report as directed by your instructor. Before beginning your laboratory work you should prepare a data sheet which contains at least the following:

(a) the date
(b) the title of the experiment
(c) ruled data tables like the ones in this manual, which contain in *logical sequence,* a list of all measured, calculated, or reference items which you will need to complete the experiment. *Do not enter any data in the tables of this manual.* They are here only for your guidance in preparing your report.

3. Record all data with a ball point or other pen. *Do not record any data on scraps of paper.* If you make an incorrect entry, rule it out with a single line. Below the table under the heading *Sample Calculations,* show only one mathematical setup for each different, calculated item which appears in the table. Do not show any longhand arithmetical calculations. All calculations, where applicable, should be done using conversion factors (factor-label method), showing all units and following the rules of significant figures. Give complete answers to all the questions in each experiment. These questions are designed to emphasize the important concepts related to the experiment, and to help you interpret and summarize the results. Since your textbook is closely integrated with your laboratory manual, you should consult it as well as other references to obtain additional information related to your laboratory problems.

LABORATORY RULES OF CONDUCT

1. Always maintain a businesslike attitude. The laboratory is a dangerous place for horseplay. There should be no loud talking. **THINK AT ALL TIMES IN THE LABORATORY.**

2. Dispose of waste chemicals as prescribed by your instructor. Corrosive liquids may be neutralized and washed down the sink with much water. Do not put any solids, paper, or matches into the sink.

3. Take only the amount of materials that you actually need for an experiment. For most test-tube reactions, 2 or 3 ml is sufficient.

4. Return all reagent bottles to their proper location, but never return any excess chemical to a reagent bottle.

5. If you are in doubt about any procedure, ask your instructor.

6. Clean and dry your laboratory bench at the close of the laboratory period. Return all borrowed equipment to the stockroom or supply shelf.

7. Check to see that the gas and water are turned off before you leave your working area.

8. Wash your hands thoroughly after a laboratory period.

SAFETY RULES

1. Perform *only* those experiments that you have been specifically authorized to do.

2. If any corrosive chemical is spilled or splashed on your skin or in your eyes, *flood with water immediately* then notify your instructor.

3. Notify your instructor of any accident, *no matter how minor.*

4. Wear *protective glasses.* (Fig. A-1).

Fig. A-1   When smelling a substance, use a gentle fanning motion to waft the vapors toward your face. Wear protective glasses in the laboratory.

5. Whenever you are asked to note the odor of any chemical, carefully waft the fumes toward your nose as shown in Figure A-1. *Do not inhale any fumes directly.* Fume hoods should be used where poisonous or irritating fumes are evolved.

6. When heating any solids or liquids in a test tube, keep the tube in constant motion and *do not* point the mouth of the test tube at anyone. Always hold the test tube at an angle and heat the sides of the tube as well as the bottom. If the bottom alone is heated, vapor can be produced at that point which will cause the entire contents to

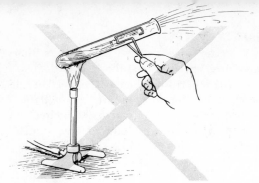

Fig. A-2 *When heating a liquid in a test tube, the flame should not be applied continuously to the bottom of the tube. The sudden formation and expansion of steam near the bottom may cause the liquid to spatter (bump).*

spurt out (Fig. A-2). Do not leave experiments which are heating or reacting.

7. *Carefully* read the label *twice* on any bottle prior to using the chemical. Many formulas and chemical names look very much alike but confusing them could be disastrous.

8. *Never use an open flame near a volatile or flammable liquid.* You should become familiar immediately with the location and use of fire extinguishers and other emergency equipment. If clothing should catch fire, smother flames with a wet towel or fire blanket, or get under a fire shower. It is important to keep calm.

9. *Never taste any chemical in the laboratory.* Not all poisonous materials in the laboratory are so labeled.

10. If you spill any acid or base on your clothing or skin, flood the part with water and then neutralize any acid with dilute ammonia-water solution or a solution of sodium bicarbonate. Neutralize any spilled alkali (base) with dilute acetic acid. Then wash with dilute sodium bicarbonate. If you are not sure if the liquid is an acid or a base, wash with dilute sodium bicarbonate, then with water. Numerous supplies of sodium bicarbonate should be available in every laboratory.

11. When diluting acids, *always pour the acid into water while stirring. Never pour water into a concentrated acid.* See Fig. A-3.

12. Be cautious of any glass that has recently been heated. Hot glass looks just like cold glass but can inflict severe burns.

13. When inserting glass tubing or thermometers through rubber stoppers, always use a cloth towel as shown in Fig. A-4. Grasp the tubing (or thermometer) close to the stopper which has been moistened with water. Devices known as "hand savers" offer the best protection and should be used if available.

14. Make sure that the vertical rod of the ring stand is securely tightened onto the base. If you fail to check your ring stand it may collapse, causing a serious accident.

15. Wear an apron at all times to protect your clothing.

16. Shoes must be worn in the laboratory at all times. Long hair should be tied back to prevent its catching fire in a bunsen burner.

Fig. A-3 *Technique for diluting concentrated acids.*

TRANSFERRING SOLIDS AND LIQUIDS

Most experiments involve the use of solid and liquid chemicals. These chemicals are stored in the laboratory in bottles known as *stock bottles*. It is of the utmost importance that you learn to obtain chemicals from these bottles for your laboratory use without contaminating them.

Solids may be transferred from a stock bottle with a *clean* spatula as shown in Fig. A-5. While you are removing the solid, you must be careful that the stock bottle cap does not become contaminated. Figure A-5 shows how to place the cap during this procedure. You may put solid reagents into a test tube by pouring the granulated solid from a stock bottle onto a paper strip and then transferring the reagent from the paper strip to the test tube, as in Fig. A-6.

Fig. A-4 *When inserting a piece of glass tubing, funnel, or thermometer into a stopper, lubricate with water or glycerine, keep your hands close together and work the glass using a gentle twisting motion. Never force glass tubing into a stopper. Use a "hand saver" if available.*

Spatula

Stopper

Fig. A-5 *Techniques for removing a sample from a stock bottle. Be sure to close the reagent bottle tightly with the correct lid or stopper. If the cleanliness of the spatula is in doubt, then use the method depicted in Fig. A-6.*

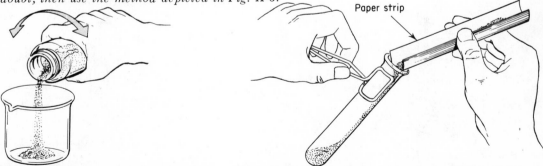

Paper strip

Fig. A-6 *Large quantities of solid may be removed from a reagent bottle by tilting and rolling the bottle. They may be transferred to test tubes or apparatus by using creased paper strips.*

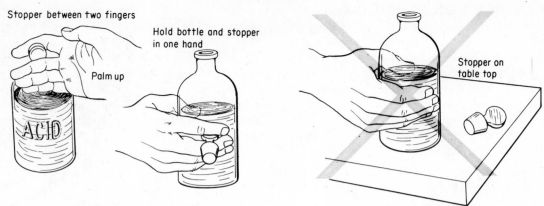

Stopper between two fingers

Hold bottle and stopper in one hand

Palm up

Stopper on table top

Fig. A-7 Care must be taken that the stopper is not contaminated while transferring a liquid from a stock bottle.

When transferring liquids from stock bottles care must be taken that the stopper not be contaminated. Figure A-7 shows the proper way to hold a bottle and stopper during this process. When transferring a liquid from one beaker to another, avoid splashing the liquid by pouring down a stirring rod as shown in Fig. A-8. After you have finished pouring a liquid from a reagent bottle, be sure to clean off any liquid that runs down the outside of the bottle. Failure to do this may cause the next person to be burned or injured by a corrosive liquid.

MEASUREMENT OF MASS

Laboratory balances are sensitive instruments which must be protected from abuse and kept clean if they are to operate properly. There are three types of balances commonly used in school laboratories: *platform balances* (Fig. A-9), *triple-beam balances* (Fig. A-10), and *single-pan balances* (Figs. A-11 and A-12). Your instructor will give you specific instructions for operating the

Fig. A-8 Pouring a liquid from a beaker into another vessel, using a clean stirring rod held against the lip of the beaker. The rod should touch the wall of the receiving vessel.

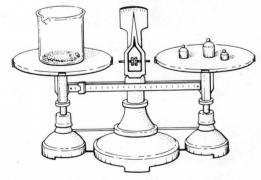

Fig. A-9 A platform balance.

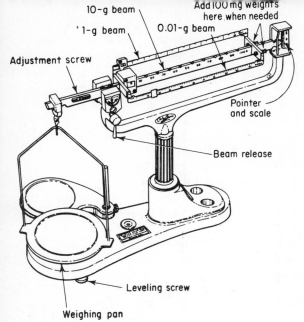

10-g beam

Add 100 mg weights here when needed

'1-g beam   0.01-g beam

Adjustment screw

Pointer and scale

Beam release

Leveling screw

Weighing pan

Fig. A-10   A triple-beam balance.

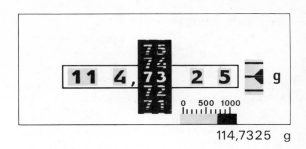

114,7325 g

Enlargement of reading scale of the balance shown below.

Fig A-12   Top-loading balance. (Mettler Instruments)

type of balance you will be using. The following precautions apply to these balances.

1. Before using a platform or triple-beam balance, place all rider weights on zero and check to see that the pointer swings freely along the scale. Note the center of oscillation of the pointer

Fig. A-11   Automatic single-pan balance. (Mettler Instruments)

when the balance is empty. The *center of oscillation* is the estimated center point of the pointer as it moves back and forth on the scale. This may not be located at the zero point or center of the pointer scale. Do not wait for the balance to stop before taking a reading. When weighing an object, the pointer should oscillate about the same center of oscillation as when the balance was empty. A newly minted five cent coin can be used as a standard for checking the accuracy of a balance since these coins weigh 5.00 grams. Some balances have the swing of the beam magnetically damped.

2. Most balances have a metal or agate knife-edge. If the balance is subjected to shock, or if the knife-edge is dirty, the balance cannot function normally. All chemicals must be placed in a proper container before being weighed. Never place any chemical directly on the pan of a balance. The beam release on most triple beam balances should be used to prevent the balance from swinging when not in use. This swinging causes unnecessary wear on the knife-edge.

3. *Hot objects should never be placed on a balance.* Besides the possibility of damaging the balance, hot objects cause convection currents of air around the pans which interfere with the operation of a balance.

4. Moisture and corrosive chemicals should be kept far from any laboratory balance. If a sample of a corrosive liquid must be weighed, it should be placed in a proper container. Care must be taken that the liquid does not come into direct contact with the balance.

5. In the case of the single-pan balance, the beam should be in the *arrest* position whenever objects are being placed on or removed from the pan and between weighings. All mass manipulation knobs should be turned slowly and only when the beam is in the *arrest* or *partial arrest* position.

MEASURING VOLUMES OF LIQUIDS

There are several types of apparatus for measuring liquid volumes. Some of these devices are calibrated to *contain* a certain volume of liquid;

others are calibrated to *deliver* a certain volume. These are often labeled with the letters TC (to contain) TD (to deliver) so that you will know how they were calibrated. The calibration is often specific at a given temperature, usually 20°C. All of these instruments require that the volume be correctly read on a scale which is usually etched into the glass. The surface of liquids as viewed in graduated glass vessels is always curved. The curved surface is called the *meniscus*. When reading the meniscus it is important to have your eye on a level line of sight along the bottom of the curved surface as shown in Fig. A-13. Some specific hints on the use of four different volume measuring devices may be helpful to you.

1. A *volumetric flask* is used for making up a certain volume of a solution. These flasks are calibrated with a single line etched on the neck of the flask. The calibration of volumetric flasks is always TC (to contain). A one-liter volumetric flask may be used for preparing a liter of solution of known concentration. Of course, when the

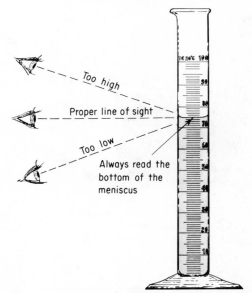

Fig. A-13 The volume of a liquid in a graduated vessel is measured by reading the bottom of the meniscus. The line of sight must be level of the meniscus.

solution is poured out of the flask the volume of solution delivered will be less than one liter because some of it clings to the inside of the flask. For most purposes, this amount is negligible.

2. A *graduated cylinder* (graduate), like a volumetric flask, is usually calibrated TC. This instrument is designed to be used only for measuring the volumes of pure liquids. *Do not mix any chemicals in a graduated cylinder.* The heat of a reaction can easily break the glass. *Never heat a graduated cylinder in a burner flame.* The thick glass of the cylinder is almost certain to break if it is heated.

3. The *transfer pipet,* Fig. A-14, is calibrated TD (to deliver). Care must be taken in using the pipet since it is possible for corrosive liquids to be drawn into your mouth. When pipeting *corrosive liquids,* a suction bulb should be attached

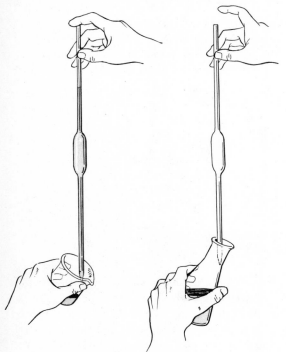

Fig. A-14 *Pipet technique. After liquid has stopped flowing, allow 15-20 seconds for drainage. Touch the tip of the pipet against the side of the flask for a few seconds. Do not blow out any liquid remaining in the pipet.*

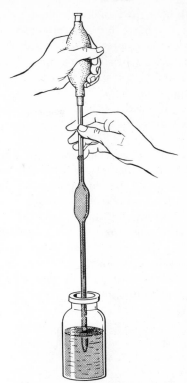

Fig. A-15 *Never use your mouth to fill a pipet with a corrosive or poisonous liquid.*

to the pipet (Fig. A-15). Like a volumetric flask, a transfer pipet has only one calibration mark and is used for measuring only a specific volume of liquid. The level of the liquid should be drawn above the calibration mark and held there by placing a finger over the top of the pipet. The level of the liquid can be lowered to the etched mark by carefully admitting air to the top. You should practice pipetting with tap water before trying to use the pipet in an experiment.

4. A *buret* is used for measuring variable amounts of liquids. Like the pipet it is calibrated TD (to deliver). Most burets have major graduation marks at each milliliter division with minor calibration marks at each 0.1 ml. Burets are equipped with several types of valves at the bottom to control the flow of liquid. The simplest valve is a piece of rubber tubing with a pinch-clamp or bead. The Teflon tip and the glass stop-

cock burets are much easier to control. The
Teflon tip buret requires no lubricant but the
glass stop-cock buret should be lubricated with a
very thin coat of silicone stop-cock grease. The
buret should be cleaned with a warm soap solution and a buret brush. If your buret has been
properly cleaned you will not notice any droplets
of water adhering to it. When you rinse a clean
buret, you will see only a uniform film of water
on the surface. After cleaning the buret, rinse it
at least three times with the solution you are
going to use to be sure that your solution does
not become diluted by residual water in the
buret. You should run a few milliliters of the
solution through the tip of the buret each time it
is rinsed. The correct way to manipulate a glass
stop-cock buret is shown in Fig. A-16. The stop-
cock is turned with the left hand and the flask is
swirled with the right hand.

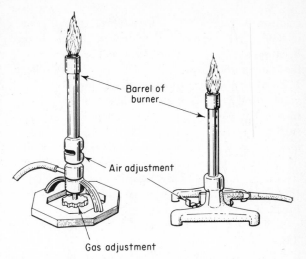

Fig. A-17 Common laboratory burners.

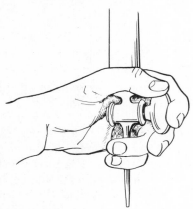

Fig. A-16 How to grasp and manipulate a glass
or Teflon stopcock buret.

THE GAS BURNER

There are many types of laboratory gas burners,
but most of them are very similar in their operation. The bunsen burner, Fig. A-17, is the one
most commonly used. It consists of a *base* and a
barrel. The gas comes through the gas inlet
through a small *jet* in the base. The adjustable
air inlet is located at the base of the barrel. The
gas mixes with air in the barrel and is ignited at
the top of the barrel. When lighting a bunsen

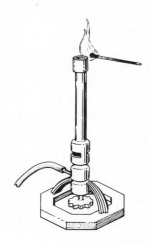

Fig. A-18 The proper technique for lighting a
burner.

burner, hold a lighted match so that the bottom
of the flame is below the top of the barrel as in
Fig. A-18. Then turn on the gas. If the lighted
match is placed directly over the burner barrel,
the rush of air may extinguish the match. After
the burner is lighted, adjust the air by rotating
the barrel so that there is an inner blue cone in
the flame and an outer almost invisible cone as
shown in Fig. A-19. If the flame is large and
luminous, admit more air. If a gap forms between

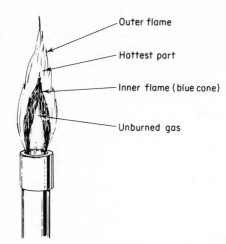

- Outer flame
- Hottest part
- Inner flame (blue cone)
- Unburned gas

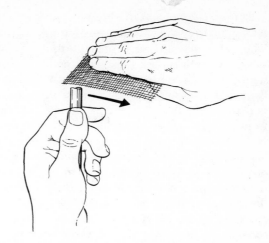

Fig. A-19   The hottest portion of a properly adjusted burner flame is located at the tip of the inner flame (blue cone).

Fig. A-21   Remove jagged edges by stroking the cut end of the glass tubing with a wire screen.

the flame and the top of the burner, decrease the amount of air being admitted. If a flame seems to be originating at the base, burning inside the barrel, turn off the flame, close the air vent slightly, and relight. **Caution:** *the barrel may be very hot.* The tip of the inner blue cone is the hottest part of the bunsen-burner flame.

GLASSWORKING

A few simple skills in glassworking will be a great aid to you in your laboratory work. The necessary skills are cutting, fire polishing, and bending glass tubing.

1. *Cutting glass.* Glass is a noncrystalline mate-

rial which does not break along regular cleavage planes as does a crystalline solid. To cut a piece of glass tubing, first make a single scratch at the desired breaking point with a glass-tubing cutter or a sharp triangular file. *Do not attempt to file a deep scratch in the tubing.* Place the scratch away from your body, holding your thumbs behind it as shown in Fig. A-20. To break the glass, press outward with your thumbs and at the same time pull inward on the piece of tubing. If the break is uneven and the ends have sharp projections, you can break off the projections evenly by lightly brushing the end of the tubing with a piece of wire screen (Fig. A-21). A glass-tubing cutter, if available, is much easier to use.

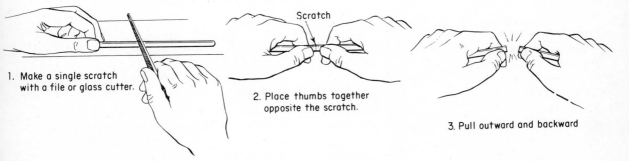

1. Make a single scratch with a file or glass cutter.

Scratch

2. Place thumbs together opposite the scratch.

3. Pull outward and backward

Fig. A-20   Proper technique for cutting glass tubing.

2. *Fire polishing.* A freshly cut piece of glass tubing has very sharp edges which are dangerous. They also make it very difficult to insert the tubing through rubber stoppers or corks. By constantly rotating the end of the glass tubing in a flame, these sharp edges can be melted into round smooth edges which are safe to handle and easy to insert into rubber tubing and rubber stoppers. *Do not heat the end of the tubing so long that the opening in the tubing becomes constricted.* See Fig. A-22. Glass is very slow to cool, so care must be taken that you do not burn yourself on the glass after it has been fire-polished. Place the hot glass on an asbestos sheet or wire screen for cooling. *Do not touch the hot portion for several minutes after heating.* The thicker the glass is, the more slowly it cools.

3. *Bending glass.* Place a wing top (flame spreader) on your bunsen burner as shown in Fig. A-23. The wing top distributes the heat over a greater length of the glass. Heat the glass at the point where you want to make a bend by gently rotating the glass in the flame. A yellow flame (caused by the sodium content of the glass) indicates that the glass is getting hot enough to be bent. Notice that the glass becomes pliable at the point where it is being heated. *Do not heat the glass so long that it sags excessively.* Remove the glass from the flame and allow it to cool for a few seconds. This allows the heat to spread evenly over the glass so that a more uniform bend may be obtained. Gently bend the glass tubing to the

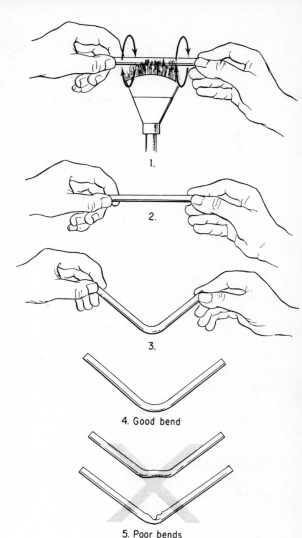

1.

2.

3.

4. Good bend

5. Poor bends

Fig. A-23   *Technique for making glass bends.*

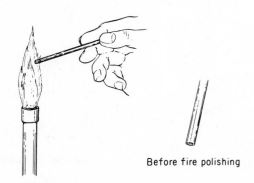

Before fire polishing

After fire polishing

Constricted tubing which has been heated too long.

Fig. A-22   *Technique for fire polishing.*

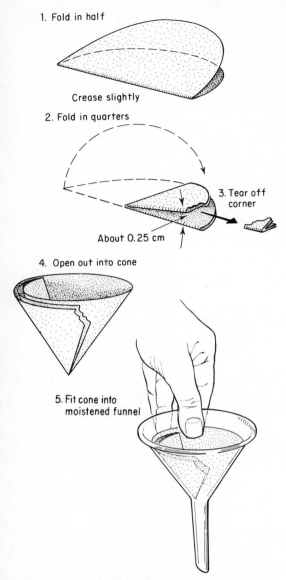

1. Fold in half

Crease slightly

2. Fold in quarters

3. Tear off corner

About 0.25 cm

4. Open out into cone

5. Fit cone into moistened funnel

Fig. A-24   How to fold and fit a piece of filter paper into a funnel.

desired angle. With a little practice you will learn the amount of heating needed. This varies with the thickness of the glass and the amount of force that must be exerted while making the bend. After two or three trials you should be able to make a good bend. (See Fig. A-23).

FILTERING PRECIPITATES AND DRYING RESIDUES

Filtration is commonly used to separate a material in the solid phase from one in the liquid phase. A filter paper is folded so that it fits into a glass funnel. A corner is torn off the filter paper to prevent air from leaking into the fold. Fit the filter paper into the funnel. Moisten the filter paper with water so that it adheres to the glass funnel (Fig. A-24). If your filter paper is properly folded and placed into the funnel, a liquid passes through it without forming bubbles in the stem of the funnel. Place a receiving beaker under the filtering funnel as shown in Fig. A-25. Pour the mixture to be filtered into the funnel using a glass stirring rod to prevent splashing. If some of the solid passes through the filter paper, you may need to heat the mixture and then cool it so that the finely divided particles coagulate into larger particles. The funnel stem

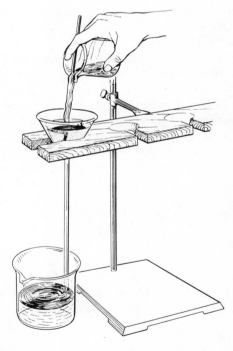

Fig. A-25   Filtration technique. When the liquid is no longer visible in the filter paper cone, more of the mixture which to be filtered may be added.

rests against the side of the receiving beaker so that the liquid flows down the side of the beaker. If a tight seal is obtained between the filter paper and the funnel, no air bubbles enter and the weight of the solution in the funnel hastens the filtration process. You may use a plastic squeeze bottle, Fig. A-26, to wash out the last remaining particles of precipitate from the beaker. You should also wash the precipitate down into the apex of the filter paper. Most precipitates should be rinsed with distilled water. The rinsing and washing down can be combined into a single operation.

Residues from filtration almost always need to be dried. To expedite drying, the filter paper should be removed from the funnel and unfolded. The time required for drying depends upon the amount and nature of residue. In most cases, 24 hours of air-drying in your locker is sufficient. If an experiment calls for oven drying, lay the open filter paper on a watch glass and place the glass in an oven at 100 to 110°C or under an infrared heat lamp. The residue should dry completely in 15 to 20 minutes.

If a *centrifuge* is available, your instructor will demonstrate its use to separate a precipitate from a solution. A centrifuge works much faster than a conventional filter. The solution in the tube is subjected to a force of 500 to 1000 times that of gravity while it is being centrifuged. Not more than 15 or 20 seconds of centrifuging are required to cause a precipitate to settle out. You should always counterbalance the tube of solution being centrifuged by placing an equal amount of liquid in the opposite tube. This prevents the centrifuge from vibrating while in operation. If a precipitate is well compacted, the supernatant liquid (liquid above the precipitate) may be decanted. If the solid is not well compacted, you may find it necessary to remove the liquid above the residue carefully with a pipet or medicine dropper.

Fig. A-26 Using a plastic squeeze bottle to wash the last bits of solid residue into a filter.

Fig. A-27 Centrifuge. (Fisher Scientific Co.)

1-1
Analysis of a Mixture

GENERAL DISCUSSION

In this experiment, you will qualitatively analyze a solution for silver and lead. The procedures and questions are designed to acquaint you with a number of basic concepts introduced in the text and in classroom discussion, and to familiarize you with laboratory equipment and operations.

You are not expected to understand the chemistry involved in the procedures but are expected to become acquainted with some concepts and terms which are an essential part of every chemistry student's vocabulary. You should note carefully the properties and names of substances with which you work. This information is important background material which can be referred to or used as a basis for later discussions.

The solution which you will analyze has been prepared by dissolving a silver compound called silver nitrate and a lead compound called lead nitrate in distilled water. The silver and lead in these compounds can be identified by converting them into different compounds which do not dissolve appreciably in water, and which have characteristic properties of their own. The process which you follow is represented by the flow diagram, Fig. 1-1. *Precipitates* are the insoluble solids

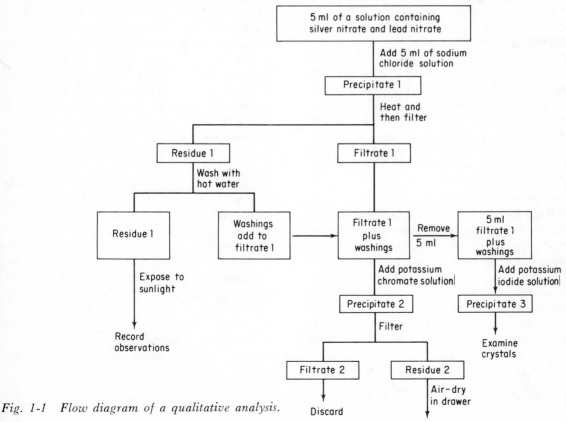

Fig. 1-1   Flow diagram of a qualitative analysis.

formed when the particles of the compounds in two different solutions react. *Filtrates* are the solutions which pass through the filter paper during filtration. *Residues* are the solids which remain on the filter paper during filtration. Before beginning the laboratory work, let us concisely state the goals we wish to achieve in this experiment.

OBJECTIVES

1. To separate and identify silver and lead compounds in a solution.
2. To learn the names and some of the characteristics of the chemicals used in this experiment.
3. To develop skill in making careful observations.
4. To attach a meaning to common chemical terms such as *system, phase, precipitate, residue,* and *filtrate.*
5. To become acquainted with the names and uses of common kinds of laboratory equipment and with laboratory procedures.

MATERIALS

Test tubes, test solution (silver and lead nitrates, 0.5 *M*), sodium chloride solution (1.5 *M*), burner, filter paper, funnel, graduated cylinder, wash bottle, potassium chromate solution, evaporating dish, 0.10-*M* potassium iodide solution, medicine dropper, glass slide or plate, magnifier, mortar and pestle, linseed oil, 6-*M* HNO_3, 6-*M* NH_3 solution.

PROCEDURE

1. Read the section on measuring and pouring liquids in Introducing the Laboratory Program, and then measure 5 ml of the test solution containing silver and lead nitrates into a test tube. Describe the characteristics (properties) of the *chemical system* in the test tube. Record this and all subsequent observations in a data table like the one shown here. Include such properties as *volume, color, odor,* and *physical phase* (solid, liquid, or gas). When describing solids, indicate their *texture* or *apparent state of subdivision.* Use terms such as *coarse, finely divided,* and *gelatinous.*

2. Measure 5 ml of sodium chloride solution into a second test tube and describe its properties. Consider the contents of the two test tubes as components of a single system which you are studying.

3. Tilt the test tube containing the test solution at a slight angle and slowly add the sodium chloride solution. Indicate the state of the chemical system in the test tube at this point by describing its characteristics. Note the apparent number of phases in the system. The solid, called a *precipitate,* is a mixture of silver chloride and lead chloride.

4. Warm the solution gently. Allow the solid to settle and then filter the solution by pouring the components of the system into a filter paper using the techniques in Introducing the Laboratory Program. Collect the filtrate in a 150-ml beaker. The *filtrate* is the liquid that passes through the filter paper. Rinse the test tube with two separate 10-ml portions of hot water. Pour each portion through the paper and collect the washings in the beaker with the filtrate. Describe the components of the system at this point.

5. Pour about 5 ml of the solution containing the filtrate and the washings into a test tube and set aside for Procedure 10. To the remainder of the filtrate and washings add 5 ml of potassium chromate solution. Describe the appearance of the system in the beaker. The precipitate is lead chromate.

6. Filter the solution. Discard the filtrate and place the filter paper with the *residue* on an evaporating dish. Allow the residue to dry in your locker until the next laboratory period.

7. Unfold the filter paper containing the residue from Procedure 4 and expose it to the sunlight or other ultraviolet light for a few minutes. Describe its appearance. This compound is called silver chloride.

8. Transfer the residue to a 150-ml beaker and slowly add 6-*M* ammonia-water until the residue just dissolves. Now slowly add 6-*M* nitric acid until the solution changes blue litmus paper to red. A white precipitate, silver chloride, confirms the presence of silver.

9. Place 5 ml of 0.1-*M* potassium iodide solution in a test tube. Warm gently but do not boil.

10. Using a medicine dropper, place 2 drops of the solution set aside from Procedure 5 on a glass plate or microscope slide. Rinse the medicine dropper several times with water and then add 2 or 3 drops of the warm potassium iodide solution to the solution on the glass plate. Allow to cool. Examine the crystals with a magnifying glass or under a low power microscope. Describe the color and shape of these crystals. These are crystals of lead iodide.

11. Crush and grind the residue from Procedure 6 to a fine powder and add a few drops of linseed oil until the mixture has the consistency of paint. The pigment in your paint, lead chromate, is commonly called chrome yellow. Paint a small square of paper with your paint. When it is dry, attach it to your laboratory report. Remove the paint from any apparatus using the remover designated by your instructor.

FURTHER EXPERIMENTATION

1. Analyze an unknown for the presence of lead and silver. This solution may contain one, both, or neither of these substances. Be aware that a white precipitate in Procedure 3 does not necessarily mean that either lead or silver is present. Suggest why.

FOLLOW-UP DISCUSSION

In this experiment you started with two solutions in two separate test tubes. The contents of these tubes constituted the chemical system which you isolated for study. The two solutions were the *initial components* of this system. The observations which you noted in Procedures 1 and 2 described the initial state of this chemical system. In subsequent experiments you will be able to give a more complete description of the state of a system by noting such characteristics as *temperature, pressure, mass,* and *chemical composition.* The observations you made in Procedure 3 indicated that two phases (solid and liquid) were present. The final state of the system at this point was therefore different from its original state. A difference between the initial and final state of a system indicates that the system has undergone a change. In the study of chemistry we are usually interested in the changes in chemical systems which we can observe and measure.

No doubt you are curious as to how and why reactions such as those you observed in this experiment take place. Unfortunately, consider-

Procedure	Observations
1. Add 5 ml of test solution to test tube.	
2. Measure out 5 ml of sodium chloride solution.	
3. Add sodium chloride solution to test solution.	
4. Filter solution and wash residue.	
5. Divide washing into 2 portions, to larger portion add 5 ml of potassium chromate.	
6. Filter the solution containing precipitate (5); set residue aside for Procedure 11.	
7. Expose residue from Procedure 4 to sunlight.	
8. Add ammonia water to residue and acidify with nitric acid.	
9. Warm 5 ml of potassium iodide solution.	
10. Add a few drops of warm potassium iodide solution to a few drops of the solution from Procedure 5.	
11. Add a few drops of linseed oil to the finely ground residue from Procedure 6.	

able chemical background is needed to understand how reactions take place. Most of the reactions in this experiment occurred spontaneously. That is, they proceed by themselves with no external energy required. Later in the course you will learn more fundamental concepts which will enable you to predict whether or not reactions are spontaneous.

FOLLOW-UP QUESTIONS

1. What were the observable differences between the initial state of the system described in Procedures 1 and 2, and the final state of the system as described in Procedure 3? Suggest other differences which you may not have been able to observe by visual inspection of the systems.

2. Is it possible that more than two phases were present in the system which you described in Procedure 3? Explain.

3. Did the system represented by the residue in Procedure 4 undergo a change when exposed to sunlight? What evidence do you have to support your answer? Does the behavior of this substance suggest any practical applications for which it might be used?

4. Is the yellow precipitate obtained in Procedure 5 identical to that obtained in Procedure 10? Explain your answer. How might you obtain evidence for your answer?

5. Suggest a reason for using hot water rather than cold water in Procedure 4.

6. Sketch the appearance of the crystals observed in Procedure 10. Identify the geometrical shape. Look up the shape of lead iodide crystals in a chemical handbook to verify your description.

7. Name three lead compounds and one silver compound which you would consider to be insoluble in cold water.

8. Look up a reference on growing crystals and list the conditions that should be controlled in order to obtain large, well-formed crystals.

9. What are the components of an oil paint? What is the function of each component? Refer to a reference book or an encyclopedia if necessary.

1-2

Measurement—

the Basis of Quantitative Chemistry

GENERAL DISCUSSION

In all scientific work, measurement is important. The *accuracy* of the result of a quantitative experiment is limited by the *precision* of the individual measurements made in obtaining the data. It is important, therefore, that you be able to use measuring instruments properly and be aware of their and your own limitations.

The equipment which you will use in chemistry usually is graduated in metric-system units. These units and their relationships to the familiar English-system units are listed in the Appendix of this manual and discussed briefly in Chapter 1 of *Foundations of Chemistry*.

This experiment is designed to make you aware of the limitations of different measuring instruments. In addition, you will become aware of some of the common errors which affect the accuracy of an experimental result. These limitations and errors become apparent when, in this experiment, you determine the density of various substances and solutions using different instruments and methods.

Density. Density is an important property of any substance. It can often be used to help identify a particular substance since it is very rare for two different types of matter to have the same density. Density is the mass of a unit volume of matter. It is a measure of the *compactness* of a sample of matter. The density of liquids and solids is usually expressed in grams per milliliter (g/ml). Since gases have relatively low densities, their densities are normally expressed in grams per liter (g/ℓ). The volume of all substances changes with temperature, so that you should always record the temperature at which density

determinations are made. It is not always convenient to measure out one liter or one milliliter of a substance and then weigh it. It is more practical to determine the mass of whatever volume is used and then find the mass of a unit volume by dividing the mass by whatever volume is used.

The mass of a substance is determined by direct comparison with a known standard mass using an equal-arm balance. The precision with which the mass can be determined depends on the type of balance you use. For example, suppose you wish to weigh a 10-g mass and have a balance which will enable you to weigh the object to the nearest 1 mg. With this balance you could attain an accuracy of 0.01% when you weigh a 10-gram object.

$$\frac{1 \text{ mg}}{10\ 000 \text{ mg}}\ (100) = 0.01\%$$

Volumes may be determined in a number of ways, depending on the substance involved and the equipment available. The volumes of liquids may be measured in graduated cylinders, burets, or pipets. The volumes of solids may be determined by several different methods. If the object is regularly shaped, its dimensions may be measured with a ruler, micrometer, or other devices used for linear measurement. The volume may then be calculated by using the formula which applies to the geometric shape of the object. For example, the volume of a rectangular solid is equal to length × width × depth and that of a cylindrical solid is equal to $\pi r^2 l$.

If the object is irregularly shaped, the volume may be determined by displacement of liquid provided the substance is insoluble and does not react with the liquid. This method is based on the principle that a body immersed in a liquid displaces its own volume of the liquid. If an insoluble object is submerged in a measured volume of liquid in a graduated vessel, the liquid level rises. The difference between the final and the original levels is the volume of the submerged object.

The third method of determining the volume is based on Archimedes' principle: a partially or completely submerged object is buoyed (lifted) up by a force which is equal to the mass of the fluid displaced by the object. A submerged object apparently weighs less in the liquid than in air. The volume of the object still is equal to the volume of the liquid displaced, but in this method the volume of liquid displaced is determined by first finding the mass of the liquid displaced, and then converting the mass to volume by substituting the data in $V = M/D$, where M is the mass of the liquid displaced and D is the density.

A *hydrometer* is a sealed tube whose bottom is weighted so that it floats vertically in a liquid. The upper portion contains a scale. The hydrometer is placed in the liquid and the scale is read at the position where the meniscus of the liquid crosses the scale. If the scale on a hydrometer is calibrated appropriately (not Baumé), the addition of the words *"grams per milliliter"* approximates the density of the liquid.

Solutions. Most of the liquids which you use in the chemistry laboratory are water solutions, composed of a dispersed substance called a *solute* and a dispersing medium called the *solvent*. Water is the solvent in *aqueous* solutions. The solute may be a solid such as sugar or salt, a liquid such as alcohol, or a gas such as carbon dioxide. The quantity of solute in a solution is sometimes expressed in terms of a mass percentage of the total mass of the solution. For example, a 20.0% solution of calcium chloride indicates that the solute calcium chloride constitutes 20.0% of the total mass of the solution. The total mass of a given volume of solution may be calculated from a knowledge of its density.

One liter $(1.00\ l)$ of a 20.0% calcium chloride solution which has a density of 1.18 g/ml has a mass of

$$1.00\ell \times \frac{1.000 \times 10^3}{\ell}\text{ml} \times 1.18\text{g/ml}$$

$$= 1.18 \times 10^3 \text{ g}$$

and contains

$$0.200 \times 1180\text{ g} = 236\text{ g}$$

of calcium chloride.

This experiment is divided into several parts. In the first part, measure the volume and mass of an object and determine its density from these measurements. Use several methods to measure the volume. This enables you to see how different procedures and apparatus affect experimental results.

In Part II experimentally determine the density of a calcium chloride solution and compare this value with the density of the solution as determined with a hydrometer. You then evaporate a specific volume of the solution to dryness and determine the mass of the residue. The theoretical mass of solute can be calculated by using data obtained from a graph. Finally, calculate and account for the percentage differences between the experimental and calculated values.

Your last problem, in Part III of this experiment, is to determine the thickness of a rectangular piece of aluminum foil. You will be given the density of aluminum. It is left to you to devise a method for making this determination. If a micrometer is available you will be able to measure the thickness and compare it with your calculated value.

OBJECTIVES

1. To gain skill in making accurate measurements.

2. To become familiar with the limitations of measuring devices and sources of experimental error.

3. To obtain a working knowledge of the concept of density.

4. To determine the density of a rectangular or cylindrical solid.

5. To determine the density of an aqueous solution.

6. To determine the thickness of a piece of metal foil.

MATERIALS

Cylindrical or rectangular metallic solid, triple-beam balance, metric ruler, graduated cylinder, thread, beaker, watch glass, calcium chloride solution, buret, hydrometer, wire gauze, ring stand, burner, aluminum foil, micrometer.

Part I · Density of a Metal

PROCEDURE

1. Obtain a small cylindrical or rectangular metallic solid.

2. Weigh the object to the nearest 0.01 gram and record the mass in Tables I, II, and III.

3. Measure the dimensions (length, width, and depth if the object is rectangular; length and diameter if it is cylindrical) of the object to the highest degree of precision permitted by your measuring instruments. Record data in Table I.

4. Calculate the volume of the object by using the proper formula.

5. Determine and record the density of the object.

Table I   Direct Measurement of Volume

Mass of object		
Length of object		
Width or diameter of object		
Depth of object (if rectangular)		
Volume of object in ml		
Density of object in grams/ml		

6. Place about 25 ml of water in a 50-ml graduated cylinder and read the volume to the nearest 0.2 ml. Record data in Table II.

7. Tilt the cylinder and carefully slide the object in so as to avoid splashing the water or breaking the cylinder.

8. Read and record the final volume.

9. Determine the volume of water displaced by subtracting the initial water level from the final level.

10. Calculate the density of the object.

11. Suspend the object from the hanger of the triple-beam balance with a thread.

12. Place a platform on the platform support of the balance and swing it over the pan of the balance. Place a beaker of water on the platform and suspend the object from the hanger so that it is completely submerged as shown in Fig. 1-2. Record the mass of the submerged object.

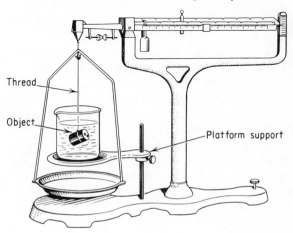

Thread
Object
Platform support

Fig. 1-2   Apparent mass of a submerged object.

13. Calculate the difference between the mass of the object in air and in water. Record this as the mass of the water displaced.

14. Assume the density of water at room temperature to be 1.00 g/ml and calculate the volume of the water displaced. Also record this value as the volume of the object.

15. Calculate the density of the object.

Part II · Density of an Aqueous Solution

16. Weigh to the nearest centigram a small beaker (50 ml) covered with a watch glass. Record data in Table IV.

17. Drain 5.00 ml of a calcium chloride solution from the buret provided.

18. Weigh the beaker containing the calcium chloride solution and the watch glass.

19. From these data calculate the density of the solution.

20. Read the hydrometer floating in the calcium chloride solution, located on the reagent table. Record the density of this solution in Table IV.

21. Cover the beaker with the watch glass, place the assembly on a wire gauze and evaporate the solution to dryness. Avoid spattering! Use a bunsen burner or a heat lamp (IR).

22. Cool and weigh the beaker, watch glass, and dry calcium chloride. If time permits, reheat, cool, and reweigh until a constant mass is obtained.

23. Determine the mass of the calcium chloride in the original 5.00 ml of solution.

24. Use the density as determined in Procedure 20 and refer to the graph, Fig. 1-3, and calculate the mass of solute that should be present in the 5.00 ml of solution.

25. Find the percentage difference between the experimental mass (Procedure 22) and the calculated mass (Procedure 24).

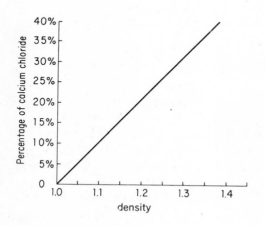

Fig. 1-3 Plot of mass percentage of CaCl$_2$ vs density.

Table II Volume by Water Displacement

Final reading of water level		
Initial reading of water level		
Volume of water displaced		
Volume of object		
Mass of object		
Density of object		

Table III Volume by Archimedes' Principle

Mass of object in air		
Mass of object in water		
Mass of water displaced by object		
Density of water		
Volume of water displaced by object		
Volume of object		
Density of object		

Table IV Density of an Aqueous Solution

Volume of solution	
Mass of beaker, watch glass, and solution	
Mass of beaker and watch glass	
Mass of solution	
Density of solution	
Density (hydrometer)	
Mass of beaker, watch glass, and dry solute	
Mass of beaker and watch glass (same as item 3)	
Mass of solute (experimental)	
% of solute in solution (from graph)	
Calculated mass of solute	
% difference between experimental and calculated mass	

Part III · The Thickness of Aluminum Foil

26. Obtain a rectangular piece of aluminum foil. The density of aluminum at 20°C is 2.70 g/ml. Measure its mass, length, and width. From these measurements determine the thickness of the foil. Record all data and calculated results in Table V. If a micrometer is available, use it to check your results.

Table V   Thickness of Aluminum Foil

Mass	
Length	
Width	
Density	2.70 g/ml
Volume	
Area	
Thickness (cm)	
Thickness (Ångstroms)	
Thickness (micrometer)	

FOLLOW-UP DISCUSSION

Whenever repeated measurements are made to the limits of precision of the measuring instrument, the values obtained are seldom in complete agreement. There may be a number of reasons for the variations in the values obtained. A few common sources of error are listed below.

1. Variations in the functioning of measuring instruments.

2. Physiological effects such as fatigue of the eye.

3. Errors in estimating fractional parts of a scale division.

4. Incorrect masses (weights) and burets that are incorrectly graduated.

5. Inability to distinguish between colors.

6. Presence of a volatile or nonvolatile impurity in a supposedly pure sample.

7. Occurrence of side reactions which are not recognized.

8. Fluctuating temperature.

9. Overheating and underheating of substances being tested.

10. Misreading and incorrectly recording masses and volumes.

11. Errors in transferring substances from one vessel to another.

12. Spattering of a solution during evaporation.

13. Incomplete drying of products.

14. Mixing up samples by improper labeling.

By exercising proper laboratory technique you can avoid many of these errors and obtain a relatively high degree of precision and accuracy in your quantitative laboratory work.

The terms *precision* and *accuracy* are widely used in any scientific work where quantitative measurements are made. Precision is a measure of the degree to which results of a given experiment "check." A high degree of precision is obtained when several results for the same experiment are in close agreement. We may consider precision to be a measure of the deviation of individual results from the average (known as the arithmetical mean) of several results. For example, suppose a student analyzed a compound to determine the percentage of water in it and obtained these results:

Trial I	14.86% water
Trial II	14.16% water

The average of the two results is 14.51%. Each of the results differs by 0.35 from the mean. The % precision is thus

$$\frac{0.35}{14.51} \times 100 = 2.4\%$$

It is not desirable to use only two results since if the precision of the results is not good, the experimenter has no way of telling which of the two results is the more reliable. Since time does not usually permit running more than two trials, report the average of the results you obtain in the experiments involving quantitative measurements.

The accuracy of a result is the degree to which the experimental value agrees with the true value. It is possible to have a high degree of precision with poor accuracy. This occurs if the same error is involved in repeated trials of the experiment.

In some experiments which you perform, you are asked to calculate the percentage error or percentage deviation of your result from some given value. This may be accomplished by applying the relationship.

% Error (deviation) =
$$\frac{\text{diff. between exp. and given values}}{\text{given value}} \times 100$$

Suppose that in the preceding example the correct percentage of water in the compound is 14.00%. The value reported by the student would be the average of the two trials, 14.51%.

The percentage error in the experimental result is

$$\% \text{ Error} = \frac{14.51 - 14.00}{14.00} \times 100 = 3.64\%$$

FOLLOW-UP QUESTIONS

1. The densities of several common metals are listed below. Compare your experimental density with the given values and try to determine which metal you tested.

- (a) Iron .... 7.86 g/ml
- (b) Copper .... 8.92 g/ml
- (c) Aluminum .... 2.7 g/ml
- (d) Lead .... 11.34 g/ml
- (e) Tin .... 7.31 g/ml
- (f) Brass (70% Cu, 30% Zn).. 8.53 g/ml

What other property could be used to help identify your sample?

2. Which method do you think gave the most accurate value for the volume in Part I? Explain your choice.

3. List sources of error for each method.

4. What measurement limited the accuracy in each case?

5. Assuming the balance used could be read to 0.01 g, what percentage error might you expect when weighing a 10.00-gram object?

6. What percentage error would you expect in using your graduated cylinder to measure 5 ml of water if you can read the graduated cylinder to 0.2 ml?

7. What percentage error would you expect in using a buret to measure 5 ml of water if you can read a buret to 0.02 ml?

8. In Part I of this experiment, all members of your class probably determined the density of the same metal. Each student probably had a sample of different mass and different volume. One way of representing the relationship between two variables such as mass and volume is by means of a graph. Assume that all the students who had samples made of the same metal pool their data as shown in Table VI. (a) Plot a graph of mass (ordinate) *versus* volume (abscissa). (b) Are the variables mass and volume inversely or directly proportional to each other? Recall from your mathematics courses that a straight line graph represents a direct proportion. (c) Express the ratio between mass and volume in terms of an equation. Represent the constant of proportionality as D. (d) Solve the equation for D and determine its value. The constant, D, is known as the *slope* or *inclination* of the line, and is equal to the density of the magnesium. See Appendix 2 for a discussion of slope.

Table VI Related Masses and Volumes of Different Samples of Magnesium

Mass (g)	Volume (ml)
3.4	2.0
6.8	4.0
10.2	6.0
13.6	8.0
17.0	10.0
20.4	12.0
23.8	14.0
27.2	16.0

9. Explain how you could use Archimedes' principle to determine the density of the aqueous solution in Part II.

10. A full barrel holds 750 pounds of gasoline.

The same barrel holds 1100 pounds of water when full. What is the density of the gasoline?

11. A solution of sodium hydroxide consisting of a solute (sodium hydroxide) and a solvent (water) has a density of 1.22 g/ml. What does 0.100 liter of this solution weigh? If the solution is 20.0 percent by mass solute, what mass of pure sodium hydroxide is in the 0.100 liter of solution?

12. Osmium metal, the densest element, has a density of 22.5 g/ml, while hydrogen gas, the least dense element, has a density of 8.90×10^{-5} g/ml. Calculate the volume occupied by 1.00 g of each element. How many times denser than hydrogen is osmium?

13. Calculate the approximate thickness of the aluminum foil in terms of atoms. Each aluminum atom has a radius of 1.48 Ångstrom units. Although aluminum atoms in the foil are stacked like cannon balls, you may assume for this calculation that they are stacked one upon another.

2-1

Separation, Purification, and Identification of the Components of a Mixture

GENERAL DISCUSSION

Most materials found in nature or produced by manufacturing concerns are mixtures. Even the purest chemicals available from chemical supply houses contain tiny traces of impurities. The separation, identification, and purification of the components of a mixture are among the everyday problems faced by both industrial and research chemists.

A number of methods for separating the components of mixtures are based on the relative solubilities of the components in different solvents or at different temperatures in a given solvent. In Part I of this experiment, you will be given a murky mixture composed of salt (sodium chloride), sand, charcoal, benzoic acid, and glycerol. Your objective will be to separate colorless, needle-like crystals of benzoic acid from the other components. The separation is based on the difference between the solubility of benzoic acid and that of the impurities in hot and cold water. Benzoic acid is quite soluble in hot water but less soluble in cold water. Both glycerol, a liquid, and sodium chloride, a solid, are relatively soluble in both hot and cold water while sand and charcoal are essentially insoluble in both hot and cold water. You can verify that the product which you isolate is benzoic acid by comparing its melting point with that of the pure compound (122.4°C).

In Part II of this experiment you will separate and identify the components of a mixture of colored dyes by paper chromatography. In this process, a solution containing the solute mixture is placed on a strip of filter paper, the end of which is then immersed in an organic solvent. The paper contains and supports an aqueous phase (called the stationary phase). As the solvent (called the moving phase) rises up the paper by capillary action, the solutes move at different rates through the stationary phase, which depend upon their relative solubility in the two phases. Each solute has a characteristic rate; thus the components distribute themselves differently on the stationary phase as the mobile phase moves over it. The components may be located by the colored zones located at different positions on the paper. If the components are colorless, some substance(s) must be placed on the final chromatogram which will react with the components and give some visible evidence of their reactive position on the paper. For example, a substance called *ninhydrin* is used to show the relative position of various amino acids when an analysis of proteins is carried out. The distance traveled by each solute and that moved by the solvent may be measured. The ratio

$$\frac{\text{Distance traveled by solute}}{\text{Distance traveled by solvent}}$$

is called the R_f value for that solute and is characteristic of that substance in a given set of experimental conditions or with a specific solvent. Thus, the components of a mixture may be identified by comparing measured R_f values with a standard R_f value for each solute.

In this part of the experiment, you will be given, or asked to determine experimentally, the R_f values for a number of food colorings (dyes) and some indicators. You will then use paper chromatography to separate and identify some of these substances present in an unknown mixture.

OBJECTIVES

1. To become familiar with techniques and principles associated with recrystallization, paper chromatography, and other processes commonly used to separate and purify the components of a mixture.

2. To separate and purify a compound (benzoic acid) from a heterogeneous mixture.

3. To determine the melting point of the compound (optional).

4. To determine the R_f values for dyes used as coloring agents in foods, and for some selected indicators used in chemistry.

5. To use standardized R_f values to identify the colored components in an unknown mixture.

MATERIALS

Heterogeneous mixture (50% benzoic acid, 20% sodium chloride, 30% sand, enough fairly coarse charcoal to color the mixture and enough glycerol to give it a mud-like consistency, 250-ml beaker, filter paper, funnel, burner, wire gauze, melting point tubes (optional), thermometer (optional), mineral oil (optional), rubber bands (optional), Whatman #1 chromatographic paper (or ordinary filter paper), scissors (if strips are not provided), wide-mouth gas-collection bottle, aluminum foil or Ditto paper, a solvent which is 2% by volume isobutyl alcohol, 2% by volume concentrated (15-M) aqueous ammonia, and 96% by volume water, washable black "Super Quink," green, blue, yellow, and red food dyes, methyl orange, methyl red, indigo carmine, bromocresol purple, and quinaldine red indicators, assorted mixtures of food dyes and indicators.

Part I

PROCEDURE

1. Place about a 2-g sample of the mixture (provided by the instructor) in a 250-ml beaker and add approximately 100 ml of water. Heat the solution to boiling.

2. Filter the hot solution through two layers of filter paper into another beaker.

3. Heat the filtrate to boiling, remove from the heat, and allow to cool slowly without disturbance.

4. After crystals form, filter and show them to your instructor. Allow the sample to dry thoroughly before melting point is taken. Go on to Part II and complete Part I later if directed to do so by the instructor.

5. Obtain a melting point tube.

6. Crush your sample to a powder and push the open end of the melting point tube into the mound to force the sample in. Shake the sample down to the closed end by tapping tube gently with your finger or by rubbing gently with a file. There should be no more than 3 mm of lightly-packed sample in the tube. Attach the tube to a thermometer with a rubber band made by cutting a slice from a piece of rubber tubing (Fig. 2-1), or with a copper wire.

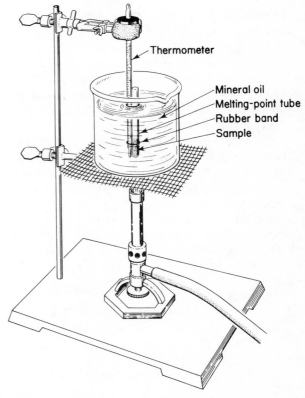

Fig. 2-1 Set-up for determining the melting point of a solid.

7. Place the bulb of the thermometer and melting point tube in a beaker of mineral oil so that the thermometer bulb and sample are in the center of the container and fully submerged. Warm the oil slowly and record the temperature at which the compound in the tube melts. Record this temperature in Table I.

Table I   Properties of Benzoic Acid

Color of crystals	
Appearance (nature) of crystals	
Melting point of your product	
Melting point of pure benzoic acid	122.4°C

Part II

PROCEDURE

1. Cut Whatman #1 chromatographic paper or ordinary filter paper into strips 1-in. wide at the bottom and slightly wider at the top.

2. Draw two *pencil* lines across each strip. One line should be 1 cm from one end and the second should be 10 cm above the first. This simplifies the calculation of R_f values.

3. Make a cap for a wide-mouth, gas-collection bottle out of aluminum foil or stiff (Ditto) paper. Make a small, slightly curved slit in the cap. The length of the slit is slightly less than the upper width of the tapered paper strips.

4. Place the solvent (isobutyl alcohol, concentrated (15-M) NH_3(aq), H_2O in a 2:2:96 by volume ratio) in the gas bottle to a depth of 0.5–1.0 cm.

5. Place the cap on the bottle after first wiping off any moisture around the top. Avoid making the slit any wider or getting the cover wet. If paper is used, attach a rubber band to hold the cover on your bottle.

6. Use a melting-point tube open at both ends and carefully spot the paper at the bottom line with washable black Super Quink. It will be necessary to restrict the opening of an ordinary melting point tube further by drawing it out in a flame. Test the opening with a piece of scrap filter paper. The spot should be about 0.5–1 mm in diameter.

7. Carefully slide the strip through the slit into the bottle, being certain that the strip does not touch the inside wall of the bottle. Have the bottom of the strip firmly "implanted" on the bottom of the bottle but be certain that the paper does not "bow" and slip to the side and touch the walls (Fig. 2-2).

8. Allow the solvent to migrate to the upper line.

Fig. 2-2   *Resolution of a mixture by paper chromatography.*

Table II R_f Values for Colored Components in Black Super Quink®

Color	Distance Traveled by Solvent (cm)	Distance Traveled by Solute (cm)	R_f Value for Solute
	10.0		
	10.0		
	10.0		
	10.0		

9. Determine the R_f value for each colored area by dividing the distance from the bottom line to the top of each colored area by 10.0 (see Fig. 2-2). Record data in Table II.

Part III

10. Use the techniques described in Part II to determine which of the food, drug, and cosmetic dyes approved by the government are present in the products listed in Table IV. The R_f values for the approved colored dyes using the developing solvent described above are given below in Table III. Dissolve each of the solid powders in a minimum of water and prepare individual chromatograms. Determine the distance traveled by each solute, calculate the R_f values, and record the data in Table IV. Compare these R_f values with the standard values given below to help identify the FD & C dye in each product.

Part IV

11. Prepare paper chromatograms for the indicators listed in Table V and determine the R_f values for the colored components.

12. Obtain an unknown mixture from your instructor and use paper chromatography to separate and identify the components. The unknown may be a mixture of (a) food dyes, (b) food dyes and indicators, or (c) indicators. You will have to refer to the R_f values in Tables III and V, and compare these values with those of the colored components in your unknown in order to identify the components of your mixture.

Table III R_f Values for Approved FD & C Dyes

Dye	R_f Value
Red 2	0.81
Red 3	0.41
Red 4	0.62
Yellow 5	0.95
Yellow 6	0.77
Green 3	1.0
Blue 1	1.0
Blue 2	0.79
Violet 1	0.79

Table V R_f Values for Indicators

Indicator	Colored Zones	R_f Value
Methyl Orange		
Methyl Red		
Indigo Carmine		
Bromocresol Purple		
Quinaldine Red		

Table VI   Unknown Mixture

Colored Zones	R_f Values	Conclusion

Table IV R_f Values for Coloring Agents in Household Products

Product	Colored Zones	Distance Traveled by Solvent (cm)	Distance Traveled by Solute (cm)	R_f Value for Solute	FD & C Dye Present
Green Food Dye					
Blue Food Dye					
Yellow Food Dye					
Red Food Dye					

FOLLOW-UP DISCUSSION

In this experiment you separated a mixture of substances by taking advantage of the differences in their solubilities. You first added water, a solvent classified as a *polar inorganic molecular substance*, to the original mixture. Sodium chloride, an *ionic inorganic compound*, and glycerol, a *polar organic molecular compound*, both readily dissolve in cold water. In general, most ionic compounds and most polar molecular solutes are soluble to varying degrees in polar molecular solvents.

You heated the solution in order to dissolve benzoic acid, another organic polar molecular substance whose solubility, unlike that of sodium chloride depends greatly on the temperature. Substances such as graphite are classified as *macromolecular* and are insoluble in all common solvents. Graphite dissolves in liquid iron but in few, if any, other liquids. Sand may be considered to be a form of impure quartz (silicon dioxide), another macromolecular solid which is insoluble in water.

The sand and graphite were first separated from your mixture by simple filtration. The filtering process permitted rapid cooling of the solution and the formation of small, poorly formed crystals of benzoic acid. In order to improve the quality of the crystals (their size, shape, and filterability) you reheated the filtrate and allowed it to cool *slowly*. This recrystallization process produces an aggregate of large needle-like crystals of benzoic acid which you then isolated by again filtering the solution. This time the filtrate contained sodium chloride whose solubility varies little with temperature. Solubility data show that approximately 35 g of sodium chloride can remain dissolved in 100 g of water at 0°C. You could verify the presence of chloride ions from the salt in the filtrate by adding dilute silver nitrate solution ($AgNO_3$) and noting the characteristics of the resulting precipitate. The purity of the benzoic acid crystals was approximated by checking the sharpness and value of its melting point. Pure compounds have a sharp, well-defined melting point.

In the second, third, and fourth parts of this experiment you effected a separation of substances by allowing the mixture to move across a sheet of filter paper. Paper, which is manufactured from wood pulp, is composed of cellulose fibers which have water molecules attached to them by hydrogen bonds. The water molecules are stationary and thus cannot move across the paper but they can attract certain polar components of various mixtures. As the developing solvent rises up the paper by capillary effect, it passes through the sample, dissolves the components of the mixture and carries them up the paper. The rate at which each component moves up the paper depends upon its relative solubility in the solvent and its tendency to be attracted to and held by the stationary water molecules. Components that are relatively soluble in the developing solvent but are not attracted greatly to the water molecules move up the paper at a rapid rate, relative to those that are relatively insoluble in the solvent and strongly attracted by the water molecules. Because the characteristics of the components differ, they move at different rates and thus become separated from one another.

FOLLOW-UP QUESTIONS

1. (a) What are the major differences between a homogeneous mixture and a compound? (b) Identify one heterogeneous mixture, one homogeneous mixture, one element, and five compounds that you encountered in this experiment.

2. Describe physical methods that could be used to separate each of these mixtures into their component compounds and/or elements.

(a) A solution of sodium chloride and water.

(b) A solid mixture of sodium chloride and iodine. Iodine is relatively soluble in carbon tetrachloride or Freon while sodium chloride is not. Also, iodine sublimes (passes directly from the solid phase to the gaseous phase before it has reached its melting point).

(c) A mixture of sodium nitrate (very soluble in both hot and cold water), lead chloride (much more soluble in hot than in cold water), iodine (relatively) insoluble in water but soluble in Freon or carbon tetrachloride), and sand.

3. A colored component of a mixture is insoluble in the developing solvent but strongly attracted by water, the stationary phase on filter paper. Would you expect to find this component near the origin or near the top of the strip (chromatogram)?

4. What are the R_f values for the components shown on the chromatogram reproduced in Fig. 2-3?

5. If two components have R_f values of 0.88 and 0.50, what is the distance of separation between the component areas after the developing solvent has risen 10.0 cm from the origin?

6. Explain why it would be unwise to use a pen to mark the origin on the paper strips used in Parts II, III, and IV of this experiment.

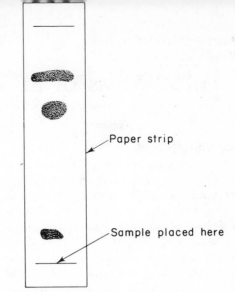

Fig. 2-3 Paper chromatogram.

2-2
Molecular Mass of an Unknown Gas

GENERAL DISCUSSION

In 1811 the Italian scientist, Amadeo Avogadro, proposed that equal volumes of gases under the same conditions of temperature and pressure contained equal numbers of molecules. Avogadro's proposal was later verified and is now a generally accepted principle. If this principle is true, it follows that the masses of equal volumes of different gases under the same conditions of temperature and pressure must be in the same ratio as the masses of the individual molecules.

In this experiment you determine the molecular mass of an unknown gas by applying Avogadro's principle. In this experimental procedure you will compare the mass of a given volume of unknown gas with the mass of the same volume of O_2. The experimentally determined masses of the two gases are in the same ratio as their molecular masses. It is not necessary to make temperature and pressure corrections since the temperature and pressure will be constant throughout this experiment. The mass of the empty flask may be determined by weighing the flask with air and then subtracting the mass of air. The mass of the air in the flask can be calculated by multiplying the volume of the flask by the density of the air which may be obtained from a table. You may wish to refer to Sections 2-13 through 2-15 in *Foundations of Chemistry* before going further with this experiment.

OBJECTIVE

Determine the molecular mass of an unknown gas by applying Avogadro's principle.

MATERIALS

250 ml erlenmeyer flask with solid stopper, paper towels, tank of oxygen, sources of other dry gases. If oxygen is not available, use hydrogen

peroxide (3%) and manganese dioxide as shown in Fig. 2-4.

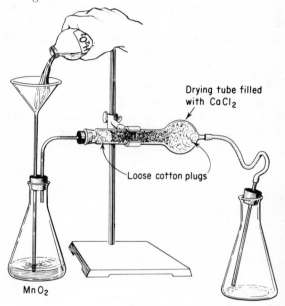

Fig. 2-4 *Apparatus for generating oxygen gas.*

PROCEDURE

1. Equip a clean, dry, 250-ml erlenmeyer flask with a solid stopper. Handle this flask with a folded paper towel to avoid getting greasy finger prints on the flask. Carefully weigh the flask, air, and stopper to the nearest 0.01 g and record the data in the table.

2. Fill the flask with dry oxygen gas. Your instructor may have a tank of oxygen gas or oxygen generator set up to supply the oxygen. The oxygen generators may be constructed by fitting a two-hole stopper, containing a delivery tube and thistle tube, into a 250-ml erlenmeyer flask (Fig. 2-4). A calcium chloride drying tube should be

attached to the generator so that the oxygen will be free of water vapor. The generator contains about 10 ml of water and a few grams of manganese dioxide. To produce a flow of oxygen, 3% or 6% hydrogen peroxide (**Caution**) *should be slowly poured into the thistle tube.* The volume of H_2O_2 required depends on its concentration. The flask should be swirled gently and the oxygen allowed to pass through the drying tube into the weighed flask. Since oxygen is more dense than air, the flask should be filled by the upward displacement of air (the flask should be upright).

3. When the flask is full of oxygen, replace the stopper and weigh. Be sure to use the same balance as in the previous weighing. Record this mass.

4. Under a fume hood, remove the bunsen burner from its rubber tubing and insert this end of the tubing into the weighed flask. Turn on the gas for a few seconds and fill the flask with the fuel gas. If the fuel gas is less dense than air the flask should be filled by downward displacement of air (inverted flask). Country bottled gas may be denser than air. Other gases may be used if lecture bottles are available.

5. Replace the stopper assembly and again weigh on the same balance. Record this mass.

6. Mark the flask at the bottom of the stopper and fill the flask with water up to the mark, so that the volume of water is equal to the volume of your gas samples. Pour the water into a graduated cylinder and record this volume.

7. Determine the mass of the air in the flask by multiplying the volume of the flask by the density of air. The density of air may be found, after taking the room temperature, by referring to the table below or a handbook. If the pressure varies much from 745 torr you will need to consult a handbook for the density of the air.

8. Determine the mass of the empty flask by subtracting the mass of the air from the mass of the flask plus air.

9. Calculate the molecular mass of the unknown gas.

Molecular Mass of an Unknown Gas

Mass of flask with air	
Volume of flask	
Room temperature	
Density of air at room temperature	
Mass of air in flask	
Mass of empty flask	
Mass of flask with oxygen	
Mass of empty flask	
Mass of oxygen	
Mass of flask and unknown gas	
Mass of empty flask	
Mass of unknown gas	
Molecular mass of unknown gas	
Class average of molecular mass of unknown gas	
Percent of deviation from class average	

FOLLOW-UP DISCUSSION

The fuel gas which is used as an unknown has a variable composition and is truly an unknown. It is largely methane (CH_4) which has a theoretical molecular mass of 16. The other gases present in fuel gas have higher molecular masses, so the

Density of Air at 745 torr

Temperature (°C)	14	16	18	20	22	24	26	28	30
Density (g/ml × 10^{-3})	1.208	1.200	1.189	1.181	1.173	1.165	1.157	1.150	1.142

average mass of all molecules present is slightly more than 16. The mean value obtained by the class is probably the best approximation of the true molecular mass.

The masses of equal volumes of two gases under the same conditions of temperature and pressure have the same mass ratios as the individual molecules. Let us carry out a sample calculation of the molecular mass of a hypothetical unknown gas.

Suppose that 250 ml of an unknown gas at a given set of conditions has a mass of 0.498 g, while an equal volume of oxygen at the same conditions has a mass of 0.332 g. We can assume that each molecule of the unknown is 0.498/0.332 times as massive as an oxygen molecule. This molecule would then have a mass 1.50 times as much as a single oxygen molecule. If we arbitrarily set the mass of an oxygen molecule as 32.0 mass units, then the unknown molecule would have a mass of 1.50 × 32.0 or 48.0 mass units. Thus, according to Avogadro's principle, 48.0 g of the unknown gas contains the same number of molecules as 32.0 g of oxygen.

The molecular mass of a substance expressed in grams is called a *gram-molecular mass* or commonly is referred to as a *mole*. The mole is a fundamental chemical unit based on mass which always contains the same number of particles. This means we can count molecules of a substance by weighing out a specific mass or by measuring a specific volume of a gaseous substance at a given temperature and pressure. Measurements on gases show that ideally, one mole of a gas occupies 22.4 liters at 0°C and 760 torr. We shall investigate this relationship in greater detail later on in the course.

In order to calculate the number of molecules in a specific mass of a substance, we must first know how many molecules (or particles) there are in one mole of a substance. There are several precise methods by which this number may be determined. In the next experiment we shall use a rather simple method to determine an approximate value of the number which is called Avogadro's number.

FOLLOW-UP QUESTIONS

1. Summarize the sources of error in this experiment. Explain briefly how each error would affect your experimental answer for the molecular mass of the unknown gas.

2. Compare your results with the class average. Calculate the percent deviation between your value and the average value.

3. Calculate the number of grams of hydrogen gas your flask would hold under the conditions of the experiment. Hydrogen (H_2) has a molecular mass of 2.0.

4. Calculate the experimental density of oxygen and of the unknown gas from the data in your table.

5. Use the data in your table to determine what volume would be occupied by one mole of (a) oxygen and (b) the unknown gas at the temperature and pressure conditions of your experiment.

6. Carbon dioxide (CO_2) is a gas which has a molecular mass of 44.0. Calculate (a) the grams of CO_2 in 0.50 mole, (b) the moles of CO_2 in 11.0 g of the gas, (c) the volume occupied by 16.8 g of the gas at 0°C and 760 torr (1 mole occupies 22.4 liters), (d) the mass of 1.12 liters of CO_2 measured at 0°C and 760 torr.

2-3
Estimation of Avogadro's Number

GENERAL DISCUSSION

In a previous experiment we used Avogadro's principle to determine the relative molecular mass of a gaseous substance. In that experiment we assumed that equal volumes of gases at the same conditions of temperature and pressure contained equal numbers of molecules. We accomplished our objective without knowing or calculating the number of molecules in the flask. In the follow-up discussion, we identified the molecular mass of a substance expressed in grams as a chemical unit called the *mole,* and deduced on the basis of Avogadro's principle that a mole of any substance must contain the same number of molecules. The number of molecules in a mole is known as *Avogadro's number.* In this experiment we shall estimate the volume of a molecule and the value of Avogadro's number.

When a benzene solution of oleic acid of known concentration is added dropwise to water, the solution spreads out. The benzene evaporates rapidly and leaves a layer of the acid on the surface of the water that has a uniform thickness and is believed to be one molecule thick. Once the surface is covered with the monolayer, the addition of more solution produces a "lens," or globule which does not spread out or disappear rapidly. From the number of drops of solution required to cover the surface with a monolayer of acid, the known concentration of the solution, and the given density of the acid, it is possible to calculate the volume of the oleic acid in the monolayer. The thickness of the layer is obtained by dividing the volume of the acid by the measured area of the water surface.

By assuming that an oleic-acid molecule has a specific shape and that one of the dimensions is equal to the calculated thickness of the monolayer, it is possible to estimate the volume of a

molecule. The volume of the monolayer divided by the volume of each molecule yields the number of molecules in the layer. Once the number of molecules in a given mass of oleic acid (in the monolayer) is known, the number of molecules in a mole (Avogadro's number) of the acid may be calculated.

OBJECTIVES

1. To become aware of the role (uses) of and limitations of assumptions made to help solve problems.

2. To gain an understanding of the relationship between quantities and dimensions on a macroscopic scale and those on a molecular scale.

3. To estimate the size (volume) of an oleic-acid molecule.

4. To estimate the value of Avogadro's number (molecules/mole).

MATERIALS

Benzene solution of oleic acid [2 drops (about 0.04–0.05 g) oleic acid per liter of benzene], capillary pipet (60–100 drops/ml), 4-in. watch glass, saucer, or plate, 10-ml graduated cylinder, benzene (C_6H_6), metric ruler, detergent, 6-M aqueous NH_3, tissue for drying glassware, test-tube brush.

PROCEDURE

1. Obtain a piece of 7-mm glass tubing and prepare a capillary dropper which delivers between 60 and 100 drops of benzene per ml. The dropper may be prepared by rotating rapidly the piece of glass tubing in the hottest part of a bunsen burner flame (no wingtop) until it begins to sag, and then removing it from the flame, pausing a couple of seconds and drawing it out steadily to arm's length. Use the sharp edge of a Carborun-

dum chip, the edge of a broken clay plate, or a very sharp file to scratch and then break the capillary tube cleanly at a place where the orifice is the proper diameter. The upper end or 7-mm section of your dropper should be about 8 to 10 cm long and fitted with the rubber bulb from your medicine dropper (Fig. 2-5). Alternatively, a disposable Pasteur-type capillary pipet may be used if available. Reduce the diameter of the orifice of this pipet further until it delivers the proper number of drops.

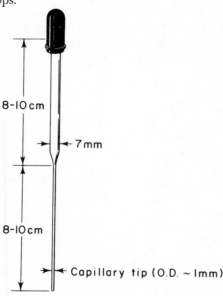

8-10 cm

←7mm

8-10 cm

←Capillary tip (O.D. ~1mm)

Fig. 2-5 Capillary pipet.

2. Use a test-tube brush and a detergent to clean a shell vial thoroughly. Then wash the inside with 6-M aqueous NH_3 and rinse several times with water. Dry with a tissue, rinse thoroughly with benzene, and finally add about 3 ml of benzene.

3. Rinse the capillary pipet with benzene (do not allow the benzene to contact the rubber bulb at any time during the experiment) and determine the exact number of drops needed to equal one milliliter. Add the benzene dropwise to a 10-ml graduated cylinder or to a calibration tube. Do not wash the graduated cylinder, calibration tube, or dropper with water before or after the

calibration. Dispose of excess benzene in a receptacle provided by your instructor. Dry the vial with a tissue.

4. Measure the diameter of a 4-in. watch glass, saucer, or small plate to the nearest 0.1 centimeter.

5. *Thoroughly* clean the watch glass by scrubbing with a detergent and brush for several minutes. Rinse well with water and then scrub thoroughly with 6-M aqueous NH_3. Rinse many times with tap water and finally with distilled water. The glass or plate should drain cleanly leaving no "beads" of water on its surface. Hold the glass in such a way that there will be no finger prints on the upper surface of the glass or on its rim.

6. Place the watch glass on a ring mounted on a ring stand. Be sure the glass is parallel to the top of the laboratory bench. Fill the watch glass to the brim with distilled water obtained from a clean and grease-free container.

7. Take the clean, lint-free glass vial to your instructor who will pour into it an oleic acid-benzene solution about 5 mm deep.

8. Draw some of the oleic-acid solution up into your capillary dropper, hold the dropper perpendicular to the surface of the water in the watch glass, and add one drop of the oleic-acid solution to the water surface. The solution should spread out rapidly across the surface of the water and disappear within a few seconds (Fig. 2-6a). If the watch glass is not properly cleaned, then an oily "lens" or globule may appear after the addition of only one or a few drops of solution. In this case, it will be necessary to clean the watch glass again. If the first drop disappears rapidly, then continue adding the solution dropwise, counting the drops. After perhaps 20 drops, as the monolayer nears completion, the drop of solution forms a circular pattern rather than flowering out (Fig. 2-6b). The circular film of solution contracts as it evaporates and disappears in a relatively short time. This pattern will be observed for a few drops until, finally, one drop strikes the surface and remains as a "lens" or globule that requires a prolonged period of time to disappear (Fig.

2-6c). At this point, the surface of the water is covered with a monolayer of oleic acid and one more drop placed at a different point on the water surface forms a second "lens". Record the number of drops and if time permits, repeat the procedure until reproducible values are obtained.

9. Obtain the concentration of the oleic acid-benzene solution (in g oleic acid per liter or ml of solution) from your instructor and calculate the mass of oleic acid on the surface of the water.

10. Calculate the volume of the oleic acid on the surface.

11. Calculate the surface area of the water surface (area of monolayer).

12. Calculate the thickness of the monolayer.

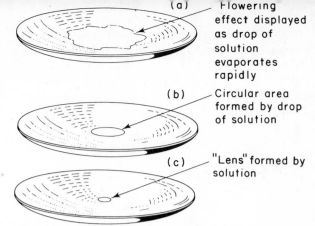

(a) Flowering effect displayed as drop of solution evaporates rapidly

(b) Circular area formed by drop of solution

(c) "Lens" formed by solution

Fig. 2-6 Different stages in the formation of a monomolecular layer of oleic acid.

Table I Estimation of Avogadro's Number

	Trial I	Trial II
Drops of benzene per ml		
Number of drops of solution required to form "lens" or globule of solution		
Volume of solution used (ml)		
Concentration of oleic acid-benzene solution (g/ml) (see instructor)		
Mass of oleic acid in monolayer on water surface (g)		
Density of oleic acid (g/ml)	0.895	0.895
Volume of oleic acid in monolayer (ml)		
Diameter of water surface (monolayer)		
Area of water surface (of monolayer)		
Thickness of monolayer (cm)		
Volume of oleic acid molecule assuming it is a rectangular solid with a width and length equal to $\frac{1}{5.44}$ of the height (t) where the height equals the thickness of the monolayer		
Number of oleic-acid molecules in the surface layer		
Molecular mass of oleic acid ($C_{18}H_{34}O_2$) (g/mole)	282	282
Number of moles of oleic acid in the surface layer		
Value of Avogadro's number (molecules per mole of oleic acid)		

13. Calculate the volume of the acid molecule assuming it is a rectangular solid with a width and length equal to $\frac{1}{5.44}$ the height, where the height is equal to the thickness of the monolayer.

14. Calculate the number of acid molecules in the surface.

15. Calculate the moles of oleic acid on the surface.

16. Calculate the value of Avogadro's number (molecules per mole).

SAMPLE CALCULATIONS

1. Volume of *oleic-acid solution* used.

$$V(ml) = \text{drops of solution} \times \frac{ml \text{ solution}}{\text{drops solution}}$$

2. Mass of oleic acid in monolayer.

$$\text{Mass} = \frac{\text{g oleic acid}}{\text{ml solution}} \times ml \text{ solution used}$$

3. Volume of oleic acid in monolayer.

$$V = \frac{M \text{ acid}}{D \text{ acid}}$$

4. Surface area of monolayer.

$$A = \frac{\pi d^2}{4}$$

5. Thickness of monolayer (h)

$$h = \frac{\text{volume of oleic acid in monolayer}}{\text{area of monolayer}}$$

6. Volume of oleic-acid molecule assuming its shape to be a rectangular solid whose width and depth are $\frac{1}{5.44}$ of its height (thickness of the monolayer)

$$V = t \times \frac{t}{5.44} \times \frac{t}{5.44} = \frac{t^3}{(5.44)^2}$$

7. Number of oleic molecules in monolayer.

$$\frac{\text{Volume of monolayer}}{\text{Volume of molecule}}$$

8. Moles of oleic acid in monolayer.

$$\text{Moles} = \frac{\text{grams of acid in monolayer}}{\text{grams per mole of acid}}$$

9. Molecules per mole of oleic acid (Avogadro's number, N).

$$N = \frac{\text{molecules of acid in monolayer}}{\text{moles of acid in monolayer}}$$

FOLLOW-UP DISCUSSION

Oleic acid is an organic compound whose formula is $C_{18}H_{34}O_2$. The carbon atoms are arranged in a long chain with the oxygen atoms attached to the carbon atom at the end of the chain as shown in the structural formula at the bottom of this page.

The $-C \overset{O}{\underset{O-H}{\big\langle}}$ group at the end of the chain

is called a *polar group* and is attracted by the water molecules, whereas the long hydrocarbon chain has little attraction for water. Both oleic acid and benzene are relatively immiscible with, and also less dense than water. Thus, when a benzene solution of oleic acid is added to water, the solution spreads rapidly across the surface of the water. The benzene evaporates rapidly leaving a surface film of oleic acid molecules oriented with their polar heads attracted to the water molecules and their hydrocarbon "tails" projecting away from the water as shown at the top of the next page.

When the surface of the water is covered with a monolayer of oleic acid, the molecules of acid are packed so closely together that the hydro-

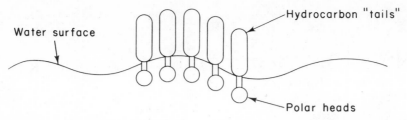

Fig. 2-7 *Assumed orientation of oleic acid molecules in monolayer on surface of water.*

carbon "tails" are practically perpendicular to the surface of the water. We can visualize the acid molecules as a cluster of tightly packed rectangular boxes. Since we know one dimension of the boxes, this assumption enables us to approximate the volume of each box (molecule) and, hence, the number of molecules in the surface film whose volume is known. Chemists have used experimental data to deduce that the length of the oleic-acid molecule is 5.44 times as great as its width or length. For simplicity of calculations, you may assume that the shape of the molecule resembles a rectangular solid. You may wish to make other assumptions as to the shape and relative dimensions of the molecule (for example, a cylinder).

It is apparent that the assumption made and technique used in this experiment limit the results. There are, of course, a number of methods available for determining an accurate value for Avogadro's number. In general, these methods involve the use of techniques and apparatus that are beyond the scope of an elementary course. Some of these methods are discussed in your text.

FOLLOW-UP PROBLEMS

1. What assumptions were made in this experiment in order to arrive at a value for Avogadro's number?

2. Itemize the factors which may have contributed to an inaccurate value for Avogadro's number.

3. In the Experiment No. 2-2, assume that your flask contained 0.30 g of oxygen gas. How many molecules of oxygen were in this flask?

4. How many grams of hydrogen would the same flask hold under the same conditions of temperature and pressure? How many molecules of hydrogen would the flask hold under these conditions?

5. (a) Using the correct value for Avogadro's number, calculate the mass of an oxygen molecule. (b) Calculate the mass of one molecule of oleic acid.

6. Use the number of moles of oleic acid calculated in Procedure 16 and the correct value for Avogadro's number to calculate the number of oleic-acid molecules in the monolayer.

7. If 1.00 mole of oleic-acid molecules were closely packed in a monolayer, what would be the diameter of a circular body of water just large enough to contain the monolayer? Base your calculations on the density of oleic acid and the calculated thickness of the film which was arrived at in Procedure 12 of the experiment.

2-4

The Mole—A Chemical Unit

GENERAL DISCUSSION

One of the most important and widely used concepts in chemistry is the *mole*. The word *mole* is derived from Latin and means "heap" or "pile." In chemistry, a mole is a specific mass of a substance and contains a given number of particles. There are 6.02×10^{23} particles in one mole. This number is known as Avogadro's number.

In terms of particles, the concept of the mole is usually applied to atoms, ions, molecules, or electrons. In terms of mass units, the mole is the number of grams numerically equal to the atomic, molecular, or formula mass of a substance. For example, one mole of oxygen atoms has a mass of 16.0 g and is composed of 6.02×10^{23} atoms. One mole of oxygen molecules (O_2) has a mass of 32.0 g and is composed of 6.02×10^{23} molecules. The total number of oxygen atoms in one mole of oxygen molecules is

$$\frac{6.02 \times 10^{23} O_2 \text{ molecules}}{1 \text{ mole of } O_2 \text{ molecules}} \times \frac{2O \text{ atoms}}{1 O_2 \text{ molecule}}$$

$$= \frac{12.04 \times 10^{23} O \text{ atoms}}{1 \text{ mole of } O_2 \text{ molecules}}$$

One mole (formula mass) of sodium chloride has a mass of 58.5 g and contains 6.02×10^{23} sodium ions and 6.02×10^{23} chloride ions.

This discussion suggests that we can count molecules, atoms, or ions of a given substance by measuring their mass and then converting the measured mass into moles.

In Part I of this experiment you will determine the number of atoms on a piece of galvanized iron (zinc-coated iron) and approximate the thickness in atoms of the coating. The procedure involves measuring and weighing the galvanized iron before and after removing the zinc coating. Knowledge of the masses of zinc and iron will enable you to calculate the relative number of moles and

of atoms of the two metals in the piece of galvanized iron. By using the known radius of a zinc atom and making the simplifying assumption that the zinc atoms in the coating are stacked directly over one another, you can approximate the thickness of the coating in atoms.

In Part II of the experiment you will observe and calculate the mass of one mole of several different substances and then observe and/or calculate their volumes and densities.

OBJECTIVES

1. To understand the mole concept.
2. To learn the relationships between moles, grams, molecules, and atoms.
3. To determine the ratio of zinc atoms to iron atoms in a piece of galvanized iron.

MATERIALS

Galvanized iron sheet, 150-ml or 250-ml beaker, 6-M hydrochloric acid, 2 graduated cylinders, mercury, sucrose, sodium chloride.

PROCEDURE

Part I · Mass of Zinc Coating on Galvanized Iron

1. Obtain a square or rectangular piece of galvanized iron which is 2 to 3 cm on an edge. Measure its length, width, and mass as precisely as your measuring instruments permit. Record data in Table I.

2. Place the metal in a 150-ml or 250-ml beaker and add about 25 ml of dilute 6-M hydrochloric acid. If necessary, warm gently to start the reaction. Cease warming as soon as a rapid evolution of bubbles is observed. When the reaction has reached the stage where only a few bubbles of gas are being evolved, remove the metal. The more

Table I   Ratio of Zinc to Iron Atoms in Galvanized Iron

Length of galvanized iron	
Width of galvanized iron	
Mass of galvanized iron	
Mass of iron core	
Mass of zinc coating (2 sides)	
Atomic mass of iron	
Moles of iron	
Atomic mass of zinc	
Moles of zinc in coating (2 sides)	
Mole ratio of zinc to iron	
Atoms of zinc on 2 sides	
Atoms of iron	
Ratio of zinc to iron atoms	
Mass of zinc on one side	
Density of zinc	7.14 g/ml
Volume of zinc on one side	
Thickness of zinc coating (cm)	
Thickness of zinc coating	
Thickness of zinc coating in atoms	
Mass of a zinc atom (g)	

reactive zinc has then been removed. Rinse the metal with water and dry it well.

3. Weigh and record the mass of the iron core.

4. Make the calculations necessary to complete Table I. Use the data in the table to approximate the mass of a single zinc atom in grams. In order to approximate the thickness of the zinc coating in atoms assume that the atoms are stacked directly one above another. (Actually they are stacked more like cannon balls.) Assume that the diameter of a zinc atom is 2.66 Ångstrom units.

Part II · Relative Masses, Volumes, and Densities of One Mole of Substances

5. On the reagent shelf, find one graduated cylinder containing one mole of water and another cylinder containing one mole of mercury. Record in Table II the physical phase, the color, and the volume of both of these substances. Calculate and record the mass and number of atoms of Hg, and the mass and number of molecules of water in the respective samples. Use the mass and volume of 1 mole of each substance to calculate their densities.

6. Two beakers on the reagent shelf contain respectively, one mole of sucrose (sugar) and one mole of NaCl (salt). Record the physical phase and color of each of these substances. Calculate and record the mass and number of molecules in one mole of sucrose. Record the grams in one formula mass of NaCl and the number of moles of Na^+ and Cl^- ions in one formula mass of NaCl.

Table II   The Mole and Its Relationship to Other Units

Substance	Physical Phase	Color	Units which Compose Solid, Liquid, or Gas	Total Number of Units in 1 Mole of Substance	Mass of Mole of Substance	Volume of 1 Mole of Substance (Room Cond.)	Density at Room Conditions
1 mole of O_2			molecules				
1 mole of Hg			atoms				
1 mole of $C_{12}H_{22}O_{11}$ Sucrose			molecules			215 ml	
1 mole of NaCl			Na^+ ions			27.0 ml	
			Cl^- ions				

FOLLOW-UP DISCUSSION

In Part I of this experiment you interpreted the quantities of zinc and iron involved in terms of atoms, and in Part II you interpreted observed quantities of several substances in terms of atoms, molecules, and ions. Scientists are always interested in explaining the macroscopic properties of aggregates in terms of the behavior of submicroscopic particles which compose the observable aggregate. In Table II we identified the units which compose the different solids and liquids which you examined. Various methods, which will be discussed later, can be used to identify the nature of the particles which compose an observable aggregate. Experiments show that, in general, substances such as NaCl, KBr, and NH_4NO_3 which we classify as *salts* or *ionic crystals* are composed of an aggregate of positive and negative particles called ions. Most pure substances, which at ordinary temperatures and pressures exist as gases or liquids are aggregates composed of molecules. There are, of course, many solid organic substances such as carbohydrates, proteins, and fats which are composed of molecules. In general, we think of metals and macromolecular substances such as diamonds as consisting of an aggregate of atoms. It is a good idea to become acquainted with the nature of the particles which compose the aggregates you encounter in this course. Such background information helps you to classify substances, to interpret their properties, and to understand their behavior.

The galvanized iron you used in Part I consists of an iron core sandwiched between two very thin layers of zinc metal. Both zinc and iron react with hydrochloric acid. Zinc is more reactive, so that the rate at which gas is liberated from the acid can be used to determine the point at which only iron remains.

The rather sudden cessation of rapid bubbling serves as an indicator that all the zinc has reacted. The reaction of both zinc and iron with hydrochloric acid are examples of what are sometimes called "displacement" reactions.

Balanced equations are useful devices for conveying both qualitative and quantitative information related to a chemical reaction. The equation for the reaction between zinc and hydrochloric acid is

$$Zn(s) + 2HCl(aq) \rightarrow ZnCl_2(aq) + H_2(g)$$

zinc   hydrochloric   zinc   hydrogen
acid   chloride

The notations in parentheses indicate the physical phase of the substance. The designations are (s) for solid, (1) for liquid, (g) for gas, and (aq) for aqueous (water) solutions of solutes.

It may be seen that the above displacement reaction consists of a free element (Zn) displacing an element (H) combined in a compound. The products are a different compound ($ZnCl_2$) and a different element in its free elemental state (H_2). Zinc chloride is an example of a salt. Almost all salts exist as ions in water solution. It would be more accurate, therefore, to write the formula of the salt showing the ions that are actually present in the solution. Experiments show that acids such as hydrochloric (HCl), nitric (HNO_3), and sulfuric (H_2SO_4) also exist as ions in aqueous solution and should be shown as ions in equations.

Following this convention, the ionic equation for the reaction between zinc and hydrochloric acid is written

$$Zn(s) + 2H^+(aq) + 2Cl^-(aq) \rightarrow$$
$$Zn^{2+}(aq) + 2Cl^-(aq) + H_2(g)$$

It can be seen from the above equation that chloride ions do not enter the reaction. They can be deleted from the equation. The remaining *net ionic equation* is

$$Zn(s) + 2H^+(aq) \rightarrow Zn^{2+}(aq) + H_2(g)$$

This equation shows that the reaction is between zinc metal and hydrogen ions, forming zinc ions and hydrogen gas. The chloride ions are nonparticipating "spectators" in the system. Note that the total number of atoms represented on the reactant (left) side of the equation equals the total number of atoms represented on the product (right) side of the equation. Also, the net ionic charge is the same (2+) on both sides of the equation so that electric balance is achieved. Writing and balancing equations is discussed in Sections 3-1 and 3-2 of *Foundations of Chemistry,* 2nd ed.

FOLLOW-UP QUESTIONS

1. Account for the observation that 7.1 ml of iron contains the same number of atoms as 14.7 ml of mercury.

2. Account for the observation that 18 g of water occupies 18 ml while 200 g of Hg occupies only 14.7 ml.

3. (a) How many grams of NaCl furnish 1 mole of Na^+ ions? (b) How many grams of $BaCl_2$ furnish 1 mole of Cl^- ions?

4. How many carbon atoms are there in one mole of sucrose molecules?

5. Write balanced word, formula, ionic, and net ionic equations for the reaction between iron and hydrochloric acid. The equations are parallel to those for the reaction between zinc and hydrochloric acid.

6. How does the mole ratio of zinc to iron compare with the atomic ratio? Explain.

2-5
Synthesis and Composition of a Compound

GENERAL DISCUSSION

All forms of matter are composed of chemical elements. Elements cannot be further decomposed by ordinary chemical means, but they can be chemically combined, forming compounds. One of the simplest types of compounds is the *binary* (two element) compound, sometimes formed when a metallic element chemically reacts with a nonmetallic element. This reaction is called a *combination* or *synthesis reaction.*

The binary compound formed when a metal combines with a nonmetal is named by first stating the name of the metal. The second part of the name is obtained by adding the suffix *-ide* to the stem of the nonmetal's name. For example, the compound composed of magnesium and oxygen is named magnesium oxide.

Each element has certain fixed combining capacities when it reacts with another element. These combining capacities may be determined by either synthetic or analytic methods. In the analytic method a known mass of a binary compound is decomposed and the mass of one of the elements obtained by the decomposition is determined. The difference between the mass of the original compound and that of one element equals the mass of the second element. These data furnish the mass ratio of the two elements in the compound. The mass percentage of each element in the compound can be determined from this ratio. It will be shown later that this ratio may also be used to determine the ratio in which the atoms of the two elements are present. This ratio can be used to construct the simplest formula of the compound.

In this experiment you use a *synthetic* method to determine the composition of a compound. You start with a fixed mass of magnesium metal which reacts with an excess of oxygen from the atmosphere. The product formed is magnesium oxide.

The mass of oxygen which combines with a fixed mass of magnesium can be determined by subtracting the mass of the metal from the mass of the magnesium oxide formed. The success of this procedure requires good technique on the part of the experimenter. You may wish to refer to Section 2-12 in *Foundations of Chemistry,* 2nd ed., before going any further.

OBJECTIVES

1. To synthesize a compound and compare its properties with those of the elements from which it is formed.

2. To determine the composition of the compound in terms of the masses and mass percentages of the elements of which it is composed.

3. To understand the Law of Definite Proportions.

4. To observe changes which occur during a chemical reaction.

5. To learn to express a reaction in terms of a simple equation.

6. To gain insight into the meaning of chemical formulas.

MATERIALS

Magnesium ribbon, crucible and cover, pipestem triangle, ring stand, burner, balance, tongs, glass stirring rod.

PROCEDURE

1. Examine and record the properties of the two reactants listed in Table I.

2. Obtain a piece of magnesium ribbon with a mass of about 0.5 g. Your instructor will tell you the approximate length to use (usually 70–75 cm of ribbon). Buff it free of any corrosion with steel wool. Wind the ribbon around a dime or penny and form it into a hollow ball. Remove the coin.

Table I   Properties of Reactants and Product

Substance	Element or Compound	Metal or Nonmetal	Physical Phase (solid, liquid, gas)	Color	Combustibility	Symbol or Formula
Magnesium						
Oxygen						
Magnesium oxide						

3. Heat a clean crucible and its cover with a hot flame for a few minutes to drive off any volatile material. Cool and weigh to the nearest 0.001 g if possible. Record the data in Table II.

Table II   Composition of Magnesium Oxide

1. Mass of crucible, cover, and magnesium	
2. Mass of crucible and cover	
3. Mass of magnesium used	
4. Mass of crucible, cover, and product	
5. Mass of crucible plus cover (Item 2)	
6. Mass of compound formed	
7. Mass of magnesium used (Item 3)	
8. Mass of oxygen in compound	
9. Percentage of oxygen in compound	
10. Percentage of magnesium in compound	
11. Average value obtained by class (Mg)	
12. Percentage deviation of your value from the average (Mg)	
13. Percentage deviation from theoretically calculated value	

4. Add the magnesium ball to the crucible and then weigh the crucible, lid, and contents to the nearest 0.001 g.

5. Place the crucible, cover, and contents on a clay triangle resting on a ring. For optimum results, it is necessary that the magnesium burn very slowly, and that the finely divided, white magnesium oxide smoke be kept from escaping. This can be accomplished by heating the bottom of the crucible and lifting the cover only momentarily to allow a fresh supply of air to enter the combustion chamber.

6. Begin by holding the crucible cover with a pair of tongs while you heat the bottom of the crucible until the magnesium ignites. At this moment, place the cover on the crucible. After a short interval lift the cover and allow enough air to enter the crucible to again ignite the magnesium. Immediately replace the cover. Repeat this procedure until the magnesium no longer ignites when you raise the cover.

7. At this point adjust the cover so that most of the crucible opening is covered but there is enough gap to allow a steady flow of air into the crucible. Heat with a hot flame for a few minutes. Allow to cool.

8. Pulverize the contents of the crucible with a solid glass stirring rod. Be sure that no powder sticks to the rod. Add 5 to 10 drops of water to the product, replace the cover and heat gently for 3 or 4 minutes. Carefully note the odor coming from the crucible. Then heat strongly for another 3 or 4 minutes. (This step will be explained briefly in the Follow-up Discussion section.) Allow crucible and contents to cool.

9. Weigh the crucible and contents to the nearest 0.001 g. Examine the product and record its properties in Table I. Read the Follow-up Discussion and make the calculations required to complete Table II. Record your experimental percentage of magnesium in the space provided on the blackboard. This tabulation enables you to compare your results with those of your classmates. The instructor will determine the arithmetical mean (average). Record this average value in Table II.

10. Clean the crucible. It may be necessary to

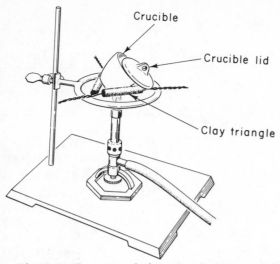

Crucible

Crucible lid

Clay triangle

Fig. 2-8   Proper technique for drying a crucible.

warm a dilute acid in the crucible for a few minutes. Then pour out the acid, rinse with water, and scrub the crucible with an abrasive cleanser.

FURTHER EXPERIMENTATION

Devise an experiment for determining the composition of a compound formed by the reaction between copper and sulfur, iron and sulfur, or lead and sulfur. Note that experiments which involve the burning of sulfur should be carried out under a fume hood.

FOLLOW-UP DISCUSSION

The percentage of magnesium should be, within experimental error, the same for all samples of magnesium oxide which were synthesized. The reaction which you actually observed is the result of an interaction between countless numbers of atoms, each far too small to be directly observed. However, the constancy of the mass relationships between the two elements in the compound suggests that the atoms of each element have a definite mass and react in a definite ratio. This ratio is expressed in terms of a formula. The formula for magnesium oxide (MgO) reveals that magnesium and oxygen atoms combine in a 1:1 ratio.

The individual atoms of different elements

have been assigned relative masses which are based on the mass of a standard carbon atom. These relative masses, expressed in atomic mass units (amu), were formerly determined by using data similar to that obtained in this experiment.

Very precise determinations of atomic masses are now made by instrumental methods. The known atomic masses listed in tables may be used to determine the ratios in which atoms combine, and hence, the simplest formulas of compounds. Atomic masses are relative and are based on the standard carbon-12 atom. On this scale, oxygen and magnesium atoms have atomic masses of 16.0 and 24.3 amu, respectively. Dividing the experimentally determined combining mass of magnesium and oxygen by their respective atomic masses gives the ratio in which the atoms combine. Using hypothetical experimental data, the ratio of magnesium to oxygen atoms in the compound formed by the reaction of 1.020 g of Mg and 0.670 g of O is

$$1.020 \text{ g Mg} \times \frac{1 \text{ mole Mg}}{24.3 \text{ g Mg}} = 0.0420 \text{ mole Mg}$$

$$0.670 \text{ g O} \times \frac{1 \text{ mole O}}{16.0 \text{ g O}} = 0.0420 \text{ mole O}$$

or a 1 to 1 mole ratio.

The known atomic masses can also be used to calculate the formula masses of compounds. For example, the formula mass for MgO is 24 amu + 16 amu = 40 amu. The known, definite mass composition of the compound allows us to calculate its percentage composition. The mass percentage of magnesium in the compound is

$$\frac{24}{40} \times 100 = 60\%$$

expressed to two significant figures.

Chemical reactions may be represented by equations which represent the reactants and products by words or symbols. The reaction which you investigated may be represented by word and formula equations.

$$\text{magnesium} + \text{oxygen} \rightarrow \quad \text{magnesium oxide}$$
$$2Mg \quad + \quad O_2 \rightarrow \quad\quad 2MgO \quad \textbf{Eq. 1}$$

Note that a coefficient of 2 is placed in front of the formula for magnesium oxide. This is added in the process of balancing the equation so that it conforms to the Law of Conservation of Matter. You can verify this law by weighing a flashbulb, firing it, and then reweighing it. The reaction within the bulb is the one described in Equation 1.

Equation 1 would convey more qualitative information if the overall energy change were noted. On the basis of your observations, you should be able to state than a large amount of energy was transferred to the surroundings during the course of the reaction. Using the symbol q to represent heat, Eq. 1 could be written

$$Mg + O_2 \rightarrow 2MgO + q$$

The positive value for q on the right hand side of the equation indicates that heat was transferred to the surroundings. The quantity of heat required to initiate the reaction was small in comparison to that evolved by the reaction.

Magnesium also reacts with nitrogen in the air forming magnesium nitride

$$3Mg + N_2 \rightarrow Mg_3N_2$$

The white powder obtained by burning magnesium is a mixture of MgO and Mg_3N_2. Water was added to convert Mg_3N_2 into MgO (Proc. 8).

$$Mg_3N_2 + 3H_2O \rightarrow 3MgO + 2NH_3(g)$$

In this way, all of the magnesium appears in the form of MgO.

FOLLOW-UP QUESTIONS

1. Does oxygen burn? Does it support combustion of other materials? Cite evidence for your answers.

2. The elements calcium, barium, strontium, zinc, cadmium, and others may combine with oxygen in the same atomic ratio as magnesium. Write the formulas and names of the oxides of these elements.

3. Explain in general terms how a homogeneous mixture such as a true solution differs from a homogeneous compound such as the magnesium oxide synthesized in this experiment.

4. Use the average of the values obtained by the class for the masses of magnesium and oxygen in the compound and calculate the atomic mass for magnesium. Assume magnesium and oxygen atoms react in a 1 to 1 ratio and that the standard for atomic masses is oxygen equals 16. Show calculation and result.

5. Use the same experimental masses to determine the ratio in which the magnesium and oxygen atoms combine. This time use the accurate atomic masses given in the table on the back cover of the manual. Since atoms generally combine in the ratio of small whole numbers, round off the numbers in your ratio to whole numbers. Write the experimentally determined formula for the compound.

6. Which had the greater energy content, the magnesium oxide or the two reactants from which it was formed? Give a reason for your answer.

7. List the possible sources of error in your determination. If possible, indicate how they would have affected the experimental percentage of magnesium which you reported.

8. You may have noted a distinctive odor when you added water to the crucible in Procedure 8. Write the name and formula of the gas responsible for this odor.

2-6
Properties of Acids and Bases

GENERAL DISCUSSION

Different substances may be distinguished from each other by the differences in their properties. When a number of different compounds have several common properties they are often classified for convenience as a distinct type of compound. Two important types of compounds are the acids and the bases. All acids have common properties and all bases have common properties.

The observable properties which describe the experimental behavior of acids (or bases) constitute an operational definition of an acid (or base). By studying the formulas, atomic and molecular structures, and reactions of substances which qualify as acids or bases under our operational definition, we can develop conceptual definitions for them. Conceptual definitions help to explain why certain substances behave in a common fashion. These definitions will help us to classify a substance as an acid or base without testing it in the laboratory.

In this experiment you study the behavior of some common acids and bases. The data which you record will enable you to develop operational definitions for acids and bases. In addition, we shall examine the formulas for the substances you use and develop a simple conceptual definition. More complete and useful conceptual definitions will be developed later in the course when your chemical background is greater.

OBJECTIVES

1. To determine the properties common to most acids and develop an operational definition for an acid.

2. To determine the properties common to most bases and develop an operational definition of a base.

3. To learn the names and formulas of a number of common acids and bases.

4. To develop a limited conceptual definition of an acid and base.

5. To learn to recognize compounds commonly referred to as salts.

MATERIALS

1-M solutions of sulfuric, hydrochloric, and nitric acids, test tubes, litmus papers (red and blue), stirring rod, calcium carbonate, splints (wood), zinc, magnesium ribbon, 1-M solutions of sodium, potassium, and calcium hydroxides, phenolphthalein, 1-M solutions of sodium hydroxide and hydrochloric acid, graduated cylinder, evaporating dish, beaker, electric conductivity apparatus, 0.1-M solutions of acetic acid, sodium chloride, sodium sulfate, sodium nitrate, sodium acetate, potassium nitrate, calcium nitrate, ammonia water, ammonium chloride. Optional: Hoffman, or other, electrolysis apparatus.

PROCEDURE

1. Pour approximately 5 ml each of 1-M hydrochloric, 1-M sulfuric, and 1-M nitric acid into separate test tubes. Separately test the reaction of each acid with blue litmus paper by placing a stirring rod in the solution and then touching the rod to the litmus paper. Record your observations in Table I.

2. Add a few large crystals (amount equal to the size of a large pea) of calcium carbonate to each of the test tubes and test the chemical properties of any gas which is evolved by holding a burning splint in the mouth of the test tube. This gas is carbon dioxide.

3. Empty and rinse the test tubes and again pour approximately 5 ml of each of the 1-M acids into separate test tubes. Drop a small piece of zinc metal into each test tube. Test any gas evolved with a burning splint. See Follow-up Discussion and write a formula for each gas evolved.

Table I   Properties of Acids

Name of Solution	Formula of Solute	Effect of Litmus	Reaction with Active Metals		Reaction with Carbonates	Effect on Properties of Bases	Electric Conductivity
			Zinc	Magnesium			
Hydrochloric acid	HCl						
Sulfuric acid	H_2SO_4						
Nitric acid	HNO_3						

4. Repeat Procedure (3) using a coiled 7-cm piece of magnesium ribbon instead of zinc.

5. Rinse out the test tubes and pour approximately 5 ml each of solutions of sodium, potassium, and calcium hydroxides into separate test tubes. These compounds form water solutions of bases.

6. Test each of the bases with red litmus paper. Record your observations in Table II.

7. Add one or two drops of phenolphthalein indicator to each of the test tubes and record your observations.

8. Place a drop of each base on your fingers and rub your fingers together. Record the feel as one of the physical properties of bases. Rinse your hand with water.

9. Place about 5 ml of 1-M sodium hydroxide solution in a porcelain evaporating dish and add 2 drops of phenolphthalein indicator.

10. While stirring constantly, add about 3 ml of a 1-M hydrochloric acid solution to the base.

11. While continuing to stir, add the acid slowly, drop by drop, from a clean dropper until one drop of the acid turns the mixture from pink to colorless. This point of the reaction is known as the indicator endpoint.

12. Pour a little of the mixture into a clean beaker. Evaporate to dryness and when cool taste the residue. Rinse your mouth. Record taste in Table III.

13. Test the remainder of the mixture in the evaporating dish with red litmus. Record your observation in Table III. Repeat, using blue litmus.

14. Moisten your finger with the mixture and rub your fingers together. Record whether the mixture has the feel of the base.

Table II   Properties of Bases

Name of Solution	Formula of Solute	Effect on Litmus	Effect on Phenolphthalein	Feel	Effect on Properties of Acids	Electric Conductivity
Sodium hydroxide	NaOH					
Potassium hydroxide	KOH					
Calcium hydroxide	$Ca(OH)_2$					

Table III Properties of Solution After Acid-Base Reaction

Effect on red litmus	
Feel	
Reaction with active metal (zinc or magnesium)	
Taste of residue after evaporation	
Electric conductivity	
Formula of solute	

15. Add a piece of zinc to the mixture. Record whether a gas is being evolved.

16. Record the effect that a base has on the properties of an acid in Table II. Record the effect that an acid has on the base in Table I.

17. **Teacher demonstration.** Use an apparatus similar to that shown in Fig. 2-9 to test the electric conductivity of the solutions listed in Tables I, II, and IV. Lower the electrodes into a beaker containing the solutions. Observe the brightness of the light. If a bright light is observed, record that the solution is a good conductor. If the light glows only dimly, then record that the solution is a poor conductor. If the light does not glow at all, record that the solution is a nonconductor. Record the conductivity of the sodium chloride solution in Table III.

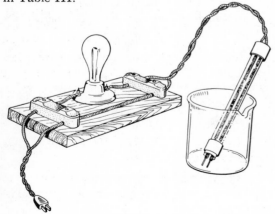

Fig. 2-9 Conductivity apparatus.

Table IV Conductivity of Acid, Base, and Salt Solutions

Solution	Light Glow	Conductivity of Solution
Distilled water		
0.1-M HC$_2$H$_3$O$_2$ (acetic acid)		
0.1-M NaCl (salt)		
0.1-M Na$_2$SO$_4$ (salt)		
0.1-M NaNO$_3$ (salt)		
0.1-M NaC$_2$H$_3$O$_2$ (salt)		
0.1-M KNO$_3$ (salt)		
0.1-M Ca (NO$_3$)$_2$ (salt)		
0.1-M NH$_3$ solution (base)		
0.1-M NH$_4$Cl (salt)		

FURTHER EXPERIMENTATION

Use a Hoffman, or other electrolysis apparatus, and a direct current to electrolyze a 3-M solution of hydrochloric acid. Collect, test, and identify the products. Use these data to help identify the particles which carry the electric charge in the solution.

FOLLOW-UP DISCUSSION

Acids, bases, and solutions of many other substances conduct an electric current. The electrolysis of a hydrochloric acid solution (suggested as an extension of this experiment), or of melted sodium chloride indicates that electrically charged atoms (called ions) are the charge-carriers in the solution or in the melted salt. During the electrolysis of a hydrochloric acid solution, chlorine gas is evolved at the positive electrode. This suggests that chloride ions must carry a negative charge, since they are attracted to the positive electrode where they are converted to chlorine atoms. The atoms combine and form chlorine molecules (Cl_2). In the electrolysis of melted sodium chloride, metallic sodium is formed at the negative electrode. This suggests that sodium ions carry a positive charge, since they are attracted to the negative electrode and converted to sodium atoms.

Pure water, pure liquid hydrogen chloride (HCl), and solid sodium chloride do not conduct a current. This suggests that many solids, liquids, and gases interact with water and form ions and hence, a conducting solution. This interaction is called *ionization* if ions form by reaction with water. The separation of ions from one another in a solvent is called *dissociation*.

In the **FOLLOW-UP QUESTIONS** section you are asked to develop operational definitions for acids and bases on the basis of the experimental data. Since the formulas of all the substances you classified as acids contain the element hydrogen, we might assume that hydrogen ions (H^+) are responsible for acid properties. Similarly, on the basis of the data in Table II we might assume that hydroxide ions (OH^-) are responsible for basic properties. It turns out that hydroxide ions *are* responsible for basic properties. It can, however, be shown that in water, hydrogen ions always combine with the polar water molecules and form hydrated hydrogen ions

$$H^+ + H_2O \rightarrow H_3O^+$$

The hydrated hydrogen ions (H_3O^+) are called hydronium ions. Thus it is the hydronium ions that impart acid characteristics to a solution. For simplicity, hydrogen ions (H^+) are often used to represent H_3O^+ ions in equations. We now have enough information to develop a simple conceptual definition of an acid or a base.

An acid is a substance which dissolves in water and yields a larger number of H_3O^+ ions than OH^- ions. A base is a substance which dissolves in water and yields a larger number of OH^- ions than H_3O^+ ions.

The data in Tables I and IV show that not all acids conduct electricity to the same degree. Acids which form highly conductive solutions are called *strong* acids. Acids which form poorly conductive solutions are called *weak* acids. Thus, the strength of an acid is determined by the extent to which it forms ions. The same principle applies to bases.

In addition to those tested in this experiment, these strong acids are often used: perchloric acid ($HClO_4$), hydrobromic acid (HBr), and hydriodic acid (HI). These three strong acids plus those you tested in this experiment constitute the majority of strong acids which we shall encounter. You may consider any other acid to be a weak acid unless we specifically state that it is strong. For our purposes assume that, in aqueous solutions, strong acids and bases are completely dissociated into ions and thus do not exist in molecular form.

All hydroxides formed by the elements in Group IA may be classified as strong bases. Many metallic hydroxides are insoluble in water.

In Table IV we identified aqueous ammonia (NH_3 aq) as a base. According to our tentative definition of a base, therefore, NH_3 reacts with water and forms hydroxide ions. Tests show that the solution also contains ammonium ions and ammonia molecules. The equation for the reaction, therefore, is

$$NH_3(g) + HOH \rightleftharpoons NH_4^+(aq) + OH^-(aq)$$

The limited conductivity of this solution suggests that there are relatively few ions so the reaction occurs only to a limited extent. The double arrow indicates that the reaction is reversible and that in aqueous ammonia there are ammonium ions, hydroxide ions, ammonia and water molecules.

The data in Table III reveal that during an acid-base reaction both the acid and the base lose their identifying characteristics. This type of reaction is sometimes termed a *neutralization* reaction. The product of this reaction is water in which the ions of a salt are dissolved. The equation for the acid-base reaction which you carried out is

$$HCl + NaOH \rightarrow NaCl + HOH$$

We have demonstrated that HCl, NaOH, and NaCl exist entirely as ions in dilute aqueous solution. A better way to represent the reaction is to show the ions that are present in the system. The ionic equation is

$$H^+(aq) + Cl^-(aq) + Na^+(aq) + OH^-(aq) \rightarrow$$
$$Na^+(aq) + Cl^-(aq) + H_2O(\ell)$$

A still better method is to use a *net ionic equation* to show only the ions that participate in the reaction. It can be seen that $Cl^-(aq)$ and $Na^+(aq)$ do not undergo any change. These so-called unreactive ions are not shown in the net ionic equation which is written as

$$H^+(aq) + OH^-(aq) \rightarrow H_2O(\ell)$$

The data in Table IV show that salt solutions are good conductors of an electric current. We may assume that, in water, most salts dissolve and form ionic solutions. Additional data reveal that salt crystals are also composed of ions. The neutralization reaction by which water is formed and the ions of a salt are left may be used as the basis for identifying a salt. That is, a salt may be described as the product other than water, formed when an acid reacts with a base. A salt may be viewed as a derivative of an acid and a base reaction. The positive ion is derived from the base "parent" and the negative ion of the salt is derived from the acid "parent." Thus, NaCl may be described as the salt of sodium hydroxide and hydrochloric acid. Salts may be formed as a product in reactions between many different substances. For example, the reaction between hydrochloric acid and sodium carbonate produces a salt, carbon dioxide, and water.

$$2HCl(aq) + Na_2CO_3(s) \rightarrow$$
$$\text{acid} \qquad\qquad \textbf{salt}$$

$$2NaCl(aq) + CO_2(g) + H_2O(\ell)$$
$$\textbf{salt} \qquad \text{carbon} \qquad \textbf{water}$$
$$\qquad\qquad \text{dioxide}$$

It is rather difficult to define a salt rigorously. Perhaps the best conceptual definition we can give at this point is that *salts are generally compounds composed of positive and negative ions.*

The data in Table I suggest that metals react with acids and produce gases. The gases may be identified by their properties. If the gas is colorless and "pops" when ignited in the presence of air, then you may assume that it is hydrogen (H_2). If it is colored and there is no "explosion", you may assume it is nitrogen dioxide (NO_2). Additional tests involving still other acids and metals

show that certain metals, sometimes called *active metals,* participate in so-called displacement reactions with all the familiar acids except nitric or perchloric acids, and yield hydrogen gas. Nitric and perchloric acids are powerful oxidizing acids which react with almost all metals and yield gases other than hydrogen as products. Active metals can be identified by referring to the activity series of the elements. This simplified series is shown and explained below. A more detailed version will be developed later in the course.

Activity Series

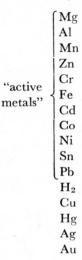

"active metals"
Mg
Al
Mn
Zn
Cr
Fe
Cd
Co
Ni
Sn
Pb
H_2
Cu
Hg
Ag
Au

In theory, the general rule is that any element causes the formation (or precipitation) of any element which lies below it in the series from a dissolved compound containing ions of the lower element. For example, Cu causes Ag to form from a solution of silver nitrate. The products are silver and a solution of copper nitrate.

$$Cu(s) + 2AgNO_3(aq) \rightarrow$$
$$2Ag(s) + Cu(NO_3)_2(aq)$$

FOLLOW-UP QUESTIONS

1. Write an operational definition for an acid.

2. Write an operational definition for a base.

3. Write word and formula equations for reactions between the following pairs of substances in

solution: (a) potassium hydroxide and sulfuric acid, (b) calcium hydroxide and nitric acid, (c) sodium carbonate and sulfuric acid, (d) magnesium and sulfuric acid.

4. Name and write the formulas for six strong acids, four strong bases, one weak acid, and one weak base. Refer to Table IV and the Follow-up Discussion section as needed.

5. Name and write the formulas for the base "parent" and the acid "parent" of the following salts: (a) potassium nitrate (KNO_3), (b) calcium sulfate ($CaSO_4$), (c) barium chloride ($BaCl_2$), (d) sodium bromide ($NaBr$), (e) magnesium iodide (MgI_2).

6. Write the formulas and charges of the ions which are primarily responsible for the flow of current through solutions of a hydrobromic acid, (b) nitric acid, (c) sulfuric acid, (d) calcium hydroxide, and (e) melted potassium iodide.

7. Predict whether or not: (a) silver reacts with hydrogen ions from hydrochloric acid, (b) zinc reacts with hydrogen ions from sulfuric acid, and (c) zinc reacts with silver ions from silver nitrate. If your prediction is affirmative, write an equation for the reaction.

8. In Tables I and II, are the solute particles, molecules or ions? Write the formulas for the solute particles in each solution.

3-1
Mole Relationships in a Decomposition Reaction

GENERAL DISCUSSION

One of the most important applications of the mole concept is for expressing mole relationships between substances in a chemical reaction. To illustrate this, let us consider the reaction between hydrogen and oxygen forming water.

$$2H_2 + O_2 \rightarrow 2H_2O$$

In this equation, the formulas of all participants represent molecules. The coefficients represent the relative numbers of each kind of molecule involved in the reaction. The number of molecules is directly proportional to the number of moles. Therefore, we can say that 2 moles of hydrogen (molecules) react with 1 mole of oxygen (molecules) and form 2 moles of water (molecules). Each mole may be expressed in terms of a gram-molecular mass. Converting the gram-molecular mass ratio (mole ratio) into gram ratios shows that 4.0 g of hydrogen react with 32.0 g of oxygen and form 36.0 g of water. This discussion is summarized in the equations below

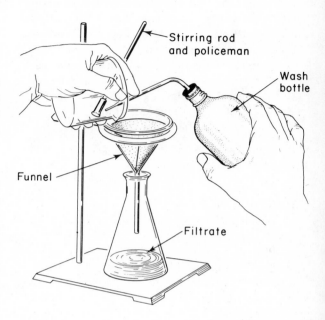

Fig. 3-1 Proper technique for transferring a precipitate from a beaker to filter paper. "Policeman" is for scrubbing particles of precipitate from walls of beaker.

Equation:	$2H_2$	$+ O_2$	$\rightarrow 2H_2O$
Moles:	2	$+ 1$	$\rightarrow 2$
Molecules:	$2(6.02 \times 10^{23})$	$+ 1(6.02 \times 10^{23})$	$\rightarrow 2(6.02 \times 10^{23})$
Grams:	4.0	$+ 32.0$	$\rightarrow 36.0$
Atoms:	$4(6.02 \times 10^{23})$	$+ 2(6.02 \times 10^{23})$	$\rightarrow 6(6.02 \times 10^{23})$

It can be seen that the total mass of product is the same as the sum of the mass of the reactants. Also, the total number of atoms of product is equal to the total number of all reactant atoms, in agreement with the Law of Conservation of Matter. Note that the total number of moles or total number of molecules of product do not necessarily equal those of the reactants. This is because atoms rearrange themselves into different combinations during a reaction.

This experiment is designed to illustrate mole relationships in chemical reactions. You will thermally decompose sodium bicarbonate (baking soda). The products are sodium carbonate, water, and carbon dioxide. From the experimentally determined masses of the sodium bicarbonate and sodium carbonate you will be able to determine the mole ratio and the coefficients in a balanced equation.

OBJECTIVES

1. To become acquainted with the use of the mole concept to express mole relationships between substances participating in a chemical reaction.

2. To determine the mole relationship between substances in a chemical decomposition reaction.

3. To convert sodium bicarbonate into sodium carbonate and then determine mass and mole relationships.

MATERIALS

Bunsen burner, ring stand, balance, nickel crucible, sodium hydrogen carbonate (bicarbonate), pipestem triangle, crucible tongs.

PROCEDURE

1. Weigh a nickel crucible to the nearest 0.01 g. Record data in Table I.

2. Place 2 to 3 g of $NaHCO_3$ in the crucible and weigh crucible and contents to nearest 0.01 g.

3. Place the crucible on a clay triangle which rests on an iron ring. Heat gently for 5 or 6 minutes. Then increase the intensity of the flame and heat very strongly for another 3 or 4 minutes. Cool crucible to room temperature and weigh.

Table I   Mole Relationships in Chemical Reactions

Mass of crucible + $NaHCO_3$	
Mass of crucible	
Mass of $NaHCO_3$	
Mass of crucible + Na_2CO_3 (after heating)	
Mass of crucible (item 2)	
Mass of Na_2CO_3	
Moles of $NaHCO_3$	
Moles of Na_2CO_3	
Mole ratio: $NaHCO_3/Na_2CO_3$	
Simplest whole-number mole ratio	

4. If time permits, reheat the sample strongly for another 5 minutes. Cool and reweigh. This second heating and cooling allows you to determine whether or not the sample has been completely decomposed.

5. Read the Follow-up Discussion and Follow-up Questions, and make the calculations required to complete Table I.

FOLLOW-UP DISCUSSION

In this experiment you carried out a reaction that is sometimes referred to as a decomposition reaction. This reaction is characteristic of many thermally unstable compounds. Examples of thermally unstable substances are a number of carbonates and bicarbonates, sulfites, and bisulfites, and compounds containing the element nitrogen. Carbonates decompose and yield carbon dioxide and a simpler compound. For example,

$$CaCO_3 \xrightarrow{\text{heat}} CaO + CO_2$$

The unbalanced expression for the thermal decomposition of $NaHCO_3$ is

$$NaHCO_3 \xrightarrow{\text{heat}} Na_2CO_3 + CO_2 + H_2O$$

You are using your experimental data to supply the proper coefficients for this expression.

FOLLOW-UP QUESTIONS

1. Assume that all of the hydrogen in the $NaHCO_3$ is evolved as H_2O. How many moles of H_2O were formed in your experiment? How does the coefficient of H_2O compare with that of $NaHCO_3$ in the equation for the reaction? Write an equation for the reaction.

2. Use the correct equation for the reaction to calculate the mass of Na_2CO_3 that should have been obtain by decomposing the original $NaHCO_3$. Calculate the percentage deviation between the experimental and the calculated value.

3. List the sources of error and, where possible, indicate how the error affects the result. Consider moisture, volatile and nonvolatile impurities.

4. Write equations for the thermal decomposition of (a) $BaCO_3$, (b) $Ca(HSO_3)_2$, (c) HgO.

3-2
Molarity and Mole Relationships in Precipitation Reactions

GENERAL DISCUSSION

Solutes in solutions react in the same mole and mass ratios as they do in any other state. The ratios in which they react may be determined from an equation. The volume of solution which contains a given quantity of solute may be calculated from the concentration of the solution. One widely used method for expressing the quantity of solute is in terms of the number of moles of solute in one liter of solution. This concentration unit is known as molarity (M). Expressing the definition in an equation we obtain

$$M = \frac{\text{moles of solute}}{\text{volume of solution}(\ell)} \qquad \text{Eq. 1}$$

$$M = \frac{\text{millimoles of solute}}{\text{volume of solution}(\text{ml})}$$

Solving Eq. 1 for volume yields

$$\text{volume of solution } (\ell), V = \frac{\text{moles of solute}}{M} \qquad \text{Eq. 2}$$

Solving Eq. 2 for moles of solute yields

$$\text{moles of solute} = MV(\ell)$$

Thus, we can calculate the volume of solution needed, the moles of solute required, or the molarity of a solution if we know two of the three factors in Eq. 1.

In this experiment you use solutions of known and equal concentration for two reactants. The two reactants are lead nitrate [$Pb(NO_3)_2$] and potassium iodate (KIO_3). Both compounds are ionic crystals (salts) which dissolve and form ionic solutions. In other words, one solution contains aquated lead ions [$Pb^{2+}(aq)$] and aquated nitrate ions [$NO_3^-(aq)$], while the other contains aquated potassium ions [$K^+(aq)$] and aquated iodate ions

[$IO_3^-(aq)$]. When the two solutions are mixed, the force of attraction between the Pb^{2+} ions and IO_3^- ions is greater than the attraction of these ions to the water molecules; thus they combine and form a solid white precipitate of lead iodate.

According to the principles of chemical combination, the lead ions and iodate ions can react only in a fixed ratio, thus forming a compound having a definite composition. If the two reactant ions are not present in the required fixed ratio, one of them will be in excess and the quantity of lead iodate formed will be limited by the one that is not in excess. In other words, for a fixed total volume of the two reacting solutions the maximum quantity of precipitate is obtained when the quantities of the two reactants are present in the mole ratio fixed by the nature of the ions.

For the purpose of this experiment the class is divided into groups and each group is assigned to mix different volumes of each solution but the same total volume is used by all groups. The mass of precipitate obtained is then determined. Because the solutions are of equal concentration (0.250 M), the volume ratio will be equal to the mole ratio of the reactant solutes. Thus, each group of experimenters can associate a fixed mass of product with a volume ratio of reactant solution and a mole ratio of reactant ions. In theory, if there were an unlimited number of student groups using the same total volume of the two solutions, then the group that obtained the greatest mass of precipitate could assume that the volume ratio which it used represented the mole ratio of the reactant ions in the compound (precipitate) and in the equation for the reaction.

Because the experiment involves only a finite number of groups, the results obtained by all of the participating groups are correlated and the *method of continuous variation* will be used to establish mole ratios. This means that each student group is asked to report the volumes of solution used and the mass of lead iodate obtained so that each student can record data from all groups in his own write-up. Each student uses these data to plot mass of precipitate obtained on the ordinate *vs* ml of $Pb(NO_3)_2$ solution used on the abscissa. He then draws two straight lines through the points and uses the volume ratio of solutions to compute the mole ratio of IO_3^-/Pb^{2+} at the point where the lines converge. The experimentally determined mole ratio can then be simplified to a whole-number ratio which should represent the ratio of the coefficients in the balanced equation for the reaction.

OBJECTIVES

1. To discover the mole ratio in which lead ions and iodate ions react and form lead iodate.

2. To react definite volumes of lead nitrate $(0.25\,M)$ and potassium iodate $(0.25\,M)$ and measure the mass of lead iodate precipitate obtained.

3. To improve the student's ability to carry out quantitative procedures in the laboratory.

4. To learn the concept of charge balance in a precipitation reaction.

5. To plot and interpret a graph by the method of continuous variation.

MATERIALS

Solutions of lead nitrate $(0.250\,M)$ and potassium iodate $(0.250\,M)$, burets, balance $(\pm0.01\,g$ sensitivity or better), 50-ml beaker, funnel, filter paper, wash bottle, "policeman" or spatula, acetone or ethanol.

PROCEDURE

1. Dispense from a buret into a 50-ml beaker, without spattering, the volumes of 0.250-M lead

Table I   Mole and Mass Relationships in Precipitation Reactions

Group no.	Vol. KIO_3 (ml)	Vol. $Pb(NO_3)_2$ (ml)	Mass of Paper (mg) Trial I	Mass of Paper (mg) Trial II	Mass of Paper + Precipitate (mg) Trial I	Mass of Paper + Precipitate (mg) Trial II	Mass of Precipitate (mg) Trial I	Mass of Precipitate (mg) Trial II	Volume Ratio of IO_3^- Solution to Pb^{2+} Solution (decimal fraction)
1	19.00	1.00							
2	18.00	2.00							
3	17.00	3.00							
4	16.00	4.00							
5	15.00	5.00							
6	14.00	6.00							
7	12.00	8.00							
8	10.00	10.00							
9	8.00	12.00							
10	6.00	14.00							
11	4.00	16.00							
12	2.00	18.00							

nitrate and 0.250-M potassium iodate assigned by the instructor. The sum of the volumes of the two solutions should be precisely 20.0 ml. Twelve suggested combinations are listed in Table I.

2. Weigh a piece of filter paper to ± 0.01 g or better and then quantitatively transfer the precipitate of lead iodate to this paper. Use a policeman or spatula and the filtrate to aid in transferring all of the precipitate and to wash out the beaker. It is imperative that this procedure be done with extreme care so that essentially *all* of the precipitate is transferred to the filter paper. Any visible traces of precipitate left in the flask or on the spatula introduce a serious error in the results.

3. After the transfer is complete, wash the filter paper and precipitate three or more times with 5- to 10-ml portions of water. Allow to drain completely, discard filtrate, and then wash twice with 5 ml of acetone. Open the filter paper and place on a piece of clean paper towel and allow paper and precipitate to dry for at least 48 hours before attempting to determine the mass of the precipitate.

4. Report the volumes of solutions used to ± 0.1 ml or better, and the mass of precipitate obtained to ± 0.01 g or better as directed by the instructor. Record all data reported by other student groups in your data table.

5. Plot mass in mg of precipitate obtained on the ordinate and volume in ml of lead nitrate solution used on the abscissa.

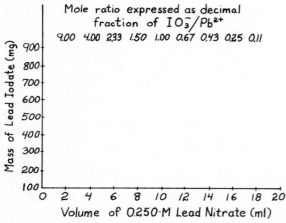

6. Draw two straight lines through the points and determine the point at which they converge. Compute the mole ratio of IO_3^-/Pb^{2+} at this point and simplify to the closest whole-number ratio.

7. Use the whole-number ratio determined in Procedure 6 to write a net ionic equation for the reaction.

FOLLOW-UP DISCUSSION

Although the solutions of $Pb(NO_3)_2$ and KIO_3 were prepared in advance, you should be able to use the concept of molarity and calculate the mass of solute required to prepare a given quantity of each solution. Let us consider the calculations and procedure used by your instructor or his assistant to prepare 0.500 liters of 0.250-M KIO_3 solution. The mass of KIO_3 required is

$$\frac{0.250 \text{ mole } KIO_3}{1.00 \ \ell \text{ solution}} \times 0.500 \ \ell \text{ solution} \times$$
$$\times \frac{214.0 \text{ g } KIO_3}{1 \text{ mole } KIO_3} = 26.8 \text{ g } KIO_3$$

The 26.8 g of KIO_3 is placed in a beaker and dissolved in distilled water. The solution is then transferred quantitatively to a 500-ml volumetric flask and enough distilled water added to reach the etched mark on the neck of the flask.

It is not practical to carry out an experiment such as this every time you wish to write an equation for a reaction. As a result of performing this experiment, however, you should have developed an insight into the principles of atom balance and charge balance as they apply to equations for precipitation reactions and which you can use to write ionic equations for other reactions.

In the next experiment you will have an opportunity to carry out and observe numerous precipitation reactions and to write ionic equations for them based on these principles.

FOLLOW-UP QUESTIONS

1. Calculate the mass of lead nitrate [$Pb(NO_3)_2$] required to prepare 0.250 liters of 0.250-M solution.

2. Calculate the mass of lead iodate that should

be formed theoretically in the experiment conducted by the group that reacted 10.00 ml of 0.250-M lead nitrate with 10.00 ml of 0.25-M potassium iodate. What is the percentage deviation between experimental and calculated value?

3. As a result of experimentally determining the coefficients in the equation for the reaction, what can you conclude about the relationship between the net ionic charge on the reactant side of the equation to that on the product side of the equation? What can you conclude about the number of each kind of atoms shown on the two sides of the equation?

4. What ions are present in the system you studied that are not shown in the net ionic equation for the reaction?

5. Calculate the mass of iron(III) hydroxide that would be produced by the mixing of 25.0 ml of 0.100-M iron(III) nitrate and 30.0 ml of 0.125-M NaOH. Assume that the precipitate has negligible solubility in the resulting mixture.

6. We usually define a 1-molar solution as a solution containing 1 mole of solute per liter of solution. We might also say that a molar solution contains 1 millimole of solute per milliliter of solution. (a) How many millimoles of $Pb(NO_3)_2$ are in a solution containing 10.0 ml of 0.250-M solution? (b) How many mg of $Pb(NO_3)_2$ are in this solution?

7. List some of the sources of error in this experiment.

3-3

Precipitation Reactions—Net Ionic Equations and General Solubility Rules

GENERAL DISCUSSION

The reactions which you carry out in this experiment involve an interaction between positive and negative ions. In many of the reactions the force of attraction between oppositely charged ions is so great that they come together and form a slightly soluble or practically insoluble substance which is called a precipitate.

A chemical reaction may be represented by a chemical equation, a clear, concise method of describing a reaction. Careful observation of the characteristics of the products will help you identify them correctly. This information and knowledge of the name of the reactants will aid you in writing the correct equations for the reactions.

In order to determine which of the products is the precipitate, you will have to know some of the ions which, in general, are found only in soluble compounds. The first part of this experiment is designed to acquaint you with some of these ions and involves only the examination of solutions on the reagent table. After carrying out the indicated reactions in the second part and tabulating the data, you should be able to develop a tentative list of general solubility rules. If materials are available, you will then organize and systematize your data by using a Periodic Table to locate the position of various positive ions that form slightly soluble compounds with selected negative ions.

OBJECTIVES

1. To carry out a series of precipitation reactions and to become acquainted with a number of substances which have very low solubilities in water.
2. To learn to write net ionic equations for precipitation reactions.

3. To develop and learn some general solubility rules.
4. To become familiar with the location in the Periodic Table of some positive ions which form slightly soluble compounds with selected negative ions.

MATERIALS

Dropper, plastic sheet or spot plate or glass plates or small test tubes and rack, if available dropper bottles containing 1-M sodium chloride, 1-M sodium bromide, 1-M sodium iodide, 0.2-M silver nitrate, 0.2-M mercury(I) nitrate, 0.2-M copper(I) nitrate, 0.2-M strontium nitrate, 0.2-M barium nitrate, 1-M sodium hydroxide, 0.2-M magnesium nitrate, 0.2-M aluminum nitrate, 0.2-M iron(III) nitrate, 0.2-M cadmium nitrate, 0.2-M mercury(II) nitrate, 0.2-M bismuth nitrate, 1-M sodium carbonate, 1-M sodium phosphate, 0.2-M zinc nitrate, 0.2-M antimony(III) chloride, 0.2-M arsenic(III) chloride, 0.2-M ammonium sulfide.

PROCEDURE

To expedite the experiment, the class may be divided into five groups, with each group testing the reactions of a specific ion or group of ions and then tabulating its data on the board and exchanging it with that from the other groups.

Part I · Ions Which Generally Form Soluble Compounds

1. Check the reagent shelf and write in Table IA the formulas of any nitrates that can be dissolved, forming a solution containing 0.1 or more mole of the solute. Any solution whose label shows

that it has a concentration equal to or greater than 0.1 M fulfills this requirement.

2. Repeat Procedure 1 for the compounds listed below.

Table IIA   Soluble chlorides, bromides, or iodides.
Table IIIA   Soluble sulfates
Table IVA   Soluble hydroxides
Table VA   Soluble carbonates and phosphates
Table VIA   Soluble sulfides
Table VIIA   Soluble ammonium compounds

Table IA
Soluble Nitrates

Table IIA
Soluble Chlorides, Bromides, and Iodides

chlorides	bromides	iodides

Table IIIA
Soluble Sulfates

Table IVA
Soluble Hydroxides

Table VA
Soluble Carbonates and Phosphates

Carbonates	Phosphates

Table VIA
Soluble Sulfides

Table VIIA
Soluble NH$_4^+$ Compounds

Part II · Chlorides, Bromides, and Iodides

2. Carry out the reactions listed in Table II. Dispense the solutions from dropper bottles onto spot or glass plates, if they are available. Use an equal number of drops of each solution in carrying out a test. Describe the colors of the solutions

as well as the color and characteristics of any precipitates. Use the data in Tables IA through VIIA to help identify and write the formula of any slightly soluble compound. Use 1-M solutions of sodium chloride, sodium bromide, and sodium iodide as a source, respectively, of Cl^- ions, Br^- ions, and I^- ions. Use 0.2-M solutions of the nitrates of the solutions of the positive ions listed in Table II. It is understood that all ions are aquated.

Table II   Reactions Involving Chlorides, Bromides, and Iodides

Reaction	Observation	Formula of Precipitate
$Ag^+ + Cl^-$		
$Hg^{2+} + Cl^-$		
$Pb^{2+} + Cl^-$		
$Ag^+ + Br^-$		
$Hg^{2+} + Br^-$		
$Pb^{2+} + Br^-$		
$Ag^+ + I^-$		
$Hg^{2+} + I^-$		
$Pb^{2+} + I^-$		

Part III · Sulfates

3. Carry out the reactions listed in Table III. Use a 1.0-M solution of Na_2SO_4 as a source of sulfate ions and 0.2-M solutions of the nitrates of the positive ions listed in Table III.

Table III   Reactions Involving Sulfate Ions

Reaction	Observation	Formula of Precipitate
$Ca^{2+} + SO_4^{2-}$		
$Sr^{2+} + SO_4^{2-}$		
$Ba^{2+} + SO_4^{2-}$		
$Pb^{2+} + SO_4^{2-}$		

Part IV · Hydroxides

4. Carry out the reactions listed in Table IV. Use a 1-M solution of sodium hydroxide as a source of hydroxide ions and 0.2-M solutions of the nitrates of the positive ions listed in the table.

Table IV   Reactions Involving Hydroxide Ions

Reaction	Observation	Formula of Precipitate
$Mg^{2+} + OH^-$		
$Ca^{2+} + OH^-$		
$Al^{3+} + OH^-$		
$Fe^{3+} + OH^-$		
$Cd^{2+} + OH^-$		
$Hg^{2+} + OH^-$		
$Pb^{2+} + OH^-$		
$Bi^{3+} + OH^-$		

Part V · Carbonates and Phosphates

5. (a) Add a few drops of 1-M Na_2CO_3 to 0.2-M solutions of the nitrates of the positive ions listed in Table VA. (b) Add a few drops of 1-M Na_3PO_4 to 0.2-M solutions of the nitrates of the positive ions listed in Table VB.

Table VA   Reactions Involving Carbonate Ions

Positive Ion	Negative Ion	Observation	Formula of Precipitate
Mg^{2+}	CO_3^{2-}		
Sr^{2+}	CO_3^{2-}		
Ca^{2+}	CO_3^{2-}		
Ba^{2+}	CO_3^{2-}		
Zn^{2+}	CO_3^{2-}		
Cd^{2+}	CO_3^{2-}		
Hg^{2+}	CO_3^{2-}		
Pb^{2+}	CO_3^{2-}		

Table VB   Reactions Involving Phosphate Ions

Positive Ion	Negative Ion	Observation	Formula of Precipitate
Mg^{2+}	$PO_4{}^{3-}$		
Sr^{2+}	$PO_4{}^{3-}$		
Ca^{2+}	$PO_4{}^{3-}$		
Ba^{2+}	$PO_4{}^{3-}$		
Zn^{2+}	$PO_4{}^{3-}$		
Cd^{2+}	$PO_4{}^{3-}$		
Hg^{2+}	$PO_4{}^{3-}$		
Bi^{3+}	$PO_4{}^{3-}$		
Pb^{2+}	$PO_4{}^{3-}$		

Part VI · Sulfides

6. Add a few drops of 0.2-M $(NH_4)_2S$ to 0.1-M solutions of the nitrates of the positive ions listed in Table VI. Ammonium sulfide has an unpleasant odor and should be used under a hood or with adequate ventilation.

Table VI   Reactions Involving Sulfides

Positive Ion	Negative Ion	Observation	Formula of Precipitate
Zn^{2+}	S^{2-}		
Cd^{2+}	S^{2-}		
Hg^{2+}	S^{2-}		
Bi^{3+}	S^{2-}		
Pb^{2+}	S^{2-}		
Sb^{3+}	S^{2-}		
As^{3+}	S^{2-}		

FOLLOW-UP DISCUSSION

Each of the compounds which you encountered in this experiment forms an ionic solution in water. The precipitates, however, have low solubilities and furnish an extremely low concentration of ions. All of the reactants were soluble. That is, they all dissolved and formed solutions which have a concentration greater than 0.1 M. Examination of the formulas of the reactants as well as observation of the names of the solutions on the reagent shelf should enable you to deduce the names of a number of positive and negative ions that generally form soluble compounds.

Knowing the ions that form soluble compounds, you should be able to deduce which of the products are precipitates in each of the reactions you investigated.

In Follow-up Question 1 you are asked to summarize the results of this experiment by preparing a table of general solubility rules. In addition, you may be asked to represent the solubility rules pictorially using the Periodic Table to locate the position of the positive ions that form slightly soluble compounds with selected anions.

The ability to write net ionic equations for reactions is an important skill that should be a part of every chemistry student's background. You will have a chance to develop this ability by writing equations for each of the reactions you observed in this experiment. Represent slightly soluble compounds (precipitates) with neutral formulas, and soluble salts as well as strong acids and bases with ionic symbols. The technique is discussed in Section 3-4 and summarized in Section 16-6 of *Foundations of Chemistry*, 2 ed.

FOLLOW-UP QUESTIONS

1. Summarize your data in the form of general solubility rules by completing the sentences below.

(1) In general, all compounds containing ions from Group IA of the Periodic Table are _____.

(2) In general, all compounds containing $NH_4{}^+$ ions are _____.

(3) In general, all compounds containing $NO_3{}^-$ ions are _____.

(4) In general, all compounds containing Cl^-, Br^-, and I^- ions are _____ except those containing these positive ions _____.

(5) In general, compounds containing SO_4^{2-} ions are soluble except those containing these positive ions _____.

(6) In general, most compounds containing hydroxide ions are _____. Exceptions are the compounds containing these positive ions _____. Assume that (a) the reaction of iron(III) ions is typical of all ions in the first series of the transition elements (#21–30), (b) the reaction of the Cd^{2+} ions is typical of the ions in the second series of transition elements (#39–48), and (c) the reaction of the Hg^{2+} ions is typical of the ions in the third series of transition elements (#71–80).

(7) In general, most compounds containing carbonate or phosphate ions are _____. Exceptions are the compounds containing the positive ions from Group _____ of the Periodic Table. Assume that (a) the reaction of Zn^{2+} ions is typical of all the ions in the first series of the transition elements, (b) the reaction of the Cd^{2+} ions is typical of the ions in the second series of transition elements, and (c) the reaction of Hg^{2+} is typical of the ions in the third series of transition elements.

(8) In general, most compounds containing sulfide ions are _____. Exceptions are the ions in Groups _____ and _____ of the Periodic Table. Again, assume the ions you tested from each of the transition series are representative of the behavior of all of the ions in the series.

2. If they are available, obtain from your instructor, two sheets of paper each containing three blank Periodic Tables. Label the tables respectively, 1, 2, 3, 4, 5, and 6. Refer to Tables IA through VIIA and Follow-up Questions 1 through 8 as well as your other data and write in Periodic Table 1, in the proper space, the symbols of the positive ions that form soluble compounds with all anions. (Below Table 1 write the formula of a negative ion that forms soluble compounds with all positive ions.) If pastel colored felt-tipped pens are available, you may wish to color the squares. In Table 2 write the symbols of the positive ions that form chlorides, bromides, or iodides having low solubilities. Use a different colored ink for these squares. In Table 3 write the symbols of the positive ions that form sulfates having low solubilities. In Table 4 write the symbols of the positive ions that form hydroxides having low solubilities. Refer to a regular Periodic Table for the symbols of the transition elements you wish to include. In Table 5 write the symbols of the positive ions that form carbonates and phosphates having low solubilities. In Table 6 write the symbols of the positive ions that form sulfides having low solubilities.

3. Write net ionic equations for each reaction recorded in Tables II through VI. Group the equations in tables that correspond to Tables II through VI.

3-4

Mole Relationships in "Displacement" Reactions

GENERAL DISCUSSION

In this experiment you carry out a reaction between metallic copper atoms and silver ions in solution and produce copper ions in solution and metallic silver atoms. The objective is to determine the mole ratio between silver and copper in the reaction.

The expression, shown without coefficients, is

$$Cu(s) + Ag^+(aq) \rightarrow Cu^{2+}(aq) + Ag(s) \qquad Eq. 1$$

Once the mole ratio is determined, it may be converted to a whole-number ratio, and the numbers placed in front of the symbols for copper and silver. The result should be a balanced chemical equation with the atoms of the product equal in number and kind to the atoms of reactant. Stoichiometric calculations are based on the coefficients in a correctly balanced equation.

OBJECTIVES

1. To determine experimentally the mole ratio between the participants in a chemical reaction.
2. To determine experimentally the coefficients in an equation for a reaction.

MATERIALS

Copper wire (#14 or larger), balance, 250-ml beaker, 0.2-M silver nitrate solution, coffee-can sand bath, burner, ring stand.

PROCEDURE

1. Obtain a heavy copper wire (#14 or ordinary electric wiring is satisfactory) about eight inches long. Form the lower part into an elongated coil, and bend it to form a hook at the opposite end. Carefully weigh the copper to the nearest 0.01 g and record the mass in the table.

1	Mass of copper coil before reaction	
2	Mass of copper coil after reaction	
3	Mass of copper used in reaction	
4	Mass of filter paper and dry silver	
5	Mass of filter paper	
6	Mass of silver produced in reaction	
7	Moles of solid copper used in reaction	
8	Moles of solid silver produced in reaction	

2. Carefully weigh a piece of filter paper to ±0.001 g.

3. Add about 150 milliliters of 0.2-M silver nitrate solution (0.2 moles of $AgNO_3$ per liter of solution) to a 250-ml beaker. **Caution:** *Silver nitrate solution will stain your hands so avoid getting any of this solution on yourself. If you should get any on your hands, immediately wash it off.* Check with the instructor for advice on removing the stain.

4. Suspend the coil of copper in the silver nitrate solution by hanging the hook over a glass rod or over the side of the beaker.

5. Place the beaker in your locker until the next laboratory period.

6. Carefully shake the silver from the copper coil into the beaker. Using your wash bottle, rinse the coil and then allow it to dry. Weigh and record its mass.

7. Decant the solution onto the weighed filter paper. Add 5–10 ml of the 0.2-M silver nitrate solution. Break up the mass of precipitate with a stirring rod and be certain that all of the particles

have come into contact with the $AgNO_3$ solution. Allow to stand 5 minutes and then transfer all of the Ag to the filter paper.

8. Wash the silver thoroughly with water at least three times.

9. Allow all of the wash water to drain off and then have the instructor wash the filter paper and silver crystals with acetone or alcohol and allow to drain.

10. Remove the filter paper from the funnel, open up on a piece of paper toweling, and dry in locker for 48 hours. Weigh and record its mass.

11. Make the calculations needed to complete the table.

12. Save your silver for use in a later experiment. You may be asked to determine its purity in Experiments 3-6 and 3-7.

FOLLOW-UP DISCUSSION

The numbers obtained for Items 7 and 8 in the table represent the mole ratio of Cu to Ag. These fractional numbers may be used as coefficients in front of the symbols in Equation 1. It is desirable to use whole-number coefficients whenever possible. A close approximation of whole-number ratios may be obtained by dividing both experimentally determined coefficients by the smaller of the two numbers: that is, the moles of copper. When a chemical equation is balanced, the number of atoms represented on the left and right sides of the equation is the same, as are the units of electric charge.

Note also that the positive charge from positive ions in a solution must be balanced by an equal quantity of negative charge contributed by negative ions. In this experiment, the negative charge was furnished by nitrate ions present in the system but not involved in the reaction. These unreactive ions are not shown in a net ionic equation.

It is not usually convenient nor practical to determine experimentally the coefficients in an equation. The coefficients for simple equations are usually obtained by equalizing the number of reactant and product atoms in a skeleton equation by inspection. It is essential that the skeleton equation contain correct formulas for all reactants and products. Refer to Section 3-2 in *Foundations of Chemistry,* 2 ed., for an explanation of balancing simple equations.

FOLLOW-UP QUESTIONS

1. Write an equation for the reaction between copper and silver ions. Include your experimentally determined mole ratios as fractional coefficients. Convert the fractional coefficients to a whole-number ratio and rewrite the equation using the whole-number ratio. How do these ratios compare with the correct whole-number ratios furnished by your instructor?

2. List some of the sources of experimental error in this experiment.

3. If the silver in the beaker contained water during your last weighing, how would this affect your results?

4. Assume that magnesium metal would act atom-for-atom exactly the same as copper in this experiment. How many grams of magnesium would have been used in the reaction if one gram of silver were produced? The atomic mass of magnesium is 24.3.

5. Account for the blue color produced in the solution.

6. Refer to the Activity Series introduced in the Follow-up Discussion of Experiment 2-6 and predict whether or not metallic silver reacts with a solution of copper(II) nitrate and yields metallic copper and a solution of silver nitrate.

3-5

Mass Relationships in an Acid-Base Reaction

GENERAL DISCUSSION

In general, we can say that a reaction goes to completion (is quantitative) if one of the reactants is completely consumed by the reaction. There are several ways that a reactant may be consumed. This occurs if (a) a precipitate is formed, (b) a weakly dissociated substance such as water or a weak acid is formed, and (c) a gas (volatile substance) is formed.

In this experiment you allow sodium bicarbonate (baking soda) to react with hydrochloric acid for the purpose of obtaining a high yield of sodium chloride.

$$NaHCO_3 + HCl \rightarrow NaCl + H_2O + CO_2(g)$$
$$\text{Eq. 1}$$

Use an accurately measured mass of $NaHCO_3$ and enough dilute HCl to react completely with it. You isolate the NaCl from the other products and determine its mass. The theoretical yield can be calculated by using the mole and mass ratios obtained from the equation for the reaction. The percentage yield can then be determined.

OBJECTIVES

1. To prepare and determine the yield of sodium chloride.
2. To gain an understanding of mass relationships in chemical reactions.

MATERIALS

Evaporating dish, watch glass, balance, sodium bicarbonate (CP), hydrochloric acid, burner, wire gauze, ring stand, wash bottle.

PROCEDURE

1. Clean and dry an evaporating dish and watch glass, and weigh the combination to the nearest 0.001 g. Record the data in the table.
2. Put about 2 g of pure sodium bicarbonate into the dish. Weigh the dish, contents, and cover to the nearest 0.001 g.
3. Cover the dish with the watch glass. Place

the convex side down and the glass slightly off center so that the lip of the dish is uncovered. Add dilute hydrochloric acid dropwise down the lip of the dish to the bicarbonate in the dish. Continue this procedure until no more reaction takes place when a drop of acid is added. Gently swirl the contents of the dish so that all of the solid contacts the liquid. Do not add excess HCl.

Table I   NaCl from $NaHCO_3$

	Trial I	Trial II
Mass of evaporating dish, cover, and $NaHCO_3$		
Mass of evaporating dish and watch glass		
Mass of $NaHCO_3$ taken		
Mass of evaporating dish, cover, and NaCl		
Mass of evaporating dish and cover (item 2 above)		
Mass of salt obtained (experimental)		
Theoretical mass of salt (calculated)		
Percentage yield		

4. Carefully rinse the underneath side of the watch glass with distilled water, a few drops at a time, and collect the washings in the dish.
5. Carefully heat the evaporating dish contents and cover with a low flame or a heat lamp until the salt is completely dry. Do not allow the contents of the dish to spatter.
6. Allow the dish to cool to room temperature and weigh it (and cover) to the nearest 0.001 g.

Repeat Steps 5 and 6 to be sure constant weight has been obtained. Two consecutive mass readings should agree within 0.02 g.

7. Calculate the mass of NaCl that should have been obtained. Show mathematical calculations in your report including proper units.

8. Determine the percentage yield.

FURTHER EXPERIMENTATION

Devise another experiment for obtaining pure NaCl.

FOLLOW-UP DISCUSSION

The reaction which you used to prepare the salt in this experiment should have proceeded to completion. This type of reaction is also used to prepare weakly dissociated acids. It may be seen from Eq. 1 that the reactants are a strong acid and the salt of a weak acid. One product of such a reaction is a weak acid. We can assume that when a strong acid reacts and forms a weak acid that ions of the strong acid are removed from solution. Hence, the reaction proceeds essentially to completion. In this reaction, the weak acid formed was carbonic acid, H_2CO_3. This compound decomposes into CO_2 and H_2O. It has never been isolated as a pure compound. For this reason it is usually written in its decomposed form as $H_2O + CO_2$. A solution of carbonic acid is acid and a poor conductor of an electric current. Tests show that the solution contains H_3O^+ HCO_3^- and CO_3^{2-} ions and CO_2. The net ionic equation for the reaction is

$$HCO_3^-(aq) + H_3O^+ \rightarrow 2H_2O + CO_2(g) \quad \text{Eq. 2}$$

One of your objectives in this experiment was to compare the experimental and calculated yield of product. We shall define the percentage yield by means of the equation shown below.

$$\text{percentage yield} = \frac{\text{experimental yield}}{\text{theoretical yield}} \times (100)$$

The theoretical yield is calculated by using the mass of reactant ($NaHCO_3$) weighed out for the experiment and the mole relationship between the reactants and products as shown by the balanced equation for the reaction. You must assume, of course, that a slight excess of HCl was present so that all of the $NaHCO_3$ was consumed. This type of calculation is described in Sec. 3-3 of *Foundations of Chemistry*, 2 ed.

FOLLOW-UP QUESTIONS

1. What was the cause of the effervescence which you used as an indication of a reaction?

2. Give two reasons why the reaction in this experiment should go to completion.

3. $NaHCO_3$ may be considered to be a salt. From what acid is it derived?

4. How can you be sure that your product was completely dry?

5. If you had added excess hydrochloric acid to the sodium bicarbonate and then evaporated the solution, you would have detected an irritating gas. What is its name and formula?

6. Suggest another chemical reaction which you could use to obtain pure NaCl. How would you know when the solution contained pure NaCl?

7. Refer to the Follow-up Discussion and suggest a reaction that could be used for the preparation of acetic acid ($HC_2H_3O_2$).

8. List all of the sources of error which you think may have influenced the accuracy of your experimental results. Wherever possible, indicate whether each error would have made your result high or low.

9. Consider the following equation and answer parts (a) to (f). Show calculations for each part.

$$3Ag(s) + 4HNO_3(aq) \rightarrow$$
$$3AgNO_3(aq) + NO(g) + 2H_2O(l)$$

(a) State the number of moles of $AgNO_3$ produced by the reaction of 3.00 moles of Ag with excess HNO_3.

(b) State the number of moles of $AgNO_3$ produced by the reaction of 108 grams of Ag with excess HNO_3.

(c) State the number of grams of $AgNO_3$ produced by the reaction of 108 grams of Ag with excess HNO_3.

(d) State the number of moles of NO produced as a product of the reaction of 108 grams of Ag with excess HNO_3.

(e) State the number of grams of NO produced as a product starting with 108 g of Ag and excess HNO_3.

(f) State the number of grams of $AgNO_3$ produced by the reaction of 324 g of silver with 126 g of HNO_3.

3-6

Gravimetric Analysis: Percentage Purity of a Sample of Silver

GENERAL DISCUSSION

An alloy contains two or more metals. Many silver alloys are composed of silver and copper. The mass of silver in a sample of an alloy may be determined by isolating the silver in the form of a pure silver compound and weighing the compound. The first step in such an analysis is to obtain a solution of copper and silver ions, using a suitable reagent such as nitric acid. A silver-copper alloy reacts with nitric acid and forms a bluish-solution which contains silver ions and copper ions. The hydrated copper(II) ions are responsible for the blue color of the solution.

The next step is to add a reagent to the solution which forms a relatively insoluble silver compound, but does not react with the copper ions. Any soluble chloride, for example sodium chloride, reacts with silver ions and forms insoluble silver chloride but does not react with copper(II) ions. The precipitated silver chloride may then be filtered out of the solution, dried, and weighed. The mass of the silver in the original alloy sample may then be determined by calculating the mass of the silver in the weighted precipitate of NaCl.

If you performed Experiment 3-4, then your objective will be to determine the percentage purity of the silver which you precipitated in that experiment. Alternatively, you may analyze a silver alloy such as dental alloy, silver solder, sterling silver, or a piece of a silver coin. Still another possibility is to determine the mg of Ag in a solution of silver ions obtained from your instructor. In this instance you may assume that the instructor has dissolved the silver sample so that you may start with Procedure 2.

OBJECTIVES

1. To determine the percentage purity of a sample of silver or to determine the mg of Ag in an unknown solution.

2. To illustrate an application of the Law of Definite Proportions.

3. To become acquainted with the procedures and calculations of gravimetric analysis.

MATERIALS

A sample of silver metal from a previous experiment or a silver alloy or a solution containing an unknown quantity of silver, filter paper, funnel, balance, 250-ml beaker, wire screen, ring stand, burner, concentrated nitric acid, 0.1-M sodium chloride solution, watch glass, stirring rod, wash bottle.

PROCEDURE

1. Weigh out approximately one-half gram of the silver precipitated in Experiment 3-4 to ± 0.001 g. Record the exact mass in your data table. If time permits, you may wish to weigh out duplicate or triplicate samples. Save the balance of your silver sample for future experiments (3-7). If you use an alloy as a sample, then weigh out enough alloy to contain about 0.5 g of silver. If silver samples are not available, then obtain some silver solution from your instructor who will dispense the solution from a buret and keep a record of the exact volume given to you.

2. Weigh a piece of filter paper to ± 0.001 g and fold it to fit a funnel. If you started with a solid sample go to Procedure 3. If your sample was a solution, add 5 ml of 6-M HNO$_3$ and then go to Procedure 4.

3. Place the sample of alloy in a 250-ml beaker. Place the beaker on a piece of iron screen supported on a ring stand (under a fume hood), and add a solution of nitric acid made by diluting 4 ml of concentrated nitric acid with 4 ml of distilled water. Warm gently to start the reaction. Allow to react until the alloy has completely dissolved.

4. As soon as the alloy has dissolved, allow the solution to cool and then dilute by slowly adding 50 ml of distilled water. Filter out and discard any precipitate that forms.

5. Add slowly, with continual stirring, 60 ml of 0.1-M sodium chloride solution. One liter of this solution may be made up by dissolving approximately 6 g of NaCl in one liter of distilled water (approximately 0.4 g per 60 ml).

6. Place the beaker on a wire screen, cover with a watch glass and heat just to boiling, stirring occasionally. Keep just at the boiling point until the precipitate coagulates and settles. Allow it to settle completely.

7. Fit a funnel with the weighed filter paper. If there is no precipitate floating on the surface of the solution or suspended in the solution, decant the clear (supernatant) liquid into another beaker. If a significant amount of precipitate is suspended, filter the entire solution through the filter paper. Finally transfer the loose precipitate to the filter paper by inverting the beaker over the funnel and guiding the precipitate from the lip of the beaker down a stirring rod into the paper. Hold the beaker and rod in this position with one hand and flush the precipitate into the paper with a stiff stream from the wash bottle (Fig. A-25 and Fig. A-26). Add a few drops of dilute nitric acid to the water in the wash bottle. This will tend to keep the precipitate in a coagulated condition.

Table I   Silver in an Alloy

	I	II
Mass of silver alloy		
Mass of filter paper + AgCl precipitate		
Mass of filter paper		
Mass of AgCl precipitate		
Fraction of silver in silver chloride		
Mass of silver in precipitate		
Experimental percentage or mg of Ag in original sample		

8. Cover the funnel with a dry filter paper to keep dust out of the precipitate. Place the funnel in your drawer and let stand until the paper and precipitate are completely dry. When they appear to be dry, weigh to the nearest milligram if possible. Return to the drawer, allow to dry another 24 hours and weigh again to be sure constant mass has been obtained.

9. Make the calculations necessary to complete the table.

FURTHER EXPERIMENTATION
Devise a method to isolate copper metal from the nitric acid solution obtained as a filtrate in Procedure 7.

FOLLOW-UP DISCUSSION
In this experiment you took a substance of unknown composition and from it you isolated and weighed a substance of known composition. This procedure is known as gravimetric analysis.

The accuracy of the results depends partially on the complete removal of the desired substance (Ag) from the alloy, and the separation of the entire precipitate (AgCl) from the solution. This means the precipitate must be in a filterable form.

The nature of the precipitate depends on the properties of the substance, and the conditions under which the reaction is carried out. Some precipitates are composed of very tiny but filterable crystals; others consist of a suspension of colloidal particles or a coagulated mass of colloidal particles.

In general, colloidal particles are too small to be seen by the eye. These particles pass right through the pores of a filter paper and are useless for quantitative gravimetric analysis. Colloidal particles often form when concentrated solutions are mixed rapidly. When substances have a tendency to form colloidal particles, it is a good idea to add one dilute solution slowly to another. Heating often causes colloidal particles to coagulate into masses which can be retained by ordinary filter paper. In this experiment, the precipitate of silver chloride is a curdy mass composed of large numbers of colloidal particles which have coagulated as a result of warming the solution for a period of time.

You probably noticed that the original white precipitate of AgCl darkened on exposure to light. This darkening is caused by a photochemical decomposition reaction which is characteristic of the silver halides (AgCl, AgBr, and AgI). The equation for the reaction is

$$AgCl \rightarrow Ag + \frac{1}{2}Cl_2$$

In most cases, where proper technique has been used, the error introduced by this decomposition is not appreciable.

The colored gas you observed during the reaction between the alloy and nitric acid was nitrogen dioxide (NO_2). The reaction between silver and nitric acid, or between copper and nitric acid probably produces colorless nitric oxide (NO).

$$3Ag(s) + 4HNO_3(aq) \rightarrow$$
$$3AgNO_3(aq) + NO(g) + 2H_2O(l)$$

$$3Cu(s) + 8HNO_3(aq) \rightarrow$$
$$3Cu(NO_3)_2(aq) + 2NO(g) + 4H_2O(l)$$

The nitric oxide produced then reacts with oxygen in air to form brown, poisonous NO_2.

$$2NO(g) + O_2(g) \rightarrow 2NO_2(g)$$

The above reactions are classified as oxidation-reduction reactions. You are not expected to complete or balance these equations at this point.

When solid silver and copper in the alloy dissolve, they form soluble compounds (salts) as indicated in the first two equations. In general, salts are composed of ions, so the solution resulting from dissolving the alloy consists of copper ions (Cu^{2+}), silver ions (Ag^+), nitrate ions (NO_3^-), and H_3O^+ ions from the acid. The important fact for this analysis is that all of the silver metal in the alloy is converted into silver ions in solution.

Silver ions react with chloride ions and form a precipitate of silver chloride (AgCl). The rest of the ions in the solution do not react with chloride ions. Therefore, when a salt solution containing chloride ions is added to the solution containing silver ions, almost all of the silver ions are converted to insoluble silver chloride.

$$NaCl(aq) + AgNO_3(aq) \rightarrow$$
$$AgCl(s) + NaNO_3(aq)$$

Since Ag^+ and Cl^- are the only two ions that react, a more concise way to express the reaction is in the form of an ionic equation

$$Ag^+(aq) + Cl^-(aq) \rightarrow AgCl(s)$$

The silver chloride precipitate containing all the silver in the original sample of alloy is filtered, dried, and weighed. Application of the Law of Definite Proportions allows us to calculate the amount of silver in the AgCl precipitate.

$$g \text{ of } Ag = \frac{Ag}{AgCl} \times (g \text{ of AgCl precipitate})$$

or

$$g \text{ of } Ag = \frac{108.0}{143.5} \times (g \text{ of AgCl precipitate})$$

Since the mass of silver ions in the silver chloride precipitate is the same as the mass of silver in the original sample of alloy, the percentage of silver in the alloy may be calculated

Percentage of Ag in alloy

$$= \frac{g \text{ of silver}}{g \text{ of alloy sample}} \times (100)$$

FOLLOW-UP QUESTIONS

1. List the sources of error that would cause the experimental percentage of silver to differ from the true percentage. Refer to the list of errors given in Experiment 1-2. If a quantitative analysis text is available, refer to the section on errors in gravimetric analysis. For each error discussed, indicate whether it would cause the experimental results to be too small or too large.

2. Brass is an alloy containing tin (Sn), zinc (Zn), and copper (Cu). The alloy may be analyzed by dissolving it in an acid and isolating the tin in the form of SnO_2 and the zinc in the form of $Zn_2P_2O_7$. The copper is electrolytically deposited as pure copper. Calculate the percentage of each metal in the brass if an 0.800-g sample yielded 0.250 g of SnO_2 and 1.00 g of $Zn_2P_2O_7$.

73

3-7

Volumetric Analysis: Percentage of Silver in an Unknown Sample

GENERAL DISCUSSION

There are two main divisions of analytical chemistry: qualitative analysis and quantitative analysis.

The methods of qualitative analysis are used to determine what constituents are present in a sample. The amounts or percentage of constituents are determined by the methods of quantitative analysis. The chemical methods used in quantitative analysis may be grouped under two general classifications: gravimetric analysis and volumetric analysis.

In *gravimetric* analysis, the compound to be determined is isolated as an element or compound of known composition. From the mass of the substance isolated and its percentage composition, the percentage of the component in the original sample may be calculated.

In *volumetric* analysis we measure from a buret the volume of a solution of known concentration (standard solution) required to react with a measured amount of an unknown substance. The process is called *titration*. The completion of the reaction is signaled by a chemical indicator which ideally changes color at the stoichiometric point. The *stoichiometric point* is the point at which the unknown has completely reacted with the standard and at which the standard and unknown have reacted in the mole ratio indicated by their coefficients in the balanced equation.

The number of moles of standard used to react with a measured quantity of unknown may be calculated from the molar concentration of the solution and the volume. The relationship is

$$\text{number of moles} = \text{molarity} \times \text{volume} \quad (1)$$

or

$$\text{number of millimoles} = \text{molarity} \times \text{volume (ml)}.$$

The number of moles in the measured amount of unknown may then be calculated from the mole ratio shown by the equation.

In this experiment you determine the percentage purity of silver in the residue from Experiment 3-4 or in an alloy such as a silver coin or dental alloy, using a standard solution of potassium thiocyanate (KSCN). As in the last analysis, you may be asked to determine the mg of silver in a solution of unknown concentration obtained from your instructor. If your sample is a solid, you first dissolve it in nitric acid, yielding silver ions in solution. The silver ions react with thiocyanate ions (SCN^-) in the standard solution and form insoluble AgSCN. When the silver ions have been removed from solution, the next drop of KSCN reacts with the ferric-ion indicator and forms a polyatomic ion which imparts a red color to the solution. The formula of this ion is $FeSCN^{2+}$.

The net ionic equation for the reaction between silver nitrate and potassium thiocyanate is

$$Ag^+ + SCN^- \rightarrow AgCNS(s)$$

The number of moles of KSCN used in the titration may be calculated as follows:

$$\text{moles} = \text{volume (liters)} \times \text{molarity (moles/liter)}$$

The equations show that Ag^+ and SCN^- ions react in a 1 to 1 mole ratio. Thus, the moles of SCN^- ions used equals the moles of Ag in the sample. The grams of silver may then be calculated by multiplying the atomic mass of silver by the moles of silver in the sample.

$$\text{grams of Ag} = \text{moles of Ag} \times \text{atomic mass of Ag}$$

Finally the percentage of silver in the sample may

be determined by dividing the grams of silver by the mass of the sample dissolved.

% Ag in sample =

$$\frac{\text{grams of Ag in sample}}{\text{mass of sample used}} \times (100)$$

OBJECTIVES

1. To determine the percentage purity of a silver sample or the mg of Ag in an unknown solution.
2. To become acquainted with the procedures and calculations of volumetric analysis.

MATERIALS

Balance, silver residue from Experiment 3-4 or a silver alloy, or a solution containing an unknown quantity of silver, 250-ml erlenmeyer flask, burner, ring stand, wire screen, 16-M nitric acid, 0.02-M iron(III) ammonium sulfate in 6-M nitric acid, graduated cylinder, standardized KSCN solution which is about 0.1 M.

PROCEDURE

1. Weigh a sample of silver saved from Experiment 3-4 or an alloy sample to the nearest mg. The sample should contain a maximum of 0.4 g of silver. If your sample is an unknown solution, add 5 ml of 6-M HNO$_3$ and go directly to Procedure 3. Otherwise go to Procedure 2.
2. Place the sample in an erlenmeyer flask and add 15 ml of 8-M nitric acid. Warm gently and agitate with a stirring rod until the sample is dissolved. Boil the solution gently for 3 or 4 minutes.
3. Cool and add 40 ml of distilled water and 5 ml of 0.02-M NH$_4$Fe(SO$_4$)$_2$ · 12H$_2$O indicator to the silver solution. Filter out any precipitate and discard it.
4. Review the section in *Introducing the Laboratory Program* on the preparation and use of a buret. Clean and rinse a buret with a few ml of standard KSCN (precise concentration will be given by your instructor). Fill the buret with the standard solution. Check to see that the tip is full and does not leak.
5. Titrate with vigorous swirling to a red-brown color which remains after 15 seconds of agitation. Record data in table.

FURTHER EXPERIMENTATION

1. Prepare and standardize a solution of approximately 0.1-M KSCN. Any book on quantitative analysis will serve as a reference. Look in the index under Volhard method.
2. Determine the mg of Cl$^-$ ions in a sample of urine by adding an excess (accurately measured) of standard AgNO$_3$, and then titrating the excess Ag$^+$ ions with standard KSCN using Fe^{3+} as an indicator.

FOLLOW-UP DISCUSSION

Many kinds of chemical reactions can be used in volumetric analysis. In general, the analysis must involve a reaction whose equation is known. The reaction should be rapid and complete (quantitative). In addition, there must be an indicator or some means of locating the stoichiometric point of the reaction. This is the point at which the reactants have been added in the mole ratios shown by the equation. We shall use indicator endpoints to signal the completion of a reaction.

The success of a volumetric analysis depends largely on the accuracy of the value for the concentration of the standard solution. Solutions may be standardized in several ways. In the first method, a pure, dry, stable nonhygroscopic solid substance may be accurately weighed and dissolved in a small quantity of distilled water. This solution may then be added to a volumetric flask and diluted to exactly 1 liter. The molarity may be calculated from the moles of solute and volume of solution.

A second method involves titrating an accurately weighed primary standard with the solution to be standardized. A primary standard is a pure, stable, nonhygroscopic solid chemical which reacts completely and rapidly with the solution to be standardized.

A third method consists of titrating the solution to be standardized with a solution that has already been standardized (secondary standard). For example, the potassium thiocyanate solution you used may have been standardized by titrating it with a previously standardized silver nitrate solution. In this case, the concentration of the thiocyanate solution cannot be any more accurate than that of the silver nitrate solution. It is pos-sible that your solution was standardized by the first method, although this is not the usual procedure since KSCN is usually not dry.

Standardized solutions may be purchased from chemical supply companies. Some alloys contain elements which might interfere with the analysis for silver. For example, dental alloy contains silver, copper, tin, and antimony. All of these metals dissolve in nitric acid. If tin is present, it forms a precipitate of a hydrated oxide which should be filtered out before titrating. The other ions do not interfere unless they are present in excessive amounts.

Table I   Volumetric Determination of Silver

	Trial I	Trial II
Mass of silver alloy sample		
Final reading of buret		
Initial reading of buret		
Volume of KSCN used		
Molarity of KSCN		
Moles of KSCN used		
Moles of silver present in sample		
Atomic mass of silver		
Grams of silver present in alloy		
Percentage purity or mg of silver in sample		

FOLLOW-UP QUESTIONS

1. List the sources of error and the effect that each might have on your result.

2. What is the molarity of a solution containing 4.86 g of KSCN per liter of solution?

3. What is the molarity of a KSCN solution, 40.00 ml of which required 37.50 ml of 0.1000-M $AgNO_3$ for titration?

4. What is the percentage of NaCl in an impure sample of salt if the sample weighs 0.500 g and requires 40.0 ml of 0.100-M $AgNO_3$ for titration to the endpoint?

4-1

Effect of Pressure Change on the Volume of a Gas

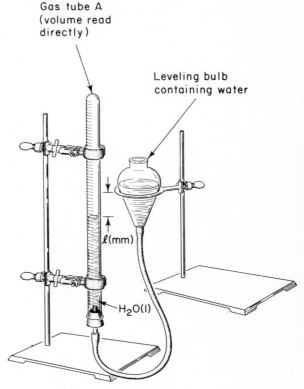

Gas tube A
(volume read
directly)

Leveling bulb
containing water

ℓ(mm)

$H_2O(l)$

Fig. 4-1   Boyle's law apparatus.

GENERAL DISCUSSION

In this experiment we shall subject a given mass of gas to changes in pressure, and observe the corresponding changes in volume. While investigating the effect of pressure changes, we shall keep the temperature constant.

After performing the experiment we shall test the data to determine what relationship exists between the variables (volume and pressure). Finally, we shall plot the data and interpret the graph.

This experiment can be done by all students (two per setup) or performed as a demonstration by students with teacher guidance and narration. In the latter case, two students can perform the demonstration while one student records the data in a table drawn on the board. Students at their seats should record the data, make calculations, and give the result to the person at the board as he requests it.

OBJECTIVE

To determine what, if any, mathematical relationship exists between the volume and pressure of a fixed mass of gas at constant temperature.

MATERIALS

Gas measuring tube, leveling bulb, rubber tubing, ring stand, iron ring, utility clamps, barometer, meter stick, graph paper.

PROCEDURE

1. Obtain or construct a piece of apparatus similar to that shown in Fig 4-1. It may be possible to borrow equipment from the physics department.

2. Read and record the room temperature and atmospheric pressure, P_1, in the table. The data table may need to be modified depending on the type of appartus used.

3. With the water levels in the two tubes *equal,* measure the volume of the gas.

4. Increase the pressure on the gas in tube A by raising the leveling bulb until the difference in water levels is greater than 0.5 meter or 500 mm. This can be done by moving the stand containing the leveling bulb up to a higher shelf, or moving the stand containing the gas tube down to the floor. Record the new distance (ℓ_2) and the new volume (V_2) in the table. The distance (ℓ_2) is the difference (in mm) between the water levels in gas tube A and the leveling bulb. Divide this

Table I   Boyle's Law

Atmospheric Pressure (torr)	Distance (ℓ) between H_2O Level in Gas Tube A and Leveling Bulb (mm)	Pressure Diff. $\dfrac{\ell}{13.6}$ (torr)	Total Pressure on Gas (torr)	Volume of Gas (ml)	$P_{(torr)} \times V_{(ml)}$	$\dfrac{P_{(torr)}}{V_{(ml)}}$

difference by 13.6 and add to the atmospheric pressure to give the total pressure P_2 which corresponds to the new volume V_2.

5. Again increase the pressure on the gas in tube A by raising the bulb until ℓ is greater than 1000 mm. Record the new volume V_3. Record the difference between water levels in the two tubes (ℓ_3), divide by 13.6 and again add to the atmospheric pressure to obtain the total pressure P_3 which corresponds to V_3.

6. Decrease the pressure on the gas in tube A by lowering the bulb until the water level in the leveling bulb is about 500 mm below the level in tube A. Measure ℓ_4 and record the new volume V_4. Divide ℓ_4 by 13.6 and this time subtract this difference from atmospheric pressure to give the total pressure P_4 on the gas in A.

7. Decrease the pressure further by adjusting the water level in the bulb so that it is about 1000 mm below the level in tube A. Measure V_5 and the difference between the levels ℓ_5. Divide ℓ_5 by 13.6 and subtract from atmospheric pressure to obtain P_5.

8. Make the calculations necessary to complete the table. Then plot a graph of pressure (torr) vs $\dfrac{1}{V_{(ml)}}$. Plot the pressures as ordinates (vertically) and the reciprocal volumes as abscissas (horizontally). Determine the slope of the line. What are

its units? Refer to Appendix 1 Part E of the Text for a discussion of the slope concept.

FOLLOW-UP QUESTIONS

1. What do you notice about the values of your PV products and your P/V quotients? What mathematical relationship between P and V do these results indicate? Express it in the form of an equation.

2. Explain why a graph of P vs $\dfrac{1}{V}$ is more meaningful in this experiment than a graph of P vs V? If you are not certain what the latter graph would be like, plot it and determine for yourself the advantage of the former.

3. Compare the value and units calculated for the slope of the graph of P vs 1/V with the values and units of the PV products calculated for each measurement.

4. Explain the observed relationship between the pressure and volume of a gas in terms of the Kinetic Molecular Theory.

5. Does the gas which you investigated in this experiment conform rigorously to the Kinetic Molecular Theory? Explain how it deviates, if it does.

6. A sample of oxygen gas occupies a volume of 500 ml at 10°C and 700 torr. Determine the volume at the same temperature and 760 torr.

4-2

Effect of Temperature Change on the Volume of a Gas—Determination of Absolute Zero

GENERAL DISCUSSION

Our molecular model of matter suggests that there may be some mathematical relationship among the variables which describe a confined gas. These variables consist of the amount of the gas sample (*i.e.* the number of moles), the volume occupied by the gas, its temperature, and pressure. In order to test for a relationship between any two of these variables, one must hold the others constant by some experimental means.

In this experiment you are to test the effect on the volume occupied by a fixed amount of gas (air), held at constant (atmospheric) pressure, as the temperature of the gas is varied. After gathering data about volume at several temperatures, you then plot volume *vs* Celsius temperature and ascertain what, if any, mathematical relationship exists between these two variables.

OBJECTIVE

To determine the mathematical relationship between volume and Celsius temperature of a fixed mass of gas at constant pressure.

MATERIALS

Thin-walled capillary tube sealed at one end, thermometer, metric ruler, No. 30 non-detergent motor oil, ice, Dry Ice, acetone or "Dowanol," burner, and assortment of beakers.

PROCEDURE

1. Obtain a piece of thin-walled capillary tubing, sealed at one end, which contains a small amount of trapped dry air which is held in by an oil plug. The tube should be at least 10 cm long. These may have been previously prepared for you, but if not, you may prepare one by this procedure: Carefully grasp the tube with forceps or tongs near the sealed end. Move the tube back and forth in a *very low* blue burner flame in order to heat and dry the air in it to a temperature above 100°C. Do *not* heat the tube so hot that the glass begins to melt. While the tube is still hot, immerse the open end in a few ml of No. 30, non-detergent motor oil. As the air in the tube cools, its pressure drops and some oil is forced into the tube by atmospheric pressure. As soon as this occurs, remove the tube from the oil and place it on a piece of paper toweling. If the tube has been prepared properly, the oil plug has trapped a column of air which, at room temperature, is at least 8 cm long.

2. With small pieces of thin copper wire, or with small rubber bands, tie the tube onto a −10 to 110-degree Celsius thermometer so that the sealed end of the tube is coincident with the base of the bulb of the thermometer. Remember that the walls of the capillary tube are quite thin. Use extreme care to avoid breakage.

3. Record the temperature reading of the thermometer and also the degree reading on the thermometer which is coincident with the inner surface of the oil plug. You will later convert this latter measurement to units of length. Record both readings as precisely as the thermometers being used allow by estimating between the graduated divisions.

4. Place the thermometer and tube in a beaker of boiling water so that the air column is submerged; however, be certain that the open end of the tube remains out of the water. Stir gently until the thermometer reading becomes constant. Read and record the temperature and position of the oil plug as in step 3.

5. Remove the thermometer and tube from the hot water, allow to cool for a minute or so, then place in an ice bath. As soon as a constant temperature is reached, read and record as above.

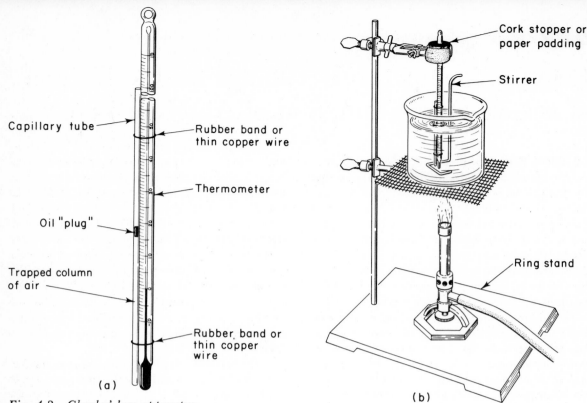

Capillary tube

Rubber band or
thin copper wire

Thermometer

Oil "plug"

Trapped column
of air

Rubber band or
thin copper wire

Cork stopper or
paper padding

Stirrer

Ring stand

(a)

(b)

Fig. 4-2   Charles' law apparatus.

6. Take the thermometer from the ice bath and carefully remove the capillary tube by loosening or clipping the copper wires. Dry the tube with a tissue. Grasp the upper (open) end of the tube with forceps or tongs and immerse it almost completely into a Dry-Ice slurry in acetone which has been prepared for you by the instructor. Hold the tube in the bath for at least two minutes. Remove the tube, lay it on a paper towel and as quickly as possible measure the length of the air column to ±0.5 mm. Note that at the temperature of the Dry-Ice slurry ($-78°C$) the oil plug congeals and its position in the tube remains stationary for sufficient time for measurements to be made.

7. Convert the degree readings made in steps 3–5 to units of length by measuring the distance from the end of the thermometer bulb to the degree marks recorded previously. Make any corrections necessary for the length of the seal at the end of the tube.

8. On graph paper, choose suitable scales and as precisely as possible, plot the lengths of the

Table II   Charles' Law

	Room Conditions	Boiling-Water Bath	Ice-Water Bath	Dry-Ice Slurry
Temperature (°C)				
Length of air column (°C)				
Length of air column (mm)				

trapped air column on the ordinate *vs* the corresponding Celsius temperatures on the abscissa. The abscissa should extend from −300°C to +100°C.

FOLLOW-UP DISCUSSION

In order to make appropriate interpretations of the data and your graph, you should consider the following: The inner portion of the capillary tube is a cylinder with constant diameter. Recalling that the volume of a cylinder equals the product of the length and its cross-sectional area ($V = \pi r^2 \ell$), you can see that any change in the length of the trapped air column is directly proportional to its change in volume. Thus, a plot of its length *vs* temperature gives the same relative information as if the actual volumes were used.

If reasonable care was used in gathering data, you should find that the points on your graph fall on a straight line. Recall that the general equation for a straight line is $y = mx + b$, where m is the slope and b is the intercept. Thus, in the case of your graph a linear relationship is indicated between volume and Celsius temperature. This result, though informative, does not show any *simple* relationship between the two variables. Recall, however, that the Celsius temperature scale is an arbitrary one and that 0°C has no special meaning with respect to gas behavior. (It is merely the melting point of ice at one atmospheric pressure.)

You can modify your graph and arrive at a simpler and more meaningful relationship between temperature and the volume of a gas. Using a broken line, extrapolate (extend beyond the experimental range) your graph downward until it intersects the abscissa. This intercept represents the Celsius temperature at which the air, if it were to remain in the gaseous state, would have zero volume. We shall now define a new temperature scale, to be called the Kelvin scale, in which the intercept is taken as zero and in which a one-degree span is equal to a one-degree span on the Celsius scale. This new zero of temperature is called *absolute* zero and has important theoretical significance.

On your graph construct a new ordinate which intersects 0°K and cross out, or disregard, the original ordinate. The graph is now in the form which has greater significance. Because the line now passes through zero on both axes, it now has an equation of the form $y = mx$. In this case the equation is $V = mT$, where V is the relative volume of the air in the tube and T is the Kelvin temperature. This, of course, indicates that these two variables are directly proportional to each other. This relationship, called Charles' law, is one of several important laws which describe the behavior of gases.

FOLLOW-UP QUESTIONS

1. Calculate the percent deviation between your value of absolute zero on the Celsius scale and the accepted value of −273°.

2. What experimental restrictions must be imposed if the direct proportionality between the volume and Kelvin temperature of a gas is to hold?

3. Charles' Law applies exactly only to ideal gas molecules, which are assumed to be dimensionless points; however, the actual radii of the gas molecules in the air are in the order of magnitude of 10^{-8} cm. (a) Calculate the approximate volume occupied by one mole of such molecules (*i.e.* the *actual* space taken up by the molecules) assuming them to be spherical in shape. (b) The volume of one mole of a gas under room conditions (25° and one atmosphere) is about 25 liters. Calculate the percentage of this volume that the molecules of the air actually occupy. (c) Based upon your answer to (b), is much error introduced if one used Charles' Law when dealing with real gases under conditions not much different from room conditions? Note that another factor, intermolecular attraction, causes real gases to deviate from ideal; however, such attractions are quite small under room conditions.

4. Commercial, "detergent-containing" motor oils contain several additives which are quite volatile at higher temperatures. Suggest the reason for a non-detergent oil being specified for this experiment. In which direction is the error in the point obtained in the boiling water bath if volatility were a problem?

4-3

Effect of Temperature Change on the Pressure of a Gas—Determination of Absolute Zero

GENERAL DISCUSSION

When a gas is heated, the speed and average kinetic energy of its molecules are increased. Consequently, they strike the sides of a container more frequently and more vigorously. If the container is flexible, like a rubber balloon, it expands. When the temperature is reduced, the balloon shrinks. If we assume the pressure is constant, we can say that as the temperature of a given mass of gas is increased, the volume of the gas will also increase.

If the container is inflexible, like a metal tank, the increased frequency of molecular impacts with the side of the container and the greater "push" exerted by each impact causes an increase in pressure. Similarly, as the temperature of the system decreases, the pressure decreases. Continued lowering of the temperature results in a decrease in pressure. A graph may be plotted to show how the pressure of a given mass of gas varies as the temperature is changed. The temperature at which the pressure of the gas would, in theory, become zero can be determined by extrapolating (extending) the curve of the graph to zero pressure. This temperature is known as *absolute zero*.

In this experiment we shall vary the temperature of a metal bulb having a fixed volume and containing a fixed amount of air. You will record the corresponding pressure changes and then plot a graph of temperature in °C versus pressure in lbs/in². By extrapolating the graph to zero pressure, you obtain an experimental value for absolute zero. If only one piece of apparatus is available, this experiment may be done as a teacher or student demonstration.

OBJECTIVES

1. To determine experimentally the relationship

between the temperature and the pressure of a fixed mass of gas held at constant volume.

2. To determine a value for absolute zero by extrapolating an experimentally derived temperature-pressure curve.

MATERIALS

Gay-Lussac apparatus (absolute zero demonstrator), 1500-ml beaker, ring stand, wire screen, burner, thermometer, ice, ammonium chloride, graph paper.

PROCEDURE

1. Immerse the metal bulb of the Gay-Lussac apparatus and a thermometer in boiling water in a 1500-ml beaker (Figure 4-3). Allow the pres-

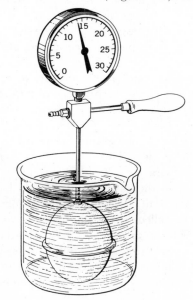

Fig. 4-3   Gay-Lussac apparatus.

sure to reach a maximum; then read the temperature and pressure. Record all data in the table.

2. Pour off about one-half of the boiling water and refill the beaker with tap water. Again read the temperature and pressure.

Reading Number	Temperature (°C)	Pressure (lb/in.²)
1		
2		
3		
4		

3. Pour off all of the warm water and fill the beaker with tap water. Take another temperature and pressure reading.

4. Place the bulb of the apparatus into a 1500-ml beaker containing a slushy mixture of ice and ammonium chloride. As soon as the pressure reaches a minimum, record both the temperature and pressure.

5. Plot a graph with temperatures (°C) as abscissas (horizontally) and pressures (lb/in.²) as ordinates (vertically). Allow space for temperature readings to −300°C. Locate the points on the graph, using the data in the table.

6. Using a broken line, extrapolate the solid line through these points to zero pressure.

FOLLOW-UP DISCUSSION

If this experiment was carefully performed, your graph should be a straight line. There are several reasons why the experimental points might not fall on the line. First of all, we are assuming that the temperature reading on the outside of the bulb also represents the temperature inside the bulb. This would be a valid assumption, provided enough time is allowed for the air in the bulb to

reach the temperature of the water outside the bulb.

We are also assuming that air acts as an ideal or perfect gas. This means that it would continue to contract upon further cooling until it had zero volume. Although this is not true, air does act, in the temperature range of this experiment, almost as if it were an ideal gas. If we had been able to continue cooling the bulb, the pressure would have suddenly dropped when the temperature was reached at which the components of air begin to liquefy.

FOLLOW-UP QUESTIONS

1. What value did you obtain for absolute zero? What is the percentage difference between your experimental value and the correct value (−273°C)?

2. Explain how, using the Gay-Lussac apparatus and your graph, you could measure temperature without a thermometer.

3. Transcribe the data from your Table into the larger Table. Test the data to see whether the proportionality between temperature and pressure is direct or inverse by completing the calculations in the Table. (a) Is the pressure of a confined gas directly, inversely, or not proportional to the Celsius temperature? Justify your answer. (b) Is the pressure of a confined gas directly, inversely, or not proportional to the Kelvin temperature? Justify your answer. (c) Express the mathematical relationship between pressure and Kelvin temperature in terms of a general equation. (d) Use the expression developed in part (c) to explain the validity of the equation $\dfrac{P_1}{T_1} = \dfrac{P_2}{T_2}$.

4. A metal tank filled with air at 20°C has a pressure of 3 atm. At what Celsius temperature does the pressure become 5 atm?

4-4

The Ideal Gas Constant

GENERAL DISCUSSION

The ideal gas law may be expressed as

$$PV = nRT \qquad \text{Eq. 1}$$

which states that the ratio R of the product of pressure and volume of a confined ideal gas to the product of number of moles of gas and its Kelvin temperature is a constant. Thus, solving Equation (1) for R, we obtain

$$R = \frac{PV}{nT} \qquad \text{Eq. 2}$$

In this experiment you will test the validity of Equation (2) for several gases and determine whether or not they deviate markedly from ideal behavior under the conditions of this experiment. The number of moles n of any substance can be calculated from its mass m and its molecular mass M. Thus, Equation (2) can be expressed as

$$R = \frac{PVM}{mT} \qquad \text{Eq. 3}$$

It is suggested that the class be divided into several groups, with each group being assigned a particular gas to investigate according to one of the procedures outlined below. Class data may then be compiled so that the constancy of R can be tested. Gases whose solubility in water is negligible may be collected by water displacement; however, those which are considerably soluble in water will have to be collected and weighed in dry flasks.

OBJECTIVES

1. To determine numerical values for R for several gases in order to test the hypothesis that it is a constant for all gases under ordinary conditions of temperature and pressure.

2. To learn several ways of making and collecting small amounts of gas in the laboratory.

MATERIALS

Part A: 200-mm Pyrex test tube, large cork with hole large enough to hold test-tube assembly, balance, sodium peroxide, 50-ml beaker, dropper, petroleum jelly, 0.1-M $CuSO_4$, rubber policeman, 500-ml flask, 400-ml beaker, two-hole stopper to fit flask, screw clamp, glass tubing, rubber tubing, thermometer, 500-ml graduated cylinder. Part B: 125-ml erlenmeyer flask, reagent grade hydrazine sulfate, 1-M H_2SO_4, reagent grade potassium iodate, shell vial, forceps, one-hole stopper to fit flask. Part C: 250-ml erlenmeyer flask with solid stopper, 250-ml erlenmeyer flask fitted with a one-hole stopper, Dry Ice. Part D: 12-M HCl, magnesium ribbon, gas tube (eudiometer), thread, large jar or beaker. Part E: lecture bottles or tanks of gases.

PROCEDURE

A. Oxygen Gas (O₂)

1. Place 2–3 grams of sodium peroxide (Na_2O_2) in a clean and *dry* 200-mm Pyrex test tube. A smaller, 150-mm tube is needed if the assembly is to be suspended by a wire hook in an analytical balance. If a top loader balance is used, the tube can be supported on a large, inverted cork which has a hole drilled through it which is of proper diameter so that the test-tube assembly fits snugly into it as shown in Fig. 4-4. The balance can be "tared" to zero with the cork on the pan alone.

2. Place about 5 ml of a 0.1-M $CuSO_4$ solution in a 50-ml beaker. Obtain, or construct, a dropper assembly as shown in Fig. 4-5 and fill it with the $CuSO_4$ solution in the usual manner. In order to remove any trapped air, invert the dropper and tap the glass and/or rubber bulb with your fingers to force the liquid down into the bulb and the air upward. When all of the liquid is in the bulb, squeeze it to force the air out. Retain pressure on

the bulb, invert and place the tip into the $CuSO_4$ solution. Release the bulb and allow the solution to finish filling the dropper. Dry the assembly completely with a tissue and insert a small amount of petroleum jelly into the dropper tip to prevent leakage of solution on the Na_2O_2 in the test tube.

3. Stopper the test tube with the filled dropper assembly as shown in Fig. 4-5, place a rubber policeman on the glass bend, and determine the mass of the entire assembly as precisely as possible using the technique outlined by your instructor. Weighing to a precision of ± 0.005 g or better is recommended.

4. Obtain a 500-ml flask, a 400-ml beaker, a two-hole stopper to fit the flask, a screw clamp, and sufficient glass tubing to construct the remainder of the apparatus shown in Fig. 4-5.

5. Adjust the height of the test tube-dropper assembly so that it can easily be connected to the intake tube to the flask. Do not connect as yet. Fill the flask with tap water. Be sure that the glass tube leading to the test tube does not touch the water and that the tube leading to the beaker

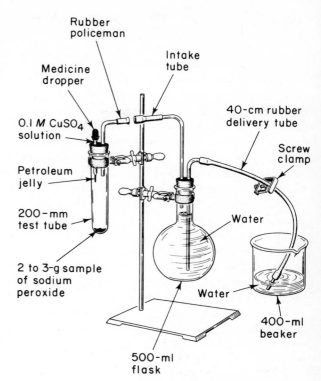

Fig. 4-5 *Apparatus for generating and measuring volume of oxygen.*

extends nearly to the bottom of the flask. Add about 150 ml of tap water to the beaker.

6. Loosen the screw clamp and blow into the intake tube until the outlet tube is completely filled with water. Immediately tighten the screw clamp to prevent loss of water by siphoning.

7. Remove the rubber policeman from the glass bend on the test tube and connect to the intake tube. Check all connections to make sure they are tight.

8. Bring the pressure of the air in the flask to atmospheric pressure by loosening the screw clamp and raising the beaker until the water level is the same as that in the flask. Tighten the clamp and empty (but do not dry) the beaker. Replace the beaker and again open the clamp. If the system is air tight, only a slight amount of water will run into the beaker; then the flow stops. *Do not discard this water!* If there is a leak in the system,

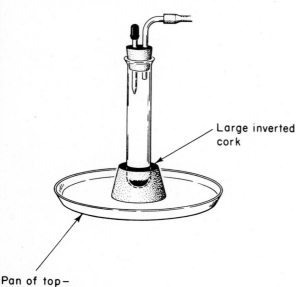

Fig. 4-4 *Set-up for weighing test tube on top-loading balance.*

check all connections until it is found; then, adjust the water levels as before.

9. With the clamp *open*, gently squeeze the rubber bulb and cause the $CuSO_4$ solution to fall onto the Na_2O_2 a few drops at a time over a period of about 5 minutes. If the test tube becomes too warm, or if the reaction becomes too vigorous, immerse the tube into a beaker of cold water. Do not allow the rubber tube to come out of the 400-ml beaker at any time before the pressures are again equalized in Step 11.

10. When the beaker is approximately ¾ full of water, discontinue the addition of the $CuSO_4$ solution and allow the system to cool to room temperature. Record the temperature.

11. Again, bring the gas in the flask to atmospheric pressure by raising the beaker until the two water levels are equal. Close the screw clamp and remove the tubing from the beaker.

12. Obtain the volume of the water in the beaker by pouring it into a 500-ml graduated cylinder. This volume represents the volume of the oxygen gas generated.

13. Disconnect the test tube-dropper assembly from the intake tube, replace the rubber policeman, dry *thoroughly* with a tissue, and determine the mass of the assembly to the same precision as in Step 3. The loss in mass represented by the difference between the original and final masses is equal to the mass of the oxygen generated.

14. Read the Follow-up Discussion for this part of the experiment and make the necessary calculations to complete Table I on page 88. Be certain to show all calculations in your final report. Use appropriate units throughout and follow the rules of significant figures.

B. Nitrogen Gas (N_2)

1. Determine the mass of a clean and dry 125-ml erlenmeyer flask to a precision of ±0.005 g or better.

2. Weigh out approximately 1.8 g of reagent-grade hydrazine sulfate ($N_2H_5^+HSO_4^-$) onto a clean piece of paper. Transfer to the flask and weigh the flask assembly and contents to ±0.005 g or better.

3. Add about 30 ml of 1-M H_2SO_4 to the flask and mix thoroughly. Some of the hydrazine sulfate remains undissolved at this point but will dissolve and react completely in Step 8.

4. Add 3 g or more of reagent grade potassium iodate (KIO_3) to a clean and dry 50×20 mm shell vial. This weighing need not be exact as long as the number of moles of KIO_3 is greater than the number of moles of hydrazine sulfate. Equation 6 in the Follow-up Discussion for this part indicates that these substances react on a 1:1 mole ratio, so it is necessary that the KIO_3 be present in excess so as to react with all of the precisely weighed hydrazine sulfate.

5. Submerge the flask about half way in a beaker of cold tap water and clamp in position as shown in Fig. 4-6.

6. Grasp the wall of the vial with clean forceps and carefully lower it into the flask, making sure that it remains upright. (If desired, you may insert a short piece of glass rod in the vial, prior to its insertion into the flask, of such a length that if the vial is accidentally tipped over, it will not tip far enough to fall prematurely into the hydrazine sulfate solution.)

7. Place a one-hole stopper, fitted with a right-angle glass bend in the neck of the flask and attach it to the intake tube leading to the 500-ml flask which was prepared according to the procedure outlined in Steps 4–8 of Part A above.

8. After the pressure of the system has been equalized to that of the atmosphere and the system has been tested for leaks, release the 125-ml flask from the clamp and mix the reactants by tilting the flask so that the hydrazine sulfate solution completely rinses the inside of the vial. The evolution of bubbles of N_2 should begin immediately.

9. Thoroughly mix the solution by gently shaking and swirling the flask, but keep the lower portion of the flask immersed in water so that the flask remains as close to room temperature as possible. By so doing, iodine, which is produced in this reaction, does not vaporize significantly. Continue mixing the contents of the flask until no more nitrogen is generated.

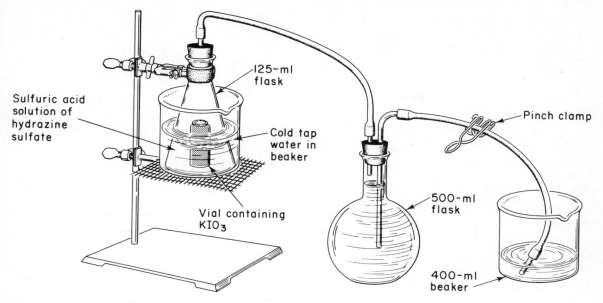

Fig. 4-6 Apparatus for generating and measuring nitrogen gas.

10. Clamp the flask back into position and then carry out Steps 11 and 12 of Part A. Record the air temperature.

11. Read the Follow-up Discussion for this part of the experiment and make the necessary calculations to complete Table II on page 89.

C. Carbon Dioxide (CO_2)

1. Equip a clean, dry 250-ml erlenmeyer flask with a one-hole stopper equipped with a thermometer. Carefully, weigh the flask stopper, and thermometer to ±0.005 g if possible. Record temperature of air in flask.

2. In a second flask, fitted with a one-hole stopper, right angle glass bend, and a one-foot length of rubber tubing, place a piece of Dry Ice [$CO_2(s)$] about 2 to 3 cm in average diameter, in the flask.

3. Close the flask with the one-hole stopper and place the end of the rubber tubing leading from it into the weighed erlenmeyer flask so that the end reaches down to the bottom. The CO_2 displaces the less dense air upward and out of the flask.

4. Allow the Dry Ice to sublime (evaporate) for at least three minutes. Remove the rubber tubing and as quickly as possible, replace the stopper and thermometer in the neck of the flask. Determine the mass of the flask, stopper, thermometer, and CO_2 to the same precision as the first weighing. Record the temperature of the CO_2.

5. Repeat the filling of the flask with CO_2, according to the above procedure until two successive weighings agree to ±0.01 g or better. By doing this, you can be reasonably certain that all of the air has been displaced by the carbon dioxide gas introduced into the flask.

6. With a felt-tipped marker, make a mark on the neck of the flask to indicate where the bottom of the stopper rests when inserted into the flask. Remove the stopper and fill the flask to this mark with tap water. Pour this water into a graduated cylinder and determine its volume to as high a precision as possible.

7. Read the Follow-up Discussion for this part and make the necessary calculations to complete Table III on page 90.

Table I Experimental Determination of *R* Using Oxygen

Name of Gas		
1. Mass of test tube, dropper assembly, and contents before reaction		g
2. Mass of test tube, dropper assembly, and contents after reaction		g
3. Mass of gas evolved		g
4. Volume of gas produced (volume of water displaced)		ml
5. Temperature (Celsius)		°C
6. Temperature (Kelvin)		°K
7. Barometric pressure		torr
8. Vapor pressure of water at above temperature (from table)		torr
9. Partial pressure of gas		torr
10. Molecular mass of gas		g/mole
11. Experimental value of *R*		$\dfrac{\text{ml} \cdot \text{torr}}{\text{°K} \cdot \text{mole}}$
12. Accepted value of *R*	6.24×10^4	$\dfrac{\text{ml} \cdot \text{torr}}{\text{°K} \cdot \text{mole}}$
13. Percentage deviation between experimental and accepted value		%

D. Hydrogen (H₂)

1. Follow the procedure outlined in Experiment 4-5 and use the known mole relationship between magnesium and hydrogen to determine the value of *R*. Modify the data table in Experiment 4-5 accordingly.

E. Other Gases

1. Follow the procedure outlined for carbon dioxide above but use lecture bottles which are available commercially as sources for the gases being tested. If possible, obtain gases of rather high molecular mass, or whose molecules have rather unsymmetrical shapes, in order to test these variables as factors which may have an effect on deviation from ideal behavior. Your instructor will suggest possible gases to test.

FOLLOW-UP DISCUSSION

A. Oxygen Gas

The experimental value for *R* can be determined by substituting items 3, 4, 6, 7, and 10 from Table I-1 into Equation 3. The accepted value may be determined by substituting the molar volume of 22 400 ml at STP (273°K, 760 torr) and 1.00 mole into Equation 2. This yields a value of

$$R = 6.24 \times 10^4 \frac{(\text{ml})(\text{torr})}{(\text{°K})(\text{mole})}$$

Note that these units must be used whenever this numerical value of *R* is used in a problem or laboratory calculation involving it.

The skeleton expression for this reaction is

$$Na_2O_2(s) + H_2O(\ell) \rightarrow NaOH(aq) + O_2(g)$$

$$\text{Eq. 4}$$

You are asked to balance this expression in Follow-up Question 1. The reaction between sodium peroxide and water may be slow at room temperature but Cu^{2+} ions catalyze the reaction. The $CuSO_4$ solution served as a source of these ions. Because a catalyst is not permanently altered in a reaction, it is usually not included in the equation for the reaction. Sometimes, however, their presence may be indicated by writing their formula over or under the arrow.

B. Nitrogen Gas

The reaction used for the generation of nitrogen gas is very complex and of a type not taken up in detail until much later in the course. The most concise and accurate form of the equation for this reaction shows it in *net ionic* form wherein the unreactive ions are left out of the equation. The equation is shown below in balanced form so that you can see the mole ratio between the hydrazonium ion and the nitrogen gas produced.

$$5N_2H_5^+(aq) + 4IO_3^-(aq) \rightarrow$$
$$5N_2(g) + 2I_2(s) + H^+(aq) + 12H_2O(\ell)$$
$$\text{Eq. 6}$$

An equation (as above) must have both charge and mass balance. One can deduce from the above equation that one mole of nitrogen gas is produced for each mole of hydrazine sulfate used.

C. Carbon Dioxide Gas

The Dry Ice is placed in a separate flask so that it will have some time to warm to room tempera-

Table II   Experimental Determination of R Using Nitrogen

1. Mass of flask plus hydrazine sulfate	g
2. Mass of empty flask	g
3. Mass of hydrazine sulfate used	g
4. Molecular mass of hydrazine sulfate ($N_2H_5^+HSO_4^-$)	g/mole
5. Number of moles of hydrazine sulfate used	mole
6. Number of moles of nitrogen gas evolved (from Equation 3 on page 84)	mole
7. Volume of nitrogen evolved (volume of water displaced)	ml
8. Temperature (Celsius)	°C
9. Temperature (Kelvin)	°K
10. Barometric pressure	torr
11. Vapor pressure of water at above temperature (from table)	torr
12. Partial pressure of nitrogen gas	torr
13. Experimental value of R	$\dfrac{ml \cdot torr}{°K \cdot mole}$
14. Accepted value of R	$6.24 \times 10^4 \dfrac{ml \cdot torr}{°K \cdot mole}$
15. Percentage deviation between experimental and accepted value	%

ture before its mass is determined. Also, it is not necessary for the Dry Ice to sublime completely before making mass measurements. If a "top loader" balance is available, it is suggested that the flask being weighed be equipped with a one-hole stopper containing a thermometer. In so doing, one can get a more accurate value of the temperature of the air and the CO_2 in the flask, and not have to *assume* that both are at room temperature.

Because the flask contained air when originally weighed, a correction for its mass must be made. Determine its mass by multiplying the volume of the flask by the density of air under the temperature and pressure conditions during the experiment. The density may be obtained from any handbook of chemistry available in your classroom or school library. Determine the mass of the empty flask plus stopper by subtracting the cal-

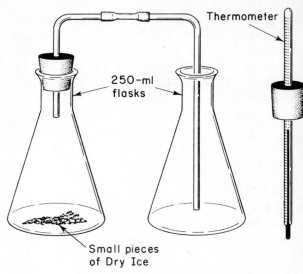

Fig. 4-7 *Apparatus for generating and measuring carbon dioxide gas.*

Table III Experimental Determination of *R* Using Carbon Dioxide

1. Mass of flask, stopper, and air	g
2. Volume of flask to bottom of stopper	ml
3. Barometric pressure	torr
4. Room temperature (Celsius)	°C
5. Room temperature (Kelvin)	°K
6. Number of moles of nitrogen gas evolved (from Equation 3 on page 00)	g/ml
7. Calculated mass of air in flask	g
8. Mass of flask, stopper, and CO_2	g
9. Mass of empty flask and stopper (1 minus 7)	g
10. Mass of carbon dioxide in flask	g
11. Molecular mass of carbon dioxide	g/mole
12. Pressure of carbon dioxide (same as 3)	torr
13. Experimental value of *R*	$\dfrac{\text{ml} \cdot \text{torr}}{\text{°K} \cdot \text{mole}}$
14. Accepted value of *R*	$6.24 \times 10^4 \dfrac{\text{ml} \cdot \text{torr}}{\text{°K} \cdot \text{mole}}$
15. Percentage deviation between experimental and accepted value	%

culated mass of air from the experimentally determined mass of the flask, stopper, and air.

D. Other Gases

If other gases are tested, which are obtained from commercially available tanks or lecture bottles, the calculations are carried out in exactly the same manner as those used in the part using carbon dioxide.

FOLLOW-UP QUESTIONS

1. Balance Equation 4 for the reaction between water and sodium peroxide.

2. Calculate the mass of sodium peroxide used in a reaction in which 375 ml of O_2 is produced at 27°C and collected by displacement of water, as in Part A, at 755 torr.

3. How many ml of dry acetylene gas, at STP can be prepared from 6.40 g of calcium carbide?

4. Summarize the sources of error in the part of the experiment which you actually performed. Explain briefly how each error would affect your experimental value of R.

5. If, in Part C of the experiment, a student weighed out 1.85 g of hydrazine sulfate and 3.00 g of potassium iodate, how many grams of KIO_3 would remain unreacted?

6. Look up the vapor pressure of iodine under room conditions in a handbook of chemistry. Is any appreciable error introduced in Part C if one doesn't correct for this vapor pressure in addition to the correction for water-vapor pressure? Explain your answer briefly.

4-5
Molar Volume of a Gas

GENERAL DISCUSSION

The volume occupied by one mole of a gas is known as its molar volume. A mole of any gas contains 6.02×10^{23} molecules. At the same conditions of temperature and pressure, equal volumes of ideal (perfect) gases contain equal numbers of molecules. It follows that the molar volume of all ideal gases is a constant at the same conditions of temperature and pressure. For convenience, the molar volume is generally referred to standard conditions of $273°K$ and 760 torr.

The molar volume of a gas at standard conditions is a convenient constant that we can use in stoichiometric calculations to determine the volume of gas that should be produced in a given reaction at a given temperature and pressure. In addition, we can use this constant and the measured density of a gas to determine an approximate value for its molecular mass.

In this experiment you will determine the value of this constant by using the data collected from a reaction between magnesium and hydrochloric acid. The formula- and net-ionic equations are

$$Mg + 2HCl \rightarrow MgCl_2 + H_2$$
$$Mg(s) + 2H^+(aq) \rightarrow Mg^{2+}(aq) + H_2(g)$$

Inspection of this equation reveals that one mole (24.3 g) of magnesium yields one mole (2.02 g) of hydrogen gas. You allow a known mass of magnesium to react with excess hydrochloric acid, and measure the volume of hydrogen evolved. The volume of hydrogen is changed to standard conditions. Knowing the number of moles of hydrogen (same as magnesium) and the standard volume of hydrogen, you can calculate the number of liters per mole.

OBJECTIVES

1. To determine an experimental molar volume for hydrogen.

2. To study mass-volume relationships in chemical reactions.

3. To become familiar with the relationship between the density and molecular mass of a gas.

4. To illustrate application of gas laws.

MATERIALS

Magnesium ribbon, meter stick or metric ruler, large beaker or jar, hydrochloric acid $(12\ M)$, buret or gas tube, thread, thermometer, barometer, balance, emery cloth or sandpaper.

PROCEDURE

1. Obtain a piece of magnesium ribbon about 5 cm long and remove any oxide coating by buffing with a piece of emery cloth. Remove any dust and weigh the ribbon to ±0.005 g. Record the mass, roll the ribbon into a loose coil, and tie it to a piece of thread or fine copper wire about 15 cm long.

2. Fill a large beaker or jar about ¾ full of water.

3. Pour 5 ml of 12-M hydrochloric acid into a buret or gas tube. Add enough water to fill the gas tube completely or just reach the zero mark on the buret. Lower the coil of magnesium into the tube to a depth of several cm.

4. Close the tube with a finger so that the thread is held firmly against the edge of the tube. Taking care that no air enters, invert the tube in the beaker and hold it against the bottom of the beaker. The acid flows down and reacts with the magnesium. If small pieces of magnesium stick to the side of the tube, wash them down by tilting the tube.

5. When the magnesium has completely reacted, pour water into the beaker or jar until its level equals that of the liquid inside the tube. Bubbles clinging to the sides of the tube should be

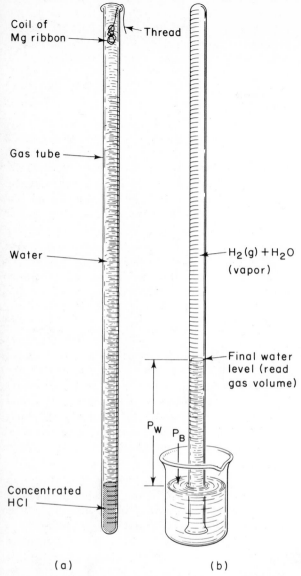

Coil of
Mg ribbon

Thread

Gas tube

Water

H₂(g) + H₂O
(vapor)

Final water
level (read
gas volume)

P_W P_B

Concentrated
HCl

(a)   (b)

Fig. 4-8 Apparatus for determining molar volume of hydrogen.

subtract it from the atmospheric pressure (depending on the relationship between the two levels). If a buret was used, it will be necessary to place your finger over the open end, remove it from the water and clamp it in an upright position. Explain why.

6. Assume that a thermal equilibrium has been established between the gas in the tube and the air outside the tube and take the temperature of the air. Record the barometric reading at this temperature. Obtain the water-vapor pressure at this temperature from the Appendix.

7. Make the calculations required to fill in all the other blanks in the table.

Table I Molar Volume

1	Mass of magnesium ribbon used	
2	Moles of magnesium ribbon used	
3	Volume in liters of hydrogen gas as collected	
4	Temperature of water and of gas (°C)	
5	Barometric pressure (torr)	
6	Vapor pressure of water (torr)	
7	Pressure of dry hydrogen gas (torr)	
8	Volume in liters of hydrogen gas (changed to STP)	
9	Moles of hydrogen gas (numerically equal to moles of magnesium)	
10	Molar volume (liters per one mole)	
11	Theoretical molar volume for perfect gas	
12	Percentage deviation between experimental and calculated value	

FOLLOW-UP DISCUSSION

The molar volume for perfect gases is constant. This value is not exactly identical for any two real gases since the degree of intermolecular attraction varies. Some molecules, because of their shape and polarity, attract each other more

dislodged by tapping the tube gently. Wait for five minutes for the system to come to room temperature, then record the volume of the hydrogen. If it is not possible to equalize the water levels, then measure the difference (in mm) between the two levels and divide this by 13.6 to convert it into torr. Either add the result to or

strongly. In this case the volume of a mole is less than for a gas whose molecules have little attraction for each other. The deviation is slight for many gases, such as hydrogen, so that the "ideal" value of 22.4ℓ can be used in many calculations without causing a significant error.

The gas that we collected in the gas tube was mostly hydrogen, but as the hydrogen passed through the water it removed some of the air dissolved in water. The collected gas also contained water vapor. We cannot easily correct for the dissolved air but it is possible to correct for the water vapor, thus mathematically "drying" the hydrogen gas. The water vapor pressure varies with the temperature. This adjustment, an application of Dalton's Law, can be made by subtracting the water vapor pressure from the total pressure of the gas. In this case the total pressure was equal to atmospheric pressure since the level inside the tube was equalized with the level outside the tube. By applying the gas laws, the volume of hydrogen collected at room conditions can be changed to standard conditions. The volume at standard conditions expressed in liters (Item 8) divided by the number of moles of hydrogen (Item 9 is the molar volume. Analysis and interpretation of the ideas and data involved in this experiment reveal that the density and molecular mass of any gas are related by a constant which is the molar volume. This relationship is unique for gases; it does not apply to materials in the liquid or solid phase. In other words, the molar volume of different liquids and solids is not equal; hence density measurements alone cannot be used to determine the molecular mass of substances in the solid or liquid phase.

One objective of this experiment was to determine the molar volume of a gas; that is, the volume of gas occupied by one gram-molecular mass (one mole) of the gas. A generalization requires more than a single experiment. If we used the data obtained for all the gases tested in Experiment 4-4 to calculate each of their molar volumes, we would find that, within experimental error, all would have approximately the same value. Thus, we shall assume that the molar

volume for all gases at the same room conditions is constant and use this value to calculate molecular masses of gases and to make stoichiometric calculations.

The density of a gas is expressed by the equation below.

$$\text{Density}_{\text{STP}} = \frac{\text{molecular mass}}{\text{molar volume}}$$

From this equation, it can be seen that the molecular mass of a gas may be determined by measuring its density. That is, molecular mass = density × molar volume. If the molar volume of 22.4ℓ at standard conditions is used, the density must be expressed at the same conditions.

We can also use this experiment to illustrate mass-volume relationships in chemical reactions. Consider the equation for the reaction between magnesium and hydrochloric acid

$$\text{Mg(s)} + 2\text{HCl(aq)} \rightarrow \text{MgCl}_2\text{(aq)} + \text{H}_2\text{(g)}$$

The coefficients in the equation show that one mole of H_2 is produced by the reaction of one mole of magnesium. This means that, in theory, 24.3 g of magnesium reacts with excess HCl and evolves 22.4ℓ of H_2 at STP. With this information you should be able to calculate the volume of hydrogen that theoretically should be evolved by reacting your sample of magnesium.

FOLLOW-UP QUESTIONS

1. Use the data in the table to help you calculate the experimental standard density of H_2.

2. Use the standard molar volume to calculate the volume of H_2 that should be evolved in this experiment. Account for any deviation between the experimental and calculated values.

3. Use the experimental data and the known mole relationship between magnesium and hydrogen to determine an experimental value for the general gas constant R.

4. A certain gas has a density of 1.34 g/ℓ at $27°$C and 740 torr pressure. Calculate the molecular mass of this gas.

5. Summarize the sources of experimental error in this experiment.

5-1

The Charge on an Electron (Demonstration)

GENERAL DISCUSSION

Many industrial chemical processes involve the passage of an electric current through a chemical system in order to bring about a desired chemical change. Electroplating operations, as well as the production of many elemental substances and useful chemical products, are examples of electrolytic processes involving the decomposition of matter by use of an electric current. An electric current or "flow of electricity" involves the transfer of an electric charge from one point to another point. Experiments such as those conducted by J. J. Thomson, which are described in your text, lead to the conclusion that a negative electric charge is carried by an electron. The magnitude of the electric charge is often measured in *coulombs,* the charge carried by a current of one ampere if it flows for 1 sec. The number of coulombs of electric charge transferred depends upon the magnitude of the current and the length of time that it flows. This may be expressed as

$$Q = I \times t \qquad \text{Eq. 1}$$

where Q represents the number of coulombs transferred, I equals the current in amperes and t equals the time in seconds. Solving Equation 1 for I, we see as stated above that a current of one ampere involves the transfer of one coulomb of electric charge per second. That is,

$$\text{amperes} = \text{coulombs/seconds}$$

Because current is easily measured with an ammeter and time with a clock, the number of coulombs of electric charge which pass through a system can be calculated readily and related to a specific volume or mass of product. In turn, the volume and mass can be related to a specific number of electrons. Thus the coulombs per electron can be calculated.

Using the data from his well-known "oil drop" experiments (see text), Millikan was able to show that an electron carries "the unit negative charge." In this demonstration, we shall experimentally determine a value for the unit electric charge in coulombs that is carried by one electron.

To accomplish this objective we shall electrolyze a solution of 1-M sulfuric acid (H_2SO_4) for a measured time, using a constant current whose value is known. From the time and current measurements we can calculate the number of coulombs of electric charge transferred into the system ($Q = I \times t$). Volume, pressure, and temperature measurments enable us to use the ideal gas equation

$$PV = nRT$$

to calculate the moles of H_2 gas evolved. The equation for the reaction at the electrode where the hydrogen gas is produced is

$$2H^+(aq) + 2e^- \rightarrow H_2(g) \qquad \text{Eq. 2}$$

The source of $H^+(aq)$ is the dissociation of the H_2SO_4 in water

$$H_2SO_4(\ell) \rightarrow H^+(aq) + HSO_4^-(aq) \qquad \text{Eq. 3}$$

Equation 2 shows that two electrons are required to produce one molecule of H_2 or that two moles of electrons (12.0×10^{23} electrons) is required to produce one mole of H_2 gas. In other words, the number of moles of electrons transferred is twice the number of moles of hydrogen produced. Thus, by calculating the number of moles of $H_2(g)$ produced, we can obtain the number of moles and hence the number of electrons which pass through the circuit. The number of coulombs divided by the number of electrons is all that is needed to obtain a value for coulombs/electron.

OBJECTIVES

1. To become acquainted with units of electric charge.

2. To understand that there is a relationship between the quantity of electric charge and the quantity of products produced in an electrolysis reaction.

3. To determine the charge on an electron.

4. To review and use the Ideal Gas Law.

MATERIALS

Eudiometer tube (with stopcock if available), 400-ml beaker, ammeter, porous cup, copper strip, 6–12 volt DC source, insulated connecting wire and alligator clips, stopwatch or clock, 1-M H_2SO_4 solution, ruler, barometer, thermometer.

PROCEDURE

1. Place an unglazed, porous cup in a 400-ml beaker and add approximately 350 ml of 1-M H_2SO_4.

2. Insert a eudiometer tube mouth downward over a piece of insulated copper wire as shown in Fig. 5-1. Be certain that a short section of bare copper is exposed.

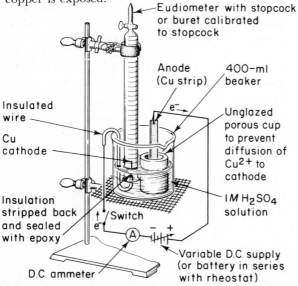

Fig. 5-1 Apparatus used for determining the charge on an electron. Alternatively, the Hoffman apparatus with platinum electrodes may be used.

3. Place a copper strip in the porous cup, and connect a piece of connecting wire to the strip with an alligator clip.

4. Place a 0 to 3-ampere ammeter in series with one of the connecting wires and connect to a variable DC source or to a variable resistor connected in series with the meter. The resistor, in turn, is connected to a 6- or 12-volt battery as shown in Fig. 5-1. Check polarity of connections carefully.

5. With a water aspirator, or other vacuum device, draw the H_2SO_4 solution into the eudiometer tube until the liquid level is just above the stopcock. Close the stopcock. If such a tube is

Table I   Charge on an Electron

Current (amperes)	
Time (sec)	
Coulombs ($Q = I \times t$)	
Volume of hydrogen (ml)	
Temperature (°K)	
R	$6.23 \times 10^4 \dfrac{\text{ml} \cdot \text{torr}}{°K \cdot \text{mole } H_2}$
Barometric pressure (torr)	
Water-vapor pressure (torr)	
Partial pressure of H_2 and P_{H_2} (torr)	
Moles H_2: $n_{H_2} = \dfrac{P_{H_2} V}{RT}$	
Moles of electrons ($2n_{H_2}$)	
Number of electrons	
Coulombs/electron	
Accepted value	1.60×10^{-19} coulomb/electron
Percentage deviation	

not available, fill an ordinary eudiometer tube to the top with 1-M H_2SO_4, place your finger over the mouth and invert, mouth downward, into the beaker. Then carefully insert the insulated copper wire into the tube as shown.

6. Simultaneously close the switch and start the timing device. *Immediately* adjust the rheostat so that the ammeter reads as close as possible to 1.00 amp. Monitor the current throughout the run by adjustment of the rheostat so that the current remains as close as possible to 1.00 amp.

7. Continue the electrolysis until approximately 45 ml of H_2 gas has been collected. Open the switch, gently tap the wire in the mouth of the tube to dislodge H_2 bubbles, and allow all gas to rise to the top.

8. Lower (or raise) the tube so that the level of the liquid in the tube is the same as that in the beaker.

9. Read the volume of H_2 collected to ± 0.1 ml and the elapsed time ± 1 second or better.

10. Record the temperature of the H_2SO_4 solution in the beaker to $\pm 1°C$ and the barometric pressure to ± 1 torr.

11. Record all data in Table I and carry out the indicated calculations, showing method clearly.

FOLLOW-UP DISCUSSION

Some students are not familiar with electric terms or devices. For this reason, we shall briefly introduce a few of the concepts frequently encountered in the study of chemistry. For an electrolytic experiment such as this, a source of electrons is required. The source may be a battery or perhaps a rectifier which converts an alternating current into a direct current. We may think of a battery as an "electron pump" which forces electrons onto one of the electrodes which is called the cathode and withdraws electrons from the other electrode which is known as the anode of the electrolytic cell. A different reaction occurs at each electrode. At the cathode, the substance being electrolyzed removes electrons and undergoes a chemical change as it is converted into a new substance. In this demonstration, if there is a high concentration of H^+ ions in the

solution, then the H^+ ions acquire electrons and become hydrogen gas.

$$2H^+(aq) + 2e^- \rightarrow H_2(g)$$

At the anode, the substance being electrolyzed gives up electrons to the electrode. The anode reaction in this demonstration is

$$Cu(s) \rightarrow Cu^{2+}(aq) + 2e^-$$

This equation shows that two moles of electrons are given up for each mole of $Cu^{2+}(aq)$ produced. Thus the quantity of electricity that produces one mole of H_2 also produces one mole of Cu^{2+} ions.

The preceding discussion shows that a unit of electric charge that involves one mole of electrons would be very convenient. This unit is known as the *faraday*. Because the number of electrons shown in the electrode equations is equal to the number of faradays of electricity, we can use the coefficients in these equations to relate directly the quantity of electricity to the moles of product evolved. Thus in the electrolysis of a solution of H_2SO_4 we can say one faraday of electric charge liberates $\frac{1}{2}$ mole of H_2 gas and produces $\frac{1}{2}$ mole of Cu^{2+} ions. In turn, the number of moles of H_2 may be converted into mass or volume units. There is, of course, a conversion factor that allows one to convert coulombs into faradays or vice versa. In Follow-up Question 2 you are asked to derive this factor on the basis of the data available in this report.

FOLLOW-UP QUESTIONS

1. Use your experimental value of coulombs per electron and calculate the number of electrons required to carry one coulomb of electric charge.

2. Calculate the number of coulombs in one faraday, that is, the number of coulombs carried by one mole of electrons.

3. How many grams of silver are deposited when a solution of silver nitrate is electrolyzed by passing a current of 0.20 amp for a period of 2.0 hr? The equation for the cathode reaction is

$$Ag^+(aq) + e^- \rightarrow Ag(s)$$

4. If one faraday of electric charge is used to electrolyze water, how many liters of hydrogen are evolved at the cathode at STP? How many liters of hydrogen are evolved at 27°C and 740 torr?

5. In an electrolysis reaction, do the products or the reactants have the greater amount of energy? Explain.

6. State the purpose of the porous cup. How would your results be affected if it were not there? Hint: the reaction $Cu^{2+}(aq) + 2e^- \rightarrow Cu(s)$ takes place more easily and rapidly than $2H^+(aq) + 2e^- \rightarrow H_2(g)$.

7. Calculate the loss in mass of the copper anode during your electrolysis.

8. List the major sources of error which would help account for the deviation between your experimental value and the accepted value.

5-2

Flame Tests

GENERAL DISCUSSION

When certain pure compounds are heated in the oxidizing or hottest portion of a small, colorless flame, they are vaporized and impart a distinctive color to the flame. The color of the flame helps to identify the nature of the compound. When the flame test is applied to a mixture of compounds, light of several different wavelengths may be emitted. In this event, one color may interfere with and mask a second color. Thus, flame tests using only the unaided eye have an extremely limited use in identifying the components of a mixture. The usefulness of flame tests is extended by the use of a spectroscope, an instrument capable of resolving light into its component wavelengths.

In this experiment you apply flame tests to a number of pure compounds and solutions of compounds, and then use the results of your tests to identify an unknown. If a spectroscope is available, you will have an opportunity to compare the flames as viewed by the unaided eye with those viewed through the spectroscope.

OBJECTIVES

1. To observe and record the colors imparted to a flame by the presence of selected ions.
2. To identify factors related to the length of time that the flame colors persist.
3. To use the flame-test technique to identify the ions in an unknown crystalline substance and in a solution containing unknown ions.

MATERIALS

Platinum, nichrome, or iron wire, emery cloth, glass tubing (7 mm), burner, lithium chloride (LiCl), calcium chloride ($CaCl_2$), potassium chloride (KCl), copper(II) chloride ($CuCl_2$), strontium chloride ($SrCl_2$), strontium nitrate

$[Sr(NO_3)_2]$, sodium chloride (NaCl), and barium chloride crystals ($BaCl_2 \cdot 2H_2O$); 1-M solutions of NaCl and KCl, a solution 1 M in KCl and 0.10 M in NaCl, a solution 1 M in NaCl and 0.01 M in KCl, 0.01-M NaCl, 0.5-M Na_2SO_4 distilled water and a spectroscope or a diffraction grating (if available).

Part I · Crystals

PROCEDURE

1. Obtain a piece of platinum, nichrome, or iron wire having a small loop in one end and attached to an insulating handle. This device may be prepared by fusing a piece of wire into a piece of glass tubing (7 mm) and then bending the end of the wire into a very small elongated

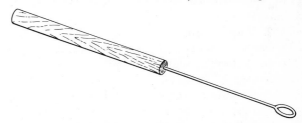

Fig. 5-2 Apparatus for carrying out flame test.

loop as shown in Fig. 5-2. The loop should not be closed. Heat the wire in the oxidizing part (hot tip of inner cone) of a burner flame until it glows yellow and then dip it into a few crystals of lithium chloride. Heat the crystals on the loop of the wire in the edge of the flame. Record the color imparted to the flame in Table I. Clean the wire with emery cloth after each test or use a different wire for each test. Do not touch the wire or you will contaminate it with Na^+ ions. Na^+-ion contamination can result also from traces of soap

Table I Color of Flames (Solid Compounds)

Name of Salt	Color of Flame
Lithium chloride	
Calcium chloride	
Potassium chloride	
Copper(II) chloride	
Strontium chloride	
Strontium nitrate	
Sodium chloride	
Barium chloride	

Table II Analysis of Unknown Crystal by Flame Test

Color of Flame	Positive Ion

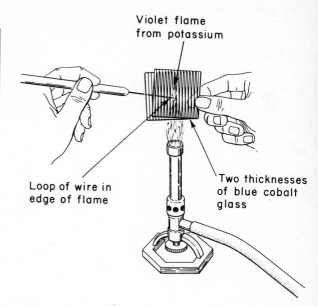

Fig. 5-3 *The two pieces of blue cobalt glass obscure the yellow sodium flame and permit the detection of potassium in the presence of sodium.*

or detergent left in the glassware used in the experiment.

2. Repeat, using crystals of calcium chloride, potassium chloride, copper(II) chloride, strontium chloride, sodium chloride, and barium chloride.

3. Obtain a crystalline "unknown" and use flame tests to identify the positive ion in the crystal. Record your observations and conclusions in Table II.

Part II · Solutions

4. Apply the flame test to the solutions listed in Table II. Record the approximate length of time that the color persists. When testing solutions containing both Na^+ and K^+ ions, observe the flame through two thicknesses of blue glass. The glass blocks the sodium color and transmits that caused by the potassium. Practice until you can identify the components and relative concentrations of the solutions.

5. Obtain an unknown solution. Use flame tests

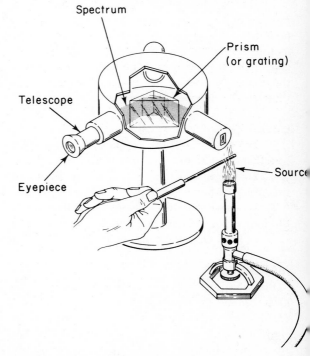

Fig. 5-4 *Cutaway diagram of a spectroscope.*

Table III Color of Flames (Solutions)

	Color of Flame	Approximate Time Color Persists
1.0-M NaCl		
0.5-M Na$_2$SO$_4$		
0.01-M NaCl		
Distilled water		
1.0-M KCl		
1.0-M KCl + 0.01-M NaCl		
1.0-M NaCl + 0.01-M KCl		

Table IV Analysis of Unknown Solution

Solution Number	Color of Flame	Positive Ion(s)	Relative Concentration of Ion(s) (High or Low)
A			
B			
C			
D			
E			

Table V Mixture of NaCl and LiCl

	Observation
Flame as observed without spectroscope	
Flame as observed through spectroscope	

to identify the positive ion in and relative concentrations of the solutions. When making the tests, you should run control experiments or blank tests with known solutions to compare with, and help identify your unknown. Record your observations and conclusions in Table IV.

6. Apply the flame test to a solution containing NaCl and LiCl. Record the color of the flame. Now observe the flame through a spectroscope or a diffraction grating. Record your observations in Table V. Sketch and identify what you observe.

FOLLOW-UP DISCUSSION

In this experiment you found that different elements when vaporized impart specific colors to a flame. The results of your tests and observations suggest that the color imparted to a flame may be used to identify an element. Ordinary flame tests using the unaided eye cannot be used to identify all 105 elements or even the components of the simplest mixtures. If you had the opportunity to use a spectroscope you found that the energized atoms of a specific element emitted light of specific wavelengths which you observed as a line spectrum. This suggests that an element is characterized by a unique line spectrum which may by used in the identification of the element.

We are now ready to measure quantitatively the wavelengths of the light emitted by the energized atoms of specific elements, to investigate the origin of these line spectra, and to relate the spectrum of an element to the electronic configuration of its atoms.

FOLLOW-UP QUESTIONS

1. What is your evidence that the color of the flame observed in a flame test is caused by the metallic ion rather than the negative ion?

2. How did the length of time the color was observed for the NaCl solution compare with that for the Na_2SO_4 solution? Suggest a reason for the difference.

3. What other factor determined the length of time the color was observed?

4. Could you tell that there was more than one compound in your mixture of a lithium and sodium compound by just looking at the flame? What was the color of the flame? How did the spectroscope enable you to tell that you were heating a mixture?

5-3

Electron Transitions in Atoms: Atomic Emission Spectra

GENERAL DISCUSSION

Much of the detailed information about the electronic structure of the atom has been obtained through spectroscopic analysis. This refers to the analysis of the light (energy) emitted or absorbed by chemical substances. You have observed the bright yellow color imparted to a flame when a little ordinary table salt is dropped into it. When this light is examined through a spectroscope, an atomic emission spectrum is observed. Every element has a characteristic spectrum by which it may be identified. In this experiment you examine the spectra of several elements. You use a diffraction grating and calculate the wavelength of one colored line in each spectrum which you observe. You are not expected to understand the theory behind the use of the diffraction grating. Neither are you responsible for the derivation of the formula that you use to calculate the wavelengths of the spectral lines. If the grating constant, d, is unknown or you suspect that it is inaccurate, you can determine its value by following the directions given in the Further Experimentation section.

OBJECTIVES

1. To observe the spectra of different elements.
2. To calculate the wavelength of spectral lines.
3. To gain some insight into the origin of spectral lines and their relationship to the electronic structure of an atom.

MATERIALS

Sodium lamp, mercury lamp, and hydrogen discharge tube, cardboard or metal shield with narrow slit, diffraction grating, meter sticks, masking tape, ring stand.

PROCEDURE

1. The instructor or an assistant will connect a sodium lamp, a mercury lamp, and a hydrogen-gas discharge tube. Each source should be shielded so that the light passes through a narrow slit. Determine the wavelength of a line in the sodium spectrum, the mercury spectrum, and the hydrogen spectrum as directed below.

2. Arrange the materials as shown in Figure 5-3 and work in groups. To obtain the data necessary to calculate the wavelength, one person must look through the grating and direct another person who locates the position of the spectral line.

3. Darken the room as much as possible and look at the light coming from the slit through a diffraction grating held against the eye. The grating should be less than one meter from the source. Move back and forth and rotate the grating until you see the colored, vertical line s. of the atomic spectrum.

4. To locate the observed line, one student should move a ruler slowly along meter stick b until the student looking through the grating sees the ruler coincide with the line being measured. Record in Table I the distance b between the line and the slit. Record the distance a from the grating to the slit.

5. Calculate the wavelength in centimeters of the line by using the formula:

$$\text{wavelength} = d \, \frac{b}{\sqrt{a^2 + b^2}} \qquad \text{Eq. 5-1}$$

where a and b are the distances measured above in centimeters and d is the distance between two lines in the grating. Gratings obtained from the Edmund Scientific Co. in Barrington, New Jer-

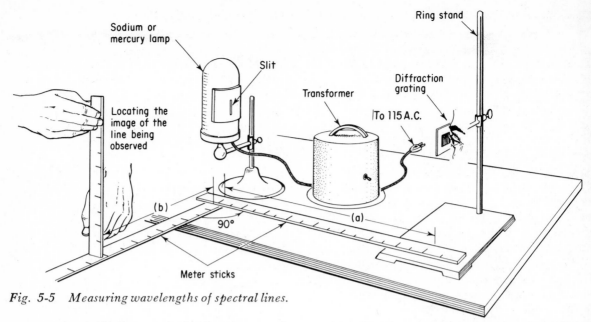

Fig. 5-5   Measuring wavelengths of spectral lines.

sey, contain 13,400 lines per inch. The distance, d, between each line is 1.9×10^{-4} cm.

6. Calculate the frequency of vibration corresponding to the measured wavelength by using the formula

$$\text{frequency} = \frac{\text{speed of light}}{\text{wavelength}}$$

where the speed of light is a constant equal to 3×10^{10} cm/sec.

7. Read the Follow-up Discussion and make the calculations needed to complete Table I.

FURTHER EXPERIMENTATION

Calibrate your grating (determine the value of d) against a source of known wavelength such as the yellow line of sodium (wavelength 5893 Å). The procedure is identical to that given above. Substitute the known wavelength in Eq. 5-1 and solve for d.

FOLLOW-UP DISCUSSION

The atomic or line spectra which you observed in this experiment are discontinuous. Each line in an atomic spectrum originates when an electron falls from one energy level to another. There are many atoms in a given sample of an element, and often many electrons and many energy levels in an atom. Therefore, the light that you observe is a result of many different electron transitions. In other words, the light observed is a mixture of components having different wavelengths. It is

Table I   Wavelength of Spectral Lines

Element	(a) cm	(b) cm	(d) cm	Wavelength		Frequency	Energy	
				cm	Ångstroms		ergs	ev
Sodium								
Hydrogen								
Mercury								

necessary to break this light up into its components in order to relate these components to specific electron transitions. The limited number of lines in the spectrum of a given kind of atom indicates a limited number of energy levels.

The energy corresponding to a given line in the spectrum of an element may be calculated by using the equation

$$E = h\nu$$

where ν is the frequency of the radiation, h is Planck's constant, and E is the energy, in ergs, of the photon of light emitted when an electron falls from a high energy level E_2 to a lower energy E_1.

In the case of a hydrogen atom, there is a relatively simple formula that enables us to calculate the energy levels involved for each line observed. This formula is

$$\frac{1}{\lambda} = R\left(\frac{1}{m^2} - \frac{1}{n^2}\right)$$

where λ is the wavelength in cm, R is a fundamental constant of nature having a value of 1.1×10^5 cm^{-1}, m is the number of the lower energy level to which the electron "jumps," and n is the higher enery level from which the electron "jumped" to give rise to the observed line. For all the lines in the visible spectrum of hydrogen, m has a value of 2. It can be shown that the red line in the hydrogen spectrum with wavelength of 6563 Å is observed when an electron goes from the 3rd energy level to the 2nd energy level. There are no simple formulas which apply to atoms more complex than hydrogen atoms.

FOLLOW-UP QUESTIONS

1. Calculate the energy in ergs corresponding to each line whose wavelength you measured. The value for h is 6.6×10^{-27} erg-sec. Record the values in Table I. Express the energy in electron volts (ev). There are 1.6×10^{12} ergs per electron volt.

2. Following are the wavelengths of a few of the main lines in the spectra of sodium, hydrogen, and mercury. Express the wavelength of the lines you measured in terms of Ångstrom units and compare with the values given below.

a. sodium	5890–5895 Å
b. hydrogen	red 6563 Å
	blue-green 4861
	blue 4342
	violet 4102
c. mercury	green 5460
	violet 4359

What is the percentage deviation between your experimental value and the accepted value?

3. Calculate the electron transition in the hydrogen atom which gave rise to the line whose wavelength you measured. If you were unable to measure the wavelength, then use the value 4861 Å for the blue-green line.

4. Approximately 14 electron volts (ev) of energy is required to remove an electron from the second energy level of a hydrogen atom. It can be shown that 10 ev is required to cause the electron to go from the first to the second level. Calculate the energy (ev) required to remove an electron completely from the second level.

6-1

Locating an Electron in an Atom by Analogy—Probability Information

GENERAL DISCUSSION

If it were possible to conduct an experiment to determine the frequency of the electron's appearance at different points in the space surrounding the nucleus, these data could be plotted on a three-dimensional graph. Boundaries could be established which would outline the regions of space in which the electron could be found 95% of the time. These regions of space, called orbitals, are commonly represented in texts as charge clouds, and physically with Styrofoam models.

Since it is impossible to conduct such an experiment, we shall perform one which, by analogy, will help give meaning to the concepts of probability distribution graphs, radii of maximum probability, maximum electron density, and orbitals.

In this experiment you will define regions of space about a bullseye in which there is a specific probability of locating a spot resulting from the impact of a dart dropped from a specific distance to the target. The spots represent the points in the space about the bullseye (analogous to the nucleus) where the dart (analogous to the electron) is observed in the experiment designed to locate the region of space within which the dart is most likely to strike (analogous to an atomic orbital).

You will also determine a radius of maximum probability (maximum spot density) by plotting the number of times the dots (analogous to places electrons might be observed) appear per cm² *vs* the distance from the bullseye (nucleus).

OBJECTIVES

1. To draw a physical analogy to some of the concepts associated with the wave-mechanical model of the atom.

2. To determine the distribution of the impacts of a dart about a bullseye.

3. To obtain and interpret probability information.

MATERIALS

Targets, typewriter carbon paper, masking tape, dart with a BB shot soldered to tip, small piece of plywood, clear plastic sheet. See Fig. 6-1 for diagrams of dart and target.

PROCEDURE

1. Obtain from the instructor or stockroom, two targets, a piece of typewriter carbon paper, masking tape, one or two darts with a BB shot soldered to the tip, a piece of plywood, and a plastic holder for your targets.

2. Place the carbon paper between the two targets so that any impression made on the front target will be reproduced on the back target. Place the carbon-paper sandwich in the plastic holder.

3. Attach the target to a piece of plywood with masking tape and place it on the floor.

4. Stand on a stool or laboratory bench with the dart in your hand. *Extend* your arm so that it is about two meters above the floor, and have your partner place the target directly below your hand. Drop the dart on the target below. Repeat 99 times. Your "electron" dart appears 100 times, and the spots represent places where it is observed.

5. Return the front target, carbon paper, plastic, plywood, and darts to the containers provided for this purpose.

6. Locate the ninety-five dots (95%) which are closest to the bullseye and using a colored pencil, draw a smooth (not wavy) curve which

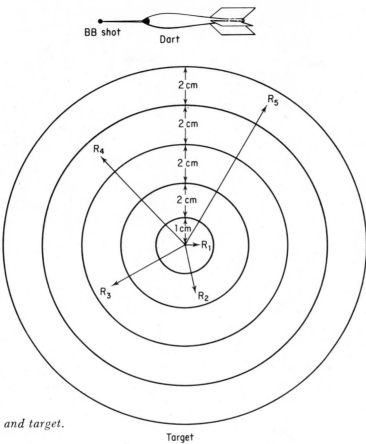

BB shot   Dart

2 cm

2 cm

R₅

R₄

2 cm

2 cm

1 cm

R₁

R₃

R₂

Fig. 6-1 Dart and target.

Target

Table I Score Card

Number of Circular Area Increment	Average Radial Distance of Area Increment from Bullseye	Area of Increment	Number of Dots in Area Increment	Dots per Unit Area Times 10
1	$R_1 = 0.5$ cm	3 cm²		
2	$R_2 = 2.0$ cm	25 cm²		
3	$R_3 = 4.0$ cm	50 cm²		
4	$R_4 = 6.0$ cm	75 cm²		
5	$R_5 = 8.0$ cm	100 cm²		

Radius of Maximum probability (from graph)_____

107

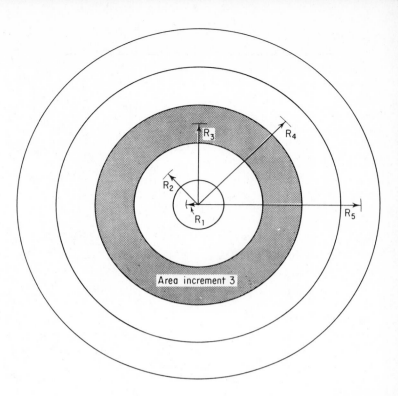

Fig. 6-2 The area increments are represented by concentric rings whose average radial distances are designated by R_1, R_2, R_3, R_4, and R_5. The outer boundary of each ring measures, respectively, 1 cm, 3 cm, 5 cm, 7 cm, and 9 cm from the center of the target. Increment 3 (shaded) has an area of 50 cm.²

encloses the region containing these dots. This region represents the two-dimensional "orbital" of your "dart electron" (analogous to the region of space where an electron might be observed 95% of the time in an experiment designed to locate it).

7. Count the dots in each concentric circular area surrounding the bullseye and record the number in the table. Divide the number of dots in each area by the area of the region given in the table. This quotient is the dots per cm². Multiply the quotient by 10 to give more easily plotted numbers. Enter your calculations in the table.

8. Plot the dots per cm² ($\times 10$) along the vertical axis, and the average radial distance of the area increment from the bullseye along the horizontal axis. Note that radial distance extends from the center of the bullseye to the mid-point of the circular area. Start the curve at 0,0 and allow it to approach the x axis asymptotically (without touching the axis).

9. Identify the radius of maximum probability

from the graph (peak of curve) and record in the space provided below the table. This is the distance from bullseye where you are most apt to find a spot (your electron) appearing when you carry on an experiment designed to locate it (drop a dart).

10. Look up the radial probability curve for an s electron and sketch it on the graph paper containing your experimental curve. Use a colored pencil for the s-electron curve.

FOLLOW-UP DISCUSSION

Bohr's model of the atom, which confined each electron to a definite orbit, did not recognize the wave nature of the electron, or Heisenberg's uncertainty principle. Despite these shortcomings, this simple model can be, and often is, used to explain simple structural concepts as well as a number of experimental observations. It fails however to explain satisfactorily spectra of many-electron atoms. More importantly for us, it also fails to explain the geometry and properties of molecular substances with covalent bonds. The directional characteristics of orbitals play an important role in determining the shape and properties of substances. It is important that you be able to represent the electron structure of an atom in terms of orbital designation.

FOLLOW-UP QUESTIONS

1. How does the shape of the curve which represents the probability of finding an *s* electron in a given volume increment compare with that representing the probability of locating your "electron" in a given area increment?

2. (a) When you drop a dart on the target, can you predict precisely where it will strike? (b) Can you predict an area within which it is likely to strike? (c) How are the answers to these questions analogous to the problem of locating an electron about a nucleus of an atom?

3. (a) Would you expect the radius of maximum probability for your target to be identical for a target of another student? Why or why not? (b) Would you predict that 1*s* orbital in a chlorine atom would enclose the same volume of space as in an argon atom? Explain.

4. What is meant by "orbital"?

5. How many electrons may one orbital have?

6. *s* orbitals are said to be nondirectional. How do you interpret this statement? Does the "orbital" outlined by your boundary line appear to be nondirectional? Explain.

7. (a) Excluding the first energy level, how many *p* orbitals are there per principal energy level? (b) What are the directional characteristics of *p* orbitals? That is, how are they oriented with respect to each other? (c) What is the maximum number of electrons that all the *p* orbitals in a given level can hold? (d) Assume that a *p* orbital is dumbbell-shaped with two major lobes and, in a certain atom, contains one electron. In which lobe is the electron most apt to be found? Explain, indicating the principle on which your answer is based.

8. Using orbital notation, write the electronic configuration for: (a) fluorine atom, (b) chloride ion, (c) potassium ion, (d) iron atom, (e) iron(III) ion.

7-1

Periodicity of Physical, Chemical, and Atomic Properties

GENERAL DISCUSSION

Oxides are sometimes classified as acid or basic depending on whether their water solution is acid (contains excess H_3O^+ ions) or basic (contains excess OH^- ions). Some oxides, however, do not dissolve appreciably in water. These oxides are classified on the basis of whether they react with acids and/or with bases. If they react with acids in a manner similar to bases, they are classified as basic oxides. If they react with bases in a manner similar to acids, they are called acid oxides. If they react with both acids and bases, they are called amphoteric oxides. A more detailed discussion of these reactions is in Chapter 15 of your text.

In this experiment you will test a number of oxides and identify them as acid, basic, or amphoteric. To determine the nature of their water solutions you use litmus paper, an acid-base indicator which turns red in acid solution and blue in basic solution. After making experimental observations, you locate in the Periodic Table the elements whose oxides you tested and ascertain, on the basis of your rather limited evidence, whether the acid or basic nature of the oxides is a periodic property, whether the metallic or nonmetallic nature of an element is related to the acidity of its oxide, and whether there is a relationship between the radius and oxidation state of the central atom and the acid nature of the oxide. You will also have an opportunity to apply the concept of periodicity when you predict the properties of substances you did not test experimentally.

OBJECTIVES

1. To determine the relative acidity or basicity of a number of oxides.
2. To determine whether or not the acid or basic nature of oxides is a periodic property.

3. To relate the metallic or nonmetallic nature of an element to the acid or basic nature of its oxide.
4. To relate the relative acidity of an oxide to the radius and oxidation state of the central atom.
5. To use the concept of periodicity to predict properties of substances.

MATERIALS

Sodium peroxide (Na_2O_2), calcium oxide (CaO), magnesium oxide (MgO), barium oxide (BaO), hydrated aluminum oxide (freshly prepared aluminum hydroxide, $Al_2O_3 \cdot xH_2O$), arsenic(III) oxide (As_4O_6), arsenic(V) oxide (As_4O_{10}), antimony(III) oxide (Sb_4O_6), hydrated bismuth oxide ($Bi_2O_3 \cdot xH_2O$) freshly prepared, 6-M aqueous ammonia [NH_3(aq)], 1-M $AlCl_3$ solution, 1-M $BiCl_3$ solution, 6-M NaOH solution, 6-M HCl solution, red phosphorus, sulfur, calcium carbonate (or bottled CO_2 or Dry Ice), copper metal (punchings), conc. HNO_3, deflagrating spoon or iron wire, 8-oz. wide-mouth bottle, cardboard square, litmus paper, test tubes, microspatula, burner.

PROCEDURE

1. Use a plastic spoon or spatula and place a small sample (size of a grain of rice) of sodium peroxide (Na_2O_2) in the center of a watch glass. This substance is highly reactive so your instructor may wish to dispense it. Add 1–2 ml of water to the peroxide and stir with a glass rod. Use litmus paper to determine whether the solution is acid or basic. Record your observations in Table I.
2. Place a small sample (not more than 0.1 g) of CaO in each of three identical test tubes. Each sample should have about the same volume, be

Table I Nature of Metallic Oxides

Formula of Oxide	Effect on Litmus	Relative Solubility in Water	Relative Solubility in 6-M HCl	Relative Solubility in 6-M NaOH	Conclusion (Nature of Oxide: Acid, Basic Amphoteric)
Na_2O_2					
CaO					
MgO					
BaO					
$As_2O(As_4O_6)$					
$As_2O_3(As_4O_{10})$					
$Sb_2O_3(Sb_4O_6)$					
Al_2O_3					
Bi_2O_3					

finely divided, and contain no lumps. Add 15 ml of water to the first test tube, 15 ml of 6-M HCl to the second test tube and 15 ml of 6-M NaOH to the third test tube. Agitate each solution vigorously and record the relative solubilities in Table I. Base your conclusion on the relative amount of solid left undissolved. Use the numeral *1* to indicate minimum relative solubility, the numeral *3* to indicate maximum relative solubility, and the numeral *2* to indicate a solubility intermediate between the two extremes. Note that in some instances it may be impossible to distinguish differences in solubility between two of the three solvents in which case you should write the same numeral in both spaces.

Test the water solution with litmus and record any color change you observe in Table I. Remember if red litmus stays red and blue litmus stays blue, then write *no effect*. In this case, you may assume that the solid had negligible solubility in water. You will then have to base your conclusion as to the nature of the oxide on its behavior in the acid and base.

3. Repeat Procedure 2 using samples of BaO MgO, As_2O_3 (As_4O_6), As_2O_5 (As_4O_{10}), and Sb_2O_3 (Sb_4O_6).

4. Prepare two samples of hydrated Al_2O_3 by adding 6-M aqueous ammonia to two separate test tubes, each containing 3 ml of 1-M $AlCl_3$ solution, until a permanent precipitate is observed. Indicate in Table I that this solid has a relative solubility of *1* in water. Test and record the relative solubility of the solid in 6-M HCl and in 6-M NaOH by adding an excess of the acid to one test tube, and an excess of the base to the other.

5. Prepare two samples of hydrated Bi_2O_3 by adding 6-M aqueous ammonia to two separate test tubes, each of which contains 3 ml of 1-M $BiCl_3$, until a permanent precipitate is observed. Indicate in Table I that this solid has a relative solubility of 1 in water. Test and record the relative solubility of the solid in 6-M HCl and in 6-M NaOH by adding an excess of the acid to one test tube, and an excess of the base to the other.

6. Use the observations recorded in Table I to classify each oxide as acid, basic, or amphoteric. If the aqueous solution turned red litmus blue, then the oxide is basic. If the aqueous solution turned blue litmus red, then the oxide is acid. If the solution did not affect litmus, and the oxide is more soluble in HCl and in NaOH

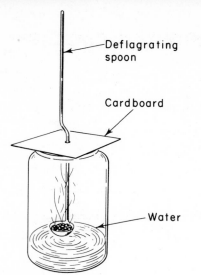

Fig. 7-1 *Burning phosphorus in a combustion spoon.*

bustion is complete, shake the contents of the bottle and remove the sample holder. Remove some of the solution with a glass rod and test it with red and blue litmus. Record the nature of the solution in Table II.

8. Repeat Procedure 7, using a sample of sulfur in place of the phosphorus. Record your observations in Table II.

9. Bubble carbon dioxide through some distilled water in a large test tube. Carbon dioxide may be prepared by adding 6-M hydrochloric acid to about one gram of calcium carbonate ($CaCO_3$) contained in a gas-generator bottle or test tube. For this experiment a stopper containing a delivery tube may be inserted into a large test tube after the acid has been added to the calcium carbonate. Dry Ice, bottled CO_2, or your breath may be also used as a source of carbon dioxide.

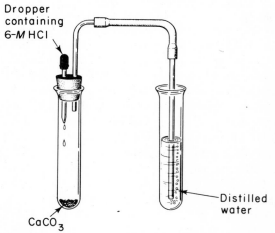

Fig. 7-2 *Apparatus for generating carbon dioxide.*

than in water, then it is amphoteric. The more basic an oxide is, the more tendency it has to dissolve in an acid. In the case of the oxides of arsenic, record their relative solubilities in acid and in base in Table III.

7. Obtain a deflagrating spoon or a piece of iron wire with a small loop at one end and insert the handle or wire through a 3 × 5-in. card. Use a spatula and place a sample of red phosphorus in the spoon or in the loop of the iron wire. Be sure that your goggles are in place and then ignite the phosphorus by heating the spoon or wire. Hold the burning sample in a wide-mouth bottle which contains about 10 ml of distilled water. Place the card over the top of the bottle so that the gas or smoke does not escape. When the com-

Table II   Nature of Nonmetallic Oxides

Oxide	Nature of Aqueous Solution	Acid, Basic, or Amphoteric Oxide
P_4O_6		
SO_2		
CO_2		
NO_2		

Table III Relationship between Periodicity in Chemical Properties and Atomic Properties

Formula of Oxide	Oxidation State of *As* in Oxide	Radius of *As* Atom in Oxide	Relative Solubility in Acid (1 = greater; 2 = lower)	Relative Solubility in Base (1 = greater; 2 = lower)
As_2O_3		0.58 Å		
As_4O_6		0.45 Å		

Group Period | IA | IIA | IIIA | IVA | VA | VIA | VIIA | O

	IA	IIA	IIIA	IVA	VA	VIA	VIIA	O
2				C 6	N 7			Ne 10
3	Na 11	Mg 12	Al 13		P 15	S 16	Cl 17	Ar 18
4		Ca 20	Ga 31	Sn 50	As 33	Se 34		Kr 36
5		Sr 38			Sb 51			Xe 54
6	Cs 55	Ba 56			Bi 83			Rn 85

acid nature of oxide increases

electronegativity of central atom increases

Basic nature of oxide increases

10. Take a large test tube half-filled with distilled water to the hood where the instructor or an assistant will bubble nitrogen dioxide (NO_2) gas through the water. Nitrogen dioxide is produced when concentrated nitric acid (HNO_3) is added to metallic copper. Test the solution with both colors of litmus paper. Record observations in Table II.

11. Identify each of the oxides in Tables I and II as acid, basic, or amphoteric, and then write the formula and the nature of each oxide in the proper space of the Periodic Table in Fig. 7-1.

12. Now, inspect the data in the Periodic Table and place arrow heads on the lines to the right of and below the Periodic Table to show the direction of the trends stated above each line.

13. On the basis of the limited evidence obtained in this experiment, propose a relationship

between the degree of acidity of an oxide, oxidation state and radius of the central atom. Complete Table III and place an arrowhead on the line to the left of the table.

14. On the basis of the limited evidence obtained in this experiment, propose a relationship between the degree of acidity of an oxide, oxidation state, and radius of the central atom. Complete Table III and place an arrowhead on the line to the left of the table.

FOLLOW-UP DISCUSSION

As a result of your observations, you should be able to draw some tentative conclusions related to periodicity in the acid or basic nature of oxides. You may find some difficulty, however, in writing correct equations for the reactions which you observed. There is no way that a beginner would know the formulas of the products of all the chemical reactions which you carried out in this experiment.

Let us use your observations to develop a few generalities which will help us to write correct equations for some of the reactions. We shall then refer to the observations and conclusions of practicing chemists to help us identify products of the more involved reactions.

In general, you found that the soluble metallic oxides of Groups IA and IIA reacted with water and formed basic solutions. Thus, the general word equation for these reactions is

$$\text{Metallic oxide} + \text{water} \rightarrow \text{base}$$

A basic solution is characterized by excess hydroxide ions (OH^-). In other words, the above reaction yields a solution of a metallic hydroxide. We may think of a metallic hydroxide as a hydrated oxide or of a metallic oxide as a dehydrated metallic hydroxide. Metallic oxides such as those noted above have sometimes been called basic anhydrides. Because many schools do not stock Bi_2O_3, it was suggested that you prepare and test hydrated bismuth oxide, $Bi_2O_3 \cdot 3H_2O$. The preparation involved reacting Bi^{3+} ions from a solu-

tion of bismuth chloride with aqueous ammonia. The neutral formula equation for the reaction is

$$BiCl_3(aq) + 3NH_3 + 3H_2O \rightarrow \\ Bi(OH)_3(s) + 3NH_4Cl(aq)$$

The net ionic equation for the reaction is

$$Bi^{3+}(aq) + 3NH_3 + 3H_2O \rightarrow \\ Bi(OH)_3(s) + 3NH_4^+(aq)$$

Note that in net ionic equations, soluble ionic salts are shown in ionic form and that unreactive "spectator" ions such as Cl^- are deleted from the equation. We may think of the hydrate as the combination of two $Bi(OH)_3$ units.

$$2Bi(OH)_3 \rightarrow Bi_2O_3 \cdot 3H_2O$$

Because aluminum oxide (Al_2O_3) which has been allowed to stand (age) for a long period of time becomes more resistant to dissolution, we substituted for it freshly prepared aluminum hydroxide.

$$Al^{3+}(aq) + 3NH_3 + 3H_2O \rightarrow \\ Al(OH)_3(s) + 3NH_4^+(aq)$$

You then use the behavior of the hydroxide to deduce the nature of the oxide which you assumed behaved in a parallel fashion.

In the case of sodium peroxide reacting with water, you may have observed a gaseous product. Tests would reveal that this gas is oxygen; hence, the general equation is

$$\text{metallic peroxide} + \text{water} \rightarrow \text{base} + \text{oxygen gas}$$

If you failed to observe the evolution of oxygen, then it is likely that the peroxide was previously exposed to moisture.

The acid solutions produced by the reaction of SO_2, NO_2, CO_2, and P_4O_6 with water suggest that nonmetallic oxides react with water and yield acids.

$$\text{nonmetallic oxide} + \text{water} \rightarrow \text{acid}$$

Thus, a nonmetallic oxide is sometimes called an acid anhydride. The formulas and names for the acids associated with several nonmetallic oxides are listed at the top of the next page.

OXIDE

Name	Formula
sulfur dioxide	SO_2
sulfur trioxide	SO_3
phosphorus trioxide	P_4O_6
phosphorus pentoxide	P_4O_{10}
carbon dioxide	CO_2

ACID

Acid Name	Formula
sulfurous acid	H_2SO_3
sulfuric acid	H_2SO_4
phosphorus acid	H_3PO_3
phosphoric acid	H_3PO_4
carbonic acid	H_2CO_3

Using the formulas given above, you should be able to write balanced equations for most of the reactions that involved nonmetallic oxides and water.

If an oxide which was insoluble in water reacted with an acid but not with a base, you classified it as a basic metallic oxide. The products of such a reaction are water and an ionic solution of a salt.

$$basic\ oxide + acid \rightarrow water + salt(aq)$$

A specific example would be the reaction of calcium oxide with hydrochloric acid. Three equations that describe the reaction are listed below.

formula equation:
$$CaO(s) + 2HCl(aq) \rightarrow H_2O + CaCl_2(aq)$$

net ionic:
$$CaO(s) + 2H_3O^+ \rightarrow 3H_2O + Ca^{2+}(aq)$$

simplified net ionic:
$$CaO(s) + 2H^+(aq) \rightarrow H_2O + Ca^{2+}(aq)$$

Note that in the net ionic equation, only the positive metallic ion is shown as a product. The chloride ions (Cl^-) from the dissociation of the strong acid (hydrochloric) is a spectator ion and is not shown in the equation. In net ionic equations, the formulas of strong acids and bases are shown in ionic form. Hydrochloric (HCl), nitric (HNO_3), and sulfuric (H_2SO_4) are the frequently encountered strong (highly dissociated) acids, while sodium hydroxide ($NaOH$) and potassium hydroxide (KOH) are strong bases.

All of the nonmetallic oxides which you tested dissolved in water and formed acid solutions. We would expect, therefore, that nonmetallic (acid) oxides would react with bases and yield water and an ionic solution of a salt.

word equation:
$$acid\ oxide + base \rightarrow water + salt(aq)$$

formula equation:
$$SO_2(g) + 2NaOH(aq) \rightarrow Na_2SO_3(aq) + H_2O$$

net ionic equation:
$$SO_2(g) + 2OH^-(aq) \rightarrow SO_3^{2-}(aq) + H_2O$$

Note that in the net ionic equation, only the oxyanion (SO_3^{2-}) is shown as a product. The oxidation state of the sulfur in the sulfite ions is the same, $(+4)$, as it is in sulfur dioxide (SO_2). The name of the anion is related to the oxidation state of the atom other than oxygen and also to the number of oxygen atoms in the polyatomic ion. Thus, in the sulfate ions, the oxidation state of sulfur is +6.

FOLLOW-UP QUESTIONS

1. (a) In general, do the metallic oxides that react with and dissolve in water form acid or basic solutions? Cite examples to justify your answer. (b) In general, do nonmetallic oxides react with water and form acid or basic solutions? Cite examples.

2. Strontium, element #38, forms an oxide which reacts with water. Would you predict the solution to be acid or basic? Explain.

3. Write a formula for gallium oxide. Gallium

115

is element #31. What is the basis for your formula?

4. Predict the formula for an oxide of selenium (element #34). Would an aqueous solution of this oxide be acid or basic? Explain.

5. Use the principle of periodicity to predict the nature of SnO_2. Tin is element #50.

6. Is ClO_2 classified as an acid or basic oxide? What is the basis for your classification? Chlorine is element #17.

7. Write a formula for cesium (element #55) peroxide.

8. Which is the more acid, As_4O_6 or As_4O_{10}? Cite your evidence. Does this observation suggest that acidity increases or decreases with an increase in oxidation number?

9. Would you predict that Sb_2O_5 is more or less acid than Sb_2O_3? Explain your choice.

10. Would you predict Sb_2O_3 to be more or less basic than As_2O_3? What is the basis of your choice? What does this suggest about the relative radii of As^{3+} and Sb^{3+}?

11. Does the acidity of an oxide of a given element increase or decrease as the oxidation state of the central atom increases? Cite your evidence.

12. Using the relative electronegativity of the central atom as a basis for your prediction, which oxide is the more acid, As_2O_3 or As_2O_5? Refer to the trends indicated in Fig. 7-1 at the top of page 112.

13. (a) $Sn(OH)_2$ is found to be insoluble in water but reacts with and is soluble in dilute HCl as well as in NaOH. Using this evidence, classify $Sn(OH)_2$. (b) $Fe(OH)_3$ is insoluble in water and in dilute NaOH but reacts with and dissolves in dilute hydrochloric acid. On the basis of these data, classify $Fe(OH)_3$.

14. Write a formula equation and a net ionic equation for the reaction that occurs when hydrochloric acid is added to barium oxide.

8-1

Shapes of Molecules and Polyatomic Ions

GENERAL DISCUSSION

One of our objectives in chemistry is to explain the properties of macroscopic samples in terms of the nature and behavior of the molecules that make up the sample. As you might expect, there are wide variations in the properties of individual molecular substances. Properties such as melting points and boiling points depend on attractions between molecules. Such properties are influenced by the polarity of the individual molecules. We would expect the properties of substances composed of polar covalent molecules to differ from those composed of nonpolar molecules. Polarity, in turn, depends on the shape of the molecule and the relative electronegativities of the atoms involved. Shapes of molecules, however, also influence the properties of nonpolar substances. Thus, structural isomers whose chemical compositions are identical, differ in structure (shape) and in properties.

The shape of a molecule depends on the angle between atoms bonded to a central atom. This angle, known as the *bond angle,* is the angle formed by two imaginary lines which join, respectively, the nuclei of each of two outlying atoms to the nucleus of the central atom. The distance between the nuclei of two bonded atoms is known as the *bond length.* The shape of the molecule is outlined by imaginary lines which join the nucleus of each of the outlying atoms to the nuclei of adjacent atoms.

One simplified theory of molecular geometry, called the "valence-shell, electron-pair repulsion theory," assumes that the shapes of molecules (and other species) are related to the positions of the valence-electron clouds on the central atom of the molecule. Each negative charge cloud, which contains two electrons of opposing spins, tends to repel all other charge clouds in the vicin-

ity. To achieve a condition of minimum potential energy, it is necessary that the charge clouds be located so that they will be as far apart as possible. In this position, the electrostatic repulsion between the clouds is at a minimum.

The spatial orientation of the charge clouds depends on the number that are present and on their size. The number is equal to the total number of electron-pairs (bonded and unbonded) in the valence level of the central atom as indicated by the Lewis structure of the species. A double or triple bond involving, respectively, two or three electron-pairs is counted as or considered equivalent to a single electron cloud for purposes of determining spatial orientation. The relative size depends on whether the electron-pair is a bonded or a lone (unbonded) pair. We would expect clouds associated with bonded electrons to be rather localized between nuclei and to take up less space than those associated with unbonded electrons.

In this activity, you will be given a set of styrofoam models and asked to identify structural features of a chemical species associated with the model. Electron-pairs are represented by a wooden splint or a pair of tacks. You should be aware, of course, that the shapes and bond angles you identify are idealized. You are to use the symmetry of the molecular models as a guide to the polarity of the species. Assume that the "atoms" attached to the central "atom" are identical. As a follow-up activity you are to construct a model for a species whose formula is furnished by your instructor.

OBJECTIVE

1. To relate the shapes and bond angles of chemical species to the number of bonded and

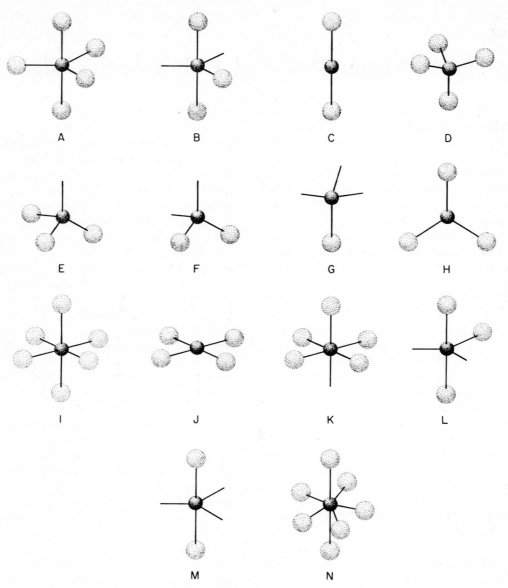

Fig. 8-1   Styrofoam models representing shapes of molecules.

unbonded electron-pairs in the valence level of the central atom in the species.

2. To relate the polarity of molecules to the shape and symmetry of the species.

MATERIALS

Sets consisting of 14 styrofoam models which

represent various molecules, white and colored styrofoam balls, wooden splints.

PROCEDURE

1. Examine each model and identify: (a) the number of electron-pairs in the valence level of the central atom (assume no multiple bonds), (b)

the number of bonded atoms (do not count the central atom), (c) the number of lone-pairs (unbonded electron-pairs), and (d) the bond angles. Record your observations in Table I. Handle the models with care and do not attempt to take them apart.

2. Write in Table I the shape of the species represented by each of the models in your set. This list may help.

Possible Shapes

linear	seesaw
trigonal planar	T-shaped
angular	octahedral
tetrahedral	square planar
pyramidal	square-based pyramid
trigonal bipyramidal	pentagonal bipyramidal

3. Assuming all the models represent neutral molecules, indicate whether each species is polar or nonpolar.

4. (a) Write the general formula for a chemical species with each of the shapes listed in the table. Use the symbol X to represent the central atom and the symbol Y to represent the atoms (all identical to each other) bonded to the central atom. (b) Write a formula showing all atoms and the number of lone pairs. Represent the lone pairs of electrons with the symbol E. For example, the formula for a species composed of two atoms of Y bonded to an X atom which still has two unbonded pairs of electrons in its valence level would be XY_2E_2.

5. Obtain the name and formula of an "unknown" from your instructor and use the styro-

Table I   Structural Characteristics of Chemical Species

Code No. of Model	No. of Atoms Bonded to Central Atom	No. of Lone Pairs of Electrons in Valence Level of Bonded Central Atom	No. of e⁻ Pairs in Valence Level of Bonded Central Atom	Bond Angle	Shape	Electric Nature (polar or nonpolar)	Formula	
							Molecu-lar	Including Lone Pairs
A								
B								
C								
D								
E								
F								
G								
H								
I								
J								
K								
L								
M								
N								

Table II   "Unknown"

Name of Unknown	Formula (from instructor)	No. of e⁻ Pairs in Valence Level of Central Atom (Include all pairs in multiple bonds)	No. of Atoms Bonded to Central Atom	No. of Lone Pairs on Central Atom	Lewis Structure	Number and Kind (Double or Triple) or Multiple Bonds	Shape

foam spheres and sticks in your set to construct a model of it. Record the information requested in Table II. Unlike the species represented by the models in your set, your unknown may involve a double bond. It is suggested that you first draw a Lewis (electron-dot) formula of your unknown. This should reveal the number of lone electron-pairs and thus, help you identify the shape of the species. Your instructor will tell whether or not the central atom follows the octet rule. Take your completed model to the instructor for his evaluation and queries. If so directed, disassemble your model and return the materials to the stock box.

FOLLOW-UP DISCUSSION

In this activity you used the number of atoms bonded to a given atom and the number of lone-pair valence electrons as a guide to the shape of a molecule. You found that the shapes of species in which there are lone pairs of valence electrons are related to the shapes of species in which all

pairs of valence electrons are involved in bond formation. For example, the shapes of all the species in which the central atom has five pairs of valence electrons can, in theory, be related to the trigonal bipyramid structure. Removal of one atom from a vertex of the equilateral triangle in the central plane of a bipyramid leaves a lone pair of electrons and yields a seesaw or teeter-totter structure. It should be noted that the angles between the atoms in the central plane of the bi-pyramid are identical but differ from the angles between the atoms at the apices of the pyramid and the atoms in the central plane. It can be shown that minimum repulsion exists when *lone pairs* of electrons in the valence level of the central atom occupy positions in the central plane of the bipyramid.

For the purpose of this experiment we assumed that some of the models represented double-bonded structures. It is possible to predict the presence of a double bond in the Lewis structure of the species by comparing the total number of valence electrons in the central atom with the sum obtained by adding the number of lone pairs to the number of atoms bonded to the central atom. For example, if there are four pairs of valence electrons, three atoms bonded to a central atom and no lone pairs, then the Lewis structure for the species must contain a double bond, be trigonal planar and nonpolar.

Another assumption we made in this activity was that identical atoms were bonded to a central atom. With this assumption, four atoms bonded to a central atom having no lone pairs gives rise to a symmetrical tetrahedral species which is nonpolar. If the attached atoms were not identical, then the symmetry would be destroyed, the molecule would be polar, and its shape would resemble a distorted tetrahedron. You should also keep in mind that the geometry of polyatomic ions can be described in the same terms as those for neutral molecules. Polarity, however, is a term reserved for describing the electric nature of neutral molecules, not ions. Although partial charges are associated with molecular dipoles, ions carry a unit charge or a multiple of the unit charge. For example, sulfate ions (SO_4^{2-}) although tetrahedrally shaped with no lone electron-pairs on the sulfur atom, carry a net charge of 2^-.

As we noted earlier, the degree of molecular polarity has an important bearing on the behavior of substances. Quantitatively, the degree of molecular polarity may be expressed in terms of a dipole moment. Dipole moments can be experimentally determined by means of electric measurements and then used to calculate the percent ionic character in a bond and to help determine the geometry of a molecule. For example, knowing that carbon dioxide has a zero dipole moment enables us to predict that the molecule is linear.

FOLLOW-UP QUESTIONS

1. Which of these species are polar? (a) CH_4, (b) CH_3Cl, (c) CCl_4, (d) C_2H_4, (e) SO_3, (f) SCl_2, (g) PH_3, (h) BCl_3, (i) SO_2, (j) $TeCl_4$. Draw a Lewis structure for each molecule.

2. Which of these involve double bonds in their Lewis structures? Assume that all atoms follow the octet rule. (a) CO_3^{2-}, (b) SO_4^{2-}, (c) SO_3, (d) CO_2, (e) SiO_3^{2-}, (f) SO_3^{2-}. Draw Lewis structures for each species.

3. What is the shape of the following species? (a) CS_2, (b) BO_3^{3-}, (c) $TiCl_4$, (d) TeO_2, (e) IO_3^-, (f) SCl_2, (g) SiO_3^{2-}, (h) SF_4, (i) AsF_5, (k) XeF_2, (l) MoF_6, (m) ICl_4^-, (n) IF_5. Draw Lewis structures for each species.

4. Hydrogen peroxide (H_2O_2) has a dipole moment of 2.2 units. Is H_2O_2 a symmetrical molecule? Explain. Is it a polar or nonpolar molecule?

8-2

Bonding Capacities of Atoms and Directional Characteristics of Hybrid Bonds

GENERAL DISCUSSION

In this "experiment" you will examine the electronic population of the outer energy levels of a number of atoms in order to explain and predict the formulas of covalent molecules. Some formulas would be difficult to explain solely on the basis of the common oxidation states which you associate with specific atoms. For example, an understanding of the concepts presented in this experiment will enable you to predict the formula of the compound formed by reaction of oxygen with fluorine, two elements which usually have negative oxidation states.

A covalent bond involves the sharing of a pair of electrons by two atoms. Although electrons in the outer levels of atoms are moving rapidly, it is possible to predict in what region of space about the nucleus of an atom they are most likely to be found. This means if an atom is going to share an electron with another atom, that the incoming atom is going to attach at the position where the bonding electron is most apt to be found. This imparts a directional characteristic to the covalent bond. Therefore, the molecules formed when two or more atoms bond to another atom have a particular geometric shape, which depends on the position of the bonding electrons. The shapes of covalent molecules can often be predicted by knowing the number and orbital location of the electrons in the outer energy level of the atoms.

In this "experiment" we are concerned only with covalent bonds formed when each of two atoms donate an electron to the shared pair. In theory, an atom with three or more principal energy levels can form as many of these covalent bonds as there are electrons in its outer energy level. In other words, the maximum number of

covalent bonds corresponds to the group number. Assume that for a given central atom all bonds distances and strengths are equivalent. Since pure atomic orbitals, that is, s, p, d, and f, differ in energies and directional characteristics, it is necessary to assume that hybrid orbitals are formed by mixing the characteristics of the pure atomic orbitals. The number of hybrid orbitals formed corresponds to the number of pure atomic orbitals mixed. The type of hybrid formed is designated by using the symbols for the pure orbitals used. The number of each pure orbital used in the hybrid is indicated by a superscript. Thus, dsp^2 represents four equivalent hybrid orbitals formed by mixing one d, one s, and two p atomic orbitals.

You will be given styrofoam models of atoms. Each set contains five colored styrofoam balls representing atoms of representative (nontransition) elements in periods 3, 4, 5, and 6 of the Periodic Table. Each "atom" has eight upholstery tacks stuck to its surface. The white tacks represent the electrons in the outer energy level of the atom, and the black tacks represent "electron vacancies."

The outer "electrons" and "vacancies" are arranged as they might be found in the isolated atoms in their lowest energy or ground state. That is, they are arranged in "orbitals." Some orbitals contain 2 electrons (2 white tacks), some contain one electron and a vacancy (1 white and 1 black tack), and others contain no electrons—a double vacancy (2 black tacks). The vacant d orbitals are not shown but you will assume that they are available for bonding.

Assume that each atom contributes one electron to the pair being shared by two atoms. Therefore, the condition for forming a regular covalent bond is that an orbital have one electron and one vacancy; that is, a white-tack-black-tack combination. Some atoms have orbitals with 2 electrons (2 white tacks) and other orbitals with no electrons (2 black tacks). When this condition exists, assume that the electrons will rearrange themselves so as to make a maximum number of orbitals available for bond formation (white-tack-black-tack combinations).

OBJECTIVES

To investigate the relationships between electron configuration, bonding capacity, hybridization of orbitals, bond angles, and shapes of molecules.

MATERIALS

Set of five styrofoam atomic models.

PROCEDURE

1. Count the number of "electrons" in the outer shell. Record data in the table. Write the outer shell orbital configuration. Show individual p orbitals; that is, the electron population of the p_x, p_y, and p_z orbitals. Do not show the principal quantum number.

2. Write in the table the maximum number of regular covalent bonds the atom is capable of forming by contributing one electron to a shared pair. Assume the atom has at least three principal energy levels.

3. Determine the type of *hybrid* orbital used

Table I Electron Data

Color	White	Blue	Green	Red	Yellow
Code letter	A	B	C	D	E
Number of electrons in outer shell					
Electron population of outer level orbitals (no principal quantum number)					
Maximum number of covalent bonds					
Type of hybrid orbital used when all outer electrons are used in single covalent bonds					
Bond angles between atoms attached to central atom					
Shape of molecule which would be formed					
Formula of covalent fluorine compound					
Polar or nonpolar bonds					
Polar or nonpolar molecule					

when the *maximum* number of other atoms bond to the given atom. Assume the models represent atoms of the representative elements from *Row 3* of the Periodic Table. Remember that *d* orbitals are available even though they are not represented on the models.

4. Write the angles you would expect to observe between atoms bonding to the given atom. These angles are the ones formed between lines drawn from the center of the sphere representing the central atom to the center of each atom bonded to the central atom. Assume that the electron clouds of the bonded atoms repel each other so they are as far apart as possible on the central atom.

5. Write the shape of the molecule formed when the atom uses all its available electrons in forming regular covalent bonds with another kind of atom. The shape refers to the shape outlined by imaginary lines which connect the centers of the atoms bonded to the central atom.

6. Assume that a covalent compound is formed when each atom reacts with fluorine, and using the code letter, write the formula of the compound. If bonded atoms are arranged symmetrically about the central atom, the molecule is nonpolar. If there is an asymmetric arrangement of atoms about a central atom, then the molecule is polar.

7. Indicate whether the covalent bonds are polar or nonpolar. Remember, the bond between any two dissimilar atoms is polar.

8. Assume all the fluorine compounds are co-valent and indicate whether the molecule is polar or nonpolar. Remember that an asymmetric arrangement of atoms about a central atom results in an electric asymmetry and a polar molecule.

9. If they are available, check out a set of molecular models or, alternatively, refer to your data table in the last experiment and identify the hybrid orbitals used by the central atoms in the selected models from the set examined in the last experiment. Record your choices in the table below. Omit this procedure if you did not do Experiment 8-1.

FURTHER EXPERIMENTATION

Prepare scale models of molecules and polyatomic ions using styrofoam balls. You will have to look up radii, bond angles, and distances. Use upholstery tacks to represent unbonded electrons. Explain the shape and properties of the species you prepare. Suggest how your model might be used as part of this "experiment" for future classes.

FOLLOW-UP DISCUSSION

In this exercise we considered only covalent bonds in which each atom contributes one electron to a shared pair. Furthermore, we assumed that in each case the central atom used all of its bonding electrons in forming bonds. In many covalent molecules, such as water, the central atom does not use all of its electrons. When lone pairs of electrons remain unbonded, they tend to distort the direction of hybrid or pure atomic orbitals

Code Letter of Ball-and-Stick Molecular Model	Code Letter of Related Model (Central Atom) in Atomic Model Set	Hybrid Orbital Used by Central Atom in the Molecular Model
D		
A		
H		
I		
C		

from their usual angles, and thus, result in a molecule with an asymmetric shape. The resulting electric asymmetry gives rise to a polar molecule. The polarity of a molecule has a pronounced effect on the properties of a substance.

It is also possible for a covalent bond to be formed between two atoms if one atom has an electron-pair and the other has a completely vacant orbital. This covalent bond is sometimes referred to as a coordinate bond. For example, we would predict that boron with 3 bonding electrons could form 3 regular covalent bonds. However, any atom in period 2 has 4 orbitals in the second energy level (one s and 3 p) and thus can form four bonds (bonding capacity equals 4). Therefore, boron can bond to 4 different atoms. This would involve three regular covalent bonds and one coordinate bond.

FOLLOW-UP QUESTIONS

1. Oxygen has a common oxidation state of 2⁻ and fluorine has an oxidation state of 1⁻. (a) How could you explain the existence of a substance with the formula OF_2, when both atoms exhibit common negative oxidation states? (b) What is the shape of OF_2? Explain. (c) Is OF_2 polar or nonpolar? Explain. (d) If polar, which end of the molecule is the negative end? Explain.

2. Do NH_3 and BF_3 have the same shape? Explain. Can both NH_3 and BF_3 form coordinate covalent bonds? Explain any differences.

3. Is it possible for iodine to form a compound such as IF_7? Can fluorine form a compound such as FI_7? Explain your answers.

4. Predict the shapes of the following molecules or ions: (a) CH_4 (b) BCl_3 (c) CaH_2 (d) PH_3 (e) H_3O^+.

5. Write the electron-dot formula for each of the covalent fluorine compounds listed in Table I.

6. Write the electron-dot formula for each of these molecules or ions and predict their shapes. All conform to the octet rule. (a) sulfur trioxide (SO_3), (b) sulfite ions (SO_3^{2-}), (c) carbonate ions (CO_3^{2-}), (d) sulfate ions (SO_4^{2-}).

7. Explain how atom A can form a molecule such as AF_4 when A has only two singly-occupied orbitals in its valence level in the ground state.

8. How many hybrid sp^2 orbitals are formed when one s and two p pure atomic orbitals hybridize? How many electrons can be accommodated by the set of sp^2 orbitals formed?

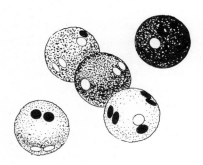

Fig. 8-2 Styrofoam atomic models.

9-1
Properties of Aggregates

GENERAL DISCUSSION

Solid crystals consist of a regular array of particles located at the lattice points in a three-dimensional lattice work. The units which occupy the lattice points in an ionic crystal are alternately spaced positive and negative ions. The force of attraction between the oppositely charged ions constitutes an ionic bond.

Some substances are composed of molecules rather than ions. Molecules are neutral species composed of atoms which are held together by covalent bonds. Covalent bonds are the result of an attraction between the positive nuclei of two atoms and the negative electrons shared by the two atoms. When molecules of gases condense, they form molecular liquids and molecular crystals. In these crystals the lattice points are occupied by molecules. The forces of attraction which hold molecules together in a molecular crystal are called van der Waals forces or bonds. If the molecule contains hydrogen and also a highly electronegative element, then the molecules may be held together by hydrogen bonds. The molecules in a molecular crystal are composed of atoms which are held together by covalent bonds.

In this experiment you examine the properties of an ionic crystal (an aggregate of ions) and those of a molecular crystal (an aggregate of molecules). The molecules of the substance which you study are classified as nonpolar. Assume that the properties of the crystals which you examine are typical of a particular class of crystal. Making these assumptions, you use your limited data to assign tentatively general properties to each type of substance. You also relate the observed properties to a type of attraction or bond between particles. In Part II you test the relative solubilities of a number of solutes in various solvents and attempt to relate the relative solubilities to the structural characteristics of the solute and solvent.

OBJECTIVES

1. To examine some of the properties associated with ionic and molecular substances.
2. To relate observed properties to the type of interaction or bond between particles.
3. To investigate the relationship between the solubility of a substance and the nature of the solute and solvent.

MATERIALS

Potassium iodide, paradichlorobenzene, graduated cylinder, evaporating dish, burner, wire screen, test tubes, electric conductivity apparatus, benzene, rock salt or marble chips, naphthalene, iodine, carbon tetrachloride or a liquid Freon, ethanol, and sucrose.

PROCEDURE

Part I

1. Use potassium iodide (KI) as a typical ionic compound, and paradichlorobenzene ($C_6H_4Cl_2$) as a typical molecular substance composed of nonpolar molecules. Subject each substance to these tests and record your observation in Table I.

(a) Smell each compound. If you detect an odor, assume that the substance is volatile. If there is no odor, assume that it is nonvolatile.
(b) Test the hardness of each compound by rubbing a small sample between your fingers. Record the hardness as either soft and waxy, or brittle and granular. Record your impression before the substance tends to dissolve in any oil or moisture on your fingers. Wash your hands after testing. Additional evidence related to this property may be obtained by using rock salt or marble chips as examples of ionic substances and a piece of a candle as an example of a molecular material.

126

Table I   Properties of Types of Aggregates

	Potassium iodide, KI (ionic)	Paradichlorobenzene, $C_6H_4Cl_2$ (molecular)
Volatility (high or low)		
Melting point (high or low)		
Solubility in water (soluble or insoluble)		
Solubility in benzene		
Electric conductivity in solid state		
Electric conductivity in liquid state		
Hardness or texture (brittle or soft)		

(c) Place a small sample of paradichlorobenzene in an evaporating dish on a ring stand. Heat the sample with a hot flame and observe the approximate time required for it to melt. **Caution:** *the vapors of paradichlorobenzene are poisonous.* Use adequate ventilation and do not inhale the vapors. As soon as it melts, remove the flame, and clean the dish (paradichlorobenzene is soluble in benzene). After removing the residue, scrub the dish with soap and water. **Caution:** *do not use benzene near a flame.*

(d) Place approximately the same size sample of KI in the dry evaporating dish and heat with a hot flame as before. Note the approximate time required for melting to occur. Use the time required for melting as a basis for identifying the melting point as relatively high or relatively low compared to paradichlorobenzene.

(e) Place 1–2 crystals (not more than 0.1 g) of each compound in separate test tubes containing water (a polar solvent). Shake or stir and record the relative solubilities of the two compounds in water.

(f) Put 1–2 crystals of each compound in separate test tubes containing benzene C_6H_6 (a non-polar solvent). Shake or stir and record the relative solubilities of the two compounds in benzene.

(g) The instructor will place samples of each compound in separate evaporating dishes or crucibles, and test the electric conductivity of each in the solid phase. He will then heat each of the solids and test the conductivity in the liquid phase. (This may be done as a demonstration.) **Caution:** *do not inhale the vapors.*

Part II · Relationship between Solubility and the Nature of Solute and Solvent

2. Add approximately 0.3 g of ordinary table sugar (sucrose) to each of two test tubes. Add approximately 0.3 g of naphthalene to each of two other test tubes.

3. Add 5 ml of water to a test tube containing the sugar and 5 ml of water to a test tube containing the naphthalene. Shake each tube for 20 to 30 seconds and record in Table II the relative solubilities of each solute in water. If the solute

Table II Effect of Solute and Solvent Nature on Solubility

Substance	Water	Benzene	Carbon Tetrachloride or a Liquid Freon	Ethanol (Ethyl Alcohol)
Sugar				
Naphthalene				
Iodine				
Water				
Potassium iodide				

appears to dissolve at all, it should be classified as soluble (s). If it appears not to dissolve appreciably, it should be classified as slightly soluble (ss).

4. Add 5 ml of benzene to the test tube containing the dry sucrose and 5 ml of benzene to the tube containing the dry naphthalene. Shake each tube for 30 seconds and record in Table II the relative solubilities of each solute in benzene.

5. Place a small crystal of iodine in the bottom of each of two test tubes. Do not touch the iodine with your hand. Add 5 ml of benzene and 5 ml of water to the first tube, and 5 ml of water plus 5 ml of carbon tetrachloride or a liquid Freon to the second test tube. Shake each vigorously. Record the color and relative solubilities of iodine in the three solvents. Base your conclusion on the color and its intensity in the various solvents. Also record the extent to which water and the other two solvents appear to dissolve in one another. Add 5 ml of ethanol (ethyl alcohol) to a crystal of iodine in another test tube, shake and record the color and relative solubility of iodine. Now add 5 ml of water to the test tube containing the ethanol and record the relative solubility of alcohol in water.

Table III Nature of Solutes and Solvents

Substance	Structural Formula	Nature of Substance (Nonpolar, slightly polar, highly polar, ionic or macromolecular)	Nature of Bonding between Particles in Aggregate
Water			
Sucrose			
Iodine			
Benzene			
Carbon tetrachloride or liquid Freon			
Napthalene			
Ethanol			
Potassium iodide			

6. Place 0.3 g of **KI** in each of four test tubes. Add 10 ml of water to the first tube, 10 ml of ethanol to the second tube, 10 ml of benzene to the third, and 10 ml of CCl_4 or liquid Freon to the fourth tube. Record the relative solubilities.

7. Look up the structural formulas and types of bonding present in all of the solids and liquids used in this part of the experiment. Record your findings in Table III.

FOLLOW-UP DISCUSSION

The electron structures of neutral atoms do not represent stable arrangements of electrons for most of the atoms. As a consequence, atoms seek to attain a more stable electron configuration. They do this through chemical combination with each other during which process electrons are rearranged and produce low-energy, more stable structures. A particularly stable structure is one in which the outer energy level of the atoms contains eight electrons. If the outer level is the only level, then two electrons represent a stable structure. The result of two atoms combining with each other is the formation of a chemical bond. A chemical bond may be defined as the attraction between the outer electrons of two atoms or groups of atoms and their nuclei, when the nuclei are spaced at a distance at which the potential energy is a minimum. This spacing is determined by three factors:

1. Attraction between the positively charged nucleus of each atom and the negative electron cloud of the other.

2. Repulsion between electron clouds of combining atoms or groups of atoms.

3. Repulsion between two nuclei of combining atoms. There are three major types of chemical bonds: ionic, covalent, and metallic.

There is no sharp dividing line between purely ionic and purely covalent bonds. Both types of bonds are fundamentally the result of electrostatic attraction between positive nuclei and negative electrons. The type of bond formed between two atoms depends on the relative attraction that the atoms have for the bonding electrons. The attrac-

tion that an atom or ion has for electrons depends to a large extent upon these factors.

1. Electronic structure of each atom or ion.

2. Effective nuclear charge (actual nuclear charge diminished by the screening effect of other electrons).

3. Radius of the particle.

The interaction of these factors results in varying degrees of attraction between two atoms and the bonding electrons. Hence, the difference between an ionic and covalent bond is simply a difference in the degree of electron-sharing. Thus, there are wide variations in the behavior of the many substances which we may classify, for convenience, as ionically or covalently bonded.

In this experiment you examined only one ionic crystal and found that the substance had a relatively high melting point and a relatively high solubility in water. Examination of other ionic crystals would reveal that they all have these same general characteristics but that their properties vary over a very large range. For example, calcium oxide (CaO) melts at 2580°C and reacts with water. The resulting $Ca(OH)_2$ is only slightly soluble in water. This variation in properties of ionic compounds can, in large part, be attributed to the differences in the electric charge and radius of the constituent positive and negative ions. Similarly, the variation in properties of molecular crystals composed of nonpolar molecules can, in large part, be attributed to differences in the sizes, shapes, and composition of the molecules that make up the crystal.

There are four principal classes of crystalline solids: ionic, molecular, macromolecular or network, and metallic.

In this experiment we did not consider either macromolecular (network) or metallic crystals. Macromolecular crystals such as asbestos, graphite, and diamond, consist of a one, two, or three-dimensional network of atoms located at the lattice points and joined by covalent bonds. The three-dimensional crystals have very high melting points, are extremely hard, and do not conduct electricity in either solid or liquid phase. In macromolecular crystals such as diamond, the lat-

129

tice points are occupied by atoms. Each atom is bonded to its nearest neighbors by covalent bonds.

Metallic crystals constitute the fourth type of solid aggregate. These crystals are excellent conductors of electricity in both the solid and liquid phases. The lattice points of these crystals are occupied by positive metallic ions surrounded by a "sea" or "gas" of delocalized, mobile electrons. The force of attraction between the positive kernels (ions) and the surrounding "sea" of electrons constitutes the metallic bond.

FOLLOW-UP QUESTIONS

1. (a) Explain in terms of type and relative strength of bonds, the presence or absence of odors of paradichlorobenzene and potassium iodide. (b) Could a substance be relatively volatile and not have an odor? Give an example.

2. Explain in terms of type and relative strength of bonds the difference in melting point of the two substances.

3. Are you comparing the relative strengths of covalent and ionic bonds when you are comparing relative melting points of potassium iodide and paradichlorobenzene? Explain.

4. Are electrons in ionic crystals tightly held by the nuclei or are they mobile and free to move throughout the crystal under the influence of an applied voltage? Cite evidence for your answer.

5. Do ionic crystals form ionic liquids? Cite evidence and explain.

6. Are the valence electrons in nonpolar covalent molecules localized or delocalized and free to move through a molecular crystal composed of nonpolar covalent molecules? Cite evidence.

7. Do crystals composed of nonpolar molecules form ionic or molecular liquids? What is the evidence?

8. How do you account for any observed differences in the hardness of the crystals you examined?

9. Are the intermolecular or intramolecular forces greater in paradichlorobenzene? Explain in terms of your observations.

10. Refer to the Periodic Table or chart of electronegativities and classify these substances as largely covalent or largely ionic (a) LiF, (b) ICl, (c) KBr, (d) SO_2, (e) Mg_3N_2.

11. Use the results of your experiment to predict the properties of the two compounds listed in Table IV.

Table IV   Predictions

	KF	CH₄
Melting point (high or low)		
Volatility (high or low)		
Electric conductivity in liquid phase		
Solubility in water		
Solubility in benzene		
Type of crystal (ionic, molecular, covalent)		
Type of bond between units at lattice points		
Type of bonds between elements shown in formula		

12. Use your observations in Part II to formulate a general rule relating the nature of the solute and nature of the solvent to the relative solubility of a solute in a solvent.

13. How can you account for the difference in color between iodine dissolved in water or alcohol or iodine dissolved in carbon tetrachloride? Remember iodine vapor is violet and is composed of I_2 molecules.

14. Predict the relative solubility of sucrose in ethanol.

15. Give reasons why you expect a wide range in the solubilities of ionic compounds in water.

16. Give reasons why you would expect a wide range in the solubilities of nonpolar molecular substances in benzene.

9-2

Metallic Unit Cells of the Cubic System

GENERAL DISCUSSION

Frequently, a knowledge of the crystalline structure of metals can help us explain variations in such properties as malleability, hardness, and density. In order to describe the makeup of a crystal on the atomic level, it is necessary to have data which allow us to determine the exact arrangement of the particles. *X-ray diffraction* enables scientists to determine the arrangement of the particles in a crystal.

As a result of their experiments, scientists conclude that the atoms, molecules, or ions in a crystalline solid vibrate about fixed positions which are arranged in an orderly fashion. The positions of the atoms or ions in a crystal are represented by **lattice points.** The three-dimensional array of lattice points is known as the **lattice structure.**

Examination of the three-dimensional arrays of lattice points reveals that each structure contains a basic pattern of ions or atoms which is repeated throughout the structure. The smallest representative building block of a crystal lattice structure is known as a **unit cell.** A unit cell is the smallest part of a crystal which resembles a single perfect crystal. Crystal structures can therefore be described in terms of the characteristics of their unit cells.

There are seven different crystal systems and fourteen different types of unit cells. In this experiment we shall consider only the three types of unit cells associated with the cubic system.

1. *Simple* or primitive cubic cells which have points at each corner.

2. *Face-centered* cubic cells which have points at the corners and at the centers of the faces of the cube.

3. *Body-centered* cubic cells which have points at the corners and in the center of the cube.

Let us imagine that identical atoms are located at the points of each of the above unit cells. Each atom in a perfect crystal has the same environment. In order to understand this environment, we must be familiar with the structure of the unit cells as well as the structure produced when unit cells are packed together. It is conventional to represent unit cells as shown in the accompanying drawings, where circles (in two dimensions) or spheres (in three dimensions) represent atoms at the lattice points. One cubic cell is that volume outlined by the lines connecting the centers of the circles or spheres. Each unit cell therefore shares its atoms with adjacent unit cells.

In Fig. 9-1 a face-centered cubic crystal is shown. The corner atoms are shared by 8 unit cells, so a given unit cell includes only $\frac{1}{8}$ of a corner atom within its volume. Atoms in the faces of the cube are shared by 2 unit cells, so that each has only one half of a face atom within its volume. In theory, packing thousands of iden-

Fig. 9-1   Styrofoam models of metallic crystals.

tical unit cells together generates an observable, perfect crystal.

Examination of unit cells and visualization of the structures produced when they are joined reveal three important features.

1. *Coordination number.* This is the number of nearest-neighbor atoms which surround a given atom.

2. *The number of atoms per unit cell.* The total number of atoms per unit cell is the sum of the *number of whole atoms* enclosed within the cube and the *fractions of atoms* at the corners, on the edges, and in the faces of the cube.

3. *The relationship between the diameter (d) of the atoms and the length (a) of the side of the unit cell.*

In this experiment, you will examine models which represent the three types of unit cells associated with the cubic system, and identify for each cell the three features noted above.

OBJECTIVES

1. To attach a meaning to the concepts of the unit cell, coordination number, and atoms per unit cell.

2. To learn to distinguish the three unit cells associated with the cubic system.

3. To learn the relationship between atomic diameters and length of sides of the different unit cells.

4. To determine the percentage of empty space in each of the unit cells.

5. To determine the relative density of the different unit cells.

MATERIALS

Models of simple, body-centered, and face-centered cubic unit cells, ruler.

PROCEDURE

1. Count and record in the table the number of closest neighbors which surround a given atom in each unit cell. This is known as the coordination number. It will be necessary to visualize each cell being surrounded by identical cells. See Fig. 9-2 (a), (b), and (c).

132

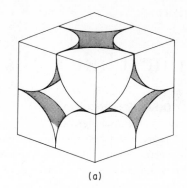

(a)

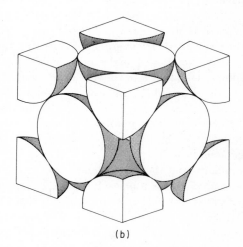

(b)

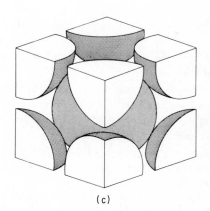

(c)

Fig. 9-2   Unit cells: (a) simple cubic, (b) face-centered, (c) body-centered.

2. Determine the number of atoms per unit cell.

3. Measure the length a of the side of each unit cell to the nearest 0.1 cm.

4. Calculate the volume a^3 of each unit cell.

5. Measure the diameter d of the "atom" in each cell. If the cells are constructed of the same size styrofoam ball, then the diameter of the "atom" is the same for each cell.

6. Calculate and record the volume ($\frac{4}{3}\pi r^3$), of an "atom" in each cell.

7. Multiply the volume of the "atom" by the number of "atoms" per unit cell to obtain the total volume occupied by all of the "atoms" in each cell.

8. Calculate the percentage of empty space in each crystal model.

9. Calculate the relative density of the three unit cells. Assume that each unit cell is composed of the same kind of atom. See the Follow-up Discussion for an explanation of the calculations.

FURTHER EXPERIMENTATION

To illustrate the arrangement of atoms in a closest-packed structure, place a layer of similar marbles or styrofoam spheres in a box so that there is a minimum amount of empty space between the spheres. Add a second layer by placing more spheres in the depressions in the first layer. Count the number of "holes" around a given sphere in the first layer. How many of these "holes" in the first layer are covered by spheres in the second layer? Notice that the "holes" in the second layer are either directly over the first-layer spheres, or over the "holes" in the first layer. Place a third layer of spheres over the "holes" in the second layer which are directly over the "holes" of the first layer. This arrangement, designated *abcabcabc* . . . is characteristic of the *face-centered cubic closest-packed structure*. Now remove the third layer of spheres and place them in the depressions of the second layer, which are directly over the atoms in the first layer. This type of packing is designated as *abababab* . . . , and classified as *hexagonal closest-packed*.

Although face-centered and hexagonal closest-packed structures are similar in many features, the face-centered structures have more planes along which atoms can glide past one another when stress is applied to the metal. These are known as *glide-* or *slip-planes*. Metals such as aluminum, silver, copper, and gold, which crystallize in face-centered structures, are more ductile and malleable than titanium and magnesium, which crystallize in a hexagonal-packed structure.

The small void or *hole* directly below and directly above each sphere in the closest-packed structures provides space for atoms to move and gives rise to properties such as ductility and malleability. When smaller atoms are added to a pure metal to form allows, they locate themselves in the

Item		Model Color		
No.	Item	Red	White	Green
1	Type of unit cell			
2	Number of closest neighbors surrounding each atom (coordination number)			
3	Number of atoms per unit cell			
4	Length a of side of unit cell in centimeters			
5	Volume of unit cell in cubic centimeters			
6	Diameter d of an atom in cell in centimeters			
7	Volume of atom in unit cell in cm³			
8	Total volume occupied by all atoms in unit cell			
9	Percentage of space occupied by atoms			
10	Percentage of empty space in unit cell			
11	Relative density of unit cells			

holes and interfere with movement along slip-planes, and thus change the characteristics of the original metal. You can observe how stress distorts slip-planes by bending a stiff wire and then attempting to bend it back in the same place.

FOLLOW-UP DISCUSSION

In this experiment, the models represent unit cells of perfect *metallic* crystals. In these crystals the lattice points are occupied by identical, positive, metallic ions. In general, *the atoms of most metallic elements tend to pack so as to achieve a maximum coordination number.* The maximum coordination number for atoms in a closest-packed structure such as a face-centered cubic crystal is 12. A few metallic elements pack in a body-centered cubic structure. In the case of the alkali metals of Group IA, which pack in the body-centered structure, the large atomic radius seems to be important in yielding a stable structure with a coordination number of 8. All the alkaline-earth metals in Group IIA except barium have a closest-packed crystalline structure as opposed to the body-centered cubic structure of the Group I-A elements. As the coordination number increases, the number of bonds to adjacent atoms increases, and, consequently, the stability of the crystal increases. The increased strength of the bonds and the differences in the crystalline structure between the I-A and II-A metals are reflected in higher melting and boiling points, increased molar heats of fusion and vaporization, and greater density of the II-A metals. Group II-A metals are malleable, but their hardness is such that they cannot easily be cut with a knife as can all Group I-A metals except lithium.

It can be shown that crystals which pack in closest-packed structures have 26 percent empty space; 74 percent of the volume is filled by atoms. Less efficient packing of atoms in the body-centered structure gives rise to softer metals with lower densities. *The density of a crystal is related to the mass of the atoms and the way in which they are packed together.* The density of a crystal is equal to the density of its unit cell and can be calculated from the dimensions of the unit cell.

(See Follow-up Problem 5.) *The value of Avogadro's number can be determined from a knowledge of the density, molecular mass, and lattice dimensions.* The lattice dimensions can be determined with the use of X-ray diffraction techniques.

In this experiment, the percentage of empty space in a unit cell (item 10) may be obtained by using the relationship:

$$\text{item } (10) = \frac{\text{item } (5) - \text{item } (8)}{\text{item } (5)} \ (100)$$

To calculate the relative densities of the unit cells (item 11), you assume the atoms in each of the unit cells are identical and arbitrarily assign the atoms a mass of 1. The density of each unit cell may be calculated by the relationship

$$D_{\text{unit cell}} = \frac{\text{mass of all atoms in cell}}{\text{total volume of cell}}$$

To determine the relative densities, divide each of the densities by that of the unit cell having the lowest density.

We can calculate the theoretical percentage of empty space in each cell by expressing the length of the side of a unit cell in terms of the diameter of the atom. For example, the relationship for the simple cubic cell is $a = d$. The volume of the unit cell is $a^3 = d^3$. There is only one atom per unit cell; thus, the volume occupied by one atom is

$$1 \times \tfrac{4}{3}\pi r^3 = 1 \times \tfrac{4}{3}\pi \left(\frac{d}{2}\right)^3 = 1 \times \tfrac{4}{3}\pi \frac{d^3}{8}$$

$$= 1 \times \frac{\pi d^3}{6}$$

Thus, the percentage of occupied space in the simple cubic cell is

$$\frac{\dfrac{\pi d^3}{6}}{d^3} \times (100) = \frac{\pi}{6} \ (100) = \frac{314}{6} = 52.3\%$$

For the purpose of calculating the theoretical relative densities of the three unit cells, the density of the simple cubic cell may be expressed as

$$\frac{M_{\text{cell}}}{V_{\text{cell}}} = \frac{1}{d^3}$$

FOLLOW-UP QUESTIONS

1. Explain why metals are malleable while ionic substances are not.

2. What factors determine the density of a metallic crystal?

3. Show using geometrical construction that the relationship between the diameter (d) of the atoms and the length (a) of the side of a face-centered cubic unit cell is

$$a = \sqrt{2}d$$

4. Show, using geometrical construction, that the relationship between the diameter (d) of the atoms and the length (a) of the side of a body-centered cubic unit cell is

$$a = \frac{2d}{\sqrt{3}}$$

5. The density of a unit cell may be expressed as

$$\text{Density} = \frac{\text{mass of unit cell}}{\text{volume of unit cell}}$$

$$= \frac{(\text{number of atoms per uc})(\text{gram atomic mass})}{(N)a^3}$$

where N is Avogadro's number and a is the length of the side of a unit cell in cm. Use the above formula and the relationships developed in problem 4 to calculate the density of chromium which has an atomic mass of 52.0, and atomic diameter of 2.53 Å, and packs in a body-centered structure. **Ans.** 6.78 g/ml³.

6. A new element has a face-centered cubic closest-packed structure. The shortest interatomic distance is 3.01 Å, and the density is 20.6 g/ml³. What is the atomic mass of this element? **Ans.** 236.

10-1
Molar Heat of Fusion of Ice

GENERAL DISCUSSION

When heat is added to a substance, its temperature usually rises. The relationship between the temperature change and the quantity of heat (Q) associated with the change is given by the equation

$$Q = \frac{\text{temperature}}{\text{change}} \times \text{mass} \times \frac{\text{specific}}{\text{heat capacity}} \quad \text{Eq. 1}$$

We shall consider the specific heat capacity to be the number of calories required to raise the temperature of one g of substance one Celsius degree. This is not a rigorous definition since specific heats of substances vary with the temperature. The specific heat of water is taken to be 1 cal/g C°. Specific heat is one of a number of *thermal properties* of matter. The determination of thermal properties requires the measurement of quantities of heat and is part of the experimental science know as *calorimetry*.

Measurements involving heat are carried out in an apparatus called a calorimeter. You will construct and use a simple calorimeter similar to that pictured in Fig. 10-1. This device is insulated so as to permit a minimum energy transfer to the surroundings.

When a process which liberates energy is carried on in the calorimeter, some of the energy will be transferred to the calorimeter and to the surroundings. The quantity of heat gained (or lost) by the calorimeter and surroundings per degree change in temperature is called the *calorimeter constant*. This constant is an important part of any calorimetric determination. In this experiment the transfer of any heat energy to or from the surroundings is minimized by the use of Styrofoam. Because of the outstanding insulating qualities of Styrofoam, the heat gained or lost by the cup is negligible compared to the uncertainty

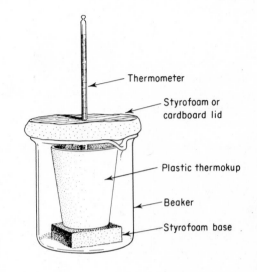

Fig. 10-1   A simple calorimeter.

of your temperature measurements so it will not be necessary to determine the calorimeter constant in this experiment. The experiment is done under conditions so that evaporation of water from the cup is negligible. This is accomplished by keeping the temperature of the water in the cup cool.

Calorimetric measurements such as those associated with this experiment are based on the assumption that the total heat lost in one part of the system equals the total amount of heat gained by another part of the system. The experiment involves adding a known mass of ice to a known mass of water whose initial and final temperature is measured. Calculation of the energy required to melt the ice is based upon the assumption that the total amount of energy lost by the water originally in the cup equals the total of the amount of energy gained by the ice as it melts at 0°C plus

Table I   Molar Heat of Fusion of Ice

Mass of dry, empty, Styrofoam cup	2.27
Mass of cup + water	76.28 g
Mass of water	74.01
Initial temperature of water in cup	39.7 °C
Final temperature of water in cup	9.7 °C
Temperature change of water ($t_i - t_f$)	30° C
Final mass of cup and contents (after melting)	105.61 g
Initial mass of cup and contents (same as item 2)	76.28 g
Mass of ice melted	29.33 g
Energy lost by water originally in cup	
Energy (cal) gained by ice as it melts at 0°C + energy gained by ice water as it warms from 0°C to t_f	
Energy (cal) gained by ice as it melts at 0°C	
Energy (cal) gained by 1.0 mole (18 g) of ice as it melts at 0°C	
Molar heat of fusion (kcal/mole)	
Accepted value	
Percent deviation from accepted value	

that which is gained as it warms from 0°C to the final temperature.

The total amount of heat gained by a mole of ice as it melts divided by the number of moles of ice melted equals the molar heat of fusion of ice.

OBJECTIVES

1. To determine the molar heat of fusion of ice.

2. To gain an understanding of the concepts of heat, temperature, specific heat capacity, and calorimetry.

3. To illustrate the Law of Heat Exchange.

MATERIALS

Styrofoam cups, large beaker to hold cups, pieces of Styrofoam or cardboard to use as insulating lids and bases, thermometer, balance, ice, paper towels, 250-ml beaker.

PROCEDURE

1. Determine the mass of an empty, dry, Styrofoam cup to the closest 0.1 g.

2. Heat some water in a 250-ml beaker until it is approximately 10–15° above room temperature. Pour some of this water into the Styrofoam cup until it is about half full. Quickly weigh the cup and its contents to the closest 0.1 g.

3. Measure and record the temperature of the water in the cup to the closest 0.1°C. *Immediately* add some small pieces of ice which have been dried with a paper towel. Stir the ice and water until the temperature has dropped to as many degrees below room temperature as the starting temperature was above room temperature. Remove any excess ice, or if only a very small amount of ice remains, stir until it has melted. Record the final temperature to the closest 0.1°C. Reweigh the cup and contents to the closest 0.1 g.

FURTHER EXPERIMENTATION

1. Design an experiment for determining the specific heat capacity of different metals. Use metallic shot or pellets for these determinations.

2. Design an experiment for determining the heat evolved when 1 g of water vapor at 100°C condenses and forms 1 g of liquid water (heat of condensation for water).

FOLLOW-UP DISCUSSION

The relationship by means of which you can determine the number of calories absorbed by the ice as it melts at 0°C is given by the generalized equation

Heat lost by one part of system
       = Heat gained by another part of system

or, more specifically

(Heat lost by original water as it cools from initial to final temperature)	=	(Heat gained by ice as it melts at 0°C) + (Heat gained by ice water as it warms to final temperature)

In formula form, the equation is

mass of original water $\times \Delta t \times$ specific heat capacity of water = mass of ice $\times$ heat of fusion (cal/g) + mass of ice water $\times \overline{\Delta t'} \times$ sp. heat capacity of water

where Δt is the change in temperature of the original water as it cools and $\Delta t'$ is the change in temperature of the melted ice as it warms to the final temperature. All but the underlined factor are known.

Although it was not necessary to determine a calorimeter constant in this experiment, it may be of value to know how such a determination is made. The procedure consists of mixing equal masses of water which, in the initial state of the system, are at different temperatures. On mixing, heat is transferred from the warm water to the cold water, calorimeter, thermometer, and surroundings. Application of the Law of Conservation of Energy shows that the energy lost by the warm component of the system exactly equals that gained by the cold component plus that gained by the surroundings. If we consider the calorimeter to be the surroundings, the relationship may be expressed as

$$\text{Heat lost by warm water} = \text{Heat gained by cold water} + \text{Heat gained by calorimeter}$$

Values for the first two terms in this equation may be calculated from experimental data. Solving for the last term gives the calories gained by the calorimeter when it undergoes a temperature change equal to the temperature change for the cold water. Dividing the total calories gained by the calorimeter by the temperature change gives the calories gained by the calorimeter per degree.

FOLLOW-UP QUESTIONS

1. List possible sources of error and the factors which limited the accuracy of your determination.

2. Does the temperature of a component of a system such as a cup of warm water depend on the quantity of matter in the sample? Explain.

3. Does the quantity of heat transferred between components depend on the quantity of matter in a component? Explain with an example.

4. What two different processes might be used to increase the temperature of a pan of cold water? Does the temperature change of a system depend on the method used to transfer energy to it?

5. What is the reason for warming the water in the cup above room temperature before adding the ice? Would a noticeable error be introduced if you had not done this? In what direction would it have shifted your final answer? Hint: Consider the direction of heat flow between the system and surroundings if at different temperatures.

10-2
Energy Changes During a Phase Change

GENERAL DISCUSSION

In a crystalline solid the atoms, ions, or molecules are arranged in a definite geometric pattern. When they absorb energy they vibrate more vigorously and, in some cases, slowly change position. Eventually the particles acquire enough energy to overcome in part the attractive forces which hold them together. When this point is reached, the particles start to slide over each other and the solid changes into a liquid. This phase change is called *melting* or *fusion*.

The melting point is an important physical property of a substance. Pure substances have definite melting points; hence, this property can be used to help identify a pure substance. In this experiment you observe temperature changes that occur when energy is transferred between a chemical system and its surroundings. You use these temperature changes to help you calculate the magnitude of the energy changes that occur when a pure liquid undergoes a solidification. You also plot time-temperature graphs for the cooling and solidification of a pure *vs* an impure solid. One of the curves is used to determine the melting point of the solid. Finally, you are asked to interpret the various regions of your graphs in terms of the types of energy changes involved.

OBJECTIVES

1. To calculate the heat of crystallization of a pure solid.
2. To plot and interpret a time-temperature graph.
3. To determine the melting point of acetamide.
4. To determine and interpret the energy changes that occur during a phase change.
5. To note the effect of a dissolved impurity on the melting point of acetamide.

MATERIALS

Acetamide, sodium iodide, watch with second hand (clock with sweep-second hand), test tube, Styrofoam cup, thermometers.

PROCEDURE

Part I · Heat of Crystallization

1. Weigh a clean and dry six-in. test tube to the closest 0.01 g. Add about 5 g of acetamide and reweigh tube and contents. Record data in Table I.

2. Weigh a dry Styrofoam cup to ±1 g. Add about 100 ml of water and quickly weigh cup and contents to ±1 g. Insert the cup in a beaker and place on the base of a ring stand. Suspend a −10°C to 50°C thermometer in the water as shown in Fig. 10-2.

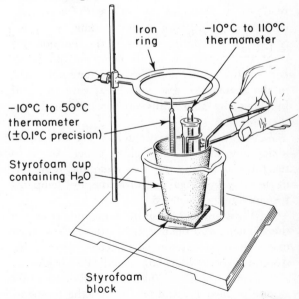

Fig. 10-2 *Apparatus for determining cooling behavior of acetamide.*

3. Melt the acetamide by heating the tube in a *low* burner flame. Monitor its temperature with a $-10°C$ to $110°C$ thermometer and do not allow the temperature of the acetamide to rise above 90°C.

4. Allow the acetamide to cool to about 83°C, measure and record the temperature of the water to $+0.1°C$, add *one* crystal of acetamide to the contents of the tube, and immediately place the tube in the water.

5. Slowly stir the water in the cup by moving the test tube about while simultaneously stirring the acetamide in the tube with the thermometer. Continue until solidification is complete and/or the water in the cup begins to cool down. Do not allow the thermometer to become embedded in the acetamide. Record the highest temperature attained by the water to the closest 0.1°C.

Part II · Cooling Behavior of Pure vs Impure Acetamide

6. Dry the tube and remelt the acetamide as in Step 3 above to about 90°C. Clamp the tube containing the thermometer onto a ring stand and record in Table II the time and temperature readings at 30-second intervals as the acetamide cools in air. Call your initial reading zero time. Stir the liquid continuously with the thermometer until solidification is nearly complete but *in no case* allow the thermometer to become imbedded in the acetamide. Also take great care to avoid breaking the thin walls of the tube with the thermometer.

7. Weigh out approximately 0.5 g of sodium iodide onto a piece of weighing paper. Add it to the tube containing the acetamide and remelt as in step 3 above. Again record time and temperature readings as in step 6.

8. When finished, wash the acetamide from the thermometer and the test tube with water. Return materials to stockroom as directed by your instructor. Process your data as indicated below.

9. Using the fact that, by definition, 1.00 calorie of heat is required to raise the temperature of 1.00 g of liquid water 1.00 C°, calculate the total number of calories absorbed by the water

Table I Heat of Crystallization of Acetamide

Mass of acetamide + test tube	
Mass of test tube	
Mass of acetamide	
Mass of cup + water	
Mass of cup	
Mass of water	
Initial temperature of water	
Final temperature of water	
Temperature change (Δt)	
Total energy absorbed by water (calories)	
Energy released by crystallization of 1.0 g of acetamide (calories)	
Energy released by crystallization of 1.0 mole of acetamide (calories)	

Table II Cooling Curve

Time (seconds)	Temperature (°C) Pure Acetamide	Temperature (°C) Acetamide + NaI
0		
30		
60		
90		
120		
150		
180		
210		
240		
270		
300		
330		
360		
390		
420		
450		
480		

in the cup in step 5. Show your method of this and all calculations clearly.

10. Calculate the amount of heat released if 1.00 g of acetamide had been used.

11. Calculate the amount of heat released if 1.00 mole of acetamide (CH_3CONH_2) had been used.

12. Plot on the same set of axes, a graph of the time-temperature data obtained from steps 6 and 7. Plot temperature along the ordinate (vertical axis) and time along the abscissa (horizontal axis). Choose appropriate scales, label the axes, label each curve, and place an appropriate title on the graph.

13. Label the melting point of acetamide on your graph.

FOLLOW-UP DISCUSSION

When energy is transferred from the surroundings to a chemical system, the system gains energy. The energy may go toward increasing the kinetic energy of the molecules or toward overcoming attractive forces which hold the molecules together. When the energy absorbed is used solely for overcoming or reducing forces of attraction, the potential energy of the system increases.

Recall that the absolute temperature of a system is directly proportional to the average kinetic energy of the molecules which compose the system. It follows that as the average kinetic energy of the molecules increases, the absolute temperature also increases. Thus, the temperature of a system as energy is transferred into or out of it may be used to determine whether the kinetic or potential energy of the system is changing.

Acetamide (CH_3CONH_2) is an organic compound. Like many other substances, it may cool to a temperature below its normal freezing point without solidifying. This phenomena is called *undercooling*. Ultimately, when the right number of acetamide molecules orient themselves in the proper geometric crystal pattern, a crystal nucleus is formed and crystallization proceeds. Because crystallization is an exothermic process, the temperature of the undercooled liquid rises to the normal freezing point and then levels off at that

temperature until solidification is complete. Undercooling is often prevented by the addition of "seed crystal" at a temperature slightly above the freezing point. This crystal furnishes the "nucleus" upon which aggregation of particles occurs.

You no doubt discovered that the freezing point of the acetamide containing the soluble impurity (NaI) in solution was lower than that of the pure solvent (acetamide). In addition, your cooling curve for the mixture does not contain a plateau. That is, in the case of the solution of NaI in acetamide, the temperature continued to drop during solidification. If the solution undercooled before crystallization, then the freezing point of the solution can be determined by extrapolating the portion of the curve following the undercooling until it intersects the first part of the curve with the large slope. Fig. 10-3 below of a cooling curve where temperature is plotted against time illustrates where the initial freezing point of the solution occurs.

In this experiment time did not permit us to use different masses of a soluble impurity as a

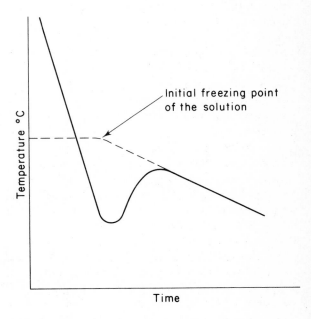

Fig. 10-3 Cooling curve for liquid acetamide.

solute. If additional experiments of this nature were carried out, you would find that there was a quantitative relationship between the number of moles of solute, the temperature change, and the mass of solvent. We shall introduce and make use of this relationship when we use a cryoscopic (freezing point) measurement to determine the molecular mass of a solute in an experiment later on in the course.

The method that you used to determine the heat of crystallization is rather crude and does not yield a very accurate value. Rest assured, however. More precise experimental methods of determining this and other heat values are available. Later in your study of chemistry you may be given the opportunity to carry out more nearly precise calorimetric determinations. The purpose here is to show that energy is evolved during the process of crystallization and that there is a relatively simple method for determining its value.

FOLLOW-UP QUESTIONS

1. Explain the origin of the energy that was released by the crystals for each segment of the cooling curve for pure acetamide.

2. Considering the shape of the cooling curve for pure acetamide, explain how a substance can remain at a constant temperature and *still* heat something else to a higher temperature.

3. Sketch what you believe a *heating* curve of a pure substance would look like if heated from 10°C below its *boiling point* to 10°C above.

4. Suggest a reason that the temperature for the solution of NaI in acetamide, continued to drop after crystallization had started. (Hint: The acetamide was solidifying and not the NaI during the early stages of crystallization.)

11-1
Additivity of Heats of Reaction

GENERAL DISCUSSION

All chemical changes are associated with energy changes. For convenience, heats of reaction may be classified according to the specific type of reaction being considered. Thus, we may refer to heat of combustion, heat of formation, heat of hydration, heat of neutralization, and others.

In this experiment you measure (1) the heat of solution of solid NaOH, (2) the heat of reaction of solid NaOH with HCl solution, and (3) the heat of neutralization of HCl solution with NaOH solution. You then use your data to show that ΔH for reaction (2) is the sum of the ΔH values obtained for reactions (1) and (3). Finally, you interpret your results in terms of ionic equations for the reactions, and show how the results constitute an application of Hess's Law, and of the Law of the Conservation of Energy.

OBJECTIVES

1. To investigate energy changes which occur during a chemical reaction.
2. To determine the heat of reaction for three separate reactions.
3. To illustrate the additivity of reactions and their heats.
4. To illustrate the Law of Conservation of Energy.

MATERIALS

Plastic Thermokup, 250-ml beaker, thermometer, sodium hydroxide pellets, triple-beam balance, 0.5-*M* hydrochloric acid, 0.5-*M* sodium hydroxide solution, graduated cylinder.

PROCEDURE

Part I · Heat of Solution of Solid NaOH

1. Use a plastic Thermokup and a beaker to construct a calorimeter similar to that illustrated in Figure 10-1.

2. Place 200 ml of water in the calorimeter. Allow the water to reach a constant temperature and read this temperature to the nearest 0.1°C, if possible. Record in Table I.

3. Obtain from the instructor or assistant two 3-in. stoppered test tubes, each of which contains approximately 2.0 g of sodium hydroxide pellets. Weigh one of the stoppered tubes, empty the contents into the calorimeter cup, replace the lid containing the thermometer, swirl the calorimeter, and stir carefully with the thermometer. Record the maximum temperature reached to the closest 0.1°C. Reweigh the empty stoppered tube.

4. Pour the contents of the calorimeter down the drain. Flush with much water. Clean the calorimeter thoroughly by rinsing several times with water.

5. Read the Follow-up Discussion and make the calculations necessary to complete Table I.

Table I   Heat of Solution of Solid NaOH

Mass of stoppered tube + NaOH pellets	
Mass of empty stoppered tube	
Mass of NaOH pellets	
Temperature of water (t_1)	
Volume of water	
Mass of water (assume density = 1 g/ml)	
Total mass of solution	
Temperature of solution after mixing (t_2)	
Heat absorbed by solution (assume specific heat capacity = 1.0 cal/g deg.)	
Moles of NaOH used	
Heat evolved per mole of NaOH	
Heat of solution for NaOH (ΔH_1)	

Part II · Heat of Neutralization of HCl and Solid NaOH

6. Place 110.0 ml of 0.50-M HCl in a beaker and add 90.0 ml of water. Allow to reach constant temperature, pour into the calorimeter and record the temperature to the nearest 0.1C° in Table II.

Table II   Heat of Reaction for HCl(aq) + NaOH(s)

1 Temperature of HCl solution (t_1)	
2 Volume of HCl solution	
3 Mass of HCl solution (assume D = 1.0 g/ml)	
4 Mass of tube + NaOH pellets + stopper	
5 Mass of empty tube + stopper	
6 Mass of NaOH pellets	
7 Total mass of solution after reaction (Item 3 + Item 4)	
8 Temperature of solution after reaction (t_2)	
9 Temperature change ($t_2 - t_1$)	
10 Heat absorbed by solution (assume specific heat capacity = 1.0 cal/g deg.)	
11 Moles of NaOH	
12 Heat evolved per mole of NaOH	
13 Heat of reaction (ΔH_2)	

7. Weigh the second stoppered tube containing approximately 2 g of NaOH pellets to the nearest 0.01 g and add the pellets to the HCl solution in the calorimeter.

8. Replace the lid, swirl the calorimeter, stir the contents with the thermometer and record the highest temperature reached to the nearest 0.1C°. Reweigh the stoppered tube.

9. Pour the contents of the calorimeter down the drain flush with excess water and thoroughly

Table III   Heat of Neutralization for HCl(aq) + NaOH(aq)

1 Temperature of acid and base solution (t_1)	
2 Volume of acid solution	
3 Mass of acid solution (assume D = 1.0 g/ml)	
4 Volume of base solution	
5 Mass of base solution (assume D = 1.0 g/ml)	
6 Total mass of NaCl solution after reaction (Item 3 + Item 5)	
7 Temperature of NaCl solution (t_2)	
8 Temperature change ($t_2 - t_1$)	
9 Heat absorbed by solution (assume specific heat capacity = 1.0 cal/g deg)	
10 Molar concentration of base solution	
11 Moles of NaOH (0.5M × 0.050 l)	
12 Heat evolved per mole of NaOH	
13 Heat of neutralization (ΔH_3)	

clean the calorimeter as in Part I. Be sure the calorimeter is dry before proceeding to Part III.

10. Make the calculations necessary to complete Table II.

Part III · Heat of Neutralization of HCl and NaOH Solutions

11. Place 50.0 ml of 0.5-M HCl in the calorimeter. Measure 50.0 ml of 0.5-M NaOH into a small beaker. Take the temperature of each solution. Be sure to clean and dry the thermometer after removing it from each solution. It is important that no base be transferred to the acid on the thermometer. The temperatures of the acid and base solutions should be the same and should not be higher than room temperature. Record the temperature of each solution in Table III.

12. Pour the NaOH solution into the HCl solution, replace the lid, swirl the calorimeter, stir the contents with the thermometer and record in Table III the maximum temperature reached.

13. Make the calculations necessary to complete Table III. Use units and conversion factors.

FURTHER EXPERIMENTATION

1. Design an experiment parallel to this one using an acid such as HNO_3 in place of HCl and a base such as KOH in place of NaOH.

FOLLOW-UP DISCUSSION

The equations for the reactions which you carried out in this experiment are shown below.

Part I $\quad NaOH(s) \rightarrow$
$$Na^+(aq) + OH^-(aq) + Q_1$$

Part II $\quad NaOH(s) + H^+(aq) + Cl^-(aq) \rightarrow$
$$H_2O + Na^+(aq) + Cl^-(aq) + Q_2$$

Part III
$$Na^+(aq) + OH^-(aq) + H^+(aq) + Cl^-(aq) \rightarrow$$
$$H_2O + Na^+(aq) + Cl^-(aq) + Q_3$$

These are thermochemical equations with a heat term (Q) on the right side which shows the heat effect on the surroundings. The positive sign indicates that in each of these reactions the surroundings gain energy; that is, heat is transferred from the chemical system to the surroundings. All three of these reactions are exothermic so that the heat of reaction (ΔH) values are all negative. This is because ΔH is *defined* as $H_{final} - H_{initial}$.

In each part of the experiment, the heat evolved by the reaction is assumed to be equal to the total heat absorbed by the solution.

The heat absorbed by the solution in each case may be calculated by using the equation

$$\begin{array}{c} \text{heat} \\ \text{absorbed} \end{array} = \begin{array}{c} \text{mass} \\ \text{of} \\ \text{solution} \end{array} \times \begin{array}{c} \text{sp. ht. cap.} \\ \text{of} \\ \text{solution} \end{array} \times (t_2 - t_1)$$

Q the heat evolved per mole of NaOH may be calculated by using the equation

$$Q = \frac{\text{total heat evolved by reaction}}{\text{moles of NaOH used}}$$

In each of the reactions, the heat of reaction, ΔH, has a value equal to $-Q$. There are a number of sources of error which might affect the experimental value obtained for ΔH. Other experimental errors such as reading the thermometer may be large. It was therefore reasonable to assume that the specific heat capacities of the solutions were all equal to 1.0 cal/g degree. Actually, the specific heat capacity of a 1-M NaCl solution is about 0.93 cal/g degree. Also the densities of the solutions are not all equal to 1.0 g/ml. In addition, we assumed that the temperature at the time of mixing was equal to the maximum temperature we observed. A more accurate value would have been obtained by plotting a time-temperature graph and extrapolating back to zero time. It should be noted that the heat of neutralization for reactions between dilute solutions of all strong acids and strong bases is very nearly the same (13.7 kcal). This evidence supports our belief that the net ionic equation for the reaction is

$$H_3O^+ + OH^- \rightarrow 2H_2O$$

Unreactive "spectator" ions such as Na^+, K^+, and Cl^- do not appreciably affect the reaction. In the case of the neutralization of a weak acid, the dissociation of the weak acid must also be considered. This endothermic process requires energy. Therefore, we would not expect the overall thermal energy release to be as great.

FOLLOW-UP QUESTIONS

1. Show that the equations for the reactions in Part I and Part III can be added algebraically to give the equation for the reaction in Part II.

2. Combine the ΔH values for the reactions in the same way you did the equations. Compute the percentage deviation between the ΔH value for reaction 2 and the sum of the ΔH values for reactions 1 and 3.

3. Draw enthalpy diagrams showing the two

145

paths which lead to the same final state of the system in Part II. Include the heat terms associated with each path.

4. Assuming there were no experimental errors, explain how the results illustrate the Law of Conservation of Energy.

5. Assume you make an error of 0.1C° in reading a thermometer. If the total temperature change of the system in one part of this experiment is 2C°, what is the percentage error in reading the thermometer?

6. List all errors which might have contributed to any inconclusive results.

7. Show how the ionic equations for the combination of protons with hydroxide ions and the dissociation of $HC_2H_3O_2$ can be added algebraically to give the net equation for the neutralization of aqueous NaOH with aqueous $HC_2H_3O_2$.

11-2

Thermochemistry: Enthalpy of Formation of $NH_4Cl(s)$

All chemical changes are associated with energy changes. For convenience, enthalpies (heats) of reaction may be classified according to the specific type of reaction being considered. Thus, we may refer to the enthalpy (heat) of combustion, the enthalpy of formation, the enthalpy of hydration, the enthalpy of neutralization, and others.

In this experiment, you determine the enthalpy (heat) of formation for one mole of solid ammonium chloride ($NH_4Cl(s)$). The standard enthalpy of formation of a substance is the difference between the enthalpy of one mole of a substance and that of the elements of which it is made. All substances are considered in their most stable form at 1.00 atm and 25°C. This quantity is symbolized by ΔH_f^0. The equation which represents the hypothetical formation of NH_4Cl directly from its elements in their most stable forms is

$$\tfrac{1}{2}N_2(g) + 2H_2(g) + \tfrac{1}{2}Cl_2(g) \rightarrow NH_4Cl(s)$$
$$\text{Eq. 1}$$

Your objective will be to determine the value of ΔH_f^0 for this reaction.

It is difficult to investigate the above reaction directly. Measured quantities of three gases are involved. Equipment available in elementary laboratories is not suitable because the gases cannot be made to combine directly at ordinary temperatures and pressures. We can, however, accomplish our objective by applying the Law of Conservation of Energy and Hess's Law of Additivity of Reaction Enthalpies to reactions which do lend themselves to laboratory investigation or to reactions for which enthalpy data are available. In short, if we can determine enthalpy changes for reactions whose equations can be combined algebraically and yield the equation for the desired reaction, we can then use these enthalpy changes to calculate the enthalpy change for the desired reaction.

To determine ΔH for Reaction (1), determine experimentally the enthalpy changes for reactions whose equations are

$$NH_3(aq) + H^+(aq) \rightarrow NH_4^+ + (1.5\text{-}M\ aq) \quad \Delta H_2$$
$$\text{Eq. 2}$$

$$NH_4Cl(s) \rightarrow NH_4^+(aq) + Cl^-(1.5\text{-}M\ aq) \quad \Delta H_3$$
$$\text{Eq. 3}$$

ΔH_2 is called the enthalpy of reaction of aqueous ammonia and $H^+(aq)$, contained in a hydrochloric-acid solution, while ΔH_3 is referred to as the enthalpy of solution of solid ammonium chloride. Standard enthalpies of solution found in reference tables are usually given for "infinite dilution." That is, diluted until the addition of more water produces no further energy effect. For the purposes of this experiment, we shall work at specific concentrations which are less than infinite dilution. Thus, ΔH_5 and ΔH_7 are not truly *standard* enthalpy changes. In addition to the experimentally determined quantities, you need to use the literature values for enthalpy changes for reactions whose equations are

$$\tfrac{1}{2}N_2(g) + 3/2\ H_2(g) \rightarrow NH_3(g)$$
$$\Delta H_4^0 = -11.0\ \text{kcal} \quad \text{Eq. 4}$$

$$NH_3(g) \rightarrow NH_3(1.5\text{-}M\ aq)$$
$$\Delta H_5 = -8.3\ \text{kcal} \quad \text{Eq. 5}$$

$$\tfrac{1}{2}H_2(g) + \tfrac{1}{2}Cl_2(g) \rightarrow HCl(g)$$
$$\Delta H_6 = -22.1\ \text{kcal} \quad \text{Eq. 6}$$

$$HCl(g) \rightarrow H^+(1.5\text{-}M\ aq) + Cl^-(1.5\text{-}M\ aq)$$
$$\Delta H_7 = -17.5\ \text{kcal} \quad \text{Eq. 7}$$

Proper combination of Equations 2, 3, 4, 5, 6, and 7 yield Equation (1) while corresponding combinations of ΔH_2, ΔH_3, ΔH_4, ΔH_5, ΔH_6, and ΔH_7 yield ΔH_f for $NH_4Cl(s)$.

OBJECTIVES

1. To investigate energy changes which occur during a chemical reaction.

2. To determine the enthalpy (heat) of formation of $NH_4Cl(s)$.

3. To determine experimentally the enthalpy of reaction for two separate reactions.

4. To illustrate the additivity of reactions and their accompanying enthalpy changes.

5. To illustrate the Law of Conservation of Energy.

MATERIALS

Plastic Thermokup, 250-ml beaker, thermometer, solid ammonium chloride, 1.5-M aqueous ammonia solution, 1.5-M aqueous hydrochloric acid solution, balance, graduated cylinder.

PROCEDURE

1. Obtain a plastic Thermokup and determine its mass to the closest 0.5 g. Construct a calorimeter similar to that illustrated in Fig. 10-1.

Table I   Enthalpy of Reaction of Aqueous NH₃ with Aqueous HCl

Temperature of 1.5-M HCl solution	
Temperature of 1.5-M NH$_3$ solution	
Average value of the above temperatures	
Mass of cup + solution after reaction	
Mass of cup	
Mass of solution after reaction	
Mass of cup + 1.5-M HCl solution	
Mass of cup	
Mass of HCl solution	
Mass of NH$_3$ solution	
Maximum temperature of solution after mixing (t_f)	
Temperature change, Δt	
Heat absorbed by solution (assume specific heat capacity = 0.96 $\left(\dfrac{cal}{g\ solution\ (C°)} \right)$	
Density of HCl solution (see instructor or handbook)	
Density of NH$_3$ solution (see instructor or handbook)	
Volume of HCl solution used	
Volume of NH$_3$ solution used	
Moles of HCl used and of NH$_4$Cl produced in reaction	
Heat evolved per mole of HCl	
ΔH_2 (enthalpy of reaction of aqueous NH$_3$ and HCl)	

148

2. From a graduated cylinder, pour 100 ml of 1.5-M HCl into the calorimeter and determine the mass of the cup plus solution. Rinse out the graduated cylinder and measure out 100 ml of 1.5-M aqueous ammonia. Take the temperature of each solution. Be sure to clean and dry the thermometer after removing it from each solution. It is important that no base be transferred to the acid via the thermometer. The temperatures of the acid and base solutions should be as close to one another as possible and should not be higher than room temperature. Record the temperature of each solution in Table I. Read thermometer to the nearest 0.1°C or to the maximum precision allowed by the thermometer which is provided.

3. Pour the ammonia solution into the HCl solution, replace the lid, stir the contents with the thermometer and record in Table I the maximum temperature reached.

4. Determine the mass of the cup plus contents.

5. Make the calculations necessary to complete Table I. That is, calculate the number of calories *absorbed by the solution* and from this, calculate the enthalpy change based upon 1.00 mole of NH_4^+(aq) ions produced. Use units and conversion factors.

6. Place 194 ml of water in the calorimeter. Allow the water to reach a constant temperature and read this temperature as precisely as possible. Record this value in Table II.

7. Weigh out 8.02 g (0.15 mole) of solid NH_4Cl. Add the NH_4Cl to the water in the calorimeter, replace the lid containing the thermometer, swirl the calorimeter and stir with the thermometer. The temperature will probably reach a minimum value momentarily and then rise slightly and level off to a temporarily constant value. Record this plateau value to the same precision as before.

8. Determine the mass of the cup and solution.

9. Make the calculations necessary to complete Table II. That is, calculate the number of calories absorbed by the solution in this experiment and from this value, calculate the enthalpy change based upon the formation of 1.00 mole of NH_4^+ (aq). Note that if the solution temperature *drops*

during the change, the value for the energy absorbed by the solution is a negative number, and indicates a positive ΔH or an endothermic reaction.

10. Use the values of ΔH obtained in Tables I and II, and those for Equations 4, 5, 6, and 7 to calculate the enthalpy of formation of solid ammonium chloride.

Enthalpy of formation of NH_4Cl:
$\Delta H_f =$ _____ kcal/mole.
Standard enthalpy of formation of $NH_4Cl(s)$
   from text: $\Delta H_f^0 =$ _____ kcal/mole.
Percentage deviation between accepted and experimental value: _____

Table II   Enthalpy of Solution of Solid NH₄Cl

Temperature of water	
Mass of cup + solution	
Mass of solution	
Mass of $NH_4Cl(s)$	
Mass of water	
Temperature after mixing (plateau value)	
Temperature change	
Heat absorbed by solution (specific heat capacity of solution = 0.96 cal/g C°)	
Moles of NH_4Cl used	
Heat absorbed or liberated per mole NH_4Cl	
ΔH_3 (enthalpy of solution for $NH_4Cl(s)$)	

FOLLOW-UP DISCUSSION

When a chemical reaction evolves energy, the heat evolved is equal to the heat absorbed by the calorimeter plus that absorbed by the solution.

$$\frac{\text{Total heat}}{\text{absorbed}} = \frac{\text{Heat absorbed}}{\text{by calorimeter}} + \frac{\text{Heat absorbed}}{\text{by solution}}$$

In this experiment we shall assume that the heat absorbed by the calorimeter is negligible. The heat absorbed by the solution may be calculated by using the equation

149

Heat absorbed

$$= \frac{\text{Mass of}}{\text{solution}} \times \frac{\text{Specific heat capacity}}{\text{of solution}} \times (t_2 - t_1)$$

Q, the heat evolved per mole of HCl, may be calculated by using the equation

$$Q = \frac{\text{total heat evolved by reaction}}{\text{moles of HCl used (MV)}}$$

If the procedures are carried out with care, then the two solutions you prepared have identical compositions. In the first case, $NH_4^+(aq)$ ions are formed by a chemical reaction between $NH_3(aq)$ and $H^+(aq)$. Chloride ions (Cl^-) were present in the HCl solution and remain as unreactive or "spectator" ions. In the second case, $NH_4^+(aq)$ and $Cl^-(aq)$ are released simply by the dissociation of the solid NH_4Cl in the water.

There are several sources of error which affect your results. Perhaps the most serious one is your inability to read the thermometer precisely. In addition, we assumed that the temperature at the time of mixing was equal to the maximum temperature observed. A more accurate value would have been obtained by plotting a time-temperature graph and extrapolating back to zero time.

FOLLOW-UP QUESTIONS

1. Show how Equations 2 through 7 can be combined to give the equation for reaction (1).

2. Assume you make an error of 0.2C° in reading a thermometer. If the total temperature change of the system in one part of this experiment is 2C°, what is the percentage error in reading the thermometer?

3. Write a thermochemical equation that represents the formation of NH_4Cl from its elements showing the heat term on the right side of the equation.

12-1
Factors Affecting Rates of Chemical Reactions

GENERAL DISCUSSION

In Part I of this experiment you investigate the general relationship between the concentration of a reactant and the time required for a reaction to occur. In Part II you examine the general relationship between the temperature and the time required to complete a given reaction. In these reactions you hold all factors constant except the one being studied.

The reaction which you will study in Parts I and II is known as the iodine "clock" reaction. This type of reaction involves several steps. The slowest step is called the rate-determining step. In this reaction an excess of iodate ions (IO_3^-) react with an acidified sodium sulfite solution. The first step in the reaction is the slow, rate-determining step.

$$3HSO_3^-(aq) + IO_3^-(aq) + 3H_2O \rightarrow$$
$$3SO_4^{2-}(aq) + I^-(aq) + 3H_3O^+ \quad Eq.\ 1$$

The I^- ions formed react with excess IO_3^- ions and form free iodine.

$$IO_3^-(aq) + 5I^-(aq) + 6H_3O^+ \rightarrow$$
$$3I_2(aq) + 9H_2O \quad Eq.\ 2$$

The I_2 liberated in reaction 2, however, reacts rapidly with HSO_3^-

$$I_2(aq) + HSO_3^-(aq) + 4H_2O \rightarrow$$
$$2I^-(aq) + SO_4^{2-}(aq) + 3H_3O^+$$

Thus the I_2 concentration never builds up until all of the HSO_3^- has been consumed. Then the blue color appears. The blue coloration is from the interaction of the molecular iodine with a starch suspension.

In Part I you hold the concentration of the HSO_3^- ions and the temperature constant, and vary the concentration of the IO_3^- ions. You measure the elapsed time from the instant of mixing to the sudden appearance of the blue color.

In Part II you hold the concentrations of all solutions constant and vary the temperature. You use your data to plot graphs and draw some general conclusions concerning the effects of concentration and temperature on the rate of a reaction.

In Part III of the experiment you react permanganate ions (MnO_4^-) with (a) iron(II) sulfate, an ionic crystal containing simple cations (Fe^{2+}), and (b) oxalic acid,

$$\begin{array}{c} O \qquad\quad O \\ \parallel \qquad\quad \parallel \\ C-C \\ / \qquad\quad \backslash \\ HO \qquad\quad OH \end{array}$$,

an aggregate composed of covalent molecules. You will use your limited observations to propose a relationship between the nature of the reactants and the rate of a reaction.

OBJECTIVES

1. To determine the effect of concentration on the rate of a reaction.

2. To determine the effect of temperature on the rate of a reaction.

3. To observe the difference in rates of reactions which involve, respectively, two ionic substances and a combination of an ionic and a molecular substance.

4. To observe the effect of a catalyst on the rate of a reaction.

MATERIALS

250-ml erlenmeyer flask, 100-ml graduated cylinders, solution B containing sulfurous acid (H_2SO_3) and starch, solution A containing 0.02-M potassium iodate (KIO_3), stop watch or watch with sweep second hand, 0.2-M iron(II) sulfate ($FeSO_4$) solution, 0.2-M oxalic acid ($H_2C_2O_4$) solution, 0.02-M potassium permanganate ($KMnO_4$) solution, 250-ml beakers, solid

$MnSO_4$ crystals, test tubes, evaporating dish, thermometer, burner.

PROCEDURE

Part I · Effect of Concentration on Rate

1. Pour 200 ml of 0.0187-M KIO_3 solution into a clean dry beaker (solution B) and 150 ml of sulfurous acid-starch solution into another clean dry beaker (solution A). These are your stock solutions.

2. Measure 60 ml of the KIO_3 solution (solution B) in a dry graduated cylinder and pour the solution into a 250-ml beaker. Add 10 ml of water and mix. Pour 30 ml of the HSO_3^--starch solution (solution A) into a second beaker. Place the beaker containing solution A on a piece of white paper. Add solution B rapidly to the beaker containing A and swirl the contents for a few seconds. Use a stop watch or a watch with a sweep second hand to record the number of seconds which elapse from the instant of mixing to the sudden appearance of the blue color. Record in Table I.

3. Rinse the reaction beaker and repeat the procedure using the other combinations of volumes shown in Table I. Be sure to use the same graduated cylinders for measuring each of the solutions that were used in the original procedure.

Part II · Effect of Temperature on Rate

4. Obtain 30 ml of solution A and 30 ml of solution B to use for these procedures. Measure 10 ml of solution A into each of three dry test tubes.

5. Now measure 10 ml of solution B into each of three separate clean dry test tubes.

6. Clean and dry a 250-ml beaker and simultaneously add 10 ml each of solutions A and B. Stir and record in Table II the time required for the appearance of the blue color.

7. Place a test tube of solution A and a test tube of solution B in a water bath (250-ml beaker 2/3 full of water) and warm to the temperature designated by your instructor. (This should be approximately 45°C to 50°C.) Let stand for 5 to 10 minutes. Record the temperature of the water. Remove the test tubes and simultaneously pour the contents into the beaker. Record the time required for the blue color to appear.

8. Repeat the procedure but cool the water to between 0°C and 2°C.

Table II   Effect of Temperature on Rate (10 ml A + 10 ml B)

Trial Number	Temperature (°C)	Time (sec)
1		
2		
3		

Part III · Nature of Reactants

9. Pour 10 ml of 0.2-M iron(II) sulfate solution into a small beaker. Pour 2 ml of 6-M sulfuric acid into the solution and add dropwise, with a

Table I   Effect of Concentration on Rate

Solution B KIO_3 (ml)	Solution A (HSO_3^--Starch) (ml)	Volume of Water Added to Solution B	Molar Concentration of IO_3^- in Solution after Mixing	Time (sec)	Reciprocal Time (1/t) (sec^{-1})
60	30	10			
50	30	20			
40	30	30			
30	30	40			
20	30	50			

medicine dropper, a 0.02-*M* solution of $KMnO_4$ and swirl the contents of the beaker. Indicate in Table III that the relative rate of reaction is *rapid* if the permanganate color disappears immediately on the addition of the permanganate solution; write *slow* if the color lingers.

10. Pour 10 ml of 0.2-*M* oxalic acid into a small beaker. Pour 2 ml of 6-*M* sulfuric acid into the solution and add dropwise, with a medicine dropper, a 0.02-*M* solution of $KMnO_4$. Record whether the reaction is rapid or slow compared to that between iron(II) sulfate and the permanganate.

11. Pour 10 ml of 0.2-*M* oxalic acid into a small beaker. Add 2 ml of 6-*M* sulfuric acid and a couple of crystals of $MnSO_4$ as catalyst. Add dropwise, with a medicine dropper, a 0.02-*M* solution of $KMnO_4$. Record whether the rate of the reaction has changed from that in Procedure 10.

12. Repeat procedure 10 only heat the oxalic acid solution to 80°C before adding $KMnO_4$.

Table III   Reactions Involving Different Types of Particles

Reaction	Relative Rate of Reaction
Iron (II) sulfate (ionic) with potassium permanganate	
Oxalic acid (molecular) with potassium permanganate	
Oxalic acid with potassium permanganate (Mn^{2+} as catalyst)	
Oxalic acid (80°C) with potassium permanganate	

FURTHER EXPERIMENTATION

1. Study the effect of a catalyst on the rate of a reaction by measuring the volume of oxygen produced in a given time by the catalytic decomposition of hydrogen peroxide. Try MnO_2, Cr_2O_3, ZnO, and other metal oxides. Also, test the effect of varying the mass of catalyst used.

FOLLOW-UP DISCUSSION

It should be pointed out that this experiment is not an example of one which is usually described by chemists as a "rate study." In the usual case, the chemist monitors the concentration of one of the reactants or products as time elapses. He must perform a series of such experiments in which the concentration of all but one of the reactants is held constant in each case. He then attempts to determine the "order" of the reaction with respect to each reactant by deducing the value of each exponent in the general rate equation

$$r = k[A]^a[B]^b$$

where [A] and [B] represent molar concentrations of reactants *A* and *B*. The method for the determination of the values of the exponents *a* and *b* is beyond the scope of the course, but can be found in most college physical-chemistry texts.

After graphing the data from Part I of this experiment you should be able to see the dependence of the term $\dfrac{1}{time}$ *vs* iodate ion concentration. As is pointed out in the General Discussion, the term 1/time is proportional to the rate of completion of reaction 1, the slow step in the overall reaction. Thus, the graph should show you a mathematical relationship between the rate of completion of reaction 1 and IO_3^- concentration. Note that in all of the runs, the IO_3^- was present in excess: that is, more than enough to react with all of the HSO_3^- present. The equation for the graph obtained should become apparent after you draw it. Hint: Recall the equations from a similar graph in which you plotted *P* *vs* $1/V$ during your study of the gas laws.

Because of the difficulty of maintaining precise temperature control in Part II, it is unlikely that you would be able to deduce any quantitative relationship between temperature (°C) and the rate of the completion of reaction 1. You should, however, have no difficulty in noting a qualitative relationship. It has been found that if the temperature is allowed to attain too high a value, certain undesired side reactions occur which interfere with the overall experiment. In addition, if the temperature gets too low, the time required becomes too long to be practical.

An attempt was made in Part III to allow you to notice a significant difference in rate between the reaction of an acidified Fe^{2+} solution with MnO_4^- compared with that of an acidified $H_2C_2O_4$ solution with MnO_4^-. The balanced net ionic equations for the two reactions are

$$5Fe^{2+}(aq)) + MnO_4^-(aq) + 8H_3O^+ \rightarrow$$
$$5Fe^{3+}(aq) + Mn^{2+}(aq) + 12H_2O \quad \text{Eq. 4}$$
$$5H_2C_2O_4(aq) + 2MnO_4^-(aq) + 6H_3O^+ \rightarrow$$
$$10CO_2(g) + 2Mn^{2+}(aq) + 14H_2O \quad \text{Eq. 5}$$

In both reactions the covalent bonds contained in each MnO_4^- ion must be broken, as well as the bonds between the water molecule and the proton in each hydronium ion. In reaction 5, however, carbon-carbon and oxygen-hydrogen covalent bonds must be broken in the oxalic acid molecules,

in order to account for the CO_2 gas which is evolved.

The above discussion indicates that both reactions are rather complex; however, reaction 4 is somewhat simpler than reaction 5. The extremely rapid overall rate of 4 would seem to indicate that in spite of its complexity, *all* of the mechanistic steps occur at a very rapid rate such that the bond breaking and any accompanying electron transfer (changes in oxidation state) present no high-energy barriers which would slow down the reaction at room temperature.

The fact that Mn^{2+} acts as a catalyst for reaction 5 has been partially explained by the fact that Mn^{2+} is found to react with MnO_4^- fairly rapidly producing low concentrations of Mn^{3+} and MnO^{2+}. These latter species must provide

some lower energy alternate pathways for the reaction to take place.

In the reaction between MnO_4^- and $H_2C_2O_4$, the situation has been found to be further complicated by the formation of oxalate complexes, which undergo several slow intermediate reactions such as

$$MnO_3^- + H_2C_2O_4 \rightarrow MnO_2C_2O_4^- + H_2O$$
$$MnO_2C_2O_4^- \rightarrow MnO_2^- + 2CO_2$$
$$Mn^{3+} + C_2O_4^{2-} \rightarrow MnC_2O_4^+$$
$$MnC_2O_4^+ \rightarrow Mn^{2+} + CO_2 + CO_2^-$$
$$Mn^{3+} + CO_2^- \rightarrow Mn^{2+} + CO_2$$

Because of the slowness of several of these steps, raising the temperature is necessary to get the reaction to go at a reasonable rate. This was illustrated when you carried out procedure 12. Because of the fact that Mn^{2+} is a product of reaction 5, its presence, after it is once formed, allows it to catalyze the reaction. Thus, one notices an increase in rate after a very slow start. Such a situation is not unique and is given the name *autocatalysis*.

The above discussion should serve to show you just how complicated most chemical reactions are. It is obvious that the mechanism of most reactions cannot be determined by merely looking at the balanced equation. It takes great patience and an exhaustive amount of time on the part of a chemist in order to unravel the puzzle of reaction mechanisms. Many chemists have spent years, and perhaps a lifetime, in the study of only one reaction, a good example being the investigation of the mechanism of photosynthesis.

FOLLOW-UP QUESTIONS

1. Using the dilutions called for in Part I, calculate the IO_3^- concentration (molarity) for each run after mixing but before the reaction takes place. The stock KIO_3 solution is 0.0187-M.

2. Find the fractional part of the reaction that took place per second (speed of reaction) by calculation of the value of reciprocal time $(1/sec)$

to the nearest thousandth for each set of conditions. This fraction is proportional to the rate of the reaction.

3. Construct a graph by plotting molar concentrations of IO_3^- on the abscissa and the reciprocal times (rates) on the ordinate.

4. What generalization can be derived from the graph? Express mathematically in terms of an equation.

5. Make a general statement regarding the effect of temperature on the time required for a reaction to occur. How does the temperature affect the rate of the reactions which you observed in Parts II and III?

6. Assuming the results you recorded in Table III are typical, would you conclude that ionic substances in solution are apt to react more or less rapidly than molecular substances? Explain in terms of the relative number and strengths of bonds that are broken during a reaction.

7. How did the presence of the Mn^{2+} ions appear to change the rate of the reaction?

Chemical Equilibrium and Application of Le Châtelier's Principle

GENERAL DISCUSSION

A system at equilibrium may be disturbed by subjecting the system to a stress, such as changing the concentration of one of the participants or the temperature. Le Châtelier's principle indicates that the system readjusts so as to minimize the stress and again restore equilibrium conditions.

In this experiment you investigate a number of equilibrium systems. You will subject these systems to stresses and explain your observations in terms of Le Châtelier's principle. In Part I you investigate a reaction whose equation may be written

$$Fe^{3+} + SCN^- \rightleftharpoons Fe(SCN)^{2+}$$

You vary the concentrations of the participants in this reaction and observe, by means of color changes, the effect on the equilibrium. Similarly, you observe and explain the changes which occur when you vary the $[H^+]$ in the reaction system whose equation is

$$Cr_2O_7^{2-} + H_2O \rightleftharpoons 2CrO_4^{2-} + 2H^+$$

Table I Colors of Ions

Ion	Color
K^+	
Cl^-	
SCN^-	
Fe^{3+}	
$Fe(SCN)^{2+}$	
Hg^{2+}	
$Hg(SCN)_4^{2-}$	Colorless
$FeCl_4^-$	Colorless

In Part II you observe the effect of changing the temperature of a system represented by the equation

$$CoCl_4^{2-} + 6H_2O \rightleftharpoons Co(H_2O)_6^{2+} + 4Cl^-$$

Your observations enable you to add a heat term to the equation.

OBJECTIVES

1. To observe and explain the effect of changing concentration on a system at equilibrium.

2. To observe and explain the effect of changing temperature on a system at equilibrium.

MATERIALS

0.1-M solutions of KCl, KSCN, BaCl$_2$, FeCl$_3$, K$_2$Cr$_2$O$_7$, K$_2$CrO$_4$, Na$_2$Cr$_2$O$_7$, Na$_2$CrO$_4$, Hg(NO$_3$)$_2$, test tubes and rack, graduated cylinder, crystals of KCl and CoCl$_2 \cdot$ 6H$_2$O; 0.1-M NaOH, 0.1-M HNO$_3$; ethanol, asbestos, beaker.

PROCEDURE

Part I · Concentration Changes and Equilibrium

1. Examine solutions of KCl, KSCN, FeCl$_3$, and Hg(NO$_3$)$_2$. Write the colors of each ion listed in Table I. You will have to perform Procedure 2 before writing the color of the Fe(SCN)$^{2+}$ ion.

2. Place a few drops of 0.1-M FeCl$_3$ in a test tube and add the same amount of 0.1-M KSCN. Swirl the mixture and add water until a transparent, orange-red solution is obtained. Provide 4 more test tubes and divide the solution into 5 approximately equal portions.

3. Use the first tube as a color standard. To tube number 2, add 1 ml of FeCl$_3$ solution; to

Table II Effect of Concentration Changes on the Equilibrium System
$Fe^{3+} + SCN^- \rightleftharpoons Fe(SCN)^{2+}$

Species Added to Equilibrium Mixture	Color Change	Direction of Equilibrium Shift	Reason for Shift
Fe^{3+} from $FeCl_3$			
Cl^- from KCl			
SCN^- from KSCN			
Hg^{2+} from $Hg(NO_3)_2$			

tube number 3, add 1 to 2 g of KCl; to tube number 4, add 1 ml of KSCN solution; and to tube number 5, add 1 ml of $Hg(NO_3)_2$ solution. Shake each tube and compare the colors with the standard. Record your observations in Table II. Use the species listed in Table I to help you explain why the equilibrium shifted. Remember that decreasing the concentration of a participant causes the equilibrium to shift. The concentration of an ion may be decreased by removing it in the form of molecular species, a polyatomic (complex) ion, or a precipitate.

4. Examine solutions of $K_2Cr_2O_7$, $Na_2Cr_2O_7$, Na_2CrO_4, and K_2CrO_4. Describe the color of the $Cr_2O_7^{2-}$ ion and the CrO_4^{2-} ion in Table III.

5. Place 5 ml of 0.1-M $K_2Cr_2O_7$ in a test tube and add 0.1-M NaOH until a color change is observed. Record your observations in Table IV.

6. Put five ml of 0.5-M K_2CrO_4 in a test tube

Table III Colors of Ions

Ion	Color
$Cr_2O_7^{2-}$	
CrO_4^{2-}	

and add HNO_3 until a color change is observed. Record observations in Table IV.

7. Add two ml of $BaCl_2$ solution to five ml of K_2CrO_4 solution. Decant solution and note color of precipitate.

8. Add two ml of $BaCl_2$ solution to five ml of $K_2Cr_2O_7$ solution. Decant and note color of precipitate. Record your observations in Table IV. Use the results of Procedures 7 and 9 to help in the identification of the precipitate and in the identification of the components in aqueous $K_2Cr_2O_7$.

Table IV Effect of Changing $[H_3O^+]$ on the Equilibrium System
$$Cr_2O_7^{2-} + 2H_2O \rightleftharpoons 2CrO_4^{2-} + 2H_3O^+$$

Original Solution	Species Added to Original Solution	Observation	Color of Precipitate (if any)	Explanation for Change
$Cr_2O_7^{2-}$	OH^- from NaOH			
CrO_4^{2-}	H^+ from HNO_3			
CrO_4^{2-}	Ba^{2+} from $BaCl_2$			
$Cr_2O_7^{2-}$	Ba^{2+} from $BaCl_2$			
Acidified $Cr_2O_7^{2-}$	Ba^{2+} from $BaCl_2$			

9. Repeat Procedure 8 but add the $BaCl_2$ solution to four ml of $K_2Cr_2O_7$ solution to which has been added one ml of 0.1-M HNO_3.

Table V Colors of Ions

Ion	Color
$CoCl_4{}^{2-}$	Blue
$Co(H_2O)_6{}^{2+}$	Red

Part II · Temperature and Equilibrium

10. Place about 0.3 g (a few crystals) of crushed $CoCl_2 \cdot 6H_2O$ in a test tube and add five ml of ethyl alcohol. Shake vigorously or stir until most of the solid has dissolved. If the solution is not pink in color, add water dropwise until the solution just turns red.

11. Heat the solution gently with a low flame until it changes color. **Caution:** *if the alcohol should ignite, smother it by placing a piece of asbestos over the top of the test tube.* Record observations in Table VI.

12. Immerse the test tube in a beaker of cold water until the color changes again.

Table VI Effect of Temperature on the Equilibrium System

$$CoCl_4{}^{2-} + 6H_2O \rightleftharpoons Co(H_2O)_6{}^{2+} + 4Cl^-$$

Procedure	Color Change	Equilibrium Shifts (L or R)
Warm solution		
Cool solution		

FOLLOW-UP DISCUSSION

Most of the procedures which you carried out in this experiment illustrated Le Châtelier's principle. You were probably able to deduce from your observations whether a given equilibrium shifted to the right or left when you imposed a stress upon it. Furthermore, you were probably able to tell whether the stress resulted from increasing or decreasing the concentration of a particular species involved in the equilibrium. The concentration of a particular ion may be decreased by transforming it into (1) a molecular species, (2) complex ion, or (3) a precipitate. An equilibrium exists between each of these three entities and its components. The equilibrium expressions for the reactions which were responsible for the decrease in ion concentration in the systems you observed are listed below. These may help you to understand and explain your observations.

$$Fe^{3+} + SCN^- \rightleftharpoons Fe(SCN)^{2+}$$

$$Hg^{2+} + 4SCN^- \rightleftharpoons Hg(SCN)_4{}^{2-}$$

$$Fe^{3+} + 4Cl^- \rightleftharpoons FeCl_4{}^-$$

$$Cr_2O_7{}^{2-} + H_2O \rightleftharpoons 2CrO_4{}^{2-} + H^+$$

$$BaCrO_4(s) \rightleftharpoons Ba^{2+} + CrO_4{}^{2-}$$

$$CoCl_4{}^{2-} + 6H_2O \rightleftharpoons Co(H_2O)_6{}^{2+} + 4Cl^-$$

Chances are that you will not have encountered before, most of the metal-centered polyatomic or complex ions whose formulas are shown above. These ions are composed of a metallic ion bonded by a coordinate bond to two or more groups called ligands. Groups that act as ligands must contain an unshared pair of valence electrons. A special nomenclature has been developed for metal-centered complex ions. This is discussed in Section 19-10 of *Foundations of Chemistry*, 2 ed. As an introduction to the nomenclature, the names of the above ions are listed.

$Fe(SCN)^{2+}$: thiocyanatoiron(III)

$Hg(SCN)_4{}^{2-}$: tetrathiocyanatomercurate(II)

$FeCl_4{}^-$: tetrachloroferrate(III)

$CoCl_4{}^{2-}$: tetrachorocobaltate(II)

$Co(H_2O)_6{}^{2+}$: hexaaquocobalt(II)

Note that negative ions end in the suffix = ate. The Roman numbers identify the oxidation state of the metallic ion. When ammonia molecules play the role of a ligand, the complex is called an ammine. Thus the name of $Ag(NH_3)_2{}^+$ is diamminesilver(I) ion. From now on you will encounter various metal-centered complex ions in both laboratory and class. These will be named and discussed whenever the opportunity arises. To help you recognize complex ions, a list of ligands is provided.

Ligand	Name
H_2O	aquo
NH_3	ammine
Cl^-	chloro
Br^-	bromo
I^-	iodo
CN^-	cyano
SCN^-	thiocyanato
OH^-	hydroxo
SO_4^{2-}	sulfato
$S_2O_3^{2-}$	thiosulfato
NO_2^-	nitro
NO_3^-	nitrato

FOLLOW-UP QUESTIONS

1. Complete Table II. Use the data in Table I and the information in the Follow-up Discussion to help you explain in which direction and why a shift in equilibrium occurred.

2. Refer to Table IV and explain what evidence indicates that hydrogen ions are a constitutent of the equilibrium mixture.

3. What evidence do you have that a water solution of $K_2Cr_2O_7$ is actually an equilibrium mixture that contains CrO_4^{2-} ions?

4. Use the data in Table V and VI to help you convert the equilibrium equation into a thermochemical equation. Write the heat term (Q) on the right side of the equation with the proper sign. As written, is the reaction exothermic or endothermic?

5. In future experiments you will encounter the complex ions whose formulas are shown below. Name these ions using the information given in the Follow-up Discussion.

Formula	Name
$Cu(NH_3)_4^{2+}$	
$Al(OH_4)^-$	

14-1
Solutes, Solvents, and Solutions

GENERAL DISCUSSION

Most of the reactions carried out in your laboratory work take place in aqueous solution. In order to explain the characteristics of solutions, to interpret the behavior of solutes involved in reactions, and to write proper equations for reactions you must first identify the type and nature of the solute particles. Electric measurements, such as those involved in this demonstration, furnish valuable clues to the nature and behavior of various solutes in different solvents.

In this demonstration, the instructor or students tests the electric conductivity of a number of solvents and solutions using the apparatus shown in Fig. 14-1 or a modification of it. The apparatus consists of a circuit containing a light bulb and an ammeter (optional) in series with a pair of testing electrodes which will be immersed in the liquids whose conductivities are unknown. When the electrodes are immersed in an electrolytic liquid containing a high concentration of ions, the bulb glows brightly and a relatively high reading will be observed on the ammeter. Record the results of the tests in tables similar to those shown later and then use the data in the tables to identify the nature of and to explain the behavior of various solute and solvent particles. Your explanations of the observed phenomena should involve structural, bonding, energy, and equilibrium concepts.

OBJECTIVES

1. To determine the electric conductivity of various solutes and solvents.

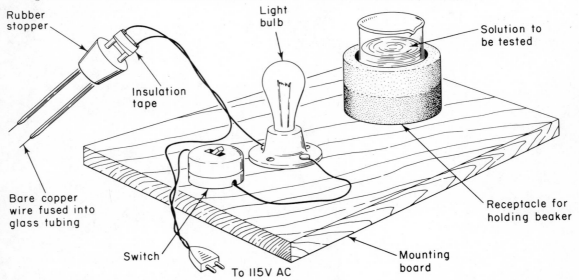

Rubber stopper

Light bulb

Solution to be tested

Insulation tape

Bare copper wire fused into glass tubing

Switch

To 115V AC

Receptacle for holding beaker

Mounting board

Fig. 14-1 Apparatus for determining relative conductivity of solutions. If relative currents are desired, then an ammeter and a variable resistor should be placed in the circuit. The current should then be adjusted for full-scale deflection for the solution of the strongest electrotype. The spacing of the electrodes and depth of immersion should be constant throughout the experiment.

2. To determine the electric nature of and the relative proportion of the different chemical species present in various solutions.

3. To explain the behavior of various solutes and characteristics of solutions in terms of bonding, equilibrium, and energy concepts.

MATERIALS

Conductivity apparatus, shell vial or 50-ml beakers, absolute or 95% ethanol, benzene, solution of dry hydrogen chloride in benzene, anhydrous (100%) acetic acid, 0.1-M acetic acid, 0.1-M aqueous ammonia, 0.1-M sucrose, 0.1-M hydrochloric acid, 0.1-M sodium hydroxide, 0.1-M ammonium acetate, solid ammonium acetate, crucible, burner, clay triangle, silver chloride, solid NH_4Cl, solid anhydrous $CaCl_2$, 0.100-M $Ba(OH)_2$, 0.100-M H_2SO_4, magnetic stirrer if available, buret, bromthymol blue.

PROCEDURE

1. Immerse the electrodes in small samples of the following liquids contained in a shell vial or 50-ml beaker. Use either separate vessels for each liquid or clean and dry them thoroughly with a tissue between tests. Rinse and clean the electrodes between tests also.

   (1) distilled water
   (2) ethanol (preferably absolute, or 100%, if available)
   (3) benzene
   (4) a solution of dry hydrogen chloride in benzene

Record your observations in Table I.

2. Add an equal volume of distilled water to the vial or beaker containing a solution of dry hydrogen chloride in benzene. Stir, allow the phases to separate, and then test the conductivity of both the water and the upper benzene layer.

3. Test the conductivity of these aqueous solutions contained in shell vials or in 50-ml beakers: (a) anhydrous (100%) acetic acid; (b) dilute (0.1-M) acetic acid; (c) concentrated (15-M) aqueous ammonia; (d) 0.1-M aqueous ammonia; (e) 0.1-M sucrose (sugar) solution; (f) 0.1-M hydrochloric acid; (g) 0.1-M sodium hydroxide

solution; (h) 0.1-M ammonium acetate solution. Record your observations in Table I.

4. Touch the electrodes to some solid ammonium acetate. Test the conductivity. Then melt the compound and test the liquid salt.

5. Place the electrodes in a sample of 0.1-M ammonia solution and add dropwise with stirring, a 0.1-M acetic acid solution. Record your observations.

6. Place a small mass of solid silver chloride in a 50-ml beaker and add 10–15 ml of distilled water. Test the conductivity of the saturated solution. Now add concentrated aqueous ammonia (15-M) with stirring until the precipitate dissolves and test the conductivity of the resulting solution.

7. In the last column of Table I indicate the nature of the solute and solvent particles.

8. Put 50 ml (± 1 ml) of water in a 100-ml gas-measuring (eudiometer) tube. Measure and record its temperature. Place 50 ml (± 1 ml) of ethanol in a second 100-ml gas measuring (eudiometer) tube. Measure and record its temperature. Add the ethanol to the water, being careful to transfer as nearly all the ethanol as possible. Mix thoroughly, then record the final volume and measure the final temperature of the solution. Record your observations in Table II.

9. Pour about five ml of distilled water into a test tube and record its temperature. Add about 2 g of NH_4Cl to the water, stir carefully with the thermometer, and record the temperature after about 20 seconds. (b) Repeat using about 2 g of anhydrous $CaCl_2$ instead of NH_4Cl. Record your readings in Table III.

10. Note the conductivity respectively of 0.100-M $Ba(OH)_2$ and 0.100-M H_2SO_4 solution. Put 25 ml of the H_2SO_4 solution in a 150-ml beaker. If a magnetic stirrer is available, insert a stirring bar in the acid solution and locate the beaker on the stirrer platform. Add two or three drops of bromthymol blue indicator (Transition color is at pH 7). Insert the electrodes of the conductivity apparatus and close the switch. From a buret add 0.100-M $Ba(OH)_2$ solution while stirring the solution until the indicator color is green. Record in Table IV your observations of any

Table I   Conductivity of Liquids and Nature of Solute and Solvent Particles

	Relative Conductivity (Brilliance of Light and/or Current Reading)	Nature of Solvent and/or Solute Particles (molecules, ions, or mixtures of both.)
Distilled water		solvent:
Ethanol		solvent:
Benzene		solvent:
Dry HCl in benzene		solvent: solute:
Water layer below benzene layer		solvent: solute:
Anhydrous acetic acid		solvent:
Dilute acetic acid		solvent: solute:
Dilute (0.1-M) aqueous NH_3		solvent: solute:
0.1-M sucrose		solvent: solute:
0.1-M $NH_4C_2H_3O_2$		solvent: solute:
0.1-M HCl		solvent: solute:
0.1-M NaOH		solvent: solute:
Sol'n from mix of $NH_3 + HC_2H_3O_2$		solvent: solute:
Solid $NH_4C_2H_3O_2$		//////////
Liquid $NH_4C_2H_3O_2$		solvent:
Saturated AgCl sol'n		//////////
Sol'n from mix of AgCl + NH_3		solvent: solute:

changes in the conductivity of the solution while the $Ba(OH)_2$ solution is *slowly* added. Record the relative conductivity when equal molar quantities of the two reactants have been reacted (pH = 7). Add a volume of $Ba(OH)_2$ solution which is significantly greater than the volume of H_2SO_4 used. Again note changes in conductivity and indicator color.

FOLLOW-UP DISCUSSION

One of the major goals of the modern chemist is to attempt to explain observed chemical phenomena in terms of bonding principles. You have already studied equilibrium principles, some of the important types of chemical bonds, and the shapes and polarities of molecules; you should therefore be in a position to make some fairly reasonable hypotheses to explain what you observed in each part of this experiment. The first task is to look up the empirical or molecular formulas of each substance used and then draw Lewis (electron-dot) structures of each. From these you should be able in most of the cases to ascertain the geometry and polarity of any of the molecular substances used. Remember that in the case of ions, the charge is the overriding property and not its geometry. For simplicity one can be reasonably correct in assuming approximate spherical symmetry for most ions and that their charge is non-directional.

In making your hypotheses, consider, in addition to shapes and polarities, such factors as relative electronegativities, charge densities, energy and entropy factors. Also, realize that your knowledge of *all* of the factors involved is still quite limited; your hypotheses, therefore, will be evaluated on the basis of the evidence of good thinking and clear reasoning, even though they may be incorrect.

FOLLOW-UP QUESTIONS

1. (a) Your conductivity apparatus may not have been sufficiently sensitive to show it, but both water and ethanol contain a measurable concentration of ions. Assume that these ions do not come from impurities and suggest a mechanism to account for their presence. (b) Benzene does not contain ions. Explain why the mechanism which you suggested in (a) would not be involved in this case. (c) Give the shape and polarity respectively of benzene, water, and hydrogen chloride molecules. In which liquid does hydrogen chloride have greatest solubility? Explain. Explain why hydrogen chloride dissolves in benzene at all.

2. In all of the cases of aqueous solutions which showed measurable conductivity, write net ionic equations to show any reaction between the solutes and water to account for a concentration of ions greater than that in pure water.

3. Explain with the use of a net ionic equation, any change in electric conductivity when 0.1-M ammonia was added to 0.1-M acetic acid.

Table II   Alcohol + Water

Volume of water	
Temperature of water	
Volume of alcohol	
Temperature of alcohol	
Volume of mixture	
Temperature of mixture	

Table III   Energy Effects Accompanying the Dissolution of Ionic Solutes

Temperature of water before adding NH_4Cl	
Temperature of solution after addition of NH_4Cl	
Temperature of water before adding $CaCl_2$	
Temperature of water after adding $CaCl_2$	

Table IV   Composition of H_2SO_4 and $Ba(OH)_2$ Solutions Before and After Reaction

Solution	Relative Conductivity	Solution Contains
0.100-M H_2SO_4		
0.100-M $Ba(OH)_2$		
After reaction of equal molar quantities of H_2SO_4 and $Ba(OH)_2$		
After addition of excess $Ba(OH)_2$		

4. What is the nature of the solute particles in an aqueous sugar solution? What is your evidence? Use energy, entropy, and bonding concepts to explain the solubility of sugar in water.

5. Refer to the Follow-up Discussion in Experiment 13-1 to obtain a hint that will enable you to explain the change in conductivity you observed in Procedure 6. Write a net ionic equation which helps to explain your observation.

6. In which direction is the solubility equilibrium represented by the equation $AgCl(s) \rightleftharpoons Ag^+(aq) + Cl^-(aq)$ shifted by the addition of aqueous ammonia to the saturated solution of AgCl? Explain in terms of differences in the rates of the forward and reverse reaction caused by the addition of the $NH_3(aq)$. Is this consistent with Le Châtelier's principle?

7. Account for the observed complete miscibility of water and ethanol as well as for the observed contraction in volume in terms of energy, entropy, and bonding concepts. Support your explanation with any experimental evidence observed. Was the process exothermic or endothermic?

8. In procedure 8 you dissolved two ionic solutes. For each solute, state which is larger, the crystal lattice energy or the hydration energy? Explain the observations in terms of bonding concepts.

9. (a) Explain with the use of net ionic equations any changes in conductivity observed when the 0.100-M Ba$(OH)_2$ was added to the 0.100-M H_2SO_4 solution. (b) Do all ionic crystals form highly conducting solutions? Support your answer with experimental evidence. Does this mean that the solute particles in a saturated solution of a slightly soluble salt such as $BaSO_4$ are molecular in nature?

10. Identify the relative concentration of the solute particles in the solutions listed below.

	Aqueous NaOH	Dilute $NH_3(aq)$	Dilute HOAc	Dilute HCl
Species present in largest concentration				
Other solute species				

11. In Experiment 9-1 you observed that naphthalene is soluble in benzene but not in water. How do you explain these observations in terms of energy and entropy effects?

14-2

Decomposition, Formation, and Reaction of a Hydrate

GENERAL DISCUSSION

In Part I of this experiment you determine the percentage of water in a barium chloride hydrate as well as the formula of the hydrate. The percentage of water is determined by heating a weighed sample of the hydrate and reweighing the anhydrous residue (anhydrate). If we assume no decomposition of the anhydrate, the mass of water in the original sample is equal to the difference between the mass of the hydrate and that of the anhydrate. The formula is determined by finding the moles of water combined with one mole of the anhydrate. The mole ratio is obtained by dividing the experimentally derived masses of anhydrate and water by their respective molecular masses.

In Part II you observe color and energy changes which occur during the formation of a specified hydrate. You will also observe changes which occur when you substitute ammonia molecules for the water molecules in the hydrate.

OBJECTIVES

1. To determine the percentage of water in a hydrate.
2. To determine the formula of a hydrate from analytical data.
3. To observe color and energy changes which occur during the formation and reaction of a hydrate.

MATERIALS

Porcelain crucible and cover, clay triangle, ring stand, burner, hydrated barium chloride, triple-beam balance, hydrated copper sulfate, mortar and pestle, thermometer, test tube, 6-M ammonia solution, 3-M sulfuric acid, graduated cylinder.

PROCEDURE

Part I · Percentage of Water in a Hydrate

1. Support a clean porcelain crucible and cover on a clay triangle on a ring stand. Heat the crucible with a nonluminous flame for two or three minutes.

2. When the crucible cools, weigh it and the cover to the nearest 0.01 g and record the data in Table I.

3. Put approximately three g of hydrated barium chloride crystals in the crucible and weigh the crucible, cover, and contents to the nearest 0.01 g. Observe the appearance of the hydrated crystals.

4. Again put the crucible and cover on the clay triangle. Heat gently at first, then use a hot full flame for 15 to 20 minutes. The bottom of the crucible becomes a dull red color. Be sure to use a nonluminous flame to avoid depositing carbon on the bottom of the crucible.

5. When the crucible has cooled to room temperature, weigh it to the nearest 0.01 g.

6. Reheat the crucible strongly for three or four minutes more to insure that the water is all driven off. Cool and reweigh. Repeat this procedure until two weighings agree within 0.01 g.

7. Observe the appearance of the anhydrous crystals and return them to the instructor.

8. Read the Follow-up Discussion and make the calculations needed to complete Table I.

Part II · Formation and Reactions of a Hydrate

9. Pulverize about one g of hydrated copper (II) sulfate in a mortar and place the powder in a crucible.

10. Heat the crucible until the contents have changed color. Record color change in Table II.

Table I Percentage of Water in a Hydrate

1	Mass of crucible, cover, and hydrated barium chloride	
2	Mass of crucible and cover	
3	Mass of hydrated barium chloride	
4	Mass of crucible, cover, and anhydrous barium chloride	
5	Mass of crucible and cover	
6	Mass of anhydrous barium chloride	
7	Mass of water in the hydrated crystals	
8	Number of moles of anhydrous barium chloride in sample	
9	Number of moles of water in hydrated crystals	
10	Percentage of water in hydrate (experimental)	
11	True percentage of water in hydrate (instructor)	
12	Percent deviation of your value from accepted value	
13	Moles of water per mole of anhydrous $BaCl_2$	
14	Formula of hydrate	

Table II Formation and Reaction of a Hydrate

Procedure	Change in	Observation
Heat $CuSO_4 \cdot 5H_2O$	color	
Add H_2O to $CuSO_4$	color	
	energy	
Add NH_3 to $CuSO_4 \cdot 5H_2O$	color	
Add H_2SO_4 to $Cu(NH_3)_4^{2+}$	color	

When cool, transfer the anhydrous copper(II) sulfate to a test tube.

11. Hold a thermometer in the anhydrous crystals and add water dropwise. Note the change in temperature. Record whether energy was transferred into or out of the chemical system.

12. After noting the temperature, add enough water to dissolve the crystals completely. Then add 6-M ammonia solution until a pronounced color change occurs.

13. Add 3- or 6-M sulfuric acid until another color change occurs.

FOLLOW-UP DISCUSSION

The hydrate used in Part I of this experiment may be represented as $BaCl_2 \cdot xH_2O$, where x stands for the moles of water combined with one mole of $BaCl_2$. The equation for the decomposition of the hydrate can be written as

$$BaCl_2 \cdot xH_2O(s) \rightarrow BaCl_2(s) + xH_2O(g)$$

The percentage of water in the hydrate may be calculated using the equation

$$\% \text{ of } H_2O = \frac{\text{mass of water}}{\text{mass of hydrate}} \times (100)$$

The moles of anhydrous $BaCl_2$ (Item 8) may be calculated by dividing the mass in grams (Item 6) by the formula mass of $BaCl_2$ (208). In a similar manner, the moles of water may be determined by dividing the mass of water (Item 7) by the molecular mass of water. The moles of water per mole of anhydrous barium chloride (Item 13) is calculated by dividing Item 9 by Item 8.

One of the objectives of Part II was to introduce another important type of nonredox reaction. This reaction is between a positive metallic ion and a coordinating group called a *ligand*. The positive ion has vacant orbitals and the ligand has unused bonding electron-pairs. The reaction involves the formation of a coordinate covalent bond in which the ligands donate both shared electrons. In this experiment a reaction between copper(II) ions and water molecules occurred because a relatively stable bond was formed between them.

$$Cu^{2+} + 4H_2O \rightarrow Cu(H_2O)_4^{2+} \qquad \text{Eq. 1}$$

central ion   ligand   complex ion

$Cu(H_2O)_4^{2+}$ is an example of a large group of polyatomic ions classed as *metal-centered complex ions*.

In general, the number of ligands attached to a central ion must be obtained from experimental data. (Complex ions are named according to a system discussed in Chapter 19 of *Foundations of Chemistry*, 2 ed.) The complex ion in Equation 1 is called tetraaquocopper(II) ion. In this experiment you saw evidence that ammonia reacted with hydrated copper(II) ions.

$$Cu(H_2O)_4^{2+} + 4NH_3 \rightleftharpoons Cu(NH_3)_4^{2+} + 4H_2O$$
$$\text{Eq. 2}$$

In this reaction, four ammonia molecules are substituted for four water molecules forming tetramminecopper(II) ions. The double arrow indicates that the reaction reaches an equilibrium condition in which all four species are present. The tetrammine complex may be destroyed by adding an acid. The hydronium ions from the acid react with NH_3 and form NH_4^+ ions. Removal of NH_3 by the acid causes the $Cu(NH_3)_4^{2+}$ to dissociate. In other words, the equilibrium represented by the equation

$$Cu(NH_3)_4^{2+} \rightleftharpoons Cu^{2+} + 4NH_3$$

shifts to the right.

FOLLOW-UP QUESTIONS

1. What was the purpose of heating the crucible before weighing it?

2. What was the reason that the crucible was cooled before weighing it?

3. How could you be sure that all the water had been removed from the hydrate?

4. How did the hydrated and anhydrous $BaCl_2$ differ in appearance?

5. Write the equation for the decomposition of hydrated barium chloride using the values you obtained for Items 8 and 9 of Table I as fractional coefficients.

6. Write the same equation using the nearest whole-number coefficients.

7. Suppose your sample contained a volatile impurity. How would this have affected your experimentally determined percentage of water?

8. List other sources of error and indicate how they might affect the experimental result.

9. In Part II, what evidence did you obtain to indicate that a reaction occurred between Cu^{2+} ions and water.

10. (a) Did the chemical system possess more or less energy after you added water to the anhydrous copper(II) sulfate? Cite the evidence. (b) How can you account for the observed energy change?

11. (a) What evidence do you have that NH_3 reacted with $Cu(H_2O)_4^{2+}$?

12. What is the evidence that the concentration of $Cu(NH_3)_4^{2+}$ changed when sulfuric acid was added?

13. Write an equation for the reaction between hydronium ions and ammonia molecules.

14-3
Preparation and Use of a Chemical Indicator

GENERAL DISCUSSION

The earliest method of determining the pH of solutions employed certain chemical compounds, called *indicators,* which change color when the hydrogen ion concentration of a solution changes. Some indicators are derived from plants which contain colored compounds that can be extracted by using the proper solvent. In this experiment you are going to extract the colored substance from the leaves of a purple (red) cabbage. You then add this to standard buffer solutions of known pH to determine the relationship between the color of the indicator and the pH of the solution. Using your indicator and its color chart, you will determine the pH of a number of solutions. If red cabbage leaves are not available you may use Yamada's indicator in this experiment.

OBJECTIVES

1. To prepare a chemical indicator.

2. To prepare a color chart for an indicator.

3. To determine the pH of a number of solutions using your indicator and its chart.

4. To learn the relationship between the pH and [H+] of a solution.

MATERIALS

Purple (red) cabbage leaves, 250-ml beaker, graduated cylinder, small test tubes, buffer solution of pH 2, 4, 6, 8, 10, and 12, 1-M HCl and 1-M NaOH solution, colored pencils, vinegar, baking soda solution ($NaHCO_3$), washing soda solution (Na_2CO_3), Drāno solution (NaOH), soap solution (sodium stearate), eye wash (0.1-M boric acid [H_3BO_3]), borax solution (sodium tetraborate [$Na_2B_4O_7$]), Spic and Span solution (Na_3PO_4), alum solution [$KAl(SO_4)_2 \cdot 12H_2O$], Clorox or other commercial bleach (NaClO), lemon juice (citric acid).

Table I pH Range and Color Changes of Cabbage Juice

pH of Buffer Solution	Color of Solution		[H+]	Condition of Solution (Acid, basic, neutral)
	Description of Color	Color Chart		
0				
2				
4				
6				
7				
8				
10				
12				
14				

PROCEDURE

1. Break the leaf of a purple (red) cabbage into small pieces and press them against the bottom of a 250-ml beaker. You may be asked to prepare this extract at home.

2. Add just enough water to cover the leaves. Do not add extra water because it requires a long period of boiling to concentrate the solution.

3. Boil the cabbage in the water until the solution is a deep purple color.

4. Add 3 to 4 ml of buffer solutions of pH 2, 4, 6, 8, 10, and 12 to separate small vials or small test tubes. Use the dilute NaOH on the bench for pH 14 and the HCl on the bench for pH 0. If buffers having a pH of 2 and 4 are not available, your instructor will tell you how to dilute 0.1-M HCl to prepare solutions with these pH values.

Similarly, you may prepare solutions having a pH of 10 and 12 by diluting 0.1-M NaOH.

5. Add enough of the cabbage-juice indicator to each of the vials or test tubes to produce a pronounced color. Shake well to obtain a uniform color throughout the solution. If colored pencils are available, match the colors and construct a tentative color chart in Table I. If colored pencils are not available, describe the colors and reproduce them at home with pencils or paints.

6. Place 3 or 4 ml of the solution labeled 0.1-M HCl into a vial or small test tube and add enough cabbage-juice indicator to give a pronounced color. Shake and compare with the colored buffer solutions which you prepared as standard. Record your observations in Table II.

7. Determine the pH of each of the solutions in

Table II pH of Common Solutions

Solution	pH	[H⁺] (approx.)	Condition (Acid, basic, neutral)	Compound Used to prepare Solution
0.1-M HCl				HCl
0.1-M $HC_2H_3O_2$ (vinegar)				$HC_2H_3O_2$
Baking soda				$NaHCO_3$
Washing soda				Na_2CO_3
Drāno				NaOH
Soap				$NaC_{17}H_{35}O_2$
0.1-M H_3BO_3				H_3BO_3
Salt water				NaCl
Borax				$Na_2B_4O_7$
Spic & Span				Na_3PO_4
Alum				$KAl(SO_4)_2$
Clorox				NaClO
Lemon juice				$CH_2(COOH)_2$
Detergent (1) mild				
Detergent (2) harsh				

Table II. If the commercial products are not available, prepare reasonable substitutes by dissolving the solutes indicated in Table II. Try other household products in which you may be interested; but avoid strongly colored ones.

8. Refer to the formula of the solute in each of the solutions and classify the compound as an acid, base, or salt.

FURTHER EXPERIMENTATION

1. Test other colored flowers and plants for possible use as indicators.

2. Use other commercial indicators to test the pH of the unknown solutions.

3. Use your indicator along with commercial indicators to determine the pH of an unknown solution furnished by the instructor.

FOLLOW-UP DISCUSSION

Many acid-base indicators are weak acids or weak bases. The dissociation of an indicator which behaves as a weak acid is shown by the equilibrium expression

$$\text{HIn} + H_2O \rightleftharpoons H_3O^+ + \text{In}^-$$
$$\text{(acid color)} \qquad\qquad \text{(base color)}$$

HIn molecules have a color different from that of In$^-$ ions. For example, if HIn represents the undissociated form of litmus, then HIn is red and In$^-$ is blue. According to LeChâtelier's principle, if a strong acid such as H_3O^+ is added to the litmus indicator system represented above in general terms, the equilibrium shifts to the left, forming more HIn. Thus, the solution turns red. If, however, a strong base such as OH$^-$ is added, the equilibrium shifts to the right thus increasing the concentration of In$^-$. Therefore, the solution turns blue. Thus the species which predominates and hence the color depends upon the pH. Different indicators vary in the color of their molecules and ions and also change color at different pH values. Phenolphthalein, for example, is a weak acid which is colorless in any solution whose pH is less than 8.3. In solutions for which the pH is greater than this, the phenolphthalein imparts a pink or red color to the solution. A great number of such substances are known and enough can be selected so that the acidity or basicity of solutions can be roughly determined over a wide range of acid concentration. A chart showing the pH ranges and color changes of some commercially available indicators is provided in the Appendix.

FOLLOW-UP QUESTIONS

1. Examine the data in Table I and indicate what characteristic most of the cleaning solutions have in common. From your knowledge about the components of basic solutions, which ions are probably involved in the cleansing process?

2. Predict from the pH values which of the cleansers would be the most and least harmful to fine fabrics or sensitive hands.

3. How can you account for the difference in the pH of 0.1-M HCl, 0.1-M HC$_2$H$_3$O$_2$, and 0.1-M H$_3$BO$_3$?

4. Account for the basic condition of the solutions containing Na$_2$CO$_3$ and Na$_3$PO$_4$. Hint: Write a proton-transfer equation for the reaction of each of the negative ions with water. The reactions of ions with water are investigated in Experiment 15-3.

14-4

Molecular Mass of Sulfur by Freezing-Point Depression Method (Molality)

GENERAL DISCUSSION

In an earlier experiment you determine the molecular mass of a gaseous substance by application of Avogadro's principle. You also learned that density measurements could be used to calculate the molecular mass of a substance in the gas phase. Many substances are not easily vaporized and thus do not lend themselves readily to vapor-density measurements. In some cases the approximate molecular mass of a substance can be determined by measuring the change in the freezing point or boiling point of a liquid that occurs when the solid substances are added as a solute to the solvent.

In your study of colligative properties you discovered that, for nonvolatile solutes, the freezing point depression of the solvent is directly proportional to the *molal* concentration of the solution. That is, to the moles of solute particles dissolved in a kilogram of solvent. This relationship is expressed by

$$\Delta T_f = k_f m \qquad \text{Eq. 1}$$

where ΔT_f is the freezing point depression, m is the molality or molal concentration of the solution, and k_f is the molal freezing point depression constant of the solvent. Thus the total molality of a solution may be determined by measuring the freezing point depression caused by a given mass of solute dissolved in a given mass of solvent. By definition

$$m = \frac{\text{moles solute}}{\text{mass of solvent (kg)}}$$

and thus

$$\Delta T_f = k_f \frac{\text{moles solute}}{\text{kg solvent}} \qquad \text{Eq. 2}$$

Substituting *g/molecular mass* for *moles of solute* in Equation 2 we obtain

$$\Delta T_f = \frac{(k_f)(\text{g solute})}{(\text{molecular mass solute})(\text{kg solvent})} \qquad \text{Eq. 3}$$

and solving Equation 3 for molecular mass of solute yields

$$(\text{molecular mass of solute}) = \frac{(k_f)(\text{g solute})}{(\Delta T_f)(\text{kg solvent})} \qquad \text{Eq. 4}$$

The units of k_f may be determined by solving Equation 1 for k_f and then substituting units for each of the factors.

$$k_f = \frac{\Delta T_f}{m} = \frac{°C}{\dfrac{\text{moles solute}}{\text{kg solvent}}} = \frac{(°C)(\text{kg solvent})}{(\text{moles solute})}$$

It is left as an exercise for you to show that proper substitution in Equation 4 yields units of g solute/mole solute.

In this experiment you dissolve a known mass of sulfur (solute) in a known mass of naphthalene (solvent) and then measure the freezing point of the solution. Knowing the normal freezing point for naphthalene you can calculate ΔT_f. The molecular mass can then be determined by substitution of the measured masses of solute and solvent, ΔT_f and k_f into Equation 2.

Once the approximate molecular mass of sulfur has been determined you can use the known atomic mass of sulfur to determine the molecular formula of sulfur. That is,

$$\frac{\dfrac{\text{g sulfur}}{\text{mole of sulfur molecules}}}{\dfrac{\text{g sulfur}}{\text{mole of sulfur atoms}}} = \frac{\text{moles of sulfur atoms}}{\text{moles of sulfur molecules}}$$

Because one mole of atoms and one mole of molecules contains the same number of particles, the above ratio equals the number of sulfur atoms in one sulfur molecule.

OBJECTIVES

1. To determine an approximate molecular mass for sulfur.

2. To determine the molecular formula for sulfur.

MATERIALS

400-ml beaker, 8-in. Pyrex brand test tube, −10 to 110°C thermometer, ring stand, wire screen, burner.

PROCEDURE

In order to finish on time, it is suggested that students work in pairs and the responsibilities be divided between partners as outlined below.

Partner 1

1. Put a 400-ml beaker about ¾ full of warm tap water on a wire screen supported by a ring and ring stand. Place a medium burner flame beneath the beaker.

2. Weigh an empty 8-in. test tube to the closest 0.01 g using a centigram or better balance. Record the mass.

3. Weigh approximately 20 g of naphthalene onto a piece of weighing paper and then pour the naphthalene into the test tube. Weigh the tube and contents to the closest 0.01 g.

4. Immerse the tube in the hot water in the beaker and clamp onto the ring stand. Carefully stir the contents with a thermometer until melting is complete.

5. Remove from the water and while stirring with the thermometer, note the temperature reading as crystals begin to form. Record the temperature which should remain fairly constant during crystallization at the freezing (or melting) point of the naphthalene.

6. Return the tube to the beaker of water, remelt the contents, and keep it melted until your partner is ready to add the sulfur.

Partner 2

1. Place about 2 g of pulverized roll sulfur in a shell vial and weigh to the closest 0.1 g. When your partner has completed step 6 above, add the sulfur to the melted naphthalene. Reweigh the shell vial and record in the data table with the original mass.

2. Heat the sulfur and naphthalene in the water until a yellow, *transparent*, single liquid phase results. If necessary, remove the tube from the water and heat with a *LOW* flame to hasten the dissolving. Do not exceed 110°C.

3. Remove the tube from the heat source and begin taking time and temperature readings at intervals of 15 seconds. Stir constantly. Continue until solidification is nearly complete.

4. Reheat the contents of the tube in hot water until melted. Remove the thermometer and wipe it as clean as possible with a paper towel. Pour the melted material in the tube into the container specified by the instructor. Clean the tube first with benzene, followed by a detergent-water solution.

Table I   Time-Temperature Readings

Time after Removing from Heat Source	Temperature °C

PROCESSING THE DATA

1. Plot a cooling curve from the time-temperature data taken for the mixture. Plot temperature on the ordinate and time on the abscissa. Draw the best straight line possible through the points

Table II   Molecular Mass and Molecular Formula of Sulfur

Mass of test tube + naphthalene	
Mass of empty test tube	
Mass (g) of naphthalene used	
Mass (kg) of naphthalene used	
Mass of vial + sulfur	
Mass of vial	
Mass of sulfur used (g)	
Normal freezing point of naphthalene (°C) (Proc. 5)	
Freezing point of solution (sulfur + naphthalene)	
Freezing point depression (ΔT_f)	
k_f for naphthalene	$\dfrac{6.9 \text{ C}° \ (1 \text{ kg naphthalene})}{1 \text{ mole solute}}$
Molality (moles of dissolved particles per kg of naphthalene, Eq. 1)	
Molecular mass of sulfur (experimental)	
Atomic mass of sulfur	32.1 g/mole S atoms
Atoms per molecule of sulfur	
Molecular formula for sulfur	

describing the cooling of the liquid mixture. Draw another straight line through the points taken after solidification began. The intersection of these two straight lines locates the freezing point of the mixture.

2. Make the calculations necessary to complete Table II.

FOLLOW-UP DISCUSSION

In this experiment you used the equation

$$\Delta T_f = k_f m$$

to determine the molality of your solution. Some simplifying assumptions are made in the derivation of this formula. One assumption is that the solution is dilute and behaves ideally; another is that the heat or enthalpy of fusion of the solvent is constant over a temperature range. Because the real solutions with which we work do not conform precisely with these and other requirements, the formula has definite limitations. Its use, however, does give approximate values that are useful in determining molecular formulas and in interpreting the behavior of solutes in various solvents.

The solute in this experiment was molecular and did not undergo dissociation or association. Measurements such as those made in this experiment can be used with ionic solutes to determine the degree or percentage of dissociation. That is, the freezing point depression can help identify the number of moles of particles formed from a given number of moles of solute. For example, if one mole of a chemical compound dissolved in 1 kg of water produced a solution which had a freezing point of −3.72°C, we would conclude that there were two moles of dissolved particles and that the original compound dissociated when dissolved in water.

FOLLOW-UP QUESTIONS

1. The freezing point of benzene is lowered from 5.48°C to 4.88°C when 1.05 grams of anthracene is dissolved in 50.0 g of benzene. What is the approximate molecular mass of anthracene?

2. What is the molality of a solution prepared by dissolving 1.71 of sucrose ($C_{12}H_{22}O_{11}$) in 10.0 g of water?

15-1
Relative Strengths of Acids and Bases

GENERAL DISCUSSION

The Brønsted theory of acid and bases states that when an acid reacts with a base, a proton is donated by the acid to the base thus, producing a new acid and a new base. As the concentration of the new acid-base pair builds up, the reverse reaction begins to take place and its effect may become significant. When the rates of the forward and the reverse reactions become equal, equilibrium is established and no further net change in concentration of any of the species occurs.

The relative concentrations of the various species at equilibrium depend largely upon the relative tendencies for the two bases to accept protons. The forward and reverse reactions can be thought of as a result of the competition of the two bases for protons. In general, the reaction between a strong acid and a strong base results in an equilibrium condition in which the "products are favored." That is, the products are present in higher concentration than the reactants. In this situation we say that the equilibrium position is displaced to the right. The reverse situation, of course, is true when a weak acid and a weak base react. These ideas are summarized in the general equation

$$HA^m + B^n \rightleftharpoons HB^{n+} + A^{n-1}$$

$$\text{strong acid} \quad \text{strong base} \quad \text{weaker acid} \quad \text{weaker base}$$

In the above equation, "m" and "n" refer to the charge of the species and can refer to a positive or negative integer or to zero.

Indicators are compounds which can behave as Brønsted acids or bases. They are useful to chemists because of the color changes they undergo when they either donate or accept a proton. Consider litmus, an organic compound whose chemical formula is quite complex. The red form of litmus, which we shall designate as HLit, is a Brønsted acid. When it donates a proton to a base, it changes to its conjugate base which is blue and is designated as Lit.

$$HLit^m + B^n \rightleftharpoons HB^{n+1} + Lit^{m-1}$$

$$\text{acid}_1\text{(red)} \quad \text{base}_2 \quad \text{acid}_2 \quad \text{base}_1\text{(blue)}$$

When a mixture of red and blue litmus, which is purple in color, is placed in a mixture of an acid and its conjugate base, the color of the resulting solution tells the chemist whether the reactants of products are there in the greater amount. In the above equation, if the base (B^n) is stronger than the basic form of litmus (Lit^{m-1}) and if the acid form of litmus $(HLit^m)$ is stronger than the conjugate acid of B^n (HB^{n+1}), then the products of the reaction are favored at equilibrium and the mixture is blue in color. If the converse is true, the mixture is red. A common example of this is the reaction of red litmus with the strong base (OH^-), resulting in a blue color.

In this experiment, you determine the relative strengths of eleven different Brønsted acids and their conjugate bases. Six of the dropper bottles labeled $HA_1 - A_1^-$, $HA_2 - A_2^-$ . . . .$HA_n - A_n^{1-}$, contain different colorless acids in equilibrium with their conjugate bases, both present in approximately equal molar concentrations. For example, a bottle might contain a mixture of acetic acid and sodium acetate. The sodium ions are inactive (spectator) ions and their presence is of no consequence in this experiment. Five other bottles, labeled $HIn_1 - In_1^-$, $HIn_2 - In_2^-$, etc., contain indicators with their acid and basic forms in equilibrium with one another. Ideally these indicators should be adjusted to the pH of their transition colors so that both the acid and base forms are present in significant concentrations. You are to mix the acid-base pairs with the indicator acid-base pairs in all possible combinations and note the color of the resulting equilibrium mixtures. From these colors you should be able to rank all of the acids in order of decreasing strength.

OBJECTIVES

1. To gain an understanding of acid-base equilibria.

2. To prepare an acid-base chart in which Brønsted acids are listed in decreasing order of strength and the conjugate bases are listed in order of increasing strength.

MATERIALS

Eleven solutions containing different conjugate acid-base pairs, 1-in. test tubes or white spot plates, 1-M NaOH, 1-M HCl.

PROCEDURE

1. Determine the colors of the acid and basic form of each indicator by placing one drop of the indicator solution into separate test tubes or on spot plates containing three to five drops of hydronium and hydroxide ions, respectively. For this test use 1-M HCl and 1-M NaOH solutions. The former will produce a solution which contains the indicator predominantly in its acid form while the latter will produce its basic form. The equation is

$$H_3O^+ + In^- \rightleftharpoons HIn + H_2O$$
$$\text{acid form}$$

The equilibrium favors the products because hy-

base possible in an aqueous solution and, hence pull protons off any of the acid forms of the indicators. Record data in the first blank horizontal row of Table I.

$$OH^- + HIn \rightleftharpoons In^- + H_2O$$
$$\text{basic form}$$

2. Determine the color produced by the addition of each indicator mixture to each colorless acid-base mixture. Use one drop of indicator mixture to four drops of the colorless mixture. Be certain that your tubes or spot plates have been rinsed thoroughly with tap water and finally with distilled water between tests. Shake off excess water. Record all data in Table I.

dronium is the strongest acid possible in an aqueous solution. Hydroxide ions are the strongest

3. From the results of your experiments, rank the eleven acids in order of decreasing strength, and their conjugate bases beside them in order of increasing strength. Your conclusions are to be based entirely upon the axiom that at equilibrium, the weaker acid and the weaker base are present in greater concentration than the stronger acid and base. Be sure to record the number of the unknown set assigned to you.

It is suggested that you first use the colors recorded in each space of Table I to identify the indicator species (HIn or In$^-$) which predominates in each equilibrium system. This informa-

Table I   Reactions of Brønsted Acids and Bases

	$HIn_1 - In_1^-$		$HIn_2 - In_2^-$		$HIn_3 - In_3^-$		$HIn_4 - In_4^-$		$HIn_5 - In_5^-$	
	acid color	base color	acid color	base color	acid color	base color	acid color	base color	acid color	base color
$HA_1 - A_1^-$										
$HA_2 - A_2^-$										
$HA_3 - A_3^-$										
$HA_4 - A_4^-$										
$HA_5 - A_5^-$										
$HA_6 - A_6^-$										

Table II

	$HIn_1 - In_1^-$	$HIn_2 - In_2^-$	$HIn_3 - In_3^-$	$HIn_4 - In_4^-$	$HIn_5 - In_5^-$
$HA_1 - A_1^-$					
$HA_2 - A_2^-$					
$HA_3 - A_3^-$					
$HA_4 - A_4^-$					
$HA_5 - A_5^-$					
$HA_6 - A_6^-$					

tion enables you to determine which of the two acids and/or which of the two bases in the system is the stronger. You should then record your conclusion in Table II using the symbols ($>$) or ($<$). For example, if your observations reveal that HA_1 is stronger than HIn_1, write $>$ in the space at the upper left of the table. Your interpretation and analysis of the conclusions shown in Table II should enable you to rank the acids and bases in the proper order.

RELATIVE STRENGTHS

BRØNSTED ACIDS	CONJUGATE BASES
1. _____	_____
2. _____	_____
3. _____	_____
4. _____	_____
5. _____	_____
6. _____	_____
7. _____	_____
8. _____	_____
9. _____	_____
10. _____	_____
11. _____	_____

FOLLOW-UP DISCUSSION

In the event you experienced some difficulty in deducing the relative strengths of the Brønsted acids or bases in this experiment, we shall illustrate the reasoning with an example. Suppose it has been established that an indicator solution which appears orange turns yellow when added to 1-M NaOH and red when added to 1-M HCl. These data indicate that the acid form of the indicator (HIn) is red and that the basic form (the conjugate base In^-) is yellow. Now suppose when this indicator is added to an unknown acid-base ($HX - X^-$) the solution turns red. This observation suggests that the equilibrium

$$HX + In^- \rightleftharpoons HIn + X^-$$

is displaced to the right. Applying the principle that *equilibrium favors the production of the weaker acid and base,* we conclude that HX is a stronger Brønsted acid than HIn and that In^- is a stronger Brønsted base than X^-. In other words, the bases In^- and X^- are competing for protons from the acid species. The stronger base In^- wins the competition and forces the equilibrium to the right. Hence, we may write

$$In^- > X^- \text{ and/or } HX > HIn$$

For each reaction you are to identify the stronger base (or acid) and itemize your conclusions as described above. You are then supposed to examine the tabulated results and arrange the bases in order of increasing strength and acids in order of decreasing strength. Once a list of bases has been established, the acids may be listed by applying the principle that *the stronger a Brønsted base, the weaker is conjugate acid.* The table or list may be used to predict the relative completeness of a reaction between any Brønsted acid and base in the table. The general principle is: *the stronger the reactant acid and base the more nearly complete the reaction;* that is, the more the equilibrium will be displaced to the right. This means that the acid at the upper left of the table reacts to the greatest extent with the base at the lower right of the table.

FOLLOW-UP QUESTIONS

1. Rewrite the following equation and identify with labels the conjugate acid-base pairs.

$$CH_3COOH + NH_3 \rightleftharpoons NH_4^+ + CH_3COO^-$$

2. The formation of products is strongly favored in this acid-base system,

$$HX + B^- \rightleftharpoons HB + X^-$$

(a) Identify the bases competing for protons.
(b) Which is the weaker acid in the above equation? Explain.
(c) Which base is the stronger? Explain.
(d) How would the equilibrium be affected by the addition of the soluble salt, NaB?
(e) Would the equilibrium constant for this reaction have a relatively large or relatively small value? Explain.

3. Barium oxide reacts with water and forms barium hydroxide. What does this observation indicate about the relative strengths of the oxide and hydroxide ions as Brønsted bases?

4. This series of reactions proceeds predominately to the right as written.

$$HC_2H_3O_2 + NH_3 \rightleftharpoons NH_4^+ + C_2H_3O_2^-$$

$$HBr + H_2O \rightleftharpoons H_3O^+ + Br^-$$

$$NH_4^+ + OH^- \rightleftharpoons NH_3 + H_2O$$

$$H_3O^+ + C_2H_3O_2^- \rightleftharpoons H_2O + HC_2H_3O_2$$

Arrange the bases NH_3, H_2O, OH^-, $C_2H_3O_2^-$, and Br^- in increasing order of basic strength. That is, place the weakest base first, the strongest base last. Beside the Brønsted bases, list the formulas of their conjugate acids.

5. Write net ionic equations for these reactions. Use an unequal double arrow to indicate in which direction the equilibrium is displaced. Refer to the table prepared in problem 4.

(a) $HBr + C_2H_3O_2^-$
(b) $NH_4^+ + Br^-$

177

15-2
Ions as Brønsted Acids and Bases

GENERAL DISCUSSION

In Experiment 4-1 you found that hydrochloric acid reacted with sodium hydroxide and produced a neutral solution. Water was the product of this reaction. Another compound called a salt remains when the water is evaporated. On the basis of this one reaction you might predict that any dry salt, when dissolved in water, would produce a neutral solution.

This experiment makes a more complete study of the characteristics of salts dissolved in water. In general, salts are composed of ions, and pure water is neutral. Therefore, if any salt solutions turn out to be acid or basic, we shall assume that a reaction has occurred between an ion of the salt and water which causes the H^+-ion concentration of water to change. The experiment is designed so that you can examine the data and determine which ion, if any, actually reacted. The reaction between a positive ion and water is called *cation hydrolysis*. That between a negative ion and water is called *anion hydrolysis*. If the solution of a salt is neutral, we shall assume that no reaction has occurred. You will write ionic equations to help explain your observations. These equations will then be interpreted in terms of Brønsted-Lowry acid-base concepts.

OBJECTIVES

1. To determine the relative acidity of different salt solutions.
2. To explain the acidity, neutrality, or basicity of salt solutions in terms of ionic equations and hydrolysis equilibria.
3. To interpret anion and cation hydrolysis in terms of Brønsted-Lowry acid-base concepts.

MATERIALS

Test tubes, graduated cylinder, red and blue litmus paper. 0.1-M solutions of Na_2CO_3, $NaCl$, KNO_3, $(NH_4)_2SO_4$, NH_4Cl, $NaC_2H_3O_2$, Na_2SO_4, Na_3PO_4, $Al_2(SO_4)_3$, $Fe(NO_3)_3$, saturated $NaC_2H_3O_2$, saturated NH_4Cl, 1-M $AlCl_3$, 1-M Na_2CO_3, 6-M HCl, 6-M $NaOH$, solid $(NH_4)_2CO_3$, NH_4HCO_3, NH_4Cl, and $(NH_4)_2SO_4$.

PROCEDURE

1. Place 2 or 3 ml of 0.1-M solutions of the salts listed in Table I in each of 10 test tubes.

2. Use litmus paper to help identify the approximate pH of the solutions. In neutral solutions, red litmus remains red and blue litmus remains blue. Record results in Table I. You should designate the condition of the solutions as (a) strongly basic, (b) weakly basic, (c) strongly acid, (d) weakly acid or (e) neutral. If the solution is either acid or basic, write *yes* in the last column of Table I. If the solution is neutral, write *No*.

3. Refer to the data in Table I and list first in Table II the ions which do not hydrolyze. Then list those which do hydrolyze. For the neutral solutions, assume that neither ion of the salt reacts (hydrolyzes).

4. In Table III write net ionic equations for the hydrolysis of each ion listed in Table II. The equations are numbered in order to relate the species in Table IV to the equations in Table III. The brief discussion of ionic equations and Brønsted-Lowry theory given in the Follow-up Discussion may help you complete this step and Procedure 5. Remember, when writing net ionic equations to eliminate unreactive ions such as Na^+, K^+, Cl^-, NO_3^-, and SO_4^{2-}.

5. Write in Table IV the conjugate acid-base pairs for each reaction listed in Table III.

6. Add 5 ml of 6-M HCl to 5 ml of saturated sodium acetate solution. Cautiously smell the contents of the test tube. If no odor is detected, gently warm the contents and identify the odor of the gas being evolved. Record your observation in Table V.

Table I   pH of Salt Solutions

Solution Number	Salt	Effect on Litmus Paper	Relative Acidity of Solution	Hydrolysis Reaction (yes or no)
1	Na_2CO_3			
2	$NaCl$			
3	KNO_3			
4	$(NH_4)_2SO_4$			
5	NH_4Cl			
6	$NaC_2H_3O_2$			
7	Na_2SO_4			
8	Na_3PO_4			
9	$Al_2(SO_4)_3$			
10	$Fe(NO_3)_3$			

Table II   Classification of Ions

Hydrolyze	Do Not Hydrolyze

Table III   Ionic Equations for Cation and Anion Hydrolysis

Equation Number	Equation
1	
2	
3	
4	
5	
6	

Table IV   Conjugate Acid-Base Pairs

Equation Number	Conjugate Acid	Conjugate Base
4		
3		
2		
1		
5		
6		

7. Add 5 ml of 6-M NaOH to 5 ml of saturated ammonium chloride solution. Cautiously smell the contents of the test tube. If no odor is detected, gently warm the contents and identify the odor of the gas being evolved.

8. Add 5 ml of a saturated sodium acetate solution to 5 ml of saturated ammonium chloride solution. Cautiously smell the contents of the test tube. If no odor is detected, gently warm the contents and identify the odor of the gas being evolved. Record your observation in Table V.

9. Add 5 ml of 1.0-M AlCl$_3$ to 5 ml of 1.0-M Na$_2$CO$_3$. The observable product is Al(OH)$_3$. Record this observation in Table V. Pour one-

Table V Acid-Base Reactions

Procedure	Reagent 1	Reagent 2	Observations
6	$NaC_2H_3O_2$	HCl	
7	NH_4Cl	NaOH	
8	$NaC_2H_3O_2$	NH_4Cl	
9	$AlCl_3$	Na_2CO_3	
10	$Al(OH)_3$	HCl	
11	$Al(OH)_3$	NaOH	
12	Ammonium compounds		

half of the contents of the test tube into another test tube. Be sure some of the $Al(OH)_3$ is in both test tubes.

10. To one test tube add 5 ml of 6-M HCl. Record your observations.

11. To the second test tube add 5 ml of 6-M NaOH. Record your observations.

12. Cautiously note the relative intensities of odor released from solid NH_4HCO_3, $(NH_4)_2CO_3$, NH_4Cl, and $(NH_4)_2SO_4$. Record your observations in Table V. Identify the substance that causes the odor.

FOLLOW-UP DISCUSSION

The experimental data show that ions may react with water and give solutions which have acid and basic characteristics. These reactions can be interpreted in terms of Brønsted-Lowry acid-base concepts. Anion or cation hydrolysis involves the reaction of the ions of a salt with water forming a stronger acid and a stronger base. The equilibrium favors the reactants; however, sufficient amounts of products are present at equilibrium to be significant and to shift the pH away from 7. Consider a solution prepared by a salt such as $Fe(NO_3)_3$ or $Al_2(SO_4)_3$. The cations in these salts are small and carry a 3+ charge. Consequently, they are highly hydrated in aqueous solution. Thus, Fe^{3+} ion exists in aqueous solution as $Fe(H_2O)_6^{3+}$. The equation for the reaction of this ion with H_2O is

$$Fe(H_2O)_6^{3+} + H_2O \rightleftharpoons$$
$$Fe(H_2O)_5(OH)^{2+} + H_3O^+ \quad \text{Eq. 1}$$

The reaction is a Brønsted acid-base reaction in which the $Fe(H_2O)_6^{3+}$ ions transfer one proton each to water molecules. Thus, $Fe(H_2O)_6^{3+}$ is a Brønsted acid (proton donor), and H_2O is a Brønsted base (proton acceptor). When a Brønsted acid donates a proton, the remaining ion is called the conjugate base of the acid. The conjugate acid-base pairs in Equation 1 are listed below.

	Conjugate Acid	Conjugate Base
Pair 1	$Fe(H_2O)_6^{3+}$	$Fe(H_2O)_5(OH)^{2+}$
Pair 2	H_3O^+	H_2O

Since the reaction in Procedure 7 is rather complicated, you are not expected to write the equation for it. The reaction was included to give you an insight into the role of hydrolysis in many chemical reactions. Knowing that most carbonates are insoluble, you might have predicted the precipitate to be aluminum carbonate. Doing so would mean that you did not consider the hydrolysis of aluminum ions or of carbonate ions. A solution of Na_2CO_3 hydrolyzes and forms a relatively high concentration of HCO_3^- and OH^- ions.

$$CO_3^{2-} + H_2O \rightleftharpoons$$
$$HCO_3^-(aq) + OH^-(aq) \quad \text{Eq. 2}$$

The second step which proceeds only slightly is

$$HCO_3^-(aq) + H_2O \rightleftharpoons$$
$$H_2CO_3 + OH^-(aq) \quad \text{Eq. 3}$$
$$\Updownarrow$$
$$H_2O \quad + CO_2(g)$$

The reaction between aluminum ions and water produces H_3O^+ ions and $Al(OH)^{2+}$ in the first step of hydrolysis.

$$Al(H_2O)_6^{3+} + HOH \rightleftharpoons$$
$$Al(H_2O)_5(OH)^{2+}(aq) + H_3O^+ \quad \text{Eq. 4}$$

Normally this is as far as the hydrolysis proceeds, but two more steps are possible. The last one is

$$Al(H_2O)_4(OH)_2^+ + H_2O \rightleftharpoons$$
$$Al(H_2O)_3(OH)_3 + H_3O^+ \quad \text{Eq. 5}$$

When the aluminum and carbonate solutions are mixed, the concentration of the hydrogen ions from Equations 4 and 5 and the concentrations of hydroxide ions from Equations 2 and 3 decrease as the ions neutralize each other. This causes Equations 2, 3, 4, and 5 to shift to the right. If the shift is complete, the products are $Al(OH)_3$ solid, H_2O, and CO_2 gas. The final products depend on the concentrations of the original solutions. The overall simplified hydrolysis equation is

$$2Al^{3+}(aq) + 3CO_3^{2-}(aq) + 3H_2O \rightleftharpoons$$
$$2Al(OH)_3(s) + 3CO_2(g)$$

It should be noted that, in some cases, both the cation and the anion of the salt hydrolyze. In this experiment we did not test any salts containing two ions that hydrolyze. We assumed that if a salt solution was neutral, there was no reaction (no hydrolysis). When both the cation and anion of the salt react with water, the condition of the solution depends on the relative degree of reaction of each kind of ions. It is possible for salts of weak acids and weak bases such as ammonium acetate to produce neutral solutions. In other words, a neutral solution does not necessarily mean that no reaction has occurred.

FOLLOW-UP QUESTIONS

1. On the basis of the data in Table I, predict which is the weaker acid, carbonic (H_2CO_3) or acetic ($HC_2H_3O_2$).

2. (a) Write a net ionic equation for the reaction observed in Procedure 6. (b) Label the conjugate acid-base pairs. (c) How would you prepare a solution of hydrofluoric acid (HF)?

3. Write a net ionic equation for the reaction between an ammonium salt and a strong base.

4. The gas evolved when sodium acetate reacted with ammonium chloride may have been difficult to identify by its odor. The reaction produced ammonia and acetic acid, both of which have strong characteristic odors. (a) Write a net ionic equation for this reaction. (b) Label the conjugate acid-base pairs.

5. What information do you need to predict the condition of a solution made by dissolving a salt that contains both a cation and an anion that hydrolyze?

6. H_2S is a weak acid and ammonia is a weak base. Does $(NH_4)_2S$ hydrolyze to a smaller or greater extent than Na_2S? Explain. Check K_a and K_b values and predict the condition of a $(NH_4)_2S$ solution.

7. Boric acid is a much weaker acid than acetic acid. Is a solution of sodium borate more or less basic than a solution of sodium acetate? Explain.

8. Some commercial cleansing powders tested in a previous experiment contained Na_2CO_3 and Na_3PO_4. How is hydrolysis related to their cleansing properties?

9. $Al_2(SO_4)_3$ and $NaHCO_3$ solutions are used in some fire extinguishers to produce CO_2 when mixed. Explain the chemistry involved in the operation of this type of extinguisher.

10. Hydroxides which react (dissolve) in either an acid or base are called amphoteric hydroxides. (a) Name an amphoteric hydroxide which you tested in this experiment. (b) Write ionic equations for the reaction of this hydroxide with HCl. (c) with NaOH (Hint: one product may be written as AlO_2^- or $Al(OH)_4^-$).

11. (a) What odor is characteristic of ammonium salts you observed in Procedure 10? (b) Write Brønsted acid-base equations, using arrows of different lengths to show the reactions which account for the production of this substance. (c) Are the results consistent with the relative basic strengths of the anions involved? Explain.

12. A solution of $(NH_4)_2CO_3$ in alcohol is known as "smelling salts." Based on observations in Procedure 10, explain their effectiveness.

15-3

Equilibrium in Solutions of Weak Acids and Weak Bases—Buffer Solutions

GENERAL DISCUSSION

This experiment is designed to provide evidence that weak acids and bases are equilibrium systems. You will subject these systems to certain stresses and see whether or not you can interpret the observed changes in terms of equilibrium principles. You will then obtain or prepare a buffer solution and compare its action with that of an unbuffered solution when a strong acid and a strong base are added to each.

OBJECTIVES

1. To obtain evidence that weak acids and weak bases are equilibrium systems.
2. To study the common-ion effect as applied to weak acids and bases.
3. To prepare a buffer and demonstrate its action.

MATERIALS

Test tubes and rack, graduated cylinder, acetic acid ($6\,M$), $NaC_2H_3O_2$, $CaCO_3$, methyl orange indicator, ammonium chloride, 6-M HCl, 6-M ammonia, phenolphthalein, ammonium chloride, sodium chloride solution, buffer solution with pH = 7, 0.1-M NaOH, bromcresol green indicator.

PROCEDURE

1. Label three test tubes A, B, and C. Add five ml of 6-M acetic acid to five ml of water in each of the three test tubes. Dissolve approximately 1.5 g of $NaC_2H_3O_2$ in B, and 3 g in C. Shake well.

2. Place three large empty test tubes in the rack and add two grams of powdered $CaCO_3$ to each tube.

3. Pour solution A into one of the test tubes containing $CaCO_3$. Shake and measure the number of seconds required for the foam to reach a height of one in. Record the time in Table I.

4. Repeat the procedure using solutions B and C.

5. Add one ml of 6-M acetic acid and three drops of methyl orange indicator to nine ml of water in each of two test tubes. Record the color in Table II. Refer to the indicator chart in the Appendix and record the approximate pH of the solution.

6. Add two g of sodium acetate to one of the test tubes. Compare the color with the other solution and record any changes.

7. Add one ml of 6-M HCl and three drops of methyl orange to nine ml of water. Record the color. Add two grams of NaCl to the solution and record any color change.

8. Add a drop of 6-M NH_3 solution to 100 ml of water. Shake and pour ten ml of this solution into each of two test tubes. Add a drop of phenolphthalein to each tube and record the color in Table III.

9. Add two g of NH_4Cl to one of the tubes and record any color change.

10. Place five ml of NaCl solution (assume pH = 7) into a small test tube and five ml of a

Table I $CaCO_3(s) + 2H^+ \rightleftharpoons H_2O + CO_2(g) + Ca^{2+}$

Reagent 1	Solution	Solute (Reagent 2)	Time for Foam to Rise
$CaCO_3$	A	$HC_2H_3O_2$	
$CaCO_3$	B	$HC_2H_3O_2$ + 1.5 g $NaC_2H_3O_2$	
$CaCO_3$	C	$HC_2H_3O_2$ + 3 g $NaC_2H_3O_2$	

Table II Common Ion Effect
$HC_2H_3O_2 \rightleftharpoons H^+ + C_2H_3O_2^-$

Solution	Indicator	Color	Approximate pH
$HC_2H_3O_2$			
$HC_2H_3O_2$ with $C_2H_3O_2^-$ as common ion			
HCl			
HCl with Cl$^-$ as a common ion			

buffer with pH 7 in another small test tube. Add two drops of phenolphthalein to each test tube. Record in Table IV the number of drops of 0.1-M NaOH needed to cause a color change in each tube.

11. Measure five ml of sodium chloride solution and five ml of a buffer solution with pH 7 into each of two small test tubes. Add two drops of methyl orange or bromcresol green to each. Record the number of drops of 0.1-M HCl required to produce a color change in each tube.

FOLLOW-UP DISCUSSION

The ionic equation for the reaction between calcium carbonate and acetic acid shows that H_3O^+ ions are reactants. According to the Law of Mass Action the rate of the reaction

$$CaCO_3(s) + 2H_3O^+$$
$$CO_2(g) + 3H_2O + Ca^{2+}(aq)$$

varies with the concentration of the H_3O^+. You observed that the rate of foaming decreased when the acid solutions treated with $NaC_2H_3O_2$ were used. This indicates that the $[H^+]$ in these

Table III Common Ion Effect
$NH_3 + HOH \rightleftharpoons NH_4^+ + OH^-$

Solution	Indicator	Color	Approximate pH
Aqueous NH_3			
Aqueous NH_3 with NH_4^+			

solutions was less than in the untreated one. The decrease in the $[H^+]$ was the result of a shift in the equilibrium

$$HC_2H_3O_2 \rightleftharpoons H^+ + C_2H_3O_2^-$$

brought about by the addition of $NaC_2H_3O_2$ which contains an ion common with the system described by the equation alone.

FOLLOW-UP QUESTIONS

1. Why did solution C listed in Table I result in the slowest reaction? Use Le Châtelier's principle to explain qualitatively the difference between the $[H_3O^+]$ in solution A and solution B. Answer this and, where applicable, all other questions in terms of net-ionic equations and equilibrium shifts.

2. Did the pH go up or down when $NaC_2H_3O_2$ was added to acetic acid? Did the concentration of undissociated $HC_2H_3O_2$ increase or decrease? Did the degree of dissociation increase or decrease? Explain using Le Châtelier's principle.

3. Refer to Table II and indicate whether addition of Cl$^-$ to the HCl solution caused a change in pH. Explain the similarity or difference between this observation and that on the $HC_2H_3O_2$-$NaC_2H_3O_2$ system.

4. Refer to Table III and indicate whether addition of NH_4Cl caused the pH to increase or decrease. Explain your observation.

5. How many drops of acid were required to change the color of the buffered solution listed in Table IV? What fraction of the total volume of buffer did it take to cause a color change? Assume 20 drops per ml. What fraction of the total volume of the unbuffered solution did it take to change its color?

Table IV Buffer Action

Solution	Drops of Base to Give Color Change	Drops of Acid to Give Color Change
Unbuffered NaCL solution, pH7		
Buffered solution with pH 7		

183

15-4

Preparation and Standardization of Acid and Base Solutions

GENERAL DISCUSSION

This experiment is another example of volumetric analysis. In this type of analysis we measure from a buret the volume of a standard solution required to react with a measured amount of an unknown substance. The process is called *titration*. The completion of the reaction is signaled by a chemical indicator which ideally changes color at the stoichiometric point. *The stoichiometric point* is the point at which the unknown has completely reacted with the standard such that the mole ratio of standard to unknown is the same as that given by the coefficients in the balanced equation for the reaction.

The number of moles of standard used to react with a measured quantity of unknown may be calculated from the molar concentration of the solution and the volume. The relationship is

number of moles = molarity × volume (ℓ)

or

number of millimoles = molarity × volume (ml)

The number of moles in the measured amount of unknown may then be calculated from the mole ratio shown by the balanced equation. This was the method used to calculate the percentage of silver in Experiment 3-7.

In this experiment you prepare and standardize a solution of NaOH. Each student or pair of students should prepare a minimum of 500 ml of approximately 0.5-M NaOH solution. The standardized NaOH solution is used to analyze a sample of vinegar in the next experiment, and to standardize a solution of H_2SO_4 if you intend to analyze a sample of household ammonia later. Alternate methods of standardizing the NaOH solution

are provided. Your instructor will designate which method to use.

If instead of, or in addition to, analyzing vinegar for the percentage of acetic acid in the next experiment, you are directed to analyze an antacid tablet or a commercially prepared impure sample of potassium hydrogen phthalate, then it is necessary to prepare 500 ml of approximately 0.1-M NaOH solution. In this case, the preparation and standardization of the solution involve different quantities of reagents but the procedures are the same in both cases.

The first method of standardizing the base involves accurately weighing a sample of a solid primary standard such as potassium hydrogen phthalate ($KHC_8H_4O_4$(KHP)), or oxalic acid dihydrate ($H_2C_2O_4 \cdot 2H_2O$) and then adding from a buret just the right volume of NaOH solution required to react completely with the acid hydrogen in the KHP or in the oxalic acid.

If there are severe time limitations, your instructor may furnish you with a standardized hydrochloric acid solution which has been standardized against a chemical such as sodium tetraborate (using methyl red as indicator). You then need two burets to measure accurately the volume of unstandardized NaOH required to react with an accurately measured volume of the standard HCl. In the event you use the second method it will be necessary to modify Table I to conform to the data you take and the calculations you make.

Your first procedure, however, involves the preparation of an unstandardized NaOH solution with a concentration of approximately 0.5 M and/or perhaps one with a concentration of approximately 0.1 M. Here again there are alternate methods for preparing the unstandardized solution. Your instructor may direct you to weigh out roughly pellets of NaOH and dissolve them in the required volume of distilled water, or he may suggest that you dilute an available concentrated stock solution to the proper concentration by adding distilled water. In some instances you may be furnished with an unstandardized solution with the required concentration.

OBJECTIVES

1. To prepare and standardize a NaOH solution.
2. To prepare and standardize a H_2SO_4 solution.
3. To become acquainted with the techniques and calculations of volumetric analysis involving acid-base reactions.

MATERIALS

Sodium hydroxide (NaOH) pellets or 6-M sodium hydroxide solution, balance, shell or weighing vial, 500-ml flask(s) with rubber stoppers or storage bottle(s), $KHC_8H_4O_4$ or

Table I(a) Standardization of NaOH Solution (Method 2a)

Mass of vial + primary standard	
Mass of vial minus fraction of solid	
Mass of solid primary standard	
Molecular mass of primary standard	
Moles in mass of primary standard used	
Moles of NaOH required to react with primary standard used	
Final reading of base buret	
Initial reading of base buret	
Volume of base used (ml)	
Volume of based used (liters)	
Molality of base	
Average molarity	

Table I(b) Standardization of NaOH Solution (Method 2b)

Final reading of acid buret	
Initial reading of acid buret	
Volume of acid used (ml)	
Molarity of acid (see instructor)	
Millimoles of acid (HCl) used	
Final reading of base buret	
Initial reading of base buret	
Volume of base used	
Millimoles of base	
Molarity of base	
Average molarity	

$H_2C_2O_4 \cdot 2H_2O$, several 125- or 250-ml erlenmeyer flasks, buret(s), wash bottle, phenolphthalein, bromcresol green, graduated cylinder, 6-M H_2SO_4 solution.

Part I · Preparation and Standardization of a NaOH Solution

PROCEDURE

1. Do either 1(a) or 1(b) as directed by your instructor.

(a) Prepare 500 ml of approximately 0.5-M NaOH solution by adding 458 ml of distilled water to 42 ml of 6-M NaOH. Mix thoroughly and store the solution in a large 500-ml flask with a rubber stopper or in a plastic-capped storage bottle. If you wish to prepare a 0.1-M NaOH solution, add about 492 ml of water to 8.4 ml of 6-M NaOH.

(b) Roughly weigh out about 10 g of NaOH pellets on a centigram balance, dissolve in distilled water, pour into container, and add water until the total volume is about 500 ml. Shake well. To prepare 500 ml of 0.1-M NaOH solution, weigh out about 2.0 g of NaOH pellets and dissolve in about 500 ml of distilled water.

2. Do either 2(a) or 2(b) as directed by your instructor.

(a) Place approximately 3 g of solid oxalic acid dihydrate in a shell vial. Weigh the vial and contents to the nearest 0.001 g, or to highest degree of precision permitted by your balance. Record the mass in Table I. If potassium hydrogen phthalate is used, then place about 9 g in the vial. Number consecutively, 3 clean 250- (or 125-) ml erlenmeyer flasks. Roll and tap out one-third of the contents of the vial into flask number 1. Reweigh the vial and contents. Record the mass in Table I. Roll and tap out another one-third of the oxalic acid or potassium hydrogen phthalate into flask number 2. Reweigh vial. Transfer the remaining primary standard into flask number 3 and reweigh the vial. To standardize a 0.1-M NaOH solution, weigh out 1/5 of the masses given above.

(b) Obtain about 150 ml of standardized hydrochloric acid from your instructor. Record its molarity in your data table.

3. Review the material in this manual on the use of burets. Obtain and clean a buret as directed by the instructor. After rinsing the buret at least three times with a few milliliters of base, fill it with the base and record the initial reading to the nearest 0.02 ml. Be sure there are no air bubbles in the tip of the buret.

4. Add 35 to 40 ml of distilled water to the acid in flask number 1 and swirl gently to dissolve the solid. Add 4 drops of phenolphthalein indicator.

5. Allow the NaOH solution to run into the acid solution fairly rapidly but with no spattering. Swirl the flask with a rotary motion to ensure thorough mixing. The rate of flow should be reduced when the pink color starts to persist (after 20 ml). At this point rinse down the sides of the flask with a stream of distilled water from your wash bottle. As the endpoint is approached, the base should be added a drop at a time and the solution thoroughly swirled. It is a good idea to note the buret reading at this time. The end point is the point at which one drop of base yields a pink color which, on swirling, lasts for 20 to 30 seconds or more. Be sure to remove any drop adhering to the buret tip. You should be careful not to go

beyond the endpoint. If you do, the titration is a failure unless a standard acid solution is available for back titration. Record the final reading of the base buret. Repeat the procedure for samples 2 and 3. With a slide rule, determine the numerical ratio of the mass of solid acid used to the volume of base used. If no manipulative error has been made in any of the three determinations, the ratios should be within a few tenths of one percent of each other. If so, calculate the molarity of the base in each case and average the results. If not, use the "best" two out of three runs.

If a standardized HCl solution is available, then titrate from a buret or deliver from a pipet, 25.00 ml or some precisely measured volume into a titration flask. Add several drops of phenolphthalein or bromthymol blue and titrate the base from a buret as directed above. In this titration it is possible to pass the endpoint. Add an additional measured amount of standard acid and then approach the endpoint more precisely. Again, in this case you may check the reproducibility of your titrations by checking the volume ratios of the acid to base.

Table II   Standardization of H_2SO_4 Solution

Final reading of base buret	
Initial reading of base buret	
Volume of base used (ml)	
Molarity of base (see Table Ia or b)	
Final reading of acid buret	
Initial reading of acid buret	
Volume of acid used (ml)	
Moles of base used	
Moles of acid required to react with moles of base used	
Volume of acid used (liters)	
Molarity of acid	
Average molarity of acid	

Part II · Preparation and Standardization of a H₂SO₄ Solution

This is to be done only if an analysis of household ammonia is to be carried out in the next experiment.

1. Prepare a solution of H_2SO_4 which is about 0.25 M by correctly diluting the stock solution (obtain approximate concentration of stock solution from instructor).

2. Titrate or pipet approximately 25 ml (exact final volume must be known) of the acid into an erlenmeyer flask, add 3–4 drops of phenolphthalein or bromthymol blue indicator, and titrate with the standardized NaOH to the endpoint. Record the data and calculate the molarity of the acid.

IMPORTANT: If you use a buret that has a ground-glass plug (stop cock), be sure to rinse it thoroughly (ten times) with water after you have used it. NaOH reacts slightly with ground glass and often causes the plug to "freeze" in place, ruining the apparatus.

FOLLOW-UP DISCUSSION

It was suggested that you use either oxalic acid dihydrate or potassium hydrogen phthalate as a primary standard. Oxalic acid is diprotic acid which dissociates in two steps

$$H_2C_2O_4 \rightleftharpoons H^+ + HC_2O_4^-$$
$$HC_2O_4^- \rightleftharpoons H^+ + C_2O_4^{2-}$$

These equations show that oxalic acid has two acid hydrogen atoms which can react with the base. Thus the equation for the reaction is

$$H_2C_2O_4 + 2OH^- \rightarrow C_2O_4^{2-} + 2H_2O$$

It can be shown that the equilibrium constant for this reaction is rather large so that, for practical purposes, the reaction may be considered complete and quantitative. Because the acid comes in the form of the dihydrate ($H_2C_2O_4 \cdot 2H_2O$) the two water molecules must be included in the molecular mass which is 126.1.

Potassium hydrogen phthalate is an acid salt which reacts with NaOH according to the equation

$$HC_8H_4O_4^- + OH^- \rightarrow C_8H_4O_4^{2-} + H_2O$$

The acid salt is derived from phthalic acid which is, like oxalic acid, a diprotic acid. The above equation shows, however, that only one hydrogen atom in the hydrogen phthalate ion is acid. Potassium hydrogen phthalate is a relatively nonhygroscopic, stable compound with a high molecular mass. It is therefore frequently used as a primary standard.

The structure of potassium hydrogen phthalate is

Notice that only one of the hydrogen atoms is bonded to a highly electronegative atom and is, therefore, the only proton that can be donated to OH^-.

FOLLOW-UP QUESTIONS

1. List the sources of error which might contribute to an inaccurate value for the molarity of the base.

2. A 0.500-M standard solution of NaOH cannot be made up by weighing out solid NaOH and dissolving it in the correct amount of water. Thus NaOH cannot serve as a primary standard. Suggest two reasons for this.

3. Why are NaOH solutions generally not used in burets with glass stop cocks?

4. Why was phenolphthalein suitable as an indicator for this experiment? Can you suggest another indicator that might have been suitable?

5. Suppose that you had prepared a standard solution by dissolving 3.000 g of oxalic acid in 100.0 ml of solution. (a) What would the molarity of the oxalic acid solution be? (b) What would be the molarity of a NaOH solution if 25.00 ml of the base were required to neutralize 30.00 ml of the standard acid solution?

187

15-5

Volumetric Analysis of Commercial Products: Vinegar, Household Ammonia, Antacids, and Impure Potassium Hydrogen Phthalate

GENERAL DISCUSSION

The Food and Drug Administration as well as other agencies and laboratories are constantly testing and analyzing consumer products and samples of unknown composition obtained from many sources. The methods and equipment now used by testing laboratories are, of course, more precise and sophisticated than those available in most school laboratories. Until recently, however, the methods and apparatus you use in this experiment to analyze several consumer products were also used by the majority of analytical laboratories. In some commercial laboratories, they are still used.

In this experiment you will use the solutions standardized in Experiment 15-4 to analyze a number of household products.

In Part I you use your standardized (0.5 M) base to analyze a sample of vinegar. Vinegar is essentially a solution of acetic acid in water. Your analysis enables you to calculate the mass percentage of acetic acid in the vinegar. You may wish to compare your result with the value given on the bottle obtained from the grocer's shelf.

In Part II you use your standardized (0.25 M) sulfuric acid to titrate a sample of household ammonia. Your data enable you to determine the mass percentage of NH_3 in the solution.

Most of you are familiar with the claims made for their product by the manufacturers of antacids. In Part III you analyze an antacid to check the validity of these claims. A more detailed discussion of the claims, problems, and analysis is given in Part III.

The final analysis described in this experiment involves samples of impure potassium hydrogen phthalate (KHP) prepared by the Thorn Smith

Company for student analysis. These samples have been analyzed by professional chemists so the compositions are known to a very high degree of accuracy.

OBJECTIVES

1. To determine the percentage of acetic acid in vinegar.
2. To determine the percentage of NH_3 in household ammonia.
3. To determine the mass of simulated stomach acid neutralized by an antacid tablet.
4. To determine the percentage of potassium hydrogen phthalate in an impure sample.

MATERIALS

150-ml and/or 250-ml erlenmeyer flasks, standardized NaOH about 0.5 M, standardized H_2SO_4 about 0.25 M, standardized NaOH about 0.1 M, bromcresol green, phenolphthalein, burets, 25-ml pipet (optional), balance, graduated cylinder, samples of vinegar, household ammonia, Rolaids® or other antacids, Thorn Smith unknown potassium hydrogen phthalate samples (if available), mortar and pestle.

Part I · Analysis of Vinegar

1. Review the material in this manual on the use of the pipet. Pipet 25.0 ml of white vinegar into a 250-ml flask. Add 3 to 4 drops of phenolphthalein indicator. If pipets are not available, you may dispense the vinegar from burets.
2. Rinse a clean buret with a 10–15 ml portion of your standard base. Drain and refill with your standardized NaOH solution. Record the initial reading in Table I.
3. Add the standardized base from the buret to

Table I   Percentage of HC$_2$H$_3$O$_2$ in Vinegar

	Trial I	Trial II
Final reading of base buret		
Initial reading of base buret		
Volume of base used		
Molarity of base		
Moles of base used (MV)		
Moles of HC$_2$H$_3$O$_2$ in sample		
Molecular mass of HC$_2$H$_3$O$_2$		
Grams of HC$_2$H$_3$O$_2$ in sample		
Volume of vinegar sample		
Density of vinegar		
Mass of vinegar sample		
Percentage by mass of HC$_3$H$_3$O$_2$ in vinegar		
Average percentage		
Percentage on label		
Percent deviation between experimental value and label value		

the flask containing the vinegar. Swirl the flask as you titrate. When the pink color starts to disappear more slowly, start adding the base dropwise. The endpoint of the reaction is that point at which the first trace of faint pink remains for 20–30 seconds after swirling. Record the final liquid level in the base buret.

4. Run a duplicate sample to check your results.

5. Clean the buret as instructed and return it to the stockroom.

6. Make the calculations necessary to complete Table I. Assume that the density of vinegar is 1.00 g/ml.

FOLLOW-UP DISCUSSION

In this part of the experiment your standard base reacted with the acetic acid in vinegar. Vinegar is a solution of acetic acid (solute) in water (solvent) and contains 3 to 6 percent of acetic acid. The Federal statutes require that all vinegar shipped in interstate commerce contain not less than 4 grams of acetic acid per 100 ml of vinegar.

The percent of acetic acid in a sample of vinegar may be calculated using the equation

$$\text{percentage } HC_2H_3O_2 = \frac{\text{mass } HC_2H_3O_2}{\text{mass vinegar}}\,(100)$$

The mass of acetic acid may be determined from the moles of acetic acid in the sample which, in turn, may be calculated from the moles of NaOH used and the mole relationship between the acid and base as shown by the equation for the reaction.

$$HC_2H_3O_2 + OH^- \rightarrow C_2H_3O_2^- + H_2O$$

The moles of NaOH used is equal to the product of the molarity times the volume in liters. That is,

$$\text{moles NaOH} = MV$$

The mass of vinegar is equal to its volume multiplied by its density.

Part II · Analysis of Household Ammonia

1. Use the standardized H$_2$SO$_4$ to titrate a 5–6-ml sample of household ammonia. The ammonia sample may be diluted with 15 to 20 ml of water before titrating. Use bromcresol green or some other indicator which changes color on the acid side (pH 4–5). Record your data in Table II and use it to calculate the percentage of NH$_3$ in the household ammonia. The calculations are similar to those you used to calculate the percentage of acetic acid in the vinegar sample. The instructor will either give you the density of the ammonia solution or ask you to determine it. The density of a 15-M NH$_3$ solution is 0.90 g/ml and that of a 6-M solution is 0.96 g/ml.

FOLLOW-UP DISCUSSION

The moles of H$_2$SO$_4$ used in the titration equals MV. The equation for the reaction between sulfuric acid and ammonia is

$$H_3O^+ + NH_3(aq) \rightarrow NH_4^+(aq) + H_2O$$

Table II   Percentage of NH₃ in Household Ammonia

	Trial I	Trial II	Trial III
Final reading of acid buret			
Initial reading of acid buret			
Volume of acid used			
Molarity of acid			
Moles of acid used			
Moles of NH₃ in sample			
Volume of NH₃ sample			
Density of ammonia solution			
Mass of ammonia solution used			
Percentage by mass of NH₃ in household ammonia			

Because H_2SO_4 is a diprotic acid, it furnishes two moles of H_3O^+ ions per mole of acid. Thus, two moles of NH_3 is required to react with one mole H_2SO_4. The g of NH_3 in the sample can be determined by multiplying the moles of NH_3 times 17 g per mole, and the mass percentage of ammonia can then be calculated by using the expression

$$\%NH_3 = \frac{g\ NH_3}{g\ NH_3\ solution}\ (100)$$

Part III · Analysis of an Antacid Tablet

Most people at one time or another, have suffered from indigestion or heartburn. In many people, these symptoms arise when the pH of the solution in the stomach falls below 3.0. This observation suggests that one way to avoid or overcome these distressing symptoms is to neutralize any excess acid with a nontoxic chemical reagent that maintains the contents of the stomach at a pH above 3.0.

A number of readily available commercial preparations have been designed to fill this need. One of the most familiar is Rolaids® whose manufacturer claims can consume "47 times its own weight in excess stomach acid." Your objective in this part of the experiment is to determine the validity of this claim. You, like the manufacturer, assume that stomach acid is approximately 0.10-M hydrochloric acid. In the stomach, some of the hydrogen (hydronium) ions combine with other species and keep the pH above 3.0. The procedures involve dissolving a weighed Rolaid tablet in an excess of simulated stomach acid (0.10-M HCl) whose volume has been carefully measured. The Rolaid tablet neutralizes a specific amount of the acid. You determine the volume of unneutralized acid by titrating the resulting solution with standardized NaOH solution. This procedure is called *back titration*. The masses of acid and base can be calculated from the given density and the volumes of the solutions used. The mass of acid neutralized by the tablet is the difference between the mass of the original acid and the mass of acid neutralized by the standard base. If the ratio

$$\frac{\text{mass of acid neutralized by the tablet}}{\text{mass of tablet}}$$

is greater than 47, then you assume that the manufacturer's claim is justified.

Obtain or prepare approximately 75 ml of 0.10-M HCl to use as simulated stomach acid for each trial. You may have a quantity of this stan-

190

dardized acid set aside from the last experiment or you may obtain it from a reserve supply in the stockroom. In the event the standardized acid is not available, then you can prepare 500 ml by appropriately diluting the 6-M desk reagent with distilled water and then determining its exact molarity by titrating it with your standardized NaOH using bromphenol blue as an indicator. Titrate to a blue endpoint and then titrate to the same color when you analyze the antacid. Assume that both the standardized HCl and NaOH have a density of 1.0 g/ml. In this part of the experiment your specific objective is to determine the mass of stomach acid (0.10-M HCl) neutralized by an antacid tablet and to compare this mass with the mass of the antacid tablet. The materials needed for this part of the experiment are dilute HCl solution (approximately 0.1-M), dilute NaOH solution (approximately 0.1-M), bromphenol blue, two 50-ml burets, Rolaids®, Tums®, Bisodol®, or other commercial antacid, 250-ml beaker, 250-ml erlenmeyer flask, mortar and pestle, balance, weighing vial. Optional, aspirator, filter flask, Buchner funnel, and filter paper to fit.

PROCEDURE

1. Grind approximately one-half of a Rolaid tablet in a mortar, put all the powdered material in a shell vial, and weigh to the nearest 0.01 g. Transfer the sample to a 250-ml erlenmeyer flask and weigh the vial again. The difference in the two masses is the mass of the antacid tablet used. Add precisely 50.0 ml of the standardized hydrochloric acid, using a buret. Refill the acid buret The solution may contain a small amount of undissolved, unreactive residue but this does not interfere with the analysis. If aspirators and vacuum filtration apparatus are available, they may be used to filter out the residue.

2. Add four or five drops of bromphenol blue indicator and back titrate the excess acid with the standard NaOH solution to a blue endpoint. If you suspect that you have passed the endpoint, then add a measured amount of standard acid and again titrate with the standard base. Record the final volumes of acid and base used.

Table III Analysis of a Rolaids® Tablet

Mass of vial + crushed Rolaid tablet	
Mass of vial after removing approximately one-half of the powder	
Mass of Rolaid used	
Final reading of HCl buret	
Initial reading of HCl buret	
Volume of HCl added to Rolaid	
Molarity of HCl solution	
Mass of HCl solution added (density = 1.0 g/ml)	
Final reading of base buret	
Initial reading of base buret	
Volume of NaOH to neutralize excess HCl	
Molarity of NaOH used to back titrate excess acid	
Millimoles of NaOH to titrate excess HCl	
Millimoles of excess HCl	
Molarity of HCl	
Volume of excess HCl neutralized by NaOH	
Mass of excess HCl (density = 1.0 g/ml) neutralized by NaOH	
Mass of acid neutralized by Rolaid	
Ratio of $\dfrac{\text{mass of acid neutralized by Rolaids}}{\text{mass of Rolaids used}}$	

3. Make the calculations necessary to complete Table III. If time permits, you may wish to analyze other antacids.

FOLLOW-UP DISCUSSION

Analytical procedures used by the Warner-Lambert Pharmaceutical Company are much more sophisticated and precise than the ones used by students in a school laboratory. The company has conducted tests using human gastric juice as well as 0.10-M hydrochloric acid. In these tests, the acid is added under controlled conditions to the tablet until the pH of the solution drops to 3.0. The results of their tests show that the company's claim is justified.

The success of a titration analysis using a visual indicator depends in part on recognizing the endpoint. For a feasible titration, the addition of one drop of standard solution near the endpoint should produce a sharp change in the color of the solution being titrated. In other words there should be a large change in pH with a small change in volume. That is, the ratio

$$\frac{\Delta \, pH}{\Delta V}$$

should be large. When, however, a solution is buffered, the pH changes very slowly and thus an indicator color change will be gradual so that no sharp endpoint is recognizable. Because Rolaids contain a buffering material, they cannot be titrated directly using a visual indicator. Thus, the obvious solution is to use an indirect approach that enables us to titrate a strong acid with a strong base. This involves reacting the Rolaid with a measured amount of excess acid and then titrating the excess acid with a standard base. In this experiment you found that bromphenol blue (color transition range of 3.0–4.6) was yellow in excess acid indicating that the solution pH was less than 3.0. At the endpoint, one drop of base caused a color change that indicated the pH increased to a value above 3.0. The change is not as sharp as that observed when you standardized your HCl solution with NaOH. In the standardization titration the endpoint solution contains only Na^+ and Cl^- ions and these ions do not affect the pH of the solution significantly.

FOLLOW-UP QUESTIONS

1. (a) Refer to the label on the Rolaids bottle and determine the qualitative composition of a Rolaid tablet. (b) Which of the substances react with the hydrochloric acid? (c) Account for the "burping" that sometimes results from ingestion of these tablets.

2. If your class analyzed other antacids, compare the neutralizing ability of those analyzed and indicate which is the best buy. (Consider cost.)

Part IV · The Percentage of Pure Potassium Hydrogen Phthalate (KHP) in an Impure Sample

If commercially prepared unknown mixtures such as those obtainable from the Thorn Smith Company are available, analyze a sample for the percentge of KHP. If you intend to make 3 trials, then place about 3 g of the unknown in a shell vial and weigh each sample into an erlenmeyer flask by difference. Each sample should weigh about one g. Record the mass in Table IV. Dissolve each sample with about 30 ml of distilled water, add three or four drops of phenolphthalein and titrate with your standard NaOH solution which should be approximately 0.1 M. It is not necessary that every bit of your unknown dissolve in the water. It will dissolve completely as you titrate. Make the calculations needed to complete Table IV and report the results of your analysis as indicated by your instructor. See Experiment 15-4 for a brief discussion of the reaction and reactants.

Table IV   Analysis of an Impure Sample of KHP

Mass of vial + original sample			
Mass of vial − sample			
Mass of sample			
Final reading of base buret			
Initial reading of base buret			
Volume of base used			
Molarity of base			
Millimoles of base used			
Millimoles of KHP in sample			
Milligrams of KHP in sample			
Mass (g) of KHP in sample			
Percentage of KHP in sample			

15-6
Dissociation Constant for Acetic Acid

GENERAL DISCUSSION

The behavior of acetic acid which you investigated and observed in Experiment 15-3 suggests that acetic acid is incompletely dissociated and exists in equilibrium with the hydrogen and acetate ions. The equilibrium existing between the molecules and the ions may be expressed

$$H_2O + HC_2H_3O_2 \rightleftharpoons H_3O^+ + C_2H_3O_2^- \quad Eq. 1$$

Application of the Law of Mass Action principles to this reaction gives the dissociation constant, K_a, for the acid

$$K_a = \frac{[H_3O^+][C_2H_3O_2^-]}{[HC_2H_3O_2]} \quad Eq. 2$$

In this experiment you prepare an acetic acid solution in which the ratio

$$\frac{[C_2H_3O_2^-]}{[HC_2H_3O_2]}$$

is known. You measure the pH of the solution and calculate the $[H_3O^+]$ from the pH. By substituting the above ratio and the (H_3O^+) in Equation 2 you can calculate a value for K_a. If time permits, you can prepare a solution with a

$$\frac{[C_2H_3O_2^-]}{[HC_2H_3O_2]}$$

ratio of 3 to 1 and measure its pH. At constant temperature the K_a calculated using this ratio and pH should be the same as before.

By measuring the pH of the original solution, you then can find the extent to which the acetic acid dissociates. The equation for the percentage dissociation is

% dissociation

$$= \frac{\text{moles of } HC_2H_3O_2 \text{ dissociated per } \ell}{\text{original molar concentration}} (100)$$

Inspection of Equation 1 reveals that one mole of H_3O^+ ions is formed for each mole of $HC_2H_3O_2$ that dissociates. Thus, the percentage dissociation may be expressed as

% dissociation

$$= \frac{[H_3O^+]}{\text{original } HC_2H_3O_2 \text{ concentration}} (100)$$

In Experiment 15-3, you found qualitatively that addition of sodium acetate to acetic acid increased the pH of the solution and decreased the percentage of dissociation. In Part II of this experiment you will determine quantitatively the effect on pH and percent dissociation of adding sodium acetate to the acetic acid solution by comparing the pH of the acetic acid before and after addition of the salt.

OBJECTIVES

1. To determine the dissociation constant for acetic acid.
2. To determine quantitatively the effect on the pH and percent dissociation of an acetic acid solution caused by the addition of sodium acetate.

MATERIALS

$NaC_2H_3O_2 \cdot 3H_2O$ or anhydrous $NaC_2H_3O_2$, 0.2-M $HC_2H_3O_2$, 0.2-M NaOH, graduated cylinder, assorted indicator solutions, and/or a pH meter if available, standard buffer solutions, burets, 250-ml erlenmeyer flasks, 150-ml beaker.

PROCEDURE

Part I · Dissociation Constant for Acetic Acid

1. Prepare a solution containing equal concentrations of $HC_2H_3O_2$ and $C_2H_3O_2^-$. This may be done by titrating 25.0 ml of 0.2-M $HC_2H_3O_2$ to

the stoichiometric point with an approximately 0.2-M solution of NaOH, and then adding exactly one-half the volume of base used in the titration to *another* 25.0-ml sample of the 0.2-M acid. Use phenolphthalein as indicator.

2. If a pH meter is unavailable, determine the pH of the half-neutralized acid solution by testing small portions of it with various indicators. Refer to the indicator range and color chart in the Appendix to help decide which indicators to use and to help you identify the pH. For example, suppose phenol red turns orange in your sample. The chart shows that phenol red is colored red at a pH greater than 8.0 and yellow at a pH less than 6.4. It is orange in a solution whose pH is between 6.4 and 8.2. You could narrow down the range by next trying an indicator such as cresol red which turns yellow at a pH of 7.0. If cresol red turns yellow, then you have identified the pH as being between 6.4 and 7.0. If they are available, standard buffer solutions may be used for comparison with the unknown. You should try to estimate the pH to the nearest 0.1 unit. A small difference in the pH value has a relatively large

effect on the value obtained for K_a. Record your data in Tables I and IA.

3. If the school has a pH meter, the instructor will show you how to determine the pH of your solution with this instrument or perhaps have an assistant determine the pH for you.

4. Prepare a solution containing acetate ions and acetic acid in a molar concentration ratio of

$$\frac{3 \text{ moles acetate ions}}{1 \text{ mole acetic acid}}$$

This may be done by adding ¾ the volume of 0.2-M NaOH used in the original titration to a fresh 25 ml portion of the 0.2-M acetic acid.

5. Determine the pH of the solution as before and record the data in Tables II and IIA.

Table I   pH of $HC_2H_3O_2$-$NaC_2H_3O_2$ Solution

Name of Indicator	Color	Conclusion (pH range)

Table IA   Dissociation Constant for Acetic Acid

pH of solution (Indicators)	
pH of solution (pH meter)	
Hydrogen-ion concentration (M)	
Ratio of $C_2H_3O_2^-$/$HC_2H_3O_2$	
Experimental K_a at _____ °C	

Table II   pH of $HC_2H_3O_2$-$NaC_2H_3O_2$ Solution

Name of Indicator	Color	Conclusion (pH range)

Table IIA   Dissociation Constant for Acetic Acid

pH of solution (Indicators)	
pH of solution (pH meter)	
Hydrogen-ion concentration (M)	
Ratio of $C_2H_3O_2^-$/$HC_2H_3O_2$	
Experimental K_a at _____ °C	

Part II · Percentage Dissociation of Acetic Acid

6. Determine the pH of the 0.2-M acetic acid solution using either indicators or a pH meter as directed in Part I. Record pH in Tables III and IIIA.

7. Dissolve 0.66 g of $NaC_2H_3O_2 \cdot 3H_2O$ *or*

Table III   pH of 0.2-*M* HC₂H₃O₂

Name of Indicator	Color	Conclusion (pH range)

Table IIIA   Percentage Dissociation of 0.2-*M* HC₂H₃O₂

pH of 0.2-M HC$_2$H$_3$O$_2$ (Indicators)	
pH of 0.2-M HC$_2$H$_3$O$_2$ (pH meter)	
Hydrogen-ion concentration (M)	
% Dissociation of 0.2-M HC$_2$H$_3$O$_2$	

Table IV   pH of Solution 0.2-M in HC₂H₃O₂ and 0.2-*M* in C₂H₃O₂

Name of Indicator	Color	Conclusion (pH range)

Table IVA   % Dissociation of 0.2-*M* HC₂H₃O₂ in 0.2-*M* C₂H₃O₂⁻ solution

pH of solution (Indicators)	
pH of solution (pH meter)	
[H$_3$O$^+$] of solution	
% Dissociation of HC$_2$H$_3$O$_2$ in 0.2-M C$_2$H$_3$O$_2^-$	
% Dissociation of 0.2-M HC$_2$H$_3$O$_2$ (Table IIIA)	

Table V   pH of Solution 0.2 *M* in HC₂H₃O₂ and 0.6 *M* in C₂H₃O₂⁻

Name of Indicator	Color	Conclusion (pH range)

Table VA   % Dissociation of 0.2-*M* HC₂H₃O₂ in 0.6-*M* C₂H₃O₂⁻ Solution

pH of solution (Indicators)	
pH of solution (pH meter)	
[H$_3$O$^+$] of solution	
% Dissociation of 0.2-M HC$_2$H$_3$O$_2$ in 0.6-M C$_2$H$_3$O$_2^-$	
% Dissociation of 0.2-M HC$_2$H$_3$O$_2$	

0.40 g of anhydrous NaC$_2$H$_3$O$_2$ in 25 ml of 0.2-M HC$_2$H$_3$O$_2$ and determine the pH of the solution as directed in Procedures 2 and/or 3. Record data in Tables IV and IVA.

8. Dissolve 2.0 g of NaC$_2$H$_3$O$_2$ · 3H$_2$O *or* 1.2 g of anhydrous NaC$_2$H$_3$O$_2$ in 25 ml of 0.2-M HC$_2$H$_3$O$_2$ and determine the pH of the solution as before. Record data in Tables V and VA.

9. Make the calculations needed to complete Tables IVA and VA.

FOLLOW-UP DISCUSSION

Although the order of magnitude of your experimentally determined K_a is probably correct, the answer itself may differ by 100% from the correct value. That is, an answer of 3.6×10^{-5} differs by 100% from the correct answer of 1.8×10^{-5}, but is still of the correct magnitude (10^{-5}). The lack of precision in our measurement of pH and concentrations is a major factor responsible for the inaccuracy of the experimental value.

Another reason for the inaccuracy is that our measurements were based on molar concentrations and did not take into account the interionic attraction which exists in solutions of relatively high ionic concentration. This interionic attraction hinders the movement of the ions so that they are less "active." This causes their effective concentration (called their activity) to be less than the measured molar concentrations. In precise measurements, activities rather than molar concentrations are used. Molar concentrations may be converted to activities by multiplying them by an experimentally determined factor known as the activity coefficient. This factor corrects for the effect of interionic attraction and other factors in the equilibrium involved. It is important that you recognize the existence of this factor, but not important that we make use of it here.

In this experiment you first prepared a solution having equal concentrations of acetic acid and sodium acetate. When these are equal, the dissociation constant

$$K_a = \frac{[H_3O^+] [C_2H_3O_2^-]}{HC_2H_3O_2}$$

becomes

$$K_a = [H_3O^+]$$

By measuring the pH of the solution and converting it to $[H_3O^+]$, you thereby obtained a measure of K_a. The equation for the neutralization of $HC_2H_3O_2$ by NaOH is

$$HC_2H_3O_2 + OH^- \rightleftharpoons C_2H_3O_2^- + H_2O$$

The one-to-one mole ratio indicates that when the acid is one-half neutralized, there are equimolar quantities of $HC_2H_3O_2$ and $C_2H_3O_2^-$. For example, if 5 millimoles of NaOH is required to neutralize 5 millimoles of $HC_2H_3O_2$ completely, then when 2.5 millimoles of base have been added, there are 2.5 millimoles of $HC_2H_3O_2$ and 2.5 millimoles of $C_2H_3O_2^-$ in solution. At this point

$$K_a = [H_3O^+]$$

When 4 millimoles of base have been added, there are 4 millimoles of $C_2H_3O_2^-$ ions and 1 millimole of $HC_2H_3O_2$ in solution. At this point,

$$K_a = [H_3O^+] \frac{4}{1}$$

Thus, the constancy of K_a may be checked by

measuring the pH of solutions with various salt/acid ratios. Other simplifying assumptions have been made in order to avoid cumbersome mathematical operations. These are mentioned in your text and need not concern us here.

The conversion of pH to hydrogen-ion concentration may require the use of logarithms. A sample calculation is present below.

Example

1. Calculate the $[H_3O^+]$ concentration of an acetic acid solution that has a pH of 2.8.

Solution

The pH is defined: $pH = -\log[H_3O^+]$
Substituting 2.8 for pH, we obtain

$$2.8 = -\log[H_3O^+] \text{ or } \log[H_3O^+] = -2.8$$

Solving for $[H_3O^+]$, we obtain

$$[H_3O^+] = 10^{-2.8} = 10^{+0.2} \times 10^{-0.3}$$

The number which is equal to ten raised to the 0.2 power is called the antilog of 0.2. The antilog may be obtained by locating in a table of logs the number whose logarithm is 0.2. This number is 1.6. The hydrogen-ion concentration therefore is $1.6 \times 10^{-3} M$.

FOLLOW-UP QUESTIONS

1 Explain why the neutralization of an acid with a standard base by the process of titration does not provide a measure of the hydronium ion concentration of the original acid solution.

2. What are the advantages of determining the $[H_3O^+]$ concentration of an HCl solution with a pH meter instead of by titration?

3. Calculate the molar concentration of the $NaC_2H_3O_2$ in the solution which you reported in Table IVA.

4. Calculate the molar concentration of the $NaC_2H_3O_2$ in the solution which you reported in Table VA.

5. In which of the three solutions which you investigated in Part II was the percent dissociation of $HC_2H_3O_2$ the greatest? Explain.

6. A 0.05-M solution of a weak acid HX gives an orange color with methyl orange. What is the approximate value for the K_a?

15-7

Equivalent Mass and Normality-Determination of the Equivalent Mass of an Unknown Acid

GENERAL DISCUSSION

To simplify the calculations of analytical chemistry, a chemical unit known as the *gram-equivalent mass* (the equivalent) and a concentration unit known as *normality* (N) are often used. The calculations involving these concepts are parallel to those involving the chemical unit of gram-molecular mass (the mole) and the concentration unit of molarity.

The principle underlying the use of equivalent mass is that *chemical substances react in a mass ratio equal to the ratio of their equivalent masses.* That is, one equivalent mass of a reactant reacts exactly with one equivalent mass of a second reactant; thus, the equivalent mass of substances is a convenient unit for comparing their reacting masses. For example, one mole (40.0 g) of NaOH reacts completely with one-half mole (98.0 g) of H_2SO_4 but one equivalent (40.0 g) of NaOH reacts completely with one-equivalent (49.0) grams of H_2SO_4. We may define the gram-equivalent mass (one equivalent) of an acid or base *that mass which donates or accepts 1 mole of protons (H^+).* One mole of an acid or base does, respectively, furnish or react with one or more moles of protons (H^+). The gram equivalent mass of an acid or base therefore is related by a small whole number to the gram molecular mass. This relationship may be expressed as

gram-equivalent mass (gem) =

$$\frac{\text{gram-molecular mass}}{\text{no. of moles of } H^+ \text{ furnished or accepted per mole of substance}} \quad \text{Eq. 1}$$

Thus an equivalent mass of a substance is either equal to or a fraction of the molecular mass. In other words, there is an integral number of equiv-

alents in one mole of a substance. The number of moles of H^+ donated or accepted is often referred to as *equivalents/mole*. Thus, in the complete neutralization of H_2SO_4, there are 2 equivalents/mole of acid, and the equivalent mass of the acid is

$$\frac{98 \text{ g}}{\text{mole}} \times \frac{1 \text{ mole}}{2 \text{ equiv}} = 49 \frac{\text{g}}{\text{equiv}}$$

Similarly, we can say that a mole of the base $Ca(OH)_2$ has a mass of 74 g and donates two moles of OH^-. Two moles of hydroxide ions are equivalent in combining power to (can accept) two moles of H^+ ions. This means there are two equiv/mole of $Ca(OH)_2$ and that the gram-equivalent mass is

$$\frac{74 \text{ g}}{1 \text{ mole}} \times \frac{1 \text{ mole}}{2 \text{ equiv}} = 37 \text{ g/equiv}$$

Thus 37 g (one equiv) of $Ca(OH)_2$ reacts completely with 49 g (one equiv) of H_2SO_4.

The concentration unit of normality is based on the concept of equivalent mass and enables us to make a direct comparison of the quantities of solute in any solution. For example, one liter of 1-N NaOH neutralizes completely one liter of 1-N H_2SO_4 because the base solution contains one equiv of OH^- ions and the acid solution contains one equiv of H^+ ions; however, one liter of 1-M NaOH does not react completely with one liter of 1-M H_2SO_4. We may define normality as

$$\text{normality} = N = \frac{\text{number of equivalents of solute}}{\text{number of liters of solution}}$$

$$\text{Eq. 2}$$

Note the parallelism to the definition of molarity. The only difference is that equivalents of solute have been substituted for moles of solute. A little reflection will show that molarity and normality are related by the same whole number that relates equivalent mass to molecular mass. For example, the normality of an 0.5-M H_2SO_4 solution is 1.0. That is,

$$\frac{0.5 \text{ moles}}{\ell} \times \frac{2 \text{ equiv}}{\text{mole}} = 1.0 \frac{\text{equiv}}{\text{liter}} = 1.0 \, N$$

By rearranging Equation 2 we can obtain an expression that enables us to calculate the number of equivalents in a given volume of any solution whose normality is known. This expression is

$$\text{equiv} = NV \qquad \text{Eq. 3}$$

If V is expressed in milliliters and N is in units of meq/ml, then the product has units of milliequivalents (meq). If the mass of a pure substance is known, then the equivalents in a given mass can be calculated by using the expression

$$\text{equivalents} = \frac{\text{mass}}{\text{equivalent mass}} \qquad \text{Eq. 4}$$

If mass is expressed in milligrams, then Equation 4 yields milliequivalents.

In this experiment, you determine the equivalent mass of an unknown acid by reacting a measured mass of the acid with a NaOH solution whose normality is known. The equivalent mass of an acid or a substance can be used to help identify the substance. Alternatively, if the instructor chooses, you may determine the normality of a base solution by titrating it into a solution containing a precisely measured mass of an acid whose equivalent mass can be calculated from its known molecular mass. In either case, the relationship between the acid and base at the stoichiometric point is

$$\text{equivalents of acid} = \text{equivalents of base}$$

Because the acid is precisely weighed and the volume of base is precisely measured, we can use Equations 3 and 4 to obtain an expression containing the measurable quantities.

$$\underset{\text{(equiv acid)}}{\frac{\text{mass}}{\text{equivalent mass}}} = \underset{\text{(equiv base)}}{NV} \qquad \text{Eq. 5}$$

OBJECTIVES

1. To become acquainted with the concepts of gram-equivalent mass, equivalents, and normality.

2. To determine the equivalent mass of an unknown acid or the normality of an unknown base solution.

MATERIALS

Balance, burets, weighing bottle or vial, 250-ml erlenmeyer flask, beakers, standardized NaOH solution about 0.2-N or an unstandardized NaOH solution to be used as unknown, several solid organic acids to be used as unknowns or oxalic acid to be used as a primary standard, phenolphthalein.

PROCEDURE (unknown acid)

1. Obtain a sample of an unknown acid from your instructor and put it in a weighing (shell) vial. Weigh two samples by difference (to the greatest precision permitted by your balance) into separate 125- or 250-ml erlenmeyer flasks. Your instructor will suggest an approximate mass for the samples. Record the data in Table I.

2. Dissolve the samples in about 50 ml of distilled water, warming slightly if needed to get the samples into solution. Some organic acids may resist dissolution in water but will dissolve as the base is added during the analysis.

Table I Equivalent Mass of an Unknown Acid

	Trial I	Trial II
Mass of vial + sample of acid		
Mass of vial − sample		
Mass of sample taken for analysis		
Final reading of base buret		
Initial reading of base buret		
Volume of base used		
Normality of base (ask instructor)		
Equivalents of base used		
Equivalents of acid used		
Equivalent mass of acid		

3. Add four to five drops of phenolphthalein and titrate the acid solution with standardized NaOH which is about 0.2 N. If necessary, review the material in the front of this manual on the care and use of a buret. Standardized NaOH may be prepared by following the directions given in Experiment 15-4.

4. Complete the calculations called for in Table I and report the results of your analysis as directed by your instructor.

FOLLOW-UP DISCUSSION

Many analyses involve only volume measurements, one of which is the volume of a standard solution (known concentration). The calculations associated with these analyses are greatly simplified by use of a titration equation developed by applying the equivalency principle. In this application, Equation 3 applies to both reactants so that the equality

equivalents of acid = equivalents of base

may be represented by

$$N_A V_A = N_B V_B \qquad \text{Eq. 6}$$

Note that the volumes on both sides of the equation must be expressed in the same units. Equation 6 can be used to *determine the concentration of an unknown solution when the concentration of the standard solution and the volumes of both acid and base are known.* Note that the equation

$$M_A V_A = M_B V_B$$

cannot be used for a titration reaction unless it is known for sure that the acid and base react in a one-to-one mole ratio.

In the analysis of an unknown we can equate the milliequivalents (or equivalents) of standard reagent used to the milliequivalents of the species being titrated. That is,

$$(NV)_{\text{standard}} = \text{meq of unknown}$$

milligrams of unknown =
$$\text{meq} \times \text{meq mass} = (NV)_s (\text{meq mass})_u$$

Substituting these factors in the analysis equation

percentage of unknown =
$$\frac{\text{milligrams of unknown}}{\text{milligrams of sample}} (100)$$

we obtain

percentage unknown =
$$\frac{(NV)_{\text{standard}} (\text{meq mass})_{\text{unknown}}}{\text{milligrams of sample}} (100)$$
$$\text{Eq. 7}$$

The data obtained from titrations may be substituted into Equation 7. Care should be taken that all the units agree. When volume is expressed in milliliters, then mass is expressed in milligrams. The Follow-up Problems are designed to provide an opportunity for you to use the equations and principles developed in this experiment.

It should be noted that there are pitfalls which must be avoided when using the concepts of gram-equivalent mass and normality. These arise primarily because some substances may have several gram-equivalent masses and a given solution may have several normalities depending on the reaction in which they are involved. For example, if two substances can react and form more than one product, then the equivalent mass depends on the extent of the reaction. Consider the reaction between sulfuric acid and sodium hydroxide which, under certain conditions of temperature and concentration, may react and form sodium bisulfate rather than sodium sulfate.

$$H_2SO_4 + NaOH \rightarrow NaHSO_4 + H_2O$$

In this reaction, a mole of H_2SO_4 donates only one mole of H^+. By definition, the equivalent mass of H_2SO_4 in this reaction is

$$\frac{98 \text{ g}}{1 \text{ mole}} \times \frac{1 \text{ mole}}{1 \text{ equiv}} = 98 \text{ g/equiv}$$

A 1-N solution made up for this reaction has 98 g of solute. If the same solution were used for a reaction in which both protons were donated, then the equivalent mass of H_2SO_4 would be 49 and the solution would have to be labeled 2 N.

Admittedly, there are logical arguments against the use of gram-equivalent mass and normality in chemical calculations. Gram-molecular mass and molarity are more fundamental. Furthermore, any analytical problem that can be solved using equivalent mass and normality can also be solved using molecular mass and molarity. Our justification in briefly developing this concept lies in its widespread use in analytical chemistry.

FOLLOW-UP QUESTIONS

1. Calculate (a) the number of equivalents in 10.0 g of $CaCO_3$ if converted to CO_2 and H_2O in a reaction with H_3O^+; (b) the eq/mole if the above were converted to HCO_3^-; (c) the number of milliequivalents in 3.7 mg of $Ca(OH)_2$; (d) the number of milliequivalents of HNO_3 (m.m. 63) that completely neutralizes 3.7 mg of $Ca(OH)_2$; (e) the number of milligrams of HNO_3 required to neutralize 3.7 mg of $Ca(OH)_2$.

2. Complete this table. Assume complete neutralization of each species.

3. What is the normality of a $Ca(OH)_2$ solution, 125 ml of which contains 74.0 mg of solute?

4. If 30.0 ml of an unstandardized NaOH solution is required to react completely with 1.00 g of $KHC_8H_4O_4$, what is the normality of the base solution?

5. An impure sample of $KHC_8H_4O_4$ weighing 2.67 g is titrated with 28.4 ml of 0.160-N NaOH. What is the mass percentage of $KHC_8H_4O_4$ in the sample?

Ans. 34.9 percent.

6. Hydrochloric acid solutions may be standardized by reaction with pure sodium carbonate (m.m. 106). What is the normality of an HCl solution if 40.0 ml is required to react with 0.445 g Na_2CO_3?

Ans. 0.210 N

7. If an impure sample of Na_2CO_3 weighing 0.804 g requires 24.2 ml of the acid standardized in Problem 6, what is the percentage of Na_2CO_3 in the impure sample?

Ans. 33.5 percent.

8. What volume of 0.100-M H_2SO_4 is needed to neutralize 25.0 ml of a 0.30-N solution of the organic base, piperidine $(C_5H_{11}N)$?

	HCl	H_2SO_4	H_3PO_4	Na_2CO_3	$Ca(OH)_2$	$Ba(OH)_2$
Molecular mass						
Equivalent mass						
Grams per liter of 0.200-M solution						
Grams per liter of 0.200-N solution						
Milligrams per ml of 0.200-N solution						
Milliequivalents in 50.0 ml of 0.200-N solution						
Milligrams in 50.0 ml of 0.200-N solution						
Normality of 0.200-M solution						

15-8
Instrumental Analysis Using a pH Meter

GENERAL DISCUSSION

You have performed several titrations in this course using indicators to determine the equivalence point of a reaction. The indicator endpoints which you observed were relatively sharp so that it was not difficult to locate them. Throughout the course you have observed many reactions which result in highly colored or turbid solutions. The use of a chemical indicator in a quantitative analysis involving such solutions is often not feasible or possible.

Instrumental analysis is especially useful in these situations. When we titrate an acid with a base, it is obvious that the hydrogen ion concentration or the pH is constantly changing. By use of dissociation constants and concentrations, it is possible to calculate the pH at any point during the titration. In other words, pH values of the solution which correspond to measured volumes of the standard may be calculated. By plotting the volume of standard solution used against the corresponding pH values, we obtain a titration curve. Titration curves contain a vertical or almost vertical section which represents a rapid change of pH with a small volume of standard. The midpoint of the vertical section (point of inflection) of this titration curve is the equivalence point for the reaction.

The pH of reacting solutions may be determined experimentally by using a pH meter on which pH values may be read directly. In practice, the electrodes of the pH meter are immersed in a known volume of a solution of unknown concentration and the initial pH is read. The known volume must often be diluted to give enough solution to cover the electrodes. The standard solution is then added from a buret and is constantly stirred. If available, magnetic stirrers should be used. pH readings are taken and re-corded after every 5 to 10 ml additions of the standard until the pH starts to rise rapidly. Close to the endpoint, readings are taken every 0.50 ml or less. The volumes are then plotted against pH values and the titration curve is drawn. The volume corresponding to the midpoint or point of inflection of the vertical section of the curve is the volume required to reach the equivalence point. See color plate II, between pages 274 and 275 of *Foundations of Chemistry, 2 ed.*

In this experiment the instructor or a student titrates a strong acid with a strong base, a weak acid with a strong base, and a polyprotic acid with a strong base. Titration curves for the three reactions are plotted, compared, and interpreted.

OBJECTIVES

1. To determine the concentration of unknown acid solutions, and examine the neutralization of a polyprotic acid with a standard base by means of a pH meter.
2. To plot and interpret titration curves.

MATERIALS

pH meter, 0.1-M HCl, 250-ml beaker, 0.100-M NaOH, magnetic stirrer, graduated cylinder, 0.1-M $HC_2H_3O_2$, 0.1-M H_3PO_4.

PROCEDURE

Part I · Titration of a Strong Acid with a Strong Base

1. Prepare and standardize the pH meter by following the directions given in the accompanying manual or as directed by the instructor.

2. Place the electrodes of the pH meter into 30.00 ml of approximately 0.1-M HCl solution in a 250-ml beaker. Add enough distilled water so

Table I

NaOH against HCl	
ml base	pH

Table II

NaOH against HC$_2$H$_3$O$_2$	
ml base	pH

Table III

NaOH against H$_3$PO$_4$	
ml base	pH

Table IA

NaOH against HCl	
Normality of base	
Volume of base to inflection point	
Volume of HCl	
Molarity of HCl	

Table IIA

NaOH against HC$_2$H$_3$O$_2$	
Normality of base	
Volume of base to inflection point	
Volume of HC$_2$H$_3$O$_2$	
Molarity of HC$_2$H$_3$O$_2$	

Table IIIA

NaOH against H$_3$PO$_4$	
Normality of base	
Volume to first inflection point	
Volume to 2nd inflection point	
Volume of base from 1st to 2nd inflection point	

that the bulb of the electrodes is covered and proper contact with the solution is made. Record the pH of the acid in Table I.

3. Fill a buret with a standardized NaOH solution which is approximately 0.100 M. This solution may be prepared by diluting a 50% NaOH solution with density 1.53 g/ml to approximately an 0.1-M concentration. The 0.1-M solution may be standardized by titrating it against commercially available standardized 0.100-M HCl, or against oxalic acid or potassium biphthalate.

4. Titrate the acid solution with standardized NaOH. It is essential that the solution be stirred

constantly. Use a magnetic stirrer if available; if not, use care not to bump the electrode.

5. Record the pH of the solution after every 5 to 10 ml of base at the start of the titration, and every 0.10 ml as soon as you observe a rapid rise in pH. After the equivalence point has been passed, continue to add base until 50.00 ml has been added. Rinse the electrodes as directed. Record data in Tables I and IA.

6. Plot the volume of NaOH used along the horizontal axis of a piece of graph paper and the pH along the vertical axis.

7. Draw a titration curve and determine the

volume which corresponds to the midpoint of the vertical portion.

8. Use this volume of standard base, the volume of unknown acid used, the concentration of the standard base, and the equations for the reaction to determine the molarity of the unknown acid.

Part II · Titration of a Weak Acid with a Strong Base

9. Repeat the procedure used in Part I, only this time place the electrodes of the pH meter in 30.00 ml of approximately 0.1-M acetic acid. Record the pH and other data in Tables II and IIA.

Part III · Titration of a Polyprotic Acid with a Strong Base

10. Repeat Part I using approximately 0.1-M H_3PO_4. The 0.1-M H_3PO_4 can be made by measuring from a buret 6.71 ml of the commercially available 85% H_3PO_4 into a 1-liter container and diluting to one liter with distilled water. Record the initial pH and other data in Tables III and IIIA. Bromcresol green and phenolphthalein may be added as indicators.

11. Titrate as before and plot a titration curve.

12. Determine the volume (ml) of base required to reach each of the two inflection points, and the volume required to go from one inflection point to the other.

FOLLOW-UP DISCUSSION

The shapes of titration curves may be interpreted in terms of the composition of the solution at various stages in the titration. The concentrations and behavior of the predominant species at these points determine the shape of the curve. For example, in the titration of a strong acid with a strong base, the product consists of ions (of a salt) which do not form a buffer solution with the remaining unneutralized acid. Hence, there is no buffering action. Near the endpoint, therefore, the pH increases very rapidly with a small change in the volume of added base. This sudden rise in pH makes the inflection point easy to locate and results in a sharp endpoint. The pH of the solution at any point in the titration is determined by the concentration of the excess acid (H^+ ion) or the excess base (OH^- ion).

When solutions of weak acids are titrated with a strong base, the salt of a weak acid is formed. That is, one or more ions formed as a product will be the anions of the weak acid. The combination of a weak Brønsted acid and its salt (conjugate base) forms a buffer solution. The buffer solution resists a change in pH so that the pH does not change as rapidly near the endpoint as with a strong acid. The inflection in this titration curve is not as easy to locate and the endpoint is not as sharp. In general, for a titration to be feasible using chemical indicators, 0.1 ml of base should cause a minimum change of 1 pH unit at the endpoint. Otherwise, one color of the indicator will fade into another so gradually that the endpoint cannot be recognized. The endpoints of these titrations can often be recognized using instrumental methods.

The two relatively steep portions of the H_3PO_4 curve can be attributed to the stepwise dissociation of H_3PO_4. Removal of the first hydrogen is represented by the equation

$$H_3PO_4 \rightleftharpoons H^+ + H_2PO_4^-$$

$$K_1 = 7.5 \times 10^{-3}$$

The equation for the second step is

$$H_2PO_4^- \rightleftharpoons H^+ + HPO_4^{2-}$$

$$K_2 = 6.2 \times 10^{-8}$$

and the equation for the third step is

$$HPO_4^{-2} \rightleftharpoons H^+ + PO_4^{3-}$$

$$K_3 = 4.8 \times 10^{-13}$$

The dissociation constant (and dissociation) for Step 3 is so small that no equivalence point is detectable. Therefore, only two practical endpoints can be used when titrating H_3PO_4 with a strong base.

FOLLOW-UP QUESTIONS

1. Which indicators could be used for the titration carried out in Part I? Which could be used in Part II?

2. The neutral point is pH 7. How do you account for the difference between the neutral point and the equivalence point in the second titration?

3. Would you expect the neutral point and the equivalence point to coincide in Part I? Explain.

4. Which titration would you consider to be more accurate, NaOH against HCl, or NaOH against $HC_2H_3O_2$? Why?

5. Why would you expect the pH to change more slowly in the case of the NaOH against $HC_2H_3O_2$ titration? Hint: Is there a buffer region in the curve?

6. Does there appear to be a relationship between the steepness of the curve and the degree of dissociation (or dissociation constant) of the acid? On the basis of the limited evidence, what is the relationship?

7. What indicators might be used to locate the first and second equivalence points in the titration of H_3PO_4 with NaOH? Explain. What are the pH ranges of the indicators you selected?

8. What is the relationship between the number of ml of NaOH needed to reach the first and second equivalence points in the H_3PO_4 titration?

9. Name the salts formed at the first and second equivalence points in the H_3PO_4-NaOH titration? Write the ionic equations.

10. What is the reason that we observe two plateaus in the H_3PO_4 analysis? What is the general composition of the solution on these plateaus? These are called buffer regions.

16-1

Reactions Involving Formation of Weakly Dissociated Molecular Species

GENERAL DISCUSSION

A weakly dissociated molecular species is a substance which in aqueous solution, exists largely as molecules. A strong electrolyte in aqueous solution exists largely in ionic (dissociated) form. When the ions of a strong electrolyte can react and form a covalently bonded weak electrolyte, they generally do so.

In this experiment you carry on a series of reactions which result in the formation of covalently bonded molecules which, in aqueous solution, are weak electrolytes. We shall assume that it is the formation of the strong covalent bonds in the weak electrolyte molecules that causes these reactions to take place. In most of the reactions which you investigate, the presence of a weak electrolyte is indicated by the evolution of a gas. The gas can be identified by its properties and related to the dissociation of a specific electrolyte.

OBJECTIVES

1. To observe the formation and properties of some weak electrolytes and become acquainted with their formulas.

2. To write ionic equations for reactions involving the formation of weak electrolytes.

MATERIALS

Ammonium chloride, test tube, 6-M sodium hydroxide, burner, litmus paper, sodium acetate, 6-M sulfuric acid, sodium bisulfite, 6-M hydrochloric acid, red flower, sodium carbonate, 6-M nitric acid, iron(II) sulfide, lead acetate, filter paper, phenolphthalein, graduated cylinder.

PROCEDURE

1. Place a small quantity (one g) of NH_4Cl in a test tube and add just enough water to dissolve the crystals. Add two or three ml of 6-M NaOH to the saturated NH_4Cl solution. Waft the gas toward your nose. If no odor is detected, gently warm the solution and again attempt to identify the odor of the gas. Hold a piece of moistened red

Table I   Results

Procedure No.	Reactant 1	Reactant 2	Observation	Formula of Gas and/or Weak Electrolyte
1				
2				
3				
4				
5				
6				

litmus paper in the gas. Record your observations in the table.

2. Place a small quantity (one to two g) of $NaC_2H_3O_2$ in a test tube and add just enough water to dissolve the crystals. Add two or three ml of 6-M H_2SO_4 to the $NaC_2H_3O_2$ solution. Attempt to identify the gas which is evolved. If no odor is detected, warm gently.

3. Place a small quantity (one g) of sodium bisulfite, $NaHSO_3$, in a test tube and add two or three ml of 6-M HCl. Cautiously note the odor of the gas which is evolved. Hold a piece of moistened blue litmus paper in the gas and record your observations. If a red flower petal (geranium, carnation, petunia) is available, moisten and place it in the upper part of the test tube where the gas can interact with it. Record your observations.

4. Place a small quantity (one g) of Na_2CO_3 in a test tube and add just enough water to dissolve the crystals. Add two or three ml of 6-M HNO_3 to the test tube. Test the gas with a flaming splint to see whether the gas is combustible. Thrust a glowing splint into the test tube to determine whether or not the gas supports combustion.

5. The instructor will set up a gas generator

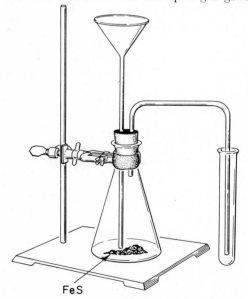

FeS

Fig. 16-1 Hydrogen sulfide generator.

under the hood (Fig. 16-1). The solid substance in the generator is iron(II) sulfide. Pour two or three ml of 6-M HCl into the thistle tube of the generator. Hold a piece of absorbent paper moistened with lead acetate in the stream of gas from the delivery tube. **Caution:** *do not attempt to smell the gas,* but merely describe its odor which will be apparent. *This gas is* **extremely** *toxic and should not be inhaled.*

6. Put five ml of 3-M HCl in an evaporating dish and add two drops of phenolphthalein indicator. Add four ml of 3-M NaOH. Continue to add 3-M NaOH dropwise with stirring until one drop of NaOH imparts a faint pink color to the solution. This color may disappear after 20 to 30 seconds. Cover the dish with a watch glass and gently evaporate the solution to dryness. When cool, taste one drop of the residue and then rinse your mouth. Record your observations in the table.

FOLLOW-UP DISCUSSION

In each of the procedures in this experiment one of the products was a weak electrolyte. You were probably able to identify most of the products by their properties. Knowing the names of the reactants and products should enable you to write equations for the reactions. Frequently, it is not convenient to carry on a reaction for the purpose of identifying a product. Therefore, it is important to know the names and formulas of common weak electrolytes which can form as a result of the interaction between ions.

Some weak acids and weak bases have such unstable structures that they have not been isolated as a pure substance. Three of these are ammonium hydroxide (NH_4OH ammonia-water), sulfurous acid (H_2SO_3) and carbonic acid. (H_2CO_3). When these substances are formed as the products of reactions, they should be shown in their more stable forms indicated below.

Unstable form	Stable form
H_2CO_3	$H_2O + CO_2$
H_2SO_3	$H_2O + SO_2$
NH_4OH	$NH_3 + H_2O$

For clarity, we have omitted some secondary reactions that occur when ions are put in solution.

In the next experiment we shall find that many precipitates (slightly soluble substances) can be dissolved by adding a chemical agent which reacts with the precipitate and forms a slightly dissociated species.

FOLLOW-UP QUESTIONS

1. Write net ionic equations for each of the reactions in this experiment.

2. What test could you use to identify hydrogen sulfide gas?

3. Which gas observed in this experiment may act as a bleach?

4. What gas observed in this experiment is odorless and neither burns nor supports combustion?

5. What gas observed in this experiment turns moistened red litmus to a blue color?

6. State a general method for preparing a weak acid.

16-2

Formation and Dissolution of Precipitates

GENERAL DISCUSSION

This experiment is designed to acquaint you with solubility equilibria. You first carry out a series of precipitation reactions and then dissolve the precipitates by applying equilibrium principles. Application of the Law of Chemical Equilibrium to saturated solutions of slightly soluble compounds gives rise to the solubility product constant, K_{sp}. The K_{sp} for the general reaction

$$AB(s) \rightleftharpoons A^{n+} + B^{n-} \qquad \text{Eq. 1}$$

has the form

$$K_{sp} = [A^{n+}][B^{n-}] \qquad \text{Eq. 2}$$

As long as the ion product $[A^{n+}][B^{n-}]$ is greater than the K_{sp}, a precipitate forms. Any reagent which reduces either $[A^{n+}]$ or $[B^{n-}]$ so that the product of their molar concentrations is $< K_{sp}$, shifts the equilibrium to the right and causes the solid AB to dissolve and establish a new equilibrium condition.

A graphical approach to this equilibrium situation for a cation and an anion of equal but opposite charge is illustrated in Fig. 16-4 on p. 516 of the *Foundations of Chemistry* text, 2nd Edition.

Some of the methods used to reduce the concentration of the ions in equilibrium with the precipitate are (1) addition of more solvent, (2) addition of a substance that forms a slightly dissociated molecule, (3) addition of a substance that forms a metal-centered complex ion, and (4) addition of a substance that forms a less soluble product. In order to explain your observations in this experiment, you must decide whether the ions furnished by the added reagent react with either of the ions furnished by (in equilibrium with) the precipitate.

OBJECTIVES

1. To prepare and dissolve a number of precipitates.

2. To explain the dissolution of precipitates in terms of equilibrium principles.

MATERIALS

Test tubes and rack, graduated cylinder, 0.1-M $AgNO_3$, 1-M $NaC_2H_3O_2$ dilute (6-M) nitric acid, 6-M NH_3, 0.2-M Na_2CO_3, 0.2-M $CaCl_2$, 0.1-M KI, 0.1-M K_2CrO_4, 0.1-M $BaCl_2$, 6-M HCl, 0.2-M $MgCl_2$, 0.1-M $CuSO_4$, 0.1-M NaOH, solid NH_4Cl, 0.1-M $Al(NO_3)_3$.

PROCEDURE

1. Place one ml of 0.1-M $AgNO_3$ in each of four test tubes. Add one ml of 1-M $NaC_2H_3O_2$ solution to each test tube. Allow to stand and record your observations in Table I.

2. To one of the test tubes containing a silver acetate precipitate, add 20 ml of water. Record your observations in Table II.

3. To the second test tube containing silver acetate precipitate, add 6-M nitric acid dropwise until a change is observed. Record in Table II.

4. To the third test tube containing silver acetate precipitate, add an excess of 6-M ammonia dropwise until a change is noted. Record in Table II.

5. To the fourth test tube containing silver acetate precipitate, add 2 ml of 0.1-M KI solution. Record observations in Table II.

6. Place 1 ml of 0.1-M K_2CrO_4 in a test tube and add 1 ml of 0.1-M $BaCl_2$. Record observations in Table I.

7. Add 6-M HNO_3 dropwise until a change is noted. Record observations in Table II.

8. Place one ml of 0.2-M sodium carbonate solution in a test tube and add 1 ml of 0.2-M calcium chloride solution. Record observations in Table I.

9. Slowly add 6-M hydrochloric acid and record observations in Table II.

Table I Formation of Precipitates

Procedure Number	Reagent 1	Reagent 2	Characteristics of Precipitate	Formula of Precipitate
1				
6				
8				
10				
12				

Table II Dissolution of Precipitates

Procedure Number	Equilibrium Number (below)	Formula of Precipitate	Species Added	Observation	Equilibrium Shifts (L or R)	Ions whose Concentration Decreases	Method Used to Dissolve Precipitate	New Species Formed
2	1	$AgC_2H_3O_2$	H_2O					
3	1	$AgC_2H_3O_2$	H^+, NO_3^-					$HC_2H_3O_2$
4	1	$AgC_2H_3O_2$	NH_3, NH_4^+, OH^-					$Ag(NH_3)_2^+$
5	1	$AgC_2H_3O_2$	K^+, I^-					$AgI(s)$
7	2	$BaCrO_4$	H^+, NO_3^-					$(HCrO_4^-)$ $Cr_2O_7^{2-}$
9	3	$CaCO_3$	H^+, Cl^-					(H_2CO_3) $H_2O + CO_2$
11	4	$Mg(OH)_2$	NH_4^+, Cl^-					$NH_3 + H_2O$
13	5	$Cu(OH)_2$	NH_3, NH_4^+, OH^-					$Cu(NH_3)_4^{2+}$

Equilibrium 1: $AgC_2H_3O_2(s) \rightleftharpoons Ag^+ + C_2H_3O_2^-$ Equilibrium 4: $Mg(OH)_2(s) \rightleftharpoons Mg^{2+} + 2OH^-$

Equilibrium 2: $BaCrO_4(s) \rightleftharpoons Ba^{2+} + CrO_4^{2-}$ Equilibrium 5: $Cu(OH)_2(s) \rightleftharpoons Cu^{2+} + 2OH^-$

Equilibrium 3: $CaCO_3(s) \rightleftharpoons Ca^{2+} + CO_3^{2-}$

10. Place two ml of 0.2-M $MgCl_2$ in a test tube and add just enough 6-M ammonia to produce a change. Record the change in Table I.

11. Slowly add solid NH_4Cl to the result of Procedure 10 and agitate until another change is noted. Record observations in Table II.

12. Place one ml of 0.1-M $CuSO_4$ in a test tube and add 0.1-M NaOH dropwise until a permanent change occurs. Record in Table I.

13. Add excess 6-M ammonia until another permanent change is noted. Record in Table II.

14. Place one ml of 0.1-M $Cr(NO_3)_3$ in each of three test tubes and add 6-M NH_3 dropwise to each test tube until a precipitate is observed.

15. To the first test tube add an additional five ml of 6-M NH_3 and record your observations.

16. To the second test tube add five ml of 6-M NaOH and record your observations.

Table III Amphoteric Hydroxides

Procedure	Observation	Net Ionic Equation
14		
15		
16		
17		
18a		
18b		
18c		
18d		

17. To the third test tube add five ml of 6-M HCl and record your observations.

18. Repeat Procedures 14–17 using one ml of 0.1-M Al(NO$_3$)$_3$ instead of 0.1-M Cr(NO$_3$)$_3$.

19. Complete Table III by writing net ionic equations for each of the reactions observed. With excess OH$^-$, chromium(III) hydroxide and aluminum(III) hydroxide form, respectively, tetrahydroxochromate(III) and tetrahydroxoaluminate(III) ions.

FURTHER EXPERIMENTATION

Determine the K_{sp} for AgC$_2$H$_3$O$_2$. This determination requires that you devise a method for determining either the [Ag$^+$] or [C$_2$H$_3$O$_2^-$] in a saturated solution of AgC$_2$H$_3$O$_2$. There are several methods you might use to determine the [Ag$^+$]. For example, you could titrate the Ag$^+$ ions with a standard SCN$^-$-ion solution as you did in Experiment 3-7. Another method would be to determine the mass of silver in a given volume of solution by precipitating it with a piece of copper as you did in Experiment 3-4.

FOLLOW-UP DISCUSSION

The dissolution of precipitates which you observed in this experiment are illustrations of Le Châtelier's principle. Your observations should enable you to tell whether the equilibria represented by the equations below Table II shifted to the right or to the left when a stress was imposed on the system by adding a reagent which reacted with a species in the reaction system. If the original precipitate disappears, then the shift is to the right.

In most instances, this observation indicates that the added reagent reacts with an ion present in the original solubility-equilibrium system forming a new species which is more stable. This new, more stable, species has less tendency to dissociate; thus the concentration of one of the ions originally present in the solution is lowered, resulting in an ion-concentration product which is less than the K_{sp}. (See graphical analysis of this situation in the General Discussion section.)

For example, you found that silver acetate dissolves when relatively large amounts of 6-M NH$_3$ are added. As indicated in Table II, Ag(NH$_3$)$_2$$^+$ is the species formed. This compound is very stable and establishes this, rather complete, equilibrium system

$$Ag^+(aq) + 2NH_3(aq) \rightleftharpoons Ag(NH_3)_2{}^+$$

The near-completeness of the forward reaction lowers [Ag$^+$](aq) to a value such that the [Ag$^+$][CH$_3$COO$^-$] product is $< K_{sp}$. The solid silver acetate now dissolves at a rate faster than that of its formation, and if sufficient NH$_3$ has been added, a balance of rates does not occur before the supply of silver acetate is exhausted.

FOLLOW-UP QUESTIONS

1. Write net ionic equations for each of the reactions recorded in Table I.

2. Complete Table II. Indicate the method used to dissolve the precipitates as (1) formation of a weakly ionized molecular species or a gas, (2) formation of a metal-centered complex ion or a new polyatomic ion, (3) formation of a less soluble substance, or (4) dilution.

3. Explain using equilibrium equations and Le Châtelier's principle why copper(II) hydroxide dissolved in an excess of 6-M NH$_3$. What is the name of the metal-centered complex ion formed in this reaction?

4. Explain why Cr(OH)$_3$(s) and Al(OH)$_3$(s) dissolve in excess 6-M NaOH but not in excess 6-M NH$_3$.

16-3

Progressive Precipitation: The Formation and Dissolution of Slightly Soluble Silver Compounds

GENERAL DISCUSSION

You have discovered in earlier experiments that slightly soluble compounds can be dissolved by adding a reagent that forms a metal-centered complex ion with the metallic ion in the solubility equilibrium. You also found that it is possible to convert one slightly soluble compound into another one provided the second compound is less soluble than the first. The latter reaction is termed a metathesis reaction. It is sometimes used in anion analysis to put the anions in a soluble form. For example, SO_4^{2-} ions in slightly soluble $CaSO_4$ may be put into solution by treating a saturated solution of $CaSO_4$ with a fairly concentrated solution of Na_2CO_3. The equation for the reaction is

$$CaSO_4(s) + CO_3^{2-}(aq) \rightarrow CaCO_3(s) + SO_4^{2-}(aq) \quad Eq. 1$$

The K_{sp} values for the two slightly soluble compounds can be used to determine the equilibrium constant for Equation 1. The relatively large value of the constant for Equation 1 indicates that the equilibrium is displaced to the right and that the conversion is fairly complete. That is, one mole of CO_3^{2-} converts almost one mole of $CaSO_4$ into $CaCO_3$.

The relative solubility of a precipitate and the extent to which it dissolves in the presence of excess complexing agent can be estimated by using solubility products and instability constants. The reactions of Ag^+ ions can be used to illustrate the relative tendencies of precipitates and complex ions, respectively, to dissolve and dissociate in aqueous solution.

In this experiment you carry out a series of reactions involving Ag^+ ions in which the product of each reaction is converted into a different product by the addition of either a precipitating or complexing agent which disturbs the original equilibrium, and establishes a new equilibrium system. In each instance you can recognize the appearance of a new product and equilibrium system by the disappearance of a precipitate or by the formation of one with a different color. Use your observations to help write net ionic equations for each reaction.

OBJECTIVES

1. To become acquainted with the behavior of Ag^+ ions in the presence of various precipitating and complexing agents.

2. To become acquainted with the names, formulas, and characteristics of chemical species containing silver ions.

3. To become acquainted with the principles which underlie the formation and dissolution of precipitates.

MATERIALS

Test tubes and test tube rack, stopper to fit test tubes, dropper bottles containing 1-M $AgNO_3$, 1-M Na_2SO_4, 0.1-M $K_2Cr_2O_7$, 1-M $NaCl$, 6-M $NH_3(aq)$, 0.1-M KBr, 0.1-M $Na_2S_2O_3$, 0.1-M KI, 0.1-M $(NH_4)_2S$ or Na_2S.

PROCEDURE

1. To five ml of 1-M Na_2SO_4, add ten drops of 1-M $AgNO_3$. Stopper the tube, shake thoroughly and allow to stand for several minutes. Record your observations and the formula of the product in the last column of Table I. Note that the product from this procedure is a reactant in Procedure 2.

2. To the mixture from procedure 1 add one drop of 0.1-M $K_2Cr_2O_7$. Stopper the tube and

211

Table I   Reactions of Precipitates and Complex Ions Containing Ag⁺ Ions

Proc. No.	Formula of Reactant 1 in Test Tube	Formula of Precipitating or Complexing Agent Added	Observation	Name of Precipitate or of Complex Ion
1	Ag^+	SO_4^{2-}		
2		$Cr_2O_7^{2-}$		
3		Cl^-		
4		NH_3		
5		Br^-		
6		$S_2O_3^{2-}$		
7		I^-		
8		S^{2-}		
9		I^-		

shake thoroughly. Record your observations and the formula of the slightly soluble product. This product is a reactant in Procedure 3.

3. To the mixture from Procedure 2, add five drops of 1-M NaCl. Stopper and thoroughly shake the tube. Record your observations and the formula of the new product.

4. To the mixture from Procedure 3, add 6-M NH₃(aq) dropwise until a permanent change is noted (about 50 drops). Shake well and record your observations. The formula of the product may be found in the table in the Follow-up Discussion. This product is a reactant in Procedure 5. The naming of complex ions is discussed in Section 19-10 of *Foundations of Chemistry,* 2 ed.

5. To the solution from Procedure 4, add 1-M KBr until a permanent change is noted (about 5 drops). Stopper the test tube, shake well and record your observations and the formula of the product.

6. To the mixture from Procedure 5 add 0.1-M Na₂S₂O₃ until a permanent change is noted (about 20 drops). Shake well and record your observations in Table I. The formula of the product may be found in the Follow-up Discussion section.

7. To the solution from Procedure 6, add three drops of 0.1-M KI. Stopper the tube, shake well and record your observations.

8. To the mixture from Procedure 7, add 100 drops (approximately five ml) of 0.1-M Na₂S. Stopper the test tube, shake well and record your observations.

9. Add five ml of 0.1-M KI to the mixture from Procedure 8 and note whether the precipitate undergoes any changes. Record any observations.

FOLLOW-UP DISCUSSION

The solubility products and instability constants related to the preceding reactions are itemized in the table. They can be used to help write net ionic equations for the reactions and to explain why certain reactions occurred and others did not. Note that the reagents added in Table I were 0.1 M except for NH₃(aq) which was 6 M.

It should be noted that a large number of salts first precipitate and then redissolve in an excess of precipitating agent. For example, hydrochloric acid is often used to precipitate Ag⁺ ions as AgCl. A large excess of Cl⁻ ions, however, causes the AgCl to redissolve because of the formation of the dicholoroargentate ion ($AgCl_2^-$).

$$AgCl(s) + Cl^- = AgCl_2^-$$

In quantitative gravimetric analysis procedures such as those you carried out in Experiment 3-6, notice that the concentration and quantity of precipitating agents must be carefully controlled. A partial list of slightly soluble salts that redissolve in an excess of precipitating agent is provided.

$$AgCl(s) \quad + Cl^- \quad = AgCl_2^-$$
$$AgBr(s) \quad + Br^- \quad = AgBr_2^-$$
$$AgI(s) \quad + I^- \quad = AgI_2^-$$
$$AgCN(s) \quad + CN^- \quad = Ag(CN)_2^-$$
$$PbI_2(s) \quad + 2I^- \quad = PbI_4^{2-}$$
$$HgI_2(s) \quad + 2I^- \quad = HgI_4^{2-}$$
$$Hg(SCN)_2 + 2SCN^- = Hg(SCN)_4^{2-}$$

The equilibrium constants in the above Table can be used to predict the relative completeness of the reactions you carried out. For example, in the second procedure you added a solution of $K_2Cr_2O_7$ to a saturated solution of Ag_2SO_4 and observed that colorless Ag_2SO_4 was converted into red $Ag_2Cr_2O_7$. You could have predicted that this conversion would be rather complete by calculating and interpreting the equilibrium constant for the equation

$$Ag_2SO_4(s) + Cr_2O_7^{2-}$$
$$= Ag_2Cr_2O_7(s) + SO_4^{2-} \quad \text{Eq. 2}$$

Equation (2) can be obtained by adding equations (3) and (4)

$$Ag_2SO_4(s) = 2Ag^+ + SO_4^{2-}$$
$$K_{sp} = 1.2 \times 10^{-5} \quad \text{Eq. 3}$$

$$2Ag^+ + Cr_2O_7^{2-} = Ag_2Cr_2O_7(s)$$

$$K = \frac{1}{K_{sp}} = \frac{1}{2 \times 10^{-7}} = 5 \times 10^6 \quad \text{Eq. 4}$$

The equilibrium constant for the net reaction (2) obtained by adding equations (3) and (4) is equal to the product of the equilibrium constants for equations (3) and (4). Thus, K for reaction (2) is

$$1.2 \times 10^{-5} \times 5 \times 10^6 = 6 \times 10 = 60$$

The magnitude of this constant suggests that the equilibrium represented by Equation 2 is displaced to the right and that a significant quantity of Ag_2SO_4 will be converted into $Ag_2Cr_2O_7$. Also keep in mind that concentration effects are important in forcing an equilibrium in a given direction and that rate effects must often be considered in explaining observations. That is, the rate at which equilibrium is achieved varies from system to system.

Precipitate or Complex Ion	Equilibrium Equation	Solubility Product or Instability Constant
Ag_2SO_4	$Ag_2SO_4(s) \rightleftharpoons 2Ag^+ + SO_4^{2-}$	1.2×10^{-5}
$Ag_2Cr_2O_7$	$Ag_2Cr_2O_7(s) \rightleftharpoons 2Ag^+ + Cr_2O_7^{2-}$	2×10^{-7}
$AgCl$	$AgCl(s) \rightleftharpoons Ag^+ + Cl^-$	1.8×10^{-10}
$Ag(NH_3)_2^+$	$Ag(NH_3)_2^+ \rightleftharpoons Ag^+ + 2NH_3$	6×10^{-8}
$AgBr$	$AgBr(s) \rightleftharpoons Ag^+ + Br^-$	4.8×10^{-13}
$Ag(S_2O_3)_2^{3-}$	$Ag(S_2O_3)_2^{3-} \rightleftharpoons Ag^+ + 2S_2O_3^{2-}$	3.5×10^{-14}
AgI	$AgI(s) \rightleftharpoons Ag^+ + I^-$	8.3×10^{-17}
$Ag(CN)_2^-$	$Ag(CN)_2^- \rightleftharpoons Ag^+ + 2CN^-$	1.6×10^{-22}
Ag_2S	$Ag_2S(s) \rightleftharpoons 2Ag^+ + S^{2-}$	1.6×10^{-49}

FOLLOW-UP QUESTIONS

1. Write net ionic equations for the reactions which you observed in each of the procedures. Refer to the Follow-up Discussion for the formulas of metal-centered complex ions and precipitates. Identify each equation with a procedure number.

2. How did you decide what the formula of the precipitate was when you added $AgNO_3$ to Na_2SO_4?

3. Which is the most insoluble silver compound in this experiment? What is the experimental basis of your choice? Explain how your answer is consistent with the K_{sp} values given in the Follow-up Discussion.

4. Which is the most stable complex ion (with respect to its dissociation) that you actually observed in this experiment? What is the experimental basis of your choice?

5. (a) What other complex ion is more stable according to the data given in the Follow-up Discussion? (b) What complexing agent (compound) could have been added to produce this complex ion? (c) For what reason was this compound omitted? (d) According to the data in the Follow-up Discussion, what precipitates could have been readily dissolved by addition of this compound?

(e) Are there any precipitates which you observed that could not be dissolved by this compound? Explain.

6. Explain in general terms why the sequence of reactions you observed in this experiment is successful while the reverse sequence does not occur.

7. In Procedure 9, you discovered that it was not possible to dissolve an appreciable quantity of Ag_2S by adding excess I^- ions. In other words, iodide ions cannot reduce the Ag^+-ion concentration in a saturated Ag_2S solution to a value below its equilibrium value and, therefore, cannot shift the equilibrium.

$$Ag_2S(s) \rightleftharpoons 2Ag^+ + S^{2-}$$

to the right. Suggest another method which might be used to shift the above equilibrium to the right and thus dissolve Ag_2S.

8. Show, using K_{sp} values given in the Follow-up Discussion that the reaction

$$Ag_2S(s) + 2I^- = 2AgI(s) + S^{2-} \qquad Eq.\ 5$$

does not occur to any extent. Hint: Calculate the K for Equation 5 using the K_{sp} values for Ag_2S and AgI.

16-4

Analysis of an Unknown Chloride Using an Adsorption Indicator

GENERAL DISCUSSION

A number of important volumetric analyses are based on ionic reactions that yield precipitates. These are known as volumetric precipitation methods. In Experiment 3-7 an impure silver sample was analyzed by titrating the dissolved silver with a standard thiocyanate solution. In the titration the silver ions reacted with the thiocyanate ions and formed a white precipitate of AgSCN. At the endpoint, the SCN⁻ ions reacted with the iron(III) ions present as an indicator and formed a colored complex ion ($FeSCN^{2+}$).

In this analysis you titrate a standardized silver-ion solution into a solution containing the unknown chloride. The reaction produces a *colloidally dispersed precipitate* of AgCl. At the endpoint an organic dye used as the indicator is *adsorbed* by the precipitate and imparts a characteristic color to the precipitate. Titrations involving *adsorption indicators* are called *Fajan's methods*. The behavior of adsorption indicators is based on the properties of *colloids*. These concepts are discussed in some detail in the Follow-up Discussion section of this experiment.

OBJECTIVES

1. To determine the percentage of chloride in an unknown compound or impure sample.
2. To become acquainted with the concepts and nature of colloids and adsorption phenomena.
3. To become acquainted with the techniques and calculations of volumetric analysis.

MATERIALS

Burets, balance, shell vial or weighing bottle, 125- and/or 250-ml erlenmeyer flasks, wash bottle, standardized $AgNO_3$ (about 0.1 M) or an unstandardized $AgNO_3$ solution and pure NaCl, dichlorofluorescein, dextrin, samples of pure compounds containing chloride ions or commercially prepared samples of unknown chlorides such as those available from the Thorn Smith Company.

PROCEDURE

1. Obtain approximately 100 ml of standardized silver nitrate (about 0.1 M) from your instructor or his assistant. Record its molar concentration to at least three significant figures. This is enough for two trials. If it is necessary to standardize your own solution, then obtain 200 ml of the unstandardized solution from the stock bottle, and standardize following the procedures given below for the analysis. Approximately 0.25 g of pure NaCl per run is required for the standardization.

2. Place your sample in a shell vial and weigh by difference (as precisely as possible) into separate erlenmeyer flasks samples of your unknown having a mass of about 0.25 g or that mass indicated by your instructor. Record data in Table I.

3. Dissolve each sample with 30–40 ml of distilled water. Add about 0.1 g of dextrin and 10 drops of dichlorofluorscein indicator to each flask.

4. Titrate with standardized silver nitrate (about 0.1 M). The white particles of AgCl that are formed by the reaction suddenly change to a definite pink at the endpoint. Record the volume of $AgNO_3$ required to reach the endpoint.

5. Compute the mass percentage of chloride ions in your sample and report it as directed by your instructor. If it was necessary to standardize the silver nitrate, it will be necessary to modify slightly the data in Table I. In this case your first task is to calculate the molarity of the $AgNO_3$ and your second is to analyze the unknown chloride sample.

Table I   Percentage of Chloride Ions in an Unknown Sample

	Trial I	Trial II
Mass of vial + sample (mg)		
Mass of vial − sample (mg)		
Mass of sample (mg)		
Final reading of buret		
Initial reading of buret		
Volume of $AgNO_3$ used (ml)		
Molarity of $AgNO_3$ solution		
Millimoles of Ag^+ used		
Millimoles of Cl^- ions in sample		
Milligrams of Cl^- in sample		
Percentage of Cl^- in sample		

FOLLOW-UP DISCUSSION

Much of your laboratory work has involved so-called true solutions in which the solute particles have molecular dimensions so small that they do not reflect light (approximately 10^{-8} cm). Colloidal dispersions are mixtures containing suspended particles which range in size from 10^1 to 10^3 Å in diameter. The range of colloidal parti-

cles is such that they may not be visible through an ordinary microscope but they are large enough to disperse light. Colloidal particles in the air are responsible for the fact that a beam of a searchlight may be seen in the night sky. When gelatin is added to water, it appears to dissolve slowly. When a beam of light is passed through the mixture, a faint opalescence is observed. This same opalescent appearance of gemstones such as opal is caused by the scattering of light by colloidal particles of one mineral dispersed in another. Likewise the blueness of the sky in the daytime is related to the dispersion of the sunlight by colloidal-sized particles high in the atmosphere. If the concentration of these atmospheric particles is particularly high, then a beautiful sunset may result. Living protoplasm, including the tissues of plants and animals, is essentially colloidal in character. Muscle tissue consists of colloid-like fibers, and skin is a colloidal dispersian of proteins. The size of blood cells is in the colloidal range and the particles contained in most foods may also be classified as colloids. Let us examine some of the characteristics of colloids which are responsible for the observed behavior.

The unique properties of colloidal substances are in large measure attributed to the extremely large surface area presented by the particles. The total surface area of a cube 1 cm on a side is 6 cm², but if this cube were subdivided into cubes

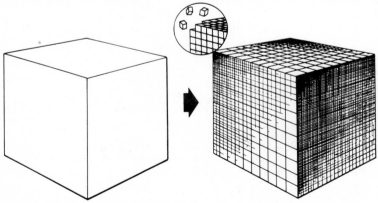

Fig. 16-2   The total surface area of a cube 1 cm on a side is 6 cm². If the original cube is divided into smaller cubes that are 1/1 000 000 cm on a side, the total surface area becomes 6 000 000 cm².

of colloidal magnitude, the total surface area would be well over 10^6 cm^2.

It can be shown that atoms contained in molecules at the surface of solids or liquids tend to attract substances with which they come into contact. This surface attraction, which is characteristic of colloidally dispersed substances, is known as adsorption. The charcoal used in gas masks and in cigarette filters has colloidal dimensions and is an excellent adsorbent, having the ability to adsorb poisonous gases, dyes, and other complex materials. The adsorbing tendency of colloidal particles results from their ability to stay suspended instead of coagulating and settling. Experiments indicate that colloidal particles tend to adsorb ions of one particular charge and thus acquire the same overall charge. The similar charges on the colloidal particles keep them separated in solution because like charges tend to repel each other. Colloidal latex particles of rubber can be "electroplated," producing thin rubber products because the latex particles carry an electric charge. The formation of river deltas can be explained in terms of this same phenomenon. Fine colloidal clay particles in rivers have a tendency to adsorb negative ions, thus, as the river flows into the ocean, the positive ions in the seawater electrically neutralize the colloidal clay particles. The clay particles then coagulate and form the deltas. Because of the absence of ions, deltas are not formed when rivers flow into fresh-water lakes.

The importance and scope of colloid chemistry may be illustrated by pointing out that paints, foods, ceramics, textiles, leather, aerosols, glues, films, soaps, jellies, adhesives, lubricants, sprays, and insecticides are all colloidal in character. The manufacture and processing of all of these materials involve colloid chemistry.

The use of an adsorption indicator requires

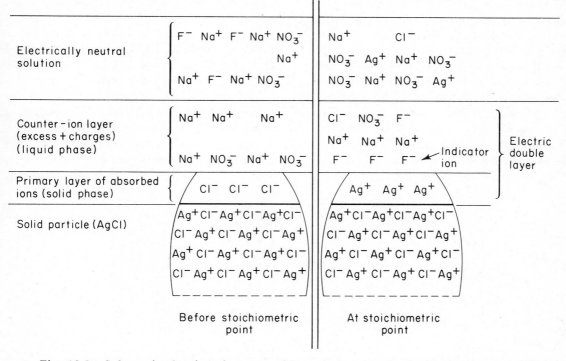

Fig. 16-3 Schematic showing the composition of the electric double layer surrounding the colloidal silver chloride before and at the stoichiometric point in the titration of a chloride solution with a standard silver solution.

that the precipitate be colloidally dispersed so that it presents a large surface area for adsorption. Surface forces of colloidal particles attract and adsorb ions from the surrounding solution. Thus, the surface of colloidal particles is charged either positively or negatively with respect to the solution. The adsorbed ions which are firmly attached to the solid comprise the so-called **primary layer.** The solution adjacent to the particle contains an excess of oppositely charged ions to balance the charge of the adsorbed ions. This excess of specifically charged ions is called the **counterion** or **secondary layer.** The net effect is that colloidal particles are surrounded by an **electric double layer** which tends to repel other colloidal particles and to stabilize the colloid.

In a colloidal system, the ions that are adsorbed as a primary layer are the ions of the colloidal particles which have the greatest concentration in the solution. For example, in the titration of a chloride solution with silver ions, the solution is treated so that colloidal silver chloride is formed. The chloride solution contains a high concentration of Cl^- ions so that these ions are adsorbed by the colloid as a primary layer. The adsorption indicator partially dissociates into hydrogen ions and negative fluoresceinate ions; thus, during the first stages of titration the negative fluoresceinate ions are repelled by the adsorbed chloride layer. At the equivalence point, however, the Cl^- ions have been quantitatively removed from solution and the next drop of silver nitrate provides an excess of Ag^+. At this point, the concentration of Ag^+ ions exceeds that of Cl^- ions; consequently, the colloid now adsorbs Ag^+ as its primary layer. This layer of Ag^+ ions now attracts the negative ions of the dye as a secondary or counter-ion layer. In solution, the negative fluoresceinate ion imparts a yellowish-green color to the solution, but when it is associated with a layer of silver ions, a reddish color is observed.

The use of adsorption indicators is somewhat limited by the relatively few substances which form colloidal precipitates rapidly. In the titration of chloride solutions, a protective colloid such as dextrin is added to help prevent coagulation of the precipitate.

FOLLOW-UP PROBLEMS

1. What is the percentage of Br^- ions in an unknown sample if 30.00 ml of 0.100-M $AgNO_3$ is required to titrate a 0.799-g sample of the unknown?

2. When a large number of samples containing the same component are to be analyzed, it is desirable to adjust the concentration of the standard solution so that the percentage of the component in the sample is equal to the volume of standard solution used in the titration. What must be the molarity of a standard $AgNO_3$ solution if the milliliters used exactly equal the percentage of Cl^- in all samples having a mass of exactly 0.500 g. **Ans.** 0.1410 M

16-5
Qualitative Analysis

GENERAL DISCUSSION

In general, the system of qualitative analysis you will use involves separating groups of positive ions on the basis of the different solubilities of their compounds. The solutions containing groups of ions are then further separated into solutions containing one kind of ion whose presence is confirmed by a specific identification test. The over- all procedure is summarized in the flow chart, Fig. 16-4. You will start with a known solution containing eight cations. These are Ag^+, Pb^{2+}, Hg_2^{2+}, Fe^{3+}, Co^{2+}, Ni^{2+}, Al^{3+}, and NH_4^+ ions.

You first add Cl^- ions and precipitate a group of slightly soluble chlorides. These are $AgCl$, Hg_2Cl_2, and $PbCl_2$. These will be separated from

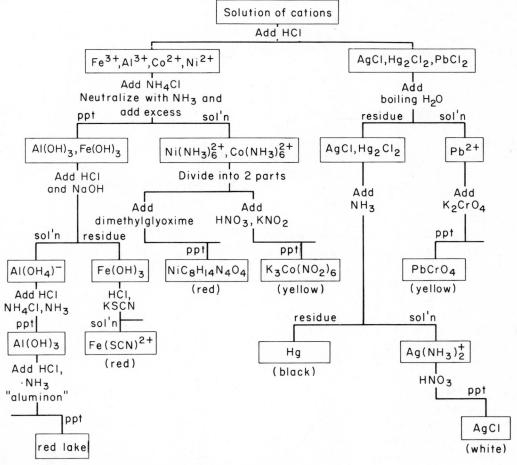

Fig. 16-4   Flow chart for cation qualitative analysis.

the solution and identified on the basis of specific reactions which they undergo. The remaining solution will then be treated with an NH_3 solution. The OH^- ions precipitate a group of slightly soluble hydroxides, while the ions which form complexes with NH_3 remain in solution. The slightly soluble hydroxides are $Fe(OH)_3$ and $Al(OH)_3$. The soluble complex ions are $Ni(NH_3)_6^{3+}$ and $Co(NH_3)_6^{2+}$. Again, specific tests are applied to help identify each ion in the individual groups. You should become acquainted with specific identification or confirmatory tests by observing the reactions of known test solutions of each ion with the reagent(s) which are used to identify it.

There are a number of advantages to using small quantities of reagents and semimicro methods. The quantities of reagents and apparatus described in the semimicro procedures assume that semimicro equipment such as 13×100 mm test tubes and centrifuges are available. If they are not, then it is necessary to use conventional filtering methods described in the macro procedures. Regardless of the method used, all equipment should be scrupulously clean and good laboratory technique employed. Record all observations such as the nature and color of precipitates, and the colors of solutions in Table I.

OBJECTIVES

1. To identify the ions in an unknown solution.
2. To observe the application of equilibrium and other reaction principles.
3. To become acquainted with the chemistry of specific ions and other substances.

MATERIALS

Test tubes (13×100 mm) and test-tube rack if centrifuge is available, funnel and filter paper if macro procedures are to be used, spatula, beaker, burner, ringstand, wire screen, triple-beam balance, regular 6-in. test tubes and rack if macro procedures are to be used, 250-erlenmeyer flask, 6-M HCl, 6-M ammonia(aq), 6-M HNO_3, 6-M NaOH, 6-M NH_4Cl, 0.1-M KSCN, 1-M K_2CrO_4, 6-M KNO_2, aluminon test reagent, dimethylgly-

Table I   Analysis of a Solution Containing Known Cations

Appearance of solution_____

Procedures	Observations	Conclusions

oxime test reagent, borax, litmus paper, test solution containing Ag^+, Hg_2^{2+}, Pb^{2+}, Al^{3+}, Fe^{3+}, Co^{2+}, Ni^{2+}, NH_4^+, unknowns containing three or four of the above ions.

PROCEDURE

A.   Semimicro Procedures

1. Place approximately one ml of the known test solution in a clean 13×100 mm test tube. Add six to eight drops of 6-M HCl. Precipitate is $AgCl$, Hg_2Cl_2, $PbCl_2$. Place test tube in a beaker of cold water for a minute. Stir gently, centrifuge and decant the supernatant liquid into another test tube. Set the solution aside for Procedure 5. Wash the precipitate by adding one ml of cold water containing a drop of HCl. Centrifuge and add the washings to the solution for Procedure 5. Treat the precipitate by Procedure 2.

2. Add two ml of water to the precipitate and place the test tube in a boiling-water bath (100 ml beaker). Stir for a minute and centrifuge for a few seconds. Pour the supernatant liquid into another test tube and immediately add two drops of 1-M K_2CrO_4 solution. Precipitate: $PbCrO_4$ (yellow) confirms lead. Discard. Whenever lead is

present, repeat the procedure two or three times using two more milliliters of water each time to insure that all the $PbCl_2$ has been dissolved. Treat the white residue by Procedure 3.

3. To the white residue from Procedure 2 add one ml of dilute 6-M ammonia-water solution. Black residue: finely divided mercury mixed with $Hg(NH_2)Cl$. Confirms presence of Hg_2^{2+} ions. Centrifuge, then decant the solution into another test tube and discard the residue.

4. Add dilute 6-M HNO_3 to the solution from Procedure 3 until the solution is acid or a permanent white precipitate is formed. Precipitate: $AgCl$(white). Confirms presence of Ag^+ ions.

5. Neutralize the solution from Procedure 1 by adding dilute (6-M) NH_3 solution until the solution is basic; then add one ml in excess. Add one ml of 6-M NH_4Cl. Colored precipitate: $Fe(OH)_3$, $Al(OH)_3$. Centrifuge and separate the solution into another test tube. If the precipitate is light and flocculent, use a medicine dropper to withdraw the solution carefully. Set the solution aside for Procedure 10. Treat the precipitate by Procedure 6.

6. Dissolve the precipitate from Procedure 5 by adding 6-M HCl dropwise. Make basic to litmus with 6-M NaOH. Then add 1-2 ml in excess. The pH rises to approximately 13. Precipitate: $Fe(OH)_3$ (rust). Centrifuge and separate the solution into another test tube. Set the solution aside for Procedure 8. Treat the precipitate by Procedure 7.

7. Dissolve the precipitate from Procedure 6 by adding dilute 6-M HCl dropwise. Add three drops of 0.1-M KSCN solution. Deep red color: $Fe(SCN)^{2+}$. Confirms Fe^{3+} ions.

8. Acidify the solution from Procedure 6 by adding dilute 6-M HCl dropwise. Add five drops of 6-M NH_4Cl and make basic by adding dilute 6-M NH_3 solution. White or grayish flocculent precipitate: $Al(OH)_3$. Centrifuge and separate the solution. Discard the solution and treat the precipitate by Procedure 9.

9. Dissolve the precipitate from Procedure 8 by adding dilute 6-M HCl dropwise. Add one ml of the aluminon test reagent. Add dilute 6-M

NH_3 solution until the solution is just basic. Warm the solution in a water bath. Red precipitate known as a "lake" is $Al(OH)_3$ which has adsorbed the aluminon dye.

10. Divide the solution from Procedure 5 equally into two separate test tubes. To the first portion add 10 to 15 drops of dimethylglyoxime and warm in a water bath. Precipitate: $NiC_8H_{14}N_4O_4$ (red). Confirms Ni^{2+} ions.

11. Acidify the second portion by adding dilute HNO_3 (6M) dropwise until there is one ml in excess. Add one ml of 6-M KNO_2 solution. Warm, let stand for 15 minutes, and then centrifuge. Precipitate: $K_3Co(NO_2)_6$ (yellowish). Confirms Co^{2+} ions in original solution. This may be further confirmed by making a borax-bead test. Prepare a borax bead and put a little of the precipitate on it. Fuse the bead in the oxidizing part of the flame. Cool and note the color. If cobalt is present, the bead is blue.

12. Test for NH_4^+ ions by taking one ml of the original known or unknown solution and adding two ml of 6-M NaOH. Heat gently and test fumes for NH_3 odor and with moistened red litmus paper which turns blue if NH_3 is evolved. This is evidence for the presence of NH_4^{+3} ions.

13. After completing the analysis of a known solution, obtain an unknown from the instructor. The solution may contain from one to four cations. Record all observations and conclusions in Table II. Report the results of your analysis as directed by your instructor.

B. Macro Procedures

1. Place approximately five ml of the known test solution in a clean six-inch test tube. Add two ml of 6-M HCl. Precipitate: $AgCl$, Hg_2Cl_2, $PbCl_2$. Place test tube in a beaker of cold water for a minute. Filter and set the filtrate aside for procedure 5. Wash the precipitate by pouring five ml of cold water containing a few drops of 6-M HCl over the precipitate. Add the washings to the filtrate to be tested in Procedure 5. Treat the precipitate by Procedure 2.

2. Pour ten ml of boiling water over the precipitate. Collect the filtrate in another test tube and

cool in a cold-water bath. Add one ml of 1-*M* potassium chromate. Yellow precipitate: $PbCrO_4$ confirms presence of Pb^{2+} ions. Whenever lead is present, repeat the procedure two or three times using ten ml of boiling water each time to insure that all the $PbCl_2$ has been dissolved, and discard the washings. Treat the white residue on the filter paper by Procedure 3.

3. Pour five ml of 6-*M* ammonia water solution over the white residue from procedure 2. White residue turning black: finely divided mercury mixed with $HgNH_2Cl$, confirms presence of Hg_2^{2+} ions in original sample. Treat the ammoniacal filtrate by Procedure 4.

4. Add dilute 6-*M* HNO_3 to the solution from Procedure 3 until the solution is acid *or* a permanent white precipitate is formed. White precipitate of $AgCl$ confirms Ag^+ ions in original.

5. Neutralize the solution from Procedure 1 by adding 6-*M* NH_3 solution until the solution is basic: then add three ml in excess. Add three ml of 6-*M* NH_4Cl. Dark precipitate: $Fe(OH)_3$, rust color; $Al(OH)_3$ grayish. Filter the solution. Set the filtrate aside for Procedure 11. Treat the precipitate by Procedure 6.

6. Dissolve the precipitate from Procedure 5 by adding 6-*M* HCl dropwise to the precipitate on the filter paper. Make the solution basic to litmus with $NaOH$: then add five ml in excess. Precipitate: $Fe(OH)_3$; rust color. Filter the solution. Set the solution aside for Procedure 8. Treat the precipitate by Procedure 7.

7. Dissolve the precipitate from Procedure 6 by adding 6-*M* HCl dropwise to the precipitate on the filter paper. Add one ml of 0.1-*M* $KSCN$ to the solution. Deep red color: $Fe(SCN)^{2+}$. Confirms Fe^{3+} ions.

8. Acidify the solution from Procedure 6 by adding 6-*M* HCl dropwise. Add one ml of 6-*M* NH_4Cl and make basic by adding 6-*M* NH_3 solution. White or grayish flocculent precipitate: $Al(OH)_3$. Filter the solution. Treat the precipitate by Procedure 9. Discard the filtrate.

9. Dissolve the precipitate from Procedure 8 by adding 6-*M* HCl dropwise to the precipitate on the filter paper. Add five ml of the aluminon test reagent to the filtrate, then add dilute NH_3 solution until the solution is just basic. Warm the solution in a water bath. Red precipitate confirms Al^{3+} ions.

10. Divide the solution from Procedure 5 equally into two separate test tubes. To the first portion add three ml of dimethylglyoxime and warm in a water bath. Precipitate: $NiC_8H_{14}N_4O_4$ (red) confirms Ni^{2+}.

11. Acidify the second portion by adding dilute HNO_3 (6-*M*) dropwise until there is one ml in excess. Add five ml of 6-*M* KNO_2 solution. Warm and let stand for 15 minutes. Precipitate: $K_3Co(NO_2)_6$. Yellowish. Confirms Co^{2+} in the original solution.

12. Test for NH_4^+ ions by taking five ml of the original known or unknown solution and adding ten ml of 6-*M* $NaOH$. Heat gently and test fumes for NH_3 (odor and with moistened red litmus paper which will turn blue if NH_3 is present). Do not hold the litmus inside the test tube nor allow any solution to splash on it.

13. After completing the analysis of a known solution, obtain an unknown from the instructor. The solution usually contains from one to four cations. Record all observations and conclusions in Table II. Report the results of your analysis as directed by your instructor.

FOLLOW-UP DISCUSSION

In this scheme of analysis, chloride ions are used to precipiate $AgCl$, Hg_2Cl_2, and $PbCl_2$. Of these three, $PbCl_2$ is the most soluble. The solution is kept as cold as possible to ensure that most of the Pb^{2+} ions precipitate with the first group. The small amount that remains in solution should not interfere with subsequent tests for the other ions. $PbCl_2$ is relatively soluble in hot water. This characteristic is used to separate it from $AgCl$ and Hg_2Cl_2. The addition of CrO_4^{2-} to a solution containing Pb^{2+} ions precipitates insoluble $PbCrO_4$. This reaction serves as a confirmatory test for Pb^{2+} ions.

NH_3 may be used to separate and help identify $AgCl$ and Hg_2Cl_2. $AgCl$ dissolves in excess NH_3 because the relatively stable, soluble, complex ion,

Table II Analysis of a Solution Containing Unknown Cations

Appearance of solution_____

Procedure Number	Observations	Conclusions

Summary

Ions present_____

Ions absent_____

$Ag(NH_3)_2^+$ forms. The AgCl reprecipitates when the solution is made acid.

$$AgCl(s) + 2NH_3 \rightarrow Ag(NH_3)_2^+ + Cl^-$$

$$Ag(NH_3)_2^+ + 2H^+ + Cl^- \rightarrow$$
$$AgCl(s) + 2NH_4^+$$

When NH_3 is added to Hg_2Cl_2, the Hg_2^{2+} ions are oxidized to Hg^{2+} ions and part is reduced to Hg atoms.

$$Hg_2Cl_2(s) + 2NH_3$$
$$Hg(NH_2)Cl(s) + Hg\ (\ell) + NH_4^+ + Cl^-$$

The $Hg(NH_2)Cl$ is white and the finely divided mercury is black. Thus, the precipitate appears black.

Mercury(I) ions are somewhat unusual in their behavior. Hg_2^{2+} is not a simple ion like most metallic ions, but is a diatomic ion composed of two mercury atoms bonded together by a covalent bond. The ion carries a 2+ charge which is equivalent to each of the bonded atoms having an oxidation number of 1+.

The ability of Ni^{2+}, and Co^{2+} ions to form soluble complex ions with NH_3 is used as a basis for separating them from Al^{3+} and Fe^{3+} which form insoluble hydroxides in NH_3 solution.

$$Ni(H_2O)_6^{2+} + 6NH_3 \rightleftharpoons Ni(NH_3)_6^{2+} + 6H_2O$$

$$Co(H_2O)_6^{2+} + 6NH_3 \rightleftharpoons Co(NH_3)_6^{2+} + 6H_2O$$

$$Fe(H_2O)_6^{3+} + 3NH_3 \rightleftharpoons$$
$$Fe(H_2O)_3(OH)_3(s) + 3NH_4^+$$

$$Al(H_2O)_6^{3+} + 3NH_3 \rightleftharpoons$$
$$Al(H_2O)_3(OH)_3(s) + 3NH_4^+$$

A low concentration of OH^- ions is essential to precipitate $Al(OH)_3$. A higher concentration such as that furnished by NaOH, a strong base, would change the hydroxide precipitate into a complex ion. The equation is

$$Al(H_2O)_3(OH)_3(s) + OH^- \rightarrow$$
$$Al(H_2O)_2(OH)_4^- + H_2O$$

The excess OH^- removes a proton from one of the H_2O molecules and forms the complex ion. It is common, however, to write the species, $Al(OH)_4^-$ without indicating the H_2O molecules bonded to Al^{3+}. The ability of $Al(OH)_3$ to form soluble ions in strongly basic solutions is used as a basis for separating it from $Fe(OH)_3$. The complex $Al(OH)_4^-$ is destroyed by treatment with HCl. The equation is

$$Al(H_2O)_2(OH)_4^- + 4H_3O^+ \rightarrow$$
$$Al(H_2O)_6^{3+} + 4H_2O$$

$Al(OH)_3$ is then reprecipitated by adding NH_3 solution. The aluminum test reagent, "aluminon," is adsorbed on the precipitate and gives the characteristic red lake.

The tests for Co^{2+} and Ni^{2+} are specific enough so that it is not necessary to separate the ions before testing. In the confirmatory test for Co^{2+} ions, nitrite ions (NO_2^-) oxidize Co^{2+} to Co^{3+} ions. The Co^{3+} ions then react with excess NO_2^- and K^+

ions forming insoluble $K_3Co(NO_2)_6$. The overall equation is

$$Co^{2+} + 7NO_2^- + 3K^+ + 2HC_2H_3O_2 \rightarrow$$
$$K_3Co(NO_2)_6 + NO + 2C_2H_3O_2^- + H_2O$$

The confirmatory test for Ni^{2+} consists of adding dimethylglyoxime $(C_4H_8N_2O_2)$. Nickel(II) ions and dimethylglyoxime react in a one-to-one ratio and yield a bright red, insoluble compound.

$$Ni^{2+} + 2C_4H_8N_2O_2 \rightarrow Ni(C_4H_7N_2O_2)_2 + 2H^+$$

FOLLOW-UP QUESTIONS

1. (a) The K_{sp} for $PbCl_2$ at room temperature is 1.6×10^{-5}. Calculate the molar solubility of $PbCl_2$ in the solution formed by adding two ml of 6-M HCl to five ml of the test solution. Hint: calculate the $[Cl^-]$ in the final solution and apply the common ion effect. (b) The test solution used is approximately 0.05 M in Pb^{2+}. Calculate the number of millimoles of $PbCl_2$ that would form in Procedure 1 of the macro procedures. (c) If the ten ml of hot water used in Procedure 2 were only 20% efficient in dissolving the $PbCl_2$ formed in Procedure 1, would you expect a precipitate of $PbCl_2$ to form upon cooling to room temperature? The solubility of $PbCl_2$ at room temperature is 1.0 g per 100 g of water. (d) Suggest the reason for the use of K_2CrO_4 in Procedure 2. Why is it necessary? (e) Calculate the minimum Pb^{2+} concentration in the wash water necessary to form a precipitate with CrO_4^{2-} in Procedure 2. The CrO_4^{2-} ion-concentrations is 1 M.

2. If in Procedure 5 (macro), the molar concentrations of the NH_3 and NH_4^+ are equal, what is the pH of the solution?

Relative Strengths of Various Oxidizing Agents

GENERAL DISCUSSION

Oxidation-reduction reactions (often called "redox" reactions) involve a change in the oxidation number of some of the elements involved in the reaction. Oxidizing agents and reducing agents differ in their strength. In general, the strongest oxidizing agents have the greatest tendency to take electrons. The strongest reducing agents have the least tendency to hold on to their own electrons. In one way, an oxidation-reduction reaction is analogous to an acid-base reaction. In the latter, two substances are competing for a proton. The strongest bases have the greatest tendency to take protons. In a redox reaction, two substances are competing for electrons. Like acids and bases, redox agents can be ranked in order of their oxidizing or reducing strength. A list of oxidizing and reducing agents in order of their strengths forms a useful table. This table can then be used to predict the tendency for a given oxidizing and reducing agent to react.

In this experiment you interpret a series of reactions in an attempt to determine the reactive strengths of several oxidizing and reducing agents. In earlier experiments you have observed that magnesium reacts with $HCl(aq)$ and produces hydrogen and magnesium chloride(aq). The net ionic equation for this reaction is

$$Mg(s) + 2H^+(aq) \rightarrow H_2(g) + Mg^{2+}(aq)$$

Bubbling H_2 gas through a solution of magnesium chloride does not produce an observable reaction. On the basis of these observations, you would conclude that $H^+(aq)$ is capable of removing electrons from magnesium atoms but that magnesium ions cannot remove electrons from H_2 molecules. You would therefore classify H^+ (hydronium) ions as a stronger oxidizing agent than hydrated magnesium ions, and magnesium metal a stronger reducing agent than H_2 gas. The two half-cell reactions can be expressed as reductions and listed in decreasing order of their relative oxidizing strengths as

$$2H^+(aq) + 2e^- \rightarrow H_2(g)$$

$$Mg^{2+}(aq) + 2e^- \rightarrow Mg(s)$$

In this arrangement the strongest oxidizing agent (H^+) is at the upper left, and the strongest reducing agent (Mg) is at the lower right. The half-cell reactions could also have been written as oxidations. In this case, the order would be

$$Mg(s) \rightarrow Mg^{2+}(aq) + 2e^-$$

$$H_2(g) \rightarrow 2H^+(aq) + 2e^-$$

Here the stronger reducing agent is at the upper left and the stronger oxidizing agent at the lower right. By interpreting the results of a number of reactions you will attempt to prepare a short table of elements and their ions in order of their relative reducing and oxidizing strengths.

OBJECTIVES

1. To carry out and interpret a series of reactions between a number of metallic elements and ions in solution.

2. To carry out and interpret a series of reactions between the halogens and their ions in solution.

3. To rank a number of oxidizing and reducing agents and their half-cell reactions in order of their oxidizing or reducing strengths.

MATERIALS

Test tubes, graduated cylinder, steel wool, sandpaper or emery cloth, copper, magnesium, lead, zinc, and silver strips (if available), 0.1-M $Zn(NO_3)_2$, 0.1-M $Pb(NO_3)_2$, 0.1-M $Cu(NO_3)_2$, 0.1-M $Mg(NO_3)_2$, and 0.1-M $AgNO_3$, chlorine water, bromine water, I_2 in 50% ethanol and water solution, carbon tetrachloride or one of the liquid Freons, 0.1-M NaCl, 0.1-M NaBr, 0.1-M NaI, unknown solid sample or solution containing one sort of halide ion for an unknown.

PROCEDURE

Part I · Relative Oxidizing Strength of Metallic Ions and Reducing Strength of Metals

1. Clean a few small pieces of magnesium, cop-per, zinc, and lead with steel wool, sandpaper, or emery cloth.

2. Place a small piece of zinc in enough 0.1-M $Cu(NO_3)_2$ solution to submerge the metal. Look for evidence of a reaction. Record your observations in Table I. If no reaction is evident, warm the solution to about 50–70°C. Do *not* boil. Repeat the procedure for all possible combinations of the metals available and the 0.1-M solutions of the ions of the other metals. (See Table I.) If strips of silver foil are used, be sure to wash them after

Table I   Metal-Metal Ion Redox Reactions

Reactants	Reaction Observed (yes–no)	Formula of New Metal and New Ion
$Zn + Mg^{2+}(aq)$		
$Zn + Pb^{2+}(aq)$		
$Zn + Ag^{+}(aq)$		
$Zn + Cu^{2+}(aq)$		
$Pb + Mg^{2+}(aq)$		
$Pb + Zn^{2+}(aq)$		
$Pb + Cu^{2+}(aq)$		
$Pb + Ag^{+}(aq)$		
$Cu + Mg^{2+}(aq)$		
$Cu + Zn^{2+}(aq)$		
$Cu + Pb^{2+}(aq)$		
$Cu + Ag^{+}(aq)$		
$Ag + Mg^{2+}(aq)$		
$Ag + Zn^{2+}(aq)$		
$Ag + Pb^{2+}(aq)$		
$Ag + Cu^{2+}(aq)$		
$Mg + Ag^{+}(aq)$		
$Mg + Zn^{2+}(aq)$		
$Mg + Pb^{2+}(aq)$		
$Mg + Cu^{2+}(aq)$		

Table II What Results of Tests Show About Relative Oxidizing Strengths

Ions	Zn^{2+}	Cu^{2+}	Pb^{2+}	Ag^+ (if available)	Mg^{2+}
Cu^{2+}					
Zn^{2+}					
Pb^{2+}					
Ag^+					
Mg^{2+}					

Relative Strengths of Oxidizing Agents

1.
2.
3.
4.
5.

use and return them to the instructor. If silver is limited, then your instructor may demonstrate and you record the behavior of the element. Alternatively, you may use about 0.1 g of the Ag crystals prepared in Experiment 3-4.

If a reaction is observed, assume that the original metal lost electrons and that the original metallic ion in solution gained electrons. Write the formulas of the products in the last column of Table I. In Table II, state what each test showed in terms of relative strengths as oxidizers. For example, if Cu^{2+} is a better oxidizing agent than Zn^{2+}, write > in the upper left space. If Zn^{2+} is a better oxidizing agent than Cu^{2+}, then write < in the upper left space.

3. Read the Follow-up Discussion and prepare a table of relative strengths containing the ions which you investigated in Part I. Use the data in Tables I and II to help you construct the table. After completing your table of relative strengths, designate with a labeled arrow the direction in which the reducing strength increases. Arrange the ion-metal couples so that the species which is the strongest oxidizing agent is located at the upper left.

Part II · Relative Oxidizing Strengths of Chlorine, Bromine, and Iodine

4. Pour five ml of 0.1-M NaBr into a test tube and five ml of 0.1-M NaI into another. To each test tube add one ml of carbon tetrachloride or one of the liquid Freons. Because carbon tetrachloride and water are immiscible, two liquid layers form with the denser carbon tetrachloride at the bottom. Add a few drops of chlorine water to each tube, stopper, and gently shake. Record your observations (color of lower layer) in Table III. Your instructor will demonstrate the color of each of the halogens when dissolved in CCl_4 or Freon.

5. Put five ml of 0.1-M NaCl and 0.1-M NaI in two separate test tubes. Add one ml of carbon tetrachloride or one of the liquid Freons to each of the test tubes. Add a few drops of bromine water to each test tube. Stopper, gently shake, and record your observations in Table III. **Caution:** *Do not allow any bromine to contact your skin.*

Table III Relative Oxidizing Strengths of the Halogens

	Halogens		
Solution	Cl_2 (observation)	Br_2 (observation)	I_2 (observation)
Cl⁻			
Br⁻			
I⁻			

Relative Oxidizing Strength of the Halogens

1.
2.
3.

It is very corrosive. Have $Na_2S_2O_3$ (hypo) solution handy to put on any Br_2 or I_2 on the skin.

6. Place five ml of 0.1-M NaCl and five ml of 0.1-M NaBr in two separate test tubes. Add one ml of carbon tetrachloride or one of the liquid Freons. Add a few drops of a water-alcohol solution of iodine to each of the two test tubes. Stopper, gently shake, and record your observations in Table III.

7. Repeat (5) using NaCl and NaBr solutions. Add I_2 (in 50% ethanol) instead of the Cl_2. Record your observations. **Caution:** I_2 *stains the skin. Avoid contact with it.*

8. Use the data in Table III to develop a list of half-cell reduction reactions for the three halogens. Put the half-cell reaction representing the strongest oxidizing ability at the top.

9. Obtain an unknown solid sample from your instructor. Use both chlorine water and Ag^+ ions to help you identify this unknown as a chloride, bromide, or iodide. Compare the reaction of known solutions with that of your unknown. Report the results as directed by your instructor.

FOLLOW-UP DISCUSSION

The observations you made in this experiment enabled you to construct a list of half-cell reactions that can be used to predict the spontaneity of selected oxidation-reduction reactions. Equations for all of your half-cell reactions were written as reductions. That is, they have the general form

$$(Oxid. Agent)^m + ne^- \rightleftharpoons (Red. Agent)^{m-n}$$

where m is the charge on the species.

In this table the strongest oxidizing agents are at the upper left. They can oxidize any species (reducing agent) on the right side of a half-cell reaction which lies lower in the series. The strongest reducing agents in such a table are at the lower right. The greater the difference in strengths between an oxidizing agent and a reducing agent in the series, the greater is their tendency to react.

The reactions in Part II provide data which allowed you to determine the relative oxidizing

strength of chlorine, bromine, and iodine. By extending the trends to the other elements in Group VIIA, you can rank fluorine and astatine in terms of their relative oxidizing ability without performing an actual experiment.

A net ionic equation which has both mass and charge balance can be obtained by adding the reduction half-cell reaction to the oxidation half-cell reaction, after first multiplying each by the necessary coefficient to equate the number of electrons gained and lost. For example:

$$3(Cu^{2+}(aq) + 2e^- \rightleftharpoons Cu(s))$$
$$\underline{2(Al(s) \qquad \rightleftharpoons Al^{3+}(aq) + 3e^-)}$$
$$3Cu^{2+}(aq) + 2Al(s) \rightleftharpoons 2Al^{3+}(aq) + 3Cu(s)$$

Note the similarity of the final equation to a Brønsted acid-base equation. Here again, the stronger reducing and oxidizing agent tends to form the weaker reducing and oxidizing agent at equilibrium.

FOLLOW-UP QUESTIONS

1. Use the concept of periodicity to rank fluorine, and astatine in their correct positions in the list of the halogen half-cell reactions.

2. Assuming that the metallic ions which are the strongest oxidizing agent tested in Part I are intermediate in strength between the two weakest halogens tested in Part II, prepare a table listing in decreasing order of oxidizing strength the half-cell reactions of all the elements and ions tested in this experiment. All other metallic ions tested in Part I are weaker oxidizing agents than the weakest halogen.

3. Using the list prepared in (2), predict whether a reaction is likely to occur (a) between Zn^{2+} and Br_2 and (b) between Cl_2 and Pb.

4. Cite a reason why you might not observe a reaction between a given element and an ion even though the location of the reactants in the reduction series indicates that a reaction is very probable.

5. Write net ionic equations for the reactions which you recorded in Tables I and III.

17-2
Oxidation-Reduction Reactions

GENERAL DISCUSSION

In Experiment 17-1 you carried on a number of oxidation-reduction reactions involving, for the most part, simple ions and elemental substances. This type of redox reaction is sometimes called a displacement reaction. In this experiment we shall extend our investigation to include redox reactions involving a number of polyatomic ions that behave as oxidizing agents. You will be asked to identify the oxidizing and reducing agents in each reaction on the basis of your observations. To help you identify products you will first note the characteristic colors of solutions and perform a series of identification tests.

In Part II you will observe a practical application of an oxidation-reduction reaction when you prepare a piece of blueprint paper and make a blueprint of some common objects.

OBJECTIVES

1. To identify, become acquainted with, and investigate the behavior of some common oxidizing and reducing agents.

2. To write net ionic equations for oxidation-reduction reactions.

3. To prepare blueprint paper and a blueprint.

MATERIALS

Test tubes, graduated cylinder, 0.1-M KCl, 0.1-M K$_2$Cr$_2$O$_4$, 0.1-M K$_2$Cr$_2$O$_7$, 0.1-M CrCl$_3$, 0.1-M MnCl$_2$, 0.02-M KMnO$_4$, 0.1-M FeCl$_3$, 0.1-M Fe(NH$_4$)$_2$(SO$_4$)$_2$, 3-M H$_2$SO$_4$, 6-M HNO$_3$, 0.1-M KSCN, 0.1-M BaCl$_2$, 0.1-M Na$_2$SO$_3$, 6-M HCl, chlorine or bromine water, 16-M (conc) HNO$_3$, 6-M NaOH, 0.1-M KI, CCl$_4$ or one of the Freons, 0.3-M K$_3$Fe(CN)$_6$, 0.3-M Fe(NH$_4$)$_3$(C$_6$H$_5$O$_7$)$_2$.

PROCEDURE

Part I · Reactions Between Selected Redox Couples

1. Observe the colors of the following stock solutions on the reagent shelf and use your observations to deduce the colors of the species listed in Table I (a) KCl, (b) K$_2$CrO$_4$, (c) K$_2$Cr$_2$O$_7$, (d) CrCl$_3$, (e) MnCl$_2$, (f) KMnO$_4$, (g) FeCl$_3$, (h) FeSO$_4$, (i) H$_2$SO$_4$.

2. Carefully observe the nature of the products in each of the following reactions. Record your observations in Table II. These reactions are intended to help you identify the ions listed in Table II which may appear as products of the redox reactions which you will subsequently carry out.

(a) Add a drop of 0.1-M potassium thiocyanate (KSCN) to two ml of 0.1-M iron(III) chloride.

(b) Add one drop of 0.3-M potassium ferricyanide (potassium hexacyanoferrate(III)) to two ml of 0.1-M iron(II) ammonium sulfate.

(c) Add one ml of 0.1-M BaCl$_2$ to two ml of 0.1-M Na$_2$SO$_3$. Record your observations and then add two ml of 6-M HCl.

3. Place three or four ml of (0.1-M) Na$_2$SO$_3$ solution in a test tube. Add one ml of dilute (6-M) HCl. Add ten drops of 0.02-M KMnO$_4$. Add a few drops of 0.1-M BaCl$_2$ solution. Record your observations in Table IV. Refer to data in Tables I and II and complete row 1 in Table III.

4. Repeat Procedure 3 using four drops of 0.1-M K$_2$Cr$_2$O$_7$ solution instead of 0.02-M KMnO$_4$.

5. Repeat Procedure 3 using a few drops of bromine or chlorine water instead of KMnO$_4$.

6. Repeat Procedure 3 using a few drops of concentrated (16-M) HNO$_3$ instead of KMnO$_4$.

7. To one ml of 0.1-M CrCl$_3$ solution, add

three ml of 6-M NaOH dropwise. Stir the solution while adding 6% H_2O_2 dropwise until a change occurs. If no color change is noted, gently warm the solution. It may be necessary to add a little more H_2O_2. Record observations in Table IV. Refer to data in Table I and complete Table IV.

8. To one ml of 0.1-M K_2CrO_4 solution add 6-M HNO_3 until the solution is orange. Then add a ml of HNO_3 in excess. Add 6% H_2O_2 dropwise with stirring and record any changes.

9. Add two drops of 3-M sulfuric acid and 4 drops of 0.02-M $KMnO_4$ to two ml of freshly prepared 0.1-M $Fe(NH_4)_2SO_4$ solution. Test for the presence of Fe(III) ions by adding one drop of 0.1-M potassium thiocyanate. Record observations in Table V.

10. Add six drops of 6-M HNO_3 to one ml of freshly prepared 0.1-M $Fe(NH_4)_2(SO_4)_2$ solution. Test the solution for iron(III) ions by adding one drop of 0.1-M potassium thiocyanate solution.

11. Add one ml of 0.1-M KI solution to two ml of 0.1-M $FeCl_3$ solution. Test for the presence of Fe(II) ions by adding a drop of 0.1-M potassium ferricyanide solution. Note any evidence of I_2. The presence of I_2 may be more readily detected by adding one ml of CCl_4 or one of the Freons and mixing.

Table I   Color of Ions

Substance	Color of Solution	Ions	Color of Ions
KCl		K^+	
		Cl^-	
$K_2Cr_2O_7$		$Cr_2O_7^{2-}$	
K_2CrO_4		CrO_4^{2-}	
$CrCl_3$		Cr^{3+}	
$MnCl_2$		Mn^{2+}	
$KMnO_4$		MnO_4^-	
$FeCl_3$		Fe^{3+}	
H_2SO_4		SO_4^{2-}	
$FeSO_4$		Fe^{2+}	

Table II   Characteristics of Fe^{2+}, Fe^{3+}, SO_3^{2-}, and SO_4^{2-} Ions

Ion to Be Identified	Reagent(s) to Be Added	Observations
Fe^{3+}	KSCN	
Fe^{2+}	$K_3Fe(CN)_6$	
SO_3^{2-}	$BaCl_2$ and HCl	
SO_4^{2-}	$BaCl_2$ and HCl	

Table III   The Sulfite Ion-Sulfate Ion Couple

Reaction	Test for SO_4^{2-} (positive or negative)	Evidence of Change in Added Reagent	Product of Oxidation	Product of Reduction	Oxidizing Agent	Reducing Agent
$SO_3^{2-} + MnO_4^- + H^+$						
$SO_3^{2-} + Cr_2O_7^{2-} + H^+$						
$SO_3^{2-} + Br_2$ (acid sol'n)						
$SO_3^{2-} + NO_3^- + H^+$						

Table IV The Chromium(III) Ion-Chromate Ion Couple

Reaction	Observation	Product of Oxidation	Product of Reduction	Oxidizing Agent	Reducing Agent
$Cr^{3+} + H_2O_2$ (basic solution)					
$CrO_4^{2-} + H_2O_2$ (acid solution)					

Table V The Iron(II) Ion-Iron(III) Ion Couple

Reaction	Observations	Product of Oxidation	Product of Reduction	Oxidizing Agent	Reducing Agent
$Fe^{2+} + MnO_4^-$ (acid solution)					
$Fe^{2+} + HNO_3 + KSCN$					
$Fe^{3+} + I^-$					

Part II · Preparation and Use of Blueprint Paper

12. Pour ten ml of a 0.3-M potassium ferricyanide solution into a test tube and add ten ml of a 0.3-M solution of ferric ammonium citrate. Stopper and invert the test tube a few times, then pour the solution into a watch glass. Protect the solution as much as possible from light.

13. Cut two or three sheets of mimeograph paper to dimensions of approximately 2 × 3 inches.

14. Fold one corner of the paper and using this corner as a handle, dip one side of the paper into the solution. Be careful that there are no air bubbles between the paper and solution, and that only one side of the paper becomes coated with the solution. Mark this coated side for future reference.

15. Place the coated paper on a paper towel, and place in your desk drawer to dry until the next laboratory period.

16. When the paper is dry, place a key, a coin, a leaf, or some other opaque object on the coated side of the paper and expose it to sunlight for 2 or 3 minutes or to artificial light for a considerably longer period of time.

17. Remove the paper from the light source and place coated side down in a watch glass filled with water. Remove from the watch glass, hold in the palm of your hand and rinse it thoroughly in a small stream of running water.

18. Press the blueprint between a folded paper towel to remove the moisture and then place it in your desk until it is dry. Paste your print on your laboratory report sheet.

FOLLOW-UP DISCUSSION

In Part I of this experiment you identified the products of a number of oxidation-reduction reactions. Since you know the names and formulas of the reactants you should be able to write ionic equations for the reactions. For reactions occurring in acid solution you will usually have to add water as a product of the reaction. However, if you use the half-cell method described in your text, the H_2O, and H^+ ion or OH^- ion will automatically appear as a consequence of the system of balancing. Your observation may not have permitted you to ascertain that one product for hydrogen peroxide reacting in the basic solution was water. It may also help you to know that in the acid solution, the end product of hydrogen peroxide was oxygen. The brownish gas which you may have observed in Procedure 6 was nitrogen dioxide, NO_2.

In Part II you prepared a piece of blueprint paper by coating a piece of white paper with a mixture of ferric ammonium citrate and potassium ferricyanide. When you exposed this mixture to sunlight, the iron(III) ions of the ferric ammonium citrate were reduced to iron(II) ions and the citrate ions were oxidized. The iron(II) ions reacted with the ferricyanide ions and formed a precipitate of insoluble Turnbull's blue $\{Fe_3[Fe(CN)_6]_2\}$. You developed the blueprint by washing in water, which removed the unreacted soluble compounds which had not been exposed to light. This is similar to the way that commercial blueprints are made.

FOLLOW-UP QUESTIONS

1. Use the data in Tables III, IV, and V, and the information in the Follow-up Discussion section to help you write balanced ionic equations for each of the reactions listed in these three tables.

2. Under what conditions did H_2O_2 act as an oxidizing agent? a reducing agent?

3. Write balanced equations for the five reactions between the species listed in Table II. Are any of these oxidation-reduction reactions? Justify your answer.

17-3
Oxidation-Reduction Analysis

GENERAL DISCUSSION

Many oxidation-reduction reactions serve as a basis for a volumetric quantitative analysis. One of the most widely used oxidizing agents in analytical chemistry is potassium permanganate. It is an inexpensive, powerful oxidizing agent which serves as a self-indicator; one drop in excess of the endpoint volume imparts a pinkish color to a large volume of solution.

The principles involved in a redox titration are the same as those for an acid-base or any non-redox titration. The moles of standard agent required to reach the endpoint are calculated using the relationship

$$\text{moles of standard} = MV$$

and the moles of unknown which react with the calculated moles of standard can be determined from the mole ratios between the two reactants obtained from the equation for the reaction.

In this experiment you titrate an approximately 0.02-M $KMnO_4$ solution which has been standardized, into a measured amount of a solution containing an unknown quantity of either iron(II) ions, H_2O_2, or $Na_2C_2O_4$.

OBJECTIVES

1. To determine the percentage of H_2O_2 in ordinary hydrogen peroxide, the milligrams of iron in an unknown iron(II) solution, or the percentage of sodium oxalate in an impure sample.
2. To become acquainted with the techniques and calculations associated with the use of volumetric oxidizing agents.

MATERIALS

Test tubes, graduated cylinder, balance, $H_2C_2O_4 \cdot 2H_2O$ or $Na_2C_2O_4$, $KMnO_4$, 3-M H_2SO_4, 250-ml erlenmeyer flasks, burner, ring stand, wire screen, thermometer, 0.1-M $MnSO_4$, burets, unknown iron(II) sulfate, household hydrogen peroxide, impure sodium oxalate samples such as those obtainable from Thorn Smith Company.

PROCEDURE

Part I · Preparation and Standardization of $KMnO_4$

If a standardized solution of 0.02-M $KMnO_4$ is available, this part may be omitted.

1. An approximately 0.02-M $KMnO_4$ solution may be prepared by dissolving 3.16 g of $KMnO_4$ in enough water to make one liter of solution.

2. If highly accurate results are desired, it will be necessary to warm the solution for 10 to 15 minutes, let it stand for at least 24 hours, filter it through glass wool and standardize it with oxalic acid dihydrate or sodium oxalate.

3. An approximate 0.05-M oxalic acid standard may be prepared by dissolving approximately 0.63 g of $H_2C_2O_4 \cdot 2H_2O$ weighed to the nearest 0.001 g in enough water to make exactly 100.0 ml of solution (use a volumetric flask). Alternatively, individual samples of oxalic acid weighing 0.200 g or samples of sodium oxalate weighing 0.250 g may be dissolved in approximately 30 ml of water and titrated.

4. Use either the individual samples or from a buret add about 30.00 ml of the standard acid to a 250-ml flask. Add 15 ml of 3-M H_2SO_4 to the titration flask and warm to 80°C or 85°C.

5. Titrate the hot acid solution with $KMnO_4$ to a slight permanent pink endpoint. Record data in Table I. Swirl while titrating and reheat if the solution drops much below 70°C.

Part II · Milligrams of Iron in an Unknown Iron(II) Solution

6. Take a clean (not necessarily dry) 250-ml flask to the instructor who will titrate a sample of freshly prepared FeSO$_4$ solution into the flask. The instructor will either record or tell you the volume delivered. Each student may receive a different volume.

7. Add enough water to your sample to make a total of about 30 ml. Add 10 ml of 3-M H$_2$SO$_4$. Titrate with standard 0.020-M KMnO$_4$ to a slight permanent pink. If time permits, obtain a second and third sample and repeat the titration. Record your data in Table II. If just one sample is analyzed, report the milligrams of iron in the sample. If you run more than one sample, you will have to determine the molarity of the original iron(II) solution received from the instructor to check the precision of your analyses. The equation is

$$M_{iron(II)} = \frac{\text{millimoles Fe(II) in sample}}{\text{ml of sample}}$$

Table I Standardization of KMnO$_4$ Solution

	Trial 1	Trial 2
Mass of H$_2$C$_2$O$_4$ · 2H$_2$O		
Molecular mass of H$_2$C$_2$O$_4$ · 2H$_2$O		
Moles of H$_2$C$_2$O$_4$ · 2H$_2$O		
Volume of H$_2$C$_2$O$_4$ · 2H$_2$O solution		
Molarity of H$_2$C$_2$O$_4$ · 2H$_2$O		
Final reading of acid buret		
Initial reading of acid buret		
Volume of acid used		
Final reading of KMnO$_4$ buret		
Initial reading of KMnO$_4$ buret		
Volume of KMnO$_4$ used		
Molarity of MnO$_4^-$		

Part III · Percentage of H$_2$O$_2$ in Ordinary Drugstore Hydrogen Peroxide

8. Weigh a clean, dry 250-ml flask to the nearest 0.01 g. Record data in Table III.

9. Add from the buret on the reagent table approximately 1.5 ml of ordinary household hydrogen peroxide. Read the volume to the nearest 0.02 ml.

10. Reweigh the flask and peroxide.

11. Add about 35 ml of water, 5 ml of 3-M H$_2$SO$_4$, and three or four drops of 0.1-M MnSO$_4$ (a catalyst) to the flask.

Table II Milligrams of Iron in an Unknown Solution

	Trial 1	Trial 2	Trial 3
Final reading of FeSO$_4$ buret			
Initial reading of FeSO$_4$ buret			
Volume of FeSO$_4$			
Final reading of KMnO$_4$ buret			
Initial reading of KMnO$_4$ buret			
Volume of KMnO$_4$ used			
Molarity of KMnO$_4$			
Millimoles of KMnO$_4$ used			
Millimoles of Fe(II) in sample			
Molecular mass of Fe(II)			
Milligrams of Fe in sample			
Molarity of FeSO$_4$ solution			
Correct value for milligrams of iron			

12. Titrate the solution with standard 0.020-M $KMnO_4$ to the faint pink endpoint.

13. Calculate the percentage of H_2O_2 in the original sample.

Table III   Percentage of H_2O_2 in Household Peroxide

	Trial 1	Trial 2
Final reading of peroxide buret		
Initial reading of peroxide buret		
Volume of H_2O_2 sample		
Mass of flask plus H_2O_2 sample		
Mass of empty flask		
Mass of peroxide sample		
Final reading of $KMnO_4$ buret		
Initial reading of $KMnO_4$ buret		
Volume of $KMnO_4$ used		
Molarity of $KMnO_4$		
Millimoles of $KMnO_4$ used		
Millimoles of H_2O_2 in sample		
Molecular mass of H_2O_2		
Milligrams of H_2O_2 in sample		
Percentage of H_2O_2 in sample (exp.)		
Percentage given on bottle		
Percentage deviation		

Part IV · Percentage of Sodium Oxalate in an Impure Sample

14. Obtain about two g of an unknown $Na_2C_2O_4$-sample from your instructor and place in a weighing or shell vial. Weigh by difference (to the greatest precision possible) into separate 125- or 250-ml erlenmeyer flasks approximately 1-g samples of the unknown. Dissolve in 30–40 ml of distilled water, add 10–15 ml of 3-M H_2SO_4,

warm to 80°C and titrate with approximately 0.020-M $KMnO_4$. Record your data in Table IV.

Table IV   Percentage of Sodium Oxalate in an Impure Sample

	Trial 1	Trial 2
Mass of vial + sample		
Mass of vial − sample		
Mass of sample		
Final reading of $KMnO_4$ buret		
Initial reading of buret		
Volume of $KMnO_4$ used		
Molarity of $KMnO_4$		
Moles of MnO_4^- used		
Moles of $C_2O_4^{2-}$ in sample		
Molecular mass of $Na_2C_2O_4$		
Grams of $Na_2C_2O_4$ in sample		
Percentage of $Na_2C_2O_4$ in sample		

FURTHER EXPERIMENTATION

1. Determine the mg of vitamin C (ascorbic acid) in fresh or canned citrus juice. This vitamin is easily oxidized, so that a mild oxidizing agent such as I_2 may be used in the analysis. Use a standard iodine solution which is about 0.005 M to titrate a 10 ml sample of juice. Add to two ml of dilute acetic acid and two to three ml of a starch indicator to the juice before titrating. At the endpoint, the starch indicator adsorbs the unreacted iodine and turns blue-black. You may assume that the iodine and vitamin C react in a ratio of one mole to one mole. The molecular mass of vitamin C (ascorbic acid) is 176.1.

FOLLOW-UP DISCUSSION

Completion of the data tables and the calculations involved in this analysis required the use of the mole concept. The experiment also provides an opportunity to extend the concepts of equivalent mass and normality introduced in Experiment 15-7. In that experiment, equivalent masses were calculated for acids and bases and were based on the number of moles of protons donated or accepted by an acid or base. The general relationship for acids and bases is expressed by

$$\text{equivalent mass} = \frac{\text{molecular mass}}{\text{moles of protons donated or accepted}}$$

The basis for calculating the equivalent mass of a redox agent differs slightly from that for a non-redox agent. The equivalent mass of a redox agent is based on a mole of electrons rather than a mole of protons. That is, one equivalent mass of a redox agent is the mass (g) of agent which gains or loses one mole of electrons. This is expressed in concise form by

$$\text{equivalent mass} = \frac{\text{molecular mass of agent}}{\text{moles of electrons gained or lost per mole of agent}}$$

The denominator in both equations is known as the *equivalents per mole*. It is a small whole number which, for an oxidizing or reducing agent, may be obtained from the appropriate half-cell equation. The half-cell equation for the reduction of the oxidizing agent in this experiment is

$$MnO_4^- + 8H^+ + 5e^- = Mn^{2+} + 4H_2O$$

According to this equation there are 5 equiv/mole of MnO_4^-. This means that for this reaction the equivalent mass of $KMnO_4$ is

$$\frac{158 \text{ g/mole}}{5 \text{ equiv/mole}} = 31.6 \text{ g/equiv}$$

The normality and molarity of the oxidizing solution are related by the same factor as the molecular and equivalent masses. Thus the normality of the 0.020-M $KMnO_4$ solution is

$$\frac{0.020 \text{ moles}}{\text{liter}} \times \frac{5 \text{ equiv}}{\text{mole}} = 0.10 \frac{\text{equiv}}{\text{liter}} = 0.10 \text{ } N$$

To gain an understanding of, and proficiency in the use of these concepts you may wish to repeat the calculations of this experiment using the concept of equivalent mass instead of molecular mass and the concept of normality instead of molarity. Your final answer should be the same for both methods. The half-cell equations for the oxidation of the reducing agents in this experiment follow.

$$Fe^{2+} \rightarrow Fe^{3+} + e^-$$
$$H_2O_2 \rightarrow O_2(g) + 2H^+ + 2e^-$$
$$H_2C_2O_4(aq) \rightarrow 2CO_2(g) + 2H^+ + 2e^-$$
$$C_2O_4^{2-}(aq) \rightarrow 2CO_2(g) + 2e^-$$

FOLLOW-UP QUESTIONS

List the sources of error which may have contributed to an inaccurate experimental result. If a quantitative analysis text is available, consult the section on permanganate titrations.

2. Write net ionic equations for the reactions described in Parts I, II, III, and IV of this experiment. The half-cell reactions found in the Follow-up Discussion section may be of some help to you.

3. (Optional) What is the equivalent mass of each of the reducing agents used in Parts I, II, III, and IV of this experiment?

4. In Table I can the formula, $(MV)_{\text{oxid. agent}} = (MV)_{\text{red. agent}}$ be used to calculate the molarity of the oxalic acid directly from titration data? Explain.

17-4
Electrochemical Cells

GENERAL DISCUSSION

In Experiment 16-1 you observed a number of oxidation-reduction reactions in which the oxidizing and reducing agents were in direct contact with each other. In these reactions electrons were transferred directly from reducing agent to oxidizing agent. Oxidation-reduction reactions may also be made to take place when the agents are not in direct contact. In this case, the electrons are transferred from the reducing agent through a wire to the oxidizing agent. This arrangement, called an electrochemical cell (Fig. 17-1), permits the system to do electric work as the electrons are transferred from one agent to another.

The reactions take place at the poles (electrodes) of the cell. The redox equation for the overall cell reaction may be expressed as the sum of two half-cell reactions. For example, the reaction

$$Zn(s) + Cu^{2+} \rightarrow Zn^{2+} + Cu(s)$$

may be obtained by adding the following two half-cell reactions.

anode (oxidation): $Zn(s) \rightleftharpoons Zn^{2+} + 2e$
cathode (reduction): $Cu^{2+} + 2e \rightleftharpoons Cu(s)$

At the anode, zinc atoms dissolve leaving electrons on the metal and forming zinc ions which go into the solution. At the cathode, copper(II) ions are removed from solution as they accept electrons and deposit on the cathode as copper atoms. The two solutions maintain their electric neutrality when positive ions (K^+) migrate from the salt bridge into the cathode compartment, and negative ions (Cl^-) migrate into the anode compartment. The flow of electrons from anode to cathode may be detected with an instrument called a galvanometer (sensitive ammeter), but we shall use a voltmeter to measure potential difference between the electrodes.

In this experiment we construct several electrochemical cells, examine the half-cell reaction at each electrode, measure the potential difference between the half-cells with a voltmeter, and investigate some factors which affect the voltage of the cell.

OBJECTIVES

1. To construct and measure the voltage of several electrochemical cells.
2. To learn the principles underlying the construction and operation of electrochemical cells.
3. To learn the significance and use of reduction or oxidation potentials.

MATERIALS

1-M solutions of $Zn(NO_3)_2$, $Cu(NO_3)_2$, 250-ml beakers, graduated cylinders, 1-M KNO_3, glass tubing, cotton, copper metal strips, zinc strips (preferably amalgamated), 0–3 D.C. voltmeter with 0 at left of dial, copper wire, alligator clamps, lead strips, 1-M lead nitrate, [$Pb(NO_3)_2$], silver strip, 1-M $AgNO_3$, K_2S or Na_2S crystals, ammonia water.

PROCEDURE

1. Prepare or obtain 200 ml of 1-M $Zn(NO_3)_2$ and 200 ml of 1-M $Cu(NO_3)_2$ solution. Place the solutions in separate 250-ml beakers.
2. Construct and fill a U-tube with 1-M KNO_3 solution. Stopper both ends with a loose cotton plug. Invert the U-tube into the two beakers as shown in Fig. 17-1. The U-tube full of a conducting solution acts as a salt bridge which keeps the solutions electrically neutral by allowing ions to migrate from one beaker to the other.
3. Place a copper strip in the copper solution

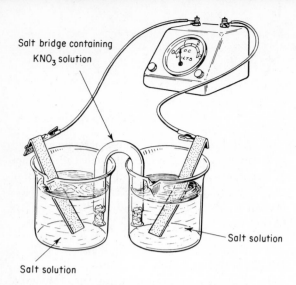

Salt bridge containing KNO$_3$ solution

Salt solution

Salt solution

Fig. 17-1   Electrochemical cell with salt bridge.

and an amalgamated zinc strip in the zinc solution. The zinc strip may be amalgamated by dipping in a solution of HgSO$_4$ for about 30 sec.

4. Obtain a 0–3 volt D.C. voltmeter with 0 at the left side. Use wires with alligator clamps to connect the electrodes to the terminals (posts) of the voltmeter. Connect the leads so that the needle deflects to the right when the circuit is completed. Read the voltage of the cell and record the value in Table I. Look at the posts on the voltmeter to identify which is the positive and which is the negative electrode. Record this information in the table. The electrons flow through the external circuit from the negative electrode (anode) to the positive electrode (cathode). In

Table I identify the anode and cathode for each cell you test.

5. Replace the beaker containing the zinc solution with one containing a lead strip in a 1-*M* Pb(NO$_3$)$_2$ solution. Save the zinc half-cell for later use. Use a different salt bridge for the lead-copper cell if one is available. Read and record the voltage of this cell.

6. Replace the beaker containing the lead strip with one containing a silver strip in 1-*M* AgNO$_3$ solution. Read and record the voltage.

7. Construct a cell using the zinc and silver half-cells and measure the voltage.

8. Reassemble the zinc-copper cell. Add small amounts of K$_2$S or Na$_2$S crystals to the Zn(NO$_3$)$_2$ solution until a voltage change is noted. Record the voltage in Table II.

Table II   Effect of Concentration on Cell Voltage of Zinc-Copper Cell

Original voltage	
Voltage after adding Na$_2$S to Zn(NO$_3$)$_2$ solution	
Change in voltage	
Change in concentration of Zn^{2+} ions	
Original voltage	
Voltage after adding Na$_2$S or NH$_3$ to Cu(NO$_3$)$_2$ solution	
Change in voltage	
Change in concentration of Cu^{+2} ions	

Table I   Voltages and Components of Electrochemical Cells

Cell	Voltage	Negative Electrode (anode)	Positive Electrode (cathode)	Theoretical Standard-State Voltage
Zn | Zn^{+2}(1M)||Cu^{+2}(1M) | Cu				
Pb | Pb^{+2}(1M)||Cu^{+2}(1M) | Cu				
Cu | Cu^{+2}(1M)||Ag$^+$(1M) | Ag				
Zn | Zn^{+2}(1M)||Ag$^+$(1M) | Ag				

9. Add Na_2S, K_2S, or NH_3 to the $Cu(NO_3)_2$ solution until a change in voltage is noted. Record this voltage in Table II.

FURTHER EXPERIMENTATION

1. Determine ΔH, ΔG, and ΔS for the reaction between zinc and silver nitrate (aq). To determine ΔH, allow zinc dust to react with aqueous silver nitrate in your calorimeter. Use your experimental value for the cell voltage to determine ΔG by substitution in the equation, $\Delta G = -nFE$. Calculate ΔS by solving the equation $\Delta G = \Delta H - T\Delta S$ for ΔS.

2. Clean and sandpaper a number of iron nails. Investigate the corrosion of these nails under different conditions. For example, check the corrosion of the nails in tap water, in salt water, and in tap water in which the nails are in contact with other metals such as copper, magnesium, and zinc. Place both bent and unbent nails in a warm solution of 1% agar containing a few drops of phenolphthalein. After a few days, carefully examine the nails and explain your observations.

FOLLOW-UP DISCUSSION

In order to calculate the standard state cell voltages for the cells listed in Table I, you must know how to use tables of reduction or oxidation potentials, representing experimental classifications of oxidizing and reducing agents according to their relative strengths. In a table of oxidation potentials, a given reducing agent reduces any oxidizing agent that lies below it in the table. In a table of reduction potentials, a given oxidizing agent oxidizes any reducing agent which lies below it in the table.

An overall equation for any oxidation-reduction reaction may be obtained by combining any two half-cell reactions in the tables in such a way that the electrons associated with each half-cell reaction cancel. When the half-cell voltages are combined in the same way as the equations, then the sign of the voltage tells whether the equation represents a spontaneous (positive voltage) or nonspontaneous (negative voltage) reaction. In the following example we shall illustrate how either reduction or oxidation potentials can be

used to calculate the theoretical standard state cell voltage for the reaction between magnesium and aqueous copper sulfate. A small portion of each table is reproduced below to show the interrelationships.

Table IIIA Standard Reduction Potentials

Oxidizing strength decreases ↓

Half-cell Reactions	E° (volts)
$Cu^{2+} + 2e^- = Cu$	0.34
$2H^+ + 2e^- = H_2$	0.00
$Zn^{2+} + 2e^- = Zn$	−0.76
$Mg^{2+} + 2e^- = Mg$	−2.34

In either table, an equation for a spontaneous reaction at standard state may be obtained by reversing a lower half-cell equation and adding it to a half-cell equation which lies above it. When the equation is reversed, the sign of its voltage must also be reversed. To obtain a balanced equation, the number of electrons in the two half-cell reactions should be balanced before adding. This can be accomplished by multiplying each species (not the voltages) in each equation by a factor that will make the electrons equal.

Example: Calculate the theoretical standard-state voltages for the reaction between magnesium and aqueous copper(II) nitrate using (a) reduction potential, and (b) oxidation potentials.

Solution: (a) From Table IIIA write the half-cell equation for the reduction of Cu^{2+} ions. Reverse the half-cell equation for the reduction of Mg^{2+} ions and write it under the copper half-cell equation. Then add the two half-cell equations.

$$Cu^{2+} + 2e = Cu + 0.34 \text{ v}$$
$$\underline{Mg = Mg^{2+} + 2e + 2.34 \text{ v}}$$
$$Cu^{2+} + Mg = Cu + Mg^{2+} + 2.68 \text{ v}$$

(b) From Table IIIB write the half-cell equation for the oxidation of Mg atoms. Reverse the half-cell equation for the oxidation of Cu atoms and write it under the magnesium half-cell equation. Then add the two half-cell equations.

$$Mg(s) \rightarrow Mg^{2+}(aq) + 2e \qquad 2.34 \text{ v}$$
$$\underline{Cu^{2+}(aq) + 2e^- \rightarrow Cu(s) \qquad 0.34 \text{ v}}$$
$$Cu^{2+}(aq) + Mg(s) \rightarrow Mg^{2+}(aq) + Cu(s) \quad 2.68 \text{ v}$$

Reducing strength decreases →

Half-cell Reactions	$E°$ (volts)
$Mg = Mg^{2+} + 2e^-$	2.34
$Zn = Zn^{2+} + 2e^-$	0.76
$H_2 = 2H^+ + 2e^-$	0.00
$Cu = Cu^{2+} + 2e^-$	−0.34

Notice that in both (a) and (b) the electrons were equal and canceled out. The positive voltage indicates the reaction goes spontaneously to the right. Thus, the standard-state cell voltage is the sum of the standard-state half-cell voltage for the oxidation half-cell reaction and that for the reduction half-cell reaction. The equation is

$E^0_{cell} = E^0_{ox}$ $+$ E^0_{red}
(for the oxidation   (for the reduction
half-cell reaction)   half-cell reaction)

The standard state voltages are based on 1-M solutions. Changing the concentration causes a change in the voltage. The effect of changing concentration can be determined by applying Le Châtelier's principle to either the half-cell or the overall cell equations. Consider the two half-reactions which occur during the operation of the magnesium-copper cell. These are

$$Mg(s) \rightarrow Mg^{2+}(aq) + 2e^- \qquad \text{Eq. 1}$$
$$Cu^{2+}(aq) + 2e^- \rightarrow Cu(s) \qquad \text{Eq. 2}$$

According to Le Châtelier's principle, increasing the concentration of Mg^{2+} ion causes the first reaction to shift left. This decreases the tendency for the reaction to occur and thus decreases the voltage. Increasing the concentration of the Cu^{2+} ions shifts the second reaction to the right. This increases the tendency for this reaction to occur and thus increases the voltage. The same result could be predicted by referring to the overall cell equation,

$$Mg(s) + Cu^{2+}(aq) \rightarrow Mg^{2+}(aq) + Cu(s)$$

This shows that as the cell continues to operate, the concentration of Mg^{2+} ion increases while that of Cu^{2+} ion decreases. These effects tend to decrease the voltage. Eventually equilibrium concentrations are established, at which point the voltage is zero.

FOLLOW-UP QUESTIONS

1. Calculate the theoretical standard state cell voltages for each cell constructed in this experiment. Refer to the table in the Appendix for standard half-cell potentials. Record the standard state cell voltages in Table I.

2. Draw a diagram to represent the zinc-silver cell which you constructed. Identify the following items with appropriate labels: (a) anode (b) cathode (c) direction of electron flow in external circuit (d) direction of anion and cation migration (e) equations for anode and cathode reaction (f) overall equation for cell reaction.

3. (a) Explain what you observed when you added Na_2S to the zinc nitrate solution. (b) What is the formula of the precipitate formed? (c) How did the formation of this precipitate affect the concentration of the Zn^{2+} ions? (d) Explain the voltage change in terms of Le Châtelier's principle.

4. (a) Explain what you observed when you added Na_2S or NH_3 to the copper(II) nitrate solution. (b) What is the formula of the substance formed? (c) How did the formation of this substance affect the concentration of the Cu^{2+} ion? (d) Explain the voltage change in terms of Le Châtelier's principle.

5. Use the table of reduction potentials to help you predict whether the reaction

$$2Ag^+ + Pb \rightarrow 2Ag + Pb^{2+}$$

proceeds spontaneously to the right, to the left, or not at all.

6. Could a solution containing zinc ions be kept in an aluminum container? Explain.

7. Iron(III) chloride is used to etch copper plates. Explain why this is possible.

17-5
Electrolytic Cells

GENERAL DISCUSSION

In an electrolytic cell, nonspontaneous oxidation-reduction reactions are made to occur by the application of an external voltage. The source of this voltage may be a dry cell. A dry cell is not really "dry." There is a moist paste inside the cell which serves as an electrolyte. When the cell is operating, the zinc container undergoes oxidation and serves as a source of electrons. When the zinc electrode (outside terminal) of the dry cell is connected to an electrode of an electrolytic cell, the electrons are forced on to the electrode (cathode) and result in the reduction of some species in the electrolytic solution. At the anode of the electrolytic cell, electrons are removed from some chemical species resulting in the oxidation of the species.

In Part I of this experiment you carry out an experiment or observe a demonstration by the instructor involving the electrolysis of several different solutions. You then identify the products and interpret them in terms of reduction potentials.

In Part II you apply electrochemical principles when you either silver plate or copper plate some common object. If time permits, you have a chance to investigate the quantitative aspects of electrolysis when you experimentally determine a value for Avogadro's number. This determination is based on the electrochemical principle that the mass of a chemical produced by an electrolytic reaction is proportional to the quantity of electricity used. This quantity, expressed in coulombs, may be determined by measuring the current and time. The relationship is

$$Q = It$$

where Q equals coulombs, I equals current in amperes, and t equals time in seconds. The electric charge carried by an electron, measured by Millikan, was found to be 1.6×10^{-19} coulombs.

Dividing the coulombs used by the charge on a single electron yields the number of electrons required to deposit the measured mass of chemical.

$$Q \text{ coulomb} \times \frac{1 \text{ electron}}{1.6 \times 10^{-19} \text{ coulombs}} = \text{electrons}$$

Knowing the number of electrons required to deposit a measured quantity of copper, we can determine the number needed to deposit a mole of copper. Finally, by relating the number of electrons associated with the deposition of one atom, we can calculate the number of atoms per mole (Avogadro's number).

OBJECTIVES

1. To electrolyze several solutions and interpret the products of electrolysis in terms of reduction potentials.
2. To silver or copper plate an object.
3. To determine Avogadro's number.
4. To become acquainted with Faraday's Laws.

MATERIALS

U-tube with side arms, several dry cells or rectifier unit as a source of D.C., platinum or carbon electrodes, copper strips for electrodes, ring stand, utility clamps, copper wire and alligator clips for making electric connections, 1-M Na_2SO_4, 1-M $CuSO_4$, 1-M KI, phenolphthalein, bromthymol blue, 1-M $CuBr_2$, 250-ml beakers, graduated cylinder, balance, 18-M (concentrated) H_2SO_4, ethyl alcohol, 0.5-M $AgNO_3$, saturated KI solution, glass rod, silver, brass, or nickel object. Additional materials needed for Part III are an ammeter, a rheostat to control current flow, a D.C. power supply, a stop watch, 1-M NaOH, 6-M HNO_3, steel wool or emery cloth, and acetone.

PROCEDURE

Part I · Electrolysis of Aqueous Solutions

1. Add 10 drops of bromthymol blue to 100 ml of 1-M Na_2SO_4 and adjust the solution to pH 7 so that the indicator color is green. Pour the solution into a U-tube with side arms (Fig. 17-2). Place either platinum or carbon electrodes in the open ends of the U-tube, connect to a source of D.C. and allow the current to pass through the solution for several minutes. Note and record in Table IA any evidence of a reaction. Use your observations and a table of reduction potentials to help identify the products of electrolysis at the electrodes and to interpret the experimental observations. Below Table IA write the equations for the anode and cathode reactions.

Table IA   Electrolysis of 1-M Sodium Sulfate Using Unreactive Electrodes

	Observations
Anode	
Cathode	

Anode reaction:
Cathode reaction:

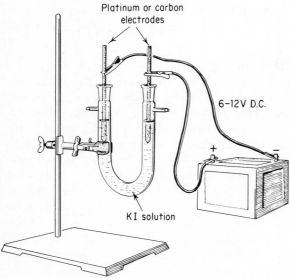

Platinum or carbon electrodes

6–12V D.C.

KI solution

Fig. 17-2   Electrolyzing a salt solution.

242

2. Pour out the contents of the U-tube, clean and refill it with 1-M $CuSO_4$. Insert platinum or carbon electrodes and again electrolyze the solution. Record your observations in Table IB and write the equations for the anode and cathode reactions below the table.

Table IB   Electrolysis of 1-M Copper Sulfate Using Unreactive Electrodes

	Observations
Anode	
Cathode	

Anode reaction:
Cathode reaction:

3. Replace both electrodes with copper electrodes and again electrolyze the 1-M $CuSO_4$ solution. Allow the current to flow until there are signs that a change is occurring at either or both electrodes and compare with the results of Part II. Record your observations in Table IC and write the electrode equations beneath the table. Note especially whether a gas evolved at either electrode.

Table IC   Electrolysis of 1-M Copper Sulfate Using Copper Electrodes

	Observations
Anode	
Cathode	

Anode reaction:
Cathode reaction:

4. Now re-insert the platinum or carbon electrodes and fill a clean U-tube with a 1-M KI solution containing ten drops of phenolphthalein. Electrolyze the solution and record your observations in Table ID. Write the equations for the electrode reactions below the table.

5. Clean the electrodes in (concentrated) 15-M HNO_3, wash, re-insert and fill a clean U-tube

with 1-M $CuBr_2$. Electrolyze the solution, record your observations and write the equations for the electrode reactions. You could pour contents of cell into a test tube, add five ml of CCl_4, shake and note color of Br_2 in CCl_4 (as distinguished from the color of I_2 in CCl_4).

Table ID · Electrolysis of 1-M Halide Solutions Using Unreactive Electrodes

Solution	Observation and Equation (anode)	Observation and Equation (cathode)
(1) KI		
(2) $CuBr_2$		

Solution (1)   Anode reaction:
                Cathode reaction:
Solution (2)   Anode reaction:
                Cathode reaction:

Part IIA · Silver Plating

6. Obtain about 200 ml of the silver iodide complex solution in a 250-ml beaker. This solution is prepared by adding a saturated solution of KI to 0.5-M $AgNO_3$ until the AgI precipitate which first forms all dissolves.

7. Fill a porous cup with the silver complex solution and place it into the beaker as shown in Fig. 17-3. This cup helps prevent contaminating the plating solution with any product formed during the plating process.

8. Using a carbon or platinum rod as the anode and a clean grease-free metallic object connected to the negative terminal of the D.C. source, attach the wires to a D.C. source as shown in Fig. 17-3 and allow the current to flow for a few minutes. Remove the object and buff with a fine abrasive such as chalk dust until a shiny metallic luster is achieved.

9. Return the silver plating solution to the container as directed by the instructor.

Part IIB · Copper Plating

10. Place about 220 ml of copper plating solution in a 250-ml beaker. If this solution is not available, you can prepare your own by dissolving 30 g of hydrated $CuSO_4$ in 200 ml of distilled water, then adding 7 ml of concentrated sulfuric acid and 11 ml of ethyl alcohol.

11. Clean the object to be plated by washing with dilute NaOH solution, then rinsing with dilute HNO_3 solution. Avoid touching the object

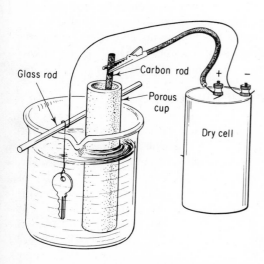

Fig. 17-3   Apparatus for silver plating.

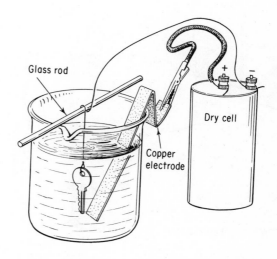

Fig. 17-4   Apparatus for copper plating.

243

with your fingers, as a greasy print will prevent the metal from adhering.

12. Place a $\frac{1}{2} \times 4$-in. strip of copper in the plating bath and bend the upper part over the top of the beaker as shown in Fig. 17-4. Obtain and clean a key or some other metallic object to be plated. Suspend the object in the plating bath by a wire wound around a glass rod which is resting across the top of the beaker. Be certain that the object to be plated is completely submerged. *Do not allow it to contact the copper strip.*

14. Remove both electrodes from the solution. Rinse, dry, and polish the object with a fine abrasive such as chalk dust. A clear light plate may be maintained if the object is dried and then sprayed with a clear lacquer.

15. Return the copper plating solution to the container directed by the instructor.

Part III · Determination of Avogadro's Number

16. Obtain two copper electrodes. A hollow cylindrical-shaped wire screen is desirable for the cathode, while a $\frac{1}{2} \times 4$-in. copper strip may be used as the anode. Fold the latter into a small cylinder. Clean the electrodes carefully with steel wool or emery cloth. Wash with water, and dilute NaOH. Then rinse well with dilute HNO_3 and

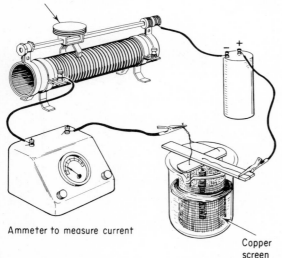

Rheostat to control current

Ammeter to measure current

Copper screen

Fig. 17-5   Determining Avogadro's number.

water. Avoid touching the electrode which is to be plated.

17. Dry and weigh the cathode to the nearest 0.01 g or better.

18. Place about 220 ml of 1-M $CuSO_4$ solution in a 250-ml beaker. Place the screen in the beaker and suspend the anode as shown in Figure 17-5. *Do not allow the electrodes to touch in the solution.*

19. Obtain a D.C. power supply which has a rheostat for adjusting the voltage. Connect the negative terminal of the power supply to the screen and the positive terminal to the copper anode.

20. Have a watch available to measure the time the current is allowed to flow. Start measuring the time at the instant you turn on the power supply. Adjust the current to about 1.00 amp and constantly adjust the voltage so that the current is maintained at 1 amp. Allow the cell to operate about 20 minutes.

21. Turn off the power supply. Remove the electrodes from the solution and record in the table the time the current was allowed to flow. Avoid dislodging any of the copper deposited on the cathode. Carefully dip the cathode in water, then in acetone and allow to dry. You may allow to dry overnight in your locker if you wish.

22. Weigh the dry cathode to the nearest 0.01 g or better and record the data in the table.

23. Read the Follow-up Discussion and make the calculations necessary to complete the following table. (Top of page 245).

FOLLOW-UP DISCUSSION

In Part I of this experiment you were asked to write the anode and cathode reactions. Your observations should help you, to some extent, write the correct equations. In some instances, however, it will be necessary for you to refer to a table of standard reduction potentials to obtain the information leading to the correct equation. For example, in the electrolysis of an aqueous solution of a sodium compound, if metallic sodium were produced it would immediately react with water and yield hydrogen gas. Thus by observation

1	Mass of cathode plus copper deposit	
2	Mass of cathode	
3	Mass of copper deposit	
4	Current (amperes)	
5	Time (seconds)	
6	Coulombs used to deposit measured mass	
7	Charge on electron (coulombs)	1.6×10^{-19}
8	Number of electrons used to deposit measured mass	
9	Mass of one mole of copper	
10	Electrons to deposit one mole of copper atoms	
11	Electrons to reduce Cu^{2+} ions to Cu^0 atoms	
12	Atoms in 1 mole of copper (Avogadro's number)	

alone you cannot distinguish between the reduction of Na^+ ions or the reduction of H_2O at the cathode. By checking the magnitude of the reduction potentials for the two processes, you find that H_2O has a higher reduction potential and therefore is more readily reduced. There are, of course, a number of factors that determine the rate at which a given product is discharged at a given electrode so that reduction potentials are not always an infallible guide to the electrode reaction. This means that you should use a combination of your observations and the values of the reduction potentials as a guide to writing electrode reaction equations. For example, if in the electrolysis of an aqueous chloride solution, you observe a yellowish, irritating gas being evolved at an electrode, you would not indicate that oxygen was the product even though the oxidation potentials indicate that water, rather than chloride ions should be the substance oxidized. Again, it should be emphasized that reduction po-

tentials are a measure of *thermodynamic* tendencies for a spontaneous reaction to occur and have no bearing on the *rate* at which the predicted reaction occurs.

In Part II of this experiment you plated a very thin coat of metal over another metal. Metals that have a tendency to alloy will probably plate easily. The opposite is also true as indicated by the fact that it is difficult to plate nickel on tin or lead. Experiments show that nickel does not alloy with either of these metals easily. The difficulty may be overcome by first plating the lead with copper, then with nickel or silver. Only a thin coat of a metal is needed to protect or beautify another metal.

The mass of metal plated may be calculated by applying Faraday's Law, which states that the mass of a substance produced by an electrolytic reaction is directly proportional to the current passing through the cell. A quantity of electricity possessed by one mole of electrons is called a faraday, approximately 96 500 coulombs. The equation for an electrode reaction shows the relationship between the number of moles of chemical species produced and the number of faradays of electricity used. For example, the equation for the oxidation of water

$$2H_2O = O_2 + 4H^+(aq) + 4e^-$$

shows that the production of one mole of oxygen gas (32.0 g) involves 4 moles of electrons (4 faradays). Thus, 1.0 faraday of electricity liberates 8.0 g of O_2 gas.

FOLLOW-UP QUESTIONS

1. Explain the color of the solution around the anode and cathode in the electrolysis of 1-M Na_2SO_4. Check the Appendix for the color of bromthymol blue in acid and basic solutions.

2. In Procedures 2 and 3 you electrolyzed a solution of 1-M $CuSO_4$ yet observed different products. Explain in terms of the anode and cathode materials used.

3. Explain the color change you observed around the cathode during the electrolysis of aqueous KI.

4. If, in the electrolysis of KI solution, K^+ were reduced to $K(s)$, then metallic potassium would react with water and produce H_2 gas according to the equation

$$K(s) + HOH \rightarrow \tfrac{1}{2}H_2(g) + K^+(aq) + OH^-(aq)$$

Explain why you do or do not believe that this is the cathode reaction.

5. The equation for the reduction of the complex ion in the silver plating bath is

$$AgI_2^- + e^- = Ag + 2I^-.$$

Explain why, although the complex ion carries a negative charge, silver ions plate out on the negatively charged cathode.

6. How could you remove the copper plate from your object (a) electrolytically, (b) chemically?

7. Does the copper(II) ion concentration of the solution increase, decrease, or remain constant during the plating process (a) when a platinum electrode is used, and (b) when a copper electrode is used? Explain.

8. Assume in Part II that 0.400 g of silver were deposited on the cathode. How many ml of O_2 gas were evolved if the temperature was $25.0°C$ and the pressure 745 torr?

9. Calculate the mass and thickness (cm) of the copper plate on your object if a current of 1 amp was allowed to flow for 3.00 min. Assume that your object was a square solid that was 2.00 cm on an edge and of negligible thickness.

18-1
Properties of the Halogens

GENERAL DISCUSSION

The single, most striking characteristic of the Group-VIIA elements is their high reactivity. Their rather high reduction potentials and high electronegativity values indicate that these elements tend to gain electrons and form stable negative ions. In Experiment 17-4 you found that all of the halogens are relatively good oxidizing agents. In this experiment you will prepare small quantities of three of these elements and observe some of their properties, as well as the properties of some of their compounds.

OBJECTIVES

1. To observe the individual halogen elements. To investigate some of their physical properties such as color, appearance, and solubility.

2. To investigate some of the chemical properties of the halogens and some of the halogen compounds.

MATERIALS

Soluble starch, solid KI, filter paper, beaker, test tube, solid $KMnO_4$, solid NaCl, 1-M H_2SO_4, graduated cylinder, colored cloth, litmus paper, solid NaBr, solid NaI, iodine, evaporating dish, burner, wire screen, ethyl alcohol, 0.2-M solutions of KI, KNO_3, NaI, 1-M $Na_2S_2O_3$, chlorine water, bromine water, 1-M KI, CCl_4 or one of the liquid Freons.

PROCEDURE

Part I · Properties of Chlorine

1. Prepare two or three strips of potassium iodide-starch paper by placing a piece of filter paper into a beaker containing a soluble starch suspension and some potassium iodide (KI). Your instructor may have prepared some KI-starch paper in advance. In this case it should be moistened before being used.

2. In a large, dry test tube, place about 12 small $KMnO_4$ crystals and about an equal amount of solid sodium chloride. To this, add about one ml of dilute sulfuric acid. **Caution:** *never add concentrated sulfuric acid to solid $KMnO_4$.* Invert a beaker over the test tube to avoid dispersing the chlorine gas into the room.

3. Observe the color of the gas produced by this reaction. **Caution:** *carefully note the odor of this gas.* Record your observations in Table I.

4. Note the behavior of any gas that escapes and compare its density with that of the air.

5. Place a strip of moistened KI-starch paper in the test tube. Observe the results and record your observation in Table I.

Table I   Properties of the Halogens

Property	Chlorine	Bromine	Iodine
Color			
Odor			
Density relative to air and to each other			
Effect on KI-starch paper			
Effect on moist colored cloth		✕	✕
Effect on moist litmus paper			
Solubility in H_2O	✕		
Solubility in CCl_4	✕		
Solubility in ethanol	✕		

6. Place a piece of moistened, dyed cloth in the test tube. Record your observations.

7. Place a piece of moist litmus paper in the test tube and record your observations.

Part II · Properties of Bromine

8. Repeat all procedures in Part I (except number 6) using NaBr crystals in place of the NaCl crystals. **Caution:** *use extreme care in smelling the gas.* Record all your observations in Table I.

9. Obtain about two ml of bromine water from your instructor. Add two ml of CCl_4 or one of the liquid Freons, shake, and observe the relative colors of the two layers. Record the relative solubility of Br_2 in H_2O and CCl_4 or the liquid Freon.

Part III · Properties of Iodine

10. Prepare a small amount of iodine using the same procedure used for preparing chlorine and bromine. Since this method may not produce enough iodine for subsequent steps, you may need to obtain a few iodine crystals from your instructor. *Avoid touching iodine crystals* since they stain your skin.

11. Place a single, small crystal of iodine in an evaporating dish and gently heat with a bunsen burner. **Caution:** *use extreme care not to inhale any vapors.* Record your observations in Table I.

12. Place a small piece of iodine in two ml of H_2O. Note its solubility. Add a crystal to two ml of CCl_4 or a liquid Freon. Note the solubility of I_2 and the color of the resulting solution. Compare the color of this solution to the color of the iodine vapor produced in (11) above. Place a second crystal in two ml of ethanol. Observe and record the relative solubility in the three solvents in Table I.

13. Place a single small crystal of iodine in each of three test tubes. To the first add two ml of 0.2-M KI solution; to the second add two ml of 0.2-M KNO_3 solution; to the third add two ml of 0.2-M NaI solution. Shake all three tubes and observe the degree of solubility of the iodine in each. Record your observations in Table II.

14. Place a single crystal of iodine in a five-ml sample of KI solution. To this add drop by drop a small amount of sodium thiosulfate. Observe and record the results in Table II.

Table II Solubility and Reaction of I_2

Procedure	Observation
$I_2 + KI$	
$I_2 + KNO_3$	
$I_2 + NaI$	
$I_2 + KI + S_2O_3{}^{2-}$	

FURTHER EXPERIMENTATION

1. Prepare a glass plate for etching by covering it with melted wax and scratching a design in the wax. Be sure to scratch the wax deep enough so that a solution can come into contact with the glass in the prepared design.

Obtain about one g of fluorspar (CaF_2) and place on the prepared glass.

Moisten the fluorspar with a few drops of concentrated sulfuric acid. **Caution:** *place in a fume hood and avoid touching the mixture. It is very corrosive.*

Allow to stand in the fume hood overnight. The etching effect of the hydrofluoric acid (HF) on the glass may be seen after the wax is removed and the glass is washed the next day.

FOLLOW-UP DISCUSSION

The preparation of the halogens in Part I is accomplished by oxidizing the halide ions with a strong oxidizing agent in the presence of an acid. The $KMnO_4$ could have been replaced by K_2CrO_4 or any other strong oxidizing agent. You can consult the Appendix to determine which other oxidizing agents could have been used. The KI-starch paper may be used as an indicator paper for any oxidizing agent stronger than I_2. By checking the Appendix you can see that such oxidizing agents as Fe^{3+}, Hg^{2+}, and $NO_3^- + 2H^+$ can oxidize I^- to I_2. The exact composition of the starch-iodide compound is not known but the blue-black compound is a specific indicator used to detect both starch and iodine.

The bleaching action of the chlorine is associated with the action of a hypochlorite which is formed when chlorine comes into contact with water.

$$Cl_2 + H_2O \rightleftharpoons HCl + HClO$$

Dry chlorine is not effective as a bleaching agent.

Bromine acts in many respects like chlorine. It has a similar odor, is very dense, and is capable of oxidizing iodide ions. The data in Table II indicate that iodide ions have some effect on the solubility of iodine in water. When I_2 is added to a KI solution, these equilibria are thought to be present.

$$I_2(s) \rightleftharpoons I_2(aq)$$
$$I_2(aq) + I^-(aq) \rightleftharpoons I^-_3(aq) \qquad \text{Eq. 1}$$

Application of Le Châtelier's principle to Equation 1 indicates that addition of I^- to an I_2 solution would shift the equilibrium to the right and cause more I_2 to dissolve. The I^-_3 ions are found to have a linear structure. An electron dot structure for these ions shows that the octet rule does not apply.

FOLLOW-UP QUESTIONS

1. Write net ionic equations for the reactions which you used to prepare the halogens.

2. Write net ionic equations for the action of chlorine water on NaBr and NaI.

3. I_2 exists as a diatomic molecule in the vapor state. In what form would you say it existed when dissolved in CCl_4? What evidence is there to support your belief?

4. Write an equation for the reaction of I_2 with sodium thiosulfate ($Na_2S_2O_3$).

5. Predict the result of adding chlorine water to a solution of NaF.

6. Use equations to explain why an aqueous solution of chlorine is slightly acid.

7. Suggest a means of removing an iodine stain from your clothing.

18-2
Nitrogen Compounds

GENERAL DISCUSSION

Although diatomic molecules of nitrogen are very stable, many compounds of nitrogen are highly unstable. In this experiment we shall not perform any chemical tests with nitrogen gas since most of these tests simply reflect the unreactive nature of nitrogen. We shall, however, investigate some of the properties of a few selected nitrogen compounds.

A study of a large number of nitrogen compounds shows that nitrogen exists in oxidation states from 3− to 5+. In ammonia (NH_3) the oxidation state is 3−; in hydrazine (N_2H_4) it is 2−; in hydroxylamine (NH_2OH) it is 1−. In elemental nitrogen the oxidation state is zero. In its oxides, nitrogen exhibits oxidation states ranging from 1+ to 4+. In nitric acid (HNO_3) and other nitrates, its oxidation state is 5+.

OBJECTIVE

To investigate some of the properties of some nitrogen compounds.

MATERIALS

Test tubes, graduated cylinder, triple-beam balance, beakers, burner, ring stand, wire screen, solid NH_4Cl, solid NH_4NO_3, solid $(NH_4)_2SO_4$, 6-M NaOH solution, solid $Ca(OH)_2$, 6-M HCl, phenolphthalein, 0.1-M $CuSO_4$, 6-M NH_3(aq), 0.1-M $ZnSO_4$, 0.1-M $AgNO_3$, 0.1-M $AlCl_3$, concentrated (16-M) HNO_3, copper wire, iron wire or iron filings, 0.1-M KCNS, white wool or egg white, solid KI, 6-M nitric acid (HNO_3), CCl_4 or a liquid Freon, $BaCl_2$.

PROCEDURE

Part I · Ammonium Compounds and Ammonia

1. In three separate test tubes, place 0.5 g samples of solid ammonium chloride (NH_4Cl), ammonium nitrate (NH_4NO_3), and ammonium sulfate [$(NH_4)_2SO_4$]. To each test tube add one ml of 6-M sodium hydroxide. Gently heat the tubes one at a time and note any odor produced. Record your observations in Table I.

2. Mix thoroughly, two g of ammonium chloride and four g of $Ca(OH)_2$. Place this mixture

Table I Ammonia and Ammonium Compounds

Procedure	Observation
NH_4Cl + NaOH	
$(NH_4)_2SO_4$ + NaOH	
NH_4NO_3 + NaOH	
NH_4Cl + $Ca(OH)_2$	
NH_3 over H_2O	
NH_3 + HCl	
NH_3 + H_2O (phenolphthalein)	
$CuSO_4$ + $NH_3 \cdot H_2O$	
$CuSO_4$ + excess $NH_3 \cdot H_2O$	
$ZnSO_4$ + $NH_3 \cdot H_2O$	
$ZnSO_4$ + excess $NH_3 \cdot H_2O$	
$AgNO_3$ + HCl	
$AgCl$ + $NH_3 \cdot H_2O$	
$AlCl_3$ + $NH_3 \cdot H_2O$	
$AlCl_3$ + excess $NH_3 \cdot H_2O$	
$AlCl_3$ + NaOH	
$AlCl_3$ + excess NaOH	

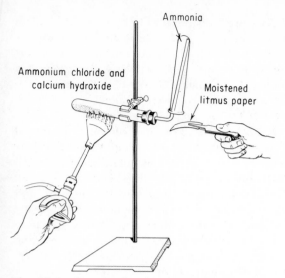

Ammonia

Ammonium chloride and
calcium hydroxide

Moistened
litmus paper

Fig. 18-1   Preparation of ammonia.

in a test tube. Equip this test tube with a delivery tube aiming upward, and fasten the assembly to a ring stand with a buret clamp. (Figure 18-1). Gently heat this mixture and collect the ammonia by placing a test tube downward over the delivery tube. Collect test tubes full of ammonia as they are needed for these tests.

(a) Invert a tube of ammonia over water in a beaker mouth of the tube in the water.

(b) Put a drop of concentrated 12-M hydrochloric acid (HCl) in a tube of the ammonia.

(c) Add two ml of water and a few drops of phenolphthalein. Stopper the tube and shake.

3. Pour about three ml of 0.1-M $CuSO_4$ into a test tube. Add a solution of 6-M ammonia (sometimes labeled ammonium hydroxide) drop by drop until a change is noted. Record your observations, then continue to add ammonia water until a second change occurs. Record this change.

4. Repeat (3) using 0.1-M $ZnSO_4$ instead of $CuSO_4$.

5. Add a drop of dilute (6-M) HCl to three ml of 0.1-M $AgNO_3$. Record your observation and then add ammonia solution until another change is noted.

6. Pour three ml of 0.1-M $AlCl_3$ or $Al(NO_3)_3$ into each of two test tubes. To one of the test tubes add 6-M ammonia-water dropwise until a change is noted. Record your observation and then add an additional five ml of 6-M ammonia solution. Record whether there has been a further change. To the other test tube add 6-M NaOH by drops until a change is noted. Record your observation and add additional 6-M NaOH (5–6 ml) until a further change occurs.

Part II · Nitric Acid

7. Place two ml of concentrated (12-M) hydrochloric acid in one test tube and two ml of concentrated (16-M) nitric acid in another. To each test tube add a *small* piece of copper wire. Record the results in Table II.

8. Put a small piece of iron wire or a few small pieces of iron filings in each of two test tubes. To the first add three ml of concentrated 12-M HCl and to the second add three ml of concentrated 16-M HNO_3. Dilute both solutions by pouring each into separate beakers containing ten ml of distilled water. Do not add water to concen-

Table II   Nitric Acid

Procedure	Observations
$Cu + HNO_3$	
$Cu + HCl$	
$Fe + HNO_3$	
$Fe + HCl$	
$Fe + HNO_3 + SCN^-$	
$Fe + HCl + SCN^-$	
$HNO_3 + protein$	
$KI + HNO_3(CCl_4)$	
$S + HCl$	
$S + HNO_3$	
$S + HCl + BaCl_2$	
$S + HNO_3 + BaCl_2$	

trated acids. To both samples add two ml of 0.1-M potassium thiocyanate. Record your observations.

9. Place a few drops of 16-M nitric acid on a sample of white wool yarn or on a sample of egg white (both of these materials contain proteins). Note and record the effect that nitric acid has on protein. If you accidentally get a drop of concentrated nitric acid on your hands you will notice the same results.

10. Dissolve about 0.5 g of KI in three ml of water in a clean test tube. Add one drop of conc 16-M HNO_3 and shake. Add about one ml of CCl_4 or a liquid Freon to this mixture and shake again. Record your observations.

11. Place a 0.5-g sample of powdered sulfur in each of two test tubes. To the first, add three ml of concentrated 12-M hydrochloric acid. To the second, add three ml of concentrated 16-M nitric acid. Warm both tubes. Gently boil for 1 minute. Allow both tubes to cool, then dilute both samples by pouring each into separate beakers which already contain ten ml of water. Decant these two solutions back into two separate test tubes (avoid getting any sulfur back into the test tubes). Add two ml of barium chloride to each tube. A white precipitate indicates the presence of sulfate ions.

FURTHER EXPERIMENTATION

1. *Preparation of nitric acid.* Put 20 g of

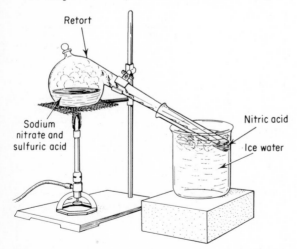

Fig. 18-2   Preparation of nitric acid.

$NaNO_3$ in a glass retort (Figure 18-2). Add 20 ml of concentrated 12-M sulfuric acid. Place this assembly under a fume hood and direct the retort into a large test tube which is immersed in a beaker of ice water. Gently heat the mixture in the retort until you have distilled several milliliters of HNO_3 into the cold test tube.

2. *Preparation of nitrated cotton.* Place ten ml of concentrated 16-M nitric acid into a 125-ml erlenmeyer flask. Carefully add 14 ml of concentrated 18-M sulfuric acid to the flask. Place about two g of absorbent cotton into this acid mixture and allow to stand for about three hours. Pour off the acid and wash the cotton several times with pure water. Continue washing the cotton and wringing it out until you are *sure that all the acid is removed.* **Caution:** *Do not allow the cotton to dry if it is not thoroughly washed.* Dry the washed cotton for one or two days. Place a piece of the nitrated cotton on an asbestos pad. Holding a match in a pair of tongs, ignite the sample of nitrated cotton. Burn a similar sample of ordinary cotton for comparison.

FOLLOW-UP DISCUSSION

Several of the observations which you made in this experiment may be explained in terms of two characteristics of NH_3. These are (a) it is a weak base in water solution and (b) it forms complex ions. Its high solubility in water and its complexing ability may in large part be attributed to the presence of the lone pair of unused electrons. The formation of hydrogen bonds between the lone electron-pair on the nitrogen atom and the hydrogen atoms of the water molecule enhances its solubility. Hydrogen bonds are also formed between the hydrogen atoms of the ammonia molecules and the lone pairs of electrons on the oxygen atom of the water molecules. Experimental evidence reveals that 700 ml of ammonia gas at standard conditions can dissolve in 1 ml of water.

The lone pair of electrons on the ammonia molecule is also available for coordinate bond formation with electronically deficient species which have vacant orbitals. Its reaction with positive ions forming complex ions is an example of a Lewis acid-base reaction. The formulas of the complex ions formed in this experiment are given in the table.

Complex Ions
$Zn(NH_3)_4^{2+}$
$Cu(NH_3)_4^{2+}$
$Ag(NH_3)_2^+$
$Al(OH)_4^-$
$Fe(SCN)^{2+}$

FOLLOW-UP QUESTIONS

1. Write a net ionic equation for the reaction between an ammonium salt and any strong base.

2. Explain why the water entered the inverted test tube filled with ammonia.

3. What is the white powder or white smoke that forms when NH_3 and HCl gas are mixed? Write an equation for the reaction.

4. Write two equations to explain your observations when you added (a) a small quantity of ammonia solution and (b) a large quantity of ammonia solution to a $ZnSO_4$ solution. (c) Use equilibrium principles to explain why the precipitate dissolved.

5. Write an equation for the reaction which occurred when you added ammonia water to the precipitate formed by the reaction between HCl and $AgNO_3$.

6. Write an equation for the reaction between aluminum chloride and ammonia solution. Did the same precipitate form when you added a drop of NaOH to the $AlCl_3$? Why did an excess of NaOH dissolve the precipitate while an excess of the ammonia solution did not? Write an equation for the reaction in which the precipitate dissolved.

7. Nitric acid and the hydrogen ions from hydrochloric acid both act as oxidizing agents. Use data obtained from this experiment to discuss their relative strengths. Why did copper react with HNO_3 but not HCl?

8. Show a net ionic equation for the oxidation of the iodide ions by nitric acid, forming iodine. Could an HCl solution have oxidized iodide ions to iodine? Refer to a table of reduction (oxidation) potentials to answer this question (Table 2 in the appendix).

9. Write a net ionic equation to show the oxidation of sulfur to sulfate ions by nitric acid.

10. Explain why red $Fe(CNS)^{2+}$ was produced by adding thiocyanate solution to the sample of iron oxidized by the HNO_3, but not by the sample oxidized by HCl.

11. What test could you use to tell whether a substance contained protein?

18-3
Sulfur and Its Compounds

GENERAL DISCUSSION

In this experiment you prepare crystals of the two allotropes of sulfur, rhombic and monoclinic. You observe some of the properties of elemental sulfur. You also investigate some of the chemistry of a few selected sulfur compounds. In compounds, sulfur is commonly found in oxidation states of 6+, 4+, 2+, and 2−. We shall briefly examine the behavior of sulfur species containing the element in its 6+, 4+, and 2− oxidation states.

OBJECTIVES

1. To prepare and observe the allotropic forms of sulfur.
2. To investigate some of the properties of sulfur and of compounds containing sulfur in its three most important oxidation states.

MATERIALS

Balance, graduated cylinder, wide-mouth bottles, test tubes, funnels, ring stand, burner, beakers, wire screen, filter paper, watch glass, magnifying glass, one-hole stoppers, copper or silver coin, flowers of sulfur, roll sulfur, CS_2, concentrated (18-M) H_2SO_4, solid $CuSO_4 \cdot 5H_2O$, sucrose, wood splint, zinc metal, copper metal, dilute (6-M) H_2SO_4, solid NaCl, solid KBr, solid KI, litmus paper, 0.1-M $Ca(NO_3)_2$, 0.1-M $BaCl_2$, 0.1-M $Sr(NO_3)_2$, 0.1-M $Pb(NO_3)_2$, 0.5-M Na_2SO_3 solution, solid Na_2SO_3, 250-ml erlenmeyer flask, two-hole rubber stopper, glass tubing, thistle tube, rubber tubing, dilute (6-M) HCl, colored flower or apple peel, 3% hydrogen peroxide, 0.1-M $KMnO_4$ solution, solid FeS, 0.1-M solutions of $Cd(NO_3)_2$, $Zn(NO_3)_2$, $SbCl_3$, $CuSO_4$, $Pb(NO_3)_2$, KCl, 0.5-M $(NH_4)_2S$, 3-M H_2SO_4, conc (12-M) HCl.

PROCEDURE

Part I · Properties of Sulfur

1. Examine a piece of sulfur. Note and record in Table I its hardness, color, and general appearance. Place a small sample in a test tube with five ml of water. Note its solubility in water.

2. Place 0.5 g of flowers of sulfur into a test tube. Add four ml of carbon disulfide, CS_2. **Caution:** *carbon disulfide is quite toxic and very flammable.* Shake the test tube until the sulfur has dissolved. Pour the solution into a watch glass and cover it with a piece of filter paper to slow the evaporation. Set this far away from any open flames and allow the CS_2 to evaporate. Examine and describe the crystals in Table I.

Table I   Properties of Sulfur

Property	Observation
Color	
Hardness	
General appearance	
Solubility in H_2O	
Solubility in CS_2	
Crystalline shape and appearance when crystallized from CS_2	
Crystalline shape and appearance when heated to melting point and recrystallized	
Properties of product formed on combustion	
Description of product formed on reaction with Ag or Cu	

3. Fold a piece of filter paper into a cone as for filtering and support it in a ring attached to a ring stand. Place about ten g of sulfur in a Pyrex test tube and gently heat the tube over a bunsen burner until the sulfur has melted. Avoid igniting the sulfur. Warm the path out and pour the melted sulfur into the conical filter paper. As a crust begins to form on the surface, break open the filter paper. **Caution:** *this sulfur is still very hot.* Spread the filter paper out flat on the table. Observe the crystals with a magnifying glass and describe them in Table I.

4. Place a sample of sulfur, the size of a pinhead, on a silver or copper coin or on a strip of copper metal. Gently heat the metal until the sulfur melts. If some of the sulfur ignites, *cautiously* note the odor of the gas given off. Describe any changes in the appearance of the metal.

Part II · Properties of Sulfuric Acid

5. **Caution:** *concentrated H_2SO_4 is extremely corrosive and should be handled carefully.* Place a single small crystal of hydrated copper sulfate, ($CuSO_4 \cdot 5H_2O$) into a test tube with two ml of concentrated 18-*M* sulfuric acid. Observe this crystal periodically for a half hour. Record your observations in Table II.

6. Add about 0.5 g of sugar (sucrose) to a test tube containing two ml of concentrated sulfuric acid.

7. Dip a wood match stick or a wood splint into a test tube with two ml of concentrated H_2SO_4.

8. Carefully add concentrated H_2SO_4 dropwise with stirring to 25 ml of water in a small beaker. Record any noticeable heat effect. **Caution:** *never pour water into the concentrated acid.*

9. Pour three or four ml of dilute (3-*M*) sulfuric acid into each of two test tubes. To one test tube add a small piece of mossy zinc; to the other add a small piece of copper. Record any evidence of a reaction. *Cautiously* smell any gas which is evolved. Also, test the combustibility of any gas which is evolved.

10. Repeat (9) using three or four ml of con-centrated H_2SO_4 in place of the dilute H_2SO_4. Heat gently.

11. Place approximately one g each of NaCl, KBr, and KI in separate test tubes. To each salt, *cautiously* add about one ml of concentrated H_2SO_4. Test any gas with moistened blue litmus paper and record the characteristics of the products of each reaction.

12. Add two ml of dilute (3-*M*) sulfuric acid to five ml samples of 0.1-*M* $Ca(NO_3)_2$, 0.1-*M* $BaCl_2$, 0.1-*M* $Sr(NO_3)_2$ and 0.1-*M* $Pb(NO_3)_2$. Record any evidence of a reaction in Table II.

Table II Properties of Sulfuric Acid

Procedure	Observation
conc. H_2SO_4 + $CuSO_4 \cdot 5H_2O$	
conc. H_2SO_4 + sucrose	
conc. H_2SO_4 + wood	
conc. H_2SO_4 + H_2O	
conc. H_2SO_4 (cold) + Zn	
conc. H_2SO_4 (cold) + Cu	
conc. H_2SO_4 (hot) + Cu	
dil. H_2SO_4 + Cu	
dil. H_2SO_4 + Zn	
conc. H_2SO_4 + NaCl	
conc. H_2SO_4 + KBr	
conc. H_2SO_4 + KI	
dil. H_2SO_4 + $Ca(NO_3)_2$	
dil. H_2SO_4 + $BaCl_2$	
dil. H_2SO_4 + $Sr(NO_3)_2$	
dil. H_2SO_4 + $Pb(NO_3)_2$	

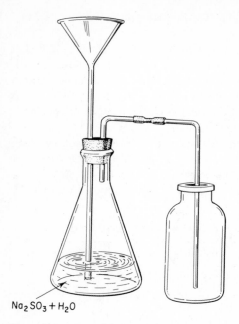

$Na_2SO_3 + H_2O$

Fig. 18-3   Preparation of sulfur dioxide.

Part III · Sulfur Dioxide and Sulfite Ions

13. Obtain two bottles of sulfur dioxide (SO_2), from a generator *under a fume hood.* Sulfur dioxide can be produced by adding a strong acid to a sulfite. To prepare the SO_2, place 0.50-M Na_2SO_3 in a flask fitted with a thistle tube and a delivery tube (Fig. 18-3). Add 6-M HCl and warm the flask. The volumes of Na_2SO_3 solution used and HCl added depend upon the amount of SO_2 needed. Collect the SO_2 under the fume hood by the upward displacement of air. The method of collection should serve as a clue to the relative densities of SO_2 and air, and to the relative solubility of the gas in water. Record these observations in Table III.

14. To one bottle of SO_2 add about ten ml of water and stopper with a one-hole stopper. Hold your finger tightly over the stopper hole and invert the bottle over a beaker of water, hole under water. Release your finger. Record your observations in Table III. Save the solution in this bottle to use in Procedures 16 and 17.

15. Place a moistened carnation, geranium, or other colored flower in the second bottle of SO_2.

If a flower is not available, use a piece of apple peel. Notice the effect of the SO_2 on these colored pigments. Remove the flower or apple peel and set it aside in the room for half an hour. Observe and record the results.

16. Divide the solution from Procedure 14 into three test tubes (10–15 ml in each). In case the solution is not available, one containing the same sulfur species may be prepared by mixing two g of Na_2SO_3, 15 ml of H_2O and one ml of dilute (6-M) HCl. To the first test tube add a few drops of concentrated (12-M) HCl and then ten ml of a 3% solution of hydrogen peroxide. Add five ml of 0.1-M $BaCl_2$ solution. Observe and record your results.

17. To the second portion of the solution, add dropwise a few ml of 0.1-M $KMnO_4$ solution. Record your observations. Test some of the resulting solution with $BaCl_2$.

18. Add a piece of mossy zinc to ten ml of dilute (3-M) H_2SO_4. To this solution add drop-

Table III   Properties of SO_2 and SO_3^{2-}

Properties	Observation
Color of SO_2	
Odor of SO_2	
Density relative to air	
Solubility in H_2O relative to H_2	
Effect on plant pigment	
Reaction of sulfur dioxide-exposed plant pigment on standing in air	
Acidified SO_2 solution + H_2O_2 + $BaCl_2$	
Acidified SO_2 solution + $KMnO_4$ + $BaCl_2$	
SO_2 solution + Zn + H_2SO_4	
Na_2SO_3 + $BaCl_2$	
Na_2SO_3 + $BaCl_2$ + HCl	

wise the SO_2 solution from the third test tube. Note the characteristics of any solid or gas which is formed as a result of the addition.

19. Add two g of Na_2SO_3 to 15 ml of H_2O in a test tube. Dissolve the crystals and add two ml of 0.1-M $BaCl_2$. Describe the product in Table III and then add five ml of dilute HCl. Record your observations.

Part IV · Hydrogen Sulfide

20. **Caution:** *hydrogen sulfide gas is extremely toxic and should be produced only in very small quantities.* To a test tube containing two ml of concentrated (12-M) HCl, add a single small crystal of FeS. Use the fume hood. *Cautiously* note the odor of the gas produced.

21. Place approximately 0.5 g of Na_2SO_3 in a test tube containing ten ml of water. Add about 0.5 ml of dilute sulfuric acid. Take the test tube to the H_2S generator located in the fume hood and saturate the solution in the test tube with H_2S. (See Fig. 16-1 for construction of the H_2S generator.) Describe in Table IV the product which is formed. Note: a solution of H_2S may be prepared by heating a water solution of thioacetamide in a water bath (fume hood not required for this).

22. Place five ml of each of the following 0.1-M solutions into separate test tubes: (a) $Cd(NO_3)_2$, (b) $Zn(NO_3)_2$, (c) $SbCl_3$ (d) $CuSO_4$, (e) $Pb(NO_3)_2$, and (f) KCl. To each solution add a few drops of 0.5-M $(NH_4)_2S$ or Na_2S. Describe each product in Table IV.

FURTHER EXPERIMENTATION

1. Obtain an unknown which may contain sulfate (SO_4^{2-}), sulfite (SO_3^{2-}), or sulfide (S^{2-}). Use procedures developed in Parts I through IV to identify this unknown.

2. Obtain an unknown solution containing a mixture of two or more of the above ions. Design a system of analysis for identifying the ions present. Carry out this scheme with your unknown.

FOLLOW-UP DISCUSSION

Sulfur, like the halogens, combines directly with several metals forming sulfides. Since most metallic

Table IV   Properties of H_2S and S^{2-} Ions

Property	Observation
Color	
Odor	
Reaction with SO_3^{2-} ions	
Reaction of S^{2-} ions with Cd^{2+} ions	
Reaction of S^{2-} ions with Zn^{2+} ions	
Reaction of S^{2-} ions with Sb^{3+} ions	
Reaction of S^{2-} ions with Cu^{2+} ions	
Reaction of S^{2-} ions with Pb^{2+} ions	
Reaction of S^{2-} ions with K^+ ions	

sulfides, except the Group I metals, are insoluble, many metals are found in nature combined with the sulfur. Soluble salts tend to be washed into streams by water and eventually end up in the sea.

You observed the dehydrating power of concentrated sulfuric acid in Part II of the experiment. This property is used in many laboratory and industrial processes. One of the most effective means of drying gases is to bubble the gas through concentrated H_2SO_4.

The qualitative test for the presence of a sulfate is to add Ba^{2+}(aq) ions to a solution. Insoluble $BaSO_4$(s) forms as a white precipitate. HCl is added to confirm that the precipitate is $BaSO_4$ and not $BaCO_3$ or $BaSO_3$. HCl dissolves $BaCO_3$ and $BaSO_3$ during the reaction which produces Ba^{2+} ions and CO_2 gas or SO_2 gas. $BaSO_4$ does not react with HCl.

FOLLOW-UP QUESTIONS

1. Sketch and label the rhombic and monoclinic sulfur crystals which you observed in Part I of this experiment.

2. Write an equation for the formation of tarnish on silverware. Name some sources of the sulfur involved in the tarnishing of silverware in the home.

3. (a) What evidence did you obtain that concentrated sulfuric acid was able to remove water from hydrated copper(II) sulfate? (b) What is the black substance that remains when concentrated sulfuric acid is added to sugar or wood? (c) Is the reaction between concentrated sulfuric acid and water exo- or endothermic? (d) Explain why it is dangerous to add water to concentrated sulfuric acid.

4. What evidence do you have that dilute or cold concentrated sulfuric acid is not a strong oxidizing agent?

5. Write the equation for the reaction between hot concentrated H_2SO_4 and copper metal.

6. Which halide ion is easiest to oxidize? What is your evidence?

7. Use the data in Table II to help you write equations for the reaction between concentrated sulfuric acid and the three halides.

8. On the basis of your observations, rank the three halogens and concentrated sulfuric acid in decreasing order of oxidizing strength.

9. Write the formulas for four sulfates which do not dissolve appreciably in water.

10. In Procedure 14 of Part III, why did the water "flow" upward into the bottle? Make a more accurate statement of what happened.

11. Explain why paper which is made from yellow wood pulp and bleached with SO_2 turns yellow with age.

12. Can SO_3^{2-} ions act as both an oxidizing and reducing agent? Cite evidence to justify your answer. What changes in oxidation state occur in each case?

13. How can you distinguish between $BaSO_4$ and $BaSO_3$?

14. Is H_2S an oxidizing or reducing agent? Cite your evidence.

15. A student has an unknown mixture which he suspects contains SO_4^{2-}, SO_3^{2-} or S^{2-} ions. He adds some 0.1-M $KMnO_4$ which immediately is decolorized. Which ion(s) are present?

19-1
Calcium and Its Compounds

GENERAL DISCUSSION

In this experiment we shall investigate some of the properties of calcium metal and a few selected calcium compounds. Calcium has very few laboratory or industrial uses in its elemental form. Compounds of calcium, however, find extensive applications.

Calcium and magnesium compounds present in small quantities in water are responsible for an objectionable property known as "hardness." Hardness in water causes problems such as boiler scale in pipes and soap scum in basins. We shall investigate the properties of both "permanent" and "temporary" hard water as well as some methods of water softening.

OBJECTIVES

1. To observe some of the properties of elemental calcium.
2. To investigate some of the properties of calcium compounds.
3. To prepare and soften "hard water."

MATERIALS

Calcium metal, beaker, test tubes, splints, phenolphthalein indicator, graduated cylinder, calcium oxide, stopper, liquid soap, medicine dropper, beakers, glass tubing, burner, ring stand, test tube clamp, $CaCl_2$, $CaSO_4 \cdot 2H_2O$, crucible, clay triangle, burner, glass plate, coin or key, mineral oil.

PROCEDURE

1. Observe the hardness, color, and general appearance of calcium metal. Record your observations in the table.
2. Break off a small piece of calcium metal and place it in a beaker of water. Place a test tube over the metal and collect the gas being evolved.

Test the gas with a lighted splint. Test the water in the beaker by adding three or four drops of phenolphthalein.

3. Place a spatula full of calcium oxide (CaO) in a test tube containing ten ml of water. Note and record any noticeable heat effects produced by this reaction. Stopper and shake the test tube to insure that the maximum amount of CaO has reacted. Pour off a few drops of the liquid into a separate test tube and add a few drops of phenolphthalein. Filter the remaining solution and save the filtrate (a solution of $Ca(OH)_2$ known as *limewater*) for Procedure 5.

	Observation
Color of calcium	
Hardness of calcium	
Ca + HOH (nature of products)	
CaO + HOH (nature of product)	
CaO + HOH (heat effect)	
Drops of soap to produce suds with distilled H_2O	
Drops of soap to produce suds with temporary hard water	
Drops of soap to produce suds after boiling temporary hard water	
Drops of soap to produce suds with "permanently" hard water	
Drops of soap to produce suds after boiling "permanently" hard water	
Drops of soap to produce suds after passing "permanently" hard water through an ion-exchange column	

4. Obtain about 30 ml of liquid soap from your instructor. Pour five ml of distilled water into a clean test tube. Add liquid soap dropwise with an eyedropper, shaking vigorously after each drop. Count the drops and continue adding drops until soapsuds form which last for two minutes. Note the thickness of the suds.

5. Add five ml of saturated limewater [$Ca(OH)_2$] from Procedure 3 to about 20 ml of distilled water in a small beaker. Using a piece of glass tubing or a straw blow through this solution until it becomes cloudy. Continue blowing through this solution until it again becomes clear. The resulting solution contains $Ca(HCO_3)_2$. This is known as "temporary" hard water. Pour five ml of this solution into each of two test tubes. Boil the first portion in a test tube for a few minutes and record any changes. Allow this sample to cool but do not confuse it with the unboiled sample. Add soap dropwise to the boiled sample (shake vigorously after each drop and count the drops) until suds remain for two minutes. Repeat the same procedure with the unboiled portion of this solution. Compare the number of drops required to produce the same quantity of suds for each sample.

6. Add about 0.5 g of $CaCl_2$ to 50 ml of distilled water in a clean beaker. Stir this solution until the $CaCl_2$ is dissolved and thoroughly mixed in solution. This solution is known as "permanent" hard water. Pour five ml of this solution into each of three test tubes. Boil one sample for a few minutes and test the sample with liquid soap for hardness. Test the unboiled sample in the same manner. Pour the third portion through an ion-exchange column set up on the reagent table. Test the water which drains from the column with liquid soap. Compare the number of drops of soap required to produce the same quantity of suds with each sample.

7. Place a five- to ten-g-sample of gypsum, $CaSO_4 \cdot 2H_2O$, in a porcelain crucible. Place the crucible in a clay triangle supported on a ring stand. Heat the crucible for 10 or 15 minutes until the bottom of the crucible is a dull red color.

When the crucible has cooled, pour the contents on a glass plate, add a few drops of water, and stir into a paste. Coat a coin or key with a thin film of oil, then press the metal object into the plaster and allow it to harden. When the plaster has hardened, remove the metal object and inspect the plaster mold.

FURTHER EXPERIMENTATION

1. Obtain a low-melting alloy, such as solder, or prepare such an alloy by melting lead, tin, and cadmium together in a nickel crucible. Pour the melted alloy into the plaster mold prepared in Procedure 7. After the metal has cooled, break off the plaster mold and inspect your casting.

2. Attempt to prepare a plaster mold from gypsum that has not been heated.

FOLLOW-UP DISCUSSION

In Procedure 3, the addition of lime (CaO), to water produces a solution of calcium hydroxide [$Ca(OH)_2$], known as limewater. This process is known as *slaking,* and the product [$Ca(OH)_2$], sometimes referred to as slaked lime. When carbon dioxide gas is passed through limewater, a precipitate, $CaCO_3$, is formed.

$$Ca(OH)_2 + CO_2 \rightarrow CaCO_3(s) + H_2O$$

The continued addition of CO_2 causes the carbonate to dissolve.

$$CaCO_3(s) + H_2O + CO_2 \underset{boil}{\overset{cool}{\rightleftharpoons}} Ca(HCO_3)_2$$

If enough CO_2 is added, the precipitate is completely dissolved and converted to soluble calcium bicarbonate [$Ca(HCO_3)_2$]. The above equilibrium not only helps to explain the fact that $CaCO_3$ is dissolved by excessive CO_2 in solution, but aids in explaining how "temporary" hard water is "softened." Thus, "temporary" hard water which contains $Ca(HCO_3)_2$ can be softened by boiling.

The use of liquid soap to test the "softness" of water is based on the fact that in pure water, soaps form thin films and produce foams consisting of small bubbles (suds) in water. If water contains calcium or magnesium ions, the soap is removed in the form of an insoluble scum, calcium stearate.

$$Ca^{2+} + 2 \text{ sodium stearate} \rightarrow$$

soap

$$\text{calcium (stearate)}_2 + 2Na^+$$

soap scum

If the soap is removed from the solution in the form of soap scum, it cannot perform a detergent action. When water contains calcium ions from a source such as $CaCl_2$, there is no chance of removing these ions by boiling and forming an insoluble carbonate. Water containing compounds like $CaCl_2$ is therefore known as "permanent" hard water. This hardness may be removed by passing the water through an ion-exchange column.

When gypsum $(CaSO_4 \cdot 2H_2O)$, is heated, some of the water of hydration is removed in a process called *calcining*. When water is added to the anhydrous calcium sulfate, another hydrate forms as the plaster of Paris "sets" into a solid mass. The "setting" of cement also involves the formation of hydrates.

FOLLOW-UP QUESTIONS

1. Write the net ionic equation for the reaction of calcium with water.

2. Write an equation to represent the slaking of lime. What is the mole ratio of lime (CaO), to limewater $[Ca(OH)_2]$?

3. Write a net ionic equation to represent the action of CO_2 on limewater.

4. List the solutes present in "temporary" and "permanent" hard water.

5. Explain, using equations, how boiling "softens" temporary hard water but does not "soften" permanent hard water.

6. Explain the operation of an ion-exchange resin.

7. Explain, using an equation, how sodium carbonate can act as a water softener. What other substance might be used to soften "permanent" hard water?

8. Why must gypsum be heated (a process called calcined) before it can be hardened into a solid?

19-2
Total Hardness in Water: Compleximetric Titration

GENERAL DISCUSSION

The quality of water is of great importance to all of us. Water, as it occurs naturally, contains many dissolved minerals as well as many types of living organisms. Standards for mineral content as well as for bacterial count have been established in order to protect the consumer. Our drinking water as well as that used by countless industries is analyzed daily to see that it conforms to established standards.

One type of impurity in water familiar to everyone is that which causes "hardness." It is Ca^{2+} and Mg^{2+} ions that are largely responsible for the hardness in water. The sum of the Ca^{2+} and Mg^{2+} ions present in water is referred to as the "total hardness" of water. Because these impurities are present to a very small extent, water analysts usually report their concentration in parts per million (ppm). For practical purposes parts per million means milligrams of impurity per liter of solution. Analysts express the hardness quantitatively in terms of dissolved $CaCO_3$. For simplicity, and to relate the calculations to principles we have already studied, we shall express the hardness in terms of millimoles per liter of Ca^{2+} plus Mg^{2+} ions.

In this experiment you determine the total hardness in a sample of water (either tap water or a typical sample of hard water) by titrating the sample with a complexing agent known as EDTA. The EDTA reacts with Mg^{2+} or Ca^{2+} in a one-to-one mole ratio. By measuring the volume of standardized EDTA required to react with a measured volume of hard water, you can calculate the total hardness in terms of millimoles of Ca^{2+} and Mg^{2+} ions per liter. The principles underlying the use of EDTA and Eriochrome black T solution as

an indicator are briefly covered in the Follow-up Discussion.

OBJECTIVES

1. To determine the total hardness in a sample of hard water.
2. To become acquainted with the concepts, principles, and calculations associated with a compleximetric titration.

MATERIALS

Burets, 250-ml erlenmeyer flasks, sample of hard water containing both Mg^{2+} and Ca^{2+} ions, freshly prepared 0.01-M EDTA solution (prepared from disodium salt sold as Versene), Eriochrome black T solution (solid + triethanolamine + absolute ethanol), special buffer with pH 10 (prepared from 6-M aqueous NH_3 and solid NH_4Cl), 1-M NaOH, 1-M HCl, litmus.

PROCEDURE

1. Pipet, or dispense from a second buret, 50.00 ml of your hard-water sample into a 250-ml erlenmeyer flask. Add a few drops of 1-M HCl until the solution is slightly acid as tested with litmus, and then boil gently for several minutes.

2. Cool the solution and add 4 drops of methyl red. Add 1-M NaOH dropwise until the red color of the indicator just disappears.

3. Add in this order, 1–2 ml of pH-10 buffer, 3 drops of Eriochrome black T indicator solution, and titrate with standard 0.01-M EDTA until one drop causes the solution to turn from red to blue. Titrate slowly. Because the color change takes place slowly, you should swirl the solution and wait a few seconds between drops as you approach the endpoint.

Table I Total Hardness of a Water Sample

	Trial 1	Trial 2
Volume of sample		
Final reading of EDTA buret		
Initial reading of EDTA buret		
Volume of EDTA to titrate sample		
Molarity of EDTA		
Millimoles of EDTA used		
Millimoles of $Ca^{2+} + Mg^{2+}$ in sample (EDTA to total ion ratio = 1:1)		

4. Record your data in Table I and calculate the total hardness of your sample in terms of millimoles of Ca^{2+} ions plus Mg^{2+} ions per liter of solutions.

FOLLOW-UP DISCUSSION

Ethylenediaminetetraacetic acid (EDTA) is known as a chelating agent. This chelate is a tetraprotic weak acid molecule with two nitrogen atoms containing an unshared electron-pair. Thus the molecule has six bonding sites and is classified as a hexadentate ligand. Two of the protons are relatively easy to remove while the remaining two are rather difficult to remove. The four K_a values are 1.0×10^{-2}, 2.1×10^{-3}, $1.4 \times 10.^{-7}$ and 1.8×10^{-11}. The structure of molecule is

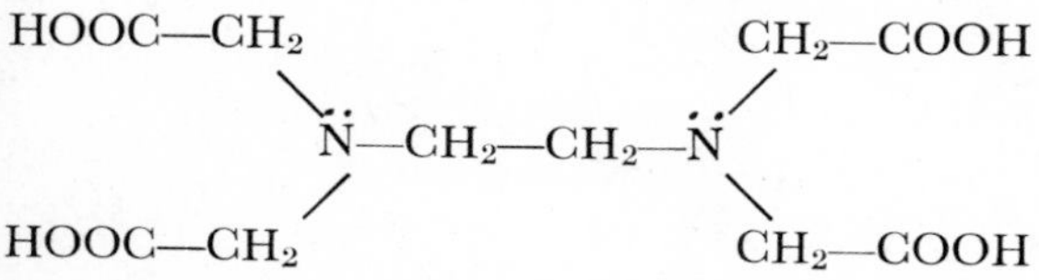

For convenience, the formulas for EDTA and its ions are abbreviated as H_4Y, H_3Y^-, H_2Y^{2-}, HY^{3-}, and Y^{4-}. Because H_4Y is not very soluble in water, and because Y^{4-} is too strong a base to exist as a stable species in water, the disodium salt ($Na_2H_2Y \cdot 2H_2O$) is usually used to prepare standard solutions for compleximetric analysis.

When EDTA reacts with metal ions, it does so in a 1:1 mole ratio. General equations for these reactions are

$$M^{2+} + H_2Y^{2-} \rightleftharpoons MY^{2-} + 2H^+$$
$$M^{3+} + H_2Y^{2-} \rightleftharpoons MY^{-} + 2H^+$$

The metal complexes are extremely stable with respect to their dissociation. This is, no doubt, caused by the six complexing groups within each EDTA molecule that bond to and surround metal ions such as Mg^{2+} and Ca^{2+}. Chelates are discussed and pictorially illustrated in Section 19-17 of *Foundations of Chemistry,* 2 ed.

Eriochrome black T is a triprotic organic dye whose equilibrium expression for the pH range in this titration is

$$\underset{\text{red}}{H_2In^-} \rightleftharpoons \underset{\text{blue}}{HIn^{2-}} + H^+$$

The species which predominates is determined by the pH of the solution. This indicator, known as a metal-ion indicator reacts with metallic ions and forms colored complexes (chelates) in the same way that acid-base indicators react with H^+ and OH^- ions and form different colored species. The reaction with Mg^{2+} may be expressed by

$$\underset{\text{blue}}{HIn^{2-}} + Mg^{2+} \rightleftharpoons \underset{\text{red}}{MgIn^-} + H^+$$

Thus, both the standard substance (EDTA) and the indicator (Eriochrome black T) react with metal ions and form chelates (complexes). In this titration when the indicator is added to the water sample containing Ca^{2+} and Mg^{2+} ions, the metal complexes form and turn the solution red. The Mg^{2+}-indicator complex is more stable with respect to dissociation than is the Ca^{2+}-indicator complex and is preferentially formed. On the other hand, the Ca^{2+}-EDTA complex is more stable than the Mg^{2+}-EDTA complex. Thus as standard EDTA is titrated into the water sample, it reacts first with the Ca^{2+} ions

$$Ca^{2+} + H_2Y^{2-} \rightleftharpoons CaY^{2-} + 2H^+$$

It next reacts with the Mg^{2+} ions

$$Mg^{2+} + H_2Y^{2-} \rightleftharpoons MgY^{2-} + 2H^+$$

Then at the endpoint, after all of the free (uncomplexed) Mg^{2+} is titrated, the EDTA displaces the indicator from the magnesium as follows

$$MgIn^- + H_2Y^{2-} \rightleftharpoons MgY^{2-} + HIn^{2-} + H^+$$
$$\text{red} \qquad\qquad\qquad\qquad \text{blue}$$

The solution is buffered at pH 10 to insure that at the endpoint the blue indicator species predominates and to prevent precipitation of insoluble metallic hydroxides. H_2In^- is red (pH < 6), HIn^{2-} is blue (pH 6–12), and In^{3-} is yellow orange (pH > 12). The pH also affects the stability of the complex formed between the indicator and the Mg^{2+} ions, as well as between EDTA and the metal ions; thus pH must be carefully controlled to get results in this experiment.

FOLLOW-UP QUESTIONS

1. Give several examples of instances where routine water analysis is essential.

2. Explain the action of the NH_3-NH_4^+ buffer in controlling pH. What mole ratio of NH_3 to NH_4^+ is necessary to buffer a solution at pH 10? $K_B = 1.8 \times 10^{-5}$.

3. Would a saturated solution of $PbCrO_4$ be safe to drink if the safe limit for lead ions in water is 0.1 ppm? Make use of the fact that the K_{sp} for $PbCrO_4$ is 1.8×10^{-14}.

4. A 100.0-ml sample of hard water requires 20.0 ml of EDTA solution to titrate the calcium and magnesium ions. Express the total hardness of the water in terms of mg of Ca^{2+} ions per liter (ppm) if 1.00 ml of the EDTA titrates the Ca^{2+} ions in 1.00 mg of dissolved Ca compounds.

20-1

Some Representative Organic Compounds

GENERAL DISCUSSION

The problem of purifying and positively identifying organic compounds is a difficult one. For the purposes of this experiment we shall attempt to identify compounds by comparing their odor and physical appearance with known compounds. Organic compounds are often classified according to characteristic functional groups such as the hydroxyl, carboxyl, and carbonyl groups. This experiment is designed to acquaint you with compounds containing some of these functional groups and to allow you to carry out a few reactions in which these compounds undergo chemical changes.

OBJECTIVES

To prepare and investigate the properties of a few organic compounds.

MATERIALS

Test tubes, graduated cylinder, methanol, 22-gauge copper wire, bunsen burner, 0.1-M $K_2Cr_2O_7$, conc. H_2SO_4, ethanol, glacial acetic acid, limewater, medicine dropper, butyric acid, salicylic acid, hot plate or oil bath, thermometer.

PROCEDURE

1. Place about two ml of methanol in a test tube. Carefully note the odor of the methanol. Prepare a spiral of fine (22-gauge) copper wire by coiling the wire around a pencil several times. Form the spiral about two cm in length, leaving about ten cm of wire for a handle. Heat the spiral in a burner flame and while it is hot, hold it just above the surface of the methanol. Observe the copper wire during this process. Note any odor produced during this process. If no change in odor was detected, reheat the copper coil and repeat the process. Record your observations in the table.

2. Put two ml of 0.1-M $K_2Cr_2O_7$ solution and two or three drops of concentrated H_2SO_4 into a test tube. To this mixture, add two drops of ethyl alcohol. Note: a green color indicates the presence of Cr^{3+}(aq) ions. Record any characteristic odor.

3. Repeat Procedure 2 using two drops of glacial acetic acid in place of the ethanol. Connect a delivery tube to the test tube. Place the other end in a solution of limewater. (A cloudy suspension is a simple test indicating carbon dioxide). After the reaction, note whether the odor of acetic acid is still detectable.

4. In a Pyrex test tube, place about three ml of ethyl alcohol and three ml of glacial acetic acid. To this mixture add about 0.5 ml (about ten drops from an eyedropper) of concentrated sulfuric acid. Warm this mixture in a water bath for five or six minutes. **Caution:** *be sure, during this warming process, not to point the test tube toward yourself or anyone else. Organic compounds such as the one being produced in this experiment may vaporize and spurt out the mouth of the test tube.* Pour the contents of the test tube into a beaker

Procedure Number	Reactants and Conditions of Reaction (temperature, catalyst, etc.)	Observation (odor and color change)	Type of Compound Formed
1			
2			
3			
4			
5			
6			
7			

containing 50 ml of cold distilled water. Cover the beaker, let stand for a minute or two and then note the odor. Compare this odor with that of ethanol and glacial acetic acid. Rinse out your dropper.

5. Repeat Procedure 4 using butyric acid instead of acetic acid. Record the odor of the compound, an ester which you prepared.

6. Repeat Procedure 4 but this time substitute methanol for ethanol and use approximately one g of salicylic acid instead of acetic acid. Record the odor of this ester. The formula for salicylic acid is HOC_6H_4COOH. The structural formula is

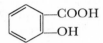

7. To three ml of ethanol in a dry, small erlenmeyer flask, add dropwise two ml of concentrated sulfuric acid. Shake the test tube after each drop has been added. Cautiously heat this with an electric hot plate or in an oil bath keeping the flask in constant motion. **Caution:** *do not point the mouth of the flask at anyone.* This reaction requires a temperature of 140–150°C so heating in a water bath will not produce the desired product. Avoid getting the test tube near any flame as the product of this reaction is extremely flammable. Cool the tube and note the odor of the product. If you are not familiar with the odor of the product, compare the odor to several known compounds placed on the reagent table by your instructor.

FURTHER EXPERIMENTATION

1. Sugars like glucose or sucrose undergo a fermentation process in the presence of a class of compounds called enzymes. The enzymes act as a catalyst. Into a 500-ml florence flask, place 275 ml of water and about 30 grams of sucrose, ($C_{12}H_{22}O_{11}$). To this mixture, add three ml of dilute (5%) disodium hydrogen phosphate, (Na_2HPO_4). Mix the contents thoroughly, then add a yeast paste made by mixing a sample of yeast with water. Place a one-hole stopper in the

flask with a delivery tube leading to a test tube containing limewater. Make sure the delivery tube is under the surface of the limewater. Allow this mixture to stand and ferment for about a week and check the condition of the limewater periodically.

After the fermentation process is complete, decant the clear liquid into a distillation flask which is fitted with a Liebig condenser. Place some boiling chips (pieces of broken porcelain) into the distilling flask to prevent bumping. Collect the distillate slowly, and in four or five fractions. Record the initial and final temperature for each fraction. Heat very slowly so that the foam does not flow over into the condenser. Note the odor and appearance of the distilled fractions. Place small quantities of each fraction in an evaporating dish and try to ignite them with a match. Note the difference in the behavior of different fractions.

FOLLOW-UP DISCUSSION

The reaction which you investigated in Procedure 1 represents a one-step oxidation of a primary alcohol. The product was an aldehyde which you should have been able to identify by its characteristic odor. In this oxidation reaction, a CuO coating on the copper metal acted as a catalyst.

The reaction in Procedure 2 represented a two-step oxidation of a primary alcohol. The product was an acid which you identified by its characteristic odor.

$$3C_2H_5OH + 16H^+ + 2Cr_2O_7^{2-} \rightarrow$$
$$3CH_3COOH + 4Cr^{3+} + 11H_2O$$

In Procedure 3 you carried the oxidation one step farther by warming the reaction mixture. The products resulting from the oxidation of the acid were CO_2 and H_2O.

The reaction in Procedures 4, 5, and 6 illustrate a method used to prepare an ester. This reaction, known as esterification, requires the presence of concentrated sulfuric acid which acts as a dehydrating agent. The equation for the reaction between acetic acid and ethanol is

$$CH_3\overset{\displaystyle O}{\overset{\|}{C}}-OH + HO-CH_2CH_3 \xrightarrow{\;H_2SO_4\;}$$

acid   alcohol

$$CH_3\overset{\displaystyle O}{\overset{\|}{C}}-O-CH_2CH_3 + H_2O$$

ester   water

Esters are frequently identified by their fragrance. The ester you prepared in Procedure 4 was ethyl acetate. This ester has a characteristic odor which differs from that of both acetic acid and ethanol. The esters which you prepared in Procedures 5 and 6 have familiar odors which you should be able to identify.

The dehydrating power of concentrated sulfuric acid which was demonstrated in Experiment 17-3 is frequently used in organic synthesis. In the production of the esters in Procedures 3, 4, and 5, and of the ether in Procedure 6, sulfuric acid acted as a dehydrating agent. The equation for the synthesis of diethyl ether is

$$CH_3CH_2OH + HOCH_2CH_3 \xrightarrow{\;H_2SO_4\;}$$

$$CH_3CH_2-O-CH_2CH_3 + H_2O$$

Note that an ether molecule is produced from two alcohol molecules.

FOLLOW-UP QUESTIONS

1. Write the equation for the oxidation of methanol to an aldehyde. Show a general heat term to indicate whether the reaction was exo- or endothermic. Identify and name the product by its odor.

2. What is your visual evidence that a reduction took place in Procedure 2?

3. Assuming that $KMnO_4$ had been used in place of $K_2Cr_2O_7$ in Procedure 2, write an equation to represent the oxidation of CH_3CH_2OH to CH_3COOH.

4. Write an equation for the reaction between acetic acid and $K_2Cr_2O_7$ in an acid solution.

5. Write an equation to represent the formation of ethyl butyrate from ethyl alcohol and butyric acid. Name and identify the odor of the ester.

6. Write an equation for the reaction between salicylic acid and methanol forming methyl salicylate. Identify the odor of methyl salicylate. The formula for salicylic acid is

7. Explain the function of concentrated H_2SO_4 in the synthesis of esters and ethers.

8. Explain how you would prepare an ether with the formula CH_3-O-CH_3.

9. How many moles of diethyl ether can be produced from one mole of ethyl alcohol?

20-2

Preparation and Properties of a Soap and a Synthetic Detergent

GENERAL DISCUSSION

The word detergent refers to any substance that is capable of cleansing metals, fabrics, or other materials. The two main cleansing agents used by all of us are often classified for convenience as *soaps* or *synthetic detergents*. In general, we shall identify soaps as cleansing agents made from natural fats and oils, and synthetic detergents as cleansing agents made from chemicals synthetically produced by the chemical industry.

There are several commercial processes for manufacturing soap. In the general commercial process an NaOH solution is added to a mixture of fats and oils such as tallow, cottonseed, coconut, and other oils. The mixture is heated and agitated by passing steam through it. The soap paste formed during this reaction is converted to small lumps by adding salt. In the last stages of the process, fillers, perfumes, dyes, antiseptics, and other ingredients may be added.

In Part I of this experiment you prepare a soap by the reaction of cottonseed oil with NaOH, using alcohol as a solvent. Alcohol is not used in commercial soap making. It is used here to bring the reacting materials into more intimate contact and thus speed up the reaction.

In Part II you prepare or obtain a synthetic detergent and compare its properties with those of the soap you prepared in Part I.

OBJECTIVES

1. To prepare and compare the properties of a soap and a synthetic detergent.
2. To relate the differences between the properties of a soap and a synthetic detergent to the differences between their structures.

MATERIALS

Evaporating dish, graduated cylinder, burner, stirring rod, wire screen, beakers, test tubes, cottonseed oil, ethanol, 30% NaOH solution, saturated NaCl solution, filter paper, litmus paper, bromthymol blue, phenolphthalein, wide range indicator paper, (12-M) HCl, mineral oil, glass plate, nonabsorbent cotton, flowers of sulfur, hard water (300 ppm), kerosene, dodecanol (lauryl alcohol), 2-M NaOH, buchner funnel, filter flask, filter paper, aspirator, household detergent.

PROCEDURE

Part I · Preparation of a Soap

1. Pour ten ml of cottonseed oil into a clean evaporating dish.
2. Add to the dish, ten ml of ethyl alcohol and five ml of 30% NaOH solution.
3. Gently heat the mixture with constant stirring until the mass becomes thick.
4. Continue heating until a drop of the mixture no longer forms a greasy spot on the surface of the liquid when added to cold water, or until you can see that all the fat has disappeared. This should take no longer than 10–12 minutes.
5. Cool the mixture in a cold water bath and add 20 ml of hot water (distilled). Cool in a cold water bath and then add 25 ml of a saturated sodium chloride solution.
6. The soap is now visible as curds in the solution. Filter or scoop off the soap and discard the filtrate which contains glycerol.
7. Add a drop or two of perfume to the soap and mold it into a small bar. Dry it between paper towels.
8. Make these tests on your sample or on a

sample of a commercially produced soap. In Part II you subject a sample of synthetic detergent to the same tests. Record your observations in the table.

(a) Add a small quantity (0.1 g or less) of

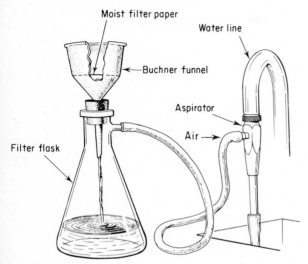

Fig. 20-1   Use of Buchner funnel and aspirator.

Property	Soap	Synthetic Detergent
Apparent solubility in H_2O		
Height of suds in distilled H_2O		
Height of suds in hard water		
Approximate pH		
Transparency of water solution		
Effect of HCl		
Effect on surface tension of H_2O		
Effect on "wetting ability" of H_2O		
Effect on oils (kerosene)		

your soap to a large test tube which is one-half full of distilled water. Shake vigorously for 15 to 20 seconds. Measure and record the height of the suds. Indicate whether your soap appears to be soluble and whether or not it produces a clear solution.

(b) Use litmus, bromthymol blue, phenol-phthalein, wide range or other indicators to determine the pH of the soap solution prepared in (a). Save the solution for use in (d).

(c) Dissolve, without shaking, another small sample of your soap in a large test tube half filled with distilled water. Add two or three ml of concentrated (12-M) hydrochloric acid to the soap solution. Record any observable changes and then shake and measure the height of the suds.

(d) Pour a few drops of mineral oil on a glass plate and wipe with a cotton cloth so as to coat the glass with a thin film of oil. Place a drop or two of distilled water on the plate. Measure the approximate diameter of the water drop. Repeat using the same number of drops of your soap solution. Note the effect of the soap on the surface tension of water. A liquid with a high surface tension forms large drops. A liquid with a low surface tension tends to spread out over a surface in the form of a film rather than to form drops.

(e) Compare the wetting ability of pure water to that of a soap solution by placing a small piece of nonabsorbent cotton on the surface of pure water and then on the surface of a soap solution. Sprinkle a little powdered sulfur (flowers of sulfur) on each liquid and record your observations.

(f) Repeat (a) using water which has a hardness of 300 ppm instead of distilled water. Record the height of the foam.

(g) Add 12 to 15 drops of kerosene or oil to a test tube which is one-quarter filled with water. Shake and note the solubility of the kerosene. Now add five ml of a soap solution and again shake the tube and its contents. If no definite changes are noted, then continue to add more soap. Record your observations.

Part II · A Synthetic Detergent

9. Place 18.6 grams of dodecanol (lauryl alco-

hol) in a 150-ml beaker. Add very slowly and cautiously, seven ml of concentrated sulfuric acid.

10. Pour 35 ml of 2-M NaOH into a 250-ml beaker. Add three to four drops of phenolphthalein. The phenolphthalein will probably be colorless in the concentrated NaOH.

11. Cautiously pour the acid solution from Procedure 9 slowly and with constant stirring into the NaOH solution. The phenolphthalein should change from colorless to red to colorless. If it does not decolorize, add small volumes of concentrated H_2SO_4 until it does. At this point you should observe a thick, white precipitate of sodium dodecylsulfate.

12. Filter, using a buchner funnel and an aspirator. See Fig. 20-1. Allow the detergent to dry.

13. Subject your detergent or a commercial sample to the tests listed in Procedure 8 of Part I. Use the same quantity of detergent as you did of soap.

FOLLOW-UP DISCUSSION

Most common soaps and synthetic detergents differ mainly in the nature of the groups which compose their ionic ends. The ionic end of common soaps contain the carboxyl group

$$-C\overset{\displaystyle O}{\underset{\displaystyle O^-}{\diagup}}$$

There are a number of types of synthetic detergents. One common form, such as the one you prepared, is called an alkyl sulfate. In this type, the ionic end is a sulfate group, $-O-SO_3^-$. The difference in the ionic ends of soaps and synthetic detergent molecules gives rise to different sets of properties. One of the most important differences is in the nature of the calcium and magnesium derivatives. These metals react with ordinary soap and form insoluble salts which precipitate out of solution and form a scum. The calcium and magnesium salts of synthetic detergents are soluble.

FOLLOW-UP QUESTIONS

1. How do you account for the pH difference between a soap and a synthetic detergent solution? Which would be more desirable for washing fine fabrics?

2. How do you account for the difference in the suds-forming ability of the two in hard water? Which is the more desirable to use for cleansing clothes in a region which is supplied with hard water?

3. How do you account for the action of HCl on the two solutions? What is your evidence that fatty acids are insoluble in water? Write an equation for the reaction of sodium stearate with HCl.

4. Why might a duck have trouble staying afloat in a tub of water containing a detergent?

5. Why did the soapy water spread out on the greased glass plate to a greater extent than the pure water?

20-3
Synthetic Rubber

GENERAL DISCUSSION

In this experiment you prepare a synthetic rubber. This particular material is a rubber substitute, but it has some properties which make it even superior to natural rubber for certain purposes. It is not dissolved by gasoline so it is used to line hoses of gasoline pumps. It has also been used as a solid rocket propellant. The commercial product that represents this particular synthetic rubber is called Thiokol. It is a member of a class of compounds called *polymers,* giant molecules composed of repeating units (*monomers*) chemically bonded together. Synthetic rubber, plastics, and many fibers such as nylon, dacron, and orlon are polymers.

OBJECTIVE

To observe a polymerization reaction by preparing synthetic rubber.

MATERIALS

250-ml beaker, graduated cylinder, burner, ring stand, wire screen, triple-beam balance, Na_2S, NaOH pellets, flowers of sulfur, 5% soap solution, ethylene dichloride, thermometer, conc. (15-M) ammonia water, 20% acetic acid.

PROCEDURE

1. Dissolve five g of Na_2S and about 2.5 grams of NaOH (25 pellets) in 50 ml of water. Heat to boiling and add seven g of flowers of sulfur with constant stirring. Allow the solution to boil for five minutes, then cool and filter through a coarse paper towel into a 250-ml beaker. Dilute this solution to about 200 ml.

2. Warm this solution with a bunsen burner to 75°C and add 10 ml of hot 5% soap solution to act as an emulsifier. Slowly add ten ml of ethylene dichloride with virogous stirring, keeping the reac-

tion below 72°C by placing the beaker in a pan of cold water. Continue to stir until the color changes from a red to a light yellow. Add five ml of conc. ammonia-water solution to stabilize the emulsion, and allow to stand overnight.

3. Pour off the upper layer and resuspend the latex by adding 200 ml of water which contains 5 ml of concentrated ammonia water. While stirring, add 40 ml of 20% acetic acid to coagulate the latex. A rubber ball forms in the bottom of the beaker. Wash before handling. **Caution:** *Be careful when squeezing the ball that the liquid does not squirt into your eye.*

4. Make any tests you can think of which will allow you to compare the physical properties of this substance with those of natural rubber.

FURTHER EXPERIMENTATION

Prepare a sheet of gum rubber from latex as directed by the instructor. Test the ability of rubber to retain its elasticity and its original shape under repeated stretching and under different temperature conditions. Describe the tests which you make and explain all of your observations. See if you can determine and explain any heat effects produced when a piece of rubber is suddenly stretched.

FOLLOW-UP DISCUSSION

Natural rubber is a polymer of isoprene which is 2 methyl-1, 3 butadiene. The structural formula for isoprene is

$$CH_2 = \underset{\underset{\displaystyle CH_2}{|}}{C} - CH = CH_2$$

Rubber has no definite molecular weight since there is really no theoretical limit as to the size of the molecules. The molecular mass of natural rubber may be as high as 5000. The following possible structure shows three repeating isoprene units of natural rubber:

$$
\begin{array}{c}
\mathrm{H} \quad \mathrm{CH_3} \ \mathrm{H} \quad \mathrm{H} \mid \mathrm{H} \quad \mathrm{CH_3} \ \mathrm{H} \quad \mathrm{H} \mid \mathrm{H} \quad \mathrm{CH_3} \ \mathrm{H} \quad \mathrm{H} \\
-\mathrm{C-C=C-C-C-C=C-C-C-C=C-C-} \\
\mathrm{H} \qquad\quad \mathrm{H} \mid \mathrm{H} \qquad\qquad \mathrm{H} \mid \mathrm{H} \qquad\qquad\quad \mathrm{H}
\end{array}
$$

The properties of rubber reflect the irregular non-crystalline structure of the substance. That is, the molecules are not aligned side by side, but are coiled and intertwined. The molecules of unvulcanized rubber can be pulled apart from each other. This is the reason that unvulcanized rubber is sticky. When rubber is vulcanized (treated with sulfur and heated in the presence of catalysts) sulfur atoms become attached to the molecular chains and bind them together with neighboring chains. During vulcanization, the sulfur molecules become attached to the rubber molecules at the site of the double bonds to form a cross-linked structure which may be represented as

$$
\begin{array}{c}
\mid \\
\mathrm{S} \\
\mid \quad\ \mid \quad\ \mid \\
-\mathrm{C-C-C-C-} \\
\mid \qquad\ \mid \\
\quad\ \ \mathrm{S} \\
\quad\ \ \mid \\
\quad\ \ \mathrm{S} \\
\mid \quad\ \mid \quad\ \mid \\
-\mathrm{C-C-C-C-} \\
\mid \quad\ \mid \quad\ \mid \quad\ \mid \\
\quad\ \ \mathrm{S} \\
\quad\ \ \mid
\end{array}
$$

This cross-linking makes the rubber more elastic and firm as the chains are no longer free to slide over each other as in raw (crude) rubber. Stretching tends to alter the characteristics of rubber by aligning the molecules. This alignment results in the formation of crystalline regions which have higher tensile strength than the amorphous (unaligned) regions.

Thiokol is a trade name for one type of polymer derived from ethylene dichloride and sodium polysulfide. Some references show its structure to be

$$
\left[-\mathrm{CH_2-CH_2-}\begin{array}{c}\mathrm{S}\\\|\\\mathrm{S}\end{array}\begin{array}{c}\mathrm{S}\\\|\\\mathrm{S}\end{array}- \right]_n
$$

and others show it to be

$$
\left[-\mathrm{S-S-}\begin{array}{c}\mathrm{H} \ \ \mathrm{H}\\|\ \ |\\\mathrm{C-C}\\|\ \ |\\\mathrm{H} \ \ \mathrm{H}\end{array}\mathrm{-S-S-} \right]_n
$$

Both structures are possible.

FOLLOW-UP QUESTIONS

1. How does the synthetic rubber you prepared compare in properties with natural rubber?

2. Compare its structural unit with that of natural rubber.

3. If this synthetic rubber were used as a reducing agent in a solid rocket propellant, list the products of oxidation.

4. What would be the effect upon natural rubber if too much sulfur were used in vulcanizing so that a very large number of links were formed from one chain to another?

5. Explain the observed properties of ordinary rubber in terms of the molecular theory.

20-4
Polymerization Reactions

GENERAL DISCUSSION

In Part I of this experiment you prepare a plastic marketed under the names Lucite or plexiglass. It is a common addition polymer. The monomer unit is methyl methacrylate, an ester of the unsaturated acid, methacrylic acid. In Part II you prepare nylon, a common condensation polymer. The monomer units which condense and form the polymer are the polyfunctional compounds, hexamethylenediamine and sebacoyl chloride.

OBJECTIVES

1. To prepare an addition and a condensation polymer.
2. To become acquainted with the preparation and the difference in structure and properties of the two types of polymers.

MATERIALS

6-in. soft glass test tube, beaker, glass stirring rod, thermometer, methyl methacrylate, benzoyl peroxide (paste form), NaOH pellets, hexamethylenediamine, triple-beam balance, sebacoyl chloride, CCl$_4$, phenolphthalein, forceps (tweezers).

Caution: *Benzoyl peroxide is a potentially dangerous reagent. It should not be stored or used as a solid.* A safe, paste form is available as BZQ-45 from U.S. Peroxygen, 850 Morton Ave., Richmond, Calif., and as Lupesco ATC from Ram Chemical Co., P.O. Box 192, Gardena, Calif. Other supply houses may also carry this product under different names.

PROCEDURE

Part I · Addition Polymerization

1. Pour 5 ml of methyl methacrylate into a clean, dry, 6-inch soft glass tube. **Caution:** *the vapors of this substance are very toxic.* Care should be taken not to inhale them.

2. Use the tip of a spatula to add a very small amount of the initiator, benzoyl peroxide paste, to the test tube. Your instructor will dispense this chemical or indicate the amount to place on the spatula.

3. Place the test tube in a hot water bath under a hood and stir the mixture with a glass rod until the benzoyl peroxide dissolves. Then allow the test tube to remain in the hot water bath for another 20 minutes until the liquid becomes viscous.

4. Add cold water to the water bath until the temperature falls to between 50°C and 60°C. Allow the polymer to cool for another ten minutes or until it is hard.

5. When the polymer is hard, break the test tube and remove the polymer. Examine the polymer and describe some of its properties such as its solubility in water and brittleness.

Part II · Condensation Polymerization

6. Place 0.7 gram (seven pellets) of NaOH into 50 ml of distilled water. To this add 1.3 g (25 drops) of hexamethylene diamine.

7. In a separate 250-ml beaker, put one ml of sebacoyl chloride into 50 ml of carbon tetrachloride. *Use caution in handling this chemical.*

8. Slowly pour the water solution onto the carbon tetrachloride solution. Avoid mixing the two solvents any more than necessary. Add a few drops of phenolphthalein solution to the water layer to make the junction more visible.

9. Using tweezers, grasp the center of the "scum" that forms at the interface of the two liquids. If the "scum" adheres to the side of the beaker, free it with a spatula. Carefully pull the nylon "rope" from the beaker.

Fig. 20-2 Extracting the nylon rope.

Caution: *extreme care should be exercised in handling the nylon so that small bubbles of occluded liquid that sometimes form will not burst and squirt into your eye.*

10. A roller apparatus for paper towels or a stirring rod may be used to reel up the string of nylon.

11. Wash the nylon thoroughly with water. Avoid getting any of the solution on your hands.

12. When the nylon has been washed and dried, examine it and describe some of its properties.

13. Place three g of phthalic anhydride, one g of glycerol and 0.05 g of sodium acetate in a 50-ml beaker. Mix with a stirring rod, cover with a watch glass and heat gently on a hot plate or with a low burner flame until the mixture melts and puffs up. Allow to cool and test its hardness, brittleness, and solubility in various solvents.

Caution: *do not expose to an open flame.*

FOLLOW-UP DISCUSSION

The monomer unit in your addition polymer is methylmethacrylate whose formula is

$$H_3C-O-\overset{\displaystyle O}{\overset{\displaystyle \|}{C}}-\underset{\displaystyle \underset{\displaystyle CH_3}{|}}{C}=CH_2$$

The initiator of the reaction is benzoyl peroxide whose formula is

It is believed that initiators form reactive species called free radicals which can add to a carbon-carbon double bond and form a new reactive species which is capable of adding on to another monomer unit. In the case of benzoyl peroxide, the oxygen-oxygen bond is weak and easily ruptured. The decomposition of this compound yields a free radical such as

This free radical may be represented as $RO\cdot$. The chain initiation step may be represented as

$$RO\cdot + H_2C=\underset{\displaystyle \underset{\displaystyle CH_3}{|}}{C}-\overset{\displaystyle O}{\overset{\displaystyle \|}{C}}-OCH_3 \rightarrow$$

$$ROCH_2\overset{\displaystyle \cdot}{C}-\underset{\displaystyle \underset{\displaystyle CH_3}{|}}{\overset{\displaystyle O}{\overset{\displaystyle \|}{C}}}-OCH_3$$

Chain propagation continues giving a polymer with the general formula

$$\left[-CH_2-\underset{\displaystyle \underset{\displaystyle CH_3}{|}}{C}-\overset{\displaystyle O}{\overset{\displaystyle \|}{C}}-O-CH_3\right]_n$$

In Part II of this experiment you prepared a condensation polymer by the reaction of a diamine with sebacoyl chloride. To help you understand this polymerization, let us consider the reaction between a simple amine and a simple acid chloride. If the two substances have only monofunctional groups the reaction does not result in polymerization. The general reaction is

$$R\text{—}NH_2 + R'\text{—}\overset{\displaystyle O}{\underset{\displaystyle |}{\overset{\displaystyle \|}{C}}}\text{—}Cl \rightarrow$$

$$R'\text{—}\overset{\displaystyle O}{\overset{\displaystyle \|}{C}}\text{—}NHR + HCl$$

This equation shows that the product consists of an amide molecule and a HCl molecule. With polyfunctional compounds such as hexamethylene diamine and sebacoyl chloride, a series of amide bonds link the monomers into a chain. The structural formula for hexamethylene diamine is

The formula for sebacoyl chloride is

During polymerization, an HCl molecule is split out between the two monomers so that the nitrogen atom from the diamine molecule can bond directly to the carbon atom of the sebacoyl chloride molecule. The linkage forms an amide. Therefore, the polymer is called a polyamide. A segment of the polyamide may be represented as shown below.

Since one monomer has six carbon atoms and the other has ten carbon atoms, the polymer is called Nylon 6-10. The formation of HCl tends to increase the acidity of the solution greatly. This tends to inhibit the reaction and hydrolyze the amide bonds. It is therefore necessary to carry the reaction out in the presence of NaOH. The sebacoyl chloride is dissolved in carbon tetrachlo-

ride, while the hexamethylene diamine is dissolved in water. Since H_2O and CCl_4 are immiscible, the monomers may unite only at the junction (interface) of the two solvents. As the polymer is removed, a new layer is constantly formed at the fresh interface.

All of the molecular chains are not the same length. In theory, there is no limit to the length of the chains. However, in a practical sense the lengths are limited by the competition of various segments for the remaining unbonded groups. In other words, all lengths are possible but only a few are most probable. The gross macroscopic properties of nylon and other polymers may be interpreted in terms of the nature, shapes and arrangement of the molecules and the forces which bond them together.

The nylon produced in this experiment is raw nylon which is not polymerized to the high degree necessary for ordinary use. It tends to have a paperlike texture when dried which is unlike the strong commercially produced threads with which you are familiar. Fibers of nylon, weight for weight, are stronger than steel wires. In order to be really useful, the raw nylon would have to be autoclaved, chopped, dissolved, forced through small orifices of a spinneret and spun on bobbins as fine fibers. Obviously, this processing is not practical to attempt in the laboratory.

The type of polymer which you prepared in Procedure 13 is known as an alkyd resin. These resins are often used in the manufacture of paints and enamels.

FOLLOW-UP QUESTIONS

1. Are there any similarities in the formation of polyethylene plastic. and plexiglass (Lucite)? Explain.

2. Dacron is a polyester formed by the condensation of a dihydroxy alcohol (ethylene glycol) and a dicarboxylic acid (1, 4-benzenedicarboxylic acid). The formulas of these monomers are

$$\underset{\text{O}}{\overset{\text{O}}{\text{HO}-\text{C}}}-\text{(benzene ring)}-\underset{}{\overset{\text{O}}{\text{C}}}-\text{OH} \quad \text{and} \quad \text{HOCH}_2\text{CH}_2\text{OH}$$

Show by analogy to the nylon condensation reaction, how these monomers combine and form dacron.

3. The Glyptal resin which you prepared in Part II is a polyester. Write an equation for the reaction. The formula of phthalic anhydride is

4. Is there any similarity between the formation of nylon fibers and protein fibers? Explain.

5. Relate the gross macroscopic properties of nylon to its submicroscopic molecular structure.

6. Could solvents other than CCl_4 be used to dissolve sebacoyl chloride? Suggest another possibility and give your reason.

7. Could a compound with the formula

$$\text{CH}_3\text{CH}_2\text{CH}_2\text{CH}_2\text{CH}_2\text{CH}_2\text{CH}_2\text{CH}_2\text{CH}_2\underset{\text{Cl}}{\overset{\text{O}}{\text{C}}}$$

be used instead of sebacoyl chloride? Explain.

21-1
Radioactivity

GENERAL DISCUSSION

There are three types of naturally occurring radioactive emissions. These emissions were first studied in the late nineteenth and early twentieth centuries. Henri Becquerel is credited with the discovery of radioactivity; however, many of the mysteries surrounding radioactivity were unravelled by Sir Ernest Rutherford of England and several of his co-workers. Rutherford identified and named the three types of emission: alpha, beta, and gamma rays. He showed that both alpha and beta rays consist of streams of charged particles, and that gamma rays are electromagnetic radiations.

Radioactive particles have been used in many experiments which have resulted in the modification of our ideas about matter. In this experiment you briefly investigate some of the characteristics of radioactive rays as well as the nature and use of radioactive materials. The small quantity of radioactive material used in this experiment is safe to handle. It represents only a fraction of the radioactivity present in some wrist-watch dials.

OBJECTIVES

1. To investigate some of the properties of radioactive rays.
2. To investigate the nature and use of radioactive materials.

MATERIALS

"Classmaster" or other radioactivity demonstrator, cobalt-60 button or other radioactive source, meter stick, lead and aluminum sheets, magnet, young tobacco or tomato plant, beaker, plastic or wood square with hole in center, 10 microcurie sample of P^{32}, X-ray film, developer, pieces of plywood, black paper, rubber bands, nickel planchets.

PROCEDURE

Part I · Characteristics of Radioactive Rays

1. Set up a radioactivity demonstration instrument such as a "Classmaster." Turn on the instrument and allow a few minutes for it to warm up at a low voltage. Slowly increase the voltage to the suggested operating level. A voltage of 900 volts is recommended for most Geiger-Müller tubes.

Table I   Absorption of Radiation

Absorber	Counts (per min)	Background Counts (per min)	Net Counts (per min)
None			
Aluminum			
Lead			

2. Set the instrument to read counts per minute. With no radioactive materials in the vicinity, determine the background radiation. Record this count as a background reading in Tables I and II. Notice the regularity (or irregularity) of the background radiation.

3. Place the cobalt-60 button, usually furnished with the instrument, or a radium-dial watch at such a distance from the G-M tube that the count rate is significantly higher than background. Read the counts per minute and record in Table I. The background count is subtracted from this reading to get the net counts per minute actually produced by the source.

4. Obtain sheets of lead and aluminum which have the same thickness. Two or three millimeters is adequate. (If necessary, pack together several sheets of aluminum to equal the thickness of

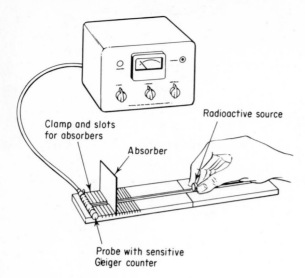

Clamp and slots
for absorbers

Radioactive source

Absorber

Probe with sensitive
Geiger counter

Fig. 21-1 Apparatus for investigating radioactivity.

the lead.) Place the aluminum sheet between the source and the G-M tube. See Fig. 21-1. Read the counts per minute and subtract the background reading to determine the net count per minute. Record in Table I.

5. Replace the aluminum sheet with the lead sheet. Record the counts per minute and calculate the net counts per minute.

6. Remove all the absorbers and hold a powerful magnet just above the level of a line between the G-M tube and the source. If a powerful magnet is used, be careful not to bring it so close as to attract the G-M tube. Note the orientation of the magnetic poles and any change in the count rate. Keeping the G-M tube at the same distance from the source, move it around to locate the direction in which the radioactive rays were deflected. Make a sketch of the setup and observations. Label poles of magnet, direction of deflection and any other relevant items.

Part II · Inverse Square Law

7. Place the radioactive source four centimeters from the G-M tube. Record the counts per minute and the net counts per minute in Table II.

278

Table II   Inverse Square Law

Distance	Counts (per min)	Background Counts (per min)	Net Counts (per min, experimental)	Net Counts (per min, calculated using 4 cm reading as reference)
4 cm				
8 cm				
12 cm				
16 cm				

8. Move the source to 8 cm, 12 cm, and 16 cm, repeating the readings at each point. Find the net counts per minute for each distance.

Part III · Uptake of Radioactive Phosphorus by Plants

9. Remove the soil from the roots of a tobacco or tomato plant, being careful to protect the fine root fibers.

10. Carefully force the roots of the plant through a hole, ¾ inch in diameter, in a plastic or wood square.

11. Place the roots of the plant in a small beaker or jar containing ten microcuries of phosphorus–32. This isotope is available in the compound $Na_3P^{32}O_4$. The amount of dangerous radiation from this sample is less than that emitted from many luminous watch dials.

12. Place a G-M tube of an instrument such as a Classmaster near the leaves of the plant and record the change in activity. See Fig. 21-2. Observe the rate meter at intervals shown in the data table up to four hours. Record the data in Table III. Plot your data on regular graph paper. Plot activity in counts per minute along the vertical axis and elapsed time along the horizontal axis.

Part IV · Radioautographs

13. After the roots of the tomato or tobacco plant have been in the solution for 24 hr, remove

Table III Uptake of P-32

Elapsed Time	Activity (cpm)
5 min	
10 min	
15 min	
20 min	
25 min	
30 min	
1 hr	

Table IV Half-Life Determination

Time (days)	Activity (cpm)	Background (cpm)	Net Counts (per min)
1			
2			
3			
4			
5			
6			
7			
8			
9			
10			
11			
12			
13			
14			
15			
16			
17			
18			
19			
20			
21			
22			
23			
24			
25			
26			
27			
28			

one of the leaves and wrap it in a plastic foil such as Saran Wrap.

14. In a dark room, place the leaf next to a piece of X-ray film held between two pieces of plywood with rubber bands. Wrap entire assembly in black paper and allow to stand for 24 hr.

15. Develop the X-ray film. The type of developer to use is usually specified by the manufacturer of the film. The developing time suggested by the manufacturer for ordinary X-rays should be shortened. The developing temperature should be approximately 18°C. After developing, the film

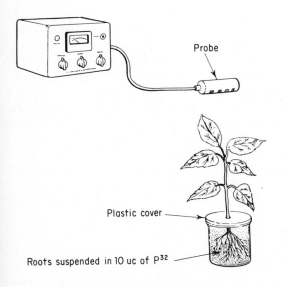

Fig. 21-2 Radioactivity in a plant leaf.

should be placed in a hypo solution for five to 10 min, washed in running water for 15 to 20 min, and then hung up and dried.

Part V · Determination of Half-Life

16. Obtain a sample of an unknown isotope from your instructor.

17. Place the sample of isotope in a nickel planchet (a small metal container) and place it at a given distance from the G-M tube. The relative position and distance of the sample with respect to the G-M tube must be carefully noted so that it can be exactly reproduced in future experiments.

18. Take count readings of your sample of isotope at 24-hr intervals and record the net counts per minute in Table IV. Be sure to take the background reading each day so that it can be subtracted from the reading with your sample to get net counts per minute. Be sure that the voltage is constant for each reading and that the distance and position of the sample from the G-M tube are constant for each reading.

19. Take readings for as many days as your instructor suggests.

20. Plot the counts per minute on the vertical coordinate and the time on the horizontal coordinate of ordinary graph paper.

21. Determine the length of time required for the net count per minute to diminish to one-half the original value. This period of time is known as the half-life. Attempt to identify the unknown isotope by using a table of known half-lives.

FOLLOW-UP DISCUSSION

The background radiation noted in Part I is apparently a random sort of a "rain" of nuclear particles and radiations. This radiation comes from a variety of sources. The plaster in the walls contains traces of radium and thorium. The atmosphere contains traces of radioactive radon gas and some radioactive particles from atomic tests. Cosmic particles are falling to earth at all times. These particles originate in outer space. Your own bodies contain traces of radioactive strontium and potassium. Many watches and instrument dials contain small amounts of radium. In order to obtain accurate count rates for measured samples of radioactive materials, it is necessary to correct for the background radiation.

The absorbing power of a material depends largely upon the concentration of electrons in that material. The fact that some radioactive particles can pass through metals such as lead and aluminum show that the atoms of these materials must not be composed of solid matter such as the billiard-ball type atom proposed by Dalton.

In general, radioactivity is described by the inverse square law which states that the intensity of radiation is inversely proportional to the square of the distance from the source. The equation is

$$I = \frac{k}{d^2}$$

where I is the intensity (counts per minute), d is the distance from the source and k is a proportionality constant. Interpretation of this formula reveals that doubling the distance from a given source reduces the intensity to one-fourth of what it was. Tripling the distance reduces the intensity to one-ninth of its original value.

Statistical variations in the emission of radioactive particles and variations in background radiation always cause some deviations from the theoretical in experiments such as this one.

The uptake of the $Na_3P^{32}O_4$ by the tomato or tobacco plant shows the specific ability of these plants to absorb a phosphorous compound. The increased count is normally noticed only a few minutes after the roots of the plant have been placed into the solution. The exposure of the tomato or tobacco plant leaf to the X-ray film shows the exact location of the radioactive material in the leaf. Photographic film is one of the oldest detectors of radioactivity. It was used by Becquerel in the discovery of radioactivity.

FOLLOW-UP QUESTIONS

1. Is it possible to predict when a given radioactive atom will decay? Explain.

2. What evidence did you see that indicates that some radioactive rays are composed of

charged particles? Did the particles you investigated carry a positive or negative charge? What was your evidence?

3. Explain how your observations support Rutherford's concept of an atom which is largely empty space.

4. How do you account for the difference in absorbing power between equal thicknesses of lead and aluminum? Name other materials which would act as good absorbers of radiation.

5. How much absorbing material would you need to insure that all radioactivity from a certain source was stopped?

6. Examine the data in Table II and state whether your experimental results indicate that radioactivity is described by the inverse square law (allow for statistical variations in count and background). Do this by comparing your experimental counts per minute with the theoretical counts per minute. To calculate the theoretical counts per minute, use four cm as the interval for "d" and the value of counts per minute at four cm as the reference reading. How can you account for the difference between the experimental and theoretical values? Show the setups for your calculations.

7. Using the four-cm reading as reference, calculate the theoretical count/minute reading at 20 cm.

8. List several methods of determining radioactivity. What are some of the advantages of each method? According to your radioautograph, where did the P–32 concentrate in the plant?

9. What is the time interval for the unknown isotope in Part V to diminish in activity to one-half the original value?

Appendix

Appendix 1
Mathematical Operations in Chemistry

SCIENTIFIC NOTATION

Scientific work frequently involves use of large and small numbers. Multiplying and dividing such numbers as 0.000 000 065 3 and 605 000 000 000 would be extremely tedious operations unless these numbers were expressed as powers of 10. A convenient method of expressing these large and small numbers in exponential form is called *Scientific Notation*. The large or small number in this system is expressed as a number between 1 and 10 with some power of 10 used to indicate the placement of the decimal point. Multiplying by a positive power of 10 indicates that the decimal point must be moved to the right.

$$1.48 \times 10^6 = 1\ 480\ 000$$
$$1.23 \times 10^2 = 123$$
$$7.66 \times 10^9 = 7\ 660\ 000\ 000$$

Multiplying by a negative power of 10 indicates that the decimal point must be moved to the left.

$$1.66 \times 10^{-4} = 1.66 \times \frac{1}{10^4}$$
$$= 1.66 \times 0.0001$$
$$= 0.000\ 166$$

Multiplication: When multiplying numbers expressed in scientific notation the exponents of 10 are added.

$$(1.40 \times 10^4)(2.00 \times 10^6) = 2.80 \times 10^4 \times 10^6$$
$$= 2.80 \times 10^{10}$$

THE SLOPE OF A LINE

The slope of a line is given by the ratio of the change in x and y coordinates from one point to another on the line. We indicate the change in the y coordinate as Δy and the change in the x coordinate as Δx. In Figure A at the top of the opposite page, points A and B are two points on line ℓ. The slope of this line is given as $\Delta y / \Delta x$ which in this case has a value of $-\frac{1}{2}$. The sign on the slope gives an indication of its direction of inclination. The slope of ℓ_1 in Figure B at the bottom of the opposite page, is negative while that of ℓ_2 is positive.

Frequently it is desirable to find the slope of a curved line such as m in Fig. *A*. Obviously, the curved line does not have a constant slope at all points. Therefore, we describe its slope at a given point. The slope at a given point on a curve can be determined by drawing a line tangent to the curve at that point, and then determining the slope of the line. In Fig. A the slope of the curved line m at the point of tangency with line ℓ is $-\frac{1}{2}$ the same as the slope of line ℓ.

The slope of a line is also defined as the value of the trigonometric function called the tangent (tan). The tan of the angle theta, θ, in Fig. A, is defined as the opposite side of angle θ, CB, divided by the adjacent side of angle θ, AC. In this coordinate system the value of CB is -9 and the value of AC is 18. Thus, $\tan \theta = -\frac{1}{2}$.

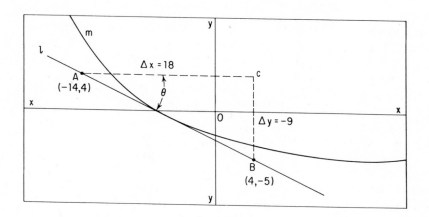

Fig. A   *The slope of the line, ℓ, is given by the relationship* $\Delta y / \Delta x$. $\dfrac{\Delta y}{\Delta x} = \dfrac{-5-(4)}{4-(-14)} = \dfrac{-9}{18} = -\dfrac{1}{2}$

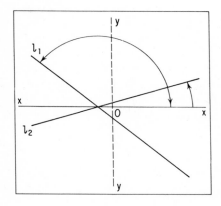

Fig. B   *If the inclination is greater than 90°, as in ℓ[1], the slope is negative. If the inclination is less than 90°, as in ℓ[2], the slope is positive.*

283

Appendix 2

Useful Tables

Table 1   Conversion Factors

1 meter (m) = 100 centimeters = 1000 millimeters = 39.370 in.
1 centimeter (cm) = 10 millimeters (mm) = 0.393 70 in.
1 Ångstrom (Å) = 10^{-8} centimeters
1 micron (μ) = 10^{-3} millimeters
1 kilogram (kg) = 1000 grams = 2.2046 pounds
1 gram (g) = 1000 milligrams (mg)
1 ounce = 28.350 g
1 pound = 453.59 g
1 atomic mass unit (amu) = 1.6604×10^{-24} g
1 liter (l) = 1000 milliliters (ml) = 1.0567 quarts
1 gallon (gal) = 3.7854 l
1 cubic inch (in.^{3}) = 16.387 ml
1 cubic foot (ft^3) = 28 317 ml
1 electron volt (ev) = 1.6021×10^{-12} erg = 23.061 kcal mole^{-1}
1 calorie (cal) = 4.1840×10^7 ergs
1 joule = 10^7 ergs
1 liter-atmosphere = 24.217 calories
$^\circ C = 5/9 \, (^\circ F - 32)$
$^\circ K = \,^\circ C + 273$
1 mm (Hg) = 1 torr = 0.019 337 lb/in.^{2}
1 lb/in.^{2} = 51.715 torr

Table 2   Standard Reduction Potentials (volts at 25°C)

Oxidizing Agents			Reducing Agents	E°
1. $F_2(g) + 2H_3O^+(aq)$	$+ 2e^- = 2H_2O$		$+ 2HF(aq)$	+3.06
2. $F_2(g)$	$+ 2e^- =$		$2F^-(aq)$	+2.85
3. $O_3(g) + 2H_3O^+(aq)$	$+ 2e^- = 3H_2O$		$+ O_2(g)$	+2.07
4. $Co^{3+}(aq)$	$+ 1e^- =$		$Co^{2+}(aq)$	+1.82
5. $H_2O_2(aq) + 2H_3O^+(aq)$	$+ 2e^- =$		$4H_2O$	+1.77
6. $MnO_4^-(aq) + 4H_3O^+(aq)$	$+ 3e^- = 6H_2O$		$+ MnO_2(s)$	+1.69
7. $MnO_4^-(aq) + 8H_3O^+(aq)$	$+ 5e^- = 12H_2O$		$+ Mn^{2+}(aq)$	+1.52
8. $H_3AuO_3(s) + 3H_3O^+(aq)$	$+ 3e^- = 6H_2O$		$+ Au(s)$	+1.45
9. $BrO_3^-(aq) + 6H_3O^+(aq)$	$+ 6e^- = 9H_2O$		$+ Br^-(aq)$	+1.44
10. $ClO_4^-(aq) + 8H_3O^+(aq)$	$+ 8e^- = 12H_2O$		$+ Cl^-(aq)$	+1.39
11. $Cl_2(g)$	$+ 2e^- =$		$2Cl^-(aq)$	+1.36
12. $Cr_2O_7^{2-}(aq) + 14H_3O^+(aq)$	$+ 6e^- = 21H_2O$		$+ 2Cr^{3+}(aq)$	+1.33
13. $MnO_2(s) + 4H_3O^+(aq)$	$+ 2e^- = 6H_2O$		$+ Mn^{2+}(aq)$	+1.23
14. $O_2(g) + 4H_3O^+(aq)$	$+ 4e^- =$		$6H_2O$	+1.23
15. $Br_2(l)$	$+ 2e^- =$		$2Br^-(aq)$	+1.06
16. $NO_3^-(aq) + 4H_3O^+(aq)$	$+ 3e^- = 6H_2O$		$+ NO(g)$	+0.96
17. $2Hg^{2+}(aq)$	$+ 2e^- =$		$Hg_2^{2+}(aq)$	+0.92
18. $HO_2^-(aq) + H_2O$	$+ 2e^- =$		$3OH^-(aq)$	+0.88

Table 2 (Continued)

	Oxidizing Agents		Reducing Agents	E°
19.	$Hg^{2+}(aq)$	$+\ 2e^- =$	$Hg(l)$	$+0.85$
20.	$O_2(g) + 4H^+(aq)\,(1M)$	$+\ 4e^- =$	$2H_2O(l)$	$+0.82$
21.	$2NO_3^-(aq) + 4H_3O^+(aq)$	$+\ 2e^- = 6H_2O$	$+\ N_2O_4(g)$	$+0.80$
22.	$Ag^+(aq)$	$+\ 1e^- =$	$Ag(s)$	$+0.80$
23.	$Hg_2^{2+}(aq)$	$+\ 2e^- =$	$2Hg(l)$	$+0.79$
24.	$Fe^{3+}(aq)$	$+\ 1e^- =$	$Fe^{2+}(aq)$	$+0.77$
25.	$O_2(g) + 2H_3O^+(aq)$	$+\ 2e^- = 2H_2O$	$+\ H_2O_2(aq)$	$+0.68$
26.	$BrO_3^-(aq) + 3H_2O$	$+\ 6e^- = 6OH^-(aq)$	$+\ Br^-(aq)$	$+0.61$
27.	$MnO_4^-(aq) + 2H_2O$	$+\ 3e^- = 4OH^-(aq)$	$+\ MnO_2(s)$	$+0.59$
28.	$H_3AsO_4(aq) + 2H_3O^+(aq)$	$+\ 2e^- = 4H_2O$	$+\ As_4O_6(s)$	$+0.58$
29.	$I_2(s)$	$+\ 2e^- =$	$2I^-(aq)$	$+0.54$
30.	$Cu^+(aq)$	$+\ 1e^- =$	$Cu(s)$	$+0.52$
31.	$O_2(g) + 2H_2O$	$+\ 4e^- =$	$4OH^-(aq)$	$+0.40$
32.	$[Fe(CN)_6]^{3-}(aq)$	$+\ 1e^- =$	$[Fe(CN)_6]^{4-}(aq)$	$+0.36$
33.	$Cu^{2+}(aq)$	$+\ 2e^- =$	$Cu(s)$	$+0.34$
34.	$Cu^{2+}(aq)$	$+\ 1e^- =$	$Cu^+(aq)$	$+0.15$
35.	$S(s) + 2H_3O^+(aq)$	$+\ 2e^- = 2H_2O$	$+\ H_2S(g)$	$+0.14$
36.	$HSO_4^{2+}(aq) + 3H_3O^+(aq)$	$+\ 2e^- = 4H_2O$	$+\ H_2SO_3(aq)$	$+0.12$
37.	$2H_3O^+(aq)$	$+\ 2e^- = 2H_2O$	$+\ H_2(g)$	0.00
38.	$O_2(g) + H_2O$	$+\ 2e^- = OH^-(aq)$	$+\ HO_2^-(aq)$	-0.08
39.	$Pb^{2+}(aq)$	$+\ 2e^- =$	$Pb(s)$	-0.13
40.	$CrO_4^{2-}(aq) + 4H_2O$	$+\ 3e^- = 5OH^-(aq)$	$+\ Cr(OH)_3(s)$	-0.13
41.	$Ni^{2+}(aq)$	$+\ 2e^- =$	$Ni(s)$	-0.24
42.	$Co^{2+}(aq)$	$+\ 2e^- =$	$Co(s)$	-0.28
43.	$Cd^{2+}(aq)$	$+\ 2e^- =$	$Cd(s)$	-0.40
44.	$Cr^{3+}(aq)$	$+\ 1e^- =$	$Cr^{2+}(aq)$	-0.41
45.	$H_2O +$	$+\ 4e^- = 4OH^-(10M)$	$+\ 2H_2(g)$	-0.44
46.	$Fe^{2+}(aq)$	$+\ 2e^- =$	$Fe(s)$	-0.44
47.	$S(s)$	$+\ 2e^- =$	$S^{2-}(aq)$	-0.48
48.	$Fe(OH)_3(s)$	$+\ 1e^- = OH^-(aq)$	$+\ Fe(OH)_2(s)$	-0.56
49.	$AsO_4^{3-}(aq) + 2H_2O$	$+\ 2e^- = 4OH^-(aq)$	$+\ AsO_2^-(aq)$	-0.67
50.	$Ni(OH)_2(s)$	$+\ 2e^- = 2OH^-(aq)$	$+\ Ni(s)$	-0.72
51.	$Cr^{3+}(aq)$	$+\ 3e^- =$	$Cr(s)$	-0.74
52.	$Zn^{2+}(aq)$	$+\ 2e^- =$	$Zn(s)$	-0.76
53.	$2H_2O(l)$	$+\ 2e^- = 2OH^-(aq)$	$+\ H_2(g)$	-0.83
54.	$Fe(OH)_2(s)$	$+\ 2e^- = 2OH^-(aq)$	$+\ Fe(s)$	-0.88
55.	$SO_4^{2-}(aq) + H_2O$	$+\ 2e^- = 2OH^-(aq)$	$+\ SO_3^{2-}(aq)$	-0.93
56.	$Mn^{2+}(aq)$	$+\ 2e^- =$	$Mn(s)$	-1.18
57.	$Al^{3+}(aq)$	$+\ 3e^- =$	$Al(s)$	-1.66
58.	$Mg^{2+}(aq)$	$+\ 2e^- =$	$Mg(s)$	-2.34
59.	$Na^+(aq)$	$+\ 1e^- =$	$Na(s)$	-2.71
60.	$Ca^{2+}(aq)$	$+\ 2e^- =$	$Ca(s)$	-2.87
61.	$Sr^{2+}(aq)$	$+\ 2e^- =$	$Sr(s)$	-2.89
62.	$Ba^{2+}(aq)$	$+\ 2e^- =$	$Ba(s)$	-2.90
63.	$Ra^{2+}(aq)$	$+\ 2e^- =$	$Ra(s)$	-2.92
64.	$Cs^+(aq)$	$+\ 1e^- =$	$Cs(s)$	-2.92
65.	$Rb^+(aq)$	$+\ 1e^- =$	$Rb(s)$	-2.92
66.	$K^+(aq)$	$+\ 1e^- =$	$K(s)$	-2.92
67.	$Li^+(aq)$	$+\ 1e^- =$	$Li(s)$	-3.04

Table 3 Solubility Product Constants

Compound	K_{sp}	Compound	K_{sp}
$PbBr_2$	6.3×10^{-6}	BaF_2	1.7×10^{-6}
$AgBr$	4.8×10^{-13}	PbF_2	2.7×10^{-8}
$MgCO_3 \cdot 3H_2O$	2.5×10^{-5}	$Mg(OH)_2$	9×10^{-12}
$CaCO_3$	4.8×10^{-9}	$Ca(OH)_2$	1.3×10^{-6}
$SrCO_3$	9.4×10^{-10}	$Sr(OH)_2 \cdot 8H_2O$	3.2×10^{-4}
$BaCO_3$	4.9×10^{-9}	$Ba(OH)_2 \cdot 8H_2O$	5.0×10^{-3}
$CdCO_3$	2.5×10^{-14}	$Cd(OH)_2$	1.2×10^{-14}
$CoCO_3$	1.0×10^{-12}	$Co(OH)_2$	2.0×10^{-16}
$PbCO_3$	1.5×10^{-13}	$Cu(OH)_2$	5.6×10^{20}
$MnCO_3$	8.8×10^{-11}	$Fe(OH)_2$	1.6×10^{-15}
Ag_2CO_3	8.2×10^{-12}	$Pb(OH)_2$	2.8×10^{-16}
$PbCl_2$	1.7×10^{-5}	$Mn(OH)_2$	7.1×10^{-15}
$AgCl$	1.8×10^{-10}	$Ni(OH)_2$	1.6×10^{-14}
$TlCl$	1.9×10^{-4}	$Pd(OH)_2$	1.0×10^{-24}
$BaCrO_4$	2.0×10^{-10}	$Pt(OH)_2$	1.0×10^{-35}
$PbCrO_4$	1.8×10^{-14}	$Sn(OH)_2$	5.0×10^{-26}
Ag_2CrO_4	1.1×10^{-12}	$Zn(OH)_2$	4.5×10^{-17}
$SrCrO_4$	3.6×10^{-5}	$Al(OH)_3$	3.0×10^{-33}
PbI_2	8.7×10^{-9}	$Cr(OH)_3$	6.7×10^{-31}
AgI	8.3×10^{-17}	$Ga(OH)_3$	5.0×10^{-37}
$CaSO_4$	2.6×10^{-5}	$Fe(OH)_3$	6.0×10^{-38}
$SrSO_4$	7.6×10^{-7}	$Sn(OH)_4$	1.0×10^{-56}
$BaSO_4$	1.5×10^{-9}	$Ca_3(PO_4)_2$	1.0×10^{-25}
Ag_2SO_4	1.2×10^{-5}	Li_3PO_4	3.2×10^{-13}
$PbSO_4$	1.6×10^{-8}	$Pb_3(PO_4)_2$	1.0×10^{-32}
MgC_2O_4	8.6×10^{-5}	Ag_3PO_4	1.6×10^{-21}
$CaC_2O_4 \cdot H_2O$	2.3×10^{-9}	Ag_2S	1.6×10^{-49}
$SrC_2O_4 \cdot H_2O$	5.6×10^{-8}	HgS	3.0×10^{-53}
$BaC_2O_4 \cdot 2H_2O$	1.1×10^{-7}	PbS	8.4×10^{-28}
$Ag_2C_2O_4$	1.1×10^{-11}	Bi_2S_3	1.6×10^{-72}
$Hg_2C_2O_4$	1.0×10^{-13}	Cu_2S	1.6×10^{-48}
$AgIO_3$	3.0×10^{-8}	CuS	8.7×10^{-36}
$Pb(IO_3)_2$	3.2×10^{-13}	CdS	1.0×10^{-28}
$Ca(IO_3)_2 \cdot 6H_2O$	1.9×10^{-6}	FeS	3.7×10^{-19}
$Ba(IO_3)_2 \cdot 2H_2O$	1.2×10^{-9}	MnS	1.4×10^{-15}
MgF_2	6.4×10^{-9}	SnS	8.0×10^{-29}
CaF_2	1.7×10^{-10}	ZnS	4.5×10^{-24}
SrF_2	3.0×10^{-9}		

Table 4 Dissociation Constants (first step only)

$SO_2 + H_2O(H_2SO_3)$	1.7×10^{-2}	H_2S	1.0×10^{-7}
HSO_4^-	1.3×10^{-2}	HS^-	1.3×10^{-13}
$H_2C_2O_4$	5.4×10^{-2}	H_2Se	1.9×10^{-4}
H_3PO_4	7.1×10^{-3}	H_2Te	2.3×10^{-3}
$H_2PO_4^-$	6.3×10^{-8}	H_2SeO_3	2.7×10^{-3}
HPO_4^{2-}	4.4×10^{-13}	HF	6.8×10^{-4}
$CO_2 + H_2O(H_2CO_3)$	4.4×10^{-7}	HBO_2	6.0×10^{-10}
HCO_3^-	4.7×10^{-11}	$HOCl$	3.2×10^{-8}
$HC_2H_3O_2$	1.8×10^{-5}	$HClO_2$	1.1×10^{-2}
HCN	4.0×10^{-10}	$NH_3 + H_2O$	1.8×10^{-5}
HNO_2	5.1×10^{-4}	NH_4^+	5.6×10^{-10}
H_3PO_3	1.6×10^{-2}	H_2O	1.0×10^{-14}
$H_2PO_3^-$	7×10^{-7}	OH^-	less than 10^{-36}
H_3AsO_4	2.5×10^{-4}		
$H_2AsO_4^-$	5.6×10^{-8}		
$HAsO_4^{2-}$	3×10^{-13}		

Table 5 Pressure of Water Vapor (Torr)

°C	Torr	°C	Torr	°C	Torr	°C	Torr
0.0	4.6	17.5	15.0	22.5	20.4	30.0	31.8
5.0	6.5	18.0	15.5	23.0	21.1	35.0	42.2
7.5	7.8	18.5	16.0	23.5	21.7	40.0	55.3
10.0	9.2	19.0	16.5	24.0	22.4	50.0	92.5
12.5	10.9	19.5	17.0	24.5	23.1	60.0	149.4
15.0	12.8	20.0	17.5	25.0	23.8	70.0	233.7
15.5	13.2	20.5	18.1	26.0	25.2	80.0	355.1
16.0	13.6	21.0	18.6	27.0	26.7	90.0	525.8
16.5	14.1	21.5	19.2	28.0	28.3	95.0	633.9
17.0	14.5	22.0	19.8	29.0	30.0	100.0	760.0

Table 6 Density and Specific Gravity of Gases

Gas	Density Grams per Liter (STP)	Specific Gravity, Air Standard	Gas	Density Grams per Liter (STP)	Specific Gravity, Air Standard
Ammonia	0.771	0.597	Hydrogen chloride	1.636	1.268
Carbon dioxide	1.977	1.529	Hydrogen sulfide	1.539	1.190
Carbon monoxide	1.250	0.968	Methane	0.714	0.554
Chlorine	3.214	2.486	Nitrogen	1.251	0.964
Dinitrogen monoxide	1.977	1.530	Nitrogen monoxide	1.340	1.037
Ethyne (acetylene)	1.169	0.906	Oxygen	1.429	1.105
Hydrogen	0.0899	0.0695	Sulfur dioxide	2.927	2.264

Table 7 Properties of Important Elements

Name	Specific Gravity		Melting Point °C	Boiling Point °C	Common Oxidation Numbers
	Water Std.	Air Std.			
Aluminum	2.70		660	2057	3+
Antimony	6.68		631	1380	3+, 5+
Arsenic	5.73		(sublimes)	(sublimes)	3+, 5+
Barium	3.78		850	1140	2+
Bismuth	9.75		271.3	1560	3+
Boron	2.34		2300	2550 (sublimes)	3+
Bromine	3.12		−7.2	58.8	1−, 5+
Calcium	1.55		842	1240	2+
Carbon	1.7–3.5		(sublimes above 3500° C)	4200	2+, 4+
Chlorine		2.486	−101.6	−34.6	1−, 5+, 7+
Chromium	7.14		1890	2482	2+, 3+, 6+
Cobalt	8.90		1495	2900	2+, 3+
Copper	8.9		1083	2336	1+, 2+
Fluorine		1.312	−223	−187	1−
Gold	19.3		1063	2600	0, 3+
Hydrogen			−259	−253	1−, 1+
Iodine	4.93		113.5	184.4	1−, 5+
Iron	7.86		1535	3000	2+, 3+
Lead	11.34		327.5	1750	2+, 4+
Magnesium	1.74		651	1107	2+
Manganese	7.3		1244	2097	2+, 4+, 7+
Mercury	13.55		−38.9	356.6	1+, 2+
Nickel	8.90		1455	2900	2+
Nitrogen			−209.9	−195.8	3−, 3+, 5+
Oxygen		0.964	−218	−183	2−
Phosphorus	1.8–2.3	1.105	44.1	280	3+, 5+
Platinum	21.45		1769.3	3825	2+, 4+
Potassium	0.86		62.3	760	1+
Radium	5(?)		700	1140	2+
Silicon	2.42		1420	2355	4+
Silver	10.5		960.8	1950	1+
Sodium	0.97		97.5	880	1+
Strontium	2.54		800	1150	2+
Sulfur	2.0		114.5	444.6	2−, 4+, 6+
Tin	7.31		231.9	2270	2+, 4+
Titanium	4.5		1677	3277(?)	3+, 4+
Tungsten	19.3		3410	5927	6+
Zinc	7.14		419.5	907	2+

Table 8 Solubility of Gases in Water

Volume of gas at STP that can be dissolved in 1 volume of water.

Gas	0° C	10° C	20° C
Air	0.0292	0.0228	0.0187
Ammonia	1298.9	910.4	710.6
Carbon dioxide	1.713	1.194	0.878
Chlorine	4.54	3.148	2.299
Hydrogen	0.0215	0.0196	0.0182
Hydrogen chloride	506.7	473.9	442.0
Hydrogen sulfide	4.670	3.399	2.582
Nitrogen	0.0235	0.0186	0.0155
Oxygen	0.0489	0.0380	0.0310
Sulfur dioxide	79.79	56.65	

Table 9 Desk Reagents

Reagent	Formula	Molarity	Density (g/ml)	Percent Solute
Acetic acid, glacial	$HC_2H_3O_2$	17 F	1.05	99.5%
Acetic acid, dilute		6	1.04	34
Hydrochloric acid, concentrated	HCl	12	1.18	36
Hydrochloric acid, dilute		6	1.10	20
Nitric acid, concentrated	HNO_3	16	1.42	72
Nitric acid, dilute		6	1.19	32
Sulfuric acid, concentrated	H_2SO_4	18	1.84	96
Sulfuric acid, dilute		3	1.18	25
Ammonia water, concentrated	NH_4OH	15	0.90	58
Ammonia water, dilute		6	0.96	23
Sodium hydroxide, dilute	NaOH	6	1.22	20

Table 10 Acid-base Indicators

pH Range	Indicator	Color Change	pH Range	Indicator	Color Change
0.4–1.8	Methyl violet	yellow-blue violet	6.2–7.6	Bromthymol blue	yellow-blue
1.2–2.8	Thymol blue	red-yellow	6.4–8.0	Phenol red	yellow-red
1.2–3.8	Benzopurpurin 4B	violet-red	7.2–8.8	Cresol red	yellow-red
3.1–4.9	Congo red	blue-red	7.4–9.0	Metacresol purple	yellow-violet
3.0–4.6	Bromphenol blue	yellow-blue violet	8.0–9.6	Thymol blue	yellow-blue
3.1–4.4	Methyl orange	red-yellow	8.2–10.0	Phenolphthalein	colorless-red
4.0–5.6	Bromcresol green	yellow-blue	9.4–10.6	Thymolphthalein	colorless-blue
4.4–6.2	Methyl red	red-yellow	10.0–12.0	Alizarin yellow	yellow-violet
5–7	Litmus	red-blue	11.4–13.0	Sodium indigosulfonate	blue-yellow
5.2–6.8	Bromcresol purple	yellow-violet	12.0–14.0	1, 3, 5-Trinitrobenzene	colorless-orange

Table 11   Four-place Logarithms of Numbers

n	0	1	2	3	4	5	6	7	8	9
10	0000	0043	0086	0128	0170	0212	0253	0294	0334	0374
11	0414	0453	0492	0531	0569	0607	0645	0682	0719	0755
12	0792	0828	0864	0899	0934	0969	1004	1038	1072	1106
13	1139	1173	1206	1239	1271	1303	1335	1367	1399	1430
14	1461	1492	1523	1553	1584	1614	1644	1673	1703	1732
15	1761	1790	1818	1847	1875	1903	1931	1959	1987	2014
16	2041	2068	2095	2122	2148	2175	2201	2227	2253	2279
17	2304	2330	2355	2380	2405	2430	2455	2480	2504	2529
18	2553	2577	2601	2625	2648	2672	2695	2718	2742	2765
19	2788	2810	2833	2856	2878	2900	2923	2945	2967	2989
20	3010	3032	3054	3075	3096	3118	3139	3160	3181	3201
21	3222	3243	3263	3284	3304	3324	3345	3365	3385	3404
22	3424	3444	3464	3483	3502	3522	3541	3560	3579	3598
23	3617	3636	3655	3674	3692	3711	3729	3747	3766	3784
24	3802	3820	3838	3856	3874	3892	3909	3927	3945	3962
25	3979	3997	4014	4031	4048	4065	4082	4099	4116	4133
26	4150	4166	4183	4200	4216	4232	4249	4265	4281	4298
27	4314	4330	4346	4362	4378	4393	4409	4425	4440	4456
28	4472	4487	4502	4518	4533	4548	4564	4579	4594	4609
29	4624	4639	4654	4669	4683	4698	4713	4728	4742	4757
30	4771	4786	4800	4814	4829	4843	4857	4871	4886	4900
31	4914	4928	4942	4955	4969	4983	4997	5011	5024	5038
32	5051	5065	5079	5092	5105	5119	5132	5145	5159	5172
33	5185	5198	5211	5224	5237	5250	5263	5276	5289	5302
34	5315	5328	5340	5353	5366	5378	5391	5403	5416	5428
35	5441	5453	5465	5478	5490	5502	5514	5527	5539	5551
36	5563	5575	5587	5599	5611	5623	5635	5647	5658	5670
37	5682	5694	5705	5717	5729	5740	5752	5763	5775	5786
38	5798	5809	5821	5832	5843	5855	5866	5877	5888	5899
39	5911	5922	5933	5944	5955	5966	5977	5988	5999	6010
40	6021	6031	6042	6053	6064	6075	6085	6096	6107	6117
41	6128	6138	6149	6160	6170	6180	6191	6201	6212	6222
42	6232	6243	6253	6263	6274	6284	6294	6304	6314	6325
43	6335	6345	6355	6365	6375	6385	6395	6405	6415	6425
44	6435	6444	6454	6464	6474	6484	6493	6503	6513	6522
45	6532	6542	6551	6561	6571	6580	6590	6599	6609	6618
46	6628	6637	6646	6656	6665	6675	6684	6693	6702	6712
47	6721	6730	6739	6749	6758	6767	6776	6785	6794	6803
48	6812	6821	6830	6839	6848	6857	6866	6875	6884	6893
49	6902	6911	6920	6928	6937	6946	6955	6964	6972	6981
50	6990	6998	7007	7016	7024	7033	7042	7050	7059	7067
51	7076	7084	7093	7101	7110	7118	7126	7135	7143	7152
52	7160	7168	7177	7185	7193	7202	7210	7218	7226	7235
53	7243	7251	7259	7267	7275	7284	7292	7300	7308	7316
54	7324	7332	7340	7348	7356	7364	7372	7380	7388	7396

Table 11   Four-place Logarithms of Numbers (cont'd)

n	0	1	2	3	4	5	6	7	8	9
55	7404	7412	7419	7427	7435	7443	7451	7459	7466	7474
56	7482	7490	7497	7505	7513	7520	7528	7536	7543	7551
57	7559	7566	7574	7582	7589	7597	7604	7612	7619	7627
58	7634	7642	7649	7657	7664	7672	7679	7686	7694	7701
59	7709	7716	7723	7731	7738	7745	7752	7760	7767	7774
60	7782	7789	7796	7803	7810	7818	7825	7832	7839	7846
61	7853	7860	7868	7875	7882	7889	7896	7903	7910	7917
62	7924	7931	7938	7945	7952	7959	7966	7973	7980	7987
63	7993	8000	8007	8014	8021	8028	8035	8041	8048	8055
64	8062	8069	8075	8082	8089	8096	8102	8109	8116	8122
65	8129	8136	8142	8149	8156	8162	8169	8176	8182	8189
66	8195	8202	8209	8215	8222	8228	8235	8241	8248	8254
67	8261	8267	8274	8280	8287	8293	8299	8306	8312	8319
68	8325	8331	8338	8344	8351	8357	8363	8370	8376	8382
69	8388	8395	8401	8407	8414	8420	8426	8432	8439	8445
70	8451	8457	8463	8470	8476	8482	8488	8494	8500	8506
71	8513	8519	8525	8531	8537	8543	8549	8555	8561	8567
72	8573	8579	8585	8591	8597	8603	8609	8615	8621	8627
73	8633	8639	8645	8651	8657	8663	8669	8675	8681	8686
74	8692	8698	8704	8710	8716	8722	8727	8733	8739	8745
75	8751	8756	8762	8768	8774	8779	8785	8791	8797	8802
76	8808	8814	8820	8825	8831	8837	8842	8848	8854	8859
77	8865	8871	8876	8882	8887	8893	8899	8904	8910	8915
78	8921	8927	8932	8938	8943	8949	8954	8960	8965	8971
79	8976	8982	8987	8993	8998	9004	9009	9015	9020	9025
80	9031	9036	9042	9047	9053	9058	9063	9069	9074	9079
81	9085	9090	9096	9101	9106	9112	9117	9122	9128	9133
82	9138	9143	9149	9154	9159	9165	9170	9175	9180	9186
83	9191	9196	9201	9206	9212	9217	9222	9227	9232	9238
84	9243	9248	9253	9258	9263	9269	9274	9279	9284	9289
85	9294	9299	9304	9309	9315	9320	9325	9330	9335	9340
86	9345	9350	9355	9360	9365	9370	9375	9380	9385	9390
87	9395	9400	9405	9410	9415	9420	9425	9430	9435	9440
88	9445	9450	9455	9460	9465	9469	9474	9479	9484	9489
89	9494	9499	9504	9509	9513	9518	9523	9528	9533	8538
90	9542	9547	9552	9557	9562	9566	9571	9576	9581	9586
91	9590	9595	9600	9605	9609	9614	9619	9624	9628	9633
92	9638	9643	9647	9652	9657	9661	9666	9671	9675	9680
93	9685	9689	9694	9699	9703	9708	9713	9717	9722	9727
94	9731	9736	9741	9745	9750	9754	9759	9763	9768	9773
95	9777	9782	9786	9791	9795	9800	9805	9809	9814	9818
96	9823	9827	9832	9836	9841	9845	9850	9854	9859	9863
97	9868	9872	9877	9881	9886	9890	9894	9899	9903	9908
98	9912	9917	9921	9926	9930	9934	9939	9943	9948	9952
99	9956	9961	9965	9969	9974	9978	9983	9987	9991	9996

Table 12 Atomic Numbers and Masses

Name of Element	Symbol	Atomic Number	Atomic Mass	Name of Element	Symbol	Atomic Number	Atomic Mass
Actinium	Ac	89	[227]	Mercury	Hg	80	200.59
Aluminum	Al	13	26.9815	Molybdenum	Mo	42	95.94
Americium	Am	95	[243]	Neodymium	Nd	60	144.24
Antimony	Sb	51	121.75	Neon	Ne	10	20.183
Argon	Ar	18	39.948	Neptunium	Np	93	[237]
Arsenic	As	33	74.9216	Nickel	Ni	28	58.71
Astatine	At	85	[210]	Niobium	Nb	41	92.906
Barium	Ba	56	137.34	Nitrogen	N	7	14.0067
Berkelium	Bk	97	[249*]	(Nobelium)	(No)	102	[254]
Beryllium	Be	4	9.0122	Osmium	Os	76	190.2
Bismuth	Bi	83	208.980	Oxygen	O	8	15.9994
Boron	B	5	10.811	Palladium	Pd	46	106.4
Bromine	Br	35	79.909	Phosphorus	P	15	30.9738
Cadmium	Cd	48	112.40	Platinum	Pt	78	195.09
Calcium	Ca	20	40.08	Plutonium	Pu	94	[242]
Californium	Cf	98	[251*]	Polonium	Po	84	[210*]
Carbon	C	6	12.01115	Potassium	K	19	39.102
Cerium	Ce	58	140.12	Praseodymium	Pr	59	140.907
Cesium	Cs	55	132.905	Promethium	Pm	61	[147*]
Chlorine	Cl	17	35.453	Protactinium	Pa	91	[231]
Chromium	Cr	24	51.996	Radium	Ra	88	[226]
Cobalt	Co	27	58.9332	Radon	Rn	86	[222]
Copper	Cu	29	63.54	Rhenium	Re	75	186.2
Curium	Cm	96	[247]	Rhodium	Rh	45	102.905
Dysprosium	Dy	66	162.50	Rubidium	Rb	37	85.47
Einsteinium	Es	99	[254]	Ruthenium	Ru	44	101.07
Erbium	Er	68	167.26	Samarium	Sm	62	150.35
Europium	Eu	63	151.96	Scandium	Sc	21	44.956
Fermium	Fm	100	[253]	Selenium	Se	34	78.96
Fluorine	F	9	18.9984	Silicon	Si	14	28.086
Francium	Fr	87	[223]	Silver	Ag	47	107.870
Gadolinium	Gd	64	157.25	Sodium	Na	11	22.9898
Gallium	Ga	31	69.72	Strontium	Sr	38	87.62
Germanium	Ge	32	72.59	Sulfur	S	16	32.064
Gold	Au	79	196.967	Tantalum	Ta	73	180.948
Hafnium	Hf	72	178.49	Technetium	Tc	43	[99*]
Helium	He	2	4.0026	Tellurium	Te	52	127.60
Holmium	Ho	67	164.930	Terbium	Tb	65	158.924
Hydrogen	H	1	1.00797	Thallium	Tl	81	204.37
Indium	In	49	114.82	Thorium	Th	90	232.038
Iodine	I	53	126.9044	Thulium	Tm	69	168.934
Iridium	Ir	77	192.2	Tin	Sn	50	118.69
Iron	Fe	26	55.847	Titanium	Ti	22	47.90
Krypton	Kr	36	83.80	Tungsten	W	74	183.85
Lanthanum	La	57	138.91	Uranium	U	92	238.03
Lawrencium	Lw	103	[257]	Vanadium	V	23	50.942
Lead	Pb	82	207.19	Xenon	Xe	54	131.30
Lithium	Li	3	6.939	Ytterbium	Yb	70	173.04
Lutetium	Lu	71	174.97	Yttrium	Y	39	88.905
Magnesium	Mg	12	24.312	Zinc	Zn	30	65.37
Manganese	Mn	25	54.9380	Zirconium	Zr	40	91.22
Mendelevium	Md	101	[256]				

A value given in brackets denotes the mass number of the isotope of longest known half-life, or for those marked with an asterisk, a better known one. The atomic mass of most of these elements are believed to have no error greater than ±0.5 of the last digit given.

Laboratory
Apparatus

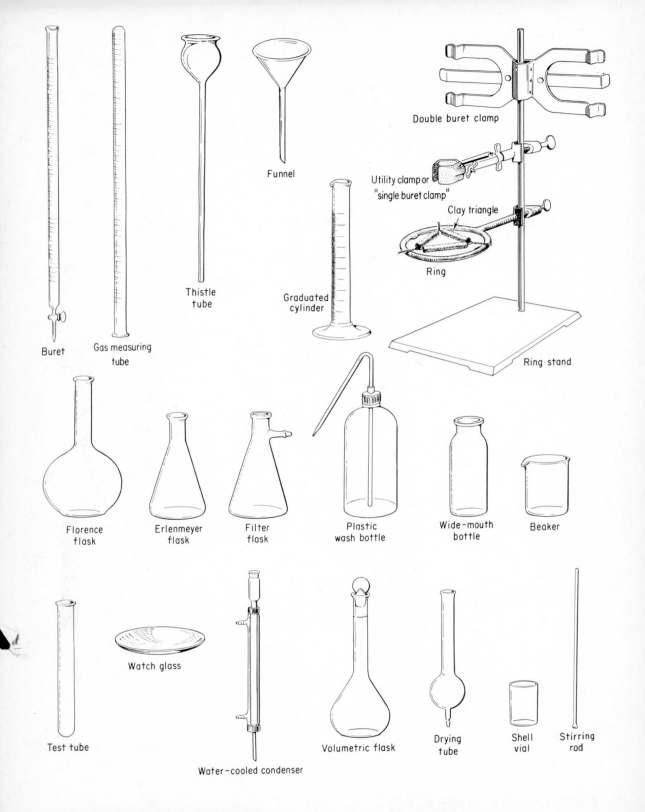

Buret

Gas measuring tube

Thistle tube

Funnel

Graduated cylinder

Double buret clamp

Utility clamp or "single buret clamp"

Clay triangle

Ring

Ring stand

Florence flask

Erlenmeyer flask

Filter flask

Plastic wash bottle

Wide-mouth bottle

Beaker

Test tube

Watch glass

Water-cooled condenser

Volumetric flask

Drying tube

Shell vial

Stirring rod

LABORATORY APPARATUS

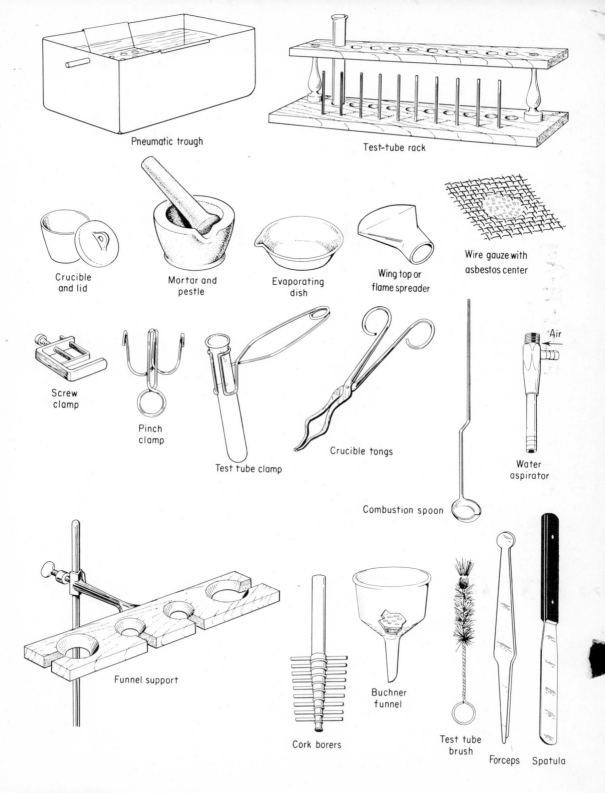

Pneumatic trough

Test-tube rack

Crucible and lid

Mortar and pestle

Evaporating dish

Wing top or flame spreader

Wire gauze with asbestos center

Screw clamp

Pinch clamp

Test tube clamp

Crucible tongs

Air

Water aspirator

Combustion spoon

Funnel support

Cork borers

Buchner funnel

Test tube brush

Forceps

Spatula

LABORATORY APPARATUS

PERIODIC CLASSIFICATION OF THE ELEMENTS

Light Metals

Heavy Metals

Nonmetals

IA	IIA	IIIB	IVB	VB	VIB	VIIB	VIIIB			IB	IIB	IIIA	IVA	VA	VIA	VIIA	VIIIA
1 *H* Hydrogen																	2 *He* Helium
3 *Li* Lithium	4 *Be* Beryllium											5 *B* Boron	6 *C* Carbon	7 *N* Nitrogen	8 *O* Oxygen	9 *F* Fluorine	10 *Ne* Neon
11 *Na* Sodium	12 *Mg* Magnesium											13 *Al* Aluminum	14 *Si* Silicon	15 *P* Phosphorus	16 *S* Sulfur	17 *Cl* Chlorine	18 *Ar* Argon
19 *K* Potassium	20 *Ca* Calcium	21 *Sc* Scandium	22 *Ti* Titanium	23 *V* Vanadium	24 *Cr* Chromium	25 *Mn* Manganese	26 *Fe* Iron	27 *Co* Cobalt	28 *Ni* Nickel	29 *Cu* Copper	30 *Zn* Zinc	31 *Ga* Gallium	32 *Ge* Germanium	33 *As* Arsenic	34 *Se* Selenium	35 *Br* Bromine	36 *Kr* Krypton
37 *Rb* Rubidium	38 *Sr* Strontium	39 *Y* Yttrium	40 *Zr* Zirconium	41 *Nb* Niobium	42 *Mo* Molybdenum	43 *Tc* Technetium	44 *Ru* Ruthenium	45 *Rh* Rhodium	46 *Pd* Palladium	47 *Ag* Silver	48 *Cd* Cadmium	49 *In* Indium	50 *Sn* Tin	51 *Sb* Antimony	52 *Te* Tellurium	53 *I* Iodine	54 *Xe* Xenon
55 *Cs* Cesium	56 *Ba* Barium	57 to 71	72 *Hf* Hafnium	73 *Ta* Tantalum	74 *W* Tungsten	75 *Re* Rhenium	76 *Os* Osmium	77 *Ir* Iridium	78 *Pt* Platinum	79 *Au* Gold	80 *Hg* Mercury	81 *Tl* Thallium	82 *Pb* Lead	83 *Bi* Bismuth	84 *Po* Polonium	85 *At* Astatine	86 *Rn* Radon
87 *Fr* Francium	88 *Ra* Radium	89 to 103															

Lanthanide series

57 *La* Lanthanum	58 *Ce* Cerium	59 *Pr* Praseodymium	60 *Nd* Neodymium	61 *Pm* Promethium	62 *Sm* Samarium	63 *Eu* Europium	64 *Gd* Gadolinium	65 *Tb* Terbium	66 *Dy* Dysprosium	67 *Ho* Holmium	68 *Er* Erbium	69 *Tm* Thulium	70 *Yb* Ytterbium	71 *Lu* Lutetium
90 *Th* Thorium	91 *Pa* Protactinium	92 *U* Uranium	93 *Np* Neptunium	94 *Pu* Plutonium	95 *Am* Americium	96 *Cm* Curium	97 *Bk* Berkelium	98 *Cf* Californium	99 *Es* Einsteinium	100 *Fm* Fermium	101 *Md* Mendelevium	102 *No* Nobelium	103 *Lw* Lawrencium	

Actinide series: 89 *Ac* Actinium

X77 85 42

Idea and Action in
American History

PRENTICE-HALL INC., Englewood Cliffs, New Jersey

Idea and Action in

American History

Marion Brady   Howard Brady

Contributing Scholars

Michael McGiffert — *Professor of History, William and Mary College*

Ronald V. Adkins — *Northeast Regional Director, University of Denver*

Richard Brown — *Chairman of History Department and Professor of History, University of Connecticut*

Bruce Stave — *Professor of History, University of Connecticut*

Carol Vogt — *Anderson Fellow, School of Education, New York University*

SUPPLEMENTARY MATERIALS
Teacher's Guide
Skills and Evaluation Package

By the same authors:

Idea and Action in World Cultures
Teacher's Guide
Skills and Evaluation Package

IDEA AND ACTION IN AMERICAN HISTORY
Marion Brady and Howard Brady

© 1977 by Prentice-Hall, Inc., Englewood Cliffs, New Jersey 07632. All rights reserved. No part of this book may be reproduced in any form or by any means without permission in writing from the publisher. Printed in the United States of America.

ISBN 0-13-450585-9   10 9 8 7 6 5 4 3 2 1

Photo Research by Mira Schachne
Maps by J & R Technical Services Inc.
Cover Art by Elissa Della-Tiana

PRENTICE-HALL INTERNATIONAL, INC., London
PRENTICE-HALL OF AUSTRALIA, PTY. LTD., Sydney
PRENTICE-HALL OF CANADA, LTD., Toronto
PRENTICE-HALL OF INDIA PRIVATE LTD., New Delhi
PRENTICE-HALL OF JAPAN, INC., Tokyo

Acknowledgments / PILOT TEACHERS

We wish to acknowledge the invaluable assistance provided by the following teachers who tried out *Idea and Action in American History* in their classrooms.

Richard Begley, *Englewood Middle School, Englewood, New Jersey*

Michael Bennett, *Hollenbeck Junior High School, Los Angeles, California*

Larry Brown, *Rocklin Elementary School, Rocklin, California*

Marilyn Curtin, *South Orange Junior High School, South Orange, New Jersey*

Nancy Hardenbergh, *Brown Junior High School, Malden, Massachusetts*

Augie Herrera, *Hollenbeck Junior High School, Los Angeles, California*

Billie Lovmark, *Marco F. Foster Junior High School, San Juan Capistrano, California*

Jean Hall, *Marco F. Foster Junior High School, San Juan Capistrano, California*

Mary Krenytsky, *Andrew Jackson Junior High School, Titusville, Florida*

Ralph Lubeck, *Glenbrook Intermediate School, Concord, California*

Carl Misener, *Edgewood Junior High School, Merritt Island, Florida*

Sherry Mollenkopf, *Andrew Jackson Junior High School, Titusville, Florida*

Russ Oliver, *Glenbrook Intermediate School, Concord, California*

Ronald Redding, *Loma Vista Intermediate School, Concord, California, New Jersey*

George Stager, *South Orange Junior High School, South Orange, New Jersey*

Jean Strickholm, *Englewood Middle School, Englewood, New Jersey*

Laura Sturrock, *La Palma Junior High School, Buena Park, California*

Acknowledgments continue page 528

Contents

Descriptions of the unit opening illustrations are on page 530.

How to Use This Book

Idea and Action in American History is divided into seven units. Each unit focuses on a concept which describes a pattern of human behavior. For example, the first unit is entitled *Exploration and Colonization/Motivation*. This double title indicates that motivation is the concept used to study reasons behind the exploration and colonization of the United States.

Activities within the unit help you investigate patterns of behavior in your own life, in American life in the past, and in the nation's life today. Here is the way the activities are organized:

Activity Title

Black type like this introduces each activity and gives background information. This will help you understand the purpose of the activity.

Brown type like this indicates activity instructions and questions. Whenever you see brown type, it means "Do this."

(a) The materials you will use in each activity are introduced by headnotes. In front of each headnote there is a letter.

Definitions, pronunciations, and questions to help you study the data appear in the margin. Sometimes they are above or below a piece of data. They are printed in this kind of type.

(a) Each activity is a puzzle or problem you must solve. Most activities include data—items such as documents, speeches, letters, maps, charts, and photographs—which you will study in order to solve the activity puzzle.

Data is enclosed within a brown frame, or box, like the one surrounding this material. Note that the headnote letter corresponds to the letter on the side of this data box.

BRANCHING OUT

Additional activities are described under this heading. The activities usually involve investigation and data-gathering outside the classroom.

Exploration and Colonization

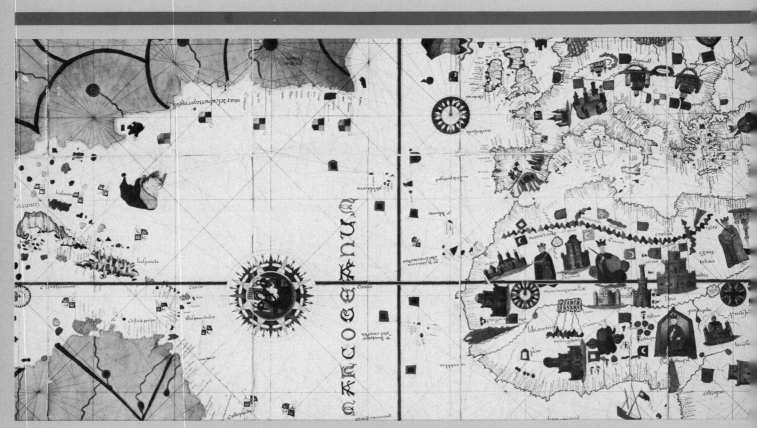

Motivation

How does motivation affect human action?

Introduction

Would you like to be somewhere else right now, doing something different—eating, listening to records, buying new clothes? Do you know why?

The things you do—your actions—grow out of ideas called **motivations.** Motivations are reasons for actions. Your action right now is reading this paragraph. Your motivating idea may be to "do what the teacher says," or "pass this course," or "find out what this book is about."

Finding out what motivates people tells you a lot about how they'll act in new situations. For example, if you know people who are motivated to "win at any price," you know something about how they're likely to act if they are losing a game. People who are motivated by a desire to have fun in a game will play differently.

People usually have at least one motivation for each action. Sometimes there are certain goals they want to reach. Sometimes certain values are important to them. The goals and values that people have are very often the motivating ideas behind their actions.

Motivation is the focus of this unit. The more you know about this concept, the better you'll understand why people act as they do today and why they acted as they did in the past.

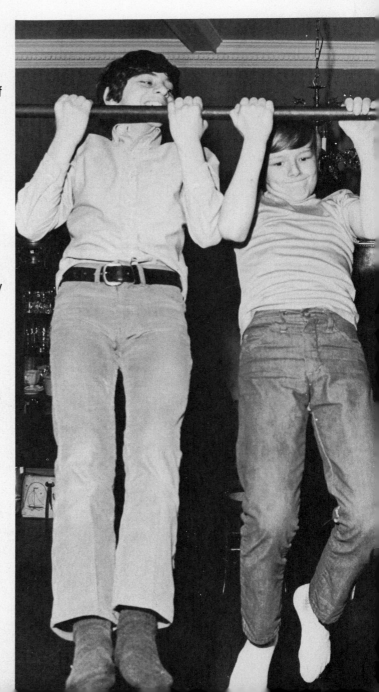

4

Why do you do what you do? Why do your friends sometimes want to do different things? Why do you sometimes disagree with your parents? These are all questions of motivation.

a Here is a list of things you might like to do.

Look over the list and select two actions—one you'd like to do and one you think a friend would enjoy doing.

a
1. Win a contest for "best-looking"
2. Spend a week in the woods alone
3. Build a vehicle (such as a racing bike, minibike, or car)
4. Fly in a hot-air balloon
5. Travel in a foreign country
6. Paint your name on a large billboard
7. Move into your own apartment
8. Be on a championship team
9. Organize and lead a club

Now try to identify possible motivating ideas for each of the actions you've chosen. Ask yourself a series of questions about why you'd like to do what you've chosen. Then pretend you are your friend and ask yourself the same questions. Keep asking questions until you've reached what seem to be "basic" reasons for your choices.

For example, if "Have a home pinball machine" had been on the list, your conversation with yourself might go something like this:

Q: Why would I like a pinball machine at home?
A: Because it would be fun.
Q: What would make it fun?
A: Seeing how high I could score.
Q: What's so great about a high score?
A: It's kind of like winning, and I like to win.

If this were your answer, "having fun" and "getting a high score" would be two motivating ideas. But your basic motivation would be a desire to win. It could also have been "having friends around," or "having something no one else has."

It's difficult to be sure that a motivating idea you've identified is really basic. As a check, ask yourself these two questions:

1. Is the motivating idea the first one you think of? If it is, then it's probably not a basic motivation. As the conversation above shows, you often have to keep asking "why" until you come up with underlying answers.

2. Does the motivating idea explain several different kinds of actions? For example, if someone said, "I like to race motorcycles," that would explain a few actions having to do with motorcycles. But "I like to compete" would explain many other actions besides those related to motorcycles.

Now go back to the two actions you chose. Did the questions you asked yourself identify basic motivating ideas? Make a list of these motivating ideas and save it for a later activity.

b Check your understanding by looking at this picture.

Make a list of possible motivations for the action shown.

Clues to Motivation

Your main motivating ideas show up in nearly everything you do. The way you spend your leisure time, the books you read, and the people you admire are examples of clues to your motivations.

● Motivating ideas also show up in what people say. On page 7 are comments parents often make to their children. (You've probably heard some of them yourself.)

Study these comments, and decide what important motivating idea each suggests.

1. "Who won? Did you score any runs?"
2. "Don't forget to clean up before you leave. You promised."
3. "It looks like rain. Did you put your bike away?"
4. "It's your allowance. You decide what to do with it."
5. "Saturday I'll take you to the game. You'll really have fun."
6. "You're as good as anyone in the class."

Think of some other comments you've often heard parents make. What do you think is the motivating idea behind each statement?

One other way to find out why people do things is to look at their decisions. When people make decisions, they base their choices on their motivations. Decisions about which product to buy, which candidate to vote for, which subjects to study in school, and which job to apply for are all evidence of important motivations.

Conduct a survey to find out some decisions of young people you know. Ask students to name choices in each category below. Also ask them to identify reasons for their choices. Record the reasons they give for their decisions—their motivations. You will need to question students carefully to identify motivations, just as you questioned yourself in the first activity.

1. Types of movies and TV shows liked best
2. Favorite items to buy
3. Spare-time activities
4. The kinds of friends chosen

Shared Motivations

Some ideas are shared by many young people. The idea "It's good to do things with my friends" is one of these. Because of this idea, many young people join clubs, have favorite meeting places, and generally spend a lot of time in groups. This activity will help you identify some other shared motivations.

1. Go through the list of motivations you made in the first activity. Group similar ideas together. (For example, "fun," "thrills," and "excitement" are similar ideas.)
2. Add to the list any other motivating ideas you can think of which are important to you or your friends.

Based on this information, what are some motivations which seem to be shared by young people you know?

The motivating ideas which are shared by most young people in this country are so familiar to you that they are easily overlooked. You probably take them for granted.

● Here are some ideas which probably differ from those of most people you know. They are ideas that are important to some young people in other countries.

Think about each idea. Then write a statement that expresses the contrasting idea you think is shared by most American young people.

1. "People should plan each day so it will be like the day before. Change is neither necessary nor desirable."
2. "The importance given to people ought to depend on the importance of their families. People reflect the qualities of their parents and ancestors. Positions of leadership should be given only to those from important families."
3. "My parents and other adults have lived a lot longer than I have. They have had much more experience in making decisions. I prefer to let adults make my really important decisions for me."
4. "It's wrong to try to be more important than those around you. By making yourself more important, you make them seem less important."

By comparing your own ideas with those listed above, you've identified four major ideas shared by many young people in America. If these ideas are motivations, they will affect people's actions. Explain how the ideas you've identified would affect these actions: 1) methods for choosing student leaders; and 2) weekend activities of young people.

How would these actions be different if most American youths shared the ideas you read about above? Do you or anyone you know agree with any of the ideas stated above?

People often act for similar reasons. Sometimes, the same motivating ideas produce different actions.

a Here are descriptions of four different actions.

What motivating idea or ideas might produce these results?

a Person A is learning to drive.
Person B is practicing to become a cheerleader.
Person C is buying new clothes.
Person D is running for a school office.

All those actions could be produced by the same motivating idea:
"It's important to be admired by the people I know."

In almost any group or society, a great many of the members'
ways of acting are motivated by a few basic ideas. If you know these
ideas, you can understand much about the people's behavior. You
can predict—in a general way—some actions in certain situations.

b The pictures below express a single motivating idea.

Identify the motivations. Explain your ideas in a few sentences about each picture.

b

THOSE HORRID AGE SPOTS
**"I was so embarrassed, I served
lunch with my gloves on."**

"Then I found Esoterica. The medicated cream that works
below the skin's surface, in the pigment-forming cells, to help
lighten and fade age spots and
other darkened skin discolorations
on hands and face. In a matter of
weeks, my skin looked clearer."
Esoterica®
HELPS FADE EMBARRASSING AGE SPOTS.

9

You've seen that one motivation can cause many different kinds of actions. It is also true that one action can be caused by several different motivations. For example, three people could have three different motivations for having a party.

List all of the motivations that could lead a person to have a party. Compare your list with those of other students and make up a "master list" of motivations for the single action of having a party.

STOP & SUMMARIZE

You've been investigating relationships between *motivation* and *action.* Now, check your understanding of these ideas.

1. What are motivating ideas? Write a definition.
2. Below are several examples of people's actions. Identify at least one possible *motivation* for each action.

a. Several students form a school photography club.
b. A group of students protest at town hall against an evening curfew for young people.
c. A group of people decide to take Karate lessons.
d. High school students begin a fund-raising effort for a local charity.
e. Parents and students get together once a week to discuss their views on different topics.

3. Below are several motivating ideas. Identify at least one *action* that might grow out of each idea.

a. It is important for me to be independent and make my own decisions.
b. It is important to associate with other young people.
c. No one should receive special privileges without earning them.
d. Competition is good.
e. Among my friends, nobody should be different.

Perspective

You have seen how a few motivating ideas shared by members of a group can explain many of the ways group members act. This knowledge is a useful tool. In studying any group—large or small, past or present—knowing just a few of that group's important ideas and goals helps you understand many of their actions.

Now you will identify the motivating ideas of some of the explorers and colonists who came to this continent. You will look at the cities and colonies they set up. You will examine the ways in which motivating ideas affected colonial growth and development. Letters, diaries, stories, town records, and pictures will describe actions and events. Your job will be to look behind these actions, events, and words. In this way you can identify the ideas and goals which help explain why the people acted as they did.

Part 1   **Spanish Exploration and Colonization**
What motivated the Spanish to explore and colonize the New World?

Part 2   **English Colonization**
What motivated the English to establish colonies in North America?
How did these motivations affect the colonists' ways of thinking and acting?

Part 3   **Colonial Growth and Development**
How did motivating ideas affect the developing American colonies?

1419
Prince Henry of Portugal founds school for sailors and navigators

1488
Diaz reaches Cape of Good Hope

1492
Columbus discovers New World

1497
Da Gama sails to India

1513
Balboa discovers the Pacific

1519
Magellan sails around the world

1521
Cortez conquers Mexico

1541
DeSoto finds the Mississippi

1577
Drake sails around the world

1607
First settlers arrive at Jamestown

1619
First blacks arrive in colonies

1620
Pilgrims land at Plymouth

1628
Puritans establish Massachusetts Bay Colony

1647
Massachusetts establishes first public school system

1651–96
Navigation Acts

1733
Georgia, last of the thirteen colonies, founded

11

Part 1

Spanish Exploration and Colonization

The years from 1450 to the early 1600s are often called the "Age of Exploration." During this time the countries of Portugal, Spain, France, the Netherlands, Sweden, and England sent ships across the Atlantic Ocean. All of these countries shared reasons for exploring unknown lands. All of them claimed territory in the Americas. However, Spain was the first to develop a great empire there. For many years it controlled the largest empire in the New World. (An **empire** is a collection of nations or territories under the control of one government. Many of the territories in the empires of Spain and other European nations were colonies. A **colony** is a permanent settlement governed by a separate, often distant, country.)

In the activities which follow, you will look at data about Spanish exploration and colonization. As you do, think about this question:

What motivated the Spanish to explore and colonize the New World?

In 1492 an Italian sailor named Christopher Columbus sailed across the Atlantic Ocean. No one knew what lay across that ocean, but Columbus thought that it led to Asia. At that time, Europeans wanted many Asian goods and had to travel difficult journeys over land or around Africa in order to buy them. Ferdinand and Isabella, the king and queen of Spain who paid for Columbus's trip, hoped that he would find a quick and easy route to Asia. This discovery would give Spain a great advantage in trade.

On October 11, 1492, after sailing for three months, Columbus reached land. Although he thought that he had reached an island off the coast of Asia, he had in fact come to a small island in what are now called the Bahamas. Columbus named the island San Salvador. (**Salvador** means "Savior" in Spanish.)

Finding a new route to Asia was one major reason why Columbus made a total of four journeys across the Atlantic. But the Spanish king and queen, Columbus, and the colonists who came to live in the newly discovered lands also had other reasons for exploring and settling the New World. Some of these important motivating ideas are made clear in the data that follows.

Analyze each piece of data. List all of the motivations for exploration and colonization that you find in the data. Include the motivations of the king and queen, explorers, colonists, soldiers, and priests.

Juan de la Cosa: WAN day lah KOH-sah

Who is Columbus carrying on his shoulders? What does this say about Columbus's motivations?

a This drawing of "Columbus Entering the New World" comes from a map drawn by Juan de la Cosa in 1500.

a

b After his first voyage to the New World in 1493, Columbus wrote a letter to Lord Raphael Sanchez, an official in the court of Ferdinand and Isabella. Here is some of what he wrote.

Raphael Sanchez: Rah-fay-EL SAN-chez

b

> March 14, 1493
>
> Knowing that it will give you pleasure to learn that I have brought my project to a successful end, I have decided to write you about all the events which occurred on my voyage.
>
> Thirty-three days after my departure, I reached the Indian Sea, where I discovered many islands, thickly populated. I took possession of them in the name of our great King, by means of a public announcement. To the first of these islands I gave the name of the blessed Savior [San Salvador], under whose protection I had reached this and other islands. To each island I gave a name, ordering that one should be called Santa Maria de la Concepcion, another Fernandina, the third Isabella, the fourth Juana [Cuba], and so on.
>
> In all the islands there is no difference in the physical appearance of the inhabitants or in their manners or language. They all understand each other clearly, a fact which should help our glorious King reach what I assume is his main goal—the conversion of these people to a belief in Christ. . . .
>
> As to the advantages to be gained from my voyage, with a little assistance from our great rulers, I can get them as much gold as they need, as much spice, cotton, and pitch as they can use, and as many men for the navy as Their Majesties require. I can bring back rhubarb and other kinds of drugs. In fact, I am sure that the men I left in the fort have already found some.
>
> Therefore, let the King and Queen, our Princes, their happy kingdoms, and all the other provinces where Christ is worshipped give thanks to our Lord and Savior Jesus Christ, who has given us this great victory and much prosperity. Let there be parades and sacred feasts, and let the churches be decorated. Let Christ rejoice on earth as he rejoices in heaven at the thought of saving so many souls in so many nations that would otherwise have been lost.

A **conversion** is a change. In this case Columbus was writing about religious conversion, a change in religious belief.

Pitch is a form of tar that was used for sealing the wooden boards of ships and barrels to make them waterproof.

Many herbs and plants such as rhubarb were used as medicine.

What does this letter tell you about the motivations of Columbus? About the motivations of the king and queen?

In 1493 Columbus left Spain on his second voyage to the New World. He took with him about 1,200 sailors, soldiers, and colonists.

In addition to exploring the area, the Spanish wanted to start a permanent settlement on the island of Hispaniola. (Columbus had discovered the island on his first trip. Today, the countries of Haiti and the Dominican Republic are on the island.)

(C) The following excerpt is part of a letter Columbus wrote to the king and queen about Hispaniola and the colonists.

*A **friar** is a member of a religious group, or order, in the Roman Catholic Church.*

*Because Columbus thought that he had reached the Indies in Asia, he called the people he found in the New World **Indians.** Europeans called all native Americans Indians, although the native Americans themselves did not use this word.*

Why do you think Columbus suggested so many rules about gold? Based on this letter, what do you think was the colonists' strongest motivation?

Most High and Mighty Sovereigns,

Concerning the island of Hispaniola: About 2,000 colonists want to go there, because the land is safe and good for farming and trading, and because it is in a good location for carrying on trade with neighboring islands.

I would suggest:

1. That three or four towns be founded in convenient places, and that each settler be assigned to one of these towns.

2. That for the rapid colonization of Hispaniola, no one be allowed to collect gold except those who have taken out colonist papers and built houses in the towns where they have been assigned.

3. That each town have a mayor and notary public, as is the custom in Spain.

4. That there be a church, and parish priests or friars to hold worship services and convert the Indians.

5. That no settler be allowed to look for gold without a license from the governor or mayor of the town where he lives, and then only when he has sworn to return to the town to register all the gold he has found.

6. That all the gold brought in be melted down immediately, and stamped with some symbol of the town. The part of it which belongs to your Highnesses should be weighed and given to the mayor for safekeeping.

7. That one percent of all gold found be set aside for building and furnishing churches, and for the support of the priests or friars.

8. Because everyone will want to look for gold instead of doing other kinds of work, it seems to me that the privilege of going to look for gold ought to be withheld during some part of the year so that the other business of the island is done.

d Queen Isabella issued this order in 1503.

The King and I first ordered that the Indian inhabitants of the island of Hispaniola are free. Now, however, we understand that the Indians have so much liberty they avoid all contact with Spaniards, wander about doing nothing, and will not even work for wages. There is so little contact with them that they cannot even be converted to Christianity.

If the Christians on Hispaniola are to maintain their farms and mine the gold, and if we are going to be able to convert the Indians to our Holy Catholic Faith, the Indians must live among the Christians. This will make it possible for them to help each other cultivate the island and take the gold.

Therefore, I command you to force the Indians to associate with the Christians, to work on their buildings, mine gold, till the fields, and produce food for the Christians and themselves. Each day, each worker is to be paid whatever you think is fair, and on feast days and at other times you shall gather them together to be taught the Faith.

This the Indians shall do as free people, not as slaves.

How did the Spaniards' motivating ideas affect their treatment of the Indians?

Spanish rule and settlement spread within the Caribbean area. Other explorers came to investigate lands beyond those Columbus had reached, and soldiers, priests, and colonists came to live in the new Spanish territory.

e The following conversation was heard and written down by a Spanish priest. The speaker Ximenes, a Spanish soldier, had been in the New World for several years. The second speaker, Zamora, had just arrived. Zamora was an assistant to the Spanish bishop Bartolome de Las Casas.

Ximenes: He-MAYN-ace
Zamora: Zah-MORE-ah

Ximenes: "You chose a poor place to stable that beast of yours for the night. The Indians will probably steal it and eat it."

Zamora: "Let them eat it, by God; we Christians owe them a lot more than that."

Ximenes: "What the devil do you mean by that?"

Zamora: "I mean that you've robbed them of their property and taken their sons from them and made them slaves in their own land."

Ximenes: "They owe us more than that, for we are Christians."

Zamora: "Christians? A Christian is known by how he acts."

Ximenes: "We are Christians, and we came to this land to make Christians of them."

Zamora: "I'll bet you came over here because you were in trouble and Spain was too hot for you. I swear, no one comes to the Indies for any other reason. That's why I came."

Ximenes: "God alone knows why each man came over, but the main thing is we conquered this country."

Zamora: "And that's why you expect the Indians to give you their food and property—because you murdered them in their own houses! Good friends you turned out to be!"

Zimenes: "You wouldn't say that if you'd lost your blood in the war."

Zamora: "I believe that even if they had killed you, they would not go to Hell, because you made war on them."

Ximenes: "They are dogs, and refuse to believe in God."

Zamora: "And a very good preacher you were, for sure. The Devil take me if I carry away a cent that I didn't earn with my shovel. The Indians don't owe me a thing."

How do you think the two men's motivations and attitudes affected their treatment of the Indians?

Complete your list of motivating ideas. In your opinion, which ideas were the strongest motivations for the Spanish king and queen? Which were the strongest for the colonists? Explain your choices.

BRANCHING OUT

Territory on the moon has been explored, but no nation has claimed any of the land as its own. Develop a program for territorial claims on the moon. The program should be one that you think would be both fair and workable.

Planning a Spanish Town

You've looked at some of the motivations that brought Spanish explorers and colonists to the New World. But motivations affect more than just the movement of people. Once the Spanish arrived, their motivating ideas affected the ways they organized, worked, and worshipped. Motivations decided the ways in which they dealt with the Indians and with each other. All their actions were based on their important ideas.

When the Spanish colonists arrived in the New World, they had to build towns in which to live. Even these towns and cities—the ways in which they were built and the ways in which people lived in them—were evidence of Spanish motivations. In this activity you'll look at Spanish rules for building colonial towns and at pictures of some of these towns.

If you were a Spanish settler who had just arrived in the New World, your first job would have been to help build a town. However, you could not have built your town just any way you wanted to build it. In July of 1573, your king, Philip II, had set up a list of ordinances, or official rules. These were to be followed in the design and construction of all new towns in Spanish America.

The rules King Philip wrote were not just his own ideas about the way towns should look. Many towns and cities in Spain were already laid out and built in ways like those described by Philip. It is likely that most Spanish people agreed with these rules of town design.

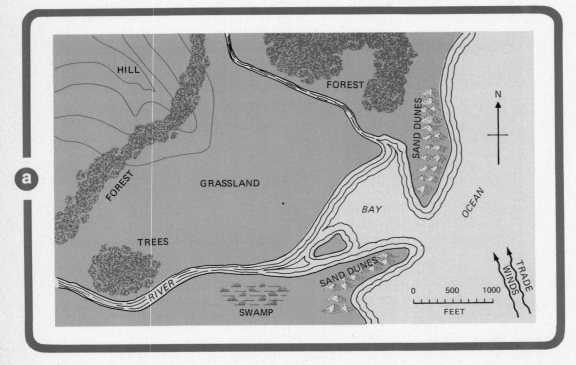

(a) → (e) The map on page 18 is of an imaginary seacoast area somewhere in Spanish America. Assume that you are a Spanish settler and this is where you've landed. On pages 19-22 are some of King Philip's "Royal Ordinances for New Towns." You must obey these rules as you design and build a town. Place your town someplace in the seacoast area where you have landed.

First, make a copy of the map on a large piece of paper. Then, read the ordinances and draw your town on your map. You may want to make changes in the town as you read the ordinances, so read all of them before you draw, or sketch lightly so that you can make changes as you read.

Study Ordinances 110 through 114 carefully before you begin laying out your design.

Royal Ordinances for New Towns

San Lorenzo, July 3, 1573

Royal Ordinance 110

When the settlers arrive at the place where the town will be built, they must make a plan for the new town. The plazas, streets, and building lots must be laid out exactly, beginning with the main plaza. Next, the settlers must lay out the streets, gates, and important roads. The plan must always leave enough open space so the town can continue to grow according to these ordinances.

Royal Ordinance 111

The town must be located on ground that is not low or swampy. There must be land for farming and pasture, fuel and wood for buildings, fresh water, and a native people nearby. The town gates should open to the north wind. If the site is on the coast, the town should be a port, but do not have the sea to the south or to the west. Lagoons or swamps in which are found poisonous animals or diseased air and water should not be nearby.

Royal Ordinance 112

If the town is on the seacoast, the main plaza should be at the ship landing place. If the town lies inland, the plaza should be in the middle of the town. The plaza must be a rectangle, with the long side equal to one and one-half times the width. This is the best shape for fiestas, especially those in which horses are used.

*A **plaza** is an open area, usually paved, surrounded by buildings.*

*A **fiesta,** or "feast," is a public celebration.*

19

Royal Ordinance 113

The plaza should be small or large depending on the number of settlers, but do not forget that in new towns the population should grow. The plaza must be no less than 200 feet wide and 300 feet long. A good size is 600 feet long and 400 feet wide.

Royal Ordinance 114

Four main streets must run from the plaza, one starting from the middle of each side. At each corner of the plaza, two streets should begin, and should line up with the sides of the plaza.

In seaport towns, because the plaza will be at the landing, there can only be three main streets. Other streets will cross all the streets going from the plaza to divide the town into blocks.

Choose a place and size for your plaza. Draw it in, and lay out the streets for the town. Follow the directions in Ordinances 116 through 118.

Royal Ordinance 116

In cold places the streets should be wide; in hot places they should be narrow. However, if horses will be used to help defend the town, the streets should be wide.

Royal Ordinance 117

The streets must go out from the main plaza in ways that will not cause problems or crowding when the town grows.

Royal Ordinance 118

If the town will be large, smaller plazas must be laid out here and there for new churches and monasteries.

Why do you think the Spaniards felt a church should have a plaza?

Add to your town plan the buildings described in Ordinances 119 through 122.

Royal Ordinance 119

If the town is on the coast, the first cathedral must be built facing the plaza, so it can be seen when arriving by sea. This building should also serve as a means of defense for the port.

Royal Ordinance 120

The building lots for the cathedral and other nearby church buildings must be assigned first. Buildings not related to the church must be kept some distance away.

*A **cathedral** is the church of a Roman Catholic bishop.*

Royal Ordinance 121

The next building lots to be chosen must be for a house for the royal council, a customs house, and an arsenal. These must

*A **customs house** is a kind of bank for collecting and storing official money and goods. An **arsenal** is a place where weapons are stored.*

be near the cathedral and port so that in times of battle they will help defend each other.

The hospital for the poor and those sick with non-contagious diseases must be built near the church buildings. The hospital for those sick with contagious diseases must be built so the wind will not blow from it toward the rest of the town.

Royal Ordinance 122

The building lots for slaughterhouses, fisheries, tanneries, and other things which cause pollution must be placed so waste is not a problem.

Add to your town plan the buildings suggested in Ordinances 126 through 129 and Ordinances 134 and 135.

Royal Ordinance 126

Building lots around the plaza must not be used for family houses. The buildings facing the plaza will be the cathedral, other buildings the church may need, buildings used for the King's business, and shops.

The first buildings to be built facing the plaza will be the shops. All the settlers must help build these shops. Anyone who buys from the merchants must pay a fair tax, to help pay for the shop buildings.

Royal Ordinance 127

The other building lots near the plaza will be given to the settlers by a lottery. The lots farther away from the plaza will be kept for later settlers, and for other buildings the town might need. The town must always keep a plan showing where new buildings and streets will be built.

Royal Ordinance 128

After the town plans are finished and each settler has a building lot, each settler must set up his tent on his lot. Those who do not have tents must build huts so they may have shelter.

As soon as possible all settlers must make a wall or ditch around the town so they may protect themselves from the Indians.

Royal Ordinance 129

An open pasture field must be prepared near the town. The pasture must be large so there will always be plenty of room for the people to go for recreation and room for the cattle to be pastured without danger.

Based on Ordinance 121, who do you think was responsible for the poor and sick?

Although other buildings were assigned lots earlier, the shops were the first buildings actually built. Why do you think this was a rule?

What does Philip's suggestion about protection from the Indians reveal about his attitude toward them?

Royal Ordinance 134

The settlers must try as much as possible to have the buildings all of one form so the town will be more beautiful.

Royal Ordinance 135

The governor assigned to the new town will pick people to lay out the town. They must follow these ordinances.

f Two Spanish colonial towns:

1 Santo Domingo, founded on Hispaniola in 1496

2 A New Mexican town

In what ways were those towns built according to King Philip's rules? Santo Domingo was laid out before the ordinances were passed. In what ways is it different from Philip's plan?

Excited by what Columbus had discovered, Spain sent other explorers to investigate the New World and its people. These men explored the great continents of North and South America.

Men like Columbus were discoverers, interested in finding out what lay in unknown places. But once new lands and people had been discovered, other kinds of Europeans came to them. Some of these were **conquistadores,** or conquerors, who wanted to overpower the Indians who lived in the discovered lands. They wanted to control the Indians so that they—and Spain—could control the land and the wealth the Indians owned. Two of the most famous of the conquistadores were Hernando Cortes, who conquered Mexico, and Fernando Pizarro, who defeated the powerful Inca empire in what is now Peru.

Other Spanish soldiers explored what is now the United States. (The map below shows the conquistadores' routes.) One of these men was Franciso de Coronado. In 1540 Coronado set out to travel north from Mexico. With him were more than 1,000 soldiers and servants. They were looking for seven "cities of gold" that they had heard about from earlier explorers. Two years later, Coronado returned to Mexico after having explored the southwestern United States. Although he had traveled as far north as the present state of Kansas, he had not found the golden cities.

conquistadores: kon-key-stah-DOHR-ace

SPANISH EXPLORERS AND CONQUERORS

- De Leon 1513
- Cabeza de Vaca 1528-1536
- Pizarro 1532
- De Soto 1539-1542
- Coronado 1541
- Coronado 1542
- Valdivia 1541-1550

The Spanish were very successful conquerors. By the year 1600 they controlled all of the land shown on the map below. Over 200 cities and towns had been established. Libraries, cathedrals, three universities, and a printing press had been built. About 160,000 Spaniards lived in the New World by the late 1500s. Among them were priests and soldiers, wealthy families and poor settlers.

Spain's empire in the New World continued to grow. In what is now the United States, settlements were established in the Southwest and as far north as San Francisco. The map below shows you the parts of North and South America held by Spain in 1784. At that time, Spain had the largest land and sea empire in the world.

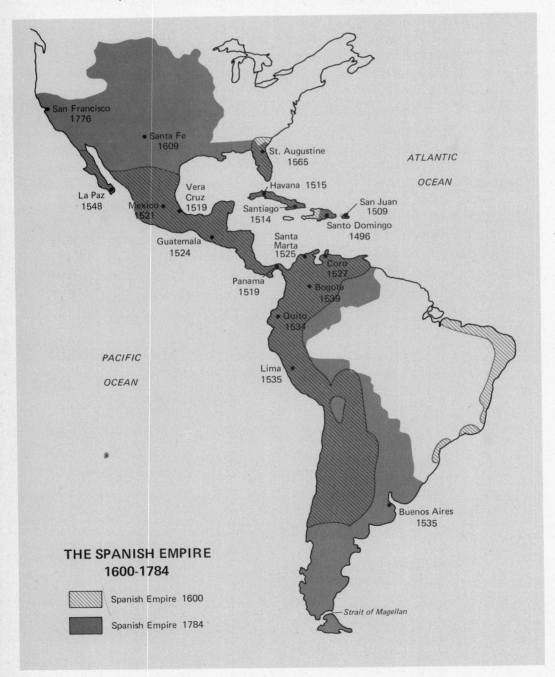

THE SPANISH EMPIRE
1600-1784

Spanish Empire 1600

Spanish Empire 1784

As you analyze the following material, identify important motivations for Spain and for the missionaries.

a The Spaniards controlled about 1.5 million Indians and most of the colonies' wealth. Great amounts of this wealth were sent back to Spain, most of it to the royal treasury. The chart below shows the number of pounds of gold and silver shipped to Spain from the New World during two ten-year periods. This was the largest amount of precious metal ever shipped back to Spain.

Find out about the present price of an ounce of gold and figure out how much this gold would be worth today.

▼

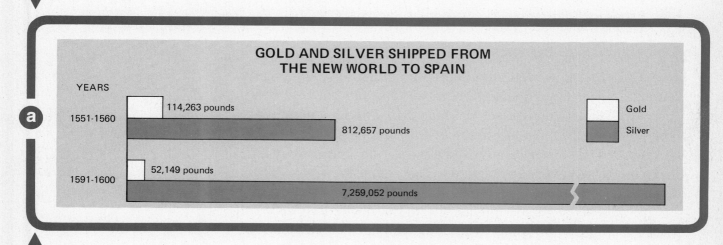

a

GOLD AND SILVER SHIPPED FROM THE NEW WORLD TO SPAIN

YEARS

1551-1560
114,263 pounds
812,657 pounds

1591-1600
52,149 pounds
7,259,052 pounds

Gold
Silver

▲

How would this amount of gold and silver affect the motivations of the Spanish government in dealing with the New World, in your opinion.

Pedro Fages: PAY-droh FAH-hace

After Spanish explorers and conquistadores found and conquered the new lands, the first to follow them were priests. Throughout the empire, the priests established religious centers, called **missions.** These priests are called **missionaries.** The following descriptions of missions were written by Pedro Fages, a Spanish colonial soldier and former royal governor.

b In this first selection, Fages described the Mission of San Gabriel. The mission is in what is now east Los Angeles.

b

The priests have built many important mission settlements in California. These settlements were built to convert the natives of this vast country to the faith of Jesus Christ and obedience to our Lord, the King of Spain.

Between San Francisco Solano and the Rio de Santa Clara is the new mission of San Gabriel. The mission was founded on September 8, 1771. The church, dwelling, and the offices are within a stockade, and are simply built. A short distance away is the village where the unconverted natives and the new Christians live. The new Christians attend Mass and religious classes regularly. Some of the unconverted natives also come so that the missionary fathers may teach them about religion.

Close to the mission stockade a few small houses were built for the five families of Christian Indians. The reverend Father-President brought these families from lower California. They work for the mission, tilling the ground and sowing wheat. It is important that the fields grow much grain. The natives of this district cannot obtain enough wild seeds of pleasant taste, and they cannot catch fish for food.

c Fages said this about the mission at San Luis Obispo.

c The mission is well supplied with land, water, and pasture. No matter how large the mission grows to be, and no matter how many Indians are converted, the land will provide enough food. The land will also support many Spanish settlers, who may wish to move here. This will help God's work, and help keep control of the country we have conquered. The Father-President told me that some settlers had offered to bring their wives and families to this country. If this happens, the Indians will stop believing that we are exiles from our own lands who have come here.

How do you think the presence of settlers' wives and children would affect the Indians' attitude toward Spanish motivations?

d In his description of another California mission, Fages said this.

d Here at Monterey the reverend fathers have tried to cultivate the soil in the best way possible. The crop of corn turned out well, and the same is hoped for the wheat crop. God will be pleased to supply the needs of these unhappy native people. If they must depend on the mission for food and the protection of a few clothes, their conversion will be easy.

What do you think Fages meant when he said that food and clothes would affect the conversion of Indians?

Most of the Indians of California were members of tribes and bands who obtained food by hunting animals and gathering wild plants. They moved around over their tribal territory to keep from exhausting the food in any location.

Based on what you have read, what changes were the missions trying to make in the lives of the Indians? What do you think were the motivations for these changes?

You've studied ways in which people's motivations are shown by their actions. The laws people write, the decisions they make, the ways they train their children, the records they keep, the towns they build—all of these show motivating ideas.

Some of the motivating ideas important to King Philip are reflected in the ordinances he wrote. These ideas were shared by many other Spanish people in the 1500s.

To identify some important Spanish motivations, follow the instructions below. Refer to the ordinances on pages 19-22.

1. Prepare a list of the various kinds of buildings and property in the Spanish town (for example, the cathedral, farms, shops, etc.).

2. Arrange the list to show the importance of various kinds of buildings and property. Begin with the most important building. Be able to explain your choices.

3. What motivating ideas are shown by the buildings and property the Spanish considered important? Name at least three of these ideas.

4. Identify all references to individuals and groups who could make decisions regulating the people in the town. When important decisions were made that affected farmers, how many of these decisions do you think the farmers made for themselves: most, some, or few?

Using all the Spanish data you've analyzed so far (pages 12-26) make a master list which summarizes the most important ideas that you think motivated the Spanish during this period.

BRANCHING OUT

Prepare a written or oral report on one of the following subjects. Whenever you can, illustrate your report with maps and drawings.

1. The life and voyages of Columbus

2. The conquistadores

3. Mission life

Exploration: An Overview

You have examined the discoveries of the explorer Columbus. But Europe's Age of Exploration began even before these daring voyages.

The Portuguese were the first to begin searching for ocean routes to Asia which would replace the long overland routes then used. Prince Henry of Portugal wanted to find these routes, and he sent many sailors out from Portugal to explore the oceans.

In 1487 the Portuguese explorer Bartholomew Diaz sailed down the coast of Africa and reached the tip of the continent. There, he saw a great ocean stretching eastward. Diaz and his exhausted crew were unable to continue the voyage any further. The Portuguese thought this ocean (the Indian Ocean) could be a route to Asia, and they were right. Ten years later, in 1497, another Portuguese navigator, Vasco da Gama, sailed even further than Diaz. After reaching the southern tip of Africa, da Gama continued up its east coast and across the Indian Ocean all the way to India. He returned to Portugal with spices, jewels, and other goods which Portugal had been eager to obtain.

As you have read, several years before da Gama's voyage, Christopher Columbus had a different plan for reaching Asia. He believed that the earth was round, and thought he could reach Asia by sailing west, instead of east, across the Atlantic Ocean. When Columbus arrived in the New World three months later, neither he nor any member of his crew realized the discovery they had made. To Columbus, the islands he had come upon were part of the Indies, near the mainland of Asia. (Today these islands are still called the West Indies.)

Columbus made four voyages in search of a westward ocean route to Asia. By his fourth voyage, he felt sure that the lands he had visited were not the Indies, but part of Asian lands unknown to Europe.

On the map find the routes of Diaz, da Gama, and Columbus. Could Columbus have reached Asia by sailing west?

Another explorer for Spain, Vasco de Balboa, discovered the Pacific Ocean. Balboa crossed the narrow land now called Panama and came to a great ocean. Balboa claimed, for Spain, the new ocean and all of the lands that it touched.

Meanwhile, the King of England also became interested in voyages of exploration. After hearing the results of Columbus's first two voyages, the King sent an Italian, John Cabot (Giovanni Cabatto), to sail in search of a westward route to Asia. Cabot set sail on his first voyage in 1497. He too reached the New World and became the first man to claim land in the New World for England. Cabot made a second voyage in 1498. Like Columbus, Cabot believed he had reached Asia.

Find Cabot's route. How was his route different from the routes Columbus took?

28

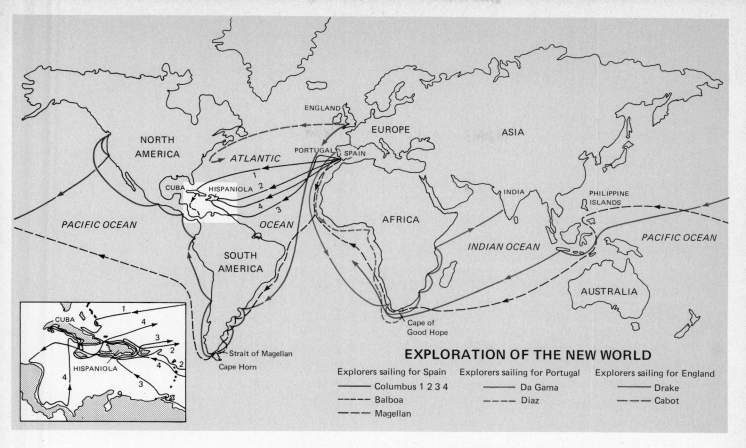

EXPLORATION OF THE NEW WORLD

Explorers sailing for Spain	Explorers sailing for Portugal	Explorers sailing for England
—— Columbus 1 2 3 4	—— Da Gama	—— Drake
---- Balboa	---- Diaz	---- Cabot
– – Magellan		

The explorer who first sailed around the world was Ferdinand Magellan, a Portuguese nobleman. He too believed that he could reach India by sailing west. With the support of the King of Spain, Magellan set sail in 1519. His fleet of ships sailed south along the coast of South America, looking for a passage through the continent.

Magellan and his men faced bad weather and many dangers. Finally they discovered a waterway at the southern end of the continent. (Today this waterway is called the Strait of Magellan.) They passed through these dangerous waters into another more peaceful ocean, the ocean Balboa had discovered. Magellan named it the Pacific Ocean. (**Pacific** means "peaceful.")

Magellan was killed before his ships returned to Spain in 1522, but it was his bravery that had led the ships around the world. The voyage established that America was not part of Asia. After Magellan's voyage, Europeans had a much more accurate idea of the world than they had ever had before.

The second complete voyage around the world was made by an Englishman, Sir Francis Drake. In 1577 Drake left England with five ships. Three years later he returned to England with only one ship, having sailed around the earth.

After Magellan's voyage, Spain controlled the water route around South America into the Pacific Ocean. Other European countries then began to explore to find a shorter way of getting to the Pacific. The routes of Magellan and Drake were too long and dangerous.

What route did Magellan's ships follow after they reached the Pacific Ocean? How far north did Drake sail? How was his route different from Magellan's?

29

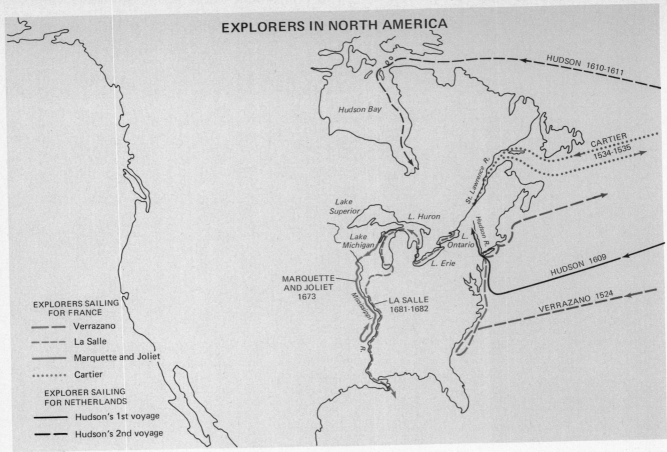

EXPLORERS IN NORTH AMERICA

HUDSON 1610-1611

Hudson Bay

CARTIER 1534-1535

St. Lawrence R.

Lake Superior

L. Huron

Lake Michigan

L. Ontario

Hudson R.

L. Erie

MARQUETTE AND JOLIET 1673

LA SALLE 1681-1682

Mississippi R.

HUDSON 1609

VERRAZANO 1524

EXPLORERS SAILING FOR FRANCE
- – – Verrazano
- – - – La Salle
- ——— Marquette and Joliet
- ········ Cartier

EXPLORER SAILING FOR NETHERLANDS
- ——— Hudson's 1st voyage
- – ■ – Hudson's 2nd voyage

In the early 1500s, France sent Giovanni Verrazano and Jacques Cartier on separate missions to search for this route. Their discoveries gave France the right to claim land and settle in the New World.

Even after the voyages of Verrazano and Cartier, the French continued their search for a way through North America to Asia. Father Marquette, a missionary, and Louis Joliet, a fur trader, explored the Mississippi in 1673, hoping this might be a passage through North America to Asia. Their explorations were continued by Robert de la Salle, who in 1682 sailed down the Mississippi River valley, hoping to build a strong French empire in the New World. He named the land Louisiana, in honor of the French king, Louis.

The Netherlands also played an active role in the New World explorations. Henry Hudson was an Englishman hired by Dutch merchants to find a passage through America to the Far East. Hudson, who set sail in 1609, was not successful in finding the route he was seeking, but he did explore the river and bay which now bear his name. His explorations gave the Dutch a claim in the New World.

The discoveries of the Age of Exploration had indeed opened up a new world. European nations now owned land thousands of miles away. They would send ships and settlers to this new world. They would become richer because of it; they would fight wars because of it. The explorers had not found quick and easy routes to the riches of Asia, but they had given their countries riches in land and people, in precious metals and new opportunities.

How were the routes of Verrazano and Cartier different from those of the Spanish explorers? What does this tell you about where the French hoped to find a route to the East?

What areas did Henry Hudson explore?

30

Part 2

English Colonization

When John Cabot returned to England after his two voyages, he was rewarded by the King for his discoveries. However, the small amount of the award showed that the King was not very excited about Cabot's discoveries.

Unlike Spain, England did nothing more about the New World for many years. Because of these voyages, however, England claimed its share of North America. This claim was later the basis for English colonization.

The activities in Part 2 will help you investigate these questions:

What motivated the English to establish colonies in North America?

How did these motivations affect the colonists' ways of thinking and acting?

Growing Interest in Colonies

The English began colonization more slowly than Spain. England was poor, and was spending much time and money struggling with other European countries. Problems within England also reduced its strength and prosperity during the 1500s. But England's power and wealth finally began to increase and the English people focused their attention on America.

⬤ England's motivations for colonization are shown in the selection that follows. These excerpts come from a document written in 1584 by Richard Hakluyt. Hakluyt was writing to the English queen, Elizabeth I, and other important English people.

Hakluyt: HACK-lut

1. Based on the data, identify
   a. Hakluyt's attitude toward colonies
   b. Important problems England was having
   c. England's religious concerns
2. Make a list of possible ways of obtaining wealth from a new colony, according to Hakluyt.

1. For a hundred years, by producing wool and wool clothing, England has raised itself to greater wealth and much higher honor, might, and power than before. But now, Spain and the West Indies are producing much wool. The wool and cloth of England must be sold for less and less money. We should plant a colony in America to give us a place to sell our wool.

2. A colony may stop the Spanish king from taking over all of America, if we begin it there immediately. Also, once England has a new colony, her Majesty will have plenty of excellent trees for masts, good timber to build ships, pitch, tar, hemp, and other things needed for a royal navy. And all these things would be free. It will be easy for England to be lord of all the seas. We can spoil King Philip's navy, and keep him from shipping his treasures from America to Spain. This will reduce the power of Spain and of Philip, the supporter of the evil Roman Catholic Church. This will stop the problems he is now causing in all Europe because he has so much treasure.

3. This voyage may be accomplished by very small ships, but large ships will increase the merchant's profits. In

What influence did Spain have on Hakluyt's thinking? Why do you think this was true?

Why would large ships increase profits? Why was this a good way for England to obtain defense?

Do you think Hakluyt believed it was wrong to trade cheap goods for valuable goods? Explain.

Flanders is an area now part of France and Belgium.

Do you think Hakluyt was concerned about the natives? About the Spanish? Explain.

this way England will gain large ships for the defense of this kingdom.

4. This new navy of large, strong ships will not be stopped by the ships of other kings or princes.

5. By shipping goods to America, (instead of Europe), we can avoid paying customs taxes to foreign princes.

6. When we trade with the natives, we will exchange cheap English goods for things of high value.

7. Great numbers of English people will be given work in the colony. This will take away from England many that are now living on welfare money.

8. If the seacoast can be used for making salt, and the inland for wine, oils, oranges, lemons, figs, etc., and for making iron, we can reduce the strength of the French, of the Spanish, of the Portuguese, of enemies, and of doubtful friends. We can reduce their wealth and power without drawing our swords.

9. From the colony we may receive metal goods that we now import from France, Flanders, Germany, etc. This will reduce the strength of these countries, and drive their people into unemployment, so our people can work.

10. By colonizing we can enlarge the glory of the Christian gospel, and from England, plant sincere religion, and provide a safe and sure place to receive people from all parts of the world that are forced to flee for God's word.

11. If we have to fight wars there, our youths will be trained in the discipline of war. They will become good soldiers for the defense of the colony and of England.

12. The Spaniards govern in the Indies by dominating and oppressing the people. When the Queen of England, who allows her people freedom, shall have a colony in America, and the news goes out that the natives are treated fairly and given freedom, the natives will revolt from the Spanish.

13. Many good men can no longer live in England because of unpaid debts or because they have done something wrong when they were young. In the colony they can find a home and serve their country.

Based on your analysis of the data, what were the two or three most important motivations for having a colony, according to Hakluyt?

Motives of the Virginia Settlers

The first English attempts at colonization failed. But in 1606 a group of London merchants formed the London Company and obtained a charter from King James I to begin another colony. (Discoverers claimed all land for the rulers of their countries. The king or queen gave individuals and companies the right to settle on land and to trade there. These rights were granted in a document called a **charter.**)

The Virginia Company, part of the London Company, sponsored England's next attempt to begin a settlement. In December 1606 the Company sent three tiny ships across the Atlantic Ocean. Five months later the ships arrived at Chesapeake Bay in Virginia and Jamestown was founded. (It was named in honor of the king.) This colony succeeded, but it first came very close to failure.

a Goals of the Virginia Company are described in the company's instructions to Sir Thomas Gates. Gates was sent as a new governor of Jamestown in 1609.

Read the document, and identify the motivations of its writers. Which of them are similar to the motivations of the Spanish? What important Spanish motivation is not mentioned?

a
We recommend four main ways to enrich the colonies and make a profit. (You must be careful that our ships do not come back empty nor filled with useless merchandise.)

The *first* way is to discover either the south seas [a route to India and China] or royal mines for gold and silver.

The *second* is to trade for valuable goods with far-off countries that you might reach by ship.

The *third* is tribute.

The *fourth* is labor of your own men—making wines, pitch, tar, soap ashes, steel, iron, pipestaves, sowing hemp and flax, gathering silk of the grass, providing the silkworm, and fishing for pearls, codfish, sturgeon, and the like.

b The group which settled Jamestown consisted of about 100 men. Others followed this first group. On page 35 there is a list of the names and occupations of the first Jamestown settlers. Following that is a list of some of the occupations of the second group of settlers.

The first English colony in America was sponsored by Sir Walter Raleigh. Raleigh was given the right to settle all of North America above Florida, an area which he named Virginia. Raleigh's colony failed.

The tribute was to be in the form of goods given to the settlers by the people they found living in Virginia.

Would Hakluyt have approved of the Virginia Company's motivations?

34

Look at the number of men listed in each occupation. Based on the list, answer these questions:

1. How well prepared were the colonists to accomplish the goals of the Virginia Company?

2. For which goals were they best prepared? Least prepared?

3. How would the colonists' occupations and preparation affect the success of the colony?

4. Why do you think these colonists wanted to come to the New World?

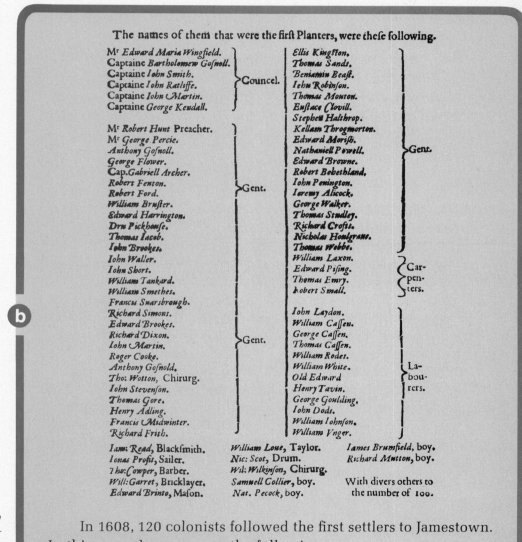

The names of them that were the first Planters, were these following.

Mr Edward Maria Wingfield.
Captaine Bartholomew Gofnoll.
Captaine Iohn Smith.
Captaine Iohn Ratliffe.
Captaine Iohn Martin.
Captaine George Kendall.
} Councel.

Mr Robert Hunt Preacher.
Mr George Percie.
Anthony Gofnoll.
George Flower.
Cap.Gabriell Archer.
Robert Fenton.
Robert Ford.
William Brufter.
Edward Harrington.
Dru Pickhoufe.
Thomas Iacob.
Iohn Brookes.
Iohn Waller.
Iohn Short.
William Tankard.
William Smethes.
Francis Snarsbrough.
Richard Simons.
Edward Brookes.
Richard Dixon.
Iohn Martin.
Roger Cooke.
Anthony Gofnold.
Tho: Wotton, Chirurg.
Iohn Stevenfon.
Thomas Gore.
Henry Adling.
Francis Midwinter.
Richard Frith.
} Gent.

Ellis Kingfton.
Thomas Sands.
Beniamin Beaft.
Iehu Robinfon.
Thomas Mouton.
Euftace Clovill.
Stephen Halthrop.
Kellam Throgmorton.
Edward Morifh.
Nathaniell Powell.
Edward Browne.
Robert Behethland.
Iohn Penington.
Ieremy Alicock.
George Walker.
Thomas Studley.
Richard Crofts.
Nicholas Houlgrane.
Thomas Webbe.
} Gent.

William Laxon.
Edward Pifing.
Thomas Emry.
Robert Small.
} Carpenters.

Iohn Laydon.
William Caffen.
George Caffen.
Thomas Caffen.
William Rodes.
William White.
Old Edward.
Henry Tavin.
George Goulding.
Iohn Dods.
William Iohnfon.
William Vnger.
} Labourers.

Iam: Read, Blackfmith.
Ionas Profit, Sailer.
Thr:Cowper, Barber.
Will:Garret, Bricklayer.
Edward Brinto, Mafon.

William Loue, Taylor.
Nic: Scot, Drum.
Wil: Wilkinfon, Chirurg.
Samuell Collier, boy.
Nat. Pecock, boy.

Iames Brumfield, boy.
Richard Mutton, boy.

With divers others to the number of 100.

The **councel** were the men chosen by the Virginia Company to run the colony. **Gent.** stands for gentleman. A **gentleman** was a person of high social position. A gentleman was not expected to do any physical labor.

In 1608, 120 colonists followed the first settlers to Jamestown. In this second group were the following:

28 gentlemen, 21 laborers, 6 tailors, 2 apothecaries, 1 jeweler, 2 metal refiners, 2 goldsmiths, 1 perfumer, 1 cooper (barrelmaker), 1 tobacco pipemaker, and 1 blacksmith.

The early years of the Jamestown colony were difficult. Unlike Spanish colonists, the Jamestown settlers found no gold or silver. The Indians supplied no valuable goods and could not be forced to work. These native Americans were sometimes friendly, but often dangerous after they had been mistreated by the settlers. One of the biggest problems, however, was the attitude of the colonists. Many, even the laborers, had to be forced to work.

Answer these questions, based on your knowledge of the Jamestown settlers:

1. Other colonists faced problems like those at Jamestown without having the poor attitudes which were typical of Jamestown settlers. How do you think the settlers' motivations affected their attitudes?

2. The environment of Virginia was suitable for farming. How could you explain the fact that many of the first Jamestown settlers died from starvation?

3. All of the land in the colony belonged to the Virginia Company. How might this fact have affected settlers' motivations?

In the first 15 years of the Jamestown colony, 10,000 settlers came to it. By 1622 only 2,000 were still alive. The others had died of disease, starvation, and Indian attack.

The Virginia Company had sent its first colonists to Virginia largely to find gold and trade routes. Although the colonists did not find gold or new routes, they did find an important product to trade. They discovered that the land was good for growing tobacco. That discovery saved the colony. Colonists shipped the tobacco back to England, where it was easily sold. With the money from this sale, they bought the manufactured goods that they needed.

In order to encourage settlers to go to Virginia, the Company allowed the colonists to own land. In this way, however, the Company gradually lost control of the colony. Finally, in 1624, King James made Virginia a royal colony. Colonists owned their own land but they were governed by the king. Jamestown had survived as England's first settled land in the New World.

BRANCHING OUT

Read about the life of Captain John Smith, one of the first Jamestown settlers. Or, read about Pocahontas, princess of the Powhatan Indians who lived in Virginia before the English arrived. Prepare a written or oral report on the life of John Smith or Pocahontas.

Another group of English colonists began their adventure north of Virginia, in New England. These settlers were "Puritans"—religious people who wished to change, or purify, the Church of England. (The Church of England was the official English church.)

The first to come to America were Puritan Separatists, called Pilgrims. The Pilgrims wanted to form a new church, separate from the Church of England. After moving to Holland, a group of Pilgrims decided that they should establish their new church and new lives in the New World. In 1620, 102 Pilgrims set sail for America on the *Mayflower.* In November 1620 these settlers founded Plymouth Colony in what is now Massachusetts. They were followed in 1630 by a large number of "Non-Conformists," Puritans who wanted to reform the English church. These Puritans settled around Massachusetts Bay and founded several communities, including Boston. The map below shows you the location of the two Puritan colonies.

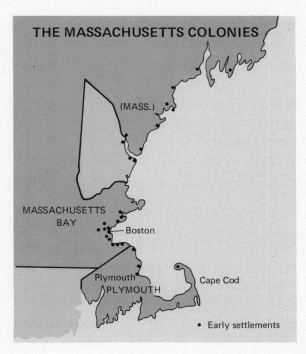

THE MASSACHUSETTS COLONIES

(MASS.)

MASSACHUSETTS BAY

— Boston

Plymouth
PLYMOUTH

Cape Cod

• Early settlements

In this activity you'll read documents which suggest motivations of the Puritans. Identify and list the motivations. In what ways are they different from those of the Virginia Company and of the Virginia settlers?

a The following reasons for colonizing come from a pamphlet published in England in 1629. The pamphlet's author, a Puritan named John Winthrop, later was governor of the Massachusetts Bay Colony.

It will be an important service of the church to carry the gospel into those parts of the world to raise a barrier against the kingdom of Anti-Christ which the Jesuits are working to establish.

England grows weary of her inhabitants, and treats them like animals because the population is too great. The towns complain about the problem of taking care of poor people. There are not enough jobs. Because of this, people have come to dislike their children, their servants, and their neighbors.

Here in England, people struggle to obtain an acre or two of land, with more work and cost than for many hundreds of acres in another country.

In England, education and religion have become evil and corrupt, and children are learning the wrong ways to live, because of the bad example of people around them.

What can be a better job for a Christian than to help establish a new church? He can join a group of faithful people, and help them succeed and prosper.

If Godly people who are wealthy give up their comfortable life and become colonists, they will be a good example for others. If they face dangers and hardships to help form a new church, they will encourage other people to join us. Then people in England will see that we are going to do what God wants, and we are not going for wrong reasons.

So many wise and faithful servants of God (ministers and others) have become interested in establishing the colony, it must be God's will for us to do this.

Anti-Christ was one way in which Puritans referred to the Catholic Church. The *Jesuits* are a group of Catholic priests.

b Captain Edward Johnson gave this version of Puritan history in 1654.

Some time ago, England began to lose its religion. Instead of getting rid of the wrong ways of the Roman Church, the people began to return to its practices and ceremonies. They failed to keep the Lord's Day holy and began celebrating it like heathens, even playing games after church service. The sinful people spread over England like grasshoppers.

For this reason, Christ, the glowing King of his churches, raised an army of good people to free his people from the priests. Because England was filled with angry and dangerous enemies, Christ created New England as a place for these good people to

A *heathen* is a person who is not religious.

go. When their enemies saw how unimportant and few the good people were, they thought they had won. But at the height of their pride, the Lord Christ brought sudden, unexpected destruction on these enemies.

Christ Jesus decided to show his power more than ever before by reforming the church to make it purer. Therefore, in 1628, he caused the people who served him to call for volunteers with this announcement:

> "Oh yes! Oh yes! Oh yes! All you the people of Christ that are here oppressed, imprisoned, and badly treated, gather yourselves together, your wives and little ones, and answer to your several names so that you can be shipped for His service, in the Western World, and plant the united colonies of New England; where you are to attend the service of the King of Kings."

The settlers of the Massachusetts Bay Colony received their charter in 1628.

*The **King of Kings** refers to Jesus Christ.*

This document shows some Puritan motivations. It also suggests other important Puritan ideas. What does the document tell you about Puritan ideas on reasons for success and failure? How would Puritans probably explain crop failure? Disease and death? What reasons would they probably give for the success and prosperity of a settlement?

c Winthrop and the Puritans believed that everyone in England and Europe was watching their actions. During the trip across the Atlantic, Winthrop said this in a sermon.

c We shall be like a city upon a hill. The eyes of all people are on us. If we deal falsely with our God in this work we are beginning, he will stop helping us. Then all the world will talk about our failure.

In what ways are Winthrop's ideas about success and failure similar to Johnson's?

The Puritan colony was definitely not a failure. Between 1630 and 1640 about 14,000 people migrated to Massachusetts. Not all were Puritans, but for many years Puritans dominated life in New England. For more than 50 years, for example, no Bay Colony resident could vote unless he was a member of the Puritan church—and only about one-fifth of the adult males were church members. (No women were allowed to vote.)

Living in a Puritan Town

For most early Puritan people, the town they lived in was far more important than the larger colony. The town was the center of religious life, the maker of rules and regulations, the source of almost everything needed from birth to death.

The founding of a Puritan town was a careful process. It usually began in England, where a group of people who wished to leave formed an organization. Often this group would send advance agents to America to find land, sometimes paying Indians for the property, sometimes obtaining it from colonial officials.

Use the data on Puritan towns to answer these questions:

1. How did Puritan towns differ from the Spanish towns you studied earlier?
2. What do Puritan towns show you about Puritan motivations?

a Once the group of colonists arrived in Massachusetts, it was necessary to set up the town. Following are some of the decisions made by the founders of what is now Springfield, Massachusetts.

a

> May the 14th, 1636
>
> We whose names are written below, being by God's help working together to make a plantation at Agawam on the Connecticut River, do mutually agree to certain articles and orders to be observed and kept by us and our successors.
>
> We intend by God's grace, as soon as we can with all convenient speed, to obtain some godly and faithful minister. We wish to join in church covenant with this minister to walk in all the ways of Christ.
>
> We intend that our town shall be composed of 40 families, or at most 50, rich and poor.
>
> Every inhabitant shall have a convenient piece of land for a house lot, suitable for each person's position and wealth.
>
> Everyone that has a house lot shall have a part of the cow pasture to the north of End Brook, lying northward from the town. Everyone shall also have a share of the Hasseky Marsh, near to his own lot if possible, and a fair part of all the woodland.
>
> Everyone will have a share of the meadow or planting ground.
>
> All town expenses that shall arise shall be paid by taxes on lands. Everyone will be taxed according to their share of land, acre for acre of house lots, and acre for acre of meadow.

*The first English settlers used the word **plantation** to describe any settlement.*

What here tells you that religion was an important motivating force for Puritans?

*A **church covenant** is an agreement among the members of a church. In it, members promise to keep the rules and beliefs of the church.*

Was cooperation important to Puritans? What kinds of cooperation are described here?

b Sudbury, Massachusetts, was a Puritan town about 20 miles west of the center of old Boston. The town was founded in 1638. It was laid out in much the same way as Springfield and other Puritan towns. Below is a map of the central part of the village, as it was in 1650.

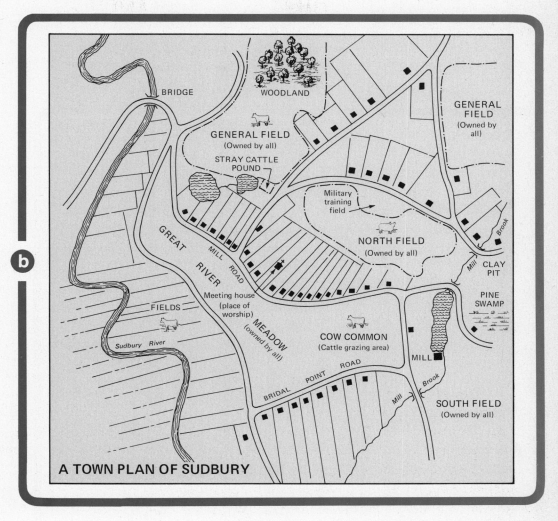

A TOWN PLAN OF SUDBURY

Answer these questions, based on the map and the Springfield data (page 40):

1. What is the main occupation of the residents of Springfield and Sudbury?

2. The land owned by each family was scattered in lots at various locations. What are the advantages and disadvantages of this layout?

3. What features shown on the map would require cooperation among residents?

4. What ideas do you think Puritans had about making a living? About ownership of property? About relationships with neighbors?

○c Most Massachusetts towns conducted business in **town meetings.** At these meetings, adult males were given a chance to speak and vote. Regular town business was handled by **selectmen**—officials elected to serve on a governing committee. Notes from Sudbury town meetings in 1649 and 1650 are below.

As you read, think about the problems the town was dealing with. Who decided how to solve the problems and how were they solved?

December 9, 1649

Edmund Goodenow and William Ward are chosen to find and mark the boundary line between Concord and Sudbury. Hugh Griffyn, John Groute and Edmund Goodenow are chosen to search the Record book to find out where Watertown's boundaries are supposed to be. They are also to see if they can find any way to prevent Watertown from claiming land that should belong to Sudbury. The town will pay them for their labors.

John Blandford has the permission of the town to claim six acres of meadow wherever he can find it. This will repay him for the meadow he gave up because it fell within the cow common.

Edmund Goodenow is requested by the town to arrange for Sergeant Wheeler to teach John Goodenow to beat the drum. Sergeant Wheeler will also feed him. The town will pay the charges.

February 7, 1650

To provide the town with a barrel of powder, 150 pounds of musket balls and 25 musket matches, the selectmen order that a 12 pounds 10 shillings tax be levied. The tax is to be paid in wheat or money at the house of Edmund Goodenow.

February 13, 1650

A public town meeting appoints Mr. Noyes, John Parminter senior, Robert Darnill and John Moore to speak with Mrs. Hunt (a widow) to decide how the town will help her.

Hugh Griffyn and John Moore are to make up a tax list for powder, balls, and matches, the minister's salary, and the town.

September 16, 1650

It is ordered that Walter Hayme, John Moore, Thomas Kinge and John Groute be authorized to repair the bridge. Some townsmen still owe the town several days roadwork. They are to use as much of this labor as they can, and if it is not enough to fix the bridge, they have permission to hire carpenters to do it. They also have permission to levy a tax to pay all the expenses.

Pounds, shillings, and *pence* were forms of English money. In 1650, for example, there were 20 shillings in one pound and 12 pence in one shilling.

● Below are several problems typical of those faced by Puritan towns. If you were attending a Sudbury town meeting, what would your opinion be on these issues?

1. More pasture land for cattle is needed. The town owns land suitable for pasture, but it is now covered by woods. The trees will need to be cleared, the land fenced, and a new road built to the pasture. How will the work be done? How will necessary expenses be paid? Will all residents contribute equally? Should costs be paid only by those who will use the new pasture?

2. The son of one of the town's families has just been married. He wishes to begin farming land of his own. Land near the village center is all distributed, but the town owns land suitable for farming in outlying areas. Should the man build his house away from the rest of the town?

3. John Howe wishes to move away from Sudbury and has found a person who wants to buy his land in Sudbury. This person is a stranger to all the Sudbury residents. Should Howe be allowed to sell his land to a stranger?

Puritan Opinions

By studying what people believe is right and wrong, you can learn a great deal about those people and their motivations. Many of a person's or a society's actions are motivated by ideas of right and wrong. These ideas can vary greatly. In some societies, for example, it is considered wrong to disagree with those in authority. An idea such as this one will affect a society in important ways.

Study the data in this activity. Identify and list actions and ideas Puritans thought were right and wrong.

ⓐ Josiah Cotton, a teacher in Plymouth, Massachusetts, wanted to teach the local Indians about the Puritan religion. In the early 1700s he prepared a *Vocabulary of the Massachusetts Indian Language.* In this *Vocabulary* Cotton translated English sentences into the language of the Natick Indians. Some of these sentences are shown on the following page.

Natick	English
Tohwaj nonkompaog ne anoohquiitcheg pumomashaog, kah matteag usseog.	Why do boys of that age run about and do nothing?
An wunnegik kuttinninumiin kah pish nunnehtuhpeh wussukquohamunat kah ogketamunat.	You had better let me have him, and I will learn him to write and read.
Nanompanissuonk wutchappehk moocheke machuk.	Idleness is the root of much evil.
Noh matteag pish quenauehhikkoo asuh metsuonk wuttattamooonk oglooonk asuh sasamitahwhuttuonk.	He shall want for nothing, neither meat, drink, clothing, or beating.
Matchee anakaussuongash kah matchee nup pooonk ussooehteomoo en matchit ayeuwonkanit.	Evil works and an evil death will lead to a bad place.

Think about the ideas Cotton was translating. What do they tell you about Cotton and his readers?

b In 1675 the Massachusetts General Court (the legislature) made the following statements.

For several years now, the most wise and holy God has warned us of our evil actions, by giving us troubles and problems. In spite of this, we did not change our ways. Finally, God made the Indians rise up in war against us. These Indians have burned several settlements and killed the people who lived there.

God did not help our army when we went to fight the Indians. He did not help us because He was punishing us and showing us our evil, and telling us to return to the Lord our God.

These laws are passed to correct our wrong actions:

1. The court sees that the churches are not keeping control of their members, nor are they giving children proper training. We recommend that the churches correct this wrong.

*From 1675 to 1677 New England colonists and Indians fought a war called **King Philip's War.** Philip was a chief who led the Indians in the war.*

2. People are showing self-pride in various ways. Some men are wearing long hair like women, either their own hair or periwigs. Some women are curling their hair or wearing immodest hair styles.

   The Court declares this is offensive to sober Christians. The County Courts are given the power to take action against such wrongdoers by warnings, fines, or punishment, according to their good judgement.

3. In spite of laws already passed, people are showing evil pride in the clothes they wear. Poorer people are buying expensive clothes. Poor and rich are both wearing vain, new, strange fashions, with uncovered arms, or decorated with ribbons. The County Court is authorized to take action against such sinful people.

4. The people have permitted and encouraged open meetings of Quakers. These people believe and teach things which are untrue and evil. This had been dangerous to religion and to the souls of the Christians, and it has made God angry.

   Every person found at a Quaker's meeting will be arrested by the police. Local officials will issue approval, and the people will be placed in jail at hard work, with bread and water only, for three days, or else they will pay five pounds fine.

5. This Court orders that children and youths must sit together in church, in some place where they can be seen by all. Those who misbehave will be warned by officials for their first offense. For a second offense the parents must pay a fine or order the children to be whipped.

6. The sin of idleness greatly increases, in spite of laws against it. This court orders that town constables shall inspect families, and present a list of names of all idle persons to the town officials, who will punish them as required. If necessary, idle people will be sent to the house of correction.

c Sometime before 1690, a Boston man named Benjamin Harris put together *The New England Primer*. This small book contained ABC's as well as religious and moral lessons. For about 150 years, *The New England Primer* was the most widely used beginning textbook in New England. Items 1, 2, and 3 come from the *Primer*.

❶ The Dutiful Child's Promises,

I will fear God, and honour the king.
I will honour my Father and Mother.
I will obey my superiors.
I will submit to my elders.
I will love my friends.
I will hate no man.
I will forgive my enemies, and pray to God for them.
I will as much as in me lies keep all God's Holy
  Commandments.
I will learn my catechism.
I will keep the Lord's Day holy.
I will reverence God's sanctuary, for our God is a
  consuming fire.

c

❷ From An Alphabet of Lessons for Youth

A Wise Son makes a glad Father, but a Foolish Son
  is the Heaviness of his Mother.

B etter is a little with the fear of the Lord, than great
  treasure with trouble.

C ome unto Christ all ye that labor and are heavy laden,
  and He will give you rest.

F oolishness is bound up in the heart of a Child, but
  the road of Correction shall drive it far from him.

L iars shall have their part in the lake which burns with
  fire and brimstone.

M any are the Afflictions of the Righteous, but the Lord
  delivers them out of them all.

P ray to thy Father which is in secret, and thy Father
  which sees in secret shall reward thee openly.

U pon the wicked, God shall rain an horrible Tempest.

W oe to the wicked, it shall be ill with him, for the
  reward of his hands shall be given him.

❸

A	In *Adam's* Fall We Sinned all.
B	Thy Life to Mend This *Book* Attend.
C	The *Cat* doth play And after flay.
D	A *Dog* will bite A Thief at night.
E	An *Eagles* flight Is out of sight.
F	The Idle *Fool* Is whipt at School.
G	As runs the *Glass* Mans life doth pass.
H	My *Book* and *Heart* Shall never part.
K	Our *K I N G* the good No man of blood.
L	The *Lion* bold The *Lamb* doth hold.
M	The *Moon* gives light In time of night.
N	*Nightingales* sing In Time of Spring.
O	The *Royal Oak* it was the Tree That sav'd His Royal Majestie.
P	*Peter* denies His Lord and cries.

Dutiful means "obedient" or "wanting to do one's duty." A **catechism** is ▲
a handbook of questions and answers that teach religious beliefs. A **sanctuary**
is a holy place. **Laden** means "loaded," and **abominable** means "evil."
The **lake which burns** refers to Hell. The **afflictions of the Righteous** are
the troubles of good people. **Father** and **Creator** refer to God. A **tempest**
is a violent storm, and **woe** means "great sorrow." Here, **ill** means "difficult."

*Did Puritans believe God was gentle or strict? What was God's attitude toward
those who did wrong? What did Puritans think were their duties toward God?*

You have investigated settlers in Spanish towns, in Jamestown, and in Puritan towns. Answer these questions, based on your knowledge of all three:

1. In which kind of town do you think status differences (differences in rank or social importance) were most important? Least important? Give reasons for your answers.

2. In which kind of town were the greatest number of decisions under the control of local people? In which kind of town did the authority and power of the king most affect the local people?

3. Based on your knowledge of their motivations, how would Puritan settlers have reacted to an order from the king redistributing their land? Do you think Spanish settlers would have reacted differently to the same order? If so, in what way? Why?

4. Compare the importance of religion as a motivation among Spanish, Jamestown, and Puritan settlers.

● Based on your list of Puritan opinions, (p. 43), consider the statements below. Puritans would agree with some of the statements, but would disagree with others. Identify the statements with which Puritans would probably agree. Explain why Puritans would not agree with the other statements.

1. "God rewards good people by giving them success."
2. "People who are proud of their personal appearance should be warned that they are doing wrong."
3. "Not everyone has the same opinion about religion. We shouldn't punish people who disagree with us."
4. If you treat children with gentleness and love, they will always do what is right."
5. If you do wrong, God will punish you severely."
6. It is wrong to be lazy. Everyone should work hard."
7. Young people should be given freedom to choose their own way of living."
8. It is man's basic nature to do evil things. People must be

careful at all times, or they will stop doing that which God expects."

9. "How people behave at home is their own business."

How do you think Puritan opinions motivated their actions? Choose one Puritan idea about right or wrong. Describe actions that idea might motivate.

Colonization: An Overview

You have read and thought about what motivated English colonization in Virginia and Massachusetts. What motivations created the other colonies?

The settlers of Virginia and the Massachusetts colonies were the first brave experimenters. After the success of their struggles, others "knew it could be done." They wanted to come to this New World for the same reasons that earlier colonists had come: to make money, to find religious freedom, and to find new lives.

John Cabot had claimed the land in North America for the king of England. At first the king gave rights to settle the land to companies who hoped to make a profit. As you read, the Virginia Company was the first to pay for and set up a colony in the new land. Later, the king gave charters to individuals who wanted to pay for colonies. These people were called **proprietors.** The proprietor was usually an important person who had done favors for the king. As a reward, the proprietor was given the right to sell land in his colony to settlers. The proprietor also had the right to control the colony's government. Colonies such as Maryland and New Jersey were proprietary colonies. That is, they were controled by proprietors.

At first the colonies were governed by the company or the proprietor or sometimes by themselves. (The Massachusetts Bay Colony began as a self-governing colony.) Colonists owed loyalty to the king but had little contact with English government. The English king and government did not pay much attention to the colonies and colonists in the New World.

As the colonies changed and grew, however, England became more interested in them. They began producing more goods that England wanted. And there were more colonists in America who could buy English products. In 1660 England passed several important laws in order to control colonial trade. By the early 1700s, England had a stronger control of colonial governments. The king had taken over the charters of many of the proprietary colonies and of self-governing Massachusetts Bay. To run his colonies he sent royal governors to America.

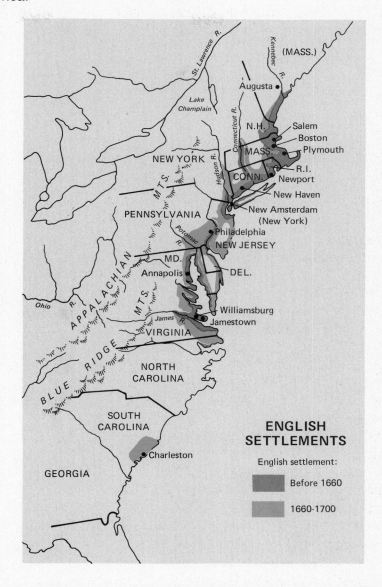

ENGLISH SETTLEMENTS

English settlement:

Before 1660

1660-1700

Why do you think the first settlements were built where they were? Look at the spread of population by 1700. Can you think of some possible reasons why it spread where it did?

The chart and map on pages 49-50 will tell you more about England's empire in North America.

The claims of French explorers had given France territory in the New World by the early 1500s. However, like England, France was slow in its efforts to colonize the land. French explorers sailed up the St. Lawrence River in the 1530s but didn't establish a permanent settlement. Another French expedition set up a post in Florida in 1562, but the Spanish destroyed it. Then, in 1608, Samuel de Champlain founded Quebec, which became the center of French power in North America.

THE COLONIES

COLONY DATE FOUNDED	FOUNDER	REASONS FOUNDED	TYPE OF GOVERNMENT
Maine 1622	Ferdinando Gorges John Mason	Profit for founders from fur trade and fishing	To 1677--proprietary 1677-1820--part of Mass.
New Hampshire 1622	Ferdinando Gorges John Mason	Profit for founders from fur trade and fishing	To 1641--proprietary 1641-1680--part of Mass. 1680--royal
Connecticut 1636	Thomas Hooker	Expand trade Religious and political freedom	Self-governing
Rhode Island 1636	Roger Williams	Religious freedom	Self-governing
Delaware 1638	Swedish settlers	Expand trade	To 1682--proprietary 1682-1704--part of Pa. 1704--self-governing
Maryland 1634	Lord Baltimore	Profit for founder from selling land Religious freedom	To 1691--proprietary 1691-1715--royal 1715--proprietary
New York 1624	Peter Minuet	Expand Dutch trade	To 1664--colony of Dutch East India Co. 1664-1685--proprietary 1685--royal
New Jersey 1664	John Berkeley George Carteret	Profit for founders from selling land Religious and political freedom	To 1702--proprietary 1702--royal
North Carolina 1663	Anthony Cooper John Colleton William Berkeley	Profit for founders Religious freedom	To 1729--proprietary 1729--royal
South Carolina 1663	Anthony Cooper John Colleton William Berkeley	Profit for founders	To 1729--proprietary 1729--royal
Pennsylvania 1682	William Penn	Profit for founder from selling land Religious freedom	Proprietary
Georgia 1730	James Oglethorpe	Profit for founder Haven for debtors Buffer zone against Spanish Florida	To 1752--proprietary 1752--royal

Most of the first Frenchmen who arrived in Canada were not interested in permanent settlement. Many were missionaries who came to convert the Indians to Roman Catholicism. Others were traders who wanted to buy valuable furs from the Indians and fishermen who wanted to fish off Newfoundland and Nova Scotia. Eventually, farmers came to settle the land, but there were always fewer

Compare the colonies to one another. Note the changes in the ways they were governed. What effect do you think this might have had on colonial life.

of these permanent settlers in New France than there were in the English colonies.

After Henry Hudson's explorations, Dutch merchants formed a company, which they called the Dutch West India Company. The merchants wanted to trade furs with the Indians and to settle the land explored by Hudson. They sent colonists to establish settlements along the Hudson River. To encourage settlers, the company promised land along the river to anyone who would bring 50 people to the colony.

The first Dutch settlers came to America in 1623. Soon afterwards, the governor of their colony bought the present-day island of Manhattan from the Indians for about 24 dollars worth of beads and trinkets. Although settlers stayed on the island, which they called New Amsterdam, others moved and established three additional settlements. These four settlements made up the Dutch colony of New Netherlands.

In 1638 Swedes settled in what is now Delaware, not knowing that the Dutch had already claimed the land. More and more Swedish settlers came, forming the colony of New Sweden. After constant conflict with the Swedes, the Dutch took over the colony in 1655.

The English colonies which grew up around New Netherlands were unhappy about the competition from the Dutch ships. England also claimed the Dutch land, based on John Cabot's original explorations. Finally, in 1664, the English sent an expedition against New Amsterdam, which surrendered without a fight. New Amsterdam became an English colony called New York. The English also took over another Dutch settlement, which became New Jersey, and the former New Sweden.

By the late 1600s, the English, the French, and the Spanish had claimed and colonized in what is now the United States. In the next 100 years, however, much of this would change.

BRANCHING OUT

For modern Americans, moving to Alaska would probably be the experience most like moving to an English colony in America 300 years ago. Read magazine articles or books written by people who have moved to Alaska. Then report on various parts of such a move: motivations for going, feelings about leaving, experiences on arrival.

BRANCHING OUT

Investigate one colony besides Massachusetts or Virginia. Prepare a written or oral report, a play, or a story in which you describe the founding of the colony. Also tell about early life in the colony.

Part 3

Colonial Growth and Development

After the first settlements, there was a long period of change and growth. More and more Europeans came to live in the colonies. They brought with them ideas and ways of living from their old worlds. But in this new world their lives and ideas often changed. The European settlers and their descendants in later generations developed a new American society. In doing this, they pushed away the first Americans—Indians. And they used the slave labor of men and women brought from Africa against their will. For the Europeans, however, life was often rewarding although difficult.

The first societies—in Virginia and Massachusetts—changed as the colonies grew. But in many ways later colonial life reflected these first beginnings. As you study Part 3, think about the motivations of the early colonists and the life created by those motivations. The activities that follow will help you answer this question about later colonial life:

How did motivating ideas affect the developing American colonies?

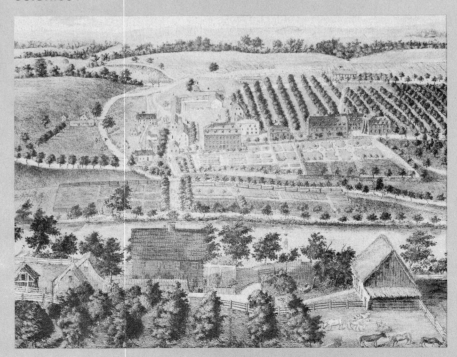

The motivations and the society of the Jamestown colonists were very different from those of the Puritans. So were the soil and climate, the kind of people who colonized, and the policies of colonial officials. And so, the society that developed in colonial Virginia was very different from that of New England. (Here, Virginia is used as an example of southern plantation colonies. South Carolina and Maryland were like Virginia in many ways.)

● The selection that follows is from the autobiography of Devereaux Jarratt, a minister in colonial Virginia.

1. As you read Jarratt's words, think about the society he described. In what way was it similar to the society in early Jamestown?

2. Think about the Puritans' ideas about sharing land and town government. Do you think that kind of sharing took place in the society Jarratt described? Give reasons for your answer.

3. Think about the gap between rich and poor in Puritan society. Do you think the differences between rich and poor in Virginia society were the same? Greater? Less?

Wealthy planters were what Jarratt called "gentle folk." How do you think Jarratt felt when he talked to a planter?

I was born in New Kent, a county in Virginia, about 25 miles below Richmond, on January 6th, 1732.

My father was brought up to the trade of a carpenter, at which he worked until the very day before he died. He was a mild, polite man, and much respected among his neighbors. None of my ancestors, on either side, were either rich or great. My parents always had plenty of plain food and clothes, wholesome and good, suitable to their humble position and the times in which they lived. All of our food was the product of our little farm; our clothes were made by my mother, except our hats and shoes. We only wore our shoes in the winter season.

We made no use of tea or coffee for breakfast, or at any other time. I did not know a single family that used them. Meat, bread and milk were the foods which we ate. I suppose rich people made use of coffee and tea, but I had no way of finding out about the lives of the rich.

We always looked on what were called *gentle folk* as people of a different and higher kind. I was quite shy of them, and kept off at a humble distance. A periwig, in those days, was a symbol that a person was one of the gentle folk. When I saw a man riding the road near our house with a wig on, I would be alarmed and afraid. It would give me such a disagreeable feeling that I would run off and hide like my life was in danger. Such ideas of the difference between gentle and simple folk were held by everyone I knew near my own age.

What did the Massachusetts General Court say about periwigs? Do you think Virginians felt the same way about people wearing wigs?

Farming in Virginia

The tobacco that had saved the Jamestown colony continued to support Virginia. In fact, Virginia's economy soon depended almost entirely on tobacco exports. (The crop was sold to merchants in England and the rest of Europe.) Tobacco was grown best on large farms, called **plantations.**

Most Virginia colonists were not wealthy planters. But the planters were the most powerful and important people in the colony; they affected everything that happened there. For this reason it is important to study their way of life.

As you study this data, think about what mattered to the men who owned plantations. Based on what you discover, make a list of motivating ideas that might have been important to a Virginia planter. Keep your list for use in the next activity.

a The drawing below was an advertisement for Virginia tobacco sold in England.

GEORGE THOMPSON, *TOBACCONIST,*
(from Mr Bury's) at the Black-Prince & Tobacco-Roll,
N.º 60 Bishopsgate Street Without, near Artillery-Lane,
LONDON.

b The selection that follows is part of a letter written by a Virginia "gentleman," William Fitzhugh. Fitzhugh wrote the letter to a friend in England who wanted to set up a plantation in Virginia for his son.

Based on this letter, was size an advantage for a plantation? If this were true, how would this affect people who wanted to set up plantations?

b

August 15, 1690

I will give you the best method for establishing a farm for your son. Place in some merchant's hand in London 150 or 200 pounds—money to buy a good convenient section of Virginia land. Then give about the same amount to someone in the Royal African Company. For that price the company will deliver Negroes here in Virginia for 16 or 18, or at most, 20 pounds per head. Horses, cattle, hogs, and so forth are easily purchased here to begin with.

Sir, a settlement made as I suggest will give your son a handsome, gentle, and sure living. If you were to give, instead, three times the above amounts, it is certain his land will yield him much tobacco, with less risk than with a smaller plantation.

c William Fitzhugh described his own plantation in a letter written in 1686.

What differences can you identify between a Virginia plantation and a New England farm?

c

*A **dovecote** is a building in which pigeons are raised.*

Based on what Fitzhugh chose to describe, what can you tell about what he valued?

The plantation where I now live contains 1,000 acres, at least 700 of it being rich underbrush. The rest is good hearty plantable land, without any waste either by marshes or great swamps. You already know how large, convenient, and pleasant it is. It is well furnished with all necessary houses, grounds, and fencing, together with a choice crew of 29 Negroes, most of them born in this country. Upon the same land is my own house. This house is furnished with all that is needed for a comfortable and gentle living. It is a very good house with rooms in it, four of the best of them hung with tapestry, and nine of them fully furnished with all things necessary and convenient. All of the houses have brick chimneys. There are four good cellars, a dairy, dovecote, stable, barn, henhouse, kitchen, and all other conveniences. There is a large orchard of 2,500 apple trees. There is a garden a hundred foot square and a yard in which are most of the houses I described.

Up the river in this country, I own three more sections of land. One of them contains 21,996 acres, another 500 acres, and one other 1,000 acres, all good land which in a few years will give a good-sized yearly income.

d Like Fitzhugh, many of the Virginia planters had thousands of acres of property. Some owned a hundred or more slaves who worked growing tobacco. William Byrd II was one of these leading planters. In a letter to an English nobleman in 1726, he describes his life.

d Besides the advantage of pure air, we who have plantations have a great supply of all kinds of materials without spending money. I have a large family of my own, and my doors are open to everybody, yet I have no bills to pay. A half-a-crown coin will stay in my pocket for many moons without being spent.

I have my flocks and herds, my slaves, and every sort of skilled trade available from my servants. Because of this I live in a kind of independence from everyone except God.

Although this life is without expense, it is still a lot of trouble. The plantation is like a machine. I must set the springs in motion, and make sure everyone does his share of the work to make the machine operate. But then, this work is an amusement in this silent country.

When Byrd said that he had "no bills to pay," did he mean that everything was free? What do you think Byrd had to buy from another person?

Based on what Byrd chose to describe, what do you think he valued?

e Virginia plantations:
1. A drawing of plantation buildings
2. Inside a Georgia plantation home
3. Westover, the home of William Byrd II

e

In your study of Spanish and Puritan towns, you looked at ways in which people's motivations affected the way they laid out their land and used it. The motivations of colonial Virginia planters also affected their use of land.

1. Review the data you have examined in this activity. What does it tell you about the planters' use of land? What does their use of land tell you about their motivating ideas?
2. Towns, churches, and schools were not very important in colonial Virginia. Why do you think that was true? How would the development of these have been different in Massachusetts?

Life in Williamsburg

Williamsburg, the capital of the Virginia Colony, was little more than a small town. Because the colonial government was there, however, planters often visited the capital.

In the descriptions that follow, identify motivations of upper-class Virginians.

ⓐ The first description was written in the 1750s by an English traveler in Virginia, Andrew Burnaby.

Williamsburg is the capital of Virginia. It consists of about 200 houses, and does not contain more than 1,000 people, whites and Negroes. It is far from being a place of any real importance.

Upon the whole, it is a pleasant place to live. There are ten or twelve gentlemen's families constantly living in it, besides merchants and tradesmen. At the time of the assemblies and general courts, it is crowded with the upper class of the country, the planters. On those occasions there are balls and other amusements. But as soon as the business of the court and assembly is finished, the people return to their plantations and the town is nearly deserted.

The trade of this colony is large and extensive. Tobacco is the main thing traded. Of this they export each year between 50 and 60 thousand hogsheads, each weighing 800 or 1,000 pounds.

*A **hogshead** is a large barrel.*

From what has been said of this colony [Virginia], it will not be difficult to get an idea of what the people are like. The climate and nature of this country make them lazy, easy-going, and good-natured. They are extremely fond of each other's company, and of eating and drinking together. They seldom show any ambition or become tired from hard work.

Their authority over their slaves makes them vain and domineering. They hardly consider Indians and Negroes to be human. If one of these unhappy creatures is hurt or even killed by a planter, it is almost impossible to bring the wrongdoer to justice.

Their public life is like their private life. They are jealous of their liberties, and can hardly stand the idea of being controlled by any superior power. Many of them consider the colonies as independent states, not connected with Great Britain, except by having the same common king. There are but few of them interested in business.

*In 1707 England, Scotland, and Wales united their governments and became **Great Britain.** The word **British** describes people or things from Great Britain.*

By being "interested in business," Burnaby means being interested in making a living as a merchant or tradesman.

Upon the whole, however, to do them justice, they have a spirit of generosity. They are loyal and never refuse any necessary supplies for the support of government when called upon.

How do you think the people Burnaby described would react to increased control by Great Britain?

b These comments on Williamsburg residents were made by a Virginia minister, Hugh Jones.

The people here live in the same neat manner, dress in the same fashions, and act exactly like the upperclass people in London. For the most part they are quite civilized, and wear the best of clothes according to their rank and position. Sometimes their clothes are too good for their circumstances.

Review the list of planters' motivations made in the preceding activity (pages 54-57). Add to the list any additional motivations you have discovered in this activity.

Putting the Pieces Together

● Below is a series of statements which describe motivations and patterns of society. Identify those that describe ideas and actions of upperclass colonial Virginians. (Use the data in the last three activities on Virginia, pages 53–59, in this exercise.)

1. "It is important that people be treated equally."
2. "The best way to make a profit is in business or manufacturing."
3. "A person's way of dress ought to show how important he is."
4. "The better people deserve a good, comfortable life."
5. "Hard work is the path to success."
6. "Good farming can be done best on large undivided sections of land."
7. "Everyone, rich and poor alike, should have an equal say in the government."
8. "It is important to help your neighbors, so they will help you when you are in trouble."

BRANCHING OUT ▶▶

George Washington was born in Virginia in 1732. Read about his youth and make a report to the class.

BRANCHING OUT ▶▶

Find out more about Colonial Williamsburg. Prepare a visual report or display on Williamsburg in the 1700s.

Slavery in the Colonies

In 1619 a Dutch ship brought about 20 Africans to Jamestown. Historians today think these first black Americans may have been brought to North America as servants, not slaves. At that time—and for many years after—many white men and women came to the colonies as **indentured servants.** They signed a contract, called an **indenture,** in which they promised to work for a certain amount of time (usually from four to seven years). At the end of this time the former servant was free to work and live independently. He or she was also given some land. The first black Americans may have been among those indentured servants.

Within 20 years, however, Virginia began to pass laws that limited the freedom of black people. Soon, blacks in all southern colonies were considered slaves. Africans were brought to the colonies as slaves and they were sold as slaves.

In this unit you have examined the motivations of some of the people who came to live in the colonies. It is not possible to do this for the black people who came. They were brought against their will, with no choice and no motivation that led them here. But what about the colonists who bought black people? What were their motivating ideas?

As you study the data and questions in this activity, identify the motivations of colonists in their relationships with slaves.

a In 1664 the General Assembly of Maryland passed this law about black people in the colonies.

a

Be it enacted that all Negroes or other slaves already within this territory, and all Negroes and other slaves that will be brought in after this will serve their masters for life.

All children born of any Negro or other slave shall be slaves as their fathers were, for all their lives.

Some free-born English women, forgetting their free condition and disgracing our nation, have married Negro slaves. In order to prevent these marriages, we order that any free-born woman who marries a slave shall also serve the owner of her husband for all her husband's life. All the children of such marriages will be slaves as their fathers were.

Based on words in this law, what do you think the lawmakers in Maryland thought about black people? What does the law suggest about the status of black people in Maryland before 1664?

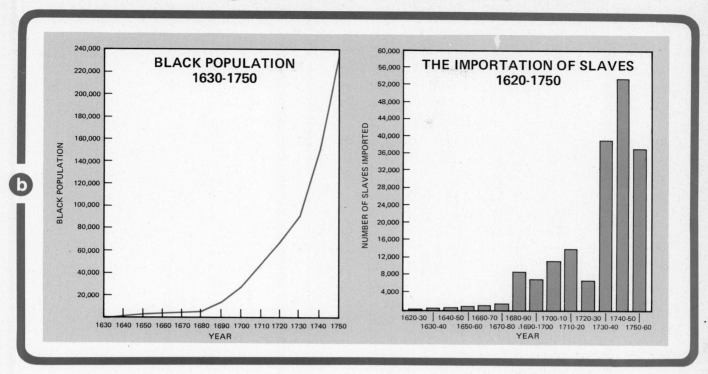

Which states had the largest number of slaves? How could the size of plantations affect the number of slaves used in a state like Virginia?

1. How might the motivating ideas of New Englanders affect the use of slaves in a state like Massachusetts?

2. How might the motivating ideas of Virginians affect the use of slaves in that state?

More People, More Land

From the first 100 settlers at Jamestown, the colonies' population grew to over 1 million in about 150 years. Naturally, as the population grew, the amount of settled land increased. To find empty land, people moved further out, away from the first coastal settlements. By 1750 the American colonies had grown a great deal, both in population and in land area.

Use the material in this activity to help you answer this question: What motivating ideas caused the growth of the colonies?

a The following chart shows the growth in population in the American colonies.

a

**COLONIAL POPULATION
1610-1750**

Year	Estimated Population American Colonies
1610	350
1620	2,300
1630	4,600
1640	26,600
1650	50,000
1660	75,000
1670	111,900
1680	151,500
1690	210,300
1700	250,800
1710	331,700
1720	466,100
1730	629,400
1740	905,500
1750	1,170,000

What effect do you think the growth had on land values? On merchants and trade? On Indians?

b → c The following two selections were written by Europeans. The first is by a Frenchman, Michel-Guillaume Jean de Crevecoeur. Crevecoeur lived in America for many years. He wrote about his experiences in *Letters from an American Farmer.* The selection below is from the *Letters.*

The second selection is from *Travels Into North America,* written by Pehr Kalm. Kalm was a young Swedish scientist who visited North America in the 1750s. In this selection he writes about Philadelphia. The writings of both men were published in Europe and read by many Europeans.

b I do not mean that everyone who comes to America will grow rich in a little time. No, but he may earn an easy, decent living by his hard work. Instead of starving he will have food, instead of being idle he will have employment; and these are riches enough for such men as come over here. The rich stay in Europe; it is only the middling and poor that leave. It is no wonder that the European who has lived here a few years is anxious to remain; Europe is not to be compared with this continent for men of middle stations or laborers.

*By **middle stations,** Crèvecoeur means the middle class.*

Provisions *are materials and supplies, such as food, clothes, wood, or tools.*

Based on what Kalm and Crèvecoeur wrote, what do you think were motivating ideas of Europeans who came to live in the colonies?

c Here is plenty of provisions, and their prices are very reasonable. There are no examples of unusual shortages.

Everyone who acknowledges God to be the creator, preserver, and ruler of all things, and does not teach or do anything against the state or against the common peace, is at liberty to settle, stay, and carry on his trade here, no matter what his religion may be. And he is so well protected by the laws and enjoys such liberties, that a citizen of Philadelphia may be said to live in his house like a king.

It is easy to understand how this city should rise so suddenly from nothing into such grandness and perfection. It has not been necessary to force people to come and settle here. On the contrary, foreigners of different languages have left their country, houses, property, and relations, and traveled over wide and stormy seas in order to come here.

d → e As the population grew, cities grew. From the first small settlements at Boston, New Amsterdam (New York), and Philadelphia, large, busy cities developed. Below, and on page 64 a chart and pictures show you something about the growth of American cities.

d

POPULATION OF COLONIAL CITIES 1630-1775

DATE	NEW YORK	BOSTON	NEWPORT	CHARLESTON	PHILADELPHIA
1630	300	–	–	–	–
1640	400	1,200	96	–	–
1650	1,000	2,000	300	–	–
1660	2,400	3,000	700	–	–
1680	3,200	4,500	2,500	700	–
1690	3,900	7,000	2,600	1,100	4,000
1700	5,000	6,700	2,600	2,000	5,000
1710	5,700	9,000	2,800	3,000	6,500
1720	7,000	12,000	3,800	3,500	10,000
1730	8,622	13,000	4,640	4,500	11,500
1743	11,000	16,382	6,200	6,800	13,000
1760	18,000	15,631	7,500	8,000	23,750
1775	25,000	16,000	11,000	12,000	40,000

▲

Find Boston, Philadelphia, New York, Charleston, and Newport on a map. Why might large cities develop in these locations? How do you think trade and immigration affected the growth of these cities?

Do you think the motivating ideas of people who live in cities are different from those of people who live in the country? Explain.

◀ **e** The growth of cities:
  1 Philadelphia, 1735
  2 Reconstruction of an early Massachusetts Bay settlement
  3 New Amsterdam, 1651
  4 Boston, 1731
  5 New York, 1719

Although cities were growing, most Americans still lived in rural areas. As late as 1775, for example, about 95 percent of the colonists lived in the country, usually on farms or in small villages.

f On page 49 you studied a map of the first stage of movement away from the coastal settlements. This expansion continued, as the map below shows.

How do you think expansion was affected by the growth in population? Describe what might have been the motivating ideas of a settler moving west in the 1700s.

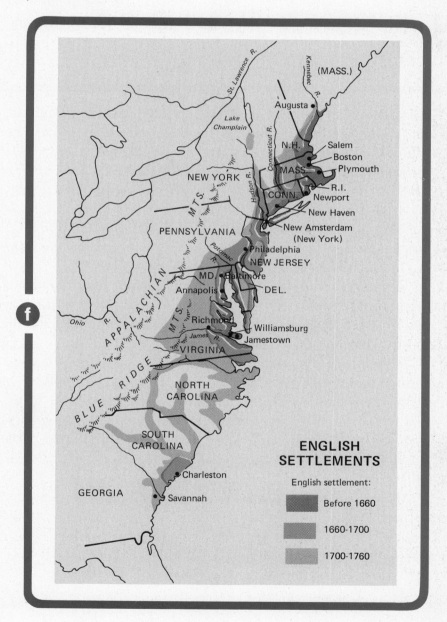

ENGLISH SETTLEMENTS

English settlement:

Before 1660

1660-1700

1700-1760

Changes in New England

By 1750 there had been many changes in New England. However, some of the basic ideas of the New England people were just about the same as the ideas of their Puritan ancestors. Some of the ways of acting might have changed. However, even these changes were related to long-held motivating ideas.

Based on your knowledge of the colonies' early Puritan society, use the following data to identify changes that had taken place in New England.

a The English traveler Andrew Burnaby describes Boston and Massachusetts in the mid-1700s.

a

Boston, the metropolis of Massachusetts Bay in New England, is one of the largest and busiest towns in North America. The length of it is nearly two miles, and the width half a mile. It is supposed to contain 3,000 houses and 18–20,000 people. At the entrance of the harbor stands a very good lighthouse. On an island, about a league from the town, there is a fairly large fort, with nearly 150 cannon. There are several good batteries about town.

The whole town is a great deal like some of our best country towns in England.

The chief public buildings are three churches; 13 or 14 Puritan meetinghouses; the governor's palace; the courthouse, or exchange; Faneuil's Hall; a linen-manufacturing-house; a workhouse; a public granary; a very fine wharf, at least a half a mile long.

The people in this province carry on quite a large trade. Among the things produced here are salted fish, and boats and ships. Of the latter they build each year a great number, and send them, loaded with fish, to England to sell. Many tons of shipping each year are sent out from Boston, Salem, Marblehead, and other ports in this area. Other than ships and salt fish, their manufactures are not large.

Arts and sciences have made greater progress here than any other part of America. Harvard College was founded more than a hundred years ago and has been very successful. The arts are definitely more advanced here than either in Pennsylvania or New York.

*A **metropolis** is a city— usually a large city—that is very important to an area.*

*A **league** is a distance of about three miles. A **battery** is a group of mounted cannon.*

__Faneuil's Hall__ was a building used as a public market and meetinghouse.

Based on Burnaby's description, what kinds of jobs do you think there were in Boston?

b Another book, by an unknown author, described New England to the English people.

b Poor, ragged beggars are hardly ever seen. All the people appear to be well fed, clothed, and housed. Nowhere are people more independent and free. There is no great difference in the ranks and classes of the people. This is unlike what we see in Britain, or other countries.

They also have the advantage of living in a country where their property is continually increasing in value. Trade, navigation, fisheries, increasing population, and other causes have helped raise the value of land.

c This map of Boston was drawn in 1743.

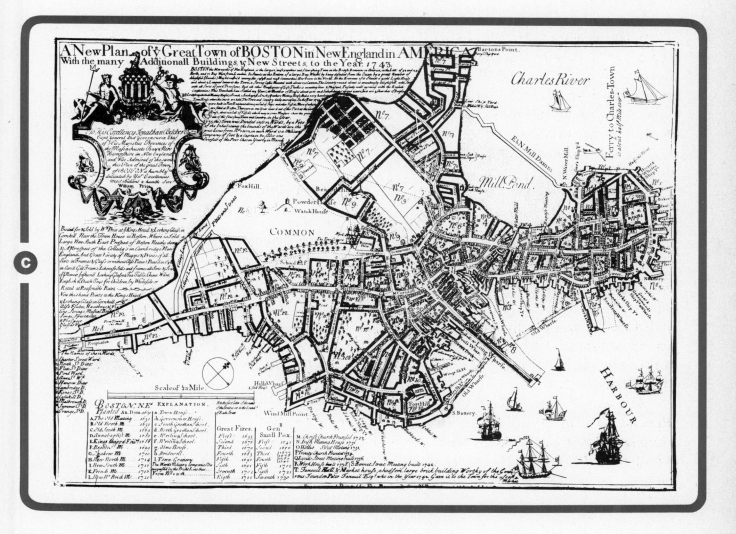

d The information on the charts below comes from reports made to the London Board of Trade in 1740 and 1752.

Based on these two charts, which of the colonies were the most active in trade? ▼

d

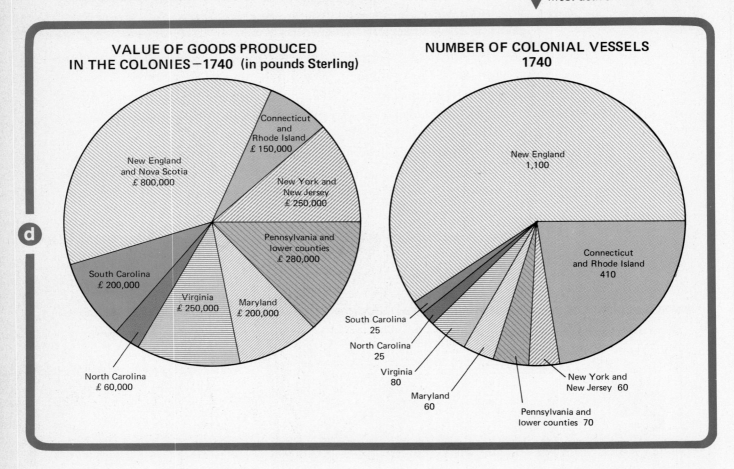

VALUE OF GOODS PRODUCED IN THE COLONIES—1740 (in pounds Sterling)

Connecticut and Rhode Island £ 150,000

New England and Nova Scotia £ 800,000

New York and New Jersey £ 250,000

Pennsylvania and lower counties £ 280,000

South Carolina £ 200,000

Virginia £ 250,000

Maryland £ 200,000

North Carolina £ 60,000

NUMBER OF COLONIAL VESSELS 1740

New England 1,100

Connecticut and Rhode Island 410

South Carolina 25

North Carolina 25

Virginia 80

Maryland 60

New York and New Jersey 60

Pennsylvania and lower counties 70

e → f By 1750 "business" and trade had become a very important part of New England life. Even though most New Englanders did not live in Boston or Newport, the busy success of these cities affected their lives—and their incomes.

As business grew in importance, what had happened to religion? The following selections were reactions to what was happening. The statement was made by John Higginson, the son of one of Massachusetts' early settlers. The drawing was part of a book called *The Progress of Sin,* published in 1744.

Do you think John Higginson was worried about the effect of trade on religion? Why?

e New England was "originally a plantation of religion, not a plantation of trades. Let merchants and such as are increasing cent per cent remember this."

*The words **cent per cent** mean "penny by penny."*

Sion means "city of God."
Beelzebub and **Lucifer** are names for the devil.

The Puritans thought their colony was a colony of God. How does this drawing show that some New Englanders were worried about what was happening to the colony?

By 1700 a man no longer had to be a member of the Puritan Church in order to vote. How do you think this fact might affect New England life?

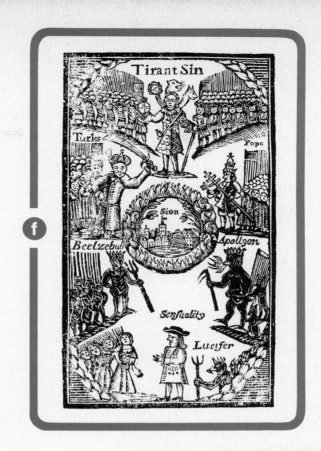

Putting the Pieces Together

Use the data you have studied in *Changes in New England* and in Part 2 to help you answer these questions:

1. What words might best describe the New England coastal economy around 1750?

2. Below is a list of categories of ideas. In each category, the Puritans shared special motivating ideas. For example, Puritans believed that "God is angry with those who do wrong, and will punish them." Recall the Puritan ideas that fit each category.

   God

   Success and failure

   Work

   Education

   Right and wrong

   Government and decision-making

   Which of these ideas and beliefs would have helped motivate New England people toward successful business and trade? Give reasons for your answers.

3. How do you think the first Puritan settlers would have reacted to the changes in their colony?

Conflict for North America

As colonists moved westward, conflict between the British and the French increased. In Europe, the two nations had been rivals for power for many years. In America, there were many areas in which they competed. Both claimed the valley of the Ohio River where there were valuable furs. Both claimed Nova Scotia where there was an important fishing industry. Also, there was religious conflict between the Catholic French and the Protestant English.

Three wars were fought in North America between 1689 and 1748. English colonists called the wars by the name of the English king or queen in power: King William's War (1689–1697), Queen Anne's War (1702–1713), and King George's War (1745–1748). In these wars, the Indians played an important part. Most of them fought with and helped the French. However, one important tribe, the Iroquois, sided with the British.

A fourth and most important of these wars has been called the French and Indian War. For nine years—from 1754–1763—British, French, Indians, and colonists fought in North America. In the end, the British defeated the French and wiped out most of France's North American empire. (Compare the two maps below.) The victories in North America, combined with victories in Europe, made Britain the most powerful nation in Europe.

Britain also became the strongest power in North America. The wars had placed more land, more people, and more power in the control of Great Britain. However, the steps the British would take to run this empire would become part of another conflict with the increasingly independent colonists.

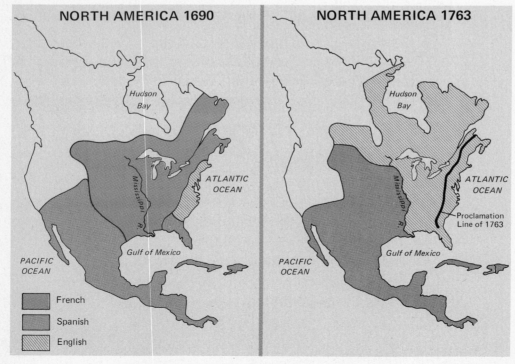

NORTH AMERICA 1690

NORTH AMERICA 1763

Hudson Bay

ATLANTIC OCEAN

Mississippi R.

PACIFIC OCEAN

Gulf of Mexico

Proclamation Line of 1763

French

Spanish

English

Application

In this unit, you've identified motivating ideas of several groups in America's early history. However, if drawing relationships between ideas and action helped you to understand only the past, you wouldn't be gaining as much as you could from your study. Understanding the relationship between ideas and actions is of greater value when you can use it to deal with events that directly affect you and others today.

In this final section, you'll apply to present-day American society what you've learned about motivating ideas.

ⓐ→ⓑ Several widely shared ideas are listed below. Not all Americans agree with every idea. However, based on the actions of Americans, these ideas are important to many people in our society. (Some people who say they disagree show by their actions that in fact they do share these motivations.)

On pages 72-73 are scenes and statements from daily American life. Match each with the motivating idea on the list below. Then give at least one other example of an action which results from each idea.

Motivating Ideas Important to Americans

1. "Nobody should be too different from the rest of us."
2. "It's good to 'move up' and 'get ahead'."
3. "It's good to own lots of things."
4. "Everybody should work for a living."
5. "Competing is good. Winning is even better."
6. "Nature should be used for our purposes."
7. "It's good to be your own boss."
8. "It's good to be young and attractive."
9. "Change is good."
10. "Everybody should have an equal chance."
11. "America is the best."

LOCAL CORPORATION PROMOTES

The Board of Directors of Mid-Continent Container Corporation yesterday appointed Lucas Donnelly president of the organization. Donnnelly, 48, began his career with Mid-Continent thirty years ago as a stockboy.

From a guide for people about to become U.S. citizens:

This Oath of Citizenship you take is a solemn statement that you call upon God to witness, that you absolutely give up of your own free will your citizenship in any other country and your allegiance to any foreign ruler whose subject you have been. You promise on your honor that you will support and defend the Constitution and laws of the United States against all enemies. You do this of your own free will, keeping back nothing in your mind.

You are not an Italian-American.

You are not a Spanish-American.

You are not a German-American, nor any other kind of hyphenated American. YOU ARE AN AMERICAN.

There is no prouder title than "Citizen of the United States of America." It is now yours. YOU ARE AN AMERICAN.

STATE SENATOR SAYS "GET CHISELERS OFF WELFARE"

A Law:

"All persons residing in this state between the ages of six and sixteen shall be required to attend school."

Get Rid of Gray Hair Some of it or all of it

1st Day   6th Day   12th Day   18th Day

Time-lapse photographs show how gradual action of Grecian Formula 16 lets you control just how much gray you slowly get rid of - some of it or all of it.

What other motivating ideas do you think are important to American society?

BIBLIOGRAPHY

Discoverers of the New World. N.Y.: American Heritage, 1960. The editors of *American Heritage* magazine have included over 150 illustrations to help make clear the motives and the achievements of the explorers of the New World.

Thomas Nelson, Inc. *Colonial Histories* series includes Gill, Harold B. Jr. and Ann Finlayson, *Colonial Virginia*, 1973, and Wood, James Playsted, *Colonial Massachusetts*, 1969. Each book contains old prints, maps, documents, photographs, a chronology of events, and a guide to historic sites.

Russell, Francis. *The French and Indian Wars*. N.Y.: American Heritage, 1962. Contemporary paintings, photographs of weapons, and maps of the battlefields are used to describe the wilderness warfare used by both sides in this war.

Clapp, Patricia. *Constance: A Story of Early Plymouth*. N.Y.: Lothrop, Lee & Shepard, 1968. Fiction. Constance Hopkins records her thoughts and feelings about life in Plymouth Plantation. Her journal begins with her arrival on the Mayflower at age 14 and ends with her marriage six years later.

UNIT **2**

Revolution and New Government

Value Conflict

How do value differences cause conflict?

Introduction

"We'll do it *my* way!"

"Are you kidding? No!"

"Oh yeah?"

"Yeah!"

"Just try to stop me, and see what happens!"

Disagreements between human beings never seem to stop. Friends disagree about what to do on Saturday. Children argue with parents about clothes. Husbands and wives differ about how they want to punish a child. Members of a club can't agree about how to spend the money in the club treasury. Disagreements like these are a part of everyday life. Other than causing hurt feelings or tension, they usually aren't problems.

There are, of course, more serious disagreements—differences of opinion between whole groups of people over questions thought to be of great importance. These sometimes lead to physical violence, hate campaigns, bitter elections, murder, and war. Your life is affected in a great many ways by these serious disagreements and the conflict that sometimes follows them.

Serious conflicts are often disagreements that involve **values.** In this unit you will define and identify values and examine the part values play in conflict.

Values are a special kind of motivating idea. They are basic ideas or beliefs that are important in a person's life. This activity will show you one way of identifying values.

a Each photograph below shows a different situation.

Decide what will happen next in each situation, and why. For each situation, answer these questions.

1. Who will react? In what way?
2. How will the person who reacts feel? Why?

77

1. Based on these photographs, write a statement that might be made by a person who would react with aroused feelings (such as anger) in each of the situations. Include in your statement a reason for the person's aroused feelings.
2. Change each of the reasons into statements which begin, "It is important to me to _____," or "I like _____."

Each of the statements you've written expresses a value. For example, "I like to be my own boss" is a value statement. So is "It is important to me to have friends." As you've just seen, looking at what makes people angry can tell you a lot about their values. If an important value is threatened, a person's feelings are aroused.

Most disagreements and conflicts grow out of value differences. If, for example, one person values peace and quiet, and another values having a noisy good time, then conflict may begin if they are both riding in the same auto.

b In the list below are situations that might be caused by value differences.

b
1. Teen-agers disagree with their parents about what to do with money they receive.
2. Friends disagree about how to act towards people in authority.
3. Club members disagree about what club activities to plan.

Choose one of these disagreements, or a similar one which you know about. Then,

1. Describe the conversation or argument that might take place.
2. Identify the values held by each of the people involved in the disagreement.

BRANCHING OUT

Conduct a survey among your friends to find out the main reasons why they become angry. Have them complete the statement, "I am angry when. . . ." Obtain several answers from each person you survey. Based on your survey, what are some of the values shared by your friends?

When members of a group have similar values there is little disagreement about what they want. However, value conflicts may grow out of differing opinions about how to get what they want. For example, everyone agrees that crime is bad, but disagreements can develop over how to prevent crime or deal with criminals. Even when people share the same values, they may disagree about strategies, or ways to accomplish a goal.

a The situation described next is one which might create strategy conflict.

Situation 1:

a The principal has decided that to save money, all the school janitorial work will be performed by students. Every student must stay one hour after school every day to clean the school.

Probably, many students would consider this unfair. They would share the value, "It is important that students' free time not be taken away by school authorities." Because this shared value is threatened, students may wish to protest.

b Listed below are some protest actions that might occur in your school. The strategies are not listed in any special order.

Strategies:

1. Taking over school auditorium for protest rally
2. Picketing in front of school
3. Wearing arm bands
4. Making a speech in classroom without permission
5. Making a speech in hallway during lunch period
6. Handing out leaflets in school hallway
7. Fighting in school with others who disagree
8. Attending evening protest meeting, off school grounds
9. Taking over school P.A. system for announcement
10. Stating personal opinion during class discussion
11. Handing out leaflets in front of school
12. Holding protest meeting in front of school during classes
13. Passing out leaflets in class without teacher's permission

Using this list of strategies,

1. Copy each item on a slip of paper. Then arrange the slips of paper in the following order. Those actions which you think would cause the least controversy should come first. Those actions which would probably cause the most controversy should be placed at the end.

2. Decide where you personally would draw the line between actions that would do more harm than good, and those that would do more good than harm.

3. Wherever you drew your line, it's probable you differ with others who feel you've gone too far or not far enough. Could these strategy differences cause conflict? If so, what kind?

C Here is another situation which could produce some strategy conflict.

C

Situation 2:

Suppose the school board is concerned about growing discipline problems in your school. They have told the principal to correct the problem or be fired. Because of this, the principal has made several new rules.

1. No student will be allowed to talk, except to answer questions by adults. This rule will apply everywhere on school property, at all times.

2. Students will not be allowed to gather in the halls or on school grounds.

3. During class changes, students must walk in single file at the right side of hallways and stairs.

4. There will be no club meetings. All school sports events will be cancelled.

Now answer these questions.

1. If Situation 2 were announced, would you "draw the line" at a different place on the list of protest strategies? Why or why not?

2. What is the relationship between the level of aroused feelings and the kind of strategy people find acceptable?

BRANCHING OUT ►►

Think of examples in which a person or a group's feelings have been aroused by a threat to their values. The examples may come from your own experiences, those of your friends or family, or from newspapers, movies, books, television. Make a poster that describes the value conflict.

STOP & SUMMARIZE ◄

1. Below are three situations in which people are expressing aroused feelings. What value is threatened in each situation?

    a. Parents are complaining about a daughter's messy room.
    b. Young people are protesting adult control of teen center music.
    c. One group of students is complaining about their treatment by other students.

2. Below are statements of values. For each value, describe a situation that would arouse the feelings of a person who holds that value.

    a. It is important that young people show respect for those who are in authority.

    b. It is important that women and girls be treated the same way as men and boys.

    c. It is important that people be allowed to speak or write about their ideas and opinions.

3. Write a statement or draw a diagram that shows how threatened values, aroused feelings, and conflict are related.

Perspective

To investigate value conflict, we could choose almost any period of American history. There have always been many issues about which Americans were willing to take sides and disagree.

In the 1630s, for example, value differences led to conflict between the Massachusetts Puritan leaders and a minister named Roger Williams. Williams left Massachusetts and founded the colony of Rhode Island. In the 1800s, value differences led to a violent civil war within the United States. Today people disagree about welfare, taxes, busing, gun control, and dozens of other issues.

Although every period of American history has had value conflicts, the disagreements that arose just before, during, and after the American Revolution seem particularly important. Our nation's independence and form of government were a result of those value conflicts. In this section you will examine the value conflicts of this period and the ways in which they were solved.

Part 1   Sources of Conflict

What value differences led to conflict between Great Britain and the colonies?

Part 2   The Growth of Conflict

How did British and colonial strategies and goals change as value conflict increased?

Part 3   Establishing Government

What value conflicts existed among the founders of our government?

How were these value conflicts resolved in the Constitution of the United States?

Part 1

Sources of Conflict

Two people in a business partnership may have different goals. The money that one partner wants to take out as profit is the same money the other wants to put back into the business to improve it.

A good many value conflicts begin for this same reason. The people involved have different goals and different motivating ideas. Events or conditions that please one person or group may be viewed as harmful by another.

In some ways, this was the situation in the American colonies in the 1700s. The policies that seemed best for English people living in Great Britain were often very unpopular with English people living in America. Disagreements between the English at home and the colonials in America frequently grew out of these differences.

As you study Part 1 of this unit, answer this question:

What value differences led to conflict between Great Britain and the colonies?

What Is the Purpose of a Colony?

In Unit 1 you investigated some of the motivations of the English colonists who came to America. Some came to avoid religious persecution. Some wished to obtain personal wealth. Others wanted to set up new and better societies. Because of their motivations, these people had clear ideas about the purposes of the colonies they were creating.

As the colonies grew, however, the ideas of the British and the colonials about colonial responsibility toward Great Britain developed in different directions. Their ideas about the purpose of a colony were not always the same.

In this activity you'll examine British ideas about the purpose of a colony. Since the British believed they had the right to govern the colonies, their attitude toward the colonies had a powerful effect on colonial life. You'll also look at one colonial response to these ideas.

As you study the material in this activity, identify the values expressed in the British attitudes.

a In 1729 Joshua Gee, an Englishman, expressed this opinion on what the relationship between the colonies and Britain should be.

a
> It seems obvious that the colonies should supply materials to Great Britain. British manufacturing will be easier if we do what other countries have done. Other countries use some people in the colonies to raise supplies and materials, and to trade with the natives. Manufactured goods from Europe are sent to the colonies to be sold. These countries are very careful to prevent any manufacturing in the colonies that might interfere with manufacturing at home. We have seen how Spain, Portugal, France, and other countries have become rich by following this policy.

The policy Gee is suggesting is called **mercantilism.** Do you believe this policy is fair? Why?

b During the later colonial period, the amount of trade between Britain and its American colonies increased greatly. At the top of page 85 is a list of the major exports that Britain and the colonies exchanged by trade.

Based on this data, make a map showing colonial trade.

*By the early 1700s the British colonies in America were well established. The people who lived in them were no longer **colonists**—people who set up a colony. So, the word **colonials** is often used to refer to the people who lived in the colonies in the 1700s.*

***Exports** are goods sent out of a country. **Imports** are goods brought into a country.*

84

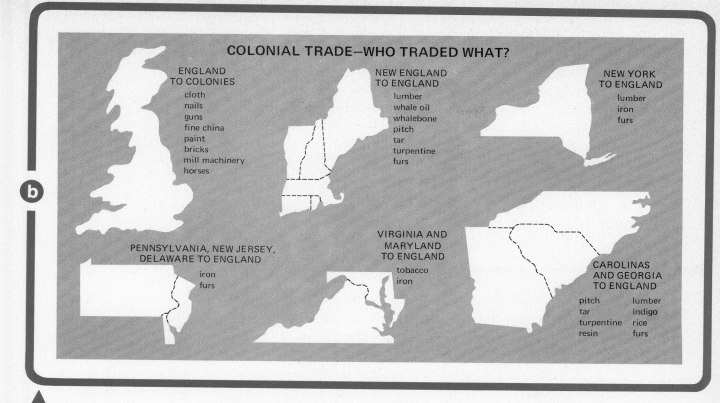

COLONIAL TRADE—WHO TRADED WHAT?

ENGLAND TO COLONIES
cloth
nails
guns
fine china
paint
bricks
mill machinery
horses

NEW ENGLAND TO ENGLAND
lumber
whale oil
whalebone
pitch
tar
turpentine
furs

NEW YORK TO ENGLAND
lumber
iron
furs

PENNSYLVANIA, NEW JERSEY, DELAWARE TO ENGLAND
iron
furs

VIRGINIA AND MARYLAND TO ENGLAND
tobacco
iron

CAROLINAS AND GEORGIA TO ENGLAND
pitch   lumber
tar   indigo
turpentine   rice
resin   furs

In the opinion of Joshua Gee, what is the purpose of a colony? According to this trade information, were the colonies serving the purpose?

c The policy of mercantilism was enforced by laws passed by Parliament. Here are some of these rules.

An Act of Parliament

June 1, 1732

The art and skill of hatmaking in Great Britain is great, and the number of hats sold in America has been enormous. In recent years, however, Americans have started manufacturing hats. They use many low-paid apprentices, their hat production is increasing all the time, and they have started to sell hats to foreign countries that once bought all their hats from Great Britain.

For these reasons, therefore, by the authority of His Majesty and of Parliament, beginning on September 29th, 1732, no hats or felts, dyed or undyed, finished or unfinished, shall be put on board ship for export in any American colony, for any reason, by anyone. Also, none shall be loaded on a horse, cart, or carriage, or anything else for the purpose of being taken from one colony to another or to anyplace else . . . .

An Act of Parliament

April 12, 1750

Pig iron from America is needed by British manufacturers, and a great deal of money now goes out of Great Britain to buy

What value conflict is suggested by the wording of the Hat Act?

Pig iron *is a crude form of iron used in manufacturing.*

pig iron from foreign countries. Because of this, after June 24th, 1750, by the authority of His Majesty and of Parliament, all taxes and duties on pig iron coming into this country from America will stop.

After June 24th, 1750, no factory will be built or continue to operate in America which can roll, slit, or forge pig iron, turn it into steel, or manufacture any product from it. Anyone building or operating any such factory will be fined 200 pounds.

Any Royal Official who knows about the operation of any factory for making iron products in America and does not close it down within 30 days, will be fined 500 pounds and removed from office.

Other trade acts of Parliament included the following rules.

1. The American colonies were not allowed to trade directly with European countries. All trade goods going between the colonies and Europe first had to be shipped to England, taken off ships, and checked. At that point taxes had to be paid on most goods.
2. Manufactured goods of the type made in Great Britain (cloth, nails, etc.) could be imported into the colonies from British manufacturers only, not from manufacturers in other countries.
3. Only British ships (including those of the colonies) could be used for colonial trade.
4. All European goods bound for the colonies had to be brought to England before being shipped to the colonies. In England they were reloaded onto British ships.

d How did American colonists react to British mercantilism? One frequent reaction is suggested by part of a letter written by William Bollan, a British official stationed in Massachusetts. Bollan wrote the letter to the British Board of Trade.

Based on this data, does Parliament agree with Joshua Gee about the purpose of a colony? What value is Parliament expressing in these acts? Why do you think the British passed each of the acts? Why might they be resented by colonists in America?

How would these laws affect an English nail manufacturer? An English hatmaker? How would they affect a colonial carpenter? A colonial hatmaker? How would they affect English dockworkers?

d Lately there has been a great deal of illegal foreign trade carried on here in Massachusetts. Large amounts of European goods are being imported directly into the colony. Some of these goods are not supposed to be imported at all, others are supposed to be shipped only from England.

There are many persons involved in this smuggling. Some of them are the richest people in this country because of the fortunes they have made in this illegal trade. They have convinced themselves that their trade should not be controlled by the laws

What rules were the colonials breaking?

Do you think that Bollan has aroused feelings? If so, what value of his is being threatened?

Look at the last two sentences in the Bollan selection. What do you think Bollan thought about the importance of trade in England's control of the colonies?

of Great Britain. They have succeeded in convincing a majority of people here that they are right. If this situation is not corrected soon, the British trade with these colonies will end. The colonies' dependence on their mother country will be lost.

Based on Bollan's letter, do you think colonists agreed with the British ideas about the purpose of a colony?

BRANCHING OUT

Assume that you are a colonial merchant and write a letter to a friend or relative in England. Describe your feelings about British trade laws and the ways that you obey or disobey them. Explain your actions.

Changing Attitudes

In Unit 1 you read that around 1700 the charters of many colonies were changed so that the king and Parliament took more direct control of colonial government. Later, there were other changes. What were the reasons for these changes? How did the colonials react?

As you study this data, list the changes in **attitude** (a way of thinking or feeling) you believe were taking place. Think about the values shown by each attitude you identify.

a The graph on page 88 shows the value of goods traded between England and the American colonies from 1695 to 1775.

Answer these questions based on the graph.
1. After 1745 the colonies imported (brought in) more from England than they exported (sent) to England. How might English merchants and manufacturers feel about this condition? Do you think the colonists would feel the same way about it?
2. How might changes in trade affect the American colonies' importance to England? How might this affect England's attitude toward controlling the colonies?

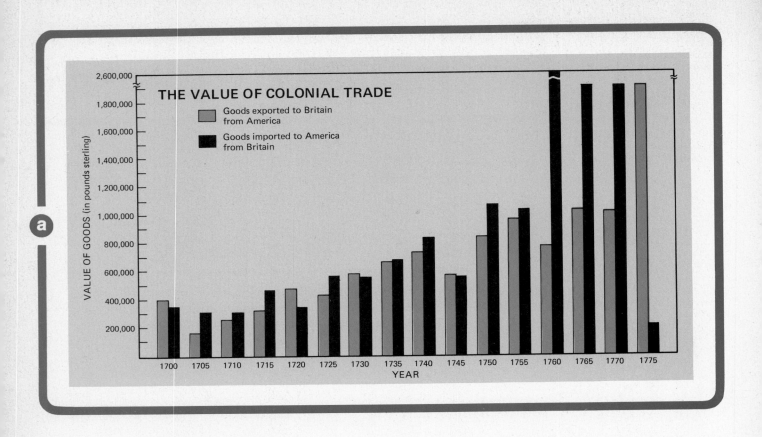

THE VALUE OF COLONIAL TRADE

Goods exported to Britain from America

Goods imported to America from Britain

VALUE OF GOODS (in pounds sterling)

YEAR

As you read in Unit 1, the British fought the French and their Indian allies to defend their empire in North America. These wars lasted, off and on, from 1689 to 1763—almost 75 years. Gaining a larger empire in America had cost Britain money. The national debt in 1675, before the war, was 72 million pounds. After the war, in 1764, the debt was 130 million pounds. About half this increase was caused by the war in the American colonies. To help pay this debt, landowners in England were being taxed about one-third of their income.

After winning the war Britain had a much larger territory than it had controlled before. (Look at the map on page 70.) Governing this land required some new decisions.

Although the French had left their old territory, their Indian allies had not. Many of these Indians were still hostile toward the British and the colonials. To prevent further conflicts, Britain passed a **proclamation,** or law, in 1763. This law said that no colonials could settle land west of a certain point in the Appalachian Mountains. Many colonies, however, had long-standing claims on land in this western area. And British colonials had already moved into areas west of the proclamation line.

b The map on the facing page shows the proclamation line and the colonial land claims.

How do you think the cost of the war in America might affect Britain's attitude toward the colonies?

By fighting with the British against the French, colonials had helped Britain gain the new western land. How do you think this fact would make them feel about the Proclamation of 1763?

Do you think that, before the proclamation, the colonies thought Britain would forbid them to settle the western land they had claimed? How would this affect their attitude after the proclamation?

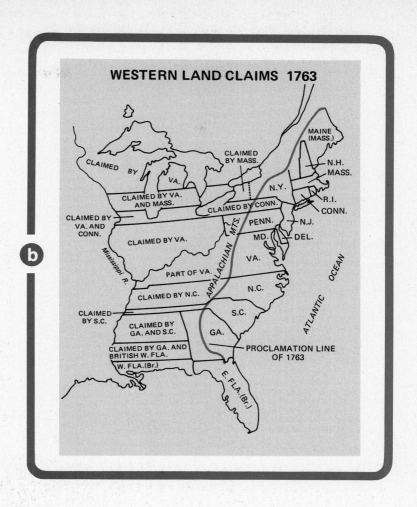

WESTERN LAND CLAIMS 1763

b

The Stamp Act

In 1765 Parliament passed a new law—the Stamp Act—to raise money from the colonies. The trade laws passed earlier had regulated colonial trade with England and other countries. This new law was the first direct tax Britain had placed on the colonies. It required colonists to buy a special stamp to put on certain official documents.

a You'll find the following materials on page 90.
A chart showing the items taxed by the Stamp Act
Pictures of actual stamps
A chart showing how long a colonist worked to earn a certain amount of money and what that money could buy

Use the information to decide how much hardship was caused by the stamp tax.

THE STAMP ACT

An Act of Parliament:

Passed March 22, 1765
Effective November 1, 1765

The purpose of this act is to establish a stamp tax in the American colonies to help pay the costs of defending and protecting them.

The tax will be paid on every piece of paper, parchment, or sheepskin used for the following purposes.

	Stamp Tax
Statements and documents used in court	Three pence
Gift transfer records	Two pounds
Entry into college or university, and diplomas	Two pounds
Ship's bills of lading and official clearances for shipping	Four pence
Certificates of appointment for officials	Ten shillings
Licenses for selling liquor	Twenty shillings
Wills	Five shillings
Bonds for future payment of money	Six pence
Leases, bills of sale, contracts, agreements	Two shillings six pence
Deeds, mortgages, notarized papers, etc.	Two shillings three pence
Deck of cards	One shilling
Pair of dice	Ten shillings
Pamphlets half sheet or smaller (incl. newspapers)	One half penny
Pamphlets larger than one-half sheet	One penny per sheet
Almanacs and calendars	Two pence

All money received by this act shall be paid into His Majesty's treasury and will be used to defend the colonies.

THE VALUE OF MONEY IN COLONIAL TIMES

  1/2 hour of work = PENNY = 1/2 lb. beef

1/2 day of work = SHILLING = 2 lbs. butter

500 days of work =   50 POUNDS =  2 cows

 (12 pence = 1 shilling)   (20 shillings = 1 pound)

a

In your opinion, is this tax a severe one? Give reasons for your opinion.

Would the stamp tax have a greater effect on farmers or merchants? How would it affect lawyers?

b Reasons for the Stamp Act were explained in a pamphlet written by British Treasury official Thomas Whatley.

As you study Whatley's words, decide whether or not you think passing the Stamp Act was a reasonable move for the British to make.

b

The colonies have lately been the darling object of their mother country's care. We are not yet recovered from a war undertaken only for their protection [the French and Indian War]. Whatever may be the value of the land gained by the war in America, the immediate benefit of this new land is to the colonies.

Even if there were no other reasons to require a tax from the colonies, the obligations they owe us for the war would be enough reason for the tax. Add to this the advantages they have gained by the peace, the national debt built up by England in fighting a war to defend the colonies, and the bad effects of the war on English government and business. It is obvious that this is the time to require the colonies to help England. The colonies have gained all the benefits, and the mother country is forced to bear the burdens. Yet all we asked of them was to support a military force in America for their own protection. Because of this need, several new taxes were laid on the colonies.

The stamp taxes are not oppressive. They are hard for nobody to pay, because they are distributed among all men, and are paid only occasionally. Stamp taxes cause less problem to the citizen than any other kind of tax.

It was never intended to make the colonists pay any part of our national debt, nor were they being asked to help pay the expenses of the government in England. All we asked was that they pay part of the expenses necessary to their own protection. The Americans are one fifth the number of the British subjects, but the aid asked of them is only about one twentieth what is asked of the people in England. This money was to be spent in their own country. The new trade and other advantages of the peace will give them far more money than the amount of tax money they will be expected to pay.

The problems of England call for every aid which any of its subjects can give. There is a special rightness in requiring it from the Americans, who have contributed so little and for whom so much has been done.

According to Whatley, why were the colonies being taxed? For what will the tax money be used?

c In a speech to Parliament, Prime Minister George Grenville spoke of Britain's right to tax. Grenville had first suggested the stamp tax to the British government.

c

When I first suggested taxing America, I asked if anyone in Parliament objected. I repeatedly asked it, and no one denied that we had that right. Protection and obedience go hand in hand. Since Great Britain protects America, America ought to be obedient.

When they want our protection, they never hesitate to ask for it, and we have always given it to them. We have run ourselves deep into debt to protect them, and now, when we call on them to help with a small amount, they deny our authority, insult our officers, and practically break out in open rebellion.

Great Britain rules America; it cannot be denied; and taxation is the right of the ruler.

Based on what you have read,
1. Predict colonial reactions to the tax.
2. Identify the values at stake for both sides.

American Strategies

The Stamp Act was passed by Parliament in March 1765, but the tax was not to go into effect until November of that year. As Prime Minister Grenville indicated, the colonials reacted strongly to the Act. The data in this activity describes some of the strategies they used to protest the Stamp Act and to try to keep the tax from being enforced.

Make a list of the strategies. Which strategies show the greatest aroused emotions? Which show less emotion? Which strategy would be most effective, in your opinion? Explain your choices.

a The following resolution was made by the landowners of Essex County, New Jersey, in 1765.

a We will hate and have contempt and disgust for every person who accepts a job having anything to do with the Stamp Act, or for anyone who will try to take advantage of this Act. We will despise and detest every stamp seller, informer, and anyone who encourages the enforcement of this Act. We will have nothing to do with these people, but to inform them of their evilness.

b Beginning in Boston, groups calling themselves "Sons of Liberty" were formed throughout the colonies. Their slogan was "Liberty, Property, and No Stamps." A royal official, Lieutenant Governor Hutchinson, describes some of the actions of the Sons of Liberty.

b

Boston, August 14, 1765

Early in the morning, a stuffed dummy was hung from a large tree in the south part of Boston. Signs attached to the dummy said that it represented the distributor of tax stamps for Massachusetts Bay, Andrew Oliver. People who were passing by stopped to view it, and soon others gathered from all parts of the town, and many from nearby towns.

Before night, the dummy was taken down and carried past the townhouse where the governor and royal council were meeting. Thousands of the mob followed the dummy down King Street to Oliver's dock, near which Mr. Oliver had recently erected a building. The mob assumed that this building would be used for a stamp office. They tore this building down within a few minutes. From there the mob headed for Fort Hill, but since Mr Oliver's house was on the way, they tried to force their way inside. They broke the windows, beat down the doors, entered, and destroyed part of his furniture. The mob continued in riot until midnight.

A short time later, mobs attacked the house of Lieutenant Governor Hutchinson. All the contents of his home were destroyed.

c On the evening of December 16th, 1765, Andrew Oliver received the following letter.

c

Sir,

The respectable inhabitants of the Town of Boston desire that you would, tomorrow, appear under Liberty Tree, at 12 o'clock, to make a public resignation. If you don't do this, Sir, you will bring about the displeasure of *The True-born Sons of Liberty.* Note this well—provided you do the above, you shall be treated with the greatest politeness and humanity. If not . . .!

(d) This poster was circulated in Boston by the Sons of Liberty.

(d)

WILLIAM JACKSON,

an *IMPORTER*; at the

BRAZEN HEAD,

North Side of the TOWN-HOUSE,

and *Oppofite the Town-Pump, in*

Corn-hill, B O S T O N.

It is defired that the Sons and DAUGHTERS of *LIBERTY,* would not buy any one thing of him, for in fo doing they will bring Difgrace upon *themfelves,* and their *Pofterity,* for *ever* and *ever,* AMEN.

*Why do you think the Sons of Liberty wanted colonials to boycott William Jackson's business. (To **boycott** something is to refuse to have anything to do with it.)*

(e) In September 1765 lawyers meeting before the New Jersey Supreme Court suggested a strategy that was adopted throughout the colonies.

The Chief Justice:

   If the stamps arrive, do you, as lawyers, intend to purchase them for any necessary legal documents?

Resolved by everyone present:

   Even if buying stamps might benefit us personally, we refuse to buy stamps. This refusal is for the public good. We will attempt to prevent riots or disorder, but by our refusal to buy the stamps, we will try to get the law repealed.

f Another strategy was adopted in October 1765 by merchants in New York who traded with Great Britain.

Resolved:

We will tell our agents not to ship to this colony any of the goods we have already ordered from Great Britain, unless the Stamp Act be repealed.

It is further agreed by everyone that no merchant will sell any goods sent from Great Britain after next January first.

Merchants in Boston, Philadelphia, and most other cities made similar agreements.

g A newspaper in Connecticut reported another strategy.

What do you think colonials hoped to gain by boycotting British cloth?

There is a tendency for many people here and in surrounding colonies to clothe themselves with cloth that they have made themselves. At Hempstead, Long Island, a company of gentlemen have set up a new wool factory. They have given notices to shopkeepers that they can supply woolen broadcloth, matching any sample, equal in fineness, color and goodness, cheaper than any imported.

It is feared by many who wish well to Great Britain, that the recent Act of Parliament will greatly distress and perhaps ruin some of the British manufacturers. It is thought that, because of this act, less of England's woolen cloth will be sold here next winter. The loss may be several thousands pounds sterling.

h In October 1765, 27 men from nine of the colonies met in New York at a Stamp Act Congress. This group, representing the legislatures of their colonies, passed a set of resolutions asking Parliament to **repeal,** or do away with, the Stamp Act. The words below are from their declaration to Parliament.

It is the right of British subjects in these colonies to petition the King, and either House of Parliament.

It is the duty of these colonies to try to get the Stamp Act repealed. To do this we will send a loyal and dutiful petition to his Majesty, and humble requests to both Houses of Parliament, asking them to repeal the Stamp Act.

The *Philadelphia Journal and Advertiser* printed this message on its front page.

Why was the closing down of the newspaper a protest against the stamp tax?

In your opinion, how would members of Parliament feel about the colonial strategies? Would these strategies threaten values of members of Parliament? If so, what values?

Why Did Americans Oppose the Tax?

Obviously the emotions of many Americans were aroused by the Stamp Act. Why? What American values were threatened by the tax? The data that follows gives the American reasons for protest.

As you study the material on American opposition
1. List reasons the colonials gave for their opposition.
2. Identify the values Americans believed to be threatened.

a John Dickinson, a Pennsylvania lawyer, wrote a series of letters that appeared in a colonial newspaper. In these letters he gave his opinions about the growing conflict with Great Britain. In the excerpt below, Dickinson discussed the Stamp Act.

a These taxes are a result of the great assistance the colonies gave to Great Britain in the late war [French and Indian], a war fought only for the benefit of Great Britain. Not one of the provinces of Canada, Nova Scotia, or Florida [places over which the war was fought] has ever paid any of the war expenses itself. In truth, only Great Britain receives any benefit from these places, and so she alone ought to pay for their defense. The old saying of the law could never be better applied that in this case: "They who feel the benefit, ought to feel the burden."

b On May 30, 1765, the Virginia legislature, the House of Burgesses, made these resolutions.

b We have always shown our loyalty and love for his Majesty. We showed it by being willing to do our part in the last war. We did it because we were certain that our King would never allow our freedom to be taken away.

We were also willing to pay our share of the expenses necessary to keep peace in America. However, because we already have heavy taxes, our ability to pay is limited. We will pay only if the method of raising these taxes is decided by ourselves.

Laws for internal government or taxation should not be passed, except by representatives chosen by the people who will be affected. People are already taxed for the expenses of the last war, to nearly half a million pounds. An increase of that tax load by Parliament would violate the most sacred and valuable principle of the English Constitution.

Such a tax will cause hard times and lack of money. The people here who could not leave would begin to manufacture the things they have imported from England up to now. Because of this, one source of wealth and prosperity for England will cease.

c The Stamp Act Congress issued a "declaration of the rights and grievances of the colonists in America."

1. His Majesty's subjects in these colonies owe the same loyalty to the Crown of Great Britain that is owing from his subjects born within England. Obedience is also due to that great body, the Parliament of Great Britain.

2. His Majesty's subjects in these colonies are entitled to all the rights and liberties of his natural-born subjects within the Kingdom of Great Britain.

3. It is necessary to the freedom of a people that no taxes be placed on them without their consent, given personally or by their representatives.

4. The people of these colonies are not and, from their local circumstances, cannot be represented in the House of Commons in Great Britain.

5. The only representatives of the people of these colonies are persons chosen in the colonies by the colonists. No taxes have been or can be imposed on them except by their own legislature.

The distance of the colonies from England make it impractical for the colonies to be represented anywhere but in their own legislatures. We humbly believe that the Parliament, following carefully the principles of the English Constitution, has never before taxed anybody unless they were represented in the Parliament.

Even if the colonies were represented legally in the House of Commons, the new taxes would still be unwise. The taxes are inconvenient, they violate the spirit of the English Constitution, and they are a poor policy for many other practical reasons. For all these reasons, we believe the new laws ought to be repealed.

What is the most important reason the Americans are giving for opposing the tax?

d At a Boston town meeting in 1766, a letter from the townspeople of Plymouth was read. Part of the letter follows.

When we think of the great efforts the first settlers made in farming and settling this land, with danger to their lives, and the great increase of strength and riches which has come to Great Britain by the expense and labor of these people, we become angry to think that there should even be any Englishmen who would seek the colonists' ruin.

Why would colonists' efforts to settle America affect their reaction to the Stamp Act?

The opposition to the Stamp Act led to a debate in Parliament in 1766. Benjamin Franklin, a well-known American from Pennsylvania, presented the American view to the British legislators. Below is part of Franklin's testimony.

Question: What is your name, and where do you live?

Franklin: Franklin, of Philadelphia.

Question: Do the Americans tax themselves?

Franklin: Certainly. They pay many and heavy taxes.

Question: What taxes do the laws of Pennsylvania require the citizens to pay?

Franklin: Taxes on land, personal possessions, a poll tax, a tax on office-holders, professions, trades, and businesses (according to their profits), a tax on wine, rum, and other spirits, a duty of ten pounds on each Negro imported, and some other taxes.

Question: For what purpose are these taxes collected?

Franklin: To support the government and the military, and to pay off the heavy debt run up during the French and Indian War.

Question: Do not all the people find these taxes easy to pay?

Franklin: No. The counties on the frontier have often been attacked by the enemy and had their property destroyed. They are poor, and can pay little tax.

Question: Are not the colonies well enough off to pay the stamp tax?

Franklin: In my opinion, there is not enough gold and silver in the colonies to pay the tax for one year.

Question: Did you know that all the money from the stamps was going to be spent in America?

Franklin: The money will be spent in America, but it will be spent in the conquered frontier territory where the soldiers are, not in the colonies that pay it.

Question: Do you think it is right for England to protect America, and America pay nothing?

Franklin: That is not the way it is. During the French and Indian war, the colonies recruited, clothed, and paid almost 25,000 men. Millions were spent.

Question: Did not Parliament pay you back?

Franklin: We were only paid back the amount you decided we had paid beyond our share. That was a very small part of what we actually spent. Pennsylvania,

*A **poll tax** is a tax paid by the voters. A **duty** is a tax paid on imports.*

e

for example, paid out about 500,000 pounds. She got back about 60,000.

Question: Do you think the Americans would pay the stamp tax if the amount of the tax was lowered?

Franklin: No, never, not unless force is used.

Question: How did most Americans feel about Great Britain before 1763?

Franklin: They had the best feelings in the world. They were obedient to the Crown and to Parliament.

Question: What if, in the future, we passed another tax like the Stamp Act. How would Americans react?

Franklin: They would not pay it.

Question: Do you know about the resolutions Parliament passed, stating that it has a right to tax Americans?

Franklin: Yes, I have heard of them.

Question: What opinion do Americans have on these?

Franklin: They think they are unconstitutional and unjust.

Question: Before 1763, did Americans believe Parliament had a right to tax them?

Franklin: I never heard any objection to taxes regulating trade, but Parliament has never had the right to tax us internally, because we have no representatives here.

Question: Can anything less than military force make the Stamp Act work?

Franklin: I do not see how military force can make it work.

Question: Why not?

Franklin: Suppose you sent the army to America. No army would meet them, so what could they do? They could not force a man to buy stamps if he chooses to do without them. They wouldn't find a rebellion. In fact, they might start one.

Question: If the Stamp Act is not repealed, what do you think will happen?

Franklin: Americans will lose all their respect and affection for England, and this country will lose the trade that depends on that respect and affection.

Question: How could trade be affected?

Franklin: In a short time, you would find that Americans would stop buying what you manufacture.

Question: Can they do without these things?

Franklin: Very easily.

Look at Franklin's figures on the cost of the French and Indian War and the number of colonial soldiers who fought in the war. How do you think this would affect the colonials' attitude toward the stamp tax? Would the colonials agree with Thomas Whatley's arguments for the tax (page 91)?

Question: How?

Franklin: What Americans buy from Britain are either necessities, conveniences, or luxuries. The necessities, with a little work, they can make at home; the conveniences they can wait for until they can provide them for themselves; and the luxuries they will do without. Americans used to be proud to wear fashions manufactured in Great Britain. Now they take pride in wearing their old clothes over and over.

1. The materials you've just read (pages 92-101) were about the strategies and arguments of the Americans opposing the Stamp Act. Based on their arguments,
   a. Do you think the Americans were justified in using all the strategies? If not, which strategies do you think were wrong?
   b. Under what conditions do you believe the use of violence is justified?
2. One of the most basic value conflicts in this period was about the question of *authority*. The British officials had one opinion of the authority of Parliament, and many Americans had a different opinion. Summarize the differences in the two views.

BRANCHING OUT

Set up a role-playing situation with other students. Role-play an argument about the Stamp Act. You might act out a formal debate between colonials and British representatives, a town meeting in Boston, an informal meeting at a New York coffee house, or some other situation. Be sure that you include supporters of and protestors against the Act.

The Stamp Act Is Repealed

In spite of American strategies, the stamp tax went into effect on November 1, 1765. However, British government officials and members of Parliament debated over the action they should take toward the colonies and their protest. They knew that the colonials were unhappy. They also knew that British merchants were concerned. Finally, in March 1766, Parliament repealed the Stamp Act.

Use the data in this and earlier activities to decide why Parliament repealed the Stamp Act.

a A Rhode Island newspaper carried this report of conditions in England before the Stamp Act was repealed.

a

We learn from those recently arrived on a ship from Bristol, that the people of England are very unhappy, and are complaining. Nearly 40,000 weavers, glovemakers, and other manufacturers appeared in London waving black flags of protest. These people even surrounded the royal palace and Parliament.

Many manufacturers are almost out of business. They believe it is because of the Acts of Parliament which have left the colonies unable to buy manufactured goods. The Norwich weavers, who a year or two ago supplied vast quantities of cloth to America, are also suffering. These weavers are now gathering and are expected to join the protest, so the law might be changed.

b On January 17, 1766, London merchants sent this petition to Parliament.

b

We have been carrying on trade between this country and the British colonies in North America for a long time. Every year we have exported very large quantities of British manufactures—woolen goods, cottons, linens, hardware, shoes, furniture, and almost everything else manufactured in Great Britain. In this trade we employed thousands of people. In return for these exports, we received from the colonies rice, tobacco, naval stores, oil, whale fins, furs, and other goods, along with payments of gold and silver the colonists earned in trade elsewhere.

This commerce now is near ruin, unless Parliament will act. The Americans already owe several millions of pounds sterling to the merchants of Great Britain. They have no money, and the taxes and laws passed by Parliament are the reason. These taxes and laws have interfered with the colonies' trade, so many people there are now bankrupt.

To save ourselves and our families from ruin, to prevent many manufacturers from going out of business, and to keep Great Britain strong, we pray that Parliament will take the action that is so badly needed.

Naval stores are materials used to build and supply ships.

How would British taxes affect the colonials' money supply?

What American strategies were affecting British manufacturers? Were the strategies effective?

c Parliament's attempt to solve the problems created by the conflict is explained in excerpts of speeches in Parliament.

c

Attorney General Yorke:

We must choose between two evils, and it seems that the best thing we can do is repeal the Stamp Act. If all we do is change the Act, we would look weak. Changing the Act would not quiet the madness in the colonies.

General Henry Seymour Conway:

The rebellion in America could be subdued—the force of this country is equal to it—but the conflict is death to both countries. Our troops in America are but about 5,000 men scattered over that immense continent. The men able to carry arms in America are great in number. If we were engaged in a civil war in America, a French and Spanish war would be the consequence, and this, connected with an American war, would be absolute ruin to this country.

d This cartoon of the "burial of the Stamp Act" appeared in an English newspaper after the repeal of the Act.

d

THE REPEAL. — Or the Funeral Procession, of MISS AMERIC-STAMP.

e This report is from the minutes of a Boston town meeting.

> At a meeting of the Selectmen, May 16, 1776:
>
> Captain Coffin arrived from London with the agreeable news that the act repealing the Stamp Act had passed and we find that the news was true as it appeared by the public papers that His Majesty had signed the said Act the eighteenth of March last.
>
> Voted that Monday next, the 19th, be the day of general rejoicing and that the inhabitants be notified thereof.

Shortly after they repealed the Stamp Act, Parliament passed another act concerning the colonies—the Declaratory Act. Its most important points are stated below.

> The colonies and plantations in America have been, are, and of right ought to be subordinate to, and dependent on the Imperial Crown and Parliament of Great Britain.
>
> Parliament has the power and authority to make laws of enough force and truth to tie together the colonies and people of Great Britain, in all cases whatsoever.

Why do you think Parliament passed the Declaratory Act? How do you think that act is related to the repeal of the Stamp Act?

Part 2

Growth of Conflict

The conflict between Britain and the colonies did not end with the repeal of the Stamp Act. The areas of disagreement which you examined in Part 1 continued to be problems. In fact, the problems became worse; the distance between the ideas of Englishmen and colonials became greater.

You have identified important values held by each side in this conflict. As you study Part 2 of the unit, think about this question.

How did British and colonial strategies and goals change as value conflicts increased?

The Townshend Acts

Many members of Parliament were unhappy that they had been forced to repeal the Stamp Act. As they stated in the Declaratory Act, they felt their authority over the colonies should be enforced—especially their authority to tax.

In 1767 Charles Townshend, Chancellor of the Exchequer (that is, "manager" of the British treasury), persuaded Parliament to pass new taxes for America. These taxes were not high, and they were not "internal" taxes such as the Stamp Act had been. They were duties on certain products colonials imported from Britain.

As you examine the Townshend Acts and the colonials' reactions to them,

1. Identify the colonial values that are threatened.
2. Evaluate the strategies of the British and the colonials concerning the taxes.

a The chart below lists the Townshend Acts.

THE TOWNSHEND ACTS

The Townshend Acts did the following:

1. Suspended the New York Assembly until it obeyed the Quartering Act. This act required colonists to provide living quarters for British troops.

2. Approved the use of Writs of Assistance. These documents allowed British officials to search any building or ship at any time.

3. Established these import taxes:

100 lbs. white glass	5 shillings 8 pence
100 lbs. green glass	1 shilling 2 pence
100 lbs. lead	2 shillings
100 lbs. paint	2 shillings
16 oz. tea	3 pence
1 ream paper	12 shillings

4. Set up an American Board of Commissioners in Boston to collect and enforce the new taxes and to prevent smuggling.

5. Used the money collected from taxes to pay royal governors and other British officials in the colonies, to help cover the cost of defending and protecting the American colonies, and to maintain the new tax system created by the act.

Do you think the British were wise to tax the colonials again? Do you think they had the right to tax them?

The Americans reacted with some of the same strategies and arguments they had used during the Stamp Act protest: nonimportation agreements, letters of protest, and violation of the new law by smugglers.

b Samuel Adams of Boston was an important leader of the colonial protest against British taxation. In a newspaper article in 1768, he expressed this opinion about the Townshend Acts.

b
When the people are unfairly ruled, when their rights are violated, when their property is invaded, when guards are put over them, when unconstitutional acts are committed before their eyes, when they are threatened every day with military troops, when the government is secret, people will be unhappy. They are not to be blamed for this feeling. Their minds will be upset as long as they care about honor, liberty, and goodness. If they have the spirit of freedom, they will boldly demand their freedom. They have the right to do this.

c John Dickinson also protested the Townshend Acts. He wrote these opinions in letters to a Pennsylvania newspaper.

Would Samuel Adams approve of the actions of the Sons of Liberty? Would John Dickinson?

In what way do taxes take away one's possessions?

In what ways are the strategies of Adams and Dickinson different? Why was Dickinson worried about colonial unity?

c
The case of liberty is a cause of too much dignity to be dirtied by violence. Those who support liberty must act with wisdom, justice, modesty, bravery, humanity, and generosity.

Let these truths be permanently in our minds:
—that we cannot be happy without being free
—that we cannot be free without being secure in our possessions
—that we cannot be secure in our possessions if other people can take them away without our consent
—that taxes imposed on us by Parliament do take away our possessions
—that duties whose only purpose is raising money are really taxes
—that attempts to place such duties on us should be instantly and firmly opposed
—that this opposition can never be effective unless it is the united effort of the colonies

d In Massachusetts the colonial legislature was suspended by Parliament because of actions objecting to the Townshend Acts. Protest was especially strong in Boston. The British officials reacted by sending two regiments of troops to Boston in 1768. These troops were under the command of British General Thomas Gage, who made this report about the situation in Boston.

d The troops were brought to Boston because of the disputes with Great Britain and this has caused the people of Boston to hate soldiers. Since all the officers and men are from Britain, they assumed the colonists were wrong, without trying to see the colonists' point of view. The soldiers have often argued and quarreled with the people of Boston and have created some problems with their attitudes.

The people are in control of things here, not the government, and they often try to make trouble with the soldiers.

Why might Boston residents feel that soldiers should not be in their city?

In March 1770 Parliament repealed all of the Townshend duties except that on tea. The tea tax was too small to make much money or to control trade for England.

Why do you think Parliament kept this small tax?

The Boston Massacre: Biased Data

When two people are questioned after they have been fighting with each other, they are likely to give very different stories of what happened. Because their emotions are aroused, their accounts may be biased. Some of these differences are not intentional. When people are angry and excited, they may remember only the things that seemed unfair to them. Other differences may be intentional; people may try to gain sympathy by telling their stories in a certain way.

This is true of historical accounts. People give different reports of a situation or event, especially if their emotions are aroused.

In Boston on the evening of March 5, 1770, something happened that has become known as the "Boston Massacre." Following are two different accounts and a drawing describing what happened.

Identify differences in the three views. Which differences do you think were created "on purpose" to influence opinion?

*A **bias** is an angle or, in thinking, it is a way of looking at facts and events. A **biased** opinion or account is one which is prejudiced. The person who has the opinion sees the facts and events only in a certain way and is not seeing or presenting the whole picture.*

a John Tudor, a Boston merchant, was an eyewitness of the event. Here is his account of it.

On Monday evening the 5th, a few minutes after nine o'clock, a most horrid murder was committed in King Street before the customhouse door by eight or nine soldiers under the command of Captain Thomas Preston.

This unhappy affair began when some boys and young fellows threw snowballs at the sentry placed at the customhouse door. At this, eight or nine soldiers came to his aid. Soon after, a number of people collected. The Captain commanded the soldiers to fire, which they did, and three men were killed on the spot and several mortally wounded, one of which died the next morning. The Captain soon drew off his soldiers up to the main guard, if he had not done this, the results might have been terrible, for when the guns fired, the people were alarmed and set the bells a-ringing as if for a fire, which drew many to the place of action.

Lt. Governor Hutchinson, who was commander-in-chief, was sent for and came to the Council Chamber, where some of the judges waited. The Governor desired the crowd to separate about ten o'clock and go home peaceably. He said he would do all in his power to see that justice was done. The 29th Regiment was then under arms on the south side of the Townhouse, but the people insisted that the soldiers should be ordered to their barracks first before they would separate. When this was done the people separated about one o'clock.

Captain Preston was arrested by a warrant given to the high sheriff by Justices Dana and Tudor. He was questioned at about two o'clock, and we sent him to jail soon after three, having enough evidence to commit him, because he ordered the soldiers to fire; so about four o'clock the town became quiet. The next day the eight soldiers that fired on the inhabitants were also sent to jail.

b Five days after the incident, General Gage described it in a letter to an official in England.

On the evening of March 5th, the people of Boston had a general uprising. They began by attacking several soldiers in a small street, near the barracks of the 29th Regiment. The noise of the attack caused several officers to come out of the barracks and investigate. They found some of the soldiers greatly hurt, but they took the soldiers into the barrack.

The mob followed them to the barrack door, threatening and waving clubs over the officers' heads. The officers tried to make peace, and asked the mob to leave.

Part of the mob then broke into a meetinghouse, and rang the bell as if there were a fire. This seems to have been a prearranged signal. Immediately many people assembled in the streets. Some of them were armed with guns, but most carried clubs and similar weapons.

Many people came out of their houses, thinking there was a fire. Several soldiers, thinking the same thing, headed for their duty posts as they were supposed to do. On the way they were insulted and attacked. Those who could not escape were knocked down and treated very badly.

Different mobs moved through the streets, passing the different barracks. These mobs tried to make the soldiers angry and urged them to come outside. One group went to the main guard and tried to stir up trouble, but they failed. The guard soldiers stood their positions quietly.

From there the mob moved to the customhouse, and attacked a single soldier on guard there. He defended himself as well as he could, and called for help. Several people ran to the main guard to tell of the danger to the soldier.

Captain Preston, who was in charge of the guard that day, was at the main guard station. When he heard of the attack on the soldier, he sent a sergeant and 12 men to aid him. The Captain soon followed to help prevent the troops from starting unnecessary trouble.

The mob attacked the group of soldiers. Some of the mob threw bricks, stones, pieces of ice, and snowballs at the soldiers. Others moved up to the soldiers' bayonets, trying to use their clubs. People in the mob called out to the soldiers to fire their guns, and used insulting language.

Captain Preston stood between the soldiers and the mob and tried to make peace by talking to them, asking them to leave. Some of the mob asked if he intended to order the soldiers to shoot at them. He answered, "Of course not. I am between you and the troops."

His words had no effect. One of the soldiers, receiving a violent blow, fired his gun. Captain Preston turned around to see who had fired. He received a blow that was aimed for his head but missed and hit his arm.

The mob did not see any damage done by the first shot, so they supposed that the soldiers had loaded only with powder and no shot to scare them. They grew bolder and attacked the soldiers with more force, continually striking the soldiers, throwing objects at them, and daring them to fire. The soldiers soon saw that their lives were in danger, and hearing the word "fire" all around them, three or four of them fired one after another. These shots were followed by three more in the same hurry and confusion. Four or five persons were unfortunately killed, and several wounded.

Captain Preston and the soldiers were soon afterward delivered into the hands of the judges, who committed them to prison.

If this poster were your only source of information about the event, what would you think about the actions of the British soldiers? Of the colonials? What was Revere's bias?

▼

C Paul Revere, a Boston silversmith and engraver, made this poster soon after the incident.

In each of these documents, what evidence of bias can you find? In your opinion, which document is most biased? Which is least biased? What additional information would help you decide about the biases of each document?

Public opinion in Boston was violently hostile to the soldiers who had been arrested, but John Adams, an important Boston lawyer and one of the leaders of the opposition to Great Britain, volunteered to act as attorney for the soldiers at their trial. He believed that the soldiers had acted in self-defense. Captain Preston and all but two of the soldiers were found not guilty. Two soldiers were convicted of manslaughter, branded on their hands, and released.

For the next five years, some colonials celebrated "Massacre Day," March 5. The Sons of Liberty held parades on that day in order to remind colonists of "what the British had done."

The Tea Business

In opposition to the British, Samuel Adams helped organize a series of "committees of correspondence." These were local groups who wrote letters to one another, spreading information about the British and encouraging opposition to British control. By 1773 there were committees of correspondence in communities throughout the colonies.

Because of these committees and other cooperative efforts, the colonies gradually became more and more unified in their opposition to British controls. This unity was put to use late in 1773 when Parliament took more action affecting trade in America.

One of England's important trading organizations was the East India Company. This company imported goods, especially tea, from China, and sold them in England, Europe, and other places. In 1773 the East India Company was almost bankrupt. So, Parliament decided to help the company sell extra tea to the American colonials. They thought that lowering the tea tax would encourage colonials to buy more tea. They set the price and tax so that the tea in America would be even cheaper than tea in England or the smuggled tea on which no tax was paid.

The colonials, however, didn't think the low price was a favor. They still objected to English taxation and thought the price was a trick to force them into paying taxes they thought were illegal.

The data that follows presents Americans' reactions to the British strategy. Use the data to answer these questions: Do you think the American strategy was justified? Do you think it was wise? Give reasons for your answers.

ⓐ Ship pilots on the Delaware Bay were given copies of this letter to present to the captain of a tea ship.

Tarring and feathering was a process in which the victim was covered with hot tar and then with feathers.

ⓐ

November 1773

To Captain Ayres of the Ship *Polly,* on a voyage from London to Philadelphia. Sir:

We have been told that you, very unwisely, are carrying a cargo of tea that the India Company and government officials sent as a test, to see if we mean what we say.

Now, because that tea is most certainly going to get you in hot water, and because you are perhaps a stranger to these parts, we have decided to let you know how things are here in Philadelphia. This may give you time to stop your dangerous errand, prepare your ship for the burning rafts we may let drift into her, and keep you out of the tar and feathers prepared for you.

In the first place, we must tell you that Pennsylvanians, every one of them, are extremely fond of freedom, the birthright of all Americans, and they intend to hang onto it.

They believe that no power on earth has a right to tax them without their permission.

They believe the tea you carry is an attempt by royal officials to enforce such a tax, and they intend to give you all the trouble they can.

They have chosen us for a disagreeable, but necessary task—to take care of anyone who offends the rights of America. Unfortunate is the man who ends up in our hands.

You have been sent on a devilish mission. If you are foolish and stubborn enough to anchor in this port, the things that happen will probably cause you (in your last moments) to enthusiastically curse those who used you to aid their own ambition and greed.

How would you like, Captain, a halter around your neck, ten gallons of liquid tar poured over your head, and the feathers of a dozen wild geese laid over that to brighten up your appearance?

Think about that—and fly back to where you came from. Fly without hesitating, without a protest, and above all, Captain Ayres, let us advise you to fly without the wild geese feathers.

Your friends,
The Committee for Tarring and Feathering

b Another letter to the Delaware Bay pilots gave additional information about Captain Ayres.

> Captain Ayres was here during the Stamp Act trouble and ought to know us better than to expect us to allow his rotten tea to be funnelled down our throats with Parliament's tax mixed with it.

The letters had their desired effect. The *Polly* returned to England without unloading the tea.

c This 1774 cartoon shows what happened to John Malcomb, who collected the British tea tax in Boston. He was tarred and feathered and forced to drink to the health of the royal family in burning hot tea.

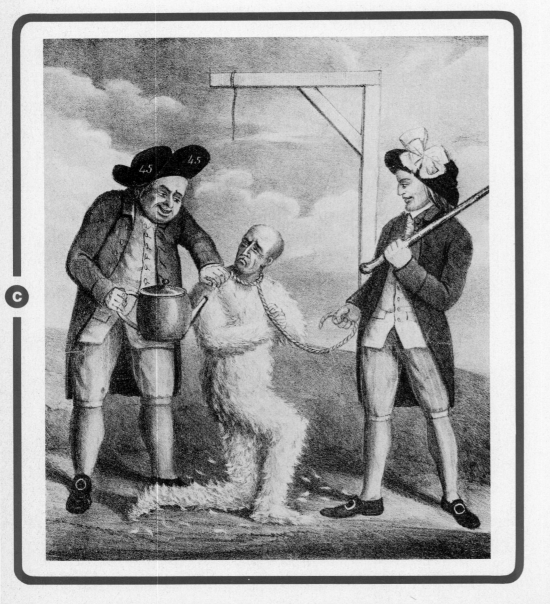

d The colonists were determined not to buy tea from the British when it did reach America. When ships loaded with tea came into Boston Harbor, some colonists took the action described below. This account of the Boston "Tea Party" is taken from a Boston newspaper of December 23, 1773.

d

Just before the end of the assembly meeting, a number of brave men dressed as Indians approached the door of the Assembly. They gave a war whoop, which rang through the house and was answered by some in the galleries. But silence was commanded, and the rest of the meeting was orderly. The "Indians" then went to the wharf where the ships were that had the tea on board. They were followed by hundreds of people who wanted to watch.

The "Indians" went on board Capt. Hall's ship, pulled the chests of tea out on the deck, broke them open, and dumped the tea overboard. Having finished the first ship, they went on to Capt. Bruce's and then to Capt. Coffin's brig. In about three hours they had broken open 342 chests (all that were on the ships) and dumped the tea overboard. When the tide came in it floated the chests and tea, covering much of the bay from the south part of town to Dorchester Neck.

Great care was taken to keep the tea from being stolen. One or two people were caught trying to pocket a small quantity, but it was taken from them and they were treated rather roughly. It should be mentioned that, although a large quantity of goods was left on board the ships, none of it was bothered. So much care was taken that when a small padlock belonging to one of the captains was broken, another was sent to him.

The town was very quiet during this evening and night. Those who had come into town from out in the country went home in a happy mood. The next day everyone seemed happy—some because the tea had been destroyed, and others because it was done so quietly.

Why do you think the protestors would care if tea—or anything else on the ships—was stolen?

BRANCHING OUT ▶▶

Throughout much of the period before the Revolutionary War, Massachusetts was the colony in which resistance to British authority was strongest. Why was resistance stronger in Massachusetts than in other colonies?

Develop a report giving the reasons you believe are important in explaining strong resistance to British authority in Massachusetts.

Choose to do one of the activities listed below, related to the Boston Tea Party.

1. With other classmates, role-play a meeting of the Board of Directors of the East India Company following the Boston Tea Party. In your role-play, be sure to include a discussion of strategies to be used in reaction to the colonists' actions.

2. With other classmates, role-play a meeting held by colonists who were planning the Tea Party. Include representatives of several points of view, including some who want to destroy everything on the ships and others who want only to threaten the ships' captains.

3. Write a newspaper article reporting the Boston Tea Party. Choose to be a reporter from either a British or a colonial newspaper. Later, compare class articles written from both points of view and discuss any bias that you find in the articles.

Putting the Pieces Together

⬤ Here is a list of possible strategies that could be used by the British government against the rebellious Americans. If you were the British Prime Minister, which of these strategies would you recommend? (You may want to use more than one.) Are there other actions you might choose besides those listed? Give reasons for your choices.

1. Send enough troops to America to enforce the trade and tax laws completely.
2. Send ships to close off all trade from Boston until the tea is paid for and the Boston people agree to obey the law.
3. Remove troops from Boston to reduce tensions.
4. Set up a committee to meet with the Americans to discuss problems and differences.
5. Attempt a compromise: If the tea is paid for, the tax will be removed. (This will help the East India Company avoid bankruptcy.)
6. Attempt a compromise: If the colonies agree to pay taxes

to Britain, the method of raising tax money can be decided by the colonial legislatures.

7. Allow the Americans to elect representatives to Parliament.
8. Round up the leaders of the rebellion, and send them to England for trial.

Further Reactions

The emotions of both colonists and British were more aroused than ever after the Boston Tea Party. Parliament took action and the colonists reacted.

As you read about the actions and opinions of both sides, identify the strategies used. Which of these are new strategies?

a Parliament responded to the colonists' actions in the tea business by passing a new series of acts to discipline the colonies. Americans called these the "Intolerable Acts." The first of them, passed in 1774, is stated below.

The Boston Port Act

The purpose of this act is to end (until certain requirements are met) the shipping or receiving of goods at the town or in the Harbor of Boston, in the Province of Massachusetts Bay, in North America.

Dangerous commotions and rebellions have been started in the town of Boston, His Majesty's government has been defied, and the public peace has been destroyed. In these commotions and rebellions, valuable cargoes of tea belonging to the East India Company were seized and destroyed.

Since it is not safe to carry on commerce there, and customs duties are not being paid, it is proper to remove the customs officers from the town.

Be it enacted, that after June 1, 1774, it is unlawful for anyone in Boston, or between Nahant Point and Alderton Point, to load any merchandise or goods on board any vessel bound for another country, province, or any other part of Massachusetts. It is also unlawful to unload any goods or merchandise from any other place within or outside the province. Anyone who does not obey must forfeit the goods or merchandise, the boat and its guns, ammunition, tackle, furniture, and supplies.

The port shall not be reopened until His Majesty has received assurance that the people of Boston have made arrangements to pay for the destruction of East India Company goods and to pay damages to his Majesty's revenue officers and others who suffered because of riots and rebellious acts in 1773 and 1774.

In your opinion, was this act a reasonable way to control the actions of the people in Boston? Why or why not?

Other acts passed at the same time gave soldiers rights to take over and live in private homes. New laws also restricted town meetings, removed many of the rights of Massachusetts' government, and stated that British officials who killed colonials in line of duty could be sent to England for trial.

Many Americans considered the Quebec Act the worst of the Intolerable Acts, even though it was not intended to affect the English-speaking colonials. This act gave the French people in Quebec, now under British control, rights to practice their Catholic religion. It also extended the territory of Quebec south and west. The rebellious colonials felt this law was a dangerous beginning. It did not give the Quebec people representative local government, or allow them to have trial by jury in civil cases.

What other reasons might Americans have for resenting the Quebec Act?

b This map shows the territory of Quebec before and after the Quebec Act.

QUEBEC
1763 and 1774

——— Quebec 1763
(after the French and Indian War)

– – – Quebec 1774
(after the Quebec Act)

British warships soon closed off Boston harbor, and the other acts were put into effect. How did Americans react? In Virginia, for example, 8,600 bushels of corn and wheat—along with hundreds of barrels of flour—were sent to help the people of Boston. Groups of citizens made resolutions of action against the British.

C These resolutions were made in Nansemond County, Virginia.

At a meeting of the citizens of the County of Nansemond, on the 11th of July, 1774, it was unanimously agreed:

That we will at all times defend, even with our lives, His Majesty's right to rule Great Britain and the colonies, and we declare our loyalty and obedience to him.

That only the General Assembly of Virginia has a right to tax Virginians.

That because we have no representation in Parliament, Parliament has no right to put a tax on tea. This is taking the colonists' property without their consent, and leads to slavery.

That the recent unfair and warlike acts of Parliament against our sister colony, Massachusetts Bay and the town of Boston proves how evil British officials are and that they intend to take away our rights.

That all the colonies should help the town of Boston.

That all the colonies should unite to fight in every legal way these threats to our liberties.

That all the colonies should agree not to buy anything from Great Britain until all our rights have been restored and Parliament repeals its cruel acts against Boston.

That all luxury and wastefulness on our part should be ended.

That manufacturing in the colonies should be encouraged.

That the slave trade is expensive, it discourages people from settling in Virginia, and also discourages manufacturing.

That wearing clothing manufactured in Virginia should be considered a sign of patriotism.

That representatives should be appointed to meet with the respresentatives of other counties at Williamsburg on the first of August to decide how best to carry out the above resolutions.

That L. Riddick and B. Baker are to represent us.

That representatives from Virginia counties should choose a committee to meet with representatives from other colonies to agree on ways to preserve our liberties.

That this colony should not trade with any colony which refuses to join in any action decided on by a majority of the colonies.

Why do you think the colonials included the slave trade in this and other non-importation agreements?

How is this document different from earlier agreements to limit trade with England?

d The attitude of some Bostonians is described in a letter written to John Adams in 1774.

d

. . . The other day I was at the North End and had this conversation with a ship carpenter.

"Very slow times, Mr. R————."

"Yes sir, very slow. The last ship built here was launched this week, and we probably won't start another, because the Admiral won't let them be sailed."

"That's discouraging. Don't you think it's about time we gave in, paid for the tea, and got the harbor opened?"

"Give up? No! It never is time to become a slave. I've still got some pork and meal, and when they are gone I will eat clams. And after we have dug up all the clams, if Congress won't let us fight, I will retreat to the woods. I can always eat acorns."

What a patriot! By heaven, it is an honor to be this man's fellow citizen.

e This cartoon, called "America in Flames," appeared in an English newspaper in 1775.

How do you think this artist felt about Britain's strategies?

e

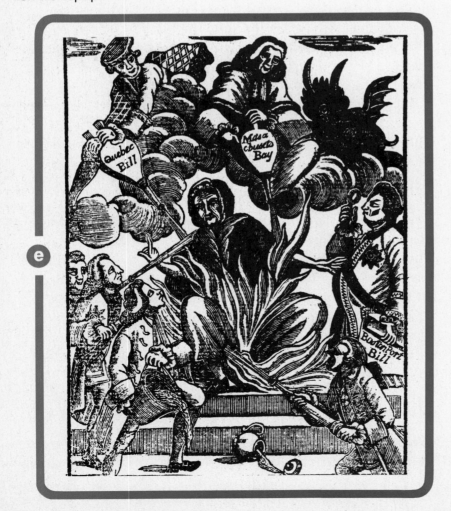

In September of 1774, the colonies sent representatives to a "Continental Congress" at Philadelphia. The purpose of the meeting was to decide on a united course of action. Fifty-five men, including Samuel Adams, John Adams, George Washington, and Patrick Henry, a Virginia patriot, thought and debated for seven weeks.

They issued petitions to Parliament and the king, a Declaration of Rights, and appeals to neighboring British colonies in Canada and and the West Indies.

f Their most effective action was the agreement which they called "The Association." Here is part of that agreement.

Oct. 20, 1774

We, his Majesty's loyal subjects, have been chosen to represent the colonies in a Continental Congress. We declare our loyalty to His Majesty, and our affection and respect for our countrymen in Great Britain.

We are anxious and alarmed at our oppression, which is the result of a system of colonial administration which began about 1763.

We believe that refusing to import or use British goods or export our goods to them is the fastest, most effective, and most peaceful method to obtain justice from Britain.

The above policies will continue until the oppressive acts of Parliament passed since the close of the last war [French and Indian] are repealed.

At this point in the conflict, what seems to be the attitude of the Americans toward

1. The king
2. Parliament
3. Taxes
4. Self-government
5. Independence as a new nation

Many of the strategies you have identified produced aroused feelings. In your opinion, which of these strategies caused the most aroused feelings for colonials? For the British? What values of each were being threatened?

g The table below lists the total imports of British goods into America between 1763 and 1776.

1. Make a graph showing the imports.
2. Based on your graph, decide how effective the non-importation agreements were in 1765–1766, 1769, 1773, and 1775–1776.

g

IMPORTS FROM GREAT BRITAIN

YEAR	VALUE OF GOODS IMPORTED TO AMERICA FROM GREAT BRITAIN (in pounds sterling)
1763	1,631,997
1764	2,249,710
1765	1,944,114
1766	1,804,333
1767	1,900,923
1768	2,157,218
1769	1,336,122
1770	1,925,571
1771	4,202,472
1772	3,012,635
1773	1,979,412
1774	2,590,437
1775	196,162
1776	55,415

The petitions of the Continental Congress were received by Parliament and Parliament's members debated, then rejected the petitions by a strong majority vote. The protests in America continued. Merchants and traders who tried to trade with England were tarred and feathered. In late 1774 and early 1775, colonials began gathering guns and practicing military drills.

Seeing the growth of hostilities, Parliament declared that Massachusetts, Rhode Island, and Connecticut were in rebellion. The British cabinet ordered General Gage to arrest the colonial leaders, break up the mobs, and use troops as needed to put down the rebellion. General Gage was also told to organize a militia of colonials who were loyal to Britain. (A **militia** is a group of citizens organized to fight in case of emergency.)

Events in the colonies convinced British authorities that an armed rebellion was very likely. The British knew that weapons, supplies, and gunpowder were stored at Concord, Massachusetts, near Boston. General Gage sent British soldiers to try to destroy the supplies and capture Samuel Adams and John Hancock, another leader of the rebellion in Massachusetts. On the night of April 18, 1775, 700 troops crossed the Charles River from Boston, beginning their march to Concord. Paul Revere, William Dawes, and other Americans rode through the surrounding area warning the colonials of the British action. Because of their warning, some of the supplies were saved, and Adams and Hancock escaped.

When the British troops arrived in Lexington at dawn on the 19th, 77 armed men greeted them. The Americans were almost persuaded to back down, but then someone began firing. (Accounts differ as to which side fired first.) In the battle that followed, eight Americans were killed and ten wounded.

The British then marched on to Concord, took the stored weapons, and destroyed some supplies. By this time hundreds of "minute men" had gathered to oppose the British. (The **minute men** were colonists who had drilled to be ready for instant action.) All along the return route to Boston the British soldiers were attacked by Americans.

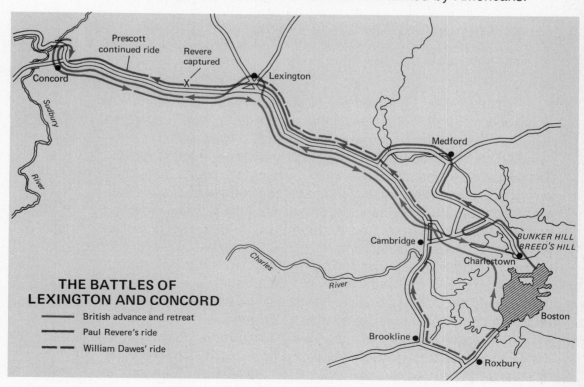

THE BATTLES OF LEXINGTON AND CONCORD

—— British advance and retreat

—— Paul Revere's ride

– – – William Dawes' ride

Here, two colonials face the British in an early battle.

Moving Toward Independence

A month after the battle of Lexington and Concord there was a second meeting of the Continental Congress. At this time, plans were made to create an army and navy and to raise money for the war that was expected. The Congress also appointed George Washington to be commander of the army.

The Second Continental Congress made one last attempt to bring peace to the colonies' relationship with Great Britain. They wrote and sent to King George the Olive Branch Petition. (An olive branch is a symbol of peace. At the time, John Adams said, "We have an olive branch in one hand and a sword in the other.") In this document the Congress told the king that they "most ardently desire that the former harmony between Britain and these colonies may be restored." The king, however, would not even read the petition.

In August 1775 the king declared that all the colonies were in rebellion. And in September he made a deal with six German princes for thousands of German soldiers, called "Hessians," to be sent to America to aid the British army.

124

The data in this activity will tell you about the colonials' feelings about independence and about their relationship with Great Britain. Use the data to answer these questions.

1. What values did the colonials support in their desire for independence?
2. How do the ideas and attitudes of Paine and the Declaration of Independence differ from earlier colonial ideas and attitudes?

Although independence from Great Britain had sometimes been suggested, most Americans had not been interested in separation from Britain. They wanted to change but not cut off the relationship. As late as January 1776, for example, officers in Washington's army were still toasting the king's health.

a John Dickinson had written this in 1768.

a If we are separated from our mother country, what new form of government shall we accept? When shall we find another Britain to fill our loss? Torn from the body to which we are united by religion, liberty, laws, affections, relations, language, and commerce, we must bleed at every vein.

b As the conflict increased and other solutions seemed impossible, many Americans began to change their minds about independence. When Thomas Paine published a small book called *Common Sense* in 1776, his ideas immediately caught on in colonials' minds.

b In the following pages I offer nothing more than simple facts, plain arguments, and common sense. . . .

Some say that because America has done well under Great Britain in the past, her future happiness depends on continuing the relationship. Nothing could be more wrong. One might as well claim that because a child has done well on milk, it should never have meat.

Others say, "England has protected us." That she has defended our continent at our expense, as well as her own, is admitted. But she would have defended Turkey for the same reasons—trade and power.

"But Britain is our parent country," some say. Then that makes her behavior all the more shameful. Even brute animals do not devour their young, nor savages make war on their families. Europe, not England, is the parent of America. This new world has been a home for mistreated lovers of liberty from every part of Europe. They have come here, not from a mother's tender embraces, but to escape the cruelty of the monster.

Any connection with Great Britain tends to involve us in European wars and quarrels, and set us against nations which would otherwise be friendly. Since all of Europe is our market, we should not favor any one part of it.

It is only right and reasonable that we separate. The blood of the dead cries, "Tis time to part." Even the distance God has placed America from England is natural proof that rule of one by the other was not what Heaven intended.

But if you say you are still willing to overlook the wrongs England has done us, then I ask, "Has *your* house been burned? Has your property been destroyed before your eyes? Are your wife and children without a bed to lie on or bread to eat? Have you lost a parent or child by their hands and you are the heart-broken survivor?" If you have not, then you are not a judge of those who have. But if you have, and can still shake hands with the murderers, then whatever be your rank in life, you are a coward.

Every quiet method to settle our differences peacefully has failed. Our plans have been turned down scornfully. So, since nothing but fighting will work, for God's sake let us come to a final separation.

In your opinion, which of Paine's arguments is the strongest? What values was Paine supporting?

C This cartoon described America's actions toward Great Britain.

THE HORSE AMERICA, throwing his Master.

d Paine's pamphlet was soon read throughout America, and sympathy for complete independence grew quickly. On June 7, 1776, Virginian Richard Henry Lee made this motion in the Continental Congress.

d

Resolved:

That these United Colonies are and should be free and independent states; that they are freed from all allegiance to the British Crown, and that all political connection between them and the State of Great Britain is, and ought to be, totally dissolved.

That it is suitable immediately to take the most effective measures for forming foreign alliances.

That a plan of confederation must be prepared and sent to all the colonies for consideration and approval.

*A **confederation** is a union of states or nations. Why would Lee suggest that the colonies create a confederation?*

On July 2nd, the Continental Congress voted unanimously to support Lee's motion. One final formal step was necessary—a legal document that declared independence and gave the reasons.

Shortly after the motion by Lee, a committee was appointed to write this document. The declaration was written by a representative from Virginia, Thomas Jefferson. It was edited by Benjamin Franklin and John Adams, and finally changed somewhat by the Congress. Signed by John Hancock, president of the Continental Congress, on July 4, 1776 this document was the final step to independence.

Other members of the Continental Congress signed the Declaration later. In your opinion, if the British had won the Revolution, what would have happened to the men who signed the Declaration of Independence?

e Some of the important ideas of the Declaration are stated here.

The original words of the Declaration of Independence are reproduced on pages 516-517.

e

When it becomes necessary for one group of people to do away with the political ties that connect them with another group of people, and become an independent country, they should give reasons for their action.

We believe that all men are created equal and that they have certain God-given rights such as life, liberty, and the pursuit of happiness. We believe governments are supposed to help people reach these goals. If a government fails in this task, the people have a right to establish a new government.

Of course, governments should not be changed for unimportant reasons, but when a great deal of evidence shows that a particular government has become dictatorial, the people not only have a right, they have a duty to end that government.

This is our situation today. Again and again, the King of Great Britain has shown his desire to have absolute power over the colonies. The wrongs are many. The facts are clear . . . .

What values are expressed in the Declaration of Independence?

Therefore, we, as representatives of the United States of America, in the name of the good people of these colonies, solemnly declare that these United Colonies are, and ought to be, FREE AND INDEPENDENT STATES and that all political connections between them and Great Britain are ended. . . .

f Having declared independence, the colonists had to increase the size of their army. Posters were used to recruit soldiers.

To what values is this recruiting poster appealing?

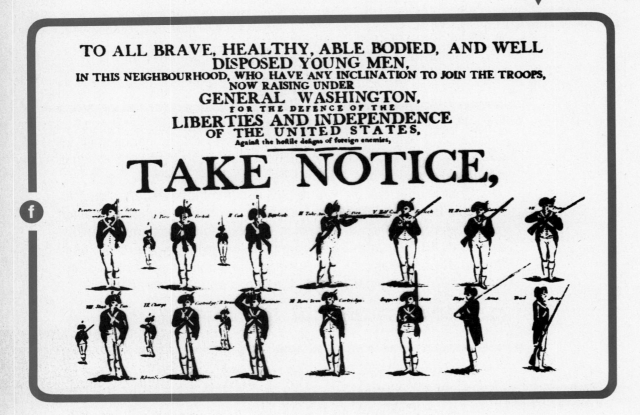

f

BRANCHING OUT

The Declaration of Independence says that under certain circumstances the people have a right to change the government or do away with it. Suppose the people in one section of the country decided that the United States government was interfering with their right to "life, liberty, and the pursuit of happiness." Do you think they ought to be allowed to declare their independence from the rest of the country? Organize a classroom debate or write a paper in which you argue one side of this question.

On a large sheet of paper, make a time line following these directions:

1. Divide the paper into two columns, labeling one "British Strategies" and the other "Colonial Strategies."
2. Beginning with events in 1765, list British and colonial strategies. Continue the list up to the date of the Declaration of Independence.
3. Next to times when emotions were especially aroused, place a star. Next to each star, list the value or values that were being threatened.

In your opinion:

1. Historians have sometimes disagreed over the most important causes of the American Revolution. What value conflicts do you think were most important?
2. Based on your knowledge of the situation, which group was legally more correct in their actions: the British officials, or the Americans who opposed the British? Give reasons for your opinions.
3. Do you think the war could have been prevented? Describe strategies that might have been used to prevent the war.

Loyalists

Not all Americans were in favor of rebellion against British rule. In fact, only about one third of all Americans solidly supported the leaders of the rebellion. Probably a little more than another one third were indifferent—they took no sides in the issue. The rest were loyal to British rule, although many of the Loyalists did not agree with everything the British officials had tried to do.

The two ruling parties in England at the time were the Whigs (who had often supported the Americans) and the Tories (who had opposed American causes). These terms came to be applied to the similar groups in America. So, those Americans loyal to British authority were called "Tories."

Tory opinions are suggested by the following excerpts from letters written by Tories in America in 1775.

You would hardly believe, without seeing it, the amount of political anger in this country. I greatly wish I was back at home in England, not among this dangerous mob of America. They claim they respect England, and want to remain joined with her. Believe me when I say that they are liars. They have been plotting to separate from Great Britain for many years now.

Nobody dares to doubt the words of the fanatics who are rebelling, unless he wishes to risk his life and property. We who doubt must keep our doubts to ourselves. If this is liberty, Good Lord deliver me from all such liberty!

If the government intends to do anything, they better do it quickly. Conceal my name, or I will be in danger of losing my life or my property.

Perhaps the whole history of empire does not give another example of forcible opposition to government with so little reason, and with such little chance of success.

Allegiance and protection should be exchanged. It is best for us to continue as a part of the British Empire and to remain under the authority of Parliament.

Many of the Loyalists took up arms to support their beliefs. About 50,000 fought in support of the British army during the Revolution. Tories were often persecuted by the American Whigs. Their property was taken away, those who refused to drink a toast of "destruction to the king" were given a coat of tar and feathers, and some were executed as traitors. Hard feelings after the war led about 80,000 Loyalists to move to Canada.

The decision to side with Whigs or Tories was not an easy one. Many who supported the rebels still had doubts about their cause. A soldier fighting in the American army wrote a poem which illustrated this problem. The poem can be read either of two ways, with two different messages.

I love with all my heart,	The Tory party here,
The Continental part,	Most Hatefull doth appear,
For their encouragement,	I rightly have denied,
My Conscience gives consent,	To be on King George's side.
Most righteous is the cause,	To fight for such a King,
To fight for nature's laws,	Would certain ruin bring,
This is my mind and heart,	In this opinion I,
Though none should take my part,	Resolve to live and Die.

Seven years of fighting followed the clash between Americans and British at Lexington and Concord. Neither side was strong enough to carry out a continuous attack. Washington was backed by a weak government, had no way to draft soldiers, and was very short of money. British General Gage had too few men, he was a long way from England, and the territory over which he had to fight was enormous.

For the British army, capturing and controlling any large part of American territory was out of the question. America's capital city could not be captured, for there was none. There were important American cities—Boston, New York, Philadelphia, and Charleston—but the colonies could survive without them. There was not even a seat of government, for Congress simply moved from one place to another if the British army got too close.

The colonists were in much the same position. Other than attacking the British army, there was no military strategy they could use which would particularly hurt the British.

The Revolutionary War, then, was mostly a story of pursuit, battle, and retreat. The map on page 132 summarizes these actions.

For the Americans, the key to success in the war was France's decision in 1778 to support the colonies. The French sent money, uniforms, soldiers, and a fleet of ships. In addition to French support, Polish and German officers aided General Washington.

The final major action of the war occurred in 1781. British General Cornwallis had moved his army to Yorktown, Virginia, on a peninsula. Washington's army, supported by French troops, bombarded Cornwallis day and night with cannon fire. With his escape by sea blocked by the French fleet, Cornwallis was forced to surrender. Minor fighting continued for several months, but Cornwallis's surrender ended major military action in the Revolutionary War. The peace treaty was signed in Paris in 1783.

BRANCHING OUT

Make a report on the life of someone who became famous during our nation's struggle for independence. Choose someone from the following list, or make your own selection. You've already read about some of the people on this list. Other names may be new to you.

Ethan Allen	Richard Henry Lee	Molly Pitcher
Crispus Attucks	Thaddeus Kosciusko	Betsy Ross
Benjamin Franklin	Marquis de Lafayette	Haym Solomon
Alexander Hamilton	George Mason	Baron von Stueben
Patrick Henry	Thomas Paine	George Washington

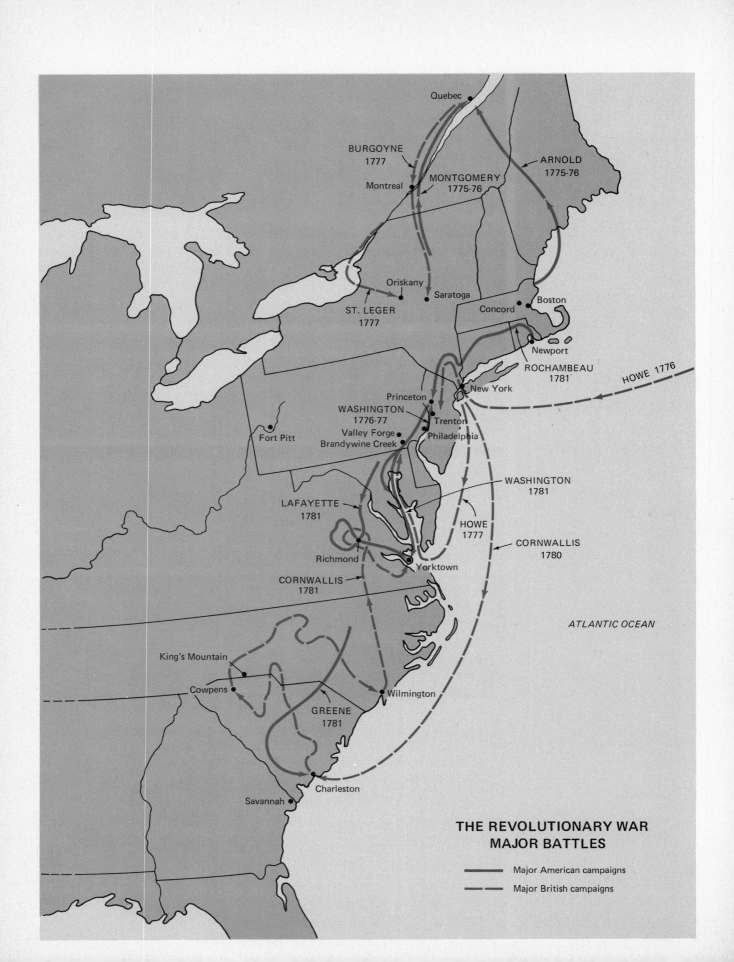

Quebec

BURGOYNE
1777

ARNOLD
1775-76

Montreal

MONTGOMERY
1775-76

Oriskany

Saratoga

Boston

Concord

ST. LEGER
1777

Newport

ROCHAMBEAU
1781

HOWE 1776

New York

Princeton

WASHINGTON
1776-77

Trenton

Valley Forge

Philadelphia

Fort Pitt

Brandywine Creek

WASHINGTON
1781

LAFAYETTE
1781

HOWE
1777

CORNWALLIS
1780

Richmond

Yorktown

CORNWALLIS
1781

ATLANTIC OCEAN

King's Mountain

Cowpens

Wilmington

GREENE
1781

Charleston

Savannah

THE REVOLUTIONARY WAR
MAJOR BATTLES

——— Major American campaigns

– – – Major British campaigns

Part 3

Establishing Government

After announcing the Declaration of Independence, the Continental Congress had begun work on a plan of government for the new nation. The plan, called the Articles of Confederation, went into effect in 1781 after all 13 states had approved it.

After the war, however, many Americans felt the need for changes in the national government. To discuss these changes, 55 delegates from 12 states met in Philadelphia in 1787. (Rhode Island did not take part.) After much discussion, these delegates wrote the Constitution, a new plan of government for the nation. Their meeting is called the Constitutional Convention. (A **constitution** is a system of laws by which a government or organization is run.)

The activities in Part 3 will help you investigate these questions:

What value conflicts existed among the founders of our government?

How were these value conflicts resolved in the Constitution of the United States?

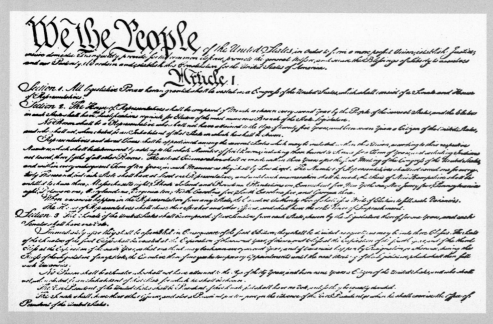

The Articles
of Confederation

When the colonies declared their independence from Britain, they became 13 independent states, called the United States of America. In claiming independence, they no longer recognized Britain's king as their ruler. Instead, each state now thought of itself as independent and free to govern itself. Each prepared its own state constitution and organized its state government. No national government existed officially for the nation until 1781, when the Articles of Confederation went into effect.

● Under the Articles of Confederation, the United States was to be governed by a single body called Congress. The diagram below shows the powers given to Congress. It also lists those powers not given to Congress.

After you study the diagram, answer these questions.
1. What values would explain why the states set up this form of government?
2. What problems might occur under this system of government?

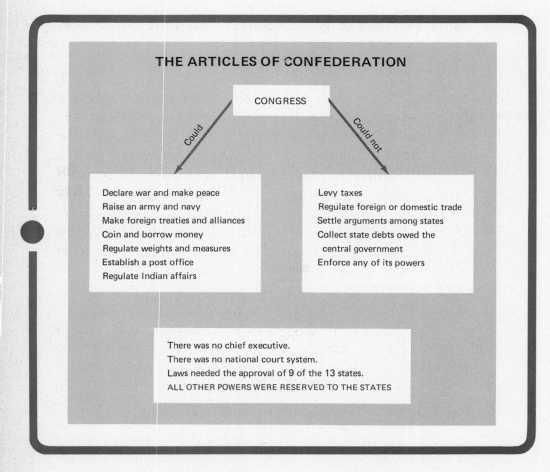

THE ARTICLES OF CONFEDERATION

CONGRESS

Could

Could not

Declare war and make peace
Raise an army and navy
Make foreign treaties and alliances
Coin and borrow money
Regulate weights and measures
Establish a post office
Regulate Indian affairs

Levy taxes
Regulate foreign or domestic trade
Settle arguments among states
Collect state debts owed the
  central government
Enforce any of its powers

There was no chief executive.
There was no national court system.
Laws needed the approval of 9 of the 13 states.
ALL OTHER POWERS WERE RESERVED TO THE STATES

Under the Articles of Confederation, where did most of the power in the government lie? How was this plan of government different from what you know about our national government today?

The Articles of Confederation did not provide a strong central, or national, government. Under the Articles, the government was a loose union among separate self-governing states. Each state regulated its own affairs and acted almost as an independent nation. For example, the central government, through Congress, could make laws, but there was no way to enforce the laws. Congress could ask the states for money to pay the expenses of government, but there was no way to force the states to pay.

The question "What kind of central government is best?" was the most important political problem faced by the new nation. The Articles had not set up a strong central government. A strong central government would mean that the states would give up certain powers to the central government.

As you study the opinions which follow,

1. Identify and list problems and advantages of strong central government.
2. Identify reasons in support of strong and less-strong central government.

a Alexander Hamilton, an important New York lawyer, wrote these ideas about government.

What problems did Hamilton predict if states were not governed the way he believed necessary?

a States which are close to each other must either be strongly united under one government, or else they will quarrel. This is human nature. In a few years, some of the larger states will be populous, rich, and powerful. Leaders within them will become ambitious. They will begin to think about separation and independence. Although it will always be to their advantage to preserve the Union, their conceit will probably be stronger. This will cause them to try to organize groups of states independently. Once this happens, differences over boundaries and competition for trade will provide plenty of excuses for going to war.

We already hear it whispered among those who oppose a stronger central government that the 13 states cover too much territory to be governed by one government. However, it seems obvious to me that if we do not strengthen the government, the Union will come apart.

If the powers of each state cannot be controlled, the powers of Congress will be defeated. There are times when acts necessary for the good of the whole nation will interfere with policies of individual states. It is too easy for the states to oppose whatever they do not like, and to form small alliances which work against larger union.

b George Washington expressed these thoughts in a letter several years before the Constitutional Convention was held.

The choice is ours. The United States can either be respectable and prosperous or worthless and miserable. We are on probation, and the rest of the world is watching. We can make the federal government strong enough to do what needs to be done. Or we can loosen the Union and become a toy of European politicians who will set states against each other to prevent any of them from becoming important.

What were Washington's views on central government? What reasons did he give for these views?

c The letter below was written to the governor of New York by two representatives to the Constitutional Convention.

We believe that a strong central government, regardless of how its constitution is worded, would very shortly begin to destroy the liberty of the citizens. The great size of the United States and the great distances separating the people, would make it almost impossible for those people to control the powerful men who hold offices in the central government.

These great distances, plus the fact that most officials would hold their positions permanently, would mean that concern for the welfare and happiness of the people would not be the same everywhere. It would also mean that obedience to the laws could not be enforced equally everywhere.

Finally, if the legislature of such a government had enough members to represent everyone, it would cost far too much to support it. If it were made up of fewer men, the interests of many citizens would be ignored.

How have modern transportation and communication affected the situation these writers feared?

d The following is from a pamphlet written by Richard Henry Lee.

Did Lee want to have a central government? What restrictions do you think he would place on that government?

d A central government which can impose and collect taxes on the people within a state, organize a militia within a state, and settle legal questions between two citizens of a state, has the means for eventually taking over almost all other power. Combined with the power to raise armies and build navies, this seems to me to include about all power. What is left to the individual states is not very important.

e A resident of Maryland wrote this in a letter to the *Maryland Gazette and Baltimore Advertiser.*

What views toward strong central government are expressed in this letter? If given a choice, would the letterwriter vote to have a central government?

e I don't doubt that a strong central government will add to the dignity and increase the splendor of the United States in other countries. I am not so sure however about the claim that a strong central government is necessary to keep us at peace with each other. I absolutely deny the claim that it is necessary in order to keep foreigners from dividing us.

We are vain, like other nations. We want to make a noise in the world. We want to cut a figure in history. Should we not consider the fact that happiness and quiet go together.

f The following selection is from a letter Samuel Adams wrote to Richard Henry Lee.

With whose views did Adams most closely agree?

f How can one central government make laws that are equally good for people who live so far apart in so many different environments, people whose habits and interests are so different? It is difficult, if not impossible. For this reason, the establishing of one strong central government will create unhappiness, distrust, suspicion of the government, and then revolt. This will make it necessary to keep a standing army.

If laws are made which consider local habits, feelings, and opinions in distant parts of the country, this favoritism will cause jealousy and envy which will also lead to war.

g This is the view of several representatives from Massachusetts.

g We must be careful that in strengthening the one or two weaknesses in Congress, we don't go to the other extreme. "More power in Congress" everyone seems to be saying. It is being said especially loudly by those who aren't interested in good government. These people want a big government that will pass out high-salaried jobs. They want to create a large bureaucracy. They would like a government which, once one gets on its payroll, would keep one secure for life.

What views did these Massachusetts representatives have toward those who supported strong central government? What reasons did they give to support their views?

Describe the value conflicts shown by the opinions you have read.

After considering views like these, the Constitutional Convention decided to set up a strong central government without completely taking away the states' powers to control their own affairs. This job was a difficult one. But after months of debate and compromise, a solution was worked out. The details of the solution are contained in the Constitution of the United States, which you will study in the next activity.

You've identified possible problems in the strength of central government. Which of these are problems today?

h Benjamin Franklin drew this cartoon during the conflict with Great Britain. It was often reprinted during the Constitutional debate.

Would this cartoon be used in support of strong central government?

What do the pieces of the snake represent?

h

JOIN, or DIE.

George Washington, Benjamin Franklin, Alexander Hamilton, James Madison, and the other political leaders who attended the Constitutional Convention agreed on many questions. All believed a stronger central government was necessary. Most felt the government should have three branches: **legislative** (Congress), **executive** (President), and **judicial** (United States courts). Each branch was to have separate powers. The leaders agreed to organize these branches so that each branch could check on the other branches and keep them from gaining too much power. This came to be called the system of **checks and balances.** In this way, the writers of the Constitution answered the question, "Who should have power?"

But the delegates to the convention didn't agree on all issues. In this activity you will read opinions on some of the important questions which were debated at the Convention. These opinions show some of the value differences among the delegates. Conflicts over these values were often heated, and emotions were strongly aroused.

For each question, choose the opinion you would have supported if you had been a delegate to the Constitutional Convention. Give reasons for your choices. If you think none of the opinions is the best answer to the problem, give and defend your own views.

Soon after the Constitutional Convention began, some of the members proposed a plan. According to the plan, the government was to be made up of three parts: (1) a Congress to make laws; (2) a president to enforce the laws; and (3) United States courts to see that justice was done.

Congress was to be divided into two houses, or sections. Soon, a major debate began over how many representatives each state should send to the houses of Congress.

ⓐ → ⓑ The opinions that follow reflect the two major views on this question. The chart shows the size of each state in 1787.

Should each state have equal representation in Congress? Or should the number of representatives from each state be based on the size of its population?

ⓐ **Wilson, from Pennsylvania:**
Since all political power comes from the people, equal numbers of people should have equal representation in Congress.

Paterson, from New Jersey:

Our present government is a confederacy. In a confederacy all members are equal. There is no more reason for a large state to have more votes in Congress than there is a reason for a rich man to have more votes than a poor one. . . .

New Jersey will never agree to give large states more power. She would be swallowed up.

According to Wilson's view, who would be entitled to more representatives in Congress —New Jersey or Pennsylvania?

Based on the chart, which states would be likely to agree with Paterson? Why? With Wilson? Why?

b

POPULATION AND LAND AREA 1787

STATE	POPULATION	AREA (in sq. mi.)
New Hampshire	141,885	9,304
Massachusetts	378,787	8,257
Rhode Island	68,825	1,214
Connecticut	237,946	5,009
New York	958,632	49,567
New Jersey	340,120	7,836
Pennsylvania	434,373	45,333
Delaware	59,096	2,057
Maryland	319,728	10,577
Virginia	747,610	64,996
North Carolina	393,751	52,712
South Carolina	249,073	31,055
Georgia	82,548	58,876

c By 1787 there were many more Negro slaves living in the South than in the North. An important debate came up over whether to count slaves as part of the population in order to figure out how many representatives a state could have in Congress.

If the number of representatives from each state is based on population, should slaves be counted in that population?

Paterson, from New Jersey:

Negro slaves are property. They have no personal freedom; they cannot enter into contracts; they cannot own property. They are themselves property and, like any other property, belong entirely to their owner. Property does not vote.

A legislature is merely a substitute—more convenient than getting all the people together. If all the people were gotten together, Negroes would not vote, so why should they be represented in Congress?

Why do you think the New Jersey representatives did not want Negroes to be counted? Why do you think the South Carolina representative wanted Negroes to be counted?

140

Butler, from South Carolina:

The main purpose of a government is to protect property. Property is the main support of government. Since the work of a slave can increase the value of property as well as the work of a freeman, the slave and the freeman are of equal value to property and should have equal representation.

Do you agree with Butler's view on the main purpose of government? Why or why not?

d An **executive** is a person whose job it is to manage the affairs of the nation, business, or organization to which he or she is responsible. Sometimes several people hold the office of executive. Delegates to the Constitutional Convention decided to have a chief executive called a president. The question below was only one of several questions about the chief executive.

How many chief executives should there be?

d

Rutledge, from South Carolina:

The executive should be a single person. He will then feel the greatest responsibility for administering public affairs well.

Sherman, from Connecticut:

The purpose of executives is to carry out the will of Congress. Since Congress will be in the best position to know what is necessary, no specific number should be set. From time to time Congress can decide how many are needed.

Randolph, from Virginia:

What is needed in the executive department is energy, speed, and responsibility. I do not see why these qualities could not be found in three as well as one man. The executive should be independent. That is all the more reason why the office should be made up of three men.

e → g The data that follows involves discussion of what role the people should play in choosing representatives to their central government. The discussions centered on the basic question, "How much democracy should the new government provide?" As you read the opinions, keep in mind that in 1787 few nations allowed their people as direct a say in government as some of the Convention delegates wished to provide.

Democracy is a government in which the people hold the ruling power, either directly or through elected representatives.

Who should choose members of the House of Representatives?

Sherman, from Connecticut:

The legislature in each state should elect that state's representatives. The ordinary people lack information and are likely to be misled.

Mason, from Virginia:

This house of the legislature should be democratic. It should be familiar with every feeling and idea in the country. It should serve the needs of every class of people. Therefore, the people should choose their representatives. The upper classes often ignore the needs of others, but they should support this idea because some of their descendents will probably end up in the lowest classes of society.

What value conflict is shown in these two opinions?

Who should choose senators?

Wilson, from Pennsylvania:

A national government should be created by all the people. If the lower house is elected by the people and the upper by state legislatures, arguments will naturally arise between them. The Senate should be elected by the people.

Morris, from Pennsylvania:

Appointment by state legislatures is the better method. The Senate must serve as a control on the House of Representatives, so they should be unlike them. They should be rich, independent, full of pride, and serve for life. With this system the two houses will watch each other very carefully.

What kind of relationship did Morris think should exist between the two houses of Congress? Do you think Wilson had the same view? Why?

Who should choose the chief executive?

Morris, from Pennsylvania:

I am against an executive chosen by Congress. He will be little more than a puppet of Congress, and will gain his office by secret bargaining.

Pinkney, from South Carolina:

Election by the general population is obviously wrong. They will be led by a few influential men. Besides, a few heavily populated states could combine and choose their own man. Congress knows its own laws best, so they should choose whom they want to carry them out.

What other ways are there to choose the chief executive besides election by the people or by Congress?

h At the Constitutional Convention, Benjamin Franklin presented his views on paying a salary to the chief executive. Although the other delegates did not agree with Franklin, they listened respectfully to his views. They did not debate the issues he raised.

Should the chief executive receive a salary?

What kind of person might be likely to seek office under Franklin's plan?

Do you agree with Franklin's views. Explain.

Franklin, from Pennsylvania:

I move that the executive's necessary expenses be paid, but that he receive no salary, fee, or reward whatever.

Men are driven by a love of power and a love of money. Separately, these drive men to action. Add them together and the effect is violent. Place before a man a post both honorable and profitable and he will move heaven and earth to get it.

What kind of men are attracted to such positions? Not the wise, not the moderate, not the lovers of peace and order. The bold, the violent and the selfish will become the rulers.

An unpaid executive is also less likely to become a king, and this protection is needed. There is a human tendency toward kingly government. Citizens will often turn to it to avoid rule by an upper class. They would rather have one dictator than five hundred. It makes them feel more equal.

i The next question was a particularly important one. The answer to it determined how democratic the new system was to be.

Who should be allowed to vote?

At that time in England and other European countries, only landowners were allowed to vote.

What value conflict is reflected in these two opinions?

Morris, from Pennsylvania:

The vote should be confined to those who own land. Give it to those who have no property, and they will sell it to the rich. The time will come when this country will be filled with people working for wages. Will they be faithful guardians of liberty? Not likely. As for merchants, if they have money and value the right to vote, let them buy land.

Mason, from Virginia:

We are borrowing old prejudices from England. In my opinion, any man who is attached to and affected by the government ought to have the vote. Are landowners the only ones who meet this qualification? Ought we to consider the merchants or the father of several children or others whose fortunes lie in this country as suspicious characters who can't be trusted with privileges their neighbors have?

143

Answers to the questions raised at the Constitutional Convention were settled after four months of debate. As you know, the new written plan of government which the delegates developed came to be known as the Constitution of the United States.

● A simplified version of the Constitution is presented on pages 144-150.

The original words of the Constitution appear on pages 518-527.

As you read the Constitution, identify the solution to each value conflict you have read about in the previous activity.

Preamble

We, the people of these United States, do now accept and adopt this Constitution for the United States of America. Its purpose is to establish justice, strengthen the bonds between our states, strengthen our defenses, improve our condition, and guarantee liberty to ourselves and our descendents.

*A **preamble** is an introduction.*

Article I Legislative Branch

Section 1 Congress

All the power to make laws is given to a Congress made up of a Senate and a House of Representatives.

__Legislative__ means lawmaking.

Section 2 House of Representatives

a. The House of Representatives will be made up of members chosen every two years by a vote of the people. In each state, voters will be those who are already allowed to vote in state elections.

b. Representatives must be at least 25 years old and citizens of the United States. They must live in the State in which they are elected.

c. The number of Representatives from a state will be based on the size of the population from that state. Indians not taxed will not be counted, and a slave will be counted as three fifths of a person.

d. In case of a vacancy, a special state election will be held.

e. Members of the House of Representatives will choose their own officers. Also, they alone will have the power of impeachment.

Amendment 13 prohibits slavery. Amendment 14 gave full citizenship rights to black Americans and did away with the three-fifths provision. Indian Americans have also been given full citizenship rights.

*The power of **impeachment** is the power—granted only to the House of Representatives—to bring accusations against federal officials that they have not properly carried out their duties.*

Section 3 Senate

Amendment 17 provides for the election of senators by the people.

Amendment 17 provides for elections to be held when vacancies occur. If the state legislature directs, the governor can make a temporary appointment until an election is held.

a. The Senate of the United States will be made up of two Senators from each state. They will be chosen by their state legislatures. Senators will be elected to six-year terms.

b. One third of the Senate will be chosen every two years. When a vacancy occurs, the state legislature will choose someone to fill the vacancy. If the legislature is in recess, the state governor can appoint someone to serve temporarily.

c. Senators must be at least 30 years old and citizens of the United States. They must live in the state in which they are elected.

d. The Vice President of the United States shall be president of the Senate. He shall vote only in case of a tie.

e. Senators shall choose all Senate officers except the president of the Senate.

Section 2e states that the House of Representatives presents charges against officials. The Senate conducts the impeachment trial.

To be **convicted** is to be declared guilty.

f. The Senate will try any federal official who is impeached. The Chief Justice (of the Supreme Court) will preside. Conviction will require agreement by two thirds of those present.

g. Individuals who are impeached and convicted may be removed from office and are disqualified from holding other offices under the United States. Convicted individuals are subject to trial and punishment under the law.

Section 4 Rules for Both Houses

a. Election procedures for members of Congress will be decided by each state.

b. Congress shall meet at least once a year.

Section 5 Rules for Each House

a. In case of an election challenge, the House and the Senate will judge the election and qualification of their own members. A majority of each is necessary to do business.

b. Each House will determine its own procedures.

c. Each House will keep and publish a record of its proceedings.

To **adjourn** is to close or put off a meeting until a later time.

d. Neither House may adjourn for more than three days without the consent of the other.

Section 6 Privileges and Restrictions

   a. Senators and Representatives shall be paid for their services. They cannot be arrested while Congress is in session, nor be questioned outside Congress for speeches made there.
   b. No Senator or Representative shall be appointed to any civil office while serving in Congress.

*A **civil office** is a nonmilitary government office.*

Section 7 Method of Passing Laws

   a. All tax bills must come from the House of Representatives.
   b. Every bill passed by the House and Senate must be signed by the President. If he refuses, and the bill is reconsidered and approved by two thirds of each House, it will become law.
   c. All orders and resolutions requiring approval by the House and Senate shall also require approval by the President.

*A **bill** is a written statement of a proposed law.*

*A **resolution** is a statement of rule or opinion adopted by an assembly or other large group.*

Section 8 Powers Granted to Congress

Congress can
   a. Set and collect taxes
   b. Borrow money
   c. Regulate foreign and interstate trade
   d. Pass naturalization and bankruptcy laws
   e. Coin money
   f. Punish those who counterfeit United States money
   g. Establish a postal service
   h. Issue patents and copyrights
   i. Establish courts lower in rank than the Supreme Court
   j. Punish crimes committed at sea
   k. Declare war
   l. Maintain an army
   m. Maintain a navy
   n. Regulate the army and navy
   o. Call out a state's militia
   p. Share with the states control of the militia
   q. Make laws for the District of Columbia
   r. Make any laws necessary to do any of the above

***Interstate** means between or among the states. **Naturalization** is the process by which a foreign-born person becomes a citizen. **Bankruptcy** is the situation in which businesses or people are unable to pay their debts. Property is sold to meet these debts.*

*To **counterfeit** is to make coins and paper bills in imitation of official United States money.*

***Patents** and **copyrights** are documents which grant to inventors and authors, for a limited time, the exclusive rights to their materials.*

Section 9 Powers Denied the National Government

a. Congress may not prohibit the states from importing any person (in other words, slave) they desire until the year 1808.

b. No one can be held or imprisoned without charges being brought, unless when during rebellion or invasion the public safety requires it.

c. No one person shall be declared guilty of a crime by action of Congress. No one can be guilty for an action which was made a crime after the action was done.

d. Direct taxes will be in proportion to the population.

e. No taxes will be placed on articles exported from one state to another.

f. The ports in every state will be treated equally, and states shall not require ships from another state to pay duties.

g. Money from the treasury can be taken out only by law. Treasury records shall be published.

h. The United States will not give out titles of nobility. No federal officeholder can accept any kind of gift from another country unless Congress approves.

Amendment 16 gives Congress the power to collect taxes on personal income.

*A **title of nobility** is a title such as count, baron, or duke.*

Section 10 Powers Denied the States

States shall not

a. Make treaties

b. Coin money

c. Pass laws declaring specific individuals guilty of crimes

d. Try individuals for actions that were declared crimes after the action was done

e. Grant titles of nobility.

f. Charge duties except to cover the cost of necessary inspections.

g. Have armies or navies in peacetime and shall not make military agreements with other states or countries. They will not make war unless actually invaded or are in such danger that they cannot delay.

Article II Executive Branch

Section 1 President and Vice President

*An **executive** has the power to see that laws and duties are carried out.*

a. The President will be the executive officer of the United

States. He and the Vice President shall be elected to four-year terms.

b. Each state will appoint electors to meet in the State to vote for President and Vice President. The number of electors from each state shall equal the state's number of Senators and Representatives. Each elector will vote for two people. Their votes shall be sealed and sent to the President of the Senate. The person having the most votes shall be President. In a tie, the House of Representatives will decide. The person having the second highest number of votes will be Vice President.

c. Congress will set the day for the electors to vote.

d. To be eligible for the office of President, a person must be a natural-born citizen of the United States, at least 35 years old, and have lived in the United States at least 14 years.

e. If the President is removed, dies, resigns, or is unable to fulfill his responsibilities, the Vice President will serve as Chief Executive. If neither can serve, Congress will appoint a President to finish the term.

f. The President will be paid for his services, but his salary may not be changed while he is in office.

g. Before entering office, an elected President must take this oath: "I do solemnly swear that I will faithfully execute the office of President of the United States, and will, to the best of my ability, preserve, protect and defend the Constitution of the United States."

Section 2 Powers of the President

a. The President shall be the Commander in Chief of the armed forces. He can require written reports from the heads of the executive departments. He can grant pardons for offenses against the United States.

b. The President can, with Senate approval, make treaties, appoint ambassadors and Supreme Court judges, and fill other positions established by law.

c. The President can fill all vacancies that occur when the Senate is not in session.

Section 3 Duties of the President

The President shall make regular reports to Congress on the State of the Union, shall recommend to them laws that he thinks

Electors are expected to vote for the candidates selected by the popular vote in their state.

Amendment 12 requires electors to cast separate votes for President and Vice President.

A *natural-born citizen* is one who is born in this country or born to American citizens who are living outside the country.

The *executive departments* are the departments in the president's cabinet (State Department, Defense Department, etc.).

To *pardon* is to release a person from punishment for a crime.

An *ambassador* is the highest ranking official representative appointed by one country to represent it in another.

should be passed, and can call them into special session. He shall faithfully enforce the laws of the United States.

Section 4 Impeachment

Any officer of the United States shall be removed from office if impeached and convicted of treason, bribery, or other crimes.

Article III Judicial Branch

Section 1 Federal Courts

Judicial matters shall be in the hands of a Supreme Court and other federal courts created by Congress. Judges shall hold office during their good behavior. They shall be paid.

Section 2 Authority of the Federal Courts

a. Federal courts will handle all legal questions arising under this Constitution and under federal laws. Controversies between two or more states and between a state and citizens of another state will be handled by federal courts.

b. Cases affecting ambassadors, ministers and consuls, and those in which a state is a party, will go directly to the Supreme Court. In all other cases under its authority, the Supreme Court will have power to review the actions of lower courts.

c. All crimes (except in cases of impeachment) shall be tried by jury and the trial shall be held in the state where the crime was committed.

Section 3 Treason

a. "Treason" means only "making war against the United States" or "supporting the enemy."

b. Congress shall declare the punishment for treason.

Article IV The States

Section 1 Official Acts

The official acts of each state shall be honored in all other states.

Treason is defined in Article III, Section 3A.

Judicial means administering justice.

Federal refers to the central government of the United States.

Amendment 11 prevents United States courts from trying cases between a state and citizens of another state.

Ministers and *consuls* are official representatives of the United States to other countries.

Lower courts are courts lower in rank than the Supreme Court.

Expanded by Amendments 5, 6, and 7.

Section 2 Privileges of Citizens

 a. The citizens in each of the states shall have the same rights.
 b. Persons charged with crimes who flee to another state shall be returned.
 c. Persons who owe others their labor and flee to another state shall be returned.

Section 3 New States and Territories

 a. New states may be admitted to the Union by Congress.
 b. Congress shall control all United States territory and property.

Section 4 Guarantees to the States

Congress guarantees to every state a republican form of government, and shall protect them against invasion. If asked by a state, Congress will also provide protection against internal violence.

*A **republican form of government** is a government in which the power rests in the citizens entitled to vote and is exercised by elected representatives.*

Article V Method of Amendment

This Constitution can be amended in this way: Two thirds of the Senate and of the House of Representatives can propose changes, or two thirds of the states can request that a convention meet to make changes. Changes from either of these two sources become a part of this Constitution when they have been approved by three fourths of the States.

*To **amend** is to change; an **amendment** is a change.*

Article VI General Provisions

 a. Debts owed by the Confederation will remain unchanged under this Constitution.
 b. This Constitution shall be the highest law of the land.
 c. All State and federal officers must swear to uphold this Constitution. No officeholder shall ever be required to pass a religious test.

Article VII Ratification

This Constitution will go into effect when it has been ratified by nine States.

***Ratify** means to give approval to.*

What checks and balances are there in the Constitution to make sure that power isn't abused? Remember that *checks and balances* is the system by which each branch of government has certain powers which allow it to *check* on the powers of the other two branches. The result is a *balance* of government.

Now, draw a diagram showing the relationship of the three branches of government to one another. In your diagram, show how the system of checks and balances works. Also, describe some of the important powers of each branch.

The Bill of Rights

The Constitutional Convention had decided that the Constitution would go into effect after nine of the thirteen states had ratified it. For several months, there were more critics than supporters, and the fate of the Constitution was in doubt.

One major argument against the Constitution was that it did not guarantee certain rights. Many people wanted laws guaranteeing specific rights to every citizen and insisted that these be made a part of the Constitution. With the promise that a bill, or list, of rights would be written and with much effort on the part of the men who had been at the Constitutional Convention, the Constitution was ratified by the states. It went into effect in 1787.

a This cartoon supported ratification of the Constitution. Its caption is "A House Divided Against Itself Cannot Stand."

In this cartoon Connecticut is being "pulled apart" by financial problems. Among these were heavy import duties paid on Connecticut goods sold in New York. How would this problem be solved by ratification of the Constitution?

▶

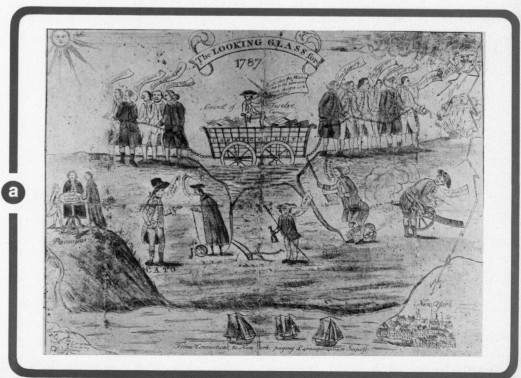

151

b A simplified version of the Bill of Rights appears below. The rights are presented in the form of amendments to the Constitution. The Bill of Rights contains ten amendments which were passed by Congress in 1789. They were ratified by the states in 1791. Since then, 16 additional amendments have been added to the Constitution.

As you study the Bill of Rights, identify the values which the amendments express.

The Bill of Rights in its original words and the additional 16 amendments appear on pages 526-527.

Amendment 1

Congress will make no laws that interfere with religion. It will make no laws that prohibit freedom of speech or of the press. It will make no laws that prevent people from gathering peaceably to ask the government to correct wrongs.

Amendment 2

Because a well-regulated military force of citizens is necessary to make a state secure, the people shall have the right to keep and carry arms.

__Arms__ are weapons.

Amendment 3

In peacetime, no soldier shall stay in any house without the owner's permission. The rule applies in time of war also, except as changed by Congress.

Amendment 4

Persons, houses, papers, and property may not be unreasonably searched or seized. Before a search warrant is issued, an oath must be taken that the reason is a good one. It must specifically describe the place to be searched or the persons or things to be seized.

A __warrant__ is a document issued by a court, giving authority, in this case, for a search.

Amendment 5

To be held for a serious crime, a person must be accused in writing by a group of citizens (a grand jury) which has examined the evidence. Military cases in wartime are an exception.

No person shall be tried twice for the same offense, or be forced to testify against himself. No person can have his life, liberty, or property taken away except through proper legal procedures. Private property taken for public use must be paid for at a fair price.

Amendment 6

In criminal cases, the accused has a right to a speedy, public trial. An impartial jury shall be chosen from the area where the crime was committed. The accused must be told the reasons why he or she is accused and must be allowed to meet the accusers. The accused must also have the power to obtain witnesses and have legal help in his or her defense.

Impartial means without prejudice.

Amendment 7

In suits involving values of more than 20 dollars, individuals have a right to a jury trial.

Amendment 8

Excessive bail will not be required. Excessive fines will not be required, nor will cruel and unusual punishment be given.

Excessive means too much or too great.

Bail is money or property deposited to guarantee that an accused person will be at his or her trial.

Amendment 9

The listing in this Constitution of specific rights does not mean that other specific rights are taken away or changed.

Amendment 10

Powers not given to the United States by this Constitution are to be kept by the states or by the people.

Putting the Pieces Together

Use all of the material in Part 3 to answer these questions.

1. What values were shared by delegates to the Constitutional Convention?
2. What were some major value conflicts which appeared in the process of writing the Constitution?
3. What methods seem to have been used to resolve these value conflicts?
4. How were they different from the strategies used against the British? Why do you think this was done?

Application

The material that you've just read might make you think there were more value conflicts than usual during the Revolutionary period. In fact, this is not true. Although those value conflicts were very important to future Americans, there were many fewer value conflicts in America then than now. This is true mainly because there were fewer "interest" groups at that time. There were no large corporations, no labor unions, no organized political parties, no great differences in social class. As America has become larger and more complex, the number of groups with special interests to protect has multiplied. Because each group works for its own goals, the number of value conflicts has increased greatly.

Some people feel this is unfortunate; but in a healthy, growing society, value conflicts are inevitable. They cause problems, but they can be useful, too. Value conflicts make us aware of social problems. They also help acquaint us with differing values and give us a kind of storehouse from which we can choose those values we think best. In recent years, for example, value conflicts have helped create important new attitudes toward war, the environment, and minority groups.

Most value conflicts have a life cycle. They begin when someone calls attention to a situation or condition—often one that is different or unfair for some part of society. The situation may have existed for a long time but gone unnoticed. The problem begins to be talked about. People take sides. Little by little, most people begin to support a particular point of view. Laws are passed to support or enforce that opinion. Finally, the conflict fades away. The whole process might take a few months or many, many years.

When an issue comes out into the open, people begin to think about it more. They talk about it and read about it. They learn other people's ideas on the subject, which may change their own ideas. In a public value conflict—like discussion of the Vietnam war—people tend to choose sides on the issue. So, getting an issue into the open helps us decide what we believe. This affects our actions, for if our ideas are unclear, our actions tend to be uncertain and unpredictable.

a → c Here are descriptions of three different issues, or questions, about which a person could have to make a decision. Although these are important issues, they are not now public value conflicts. There is not a public controversy or debate over which side, which values, are the best.

Read each of the value problems that follow. Identify the values involved in the problem and decide how you would act in the situation.

Who should be responsible for maintaining order in a society?

a You are a private citizen. Returning to your car late one night, you see another car backed into a blind alley beside a small appliance store. In the dim light, you can see a smashed window, and the last of several boxes being loaded into a car by a young man. You know that by endangering your car but not yourself, you could block the alley and run to a nearby police station.

Do you drive away, taking the position that maintaining order in society is the responsibility of the police? **OR** Do you block the alley, taking the position that maintaining order in society is everyone's responsibility?

Does an elected representative have a greater responsibility to the people or to his or her own ideas of what is right?

b You are a member of a city council, an elected representative of the people. The city's sewage-disposal plant is old, and the harmful-bacteria count in water being dumped into the river near your town is at a dangerous level. You are sure that the least-expensive time to build a new plant is now, but a majority of the residents are opposed to new taxes.

Do you do what the people who elected you want you to do—vote against a new plant and new taxes? **OR** Do you do what seems to be best for the people you've been elected to represent—vote for a new plant and new taxes?

To what degree is a person responsible to a superior?

c You are a corporal in the army, working overseas. Your job is keeping track of gasoline and diesel fuel needs for your unit. Your commanding officer, whom you think has been selling fuel to a civilian dealer, tells you to add to your monthly fuel request 10,000 gallons over the amount actually used.

As a member of the armed forces, do you obey the orders of your superior officer, as you have sworn to do? **OR** Do you refuse to falsify your monthly report?

If these three value issues became the subject of general public debate, what positions do you think the majority of Americans would take?

d Each of these pictures shows value conflict.

Write a statement of the conflict. Then write a description of the situation and the alternatives of action. As your model, use the three descriptions you have just studied.

d

BIBLIOGRAPHY

Hirsch, S. Carl. *Famous American Revolutionary War Heroes.* Chicago: Rand McNally, 1974. The author considers the major reasons and the strong feelings which inspired heroes such as George Washington, Nathan Hale, and Abigail Adams.

Forbes, Esther. *Johnny Tremain.* Boston: Houghton Mifflin, 1943. Fiction. A popular and exciting story about the years 1773-75 when the city of Boston was the center of revolutionary activity. Johnny is a 14-year-old apprentice who becomes a dispatch rider and takes part in the Battle of Lexington.

Leckie, Robert. *The World Turned Upside Down.* N.Y.: G. P. Putnam's, 1973. This book about the Revolution focuses on the men who shaped the victory against the powerful British army.

Taylor, Theodore. *Rebellion Town, Williamsburg, 1776.* N.Y.: T. Y. Crowell, 1973. A lively account of the independence movement in Virginia and the drafting of Virginia's Declaration of Rights and the Constitution. Patrick Henry, James Madison, and George Mason are the leading figures in these events.

Hayman, Le Roy. *What You Should Know About the U.S. Constitution and the Men Who Wrote It.* N.Y.: Four Winds Press, 1966. The story of the Constitutional Convention with capsule biographies of the leading figures who attended. Also included is the Constitution with helpful commentary about its contents.

157

North, South, West

Cultural Differences

How do shared experiences affect ideas and ways of acting?

Introduction

The families in your community may be similar in many ways. But you've probably learned by now that the ideas and ways of acting of other families are not *exactly* like those of your own family. In fact, families in the next town, "down South," "up North," or "out West" may think and act somewhat differently than your family does.

Why do families differ from one another? They differ for the same reason individuals differ—mostly, because their experiences have been different. Events and conditions of living affect people in many important ways. The house and town in which you live, the friends you have, the amount of money you have, the school or job you go to, the things that have scared or pleased you—all of these experiences make you think and act in certain ways. When many people in a society have shared similar experiences, they usually share ideas and ways of acting. These shared ideas and ways of acting form a society's **culture.**

In this unit you'll examine the ways in which experiences have affected your own ideas and ways of acting. And you'll look at the ways in which shared experiences have affected sections of the United States in the past and American society today.

160

The Effects of Experiences

Ideas and ways of acting often can be traced back to earlier experiences. One way of showing this is in the following diagram.

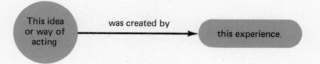

This idea or way of acting —— was created by ——> this experience.

a Here are three ways of thinking and acting.

For each, describe one or more experiences which could explain why someone might think or act in this way.

> **a**
> 1. Being neat. Keeping everything in its place.
> 2. Wishing that things were "like the good old days."
> 3. Believing that it's important to have lots of friends.

b Now let's reverse the situation. These two photographs show situations which could have lasting effects on a person.

Describe some ideas, feelings, or ways of acting that could result from each experience, especially if it occurs often. Think of each situation in terms of this diagram.

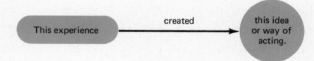

This experience —— created ——> this idea or way of acting.

b

161

Outward Bound

In 1941 a British educator named Kurt Hahn set up a training program for British young people. He called it "Outward Bound." In his Outward Bound courses, Hahn took the young people on expeditions into the wilderness. Although the course he created took only a few weeks to complete, it was a very challenging program. In it, a person was put into new and difficult situations and was required to deal successfully with these situations.

In 1962 an Outward Bound school opened in Colorado. Since then several more schools have opened in the United States, each in an isolated mountain, desert, or coastal area.

● Below is an account written by a student who completed an Outward Bound "Standard Course."

How could the experiences described have changed a person's ways of acting and thinking?

"Up! Up! Everybody up!" The instructor's voice leaves no doubt about what to do and when to do it.

Dawn filters through the forest and ends in a sunny patch on your dark blue sleeping bag. Crawl out . . . stand up . . . shiver into shorts and sneakers.

"Follow me!" The instructor's voice—self-assured, enthusiastic—orders you again. He's running, his feet are scarcely heard on the pine-needled forest floor. You and your ten companions follow, your chests heaving with the pace, the warmth of the activity making up for the cold air. Who are these strangers in your group? How will you get along with them?

Suddenly the instructor stops at the edge of a stream. He yanks off his sneakers and plunges ungracefully in.

You hesitate on the banks.

"Everybody in! Quick! Before you cool off!"

You wade, stumble on a rock, fall forward. Instinctively you plant your feet on the bottom, surface, and holler. Your yell rings through the forest, and another shiver, this one violent and magnificent, runs the length of your body.

You have begun your first day at Outward Bound.

Breakfast is over, gear divided. Your pack weighs 40 pounds or more and you wobble under it, up, up, up a steep and rocky trail. Mosquitoes ignore your generous coating of bug dope. Between swats you sop the sweat from your forehead.

There are three or four weeks of this ahead and you wonder whatever made you sign up for Outward Bound.

A few days go by: sun, rain, wind, bone-chilling cold, muggy heat, meadows of wildflowers, mud, sand, cinders, blisters, more bugs, sails, oars, paddles, lifejackets, hardhats, climbing ropes. Wilderness life is becoming almost comfortable. Your instructor can tell. So he announces that it's time to rappel.

The instructor's matter-of-fact voice is confident: "A rappel is a controlled descent by rope down a vertical rock face."

It's 100 feet from here to there, straight down. Your heart beats big and hollow, as if through a stethoscope. The sweat of fear drenches your body and it takes all your concentration to control your shaking hands.

You lean back. Two tentative, vertical steps and the faces of your instructor and your companions are gone. On the other end of those ropes is your belayer, one of the folks who was a stranger a week ago. Now your life depends on him.

You know he's up there, above the cliff, but the whole real world consists right now of you and the rock. Down, down, slowly tiptoeing against the rock, leaning back, until at last you touch the bottom.

You can feel your smile spread and your voice is clear as you shout upward, "Off belay! Off rappel!"

The days go on. Night hikes. Ecology. Bivouacs. Re-supply. Service projects. The Marathon. For Final Expedition your group is divided for the first time since the course began. It makes you feel like something's missing.

Then Solo, the mystery that causes more wondering than all the rest of Outward Bound. It's not a survival experience in the physical sense. But for most people Solo—with only clothing, basic shelter, a minimum of food—is their first absolute solitude.

Your instructor outlines your boundaries of a few hundred yards. Don't wander. Build a shelter. I'll check on you daily and be back for you in about three days.

Suddenly he's gone. You feel you must do something. Build your shelter, explore your territory. It all takes maybe an hour, but you aren't sure. Your instructor has taken your watch.

A breeze makes the lake lap at the shore, and fat, black tadpoles wiggle in the shallows. At last the sun drops behind a hill and you pull on your parka and try to sleep.

All night you doze, waking with cold and hunching down in your bag. Finally the stars and half-moon are gone. The sun isn't up, but morning is as good as here. The longest night of your life has ended.

In your opinion, how might an Outward Bound experience affect a person's feelings about the following? Explain.

1. Self-confidence
2. Personal problems
3. Others in the group
4. Ways of working
5. Desire to hide feelings from others
6. Nature
7. Feelings that one is inferior or superior to others

STOP & SUMMARIZE

Some experiences will affect ideas and action more than others. Those that a person has over and over again probably affect his or her life more than a single experience. However, something like Outward Bound or winning an important award can have a powerful affect on a person's life.

Based on your own life or the life of someone you know, describe an experience (or experiences) and a way of acting or thinking which seem to be related.

Perspective

Today, modern methods of transportation and communication make it possible for millions of Americans to share the same experiences. Network television takes into American homes the same news, jokes, clothing styles, habits of speech, and the same commercials for the same products. Marketing techniques make it possible to release the same books, films, and records all over the United States at the same time. Automobiles, trains, and airplanes carry Americans from every state into every other state. People all over the country can see many of the same sights, eat the same foods, and sleep in motels that look just about the same in Maine, Montana, and New Mexico.

This development is fairly recent. Until the second half of the 1800s, transportation and communication among the regions of the United States were very slow. Separated by hundreds or even thousands of miles, Americans in the Northeast, the South, and the West had somewhat different experiences. And so they had somewhat different ideas, attitudes, values, and ways of acting. These cultural differences help explain some of the events and problems Americans faced in the 1800s. In the material that follows you will learn about experiences which affected people in the northeastern, southern, and western regions from 1800 to 1850.

Part 1   The Northeast
How did the experiences shared by people in the Northeast affect their ideas and ways of acting?

Part 2   The South
How did the experiences shared by people in the South affect their ideas and ways of acting?

Part 3   The West
How did the experiences shared by people in the West affect their ideas and ways of acting?

Part 4   Comparing Regions
How can different experiences lead to different ideas and ways of acting?

1790
Slater builds first textile mill in U.S.

1793
Whitney invents cotton gin

1803
Louisiana Purchase

1804
Lewis and Clark explore Louisiana territory

1807
Fulton's *Clermont* steams up the Hudson

1808
Slave trade banned by Constitution

1811
National Road begun

1814
War of 1812 ends

1819
U.S. purchases Florida

1823
Monroe Doctrine

1825
Erie Canal opens

1831
McCormick invents reaper

1836
Morse invents telegraph

1845
U.S. annexes Texas

1846
War with Mexico ● Oregon Treaty with Britain

1848
Gold found in California ● Mexican Cession

1853
Gadsden Purchase

Part 1

The Northeast

The material in Part 1 will tell you about the northeastern region of the United States in the period from 1800 to 1850. In this region were New York, New Jersey, Pennsylvania, and the states of New England, including Maine. (Maine, which had been part of Massachusetts, became a separate state in 1820.)

From the data, you'll be able to identify patterns in the way people lived, worked, and governed themselves. You'll then have information to answer this question:

How did the experiences shared by people in the Northeast affect their ideas and ways of acting?

What was the northeastern part of the United States like during the first half of the 1800s? The reports of residents, notes of travelers, pictures, and government records can give you a good general picture of this region.

Below are four different areas to investigate in this activity. To keep your job simple and your thoughts organized, work in the following manner: After you study each selection, turn back to the four categories below. For each category, decide whether or not the selection gives information. Then make notes on the information, which will help you summarize the Northeast when you've studied all the material in this activity.

1. Decide how the population was generally distributed within the region (For example, answer "Most people lived in large cities," or "The population was spread fairly evenly throughout the region.")

2. Decide what social classes there seemed to be, and how large each class was in comparison to the others. (For example, "Most people were poor, so there was a large lower class.")

3. Decide how people earned a living. (For example, "Most people were farmers.")

4. Identify the region's important social organizations, if any. **Social organizations** are organized groups such as schools, churches, and clubs. (For example, "Schools were important.")

a Timothy Dwight, a Congregationalist minister and President of Yale University, was a leading citizen of New England. He traveled throughout the Northeast in the early 1800s. Dwight wrote his impressions of the region in the form of letters which he kept in notebooks. The selections below come from those notebooks.

a

Dear Sir,

I will mention some facts concerning the state in which I live.

Connecticut is divided into eight counties and 119 towns.

Every community in Connecticut has its church. Connecticut contains 216 Presbyterian or Congregational, 9 Independent, 61 Episcopal, and 67 Baptist congregations. In addition to these, there are a few Methodists scattered over the state.

There is a schoolhouse near enough to every man's door in this state to allow his children to go conveniently to school throughout most of the year. The number of schoolhouses cannot be determined. In the community of Greenfield, containing a little more than 14 square miles and 1,440 people in the year 1790, there were eight schools, besides an academy.

Children who live at a distance from school are usually not sent until after they are four years of age. Those who are near are frequently sent at two, and generally at three. A considerable number of boys, after they have arrived at eight, nine, or ten years of age, are employed during the warm season in the family business. Girls often leave the school at 12 years of age and most commonly at 14.

But whatever may be the number of students at any given time, there is scarcely a child in this state who is not taught reading, writing, and arithmetic. Poverty here does not exclude anyone from this degree of education.

Based on this account, what is the attitude toward education in the region?

I have given you a view of the schools in Connecticut. The picture is about the same in the rest of New England. In Massachusetts, New Hampshire, and Vermont, schools are everywhere established. Each area has enough schools to admit all the children which it contains.

We rode the first day to Middletown, Connecticut. This town has excellent land. It is well cultivated and produces an excess of the necessities and comforts of life. The New Haven market allows the farmers to sell everything they raise. There is a nice but small village on the hill upon which their church is built, extending along the road perhaps a mile. The houses are generally good and their owners are obviously well-to-do.

I say *their owners,* for you are to understand that every man, almost without an exception, lives on his own ground. Every farmer in Connecticut and throughout New England is, therefore, dependent for his enjoyments on none but himself, his government, and his God. Every farmer is the ruler of a kingdom large enough to supply all his needs. If he is not in debt because of sickness or weakness, he is absolutely his own master.

The legislature of each town is made up of the inhabitants, personally present in town meetings. A majority of them decide every question. The proceedings of this legislature are all controlled by exact rules and are under the direction of the proper officers. There is no confusion.

What does Dwight mean when he refers to "public business"?

How do you think town meetings and owning one's own land would affect a person's feelings of independence?

Many people in New England lived in towns. How would this fact affect the success of town meetings as a form of local government? Living in towns is one pattern of settlement. Under what patterns of settlement would the town meeting be a poor form of government?

Men learn to do public business by being involved with the affairs of towns. You will remember that every town annually elects a considerable number of officers. Even the humblest of these jobs offers chances for information and wise decision-making.

The public business done here is so varied, so similar in many ways to that of a state or national legislature, so connected with the public good, occurs so often, involves so many people and so many offices, that the inhabitants become quite well acquainted with public affairs.

On the 20th of September, 1815, I set out upon a trip to the western parts of the state of New York.

On the 28th, in company with several gentlemen, I ascended the Catskill Mountains. From a height of 3,000 feet, we could see several counties. The whole area was settled, cultivated, and beautifully spotted with farms and groves. There seemed to be scarcely room left for a single additional farmer. At the bottom of this valley, the Hudson stretched in clear view over a length of 50 miles. On its waters were moving in various directions many vessels that looked like dim white spots. With a telescope, we discovered one of these to be a steamboat, making rapid progress. In this great view, a series of towns and villages met the eye.

Based on the occupations and businesses in New Haven, what do you think was the general level of wealth of the people who lived there? Explain your answer. ▼

b A general view of the business life in New Haven is given in this 1811 list reported by Dwight.

There were in New Haven:

29 businesses dealing in foreign commerce	16 schools	14 makers of barrels and corks
41 stores of dry goods	12 inns	3 stonecutters
42 grocery stores	5 candlemakers	7 curers of leather
4 ship equipment stores	2 brass founders	2 blockmakers
2 wholesale hardware stores	3 brass workers	5 barbers
3 wholesale dry goods stores	29 blacksmiths	3 tinners
1 wholesale glass and china store	1 bell founder	1 maker and repairer of wheels
1 furrier's store	9 tanners	1 leather dresser
10 apothecaries stores	30 shoe and bootmakers	1 nailer
6 traders in lumber	9 carriagemakers	2 papermakers
1 trader in paperhangings	7 goldsmiths	5 painting offices
6 shoe stores	4 watchmakers	2 bookbinders
7 manufacturers of hats	4 harnessmakers	5 bakers
5 hat stores	5 cabinetmakers	2 newspapers published
4 bookstores	50 carpenters and joiners	*There were also*
3 ropemakers	3 combmakers	6 clergymen
2 sail lofts	4 Windsor-chair makers	16 lawyers
1 shipyard	15 masons	9 practising physicians
17 butchers	26 tailors	1 surgeon

C Here are scenes of villages and farm life in the Northeast in the first half of the 1800s.

    ❶ A Fourth of July celebration
    ❷ The village square, South Reading, Massachusetts
    ❸ Harvest time

d Charles A. Murray, another English traveler, visited the United States in 1837. He reported on his treatment while staying at a country farm in New York State.

What does Murray think is strange about American behavior?

Would life in the Northeast tend to encourage or discourage the idea of equality? Why?

d The very first evening that I passed under the roof of my worthy host, not only he, but his farm assistants and laborers, called me "Charlie." To most English travelers, this use of my name would have seemed too personal and impolite, especially when we had just met. On the other hand, a traveler may find in the first village to which he comes, that the small tavern is run by a general, the broken wheel of his wagon is mended by a colonel, and the day-laborers and mechanics speak of one another as "this gentleman" and "that gentleman."

e An English traveler to the United States, Frederick Marryat, wrote *A Diary in America.* In it he describes this scene in northern New Jersey. Similar scenes could be seen all over the Northeast.

Waterfalls were oftern used as a source of power for factories. Look at the picture on page 166.

e I crossed over to New Jersey and took the railroad to view the falls of the Passaic River, about 15 miles from New York. This water power has given birth to Paterson, a town with ten thousand people, where a variety of manufactures is carried on.

Below the falls one can see manufacturing in full activity—millions of reels whirling in their sockets—the bright polished cylinders forever turning, and never tiring. What used to be the work of thousands of women, who sat with their children at the cottage door spinning thread, is now done in a hundredth part of the time. The machines that do this require only the attention of one child to several hundred machines. But machinery cannot perform everything, and so the romantic falls of the Passaic provides jobs for thousands of people.

How do you think this form of manufacturing might change life in the Northeast? How would it affect life and work in the home?

f The information in the chart on page 172 was reported by the Secretary of the Treasury of Massachusetts to the House of Representatives of Massachusetts on April 9, 1810.

GENERAL SUMMARY OF THE MANUFACTURES OF MASSACHUSETTS

		Estimated value			Estimated Value
54	Cotton factories	$931,906	7,050	dozen whips	$7,990
1	Woolen cloth factory	$2,060,576	1,666	dozen brushes	$5,000
4	Wool carding factories	$78,998	49,905	dozen combs	$80,625
180	Carding machines	$236,193	123	tons ashes	$20,619
221	Fulling mills	$442,401	44,460	gallons oil mills	$46,982
9	Spinning jennies	$28,600		Wire factories	$24,912
6,393	Spinning wheels	$17,982		Soapstone factory	$13,000
142,645	Hats	$415,167		Ores, ocher and nitrous bed	$1,350
261,800	Moroccan skins	$130,160		Wrought iron	$521,718
174,596	Hides	$1,022,661		Lead mines	$200
65,888	Calves' skins	$129,078		Edge tools	$44,000
62,536	Sheepskins	$52,140		Small and wrought nails	$70,595
105,276	Sheep	$399,182		Earthenware	$18,700
2,800	Hog skins	$9,100		Lace for coaches	$10,000
63,307	pairs leather boots	$412,509		Glass	$36,000
844,864	pairs men's shoes	$973,033			
1,310,500	pairs women's shoes	$816,250	23,600	Saltpeter	$9,303
3,225	pieces hemp	$86,813	334,238	pounds Glauber's salt	$13,369
60,000	yards bagging and tow cloth	$33,000	2,043,720	pounds hardsoap	$239,697
35,000	pounds sheep's wool	$14,175	4,190	barrels softsoap	$18,400
37,951	pairs woolen stockings	$28,453	6,000	gallons essence of turpentine	$18,000
103	pounds sewing silk	$618	1,250	pounds spruce essence	$2,500
4,875	dozen gloves	$14,625			
1	year's supply spectacles	$10,000	716,805	Breweries	$86,450
	Steel thimbles	$10,000	316,480	gallons cider	$181,386
	Straw bonnets	$551,988	118,757	bushels salt	$79,526
	Buttons	$20,000	422,000	pounds loaf sugar	$82,400
			255,500	pounds chocolate	$73,100
1	Rake factory	$1,870	49,054	bushels corn and oats	$35,273
1	Steel factory	$4,000	2,472,000	gallons molasses	$1,404,350
1	Fire engine factory	$4,000	460,476	bushels wheat and rye	$350,896
6	Powder mills	$72,000	63,730	gallons grain	$42,590
16	Marble works	$38,000	5,400	barrels mackerel	$44,550
25,295,000	Bricks	$139,067			
19,095	Muskets	$229,085	10,725,000	feet pine	$80,480
12,976	Brass guns	$7,136	490,000	feet oak	$6,855
32,159	Copper	$22,828	2,851 1/10	tons twine and cordage ropewalks	$1,068,044
11,000,000	Tacks	$2,000	23,410	tons shipbuilding	$1,656,095
2,260	Wagons	$43,600	1,694	dozen chairs	$96,060
667	Coaches and chaises	$122,674		Cabinet work	$318,622
70,000	Corn brooms	$4,000		Clocks and watches	$46,185
1,901,550	Wax	$217,060		Catgut	$2,000
327,424	Whale oil	$240,510			
440	tons anchors	$92,712	6,000	pounds printing ink	$3,000
2,925½	tons cut nails	$664,990	95,129	reams writing paper	$257,451
21,410	pounds bells	$8,555	63,000	rolls hanging paper	$33,500
99,288	pounds brass and pewter	$41,700	251,503	pounds composition	$109,781
978	tons bar iron	$121,930			
37,995	casks cooperage	$69,318	118,400	pounds snuff	$37,281
2,340½	tons hollow ware	$132,200		Musical instruments	$17,880
				Playing cards	$97,500

Do you think Massachusetts needed many highly skilled workers? How do you think manufacturing would affect the later development of factories in the region?

g Business life in the Northeast
1 A Massachusetts factory
2 The South Street port in New York City, where trading ships docked

h American author James Fenimore Cooper described Philadelphia and the Pennsylvania countryside in 1828.

h Philadelphia resembles a good English town. It is well-constructed, and quiet, with architecture superior to New York.

New York is a great commercial town; but Philadelphia is more devoted to manufacturing and is likely to remain so. There is plenty of investment money, and it is probable that it shall soon become a modified or improved Manchester or Birmingham. Its present population is about 140,000.

Instead of following the river south out of Philadelphia, we went by an interior road. This first day's journey was through one of the most highly cultivated and richest agricultural districts of this or of any other part of the world. The countryside looks much like that in England, though I have seen no part of England where such farmhouses and barns are to be seen as we saw here. The villages are few and small, though there are two or three market-towns of some size on the route.

The Susquehannah River was crossed by a noble wooden bridge, which was said to be a mile long. This was the twentieth of these immense constructions in wood that I have seen since my landing. The great enterprise and inventiveness of the people are here shown very well. It is only necessary to mention the need for a bridge, or a canal, and someone will try, usually successfully, to build it. A bridge a mile long is no problem for a people who live in a country that was wilderness 40 years ago.

Manchester and Birmingham were—and are—important English manufacturing cities.

In what way was the pattern of settlement in Pennsylvania farming country different from the pattern in New England? How do you think this wouuld affect social organizations?

i Charles Dickens, a famous English author, visited the United States in 1842. Here he describes Boston.

i Boston is a beautiful city. It cannot fail to impress all strangers very favorably. The private dwelling-houses are, for the most part, large and elegant; the shops extremely good; and the public buildings handsome.

The intellectual refinement and superiority of Boston is probably due to the quiet influence of the University of Cambridge [Harvard], which is within three or four miles of the city. The professors at that university are gentlemen of learning and varied accomplishments. They are men who, without exception, would shed grace on and do honor to any society in the civilized world. Many of the gentry in Boston and its neighborhood and many who are professional men have been educated at this same school.

*The word **gentry** refers to the upper class in a society.*

j The Northeast's largest cities
1 A view of Boston, 1850 **3** Philadelphia scene, 1848
2 State Street in Boston, 1801 **4** Broadway in New York, 1836

k Henri Herz, a French traveler in America, gave this description of a well-to-do Philadelphia lady's day.

k

Mrs. G., as is the custom in Pennsylvania, gets up very early through the year, and does not leave her bedroom unless fully dressed, as if for going out. Her daughters, well brought up and elegant without affectation, come down a little later. Promptly at eight, whether in January or July, breakfast is on the table. Eight times in ten they will have ham fried with eggs, and drink coffee in large cups.

After breakfast the girls take their books and go by themselves to school. Mrs. G. then puts an apron, white as snow, around her waist, and gives her orders to the servants, setting an example by her own hard work. Every day the house is cleaned and set in order from cellar to attic.

After this Mrs. G. almost always goes out, either in a carriage or on foot, for two to five hours, touring the stores. Generally without any intention of making a purchase, she has 20 bolts of cloth pulled down, looks through box after box of ribbons and tries on a dozen shawls. This manner of passing time, to the despair of the salespeople, is usual among American women who have given it a special name, "shopping."

l In his *Diary in America,* Frederick Marryat wrote this about New York City.

l

Fifty years ago [1789], New York was little more than a village. Now it is a fine city with 300,000 inhabitants. I have never seen any city so well suited for commerce. It is built upon a narrow island, between Long Island Sound and the Hudson River. Each street runs to the river, on which you can see a forest of masts.

New York is not equal to London, although the Americans compare them. Still, New York is very superior to most of England's less important towns.

New York has certainly great capabilities and every chance of improvement as a city; for, about one house in twenty is burnt down every year, and is always rebuilt in a superior manner.

m The data on page 177 tells you more about the Northeast.

NORTHEASTERN STATISTICS
1840-1850

■ White population

● Free black population/
Slave population

▲ Number of people who lived
in 1 square mile

MAINE
■ 581,813
● 1,356/0
▲ 18.4

VERMONT
■ 313,402
● 718/0
▲ 30.8

NEW HAMPSHIRE
■ 317,456
● 520/0
▲ 34.3

NEW YORK
■ 3,048,325
● 49,069/0
▲ 65.9

MASSACHUSETTS
■ 985.450
● 9.064/0
▲ 127.5

PENNSYLVANIA
■ 2,258,160
● 53,626/0
▲ 50.3

NEW JERSEY
■ 465,509
● 23,810/236
▲ 58.8

CONNECTICUT
■ 363,099
● 7,693/0
▲ 79.3

RHODE ISLAND
■ 143,875
● 3,670/0
▲ 113.0

WORKERS IN THE NORTHEAST 1840

Learned professions 1.9%

Navigation 2.1%

Mining .3%

Commerce 4.2%

Manufacturing 27.3%

Agriculture 64.2%

THE PERCENT OF LAND BEING FARMED IN THE NORTHEAST 1850

PERCENT

100
90
80
70
60
50
40
30
20
10
0

Maine
Vermont
New Hampshire
Rhode Island
Massachusetts
Connecticut
New York
New Jersey
Pennsylvania

Putting the Pieces Together

1. Using your notes, summarize life in the Northeast in the period from 1800 to 1850. Include information on the four categories you have investigated: population distribution, social class, occupations, and social organizations.

2. Describe the opinions and attitudes you'd expect the average person in the Northeast to have had about
   a. Slavery
   b. A high tariff on goods manufactured in other countries and sold in the United States
   c. Working as a laborer
   d. Cheap land for sale in the West

3. Describe the opinions and attitudes you'd expect a factory owner in the Northeast to have had about
   a. A high tariff on goods manufactured in other countries and sold in the United States
   b. Immigrants
   c. Cheap land for sale in the West

4. Think about what you learned about people and events in the Northeast in Units 1 and 2. In what ways do you think the Northeast from 1800 to 1850 was the same as it was before 1800? In what ways was it different? What caused the changes, in your opinion? What characteristics of the Northeast in the late 1700s led to the development of factories in the 1800s?

*A **tariff** is a tax on imported foreign products.*

*An **immigrant** is a person who enters a country with the intention of settling there.*

BRANCHING OUT

Investigating Habitat: The Northeast

Throughout the data you've just studied is information about the habitat in the Northeast—the land, rivers, climate, etc. Use atlases and other resources to find out more about the northeastern habitat.

Trace or draw a simple outline map of the Northeast. On the map put information about the Northeast's mountains, navigable rivers, waterpower, farmland, soil quality, harbors, growing season, natural resources, and other important facts.

Then tell how you think the habitat of the Northeast is related to the ideas and ways of acting of the people who lived there in the period from 1800 to 1850.

Part 2

The South

In 1763 Charles Mason and Jeremiah Dixon surveyed and established the boundary line between the colonies of Maryland and Pennsylvania. This boundary line came to be called "the Mason-Dixon line." It also became an imaginary line separating "the North" and "the South." In the first half of the 1800s, states lying south of this Mason-Dixon line along the Atlantic coast were generally considered the "Old South." The present southern states bordering the Gulf of Mexico were sometimes called the "New South." This land had been divided into territories which became states in the 1800s: Louisiana (1812), Mississippi (1817), Alabama (1819), and Texas (1845). Kentucky, Tennessee, Arkansas, and Missouri, although later considered "southern," were then thought of as "western" lands.

By analyzing the way of life in the southern region, you can answer this question:

How did the experiences shared by people in the South affect their ideas and ways of acting?

179

Analyzing the South

Letters, documents, pictures, statistics, and accounts of the South during the first half of the 1800s can give you a general picture of life in this region. As in other regions, there were many different styles of living in the South. However, most people lived in one of the ways you'll learn about in Part 2.

As you analyze the data below, organize your information in the same categories you used to summarize the Northeast.

1. Decide how the population was generally distributed within the region.
2. Decide what social classes there seemed to be, and how large each was, compared to the others.
3. Decide how various groups of people earned a living.
4. Decide what important social organizations there were.

Once, again, you have many pieces of data to consider in one activity. Study one piece at a time and make notes on information that piece contains for any of the four categories above.

a Robert Russell, an English gentleman and writer for the London *Times* traveled throughout the South in the 1850s and made these observations.

a

Traveling through a fertile district in any of the southern states, the appearance of things is very different than that in the Free States. During two days' sail on the Alabama River from Mobile to Montgomery, I did not see enough houses in any one spot to call it a village. There were many places where cotton was shipped and supplies were landed. Still, there were no signs to show that we were in the heart of a rich cotton region. In fact, the more fertile the land, the fewer villages and towns there are. And how can it be any other way? The system of management which is recommended as the most economical and profitable is to raise and to manufacture on the plantations everything which the slaves require. This is seldom accomplished, but a great part of the clothing is homemade. The chief articles imported are bacon and mules from the northern states. The only article sold is cotton, which is taken to the nearest point on a navigable river and shipped out to an agent in an exporting town. The bacon all comes in through the same channel.

Certain states, called **Free States,** no longer allowed slavery to exist within their borders. States in which slavery was permitted were called **Slave States.**

What settlement pattern is described here? How is it different from that in the Northeast? How do you think settlement patterns of the South affected education? Religion? Law enforcement? Roads? Businesses?

b The chart below gives you information about the amount and value of cotton and slaves in the South form 1800 through 1859.

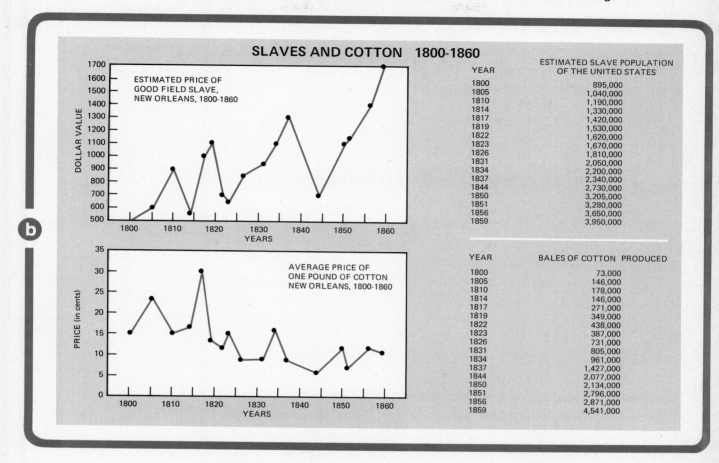

SLAVES AND COTTON 1800-1860

ESTIMATED PRICE OF GOOD FIELD SLAVE, NEW ORLEANS, 1800-1860

AVERAGE PRICE OF ONE POUND OF COTTON NEW ORLEANS, 1800-1860

YEAR	ESTIMATED SLAVE POPULATION OF THE UNITED STATES
1800	895,000
1805	1,040,000
1810	1,190,000
1814	1,330,000
1817	1,420,000
1819	1,530,000
1822	1,620,000
1823	1,670,000
1826	1,810,000
1831	2,050,000
1834	2,200,000
1837	2,340,000
1844	2,730,000
1850	3,205,000
1851	3,280,000
1856	3,650,000
1859	3,950,000

YEAR	BALES OF COTTON PRODUCED
1800	73,000
1805	146,000
1810	178,000
1814	146,000
1817	271,000
1819	349,000
1822	438,000
1823	387,000
1826	731,000
1831	805,000
1834	961,000
1837	1,427,000
1844	2,077,000
1850	2,134,000
1851	2,796,000
1856	2,871,000
1859	4,541,000

▲ *What happened to cotton production between 1800 and 1859? Based on the prices given, did Southern planters earn more money in 1800 or in 1859?*

▲ *Compare the value of slaves to the value of the total cotton crop. What does this tell you about slaves' importance to Southerners? About their importance to cotton production?*

▲ *Based on the price of slaves, do you think most Southerners could afford to own many slaves? How would this affect social classes?*

c Joseph H. Ingraham, a young New Englander, toured south-western Mississippi. His book, *The South-West,* describes what he saw. It was published anonymously in 1835, signed "By a Yankee."

The pod in which the cotton grows is called a **boll.**

A plantation well-stocked with workers is the ambition of every man who lives in the South. Young men who come to this country "to make money" soon want this. A broad plantation, waving with snow-white cotton bolls, fills their dreams. This is the reason for the great number of planters and the few professional men. In such a state of things, no men grow old or gray in their profession if they are at all successful. As soon as the young lawyer makes enough to purchase a few hundred acres of rich land and a few slaves, he quits his profession at once, though perhaps just rising into prominence, and turns cotton planter. The legal profession at Natchez is composed entirely of young men. Ten years from now, probably not four out of five of these will still work as lawyers.

Physicians make money much more rapidly than lawyers, so they turn planter even sooner. They, however, keep their titles, so that doctor-planters are now numerous. They far outnumber the regular doctors, who have not yet climbed high enough up the wall to leap down into a cotton field on the other side.

Incomes of $20,000 are common here. Several individuals possess incomes of from $40,000 to $50,000 and live in a style equal to their wealth. The amount is generally expressed by the number of their Negroes and the number of "bales" they make at a crop.

To sell cotton in order to buy Negroes, to make more cotton to buy more Negroes, etc., is the aim of all the operations of the cotton planter. His whole world is wrapped up in it.

The towns and villages of Mississippi, as in European states, are located perfectly independent of each other, isolated among forests, and often many miles apart. In between are large areas of country with no other division except counties. Natchez, for instance, is a town one mile square, but from its boundaries to Woodville, the next incorporated town south, it is 38 miles.

In your opinion, why would the ownership of a cotton plantation and slaves be such an important goal for white Southerners? Give several reasons.

A great deal of cotton grown in the South was exported to textile factories in England. From 1840 to 1860 cotton made up over half of all United States exports. How would this fact affect cotton's importance in the economy of the South? Of the United States?

Picked, clean cotton was packed in large bundles called **bales.**

Based on what you know about the price of slaves, could many people afford to buy them? How would this affect the size of plantations?

d C. C. Clay, Jr., an Alabama legislator, made the following speech to an agricultural club in his state in 1855.

d

I can show you, with sorrow, in the older portions of Alabama, the sad results of the exhausting culture of cotton. Our small planters, after taking the best off their lands, are unable to restore them with rest, fertilizer, or otherwise. So, they are moving further west and south, in search of other fresh lands which they will also ruin. Our wealthier planters with more money are buying out their poorer neighbors, extending their plantations and adding to their slave force. The wealthy few, who are able to live on smaller profits and give their fields some rest, are thus pushing off many of the small independent planters.

When cotton is planted in the same fields year after year, nitrogen is taken out of the soil and the land is no longer fertile.

Of the $20,000,000 annual profit from the sales of the cotton crop of Alabama, nearly all not used to support the producers is reinvested in land and Negroes. Thus, the white population has decreased and the slave population increased. In crossing Madison County, one will discover numerous farmhouses, once the houses of freemen, now occupied by slaves. Others are deserted and run down. One will see fields, once fertile, now unfenced and abandoned. He will see the moss growing on the walls of once-thrifty villages. He will find that "one master grasps the whole domain" that once furnished happy homes for a dozen white families. Indeed, a country where, 50 years ago, hardly a tree had been felled by the axe of the pioneer, is already showing signs of the decay apparent in Virginia and the Carolinas. The freshness of its agricultural glory is gone; the energy of its youth is extinct and the spirit of desolation seems hanging over it.

e One of the problems faced by Southern plantations was erosion of the soil. (**Erosion** can take place when land has been planted too often and when all trees have been cut down. Rain then washes away all of the valuable, rich topsoil.) Frederick Law Olmstead, a northern traveler in the South, reports on the erosion problem in Louisiana in 1854.

e

During the day I passed four or five large plantations. The hillsides were worn, cracked, and channelled like icebergs; the stables and Negro quarters were all abandoned—everything was given up to nature and decay.

In its natural state, the soil that has never been cultivated appears the richest I have ever seen, the growth upon it from weeds to trees being dense and rich in color. At first the soil is expected to bear a bale and a half of cotton to the acre, making eight or ten bales for each able fieldhand. But the soil's productivity rapidly decreases.

If these slopes were made into permanent terraces, the fertility of the soil might be preserved, even with constant use. In this way the hills would continue for ages to produce annual crops of greater value than those which are now obtained from them at such destructive expense. From ten to twenty crops of cotton turns fields into absolute deserts. But with Negroes at $1,400 a head and fresh land in Texas at half-a-dollar an acre, nothing of this sort can be thought of.

According to Olmstead, how was the price of land in Texas affecting care of Southern land?

f In the Old and the New South
  1 A farm in the New South
  2 A Mississippi River plantation

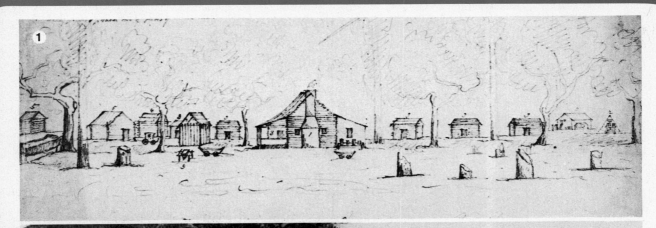

g The following letter was written by Henry Barnard to his sister in New England. In the letter Barnard tells about his visit to the Carter plantation in Virginia in 1833.

Petersburg, Virginia
March 15, 1833

My Dear Betty,

I think you would delight to visit this region, if only to observe the difference of manners and habits from what you have been accustomed to, and to experience the princely hospitality of the gentle-born families. Now, so that you may understand how we lived there and how one of these large establishments is carried on, I will describe a single day there. I will suppose also that it is a day upon which company is expected.

When you wake in the morning, you are surprised to find that a servant has been in and, without disturbing you, built up a large fire, taken out your clothes and brushed them and done the same with your boots, brought in hot water to shave you, and indeed stands ready to do what you ask. As soon as you are dressed, you walk down into the dining room. At eight o'clock you take your seat at the breakfast table of rich mahogany—each plate standing separate on its own little cloth. Mr. Carter will sit at one end of the table and Mrs. Carter at the other. Mrs. Carter will send you, by two little black boys, as fine a cup of coffee as you ever tasted, or a cup of tea. It is fashionable here to drink a cup of tea after coffee. Mr. Carter has before him a fine cold ham of the real Virginia flavor—this is all the meat you will get in the morning, but the servant will bring you hot muffins and corn batter cakes every two minutes. You will find on the table also, loaf wheat bread, hot and cold, and corn bread.

After breakfast, if visitors wish to ride, horses are ready at their command. If they wish to read, there are books enough in the library. For writing, materials are ready in his room. The Master and Mistress of the house are not expected to entertain visitors till an hour or two before dinner, which is usually at three. If company has been invited to the dinner, they will begin to come about one—ladies in carriages and gentlemen on horseback. After freshening up, the company amuse themselves in the parlor. About a half-hour before dinner, the gentlemen are invited out for a drink. When dinner is ready (and by the way, Mrs. Carter has nothing to do with setting the table; an old family servant, who for 50 years has supervised the matter, does all that), Mr. Carter politely takes a lady by the hand and leads the way into the dining room. They are followed by the rest, each lady led by a gentleman. Mrs.

How do you think seeing this kind of life would affect poorer white people? Slaves?

185

Carter is at one end of the table with a large dish of rich soup and Mr. Carter at the other, with a cut of fine mutton. Scattered round the table, you may choose for yourself: ham, beef, turkey, duck, eggs with greens, etc., etc.; for vegetables—potatoes, beets, hominy. This last you will find always at dinner. It is made of their white corn and beans and is a very fine dish. After you have dined, there circulates a bottle of sparkling champagne. After that, off pass the things and the upper tablecloth, and there is placed on the table the dessert, consisting of fine plum pudding, tarts, etc., etc. After this comes ice cream, West India preserves (peaches preserved in brandy), etc. When you have eaten this, off goes the second tablecloth, and then upon the bare mahogany table are set the figs, raisins, and almonds, and before Mr. Carter are set two or three bottles of wine—Madeira, Port, and a sweet wine for the ladies. After the glasses are all filled, the gentlemen make toasts to the ladies and down goes the wine. After the first and second glass, the ladies retire, and the gentlemen begin to circulate the bottle pretty briskly. The gentlemen may join the ladies as soon as they please. After music and a little chit-chat, the ladies prepare for their ride home.

h English traveler Harriet Martineau visited a Southern plantation in 1834 and reported on daily life.

h

Our settled rural life in the South was various and pleasant enough; all shaded with the presence of slavery, but without any other drawback.

You are awakened in the morning by black women. Perhaps, before you are half dressed, you are summoned to breakfast. You look at your watch, and listen whether it has stopped, for it seems not to be seven o'clock yet. You hurry, however, and find your hostess making the coffee. The young people drop in when the meal is half done, and then it is discovered that breakfast has been served an hour too early. The clock has stopped, and the cook has ordered affairs according to her own guesses about the time. Everybody laughs, and nothing happens.

After breakfast, a farmer in homespun—blue trousers and an orange-brown coat, or all-over gray—comes to speak with your host. A drunken white has shot one of his Negroes, and he fears no punishment can be obtained, because there were no witnesses of the deed but blacks. A consultation is held whether the affair shall go into court. Before the farmer departs, he is offered cake and liqueur.

What attitudes do you think these people had about the use of time? About education? How would their attitudes differ from attitudes in the Northeast?

Your hostess, meantime, has given her orders, and is now busy in a back room, or out on the porch behind the house, cutting out clothes for her slaves; very hard work in warm weather. The young people may pretend to study lessons, and may do more than pretend if they happen to have a tutor or governess. But it is likely that their occupations are as various as their tempers. Rosa cannot be found; she is lying on the bed in her own room reading a novel; Clara is weeping for her canary, which has flown away while she was playing with it; Alfred is trying to find out how soon we may all go out to ride; and the little ones are lounging about outside, with their arms round the necks of blacks their size. You sit down to the piano or to read, and one slave or another enters every half hour to ask what time it is.

ⓘ The growth and sale of cotton was the South's major business activity.
❶ The cotton dock at New Orleans
❷ The fields of a cotton plantation

❷

j Frederick Law Olmstead summarized some of his experiences traveling in the South.

j I went on my way into the cotton states, within which I traveled over at least three thousand miles of roads. The people living by the side of the road certainly had not been made rich by cotton or anything else. And for every mile of roadside upon which I saw any evidence of cotton production, I am sure that I saw a hundred of forest or wasteland. For every rich man's house, I am sure that I passed a dozen shabby and half-furnished cottages, and at least a hundred cabins that were mere hovels. And I think that for every man of refinement and education with whom I came in contact, there were a score or two who completely lacked the things that in the North would show that a man had begun to acquire money.

How do Olmstead's comments compare to the descriptions by Barnard and Martineau?

*A **hovel** is a small, miserable dwelling. A **score** is twenty.*

k James D. B. DeBow was the publisher of a commercial magazine in New Orleans. He was one of the South's leading supporters of industrial growth and commerce. The excerpt that follows is taken from a speech DeBow made in 1852.

k What shall we say of the South—the old South, which fought the battles of the Revolution—which gave the statesmen, the generals, and the wealth of those early times? At one time, it was the center of agriculture, commerce, and even to some extent, the manufactures of the continent. But it has lost everything except agriculture; and even this is growing less and less profitable. How much has the South promised and how little has she fulfilled? Her manufacturing began at the same time as in the North. There were not 15 cotton factories in the whole Union when an enormous factory was constructed in the South. Nearly half a century has passed since then. Now, the South leaves to others 29 to 30 percent of the profitable business of making cotton into fabrics.

And how has it been with our commerce? When New Englanders were still fishing, the rich ships of the South (filled with many products) were seeking the markets of all Europe. Seventy years before the Revolution, Maryland, Virginia, and Carolina furnished the entire exports of the colonies and imported more than New England or New York. Fifty years before the Revolution, the exports of New York, New England, and Pennsylvania together were less in amount than those of the single colony of Carolina.

The South had within her limits the longest railroad in the world and actually began the construction of the first great railroad across the mountains to the teeming West. How has she followed this movement? The North has opened innumerable communications with the Mississippi Valley and is enriching herself beyond the dreams of her own enthusiastic supporters.

The North has 12 times the extent of railroads to the square mile that the South has.

We have been content to be only agriculturists and to exhaust the fertility of an abundant soil, believing that all other pursuits were of less importance and dignity. The fashion of the South has been to think that the production of cotton and sugar and rice are the only proper occupation of gentlemen and to think that trading and manufacturing are lower class.

Where, then, shall we look for a practical remedy? We must diversify or find new employment for labor. And how is this to be done? I answer: In the construction of a system of railroads through the South. Then the South and West will naturally turn to manufacturing, which is the second great remedy for our problems.

The South has only to make a systematic and combined movement to break down Northern supremacy.

Our surplus Negro labor has here a wide field open. Everyone familiar with the operation of the machinery of a cotton mill will admit that Negro labor, properly organized and directed, can be as effective as the ignorant and miserable workers of Great Britain.

Commerce *is the buying and selling of goods, especially sales that involve the transportation of goods from one place to another.*

Why might Southern white people consider trading and manufacturing as lower-class occupations? In what way might this attitude be a result of the attitudes in the first Southern colonial settlements? How does this attitude compare to that in the Northeast?

How does this view of the South compare to what you have read about the Northeast?

❶ Charleston and New Orleans were the most important cities in the South.
   ❶ A view of Charleston, 1831
   ❷ A view of New Orleans from the harbor, 1840

m As DeBow reported below, the majority of white people in the South did not own slaves.

If most white families did not own slaves, why were slaves so important in the South?

m I believe that, in the South, the non-slaveholders far outnumber the slaveholders, perhaps by three to one. In the more Southern portion of this region ("the South-West" of which Mississippi is the center) the non-slaveholders have very little money. The land which they own is generally poor. It is so poor that a small livelihood is all that can be gotten from it. The more fertile soil is in the hands of the slaveholders and will never be available to anyone else. I am sorry to say that I have observed an evident deterioration taking place in this poorer part of the population—the younger portion of it being less educated, less industrious and less worthy of respect than their ancestors.

n The chart below shows statistics on slave ownership in 1850.

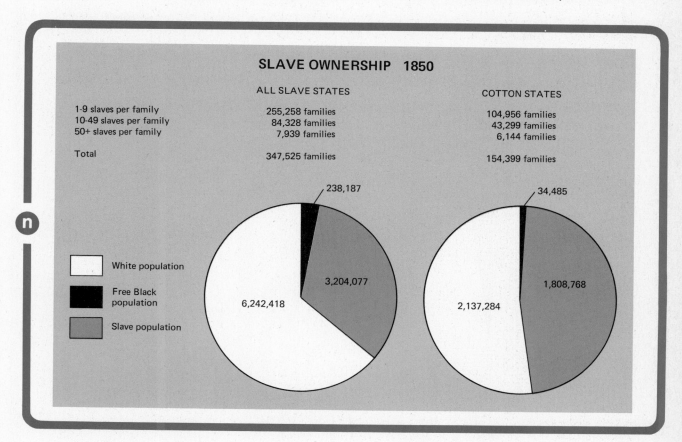

SLAVE OWNERSHIP 1850

	ALL SLAVE STATES	COTTON STATES
1-9 slaves per family	255,258 families	104,956 families
10-49 slaves per family	84,328 families	43,299 families
50+ slaves per family	7,939 families	6,144 families
Total	347,525 families	154,399 families

ALL SLAVE STATES: 238,187 · 3,204,077 · 6,242,418

COTTON STATES: 34,485 · 1,808,768 · 2,137,284

- White population
- Free Black population
- Slave population

o The data on page 192 tells you more about the South.

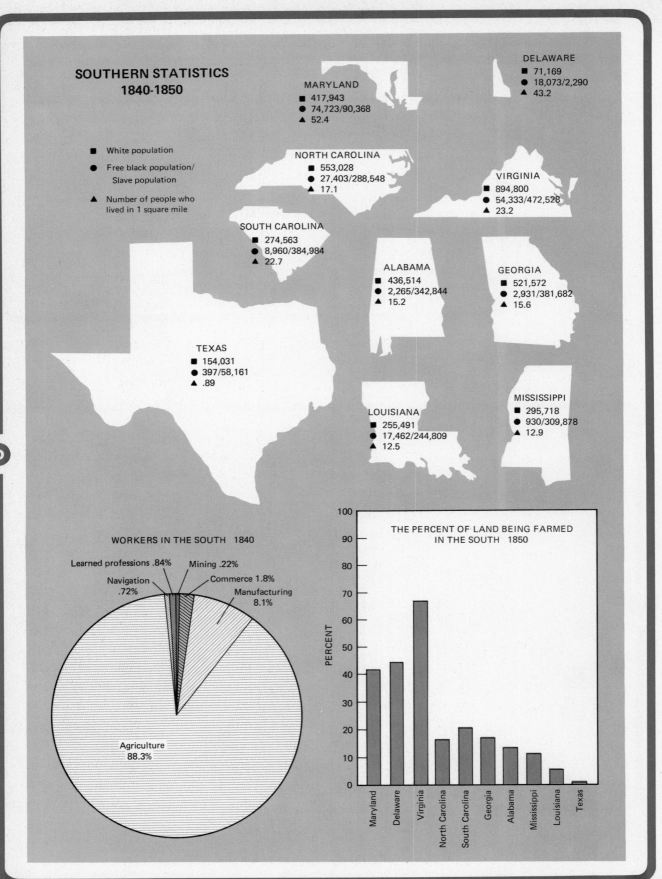

SOUTHERN STATISTICS
1840-1850

■ White population

● Free black population/
   Slave population

▲ Number of people who
   lived in 1 square mile

DELAWARE
■ 71,169
● 18,073/2,290
▲ 43.2

MARYLAND
■ 417,943
● 74,723/90,368
▲ 52.4

NORTH CAROLINA
■ 553,028
● 27,403/288,548
▲ 17.1

VIRGINIA
■ 894,800
● 54,333/472,528
▲ 23.2

SOUTH CAROLINA
■ 274,563
● 8,960/384,984
▲ 22.7

ALABAMA
■ 436,514
● 2,265/342,844
▲ 15.2

GEORGIA
■ 521,572
● 2,931/381,682
▲ 15.6

TEXAS
■ 154,031
● 397/58,161
▲ .89

LOUISIANA
■ 255,491
● 17,462/244,809
▲ 12.5

MISSISSIPPI
■ 295,718
● 930/309,878
▲ 12.9

WORKERS IN THE SOUTH   1840

Learned professions .84%   Mining .22%
Navigation .72%   Commerce 1.8%
Manufacturing 8.1%
Agriculture 88.3%

THE PERCENT OF LAND BEING FARMED
IN THE SOUTH   1850

PERCENT

Maryland, Delaware, Virginia, North Carolina, South Carolina, Georgia, Alabama, Mississippi, Louisiana, Texas

The experiences of slaves in the South were far different from those of any other American group. These experiences had powerful effects on the ideas and ways of acting of black people.

Read the accounts of slave experiences in this activity, and try to determine how you would act and feel if you had the same experiences.

a Solomon Northrup was a free black man who was kidnapped and held as a slave for 12 years. Here he describes the New Orleans slave auction at which he was sold in 1841.

In the first place we were required to wash thoroughly, and those with beards were required to shave. We were then given a new suit of clothes, cheap but clean. The men each were given a hat, coat, shirt, pants, and shoes. The women were given dresses of calico and a handkerchief to tie around their heads.

We were then taken to a large room in the front of the building, and told where to stand and how to act.

A planter of Baton Rouge purchased Randall. The little fellow was made to jump and run across the floor and perform many other feats to show his activity and condition. All this time Eliza (his mother) was crying aloud and wringing her hands. She pleaded with the man not to buy him unless he also bought her. She promised to be the most faithful slave that ever lived.

The man answered that he could not afford to buy both of them. Then Eliza burst into total grief, weeping and pleading. The owner of the slave-pen turned round to her savagely and ordered her to stop her noise or she would be whipped. If she didn't stop crying immediately, he would take her to the yard and give her a hundred lashes. Yes, he would take the nonsense out of her!

Eliza shrunk before him and tried to wipe away her tears, but she failed. She wanted to be with her children, she said, the little time she had left. All the threats and frowns of the owner would not stop her. She continued to plead and cry, and ask that she not be separated from her boy.

It did no good. The man could not afford to buy both of them. Randall must go alone. Then Eliza ran to him, hugged him, and kissed him again and again. She told him to remember her—with her tears falling on the boy's face like rain.

"Don't cry, mama. I will be a good boy. Don't cry," said Randall, looking back as they went out the door.

b When he was 90 years old, David Blount recalled his days as a slave.

The master made us work through the week, but on Saturdays we used to go swimming in the river and do a lot of other things we liked to do.

We didn't mind the work so much because the ground was soft as ashes and the master let us stop and rest when we got tired. We planted potatoes on the uplands and corn on the low ground next to the river.

I worked for awhile on Cape Fear in North Carolina. Sometimes on hot days when we were cutting fodder, we'd all stop work about three o'clock in the afternoon and go swimming. After we came out of the water we'd work harder than ever. The master was good to us because we worked hard and did what he told us to do.

Usually the master hired good overseers, and lots of times he let slaves oversee, but I remember once when he hired a man who was really mean. He beat some of the half-grown boys until the blood ran down to their heels, and he told the rest of us that if we told on him he would kill us. We didn't dare ask the master to get rid of him, so this went on for a long time.

*An **overseer** directed the work of the slaves.*

c Slave life in the South.
  1 Slaves working in a cotton field
  2 Slaves in front of their quarters on a plantation
  3 An advertisement for a slave auction

RAFFLE

Mr. Joseph Jennings respectfully informs his friends and the public that, at the request of many acquaintances, he has been induced to purchase from Mr. Osborne, of Missouri, the celebrated

DARK BAY HORSE, "STAR,"

Aged five years, square trotter and warranted sound; with a new light Trotting Buggy and Harness; also, the dark, stout

MULATTO GIRL, "SARAH,"

Aged about twenty years, general house servant, valued at *nine hundred dollars*, and guaranteed, and

Will be Raffled for

At 4 o'clock P. M., February first, at the selection hotel of the subscribers. The above is as represented, and those persons who may wish to engage in the usual practice of raffling, will, I assure them, be perfectly satisfied with their destiny in this affair.

The whole is valued at its just worth, fifteen hundred dollars; fifteen hundred

CHANCES AT ONE DOLLAR EACH.

The Raffle will be conducted by gentlemen selected by the interested subscribers present. Five nights will be allowed to complete the Raffle. BOTH OF THE ABOVE DESCRIBED CAN BE SEEN AT MY STORE, No. 78 Common St., second door from Camp, at from 9 o'clock A. M. to 2 P. M.

Highest throw to take the first choice; the lowest throw the remaining prize, and the fortunate winners will pay twenty dollars each for the refreshments furnished on the occasion.

N. B. No chances recognized unless paid for previous to the commencement.

JOSEPH JENNINGS.

d Solomon Northrup described slaves' work in the cotton fields.

During all the cotton hoeings, the overseer or driver follows the slaves on horseback with a whip. The fastest hoer takes the lead row. He is usually about a rod ahead of the others. If one of them passes him, the lead hoer is whipped. If a hoer falls behind or stops for a moment, he is whipped.

Near the end of August the cotton picking season begins. Each slave is given a long sack to carry, with a strap that goes over his head. Large baskets are placed at the beginning of the rows, each holding about two barrels. The sacks are emptied into the baskets when they are filled.

When a new man—one not used to picking—is sent for the first time into a field, he is whipped frequently and made to pick all day as fast as he possibly can. At night the cotton he has picked is weighed, to find out how much he has picked. He must bring in the same amount each night following. If he falls short, he is given a number of lashes as a penalty.

An ordinary day's work is two hundred pounds. A slave used to picking cotton is punished if he brings in less.

The hands must be in the cotton fields as soon as it is light in the morning. Except for ten or fifteen minutes given at noon for them to eat their cold bacon, they are not permitted a minute's rest until it is too dark to see. When the moon is full they often work until the middle of the night. They dare not stop until the overseer gives the order.

Once the day's work is over, the slaves carry the cotton to the gin-house, where it is weighed. No matter how tired the slave is, he comes to the gin-house afraid. If his weight is short, he knows he will be punished. If his weight is ten or twenty pounds over what he usually picks, he will probably be expected to pick that much more cotton the next day. No matter how much he has picked, the slave is afraid. After the cotton is weighed, the slaves who did not pick enough cotton are whipped.

*A **gin house** was the building in which a cotton gin was housed. A **cotton gin** is a machine that removes seeds from picked cotton.*

If you were a slave, experiencing the things described in this section, how would this probably affect your

1. Attitudes toward the future?
2. Way of acting toward overseers and toward others with authority?
3. Attitudes toward religion?

1. Using your notes, summarize life in the South in the period from 1800 to 1850. Include information on the four categories you have investigated.

2. Describe the opinions and attitudes you'd expect a plantation owner in the South to have had about
   a. Slavery
   b. A high tariff on goods manufactured in other countries and sold in the United States
   c. Working as a laborer
   d. Cheap land for sale in Texas
   e. Equality of various kinds and classes of people

3. In what ways do you think opinions of non-slaveowning white people were similar to the opinions of slaveowners? Do you think there would have been important differences in their opinions?

4. In what important ways was Southern society different from society in the Northeast?

5. Think about what you learned about people and events in the South in Units 1 and 2. In what ways do you think the South, from 1800 to 1850, was the same as it was before 1800? In what ways was it different? Do you think there were as many changes in the South as in the Northeast? Explain.

BRANCHING OUT

Investigating Habitat: The South

Throughout the data you've just studied is information about the habitat in the South—the land, rivers, climate, etc. Use atlases and other resources to find out more about the southern habitat.

Trace or draw a simple outline map of the South. On the map put information about the South's mountains, navigable rivers, waterpower, farmland, soil quality, harbors, growing season, natural resources, and other important facts.

Then, tell how the habitat of the South is related to the ideas and ways of acting of the people who lived there from 1800 to 1850.

Part 3

The West

In the early 1800s when Americans talked about the "West," they usually meant the area which we now call the Middle West. This is the territory now occupied by the states of Ohio, Indiana, Illinois, Michigan, Wisconsin, Minnesota, and Iowa.

Some states later considered part of the American South were also thought of as "western" during the early 1800s. These were the present Kentucky, Tennessee, Arkansas, and Missouri. As these areas became more heavily settled, they became more like the South.

Like other regions of the growing United States, the West varied from place to place and from time to time. Westerners who lived in Cincinnati, for example, didn't have a great deal in common with hunters, trappers, and settlers on the frontier. Most of the data in Part 3 deals with the more-settled sections of the western region.

As you study the material, think about this question:

How did the experiences shared by people in the West affect their ideas and ways of acting?

The material which follows will give you a general picture of the ideas and ways of acting of the people who moved west in the early 1800s.

Analyze the data, organizing your information in the same categories you used in Parts 1 and 2.

1. Population distribution in the region
2. The social classes that were present, and the size of each
3. The ways various groups of people earned a living
4. The important social organizations, if any

Again, you have many pieces of data to work with. After studying each one, make notes on information for the correct categories before proceeding to the next piece.

a Under the Articles of Confederation, Congress passed two laws dealing with the western lands shown on the map below. At that time, this area was called the Northwest. Colonists had moved into these lands and colonies claimed them (see map, page 89), but they were not really part of any specific colonies. How this land was to be settled and how these people were to be governed were important questions to be answered.

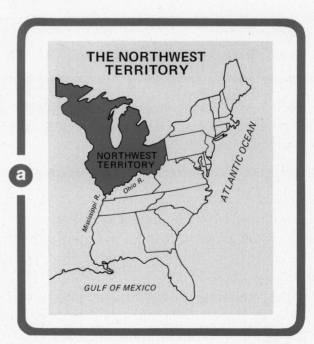

THE NORTHWEST TERRITORY

NORTHWEST TERRITORY

Mississippi R.

Ohio R.

ATLANTIC OCEAN

GULF OF MEXICO

b Congress answered the questions with two laws. The first was the Land Ordinance of 1785. This law made rules about the sale of northwestern land to private owners. First, the entire Northwest was divided into six-mile squares. Each square became a township. Each township was divided into sections. This division is shown in the diagram below.

Most of the income from the sale of land was used to supply Congress with much-needed money to pay national debts. However, the income from the sale of Section 16 in each township was to be used to support township schools.

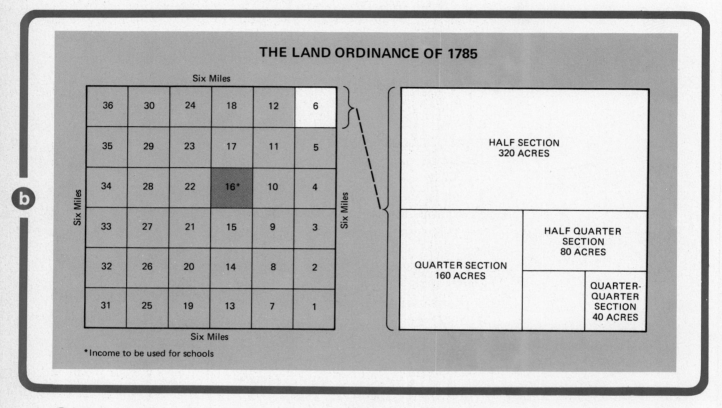

THE LAND ORDINANCE OF 1785

*Income to be used for schools

c The sale of land in the Northwest is described in the following letter. Written by an Italian priest in 1810, it was meant to tell Italians about life in America.

The land is sold by the government in a way that allows almost everyone to own property. The plan is as follows:

Before the land given up by the Indians to the government is put up for sale, it is surveyed, divided into townships, and subdivided into sections.

The smallest quantity the government will sell is 160 acres [a quarter section] at two dollars an acre. A quarter of the total amount is payable at once and the rest over four years. Whoever can purchase for cash can buy at the cost of $1.64 an acre.

How do you think the sale of land affected immigrants to the United States? How could it have affected the attitudes of people in the Northeast? In the South?

This is the plan—now let us see the effects. Every person able to pay the small sum of $80 can become a free owner of land; and even if he has not a dollar more, he always succeeds in paying the rest before the end of four years by selling the timber that he cuts to prepare the land for cultivation. He then becomes a peaceful landowner, with nothing further to pay except a tiny tax on his holdings. He can live on happily.

The second law passed by Congress under the Articles of Confederation was the Northwest Ordinance. This law made rules about the way in which the territory was to be governed. It also stated that whenever any part of the territory had 60,000 free inhabitants, it could become a state "on an equal footing with the original states." (The map on pages 512–513 shows the year which each state joined the Union.) With this law, the growth of the United States began.

d Frances Trollope, a well-known English writer, toured America in the 1820s. In her book, *Domestic Manners of the Americans,* she described her views of life in Ohio in 1828.

Mohawk, as our little village was called, gave us an excellent opportunity to compare the peasants of the United States with those of England and to judge the average degree of comfort enjoyed by each. I believe Ohio is typical; if they have the roughness and inconveniences of a new state to deal with, they also have higher wages and cheaper supplies.

Laborers, if they are good workmen, are certain to find a job with good wages, higher than in England. The average wage of a laborer is $10 a month, with lodging, boarding, washing, and mending. It appears to me that the necessities of life—meat, bread, butter, tea, and coffee (not to mention whiskey), are within the reach of every sober, industrious, and healthy man who chooses to have them.

There was one man whose progress in wealth I watched with much interest and pleasure. When I first became his neighbor, he, his wife, and four children were living in one room. They had plenty of beef-steaks and onions for breakfast, dinner, and supper, but very few other comforts. He was one of the finest men I ever saw. He was intelligent and active of mind and body, but he could neither read nor write. He drank very little whiskey and rarely chewed tobacco. (He was therefore more free from that spitting which made male conversation so difficult to bear.) He worked for us frequently and often used to walk into the drawing room and seat himself on the sofa and tell me all his plans. He made a deal with the owner of a wooded hill, by which half the wood he could cut was to be his own. His hard work made this a good bargain. From this earning he bought the materials for building a comfortable wooden house. He did the work almost entirely himself. He then got a job cutting rails and because he could cut twice as many in a day as any other man in the neighborhood, he did well. He then rented out half his pretty house.

He hopes to make his son a lawyer. I have little doubt that he will live to see him sit in Congress. When this time arrives, the woodcutter's son will rank with any other member of Congress, not of courtesy, but of right. The idea that his origin is a disadvantage will never occur to the imagination of his fellow-citizens.

How is the attitude toward work shown in this selection different from the attitude in the South? How would you explain the difference?

How do you think Westerners felt about equality?

e William Cooper Howells lived in Ohio during its pioneer days. He wrote the book *Recollections of Life in Ohio from 1813 to 1840*, from which the following selection is taken.

The life of the people was rather primitive and simple. None of them was wealthy. The possession of a quarter section or two of land, pretty well cleared up—about a third or half of it under cultivation with a log-house and barn—was thought to make a man well off. Nearly every man lived in a piece of land he owned and this was usually in 80- or 160-acre tracts. Their stock was small in number; their families were usually large. Almost every man was the son of a farmer in an older settlement who had come into this area in order to have a farm of his own. Or else, some man who had been a farm laborer or renter in an older place had bought land here and was beginning a home. Among such people there were no rich and none was very poor. Most of them lived very plainly. They usually had enough to eat, though they were likely to run short a while before harvest. All that would bring money was sold to provide for taxes and such payments as only money would make. Those who had payments to make on their land were pretty sure to sell themselves bare, and often found it hard to keep themselves in supplies.

As for clothing—that was very plain. Fortunately, there was little temptation to be extravagant in this way. The women of the family, in almost every case, produced something to wear.

Particularly remarkable was the general dependence of all upon the neighborly kindness of others. Their houses and barns were built of logs and were raised by a group of as many neighbors

In what ways did Ohio seem to differ from the South?

*To **raise** a house or barn means to build it.*

as was necessary to handle the logs. Since every man was ready with the ax and understood this work, all came together where the raising was to be done and all worked together with about equal skill. The men understood handling timber, and accidents seldom happened, unless the logs were icy or wet. I was often at these raisings. We had raisings of the same kind to do, and it was the custom always to send one from a family to help, so that you could claim assistance in return.

This kind of help was needed in many kinds of work, such as rolling up the logs in a clearing, grubbing out the underbrush, splitting rails, cutting logs for a house, and the like. When a gathering of men for such a purpose took place, there was usually some sort of cooperative job laid out for the women, such as quilting, sewing, or spinning up a lot of thread for some poor neighbor.

f An early resident of Illinois wrote this account.

My store was the first built in Springfield, or in the county. I was the first one to sell goods in Springfield. For some time my sales were about as much to Indians as to whites. For the first two years I had no competition, and my customers were widely and thinly scattered.

Soon after opening my store, my father sent to me from Kentucky a youth, 16 years old, to act as store boy and clerk. This youth was John Williams, now better known as Col. Williams. He proved to be a very valuable assistant and lived with me as one of the family until 1831. At that time I sold my goods to him and started him in business. He was very successful and soon had a large farm in connection with his store. In later years, he established the First National Bank in Springfield, of which he was president and the principal stockholder. He also built and owned the Northwestern Railroad.

After moving to my farm, I soon found myself much in need of another plowman. A boy came to me and said he wanted to work. He had the chills every other day and could only plow on his well days. His name was Robert North. He was about the most scrawny looking chap I ever saw and could neither read nor write. He soon got well of the chills and made me a most valuable helper. I taught him to read and write. He lived with me ten years, got married, and went to farming on his own hook, in which he was successful. He died two years ago, at the age of 70, after accumulating in land and cash more than $150,000.

Based on the data so far, what were the main advantages of life in the West?

In your opinion, what kind of people might not have succeeded on the frontier?

g In the shipping season of 1830–1831, these goods arrived in Buffalo from the West.

g

GOODS SHIPPED TO BUFFALO FROM THE WEST
1830—1831

267,900 bushels	wheat	86,900 barrels	flour
4,319 kegs	butter	11,800 barrels	ashes
3,500 packs	furs and pelts	4,800 barrels	whiskey
149 tons	hemp	6,900 barrels	pork
243 bales	feathers	1,600 barrels	beef
4,206 boxes	glass	1,273 barrels	lake fish
359,000 single	pipe staves	29,000 pounds	wool
		5,760 pounds	western bar iron, lumber, stone, rags, etc.

h Moving west across America.
1. Boats on the Ohio River
2. Bellvue, a trader's outpost

h

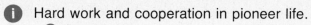

i Hard work and cooperation in pioneer life.
1 Clearing the woods   **3** A frontier farm
2 Building a fence

j Frederick Marryat, the English traveler, described a typical Western religious meeting.

j

Handkerchiefs were raised to bright eyes, and sobs were mingled with prayers and cries. Soon more than 20 men and women were crying out at the highest pitch of their voices and trying to be heard above the others. Every minute the excitement increased. Some wrung their hands and called for mercy; some tore their hair; boys laid down crying bitterly with their heads buried in the straw; there was sobbing almost to suffocation, hysterics, and deep agony.

When it was at its height, one of the preachers came in, and raising his voice high above the noise, asked the Lord to receive into his fold those who now repented and wanted to return to him. Another of the ministers knelt down by some young men, whose faces were covered up and who appeared to be almost in a state of frenzy. Putting his hands on them, the minister poured forth an energetic prayer. Groans, cries, broken sobs, frantic motions, and convulsions followed. Some fell on their backs with their eyes closed, waving their hands with a slow motion and crying out, "Glory, glory, glory!"

When the area was first settled, the people were widely scattered. The truths of the Gospel were seldom heard, because there were only a few preachers. It was because of this problem that they agreed, like the Christians in earlier times, to come together from all quarters and pass many days in meditation and prayer, helping each other. Even now it is not uncommon for the settlers in Indiana and Illinois to travel 100 miles in their wagons to attend one of these meetings.

k Frithjof Meidell, a Norwegian immigrant, described Western life to his family in Norway.

k

Springfield, Illinois

Dear Mother,

I was indeed glad to hear that all of you are getting along so well. The same is true of Christian and me.

How is the railroad getting along? Here in America it is the railroads that build up the whole country. Because of them the farmers get wider markets and higher prices for their products. They seem to put new life into everything. Even the old apple woman sets off at a dogtrot when she hears that whistle to sell her apples to the passengers. Every ten miles along the railways there are stations, which soon grow up into towns. "Soon," did I say? I should have said "immediately," because it is really remarkable how rapidly the stations are transformed into little towns.

Here you can buy houses all ready to be placed on the freight car, and in half a day's time they can be nailed together.

Since I have nothing else to write about this time, I shall attempt to describe how these towns spring up. First, the railroad company builds a depot. Next, a speculator buys the surrounding 100 acres and lays it out in lots, streets, and a marketplace. Then he gives the future town the name of an early President or a famous general—or his own name—holds an auction, and earns many hundred percent on his investment.

A young wagonmaker who has just completed his apprenticeship hears about the station, that it is beautifully located in a rich farming country, is blessed with good water, and, most important of all, that it has no wagonmaker. Making a quick decision, he buys the barest necessities for setting up in his profession, hurries off to the place, rents one of the old log houses, and is soon at work. One absolute necessity he still lacks, however: a sign, of course, which is the most important part of a man's equipment here in America. The next day he hears that there is a tramp painter aboard the train; he gets him off, puts him to work, and the very next day the farmers are surprised to see a monstrous sign straddling the roof of the old log house.

The sign is an immediate success, for the farmers rush to the shop and order wagons, wheels, and the like. The poor man is overwhelmed with more work than he can handle for ever so long. He is about to regret that sign notion of his, but suddenly he has another idea. He accepts every order, and no sooner are the customers away than he seizes his pen and writes to the editors of three different newspapers that three good apprentices can secure steady work with high wages in the "flourishing town of L." Within two days he has help enough and the work goes "like a song."

The train stops again and off steps a blacksmith who went broke in one of the larger towns. He saunters over to the wagonmaker's shop as unconcerned as if he only wished to light his cigar. In a casual way he inquires about the neighborhood and wonders what its prospects are, without indicating that he intends to settle there—by no means! But the wagoner, with his keen Yankee nose, soon smells a rat and starts boosting the place with all his might. This inspires the smith with ecstasy; he starts jumping around and making sledge-hammer motions with his arms. Off he goes and rents the other log house and nails a horseshoe over the door as a sign. The horseshoe, to be sure, cannot be seen any great distance, but the smith has a remedy for this, and he starts to hammer and pound away at his anvil so that the farmers for miles around can hear the echoes. They immediately flock to his door and there is work enough for the blacksmith.

Within a short week, a carpenter, a tailor, and a shoemaker also arrive in town. The wagoner orders a house from the carpenter and rents the second story to the tailor and the shoemaker. Soon the blacksmith also builds a house and things progress with giant strides toward the bigger and better.

Again the train stops. This time two young fellows jump off, look around, and go over to have a chat with the blacksmith. One of them is a doctor, the other a lawyer. Both of them rent rooms from the blacksmith and start business.

Once more the locomotive stops. But—what's this getting off? Be patient! Just let it come closer. It is nothing more nor less than a mustachioed, velvet-frocked German with an old, overworked hurdy-gurdy strapped to his back. On the hurdy-gurdy perches a measly little monkey dressed in red. The German goes over to the blacksmith shop and begins to crank his music box while the monkey smokes tobacco, dances a polka, and grinds coffee. But the German receives no encouragement for his art, nor does the monkey—except some rusty nails which the smith tosses to him. The artist realizes that his audience is very unappreciative and the poor man's face is overcast with sorrow.

Then he looks about inquiringly as if searching for something and steps up to the doctor to ask if there is a restaurant in town. On receiving a negative reply, his face brightens again; and, after a short conversation with the doctor and the lawyer, he steams off with the next train and jumps off at the first big town, where he sells his hurdy-gurdy and monkey and buys a barrel of whiskey, another barrel of biscuits, two large cheeses, tobacco, cigars, and sausages—miles of them. Thereupon, he engages a painter to make an appropriate sign, and in three days he is back again in the new town. Now he rents the blacksmith's old log house and fixes it up as a shop. Soon the sign swings over the door and fortune smiles upon the German innkeeper.

The German, the blacksmith, and the tailor do a rushing business. The train stops again, and this time it is a printer who makes his appearance. He gets in touch with the doctor and lawyer; an old printing press is for sale in the next town; they buy it, and with this new event we can really say that the town has "arrived." There is some little trouble, to be sure, over the political affiliations of the paper, but a compromise is soon reached and the paper announces itself as "independent." The lawyer volunteers to write the editorials, while the doctor promises a wealth of death announcements, and the German and the blacksmith undertake to fill the rest of the paper with advertisements.

Within a few years the town is very large. The wagonmaker owns practically half of it. The German deals only in wholesale. The lawyer is mayor of the town, and the blacksmith does nothing but smoke cigars, for he is now a wealthy man.

Summarize the way in which railroads affected the West.

I 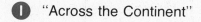 "Across the Continent"

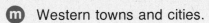

m Western towns and cities.
1. Pittsburgh, 1826
2. Cincinnati, Ohio, 1802
3. Cincinnati, Ohio, 1846
4. Galena, Illinois, 1840

n Eleven years ago, [1813], this was the only place that could properly be called a town on the Ohio and Mississippi from Steubenville to Natchez. It is far different now. But even then it was a large and compact town, with fine buildings rising on the opposite shore and with the steam-factories darting their columns of smoke into the air. All this wealth, large population, and activity has been won from the wilderness within 40 years. In 1815–16 Cincinnati contained between 8,000 and 9,000 inhabitants, handsome streets, a number of churches, and two large market houses. It now is supposed to contain between 16,000 and 20,000 inhabitants. It now has the fourth largest population in the Union.

What value differences are expressed in the two selections?

o Cincinnati is delightful to anyone who loves labor more than anything else. But whoever has a taste for pleasure and expense, amusements and gaity, would find this beautiful city, with its pure sky and beautiful scenery, a wearisome place. It would be even worse for men of leisure interested in the fine arts. For a person like that, life in Cincinnati would be miserable. He would be attacked, because there is a feeling in the United States that men of leisure are the foundations for an aristocracy.

p An Ohio resident made the following statement in 1827.

How does this attitude compare to the attitude of Clay (pages 182–183) and DeBow (pages 188–189) about the South?

p We of this generation are only pioneers. We have done much, but nothing in comparison with what the next generation will do. We are their "cutters of wood and drawers of water"; we came and saw and conquered, but the profit will be theirs. The state of Ohio has progressed at a rate that has far outstripped the most optimistic predictions. Everything around us—improvement in building, the bustle of business in the villages, the emigration of intelligent and enterprising men, the successful work on the canals, the improvement in roads, the increased travel and facilities available to travelers, the increased attention to education, a higher tone of moral feeling in the community—these and a variety of other facts show clearly that Ohio is rapidly progressing in all that make a people happy and respectable.

q The data on page 212 tells you more about the West.

WESTERN STATISTICS
1840-1850

MINNESOTA
- 6,038
- 39/0
- ▲ .04

WISCONSIN
- 304,756
- 635/0
- ▲ 5.7

MICHIGAN
- 395,071
- 2,583/0
- ▲ 7.1

- ■ White population
- ● Free black population/ Slave population
- ▲ Number of people who lived in 1 square mile

IOWA
- 191,881
- 333/0
- ▲ 3.8

ILLINOIS
- 846,034
- 5,436/0
- ▲ 15.4

INDIANA
- 977,154
- 11,262/0
- ▲ 29.2

OHIO
- 1,955,050
- 25,279/0
- ▲ 49.5

KENTUCKY
- 761,413
- 10,011/210,981
- ▲ 26.1

MISSOURI
- 592,004
- 2,618/87,422
- ▲ 10.1

ARKANSAS
- 162,189
- 608/47,100
- ▲ 4.1

TENNESSEE
- 756,836
- 6,422/239,459
- ▲ 21.9

WORKERS IN THE WEST 1840

Learned professions 1.3%
Mining .3%
Navigation .7%
Commerce 1.8%
Manufacturing 12.0%
Agriculture 83.9%

THE PERCENT OF LAND BEING FARMED IN THE WEST 1850

PERCENT

Ohio, Indiana, Illinois, Michigan, Wisconsin, Minnesota, Iowa, Kentucky, Tennessee, Arkansas, Missouri

q

In 1800 France obtained from Spain the vast territory of Louisiana. Because the French restricted American trade down the Mississippi River through New Orleans, President Thomas Jefferson had decided to try to buy New Orleans from France. Napoleon, the ruler of France, needed money and so, sold all of the Louisiana territory to the United States for 15 million dollars. The addition of this territory more than doubled the size of the United States—a great bargain at that price. (The map below shows the Louisiana Purchase.) Treaties for the Louisiana Purchase were signed April 30, 1803, and quickly approved by the U.S. Senate.

A series of government-sponsored explorations helped the United States find out just what it had bought. Between 1804 and 1806, two army officers, Meriwether Lewis and William Clark, led an expedition to explore the territory. Their routes are shown on the map. The explorers described the new territory, Indians, the animals, and the plants of the far West. Their explorations later were the basis for American claims to the Oregon country.

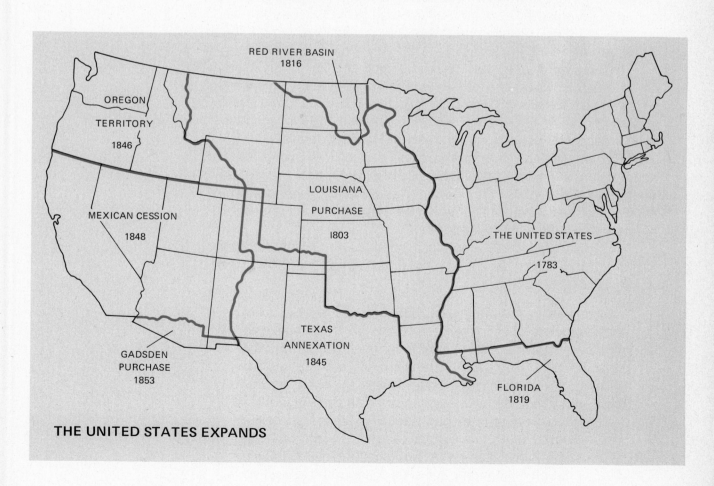

THE UNITED STATES EXPANDS

In other expeditions, Zebulon M. Pike explored the northern Mississippi River and the central plains as far west as the Rockies. In the Rockies he found the peak that now bears his name.

In a short time, Americans began moving into the west, including the Louisiana territory, Oregon country, and the vast land claimed by Mexico in the Southwest and California. Soon, the area that is now Texas was occupied by thousands of Americans, and there were clashes between the Mexican government and the settlers from the United States. In 1836 the dissatisfied Americans declared Texas independent. Finally the Texans defeated the Mexican army. Texas was an independent republic until it became a state in 1845.

Mexico still claimed the territory of Texas as its own, however, and the legal border was not clearly established between Texas and Mexico. President James K. Polk offered to buy California from Mexico but was refused. Because of this border dispute, and because he wanted California, President Polk was eager to find an excuse to go to war against Mexico.

Finally, after being provoked, Mexican troops attacked and Congress declared war. The United States troops won many victories and finally occupied Mexico City. In the peace treaty of 1848 the United States received about half of Mexico's land, including California, the disputed area of Texas, and all the land between. (See the map on page 213.) In exchange, the United States paid Mexico more than 18 million dollars.

The Oregon country was claimed by both the United States and Great Britain. However, the territory was occupied by many Americans, who wished it to belong to the United States. The issue of ownership was settled in 1846, when the border between the United States and Canada was established by treaty at the 49th parallel.

Not long before California became part of the United States, an important event took place there. Early in 1848, near present-day Sacramento, California, men working at a water-powered sawmill accidentally discovered gold. Within the next two years, thousands of fortune seekers went to California.

The gold rush made enormous changes in California. Writer Richard Henry Dana described San Francisco Bay in 1835, then again in 1859.

It was in the winter of 1835–6 that the ship *Alert,* in the process of her voyage for hides on the remote and almost unknown coast of California, floated into the vast solitude of the Bay of San Francisco. All around was the stillness of nature. One vessel, a Russian, lay at anchor there, but during our whole stay not a sail came or went.

Our anchorage was between a small island, called Yerba Buena, and a gravel beach in a little bight, or cove, of the same name, formed by two small projecting points. Over a region far beyond our sight there were almost no human dwellings. There were no settlements, and the few ranchos and missions were remote and widely separated. Not only the neighborhood of our anchorage, but the entire region of the great bay was a solitude. On the whole coast of California there was no lighthouse, beacon, or buoy.

On the evening of Saturday, the 13th of August 1859, the superb steamship *Golden Gate,* gay with crowds of passengers, neared the entrance to San Francisco, the great center of a worldwide commerce. Miles out at sea gleamed the powerful rays of one of the most costly and effective lighthouses in the world. As we drew in through the Golden Gate, on the right was a large fortification protecting the narrow entrance, and just before us the little island of Alcatraz confronted us—one entire fortress. We bore round the point towards the old anchoring-ground of the hide ships, and there, covering the sand hills and the valleys, stretching from the water's edge to the base of the great hills, and from the old presidio to the mission, flickering all over with the lamps of its streets and houses, lay a city of 100,000 inhabitants. Clipper ships of the largest size lay at anchor in the stream, or were tied to the wharves; and spacious high-pressure steamers, as large and showy as those of the Hudson or Mississippi, bodies of dazzling light, awaited the delivery of our mails, to take their cruises up the bay.

The dock into which we drew and the streets about it were densely crowded with express wagons and handcarts to take luggage, and coaches and cabs to take passengers. There were agents of the press and a great crowd eager for newspapers and verbal intelligence from the great Atlantic and European world. Through this crowd I made my way, along the well-built and well-lighted streets, as alive as today, where boys in high-keyed voices were already crying the latest New York papers; and between one and two o'clock in the morning found myself comfortably abed in a comfortable room in the Oriental Hotel, which stood, as well as I can learn, not far from the spot where we used to beach our boats from the *Alert.*

In the 1840s and 1850s, Americans, especially from the Northeast and from the old Western region, began to move further west across the continent. Pioneers made the long journey to Iowa, Indiana, and Kansas. There, they found huge stretches of flat land on which they planted grain, especially wheat. Others made even longer journeys to Oregon, to California, to Texas. They found open land on which to raise stock, great forests and rivers, and even gold.

As these pioneers settled new areas, the United States grew. In 1800 there had been just 16 states. By 1850 there were 31.

The "Golden Gate" is the name of the entrance to the harbor at San Francisco. Golden Gate was also the name of Dana's ship.

Putting the Pieces Together

1. Using your notes summarize life in the Western region. Include information on the four categories you have investigated.

2. Describe opinions and attitudes you'd expect the average person in the West to have had about
   a. Slavery
   b. Working as a laborer
   c. Equality of various kinds and classes of people
   d. The future

3. In what important ways do you think the society of the Western region was different from that of the other two regions you've studied?

Choose one of these activities:

1. Investigate the early history of your state. Find out who settled the area and when and how it became a state.

2. Read about the lives of Marcus and Narcissa Whitman, early settlers of the Oregon country.

3. Make a map showing the trails pioneers took to the West.

Investigating Habitat: The West

Throughout the preceding data is information about the habitat in the West—the land, rivers, climate, etc. Use atlases and other resources to find out more about the West's habitat.

Trace or draw a simple outline map of the West. On the map place information about mountains, navigable rivers, waterpower, farmland, soil quality, growing season, natural resources, and other important facts.

Tell how you think the habitat of the West is related to the ideas and ways of acting of the people who lived there in 1800–1850.

Part 4

Comparing Regions

You've studied writings, pictures, and statistics on the three main regions of the United States in the period from 1800 to 1850. You've thought about the ways in which people in those regions thought and acted, and you've examined the events and conditions—experiences—that affected those thoughts and actions.

In certain ways, of course, the three regions were alike. All were part of the United States. All were affected by the same national laws and decisions. But in other important ways the regions were not alike. Different events and conditions in a region led to ideas and actions that were different from those of people in other regions.

As you compare the three regions, try to answer this question. **How can different experiences lead to different ways of thinking and acting?**

Technology and Regional Difference

Technology is all of the machines, tools, and methods by which a group of people make the things that they need and want. Important changes in technology affected all sections of the United States in the first half of the 1800s. Some of the new machines affected the Northeast, some the South, others the West. In every case, new technology was important in the development of these regions.

● Below are brief descriptions of inventions or developments that became important between 1800 and 1850.

For each invention or development:
1. Identify the region or regions you think it most affected.
2. Describe, in a sentence or two, the effects you think it had on the region.

Cotton Gin

One of the early problems with growing cotton was separating the seeds from the fibers. This was a slow, difficult, and expensive job. Hand-picking one pound of fibers from three pounds of seed had been a full day's work for one slave. Because of this, very little cotton was grown, and cotton cloth was rare. In 1793 Eli Whitney developed a machine for this job. Even in its first crude form, it could clean cotton fifty times faster than work by hands. Later, larger cotton gins (**gin** is short for engine) could clean hundreds of pounds each day.

Spinning Machine

English textile factories were more advanced than factories in America. Machines for spinning fibers into thread were developed in England, but the design of these machines was kept secret. Americans offered money to anyone who would bring the secret of the design to America. Samuel Slater, a young textile mechanic familiar with the machines, came to America and succeeded in building a spinning machine here in 1791. Many cotton-spinning mills were soon established.

Power Loom

Weaving thread into cloth was originally done slowly on hand looms. After several years of experiments, a successful power-driven loom was built around 1814. By 1840 one American town had nine mills with 4,000 power looms.

Railroads

The first practical steam locomotive was built in England in 1812. By 1825 John Stevens had opened the first railway in America. The use of steam-powered locomotives grew extremely rapidly, and by 1840 there were 2,800 miles of railroad track in the United States. At first most railways were local operations. It was not until 1850 that long-distance runs began.

Steamboats

In 1807 a steam-powered boat called the *Clermont* steamed up the Hudson River from New York City to Albany. It traveled 150 miles in 32 hours, against the current. Steamboats had been built earlier but Robert Fulton was the first to build one powerful enough to convince people of its success. By 1860 over 1,000 steamboats were in use in America.

Reaper

Producing large quantities of wheat and other grain was difficult because of the labor needed to harvest the grain. Cyrus Hall McCormick solved this problem for wheat growers in 1834 when he developed the reaper. This machine cut the wheat stalks evenly, which made it far easier to remove the grain. With a reaper, one man and a team of horses could do the work of 20 or more men cutting grain by hand.

Canals

Water transportation was the cheapest way to move large quantities of freight, but some parts of the country did not have navigable rivers. This problem was solved by building canals. Boats were lifted from one level to another by changing the water level in compartments called **locks.**

Best known and most successful of the canals built during this period was the Erie Canal. By using the Erie Canal, a shipper could reduce the cost of shipping a ton of grain from Buffalo to New York City from 100 to 5 dollars. The shipping time was cut from about twenty days to six.

1. Which of the technological developments described would have been most important in changing regional development? Why?
2. How would the technology have affected regional differences? Explain.

New Americans

Since the first Jamestown colonists, immigrants had continued to come to America. However, about 1815 the flow of newcomers began to increase, as indicated on the chart below.

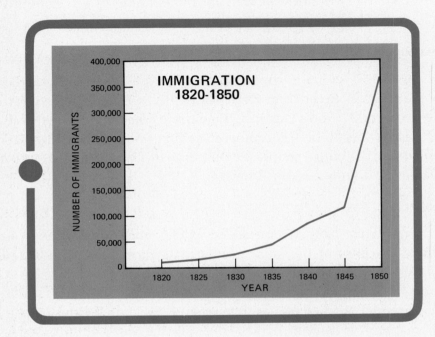

Based on what you know about the three regions of the United States between 1800 and 1850,

1. Where would you expect most immigrants to settle? Why?
2. In what region would you not expect immigrants to settle? Why?
3. In what region would you have settled if you had been a skilled laborer in Europe?
4. In what region would you have settled if you had been a farmer and arrived in the United States with no money? With a little money?

Putting the Pieces Together

Now that you've studied the regions of the Northeast, South, and West, you should have a picture of some of the more important qualities of these three regions. This activity will give you a chance to check yourself.

a → g   Each of the following selections suggests one or more of the ideas shared by the people of one region.

For each selection, identify
1. The shared idea or ideas
2. The region in which the idea was held
3. The experiences which probably helped the idea develop

a During the summer months they take tours. The winter months are the season of gaiety. Their parties are unequaled in the elegance, refinement, and the loveliness of the individuals who compose them. If you will remember that these females are educated in the most finished style, at the finest female private schools and sometimes in Europe; and remember their personal beauty, sprightliness, and extreme refinement, you will not be surprised that elegant women grace the private circles and parties.

Less attention is paid to the mental or personal development of the male youth of this state than to that of the females.

b Any man's son may become the equal of any other man's son, and knowing this makes them work harder. On the other hand, it also encourages that coarseness and lack of respect for their betters they often display.

c Towns in this area provide for all sick strangers not otherwise provided for within their limits. The expense is paid back from the public treasury.

Every town is required to support its own inhabitants when they are unable to support themselves.

d When Israel was in Egypt's land,
  Let my people go;
Oppressed so hard they could not stand,
  Let my people go.

Chorus:
Go down, Moses, way down in Egypt's land;
Tell old Pharoah, to let my people go.

Thus saith the Lord, bold Moses said,
    Let my people go;
If not I'll smite your first-born dead,
    Let my people go.

No more shall they in bondage toil,
    Let my people go;
Let them come out with Egypt's spoil,
    Let my people go.

We need not always weep and moan,
    Let my people go;
And wear these slavery chains forlorn,
    Let my people go.

What a beautiful morning that will be,
    Let my people go;
When time breaks up in eternity,
    Let my people go.

Would it do a horse or an ox any good if you gave him a cultivated understanding, or an appreciation of fine things? If a mere laborer has pride, knowledge, or if he desires to improve himself, he is not suited to be a laborer.

If there are nasty, servant-like, and laborious jobs to be done, it is better that there are nasty, servant-like, and laborious beings to do them.

I wish I could give you an idea of the perfect equality that exists among these people. A judge leaves the courthouse, shakes hands with his fellow citizens, and retires to his house. The next day you will find him holding his own plow. The lawyer has the title of captain and serves in his military capacity under his neighbour, who is a farmer and a colonel. The shopkeeper sells a yard of tape; he travels 2,000 miles in a year, is a good hunter, and has been a soldier. He dresses and talks as well as a London merchant. One prejudice, however, nothing will convince him to give up. He thinks the Americans in general, and particularly those of his own state, are the best soldiers in the world. Such is the native shopkeeper.

I have not seen a weak man, in mind or body. The most

ignorant, compared with men of the same standing in England, are well informed. Their manners are coarse; but they have amongst themselves a code of politeness, which they generally observe.

g When the efforts of one group to oppress another group have become too obvious to ignore and too harmful to endure, it has often been necessary for those who feel wronged to band together for mutual protection.

We, the workers of this city and county, knowing that our social position is lower than is fair, feel that we have no power as individuals to right the wrongs that result when most of the wealth and power is in the hands of a few. For this reason, we desire to band together to try and solve those problems which poverty and unending hard work have created for us, and which threaten to destroy us.

h During the years 1800 to 1850, in which region or regions of the United States would you be most likely to hear the following opinions? What group of people in the region would most likely express these? Give reasons for your answers.

h
1. "What this country needs is a tariff on foreign manufactured goods. This will give American industry a chance to grow."
2. "Gentlemen don't engage in physical labor."
3. "We need to move to new farmland. Let's take over more land in the Southwest."
4. "For lower-class people, education is mostly a waste of time."
5. "For ordinary people like me, this is really a land of opportunity."
6. "A magazine of essays and poetry would probably sell best in this part of America."
7. "We're all about alike, so we should all have the vote."
8. "Senator, I hope you'll vote to keep the price of 'Western' land high."
9. "Around here, a new town is organized just about every day."
10. "In this part of the country, you either have it or you don't. There aren't many in the middle."

Answer these questions about regions of the United States:

1. One of the political changes important in this period was the development of political conventions—large meetings of political party delegates who met to nominate candidates for elections to public office. This gave the average citizen a greater share in choosing candidates. In which section or sections do you think this idea was most strongly supported?

2. Who would be considered a "successful man" in the West? How was this different from the idea of a "successful man" in the South?

The War of 1812

In the first years of the 1800s, France and Great Britain were fighting a full-scale war. France, led by Napoleon, was trying to conquer all of Europe. Great Britain was France's most powerful enemy.

As a neutral country, America hoped to continue to trade with both countries, but this soon became very difficult. The French navy did all it could to keep American ships from reaching Great Britain, and the British navy interfered with American ships trying to reach French ports.

American shippers were hurt by the blockades. However, what most aroused American feeling was a British practice called "impressment"—forcing sailors, including Americans, to serve on British navy ships. The British had built a powerful navy of over 700 ships, but British sailors were so poorly paid and so unpleasantly treated they often deserted to American ships. This caused British officers to feel they had a right to stop all American ships and search for deserters. This they did, sometimes recapturing British sailors but frequently taking American seamen too.

To try to get England and France to treat the United States fairly, President Jefferson had Congress pass a measure called the Embargo Act, forbidding all foreign trade. It was a painful experience. Shippers in New England and New York were almost ruined, and farmers in the South and West began to suffer from the loss of their overseas market.

The Embargo Act was so unpopular that Jefferson and Congress replaced it with another law. This law stated that trade between the United States and Great Britain and France was forbidden. Trade would be renewed only when those countries changed their policies toward the United States and its ships and sailors.

Relations with England rapidly grew worse, and many Americans urged Congress to declare war. Westerners especially favored war. Farm prices had been falling, and Westerners blamed their troubles on the loss of foreign markets and the British sea policies. Westerners also were land-hungry. They wanted to push further and further west and north and wanted no foreign powers standing in their way (as they felt the British did in Canada).

Most New Englanders, on the other hand, were violently against a war with Great Britain. New England's economy depended heavily on trade. Since much of the trade was with Canada and England, conflict with Britain would hurt New England.

Finally the War Hawks (the name given to war supporters) won and Congress declared war on Great Britain. For two years battles were fought on land and sea. Neither side fought well and few gains were made. Finally, both sides agreed to discuss peace terms. A treaty, signed in Ghent, Belgium, on December 24, 1814, simply ended the fighting. Although the British stopped their tactics on the seas, the most important benefit of the war was a change in attitudes. Americans came out of the war feeling less like a collection of states and more like a nation. The War of 1812 helped the United States grow up.

The war's last battle was fought at New Orleans (below).

Application

What about Americans today? How do shared experiences affect their lives, their ways of thinking and acting? Geographical differences are no longer as important as they were 150 years ago. Although not all Americans share the same experiences or have the same ways of thinking and acting, some experiences are shared by many Americans today, in all regions of the United States. Now you'll examine one of those experiences.

Fourteen times! That's the average number of times Americans change residence during their lifetimes. Moving is so common that it's easy to forget that frequent moving is new to the American way of life. In earlier times, Americans did not have the **mobility**—that is, the opportunity and ability to move—that they have today. Today, improvements in transportation make it possible for Americans to move quickly and relatively easily.

● The experience of moving from one community to another affects people in different ways. Here are some comments about moving, taken from Vance Packard's book *A Nation of Strangers*.

"I think sooner or later every family has to decide what is more important—money and position or roots".

"You feel you are not really here because they expect you to move and so they don't care about getting acquainted."

"Roots are ruts."

"There's no morality here and I guess it's because nobody knows anybody. You can get away with stuff you couldn't in the old days."

"It was painful when I had to leave. Now I have a tendency not to get too close."

"Moving forces you to extend yourself as a person in order to meet people in a new location."

"If you are ambitious, moving is a part of the package. Most of my friends seem to thrive as long as they are moving up."

"I move to a new area with the feeling I will meet new people and will have many happy experiences—and I usually do."

"I worry about the kids. When we move to a new place, they're so anxious to make friends they'll take up with anyone."

Based on these comments, what seems to be the greatest disadvantage in moving? What is the main advantage?

1. Examine the ideas and actions listed below. Decide how you think frequent moving would affect each of these ways of thinking or acting.
   a. Interest in local or state government
   b. Family life
      Marriage
      Parent-child relationships
   c. Social organizations
      Schools
      Churches
      Clubs
   d. Obeying laws
2. How do you think you would be affected by frequent moving?
3. In your opinion, how would great mobility within a nation affect regional differences? Why?

BIBLIOGRAPHY

Chidsey, Donald Barr. *Lewis and Clark: The Great Adventure.* Crown, 1970. An exciting account of the expedition President Jefferson sent out to explore the unknown territory west of the Mississippi. The two-year trip included great hardships and thrilling adventures. Lewis and Clark gained valuable information about the Indians, the lands, rivers, climate, plants, and animals of this vast region.

Wright, Louis B. *Everyday Life in the New Nation, 1787-1860.* N.Y.: G. P. Putnam's, 1972. Describes clearly and concisely the social life of a growing nation between the end of the Revolutionary War and the years preceding the outbreak of the Civil War.

Meltzer, Milton. *Bound for the Rio Grande.* N.Y.: Alfred A. Knopf, 1974. Letters, diaries, maps, songs, speeches, and illustrations are combined to tell the story of the Mexican War, 1845-1850.

Tunis, Edwin. *The Young United States, 1783 to 1830.* N.Y.: World, 1969, and *Frontier Living,* N.Y.: World, 1961. Two books by a very talented writer-artist. Both have black-and-white drawings to illustrate the tools, fashions, and everyday items of the times.

UNIT 4

Civil War

Polarization

How does polarization lead to conflict?

Introduction

"Fight!" "Riot!" "Rebellion!" "War!"

Every day, stories of violent conflict fill the newspapers and news programs. Violent conflict takes the lives of men, women, and children, destroys property, ruins the earth's resources, and creates sadness and pain. Violent conflict is one of the most serious problems human beings face.

How and why does violent conflict start? Riots and wars don't just suddenly happen. Almost always they can be traced back to some small beginning—a minor disagreement or a slight misunderstanding. In steps almost too small to notice, friction between groups grows, hostility increases, and finally violence becomes almost impossible to avoid.

This gradual step-by-step increase in hostility between two groups is called **polarization.** If violent conflict is ever to be controlled, an understanding of this process is necessary. That is the purpose of this unit.

"How did the fight start, boys?"
"He hit me first!"
"Well, he shoved me."
"I only shoved you easy. Anyway, you smashed my frisbee."
"It was an accident."
"It was not. You did it on purpose!"

With only minor differences, conversations like this one occur many times every day. Beginning with a small misunderstanding, friction can grow between two people or groups. Feelings become stronger, actions become more forceful, and the two sides move farther and farther apart. This is polarization.

Based on a personal experience, or the experience of someone you know, think of a conflict which ended in a fight. Use this experience to make a chart, following the directions below.

1. In the lower right corner of a sheet of paper, describe the last action taken in the fight. Above this, on the left, describe what the other side did which caused the action on the lower right. For example, in the conflict shown on the sample chart, "calling the police" was the last thing that happened.

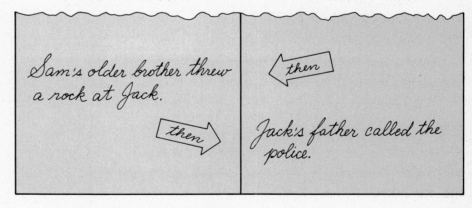

2. Continue making the chart in this way. List the actions which occurred, until you reach what seems to be the beginning of the situation. Draw arrows showing which action caused another.

3. Now study your chart. In the situation you've just described, which side would probably say, "They started it"?

As polarization continues, several things usually happen. Each of these is a specific element, or part, of the process of polarization.

1. Members within each group begin to feel closer to each other. They tend to forget their differences and think mostly of ways they are like each other and unlike the "other side." The result is sometimes called **in-group cohesion.** "Cohesion" is the act or process of sticking tightly together. What do you think "in-group" means?

2. Each group begins to think that members of the "other side" (the out-group) are very much alike. Even though the other side is made up of separate individuals, all different, their variety is forgotten. All members of the group are seen as having the same qualities, which are usually considered bad. This way of thinking is called **stereotyping.**

3. The argument between the two sides becomes more and more simple. In the beginning, the issues may have been complicated, with many points of disagreement. However, as the situation heats up, each side begins to focus on one or two ideas. They use these ideas as reasons for their actions. The ideas are sometimes called the group's **ideology.**

Think of a conflict in your own experience. From this conflict give examples of one or more of these three elements of polarization—in-group cohesion, stereotyping, and ideology.

Polarization in Camp

In this activity you'll read about events that took place at a summer camp. The camp is located on 125 acres of woods and hills in New England. It includes two bunkhouses, an open dining hall, an athletic area, and other facilities. Twenty-four boys—all about 12 years old—attended the camp for three weeks. None of the boys knew one another before meeting that summer.

ⓐ→ⓘ   What you are about to read reports the camp counselors' observations of what happened among the boys at the camp.

Use the questions to help you see how polarization developed that summer.

Days 1-3

ⓐ All the boys lived in the same bunkhouse. They ate and joined in activities together. They were allowed to plan most of their own activities.

Day 4

After breakfast, the staff divided the boys into two groups. One group was assigned the color red and the other the color blue. The groups were asked to decide which of the two bunkhouses they wanted.

The Red Group decided to stay in the old bunkhouse. The Blue Group voted to move to the new bunkhouse. One boy, Thomas, cried for ten minutes because he was going to be separated from Taylor, his special friend.

Bulldogs

On arriving at the bunkhouse, the Blue Group decided to decorate their bunkhouse blue and white. They called themselves the "Bulldogs." They decided to put the letter "B" on the door and build a chinning bar.

Immediately after the bunkhouse choices were made, cars took each group from the camp for a separate hike and cookout. The groups did not have much contact with each other for the next few days.

At the end of Day 4, how do you think each boy felt about his own group? About the other group?

Reread the discussion of stereotyping on page 232. Why do you think it's easier to stereotype a group of people when they have a label or name?

Day 5

Each group was given ten dollars to spend as it pleased.

Red Devils

b After much discussion over how to spend their money, one boy suggested buying a tetherball game for outside their bunkhouse.

"Good idea," the others said. "What about the other group? Wouldn't they use it?"

Bulldogs

After some discussion, the Bulldogs decided to buy a basket of fresh fruit for their bunkhouse and blue hats with the letter "B" on them.

"Let's build a fence around it."

"Yeah. Let's set boundaries around our territory and mark them with stakes."

During the discussion of their territory that followed, one boy said, "Let's call ourselves the Red Devils and all these things are ours."

The Red Devils set up their boundaries.

Day 5 (continued)

Red Devils	Bulldogs
	While the Red Devils were swimming, the Bulldogs went to the Red Devil bunkhouse and messed up some of the Red Devil decorations.
When the Red Devils returned and found that the Bulldogs had invaded their property, they wanted to raid the Bulldog bunkhouse. One of the counselors stopped this, saying, "They were only playing. Aren't they your friends?"	The Bulldogs went swimming and picked a secret spot for their swimming hole. It was away from the Red Devil swimming spot.
Shaw, a Red Devil leader, ordered new crepe paper decorations from a camp official. He specified red. The official asked, "How about some other color, like green or blue?" Shaw sneered, "Not blue! Not that color. We just want red and white."	During mail call, Thomas of the Bulldogs received a letter. A boy he had been friendly with—Taylor of the Red Devils—was right beside him. However, Thomas moved to his own group and sat down among them to read his letter.
	Bulldog members took an oath of secrecy: "I swear not to tell our secret swimming hole or any of the secrets of the Bulldog cabin."

What evidence of in-group cohesion can you see in the actions of the two groups?

Day 6

Red Devils	Bulldogs
Red Devils built a shelter in the woods.	Bulldogs began to improve their swimming hole by removing rocks.
Three of the Red Devils were still friendly with some of the Bulldogs. The rest of the Red Devils called them "traitors" and threatened to rough them up if they didn't stop associating with the Bulldogs.	While the rest of the Bulldogs were swimming, a few of them worked hard at the hideout to build a latrine, with no complaining.

At this point, how do you think each boy felt about his own group? About the other group?

On Days 9 to 11, the two teams took part in competition against each other. As you read, think about how team competition affected the development of polarization.

Day 9

This notice was posted on the camp bulletin board.

SPECIAL TEAM COMPETITION

MONDAY	TUG OF WAR:	5 points to winner
	SOFTBALL GAME:	15 points to winner
	BUNKHOUSE INSPECTION:	10 points to winner
	K.P. AND SWEEPING:	1 to 10 points to each team.

TUESDAY	TUG OF WAR:	5 points to winner
	SOCCER GAME:	15 points to winner
	BUNKHOUSE INSPECTION:	10 points to winner
	K.P. AND SWEEPING:	1 to 10 points to each team.

WEDNESDAY	TUG OF WAR:	5 points to winner
	TOUCH FOOTBALL:	15 points to winner
	TREASURE HUNT:	5 points to winner
	BUNKHOUSE INSPECTION:	10 points to winner
	K.P. AND SWEEPING:	1 to 10 points to each team.

ALL MEMBERS OF THE WINNING TEAM WILL RECEIVE
4-BLADED CAMPING KNIVES

Red Devils	Bulldogs
	The Bulldogs won Monday's tug of war.
Red Devils said, "They won because they had better ground." The Devils spent much of the rest of the morning discussing the loss and planning strategy for the next day.	
Near the end of the softball game, the Red Devils were behind with two outs and nobody on base. Fenwick came to bat and was tagged out on a ground ball. He cried, going off by himself and saying, "I lost the game for us."	
When Fenwick returned to the cabin, the rest of the group treated him normally and did not mention his part in the game.	Immediately after the game, Bulldogs gave a cheer, "2—4—6—8, who do we appreciate? Red Devils!" Bulldogs said, "We won because we've got organization. Yeah, those Red Devils don't pull together."

At the end of the ninth day, the Red Devils had 16 points and the Bulldogs had 26.

Day 10

The Red Devils almost won the tug of war, but the Bulldogs managed to pull ahead at the last minute.

Red Devils	Bulldogs
Red Devils said, "They must have done something to the rope."	The Bulldogs cheered, "2—4—6—8, who do we appreciate? Red Devils!"
The Red Devils won the soccer game. The Red Devils cheered, "2—4—6—8, who do we appreciate? Bulldogs!"	

The cheer was answered by the Bulldogs, and then changed to: "2—4—6—8, who do we appreci-HATE? Red Devils!"

At the end of the tenth day, the Red Devils had 41½ points, and the Bulldogs had 46½ points.

Day 11

The Bulldogs won the tug of war.

Red Devils	Bulldogs
"You guys are dirty players." "Yeah, you guys cheat." "2—4—6—8, who do we appreci-HATE? Bulldogs!"	"2—4—6—8, who do we appreci-HATE? Red Devils!"

g

During the touch football game, Red Devils called Bulldogs, "dirty players" and "cheats." "We could win easy if you guys didn't cheat," Red Devils said.

"We don't cheat. You guys are lousy players. We got organization," Bulldogs said.

At the end of the three-day competition, the Red Devils had 49½ points. The Bulldogs had 89½ points. The Bulldogs were awarded camping knives as prizes.

The Bulldogs said several times that they won because they had organization. This is a very simple kind of ideology. See page 232.

How has competition affected attitudes toward out-groups? Identify words and expressions that are stereotypes.

Day 11 (continued)

h

During the evening both groups were asked to attend a party in the dining hall. On a table were refreshments—ice cream and cake. When the boys arrived, some of the food was already crushed and messy.

Red Devils	Bulldogs

The Red Devils arrived first, picked the best refreshments, and carried them to their own table.

The Bulldogs arrived and saw what had happened. They called the Red Devils "pigs," "bums," and other nastier names.

Red Devils said, "First come, first served."

Bulldogs said,
"Let's throw our beat-up cake at the Red Devils!"
"Yeah, let's!"
"Naw, let's eat it. It will taste O.K., even if it is beat up."
"You Red Devils are pigs!"
"Yeah, dirty, rotten pigs!"
"2—4—6—8, who do we appreci-HATE? Red Devil pigs!"

"You guys are cheaters!" "Dirty players!"

One Bulldog sauntered over to the Red Devil table and showed his prize knife, saying, "I got something you guys don't."

"You guys are dirty rotten cheats!" "Cheaters, cheaters, cheaters!"

"Pigs!" "Jerks!" "Bums!"

After eating, most of the Red Devils ran out of the dining hall and down to the river.

The Bulldogs dumped their dirty plates and empty ice-cream cartons on the Red Devils' table.

One Red Devil saw this, complained, and began a fight with one Bulldog.

Another Bulldog pulled out his knife, opened it, and started to threaten the Red Devil with it. A counselor stopped the fight and made the boy put the knife away.

These posters show attitudes each group had toward the other.

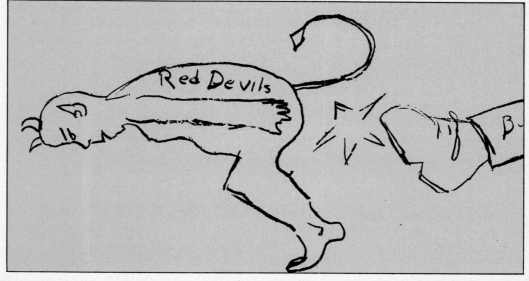

Day 12

Red Devils	Bulldogs

During breakfast, the Red Devils dirtied their table by spilling cocoa, milk, crumbs, etc., to make cleanup work hard for the Bulldogs, who had K. P. that day.

The Bulldogs found the messy table and decided to mess it up more and leave it. They smeared the table with more cocoa, sugar, syrup, etc. The table was soon covered with insects.

They also hung signs on the walls around the table.
—The Red Devils are Pigs.
—The Red Devils are Bums.
—We have a team.

The Bulldogs set the table for lunch, putting the Red Devils' plates and silver on the dirty, insect-covered table.

The Red Devils found the table, tore down the signs, and moved their plates to a different table.

They called the Bulldogs names during the meal: "Dirty cheats!" "Bums!" Other stronger names followed.

They called the Red Devils names during the meal: "Dirty rotten pigs!" "Jerks!" "Bums!"

At the end of the meal, a fight started between the two groups. Both sides threw sponges, food, and finally dishes and table knives at each other. With some difficulty, the fight was stopped by the staff.

Red Devils	Bulldogs

"They started it!"

"They started it!"

K.P. stands for "kitchen police." People on K.P. assist with duties in the kitchen.

240

Upstairs in their bunkhouse, the Red Devils started calling names at a few Bulldogs outside.

The Bulldogs responded with other names and taunts.

Both sides soon started throwing green apples, and another fight broke out. Two windows were broken. The fighting was finally stopped by a counselor.

For the remainder of camp, counselors worked to patch up the trouble. Camping activities were designed to mix up the groups. They emphasized individual competition rather than competition between the groups. Some strong feelings between the groups lasted until the end of camp, however.

Make a chart for this conflict, following the directions on page 231. Work backward through the account, event by event, explaining why the Bulldogs and Red Devils acted the way they did. Explain how you think each group felt at each point in the conflict.

Do you feel that each group's actions were understandable and reasonable considering the other group's actions? Explain.

STOP & SUMMARIZE

● On page 242 are five statements often made when people are involved in conflict.

1. Identify elements of polarization—in-group cohesion, stereotyping, ideology—in each.
2. Choose one of the statements and then make up a story about it. Write a dialogue, or short play, describing how the conflict develops. Include in your dialogue the statement you've chosen from those below. Also be sure to include examples of the elements of polarization.

a. "You just can't trust those people. They act nice until you turn your back. Then they take advantage of you."

b. "It's up to us to teach them a lesson they won't forget. They don't have a right to push us around."

c. "We were here first!"

d. "Joe, you and the others defend the strip along the stream and we'll watch the road. If everyone works together, we won't let anyone reach our spot without being seen."

e. "They won't be able to figure out our plans. They aren't smart enough."

BRANCHING OUT

Although polarization and conflict cause many problems, polarization is not necessarily all bad. In-group cohesion, for example, may help group members cooperate to protect each other.

Based on your own experiences and ideas, describe a situation in which polarization has led or might lead to a good outcome.

Perspective

Polarization has always been a part of life in America. The process of polarization helps explain the conflict between the Puritans and the Church of England, and it helps explain the Puritan decision to move to North America. Polarization helped bring about the French and Indian War and explains some of the events that led to the American Revolution. The list could go on, for there are hundreds of historical examples which show polarization's important effect on events in this country.

In this section you'll see how polarization helped bring about the Civil War—the most violent and bloody conflict fought in this country.

Part 1   Background for Conflict

What were the main issues which triggered polarization within the nation?

What were the Northern and Southern positions on these issues?

Part 2   Increasing Hostility

How did events and actions further polarize the North and South?

Part 3   War and Reconstruction

What effects did the Civil War and Reconstruction have on polarization within the nation?

1820
Missouri Compromise

1850
Compromise of 1850
Fugitive Slave Law

1854
Kansas-Nebraska Act

1857
Dred Scott decision

1860
Lincoln elected   South Carolina secedes

1861
Confederacy formed   Civil War erupts at Fort Sumter

1862
Monitor v. *Merrimac*

1863
Emancipation Proclamation   Gettysburg Address

1864
Sherman's march through Georgia

1865
Lee surrenders   Lincoln assassinated   13th amendment abolishes slavery

1868
14th amendment gives blacks citizenship

1870
15th amendment protects blacks' voting rights

1877
Military reconstruction ended

Part 1

Background for Conflict

The years following the War of 1812 are often called the "Era of Good Feelings." As you learned in Unit 3, America's population grew rapidly during this time. Industry expanded. Roads and canals were built. Settlers moved west. More and more citizens began to think of themselves as "Americans" as a national spirit developed.

But under the surface, feelings weren't all good. As you've seen, the Northeast, the South, and the West were all different. Each section had its own problems. As you'll read, federal laws and programs which helped one section made the problems in another section worse. These differences were a background and beginning for polarization.

The activities in Part 1 will help you answer these questions:

What were the main issues which triggered polarization within the nation?

What were the Northern and Southern positions on these issues?

The different needs and interests of the Northeast, South, and West made friction between them unavoidable. Trouble took place not in the sections, however, but in Congress. There, representatives from states in each section argued for laws they believed would help the people they represented. Unfortunately, it often happened that a law which the people of one section felt they needed created serious problems for people in another part of the country.

This sectional struggle continued for years. Gradually, however, the Northeast and the West moved closer to agreement with each other. They became simply the "North" in the struggle for power with the South.

The materials in this activity present the most important disagreements between the sections during the early 1800s.

The Tariff

As you have learned, a **tariff** is a tax placed on imported foreign products. The purpose of a tariff is to raise the price of the foreign products when they are sold in this country. The tariff issue became the subject of much debate and dispute between Northern and Southern representatives in Congress in the early 1800s.

Based on the comments which follow, answer these questions:

1. What was the disagreement over the tariff?
2. What was the Northern position on the issue? The Southern position?
3. What reasons did each side give for its position?

a Representative Gold expressed the following opinion during a debate in the House of Representatives in 1816.

New machinery has revolutionized the manufacture of cotton cloth. Five or six men can now operate a factory having 2,000 spindles. Any country which doesn't make use of this machinery, and buys its cloth from another country, is throwing money away. Sir James Stewart, an expert on these matters, has said, "A nation should manufacture everything it can at home, and control the competition from other nations by taxing foreign products brought into the country."

No friend of this country can look at the enormous amount of manufactured products brought into America last year and not be worried. We paid over 130 million dollars for British products. They paid us only about 91 million dollars for ours.

In fairness to all parts of the country, manufacturing should be encouraged. The South sold her cotton and tobacco for about 30 million dollars last year, but the North can produce no huge, profitable crop. The North must either turn to manufacturing or become poor.

Which section of the United States do you think Representative Gold was from? What reasons did he give in support of manufacturing?

b Representative Telfair offered these comments in 1816.

In my opinion, manufactured products coming into this country should be taxed only for the purpose of raising money to operate the government. We should not get involved in trying to protect American manufacturers. I believe it is dangerous to pass laws which favor certain small groups or classes.

At the present time, the small profits and great skill of foreign manufacturers keep the price of their products low. If a bill protecting American manufacturers is passed, it will mean that the planters will be able to choose only between high-priced American and high-priced foreign products.

Let us leave the manufacturers alone. We have in this country vast areas of land. The soil is rich. The people are healthy, strong, and independent. Considering these facts, it is obvious that for years to come Americans should be farmers and traders. We should not get ahead of ourselves by pushing the development of manufacturing too soon.

Which section of the country do you think Telfair represented?

What was Telfair's position on protecting American manufacturers? What reasons did he give?

After Northern and Southern sides of the issue had been debated, Congress passed a tarriff law in 1816. In 1824 and again in 1828, Congress passed laws that raised the tariff.

c Here are John C. Calhoun's reactions to the 1828 tariff. These remarks were prepared when Calhoun, a native of South Carolina, was Vice President of the United States.

We are slaves of this system. Out of our labor the manufacturers get rich. Whatever helps them, hurts us. The taxes on imports raise the costs of what we buy, and we cannot increase the price of what we sell enough to make up the difference.

God has given our section of the country a warm sun and a rich soil which produces much. Is it not strange then that we struggle in poverty while the rest of the country, with fewer natural advantages, is becoming ever richer?

My claim that what helps the manufacturers hurts us can be proven. We raise crops for the whole world, so our concern is for world trade. Northern manufacturers sell almost entirely within the country. They want taxes on foreign products high enough to keep those products out of the country. That forces us to buy from them at whatever price they ask. It means we must sell our crops at higher prices, and then our foreign competitors undersell us. This tariff makes it easy for the manufacturing states to compete against foreigners here in the home market, but it makes it hard for us to compete against foreigners in the foreign market.

Worse yet, in the past we have always traded Europe raw cotton for finished cloth. Now, with this tariff, European cloth will not sell here. This means that Europe must pay cash for our cotton, and this involves so much money they will refuse to do it. We will then have to depend entirely on our sales within this country, which will amount to only one fourth of our total production.

It is easy to see what will happen to us. Instead of supplying the world with cotton, as we could do if there were no tariff and trade was free, we will have to cut our production by three quarters. That will ruin us.

Who are the "we" and "they" of whom Calhoun speaks?

How were the trading concerns of the North and South different?

Explain how raising taxes on British products coming into the United States would help American manufacturers.

States' Rights

d The following statements are from a famous 1830 Senate debate between Daniel Webster from Massachusetts and Robert Hayne from South Carolina. Their debate was over the issue known as **states' rights.**

After reading the material, describe in your own words what states' rights means.

Constitutional means in agreement with or authorized by a constitution.

d

Daniel Webster: The honorable gentleman from South Carolina seems to be saying that state legislatures have the right to decide whether or not a federal law is constitutional, and to disobey it if they think it is not.

He seems to be saying that the states have a right to force the federal government to do whatever the states decide it ought to do.

He seems to be saying that the right to decide what powers the federal government has does not belong to that government or to one of its branches. He seems to think that each state can lawfully decide for itself when the federal government has acted unconstitutionally.

As I know it, this is the "South Carolina doctrine."

[Mr. Hayne rose and said that to avoid misunderstanding, he would restate his position by quoting from a resolution passed by the Virginia legislature.].

Robert Hayne: This Assembly [the Virginia legislature] absolutely declares its position that the federal government has only those powers specifically given to it, and listed in, the Constitution. If the federal government deliberately tries to exercise any power not specifically named in the Constitution, the states have a right and a duty to interfere.

Daniel Webster: We, sir, who oppose this "Carolina doctrine" do not deny that the people can, if they wish, overthrow the government and set up a better one. That is revolution, and the people have that right. But the gentleman does not seem to be talking about revolution. He seems to be saying that without revolution, without rebellion, without disorder, the solution to an abuse of power by the federal government is for the state governments to interfere.

Robert Hayne: I do not argue for the simple right to revolt. I only say that, in case of an obvious violation of the Constitution by the federal government, a state may reject the federal position.

Daniel Webster: I am happy to find that I did not misunderstand the gentleman. The great question is, then, who has the right to decide whether or not a law is unconstitutional? This leads us to the question of where the federal government gets its power. Who created that power—the state legislatures or the people?

What was Hayne's position on the right of states to declare federal actions unconstitutional? What do you think was Webster's position on the issue?

The states' rights issue grew out of the tariff disagreement between North and South. As you've read, the Southern states were unhappy with the tariff laws and looked for ways to protect their interests. They tried to declare tariff laws unconstitutional by claiming that states had the right to decide this issue for themselves.

What dangers is this cartoon warning against? What reactions might Webster, Hayne, and Calhoun have had toward this cartoon?

▼

e The cartoon below is about the issue debated by Webster and Hayne. The man at the top of the steps is John C. Calhoun. The man on the bottom right is President Andrew Jackson. This cartoon presents an opinion about the states' rights issue.

Despotism refers to a system of government in which the ruler has unlimited power.

Nullification was the policy described by Hayne. According to this policy, a state could **nullify,** or refuse to obey, federal laws which it regarded as unconstitutional.

e

Internal Improvements

Representatives from the Western states asked Congress to help meet the needs of the West. Settlers had to pay for the land they settled on, so one Western demand was for cheap land. The West also wanted internal improvements, especially improved transportation.

f In 1817 the following speech about internal improvements in the West was made in the House of Representatives.

As you read, think about why improved transportation was important to the West.

f This seems to me to be the best possible time to make some needed improvements in our country. We are at peace with the world, we have wealth, and most citizens are willing to put the good of the country ahead of political and sectional feelings.

Considering these favorable conditions, we ought to promote the construction of internal improvements, particularly roads and canals. This is by far the best way we have of increasing the wealth, strength, and political health of this nation. So much has been written about the advantages of convenient and inexpensive trade and travel that I do not need to discuss the matter at length. I will simply remind you that every important part of our economy —agriculture, manufacturing, and commerce—is helped by internal improvements.

Internal improvements tend to spread wealth among the population. They give to inland locations the same advantages enjoyed by trading centers on the coasts. Internal improvements also help keep prices in rural areas about the same as they are in the towns. In fact, investigation will prove that building roads and canals will cause wealth to grow faster than money spent in any other way.

Some people think that internal improvements are the responsibility of the states and of individuals. Now, I know that they can accomplish a great deal, but in a country as new and as large as this, even more is needed. Some of the necessary projects are simply too large and too expensive to be done by the states or by individuals. Only the federal government is in a position to plan them and complete them.

We can accomplish a great deal. If, however, we don't make use of our advantages, if we let selfish sectional jealousies divide the Representatives, our great opportunities will disappear.

What are some reasons given to support federal responsibility for internal improvements?

Based on what you know about the North and South, which of these sections would have the most to gain if the federal government paid for the construction of major roads and canals? Why might the other section be against internal improvements?

Slavery

g The following excerpts are from the diary of John Quincy Adams. The diary entry was written while Adams was Secretary of State under President Monroe. In 1825 John Quincy Adams became the sixth president of the United States.

As you read, identify the major issue which Adams was asked to respond to.

John Quincy Adams was the son of John Adams, whom you read about in Unit 2.

March 3, 1820

When I got to the office today, there was a note from the President calling a meeting of administration leaders for one o'clock.

The President expected a bill to be sent up from Congress starting Maine and Missouri on their ways to statehood. Before he signed the bill, he wanted written opinions on whether Congress had a right to prohibit slavery in a territory.

I said there was no doubt in my mind that Congress had that right. During the discussion, I maintained that, according to the Constitution, our final duty was to "establish justice." What could be more just than to keep slavery from spreading?

After the meeting, I walked home with Calhoun. He said he thought my views about what was right and just were noble, but that in the South, it was believed they applied only to white men.

We talked about slavery, and he told me that Southerners felt no white man should do manual labor. That is the proper work of slaves, he said, and no white man should stoop to that.

It seems to me that Southerners see themselves as better than ordinary free men who work for a living. They look down on Yankees, because they are not arrogant and do not treat Negroes like dogs. Slavery blinds its defenders to what is right and wrong. What could be more wrong than to have a man's fate depend on the color of his skin?

If the Union must be dissolved, slavery is the best possible reason.

What reasons did Calhoun give for his position? What reasons did Adams give for his position?

As you've just seen, polarization between North and South had its beginnings in the early 1800s. Disagreements over western land, tariffs, and the division of power between the state and federal governments contributed to a growing tension.

Of all the issues that separated the two sections, slavery was by far the most difficult to solve. As the years passed, North and South grew farther and farther apart on the subject. In the next few activities, you'll examine how polarization over slavery occurred.

BRANCHING OUT

Prepare your own version of a discussion which three representatives (one each from the Northeast, South, and West) might have had in 1830. Their conversation should include discussion of the needs and problems of each section. If possible, role-play the discussion.

Balance of Power

The North-South struggle for power in Congress lasted for over 40 years, from before 1820 until the start of the Civil War. The heavily populated North already controlled the House of Representatives. Control of the Senate would allow them to pass any law they wanted. Southerners knew they could never control the House, but a majority of votes in the Senate would at least allow them to block those laws they did not want.

a The drawing below shows how power was divided in the Senate in 1819.

How many Senators were from the North? The South?

*This situation between the North and the South was called a **balance of power.** Why?* ▼

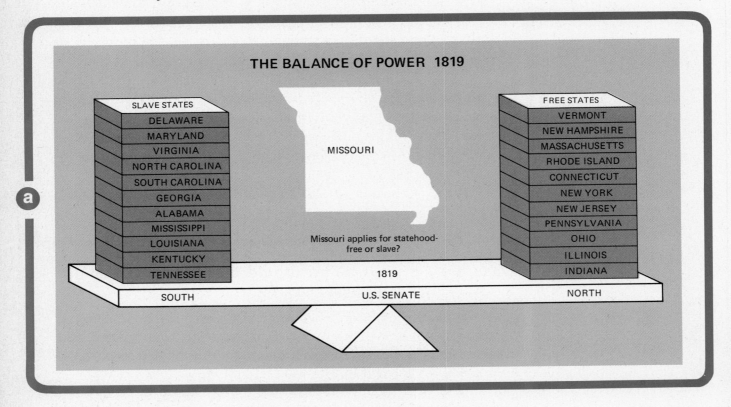

THE BALANCE OF POWER 1819

SLAVE STATES		FREE STATES
DELAWARE		VERMONT
MARYLAND		NEW HAMPSHIRE
VIRGINIA	MISSOURI	MASSACHUSETTS
NORTH CAROLINA		RHODE ISLAND
SOUTH CAROLINA		CONNECTICUT
GEORGIA		NEW YORK
ALABAMA		NEW JERSEY
MISSISSIPPI	Missouri applies for statehood— free or slave?	PENNSYLVANIA
LOUISIANA		OHIO
KENTUCKY		ILLINOIS
TENNESSEE	1819	INDIANA
SOUTH	U.S. SENATE	NORTH

The struggle between North and South for control of the Senate came to a head in 1820. The territory of Missouri had applied for admission as a state two years before. Most of the settlers of Missouri were Southerners, and many had brought their slaves into the territory. The question was, Should Missouri be admitted as a free state or as a slave state? A bitter congressional debate began.

The drawing illustrates the nature of the problem. What effect would Missouri's statehood have on the balance of power in the Senate?

Eventually a compromise on the Missouri question was worked out, keeping the power of the North and South equal in the Senate. Missouri was to be admitted as a slave state, and Maine was to be admitted as a free state. However, slavery was to be forbidden in all remaining territory above an imaginary line at 36°30′—the southern boundary of Missouri. Slavery was permitted south of this line.

b The map below shows the terms of the agreement, which is called the Missouri Compromise.

What effect do you think this had on polarization?

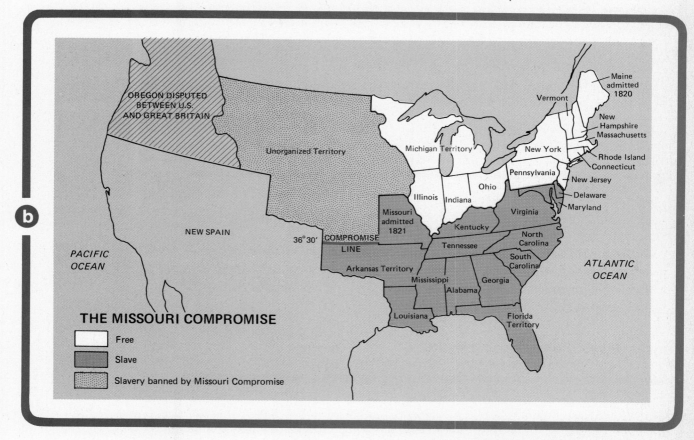

THE MISSOURI COMPROMISE

☐ Free

■ Slave

▨ Slavery banned by Missouri Compromise

Opposition to Slavery

Opposition to slavery started during the colonial period. Efforts to abolish it were led by a few religious groups who felt that slavery was wrong. Even in the South there had been opposition to slavery.

In the 1830s more and more people began to speak out in favor of **abolition,** or the ending of slavery. Abolition soon became a "movement" in the North. Abolitionists organized societies. They gave speeches, published articles, and mailed literature throughout the country, including the South.

As you study the materials which follow, make a list of the arguments against slavery given by abolitionists.

a The statement below presents the views of the American Anti-Slavery Society. This abolitionist group was founded in 1833.

a

We believe that no man has the right to enslave his brother, or to hold him as a piece of merchandise. No man has a right to earn wages for someone else's work. No man has the right to deny another a chance to improve his mind, his way of life, or his morals.

The right to liberty cannot be taken away without violating God's laws. We believe:

That the slaves ought to be set free immediately and protected by law.

That those who are colored ought to possess all the privileges and rights as anyone else.

Theodore Weld was a member of the American Anti-Slavery Society. In 1839 he published a book called *Slavery As It Is: Testimony of a Thousand Witnesses.* In the book, Weld supported his argument against slavery by using parts of articles and advertisements for runaway slaves. These articles and advertisements had first appeared in Southern newspapers.

b Portions from Weld's book follow.

b

I. Floggings

The slaves are terribly beaten with whips, paddles, etc.; red pepper and salt are rubbed into their mangled flesh; hot salt water and turpentine are poured into their gashes; and many other tortures are inflicted on them. I can prove with a cloud of witnesses that slaves are whipped inhumanly, leaving scars and ridges. After this, we will present testimony concerning a great many other kinds of tortures. For the most part, the testimony will come from the slaveowners themselves, in their own words. Much of it will be taken from advertisements in their own newspapers.

In the column under the word "witnesses" is the name of the person who placed the advertisements. Opposite the name of the witness is an excerpt from their advertisement.

Other examples were also given. What do you think Weld hoped to accomplish by publishing this material?

Witnesses	Testimony
Mr. Robert Nicoll, Dauphin St., Mobile, Alabama, in the *Mobile Commercial Advertiser.*	"Ten dollars reward for my woman Siby, very much scarred about the neck and ears by whipping."
Mr. Bryant Johnson, Fort Valley, Georgia, in the *Standard of the Union,* Milledgeville, Georgia.	"Ranaway, a Negro woman named Maria, some scars on her back from the whip."
Mr. James Noe, Red River Landing, La., in the *Sentinel,* Vicksburg, Miss.	"Ranaway, a Negro fellow named Dick—has many scars on his back from being whipped."

III. Brandings, Maimings, Gunshot Wounds, etc.

The slaves are often branded with hot irons, chased with firearms and shot, hunted with dogs and torn by them, shockingly maimed with knives, have their ears cut off, their eyes knocked out, their bones dislocated and broken, their fingers and toes cut off.

Witnesses	Testimony
Mr. Micajah Ricks, Nash County, North Carolina, in the Raleigh *Standard.*	"Ranaway, a Negro woman and two children; a few days before she went off, I burnt her with a hot iron, on the left side of her face. I tried to make the letter M."
Mr. R. P. Carney, Clark County, Alabama, in the *Mobile Register.*	"One hundred dollars reward for a Negro fellow, Pompey, 40 years old. He is branded on the left jaw."

c Abolitionists spoke out against slave conditions such as those shown in the following drawings.

c

The Underground Railroad

For many years before the Civil War, a small number of slaves escaped from their owners. These slaves moved at great risk through the Northern states to freedom in Canada. They were assisted by the **underground railroad.** This was neither underground nor a railroad. It was a network of Northern people, black and white, who provided places, or "stations," where escaped slaves were protected until they could be taken to the next "station" on the way to Canada.

● When slaveowners discovered that their slaves had run away, they frequently placed ads such as these in newspapers.

What do these ads tell you about the importance of slaves to slaveowners? ▼

$2,500 REWARD!

RANAWAY, from the Subscriber, residing in Mississippi county, Mo., on Monday the 5th inst., my

Negro Man named GEORGE.

Said negro is five feet ten inches high, of dark complexion, he plays well on the Violin and several other instruments. He is a shrewd, smart fellow and of a very affable countenance, and is twenty-five years of age. If said negro is taken and confined in St. Louis Jail, or brought to this county so that I get him, the above reward of $1,000 will be promptly paid.

JOHN MEANS.

Also, from Radford E. Stanley,

A NEGRO MAN SLAVE, NAMED NOAH,

Full 6 feet high; black complexion; full eyes; free spoken and intelligent; will weigh about 180 pounds; 32 years old; had with him 2 or 3 suits of clothes, white hat, short blue blanket coat, a pair of saddle bags, a pocket compass, and supposed to have $350 or $400 with him.

ALSO---A NEGRO MAN NAMED HAMP,

Of dark copper color, big thick lips, about 6 feet high, weighs about 175 pounds, 36 years old, with a scar in the forehead from the kick of a horse; had a lump on one of his wrists and is left-handed. Had with him two suits of clothes, one cassinet or cloth coat and grey pants.

Also, Negro Man Slave named BOB,

Copper color, high check bones, 5 feet 11 inches high, weighs about 150 pounds, 22 years old, very white teeth and a space between the centre of the upper teeth. Had a blue blanket sack coat, with red striped linsey lining. Supposed to have two suits of clothes with him; is a little lame in one ancle. $1,000 will be given for George—$600 for Noah—$450 for Hamp—$450 for Bob; if caught in a free State, or a reasonable compensation if caught in a Slave State, if delivered to the Subscribers in Miss. Co., Mo., or confined in Jail in St. Louis, so that we get them. Refer to

**JOHN MEANS &
R. E. STANLEY.**

ST. LOUIS, August 23, 1852. (PLEASE STICK UP.)

$150 REWARD

RANAWAY from the subscriber, on the night of the 2d instant, a negro man, who calls himself *Henry May*, about 22 years old, 5 feet 6 or 8 inches high, ordinary color, rather chunky built, bushy head, and has it divided mostly on one side, and keeps it very nicely combed; has been raised in the house, and is a first rate dining-room servant, and was in a tavern in Louisville for 18 months. I expect he is now in Louisville trying to make his escape to a free state, (in all probability to Cincinnati, Ohio.) Perhaps he may try to get employment on a steamboat. He is a good cook, and is handy in any capacity as a house servant. Had on when he left, a dark cassinett coatee, and dark striped cassinett pantaloons, new—he had other clothing. I will give $50 reward if taken in Louisvill; 100 dollars if taken one hundred miles from Louisville in this State, and 150 dollars if taken out of this State, and delivered to me, or secured in any jail so that I can get him again.

WILLIAM BURKE.

Bardstown, Ky., September 3d, 1838.

How do you think the abolitionist movement, including the underground railroad, affected Southern feelings toward the North? What effect would this have on polarization?

BRANCHING OUT

One of the bravest leaders of the underground railroad was Harriet Tubman. Write a report about her life and her involvement in helping slaves reach freedom.

Abolitionist Leaders

The abolitionist movement in the North had a number of important leaders. Benjamin Lundy was an early abolitionist who believed in gradually freeing slaves and sending them to Liberia in Africa. Many of the best-known leaders were from New England, including the poets James Russell Lowell and John Greenleaf Whittier. Women were active in the movement. Lucretia Mott and the sisters Angelina and Sarah Grimké were active abolitionists. These women reformers, like the men, organized antislavery groups and made speeches for abolition.

Many free Negroes also joined the abolitionists. The most famous black abolitionists were Frederick Douglass and Sojourner Truth. Douglass was born into slavery but escaped to freedom in the North. Unlike most slaves, he had been taught to read and write as a child. He became a powerful public speaker and published his own abolitionist newspaper. Sojourner Truth was born a slave in New York. She became free in 1828 under a New York law that ended slavery in that state. An impressive public speaker, she traveled widely on speaking tours.

Abolitionists such as Theodore Weld and Harriet Beecher Stowe made their voices heard through the books they wrote. You've already read excerpts from Weld's book *Slavery As It Is: Testimony of a Thousand Witnesses.* In 1852 Harriet Beecher Stowe published *Uncle Tom's Cabin,* which was a fictional story of life on a Southern plantation. The book caused strong reactions in the North as well as in the South. It strengthened Northern feeling against slavery, while at the same time it angered Southerners, who felt the story was exaggerated and unfair.

Of all the abolitionists, the one who aroused the most controversy was a New Englander named William Lloyd Garrison. In 1831 Garrison began publication of a newspaper called *The Liberator.* Through his newspaper, Garrison spoke out strongly, and sometimes shockingly, against slavery.

Below are pictures of some abolitionist leaders.
1 Sojourner Truth   3 William Lloyd Garrison
2 Frederick Douglass   4 Harriet Beecher Stowe

Part 2

Increasing Hostility

A great many writers and historians have disagreed over whether the Civil War could have been prevented. Of course, there is no definite answer to this question. Many of those who believe that it could have been prevented have ignored the way that polarization gradually increased anger and violence on both sides. Once polarization begins, it is very difficult to stop its growth.

In Part 2 you will look at the struggles, harsh words, and threats that finally brought on the Civil War. The activities in this part will help you answer this question.

How did events and actions further polarize the North and South?

Events and Polarization

You've already seen what issues were behind the growing conflict between North and South. Once there is a conflict between two sides, actions and words which irritate either or both sides further polarize the situation. This is what happened between North and South in the years before the Civil war. A series of events related to slavery increased hostilities and bad feelings between the sections.

As you read about the following events, answer these questions.

1. Which events angered and upset people in the South? How did they react?
2. Which events angered and upset people in the North? How did they react?

Nat Turner's Rebellion

During the years of slavery, probably as many as 200 slave revolts took place in this country. Although few resulted in freedom, the revolts were attempts to break away from enslavement.

One of the most violent rebellions was led by slave Nat Turner in Virginia in 1831. Turner's band of slaves killed 57 white people. In putting down the revolt, the federal militia killed perhaps 100 blacks, many of whom had not been involved in the uprising. Turner and 19 other slaves were captured and hanged.

In a confession dictated before his death, Turner claimed that he had received visions from God instructing him to kill white people. He had taught himself to read and write, and many people blamed his rebellion on this ability.

What opinion do you think the artist had of Nat Turner? Why?
▼

a Below is a drawing of Nat Turner and his followers.

Partly as a result of Turner's rebellion, several states passed new laws. What kind of laws do you think were passed? Predict other reactions to Turner's rebellion.

A **fugitive** is a person who runs away from danger or justice.

As explained in Unit 3, the United States had obtained California (as well as Texas and other territories which now make up the southwestern United States) from Mexico in 1848.

The other important terms of the Compromise of 1850 were as follows:
- The rest of the territory obtained from Mexico (that is, excluding Texas and California) was divided into the New Mexico Territory and Utah Territory. The question of slavery was left to those who settled there. The people were to decide for themselves whether slavery should be permitted.
- Slaves were not to be bought or sold in the District of Columbia.

Why was the Fugitive Slave Law written?

Fugitive Slave Law

By 1850 there were 15 Northern and 15 Southern states in the Union. Gold had been discovered in California in 1848 and thousands of Americans had gone there looking for riches. Now California was requesting admission as a state—a *free* state.

As in the case of Missouri, this created a problem between Northern and Southern states in Congress. California's admission would upset the balance of power in the Senate. This problem was solved—temporarily—by the Compromise of 1850. According to this agreement, California was admitted as a free state.

b Another important part of this compromise was a new, strict Fugitive Slave Law. This law applied everywhere in the United States.

b

September 18, 1850

Section 5:

All marshals and deputy marshals must obey this act and issue warrants as required. If a fugitive in the custody of a marshal or deputy marshal escapes, with or without the help of the marshal or deputy, the marshal will be prosecuted for the full price of the service of the slave.

Marshals, officers, or others authorized to capture fugitives may, if necessary, order bystanders or other persons to help capture fugitives. All good citizens are commanded to assist whenever their services may be needed.

Section 7:

Any person who hinders the capture and arrest of a fugitive, or tries to rescue any fugitive after he is captured, or hides and helps any fugitive, shall be fined not more than 1,000 dollars. Such person will be imprisoned for not more than six months, and will forfeit, to the person claiming the fugitive, 1,000 dollars for each fugitive lost.

Explain how both North and South gained by the Compromise of 1850. What effect do you think Congress hoped the compromise would have on polarization between North and South?

Kansas and Nebraska

c In 1854 the question of whether slavery should be allowed in the territories of Kansas and Nebraska was raised in Congress. A solution was proposed by Senator Stephen A. Douglas of Illinois. His plan, described below, came to be called **popular sovereignty.**

c Whenever it becomes necessary, in our growth and progress, to add more territory, I am in favor of it, without considering the question of slavery. When we have added it, I will leave the people in the territory free to do as they please, either to make it slave or free territory, as they prefer.

The Kansas and Nebraska Territories were part of the Louisiana Purchase.

*In the expression **popular sovereignty,** popular refers to "the people." Sovereignty means independent political power.*

How did the Douglas plan affect the Missouri Compromise? (Refer to page 253 for a review of the Missouri Compromise.)

In the Kansas-Nebraska Act of 1854, Douglas's plan was adopted for the territories. Shortly after the act was passed, both North and South sent settlers into Kansas to try to gain control of the territory. Most of the people who moved there were opposed to slavery. In 1855 the first territorial election was held to select a legislature. With the help of proslavery men from Missouri who crossed into Kansas and voted illegally, the candidates who favored slavery were elected.

d Tension grew between proslavery and antislavery settlers, and violence soon developed. So much fighting and bloodshed occurred that the territory became known as "Bleeding Kansas."

What elements of polarization can you see in the results of the Kansas-Nebraska Act?

The Dred Scott Decision

In 1857 the United States Supreme Court made a decision which it hoped would solve the problem of slavery in the territories.

Dred Scott was a slave who had lived with his owner on the free soil of Illinois and Wisconsin territory for five years. When his master took him back to the slave state of Missouri, Scott sued for his freedom. Because he had lived in free territory, he believed he ought to be considered a free man. Supported by abolitionists, Scott carried his case to the Supreme Court.

e In its decision, the Supreme Court made this statement.

There are two clauses in the Constitution which refer to the Negro race as a separate class of persons. They show clearly that Negroes were not considered citizens of the government then formed.

Upon careful consideration, the court is of the opinion that, based on the facts stated, Dred Scott was not a citizen of Missouri within the meaning of the Constitution of the United States. He was therefore not entitled to sue in its courts.

Also, the right to hold slaves as property is distinctly recognized in the Constitution. The Constitution protects the rights of individuals to private property. An act of Congress which takes away the property of a citizen merely because he brought his property into a particular section of the United States is certainly not legal.

It is the opinion of the court that the Act of Congress which prohibited a citizen from holding and owning slaves in the northern United States is not supported by the Constitution. Therefore, this law is declared void. Neither Dred Scott himself, nor any of his family, were made free by being carried into Northern territory, even if their owner had taken them there intending to become a permanent resident.

Something that is void is no longer in effect.

How did the Dred Scott decision affect the outlawing of slavery in Northern states and territories? How did Southerners probably react to this decision? What do you suppose Northern reactions were?

State in your own words the decision of the Supreme Court. In your opinion, would this decision decrease or increase polarization? Why?

John Brown's Raid

In October of 1859 abolitionist John Brown led a group of men to capture the federal arsenal at Harper's Ferry, Virginia. He hoped to obtain weapons to start a slave revolt. Brown took control of the arsenal, and several people were killed in the process.

*An **arsenal** is a storehouse for military arms and equipment.*

After seizing control of the arsenal, Brown waited for the slave uprising. It never came. Instead, federal troops captured Brown two days after the takeover.

f After his capture, Brown was interviewed by officials and reporters. Below is the text of part of the interview.

Mr. Mason: What was your object in coming?

Mr. Brown: We came to free the slaves, and only that.

A Young Man (in the uniform of a volunteer company): How many men had you in all?

Mr. Brown: I came to Virginia with 18 only, besides myself.

Bystander: Do you consider this a religious movement?

Mr. Brown: It is, in my opinion, the greatest service a man can give to God.

Bystander: Do you consider yourself an instrument in the hands of Providence?

Mr. Brown: I do.

Bystander: Upon what principle do you justify your acts?

Mr. Brown: Upon the golden rule. I pity the poor in bondage that have none to help them; that is why I am here; not to satisfy any personal hate or revenge. It is my sympathy with the oppressed and the wronged, that are as good as you and as precious in the sight of God. I don't think the people of the slave states will ever consider the subject of slavery in its true light till some other argument than a moral one is used.

Mr. Vallandigham: Did you expect a general rising of the slaves in case of your success?

Mr. Brown: No, sir, nor did I wish it; I expected to gather them up from time to time and set them free.

Reporter of the Herald: I do not wish to annoy you; but if you have anything further you would like to say I will report it.

Mr. Brown: I have nothing to say, only that I claim to be here in carrying out a measure I believe perfectly justifiable. I wish to say, furthermore, that you had better—all you people at the South—prepare yourselves for a settlement of that question that must come up for settlement sooner than you are prepared for it. You may get rid of me very easily. I am nearly gotten rid of now. But this question is still to be settled—this Negro question, I mean; the end of that is not yet.

Providence refers to divine guidance or care.

Bondage is another word for slavery.

Treason *is the offense of trying to overthrow the government to which one owes one's loyalty.*

John Brown was tried and hanged by the state of Virginia for treason, murder, and conspiracy. Although Northern opinion condemned Brown's actions, there were many who admired him as a brave man. The Southern view was a different one.

How do you think the South reacted to Brown's raid and to Northern opinion of Brown?

g This song became popular in the North after Brown was hanged.

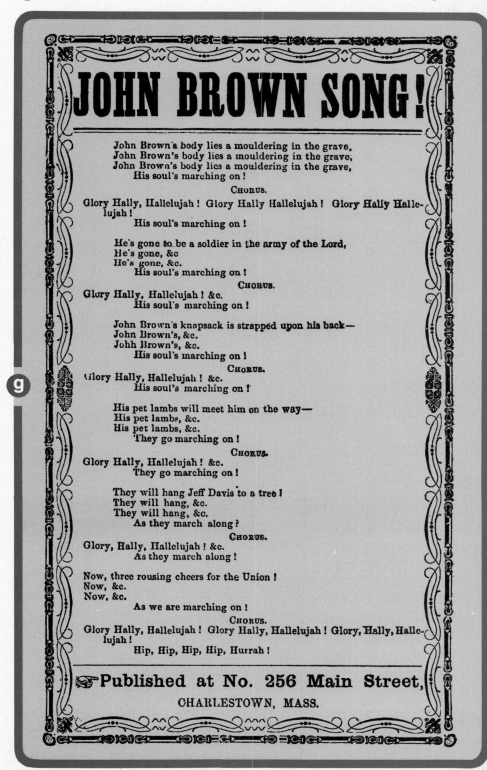

Other major slave uprisings in the early 1800s were led by Gabriel Prosser in Virginia; Denmark Vesey, a freed Negro in South Carolina; and Madison Washington. Washington's revolt took place on board a ship. Write a report on one or more of these uprisings.

Some people have said that John Brown was a madman. Others think he was a brave person who acted according to his beliefs.

Prepare a report on the beliefs and activities of John Brown. Review the facts and come up with your own conclusion as to whether he was a madman or a hero.

Feelings and Language

As people and groups polarize, their feelings become more and more aroused. A way to determine the degree of polarization is to listen to what is said or read what is written. If feelings are aroused, this will show up in the words and expressions people use. Excited or angry people use excited or angry words.

ⓐ → ⓑ Here are excerpts from two different speeches by the same man—Representative Joshua Giddings from Ohio. Both deal with the slavery issue. The first speech was made in 1844, when Congress was debating the admission of Texas as a slave state. The second speech was made six years later, in 1850, after Congress had passed the Fugitive Slave Law. Because of differences in Giddings's feelings, there is a great deal of difference between the two speeches.

Compare the speeches and identify ways in which they are different.

ⓐ It is well known, Mr. Chairman, that since the formation of this country there has been a supposed conflict between the interests of free labor and of slave labor, between the Southern and Northern states. I do not say that the conflict is real; I only say that in the minds of the people, both North and South, and in this hall, such conflict exists. This supposed conflict has given rise to difference of policy in our national councils.

What protection does this law lend to the poor, weak, oppressed, degraded slave, whose flesh has often quivered under the lash of his inhuman owner, whose youth has been spent in labor for another, whose intellect has been nearly blotted out? When he seeks safety in a land of freedom, this worse-than-barbarous law sends the officers of government to chase him down. The people are forced to become his pursuers. Starving, fainting, and numbed with the cold, he drags his weary limbs forward, while the whole power of the government under the President's command, the army and navy, and all the freemen of the land are on his track to drag him back to bondage, under this law.

Everyman here (House of Representatives) and every intelligent man in the free states knows that if he delivers a fugitive into the custody of his pursuers the fugitive will be carried to the South and sold to the sugar and cotton plantations. And the slave's life will be sacrificed in five years on a sugar plantation and in seven years on a cotton plantation.

Which events and actions might have contributed to Giddings' aroused feelings over slavery?

We will not commit this crime. Let me say to the President, no power of government can force us to involve ourselves in such guilt. No! The freemen of Ohio will never turn out to chase the panting fugitive—they will never be made into bloodhounds, to track him to his hiding-place, and seize and drag him out, and deliver him to his tormentors. Rely upon it, they will die first. They may be shot down. The cannon and bayonet and sword may do their work upon them. They may drown the fugitives in their blood. But never will they stoop to such degradation.

List several words and phrases which are especially descriptive of Giddings's feelings. Which of his expressions are stereotypes?

BRANCHING OUT

Choose a speech you read in the newspaper or heard on radio or television. What does the way the speech is written tell you about feelings on the subject discussed? How do you think the speaker wanted people to react? How do you think they will (or did) react?

If possible, conduct a survey among people who heard or read the speech to get their reactions to these same questions.

Or, choose a topic that is important to you. Write a speech putting forth your views. Which words and phrases in your speech are especially effective in getting your ideas and feelings across?

Changing Arguments About Territories

Every time a new territory was occupied in the West, there was the question of whether slavery would be allowed there. When the territory became a state, two more senators would sit in Congress, possibly upsetting the balance of power.

Beginning with Missouri in 1820, every discussion of government or statehood for western territories became a problem for Congress. However, as polarization between North and South increased, the arguments of both sides changed.

(a) → (d) Following are four different arguments—two by Northerners and two by Southerners.

1. Decide whether each statement was made by a Southerner or a Northerner.
2. Which of the Southern statements is most polarized? Least polarized? Which words and phrases are evidence?
3. Which of the Northern statements is most polarized? Least polarized? Which words and phrases are evidence?
4. Summarize one or two important changes in the arguments as polarization increased.

(a) The people who wish to keep slaves out of the territory say they want to do this because they love humanity. This is just an excuse so they can gain their political goals.

They are resisting the only possible way of freeing slaves in the future. Can we expect the slaves to be set free in the Southern states, when there are many more of them than whites?

If many slaves are sent into the West to reduce the excess population, someday they might be set free.

(b) Everything said or done in this vast circle of crime comes from the one idea that this territory, at any cost, must be made a slave state.

To accomplish this result, these three things were attempted: first, by outrages of all kinds to drive the friends of freedom already there out of the territory; second, to keep others from coming; and, third, to gain the complete control of the government.

Thus was the crime committed. Slavery now stands erect, clanking its chains on the territory, surrounded by a code of death, and trampling upon all cherished liberties, whether of speech, the press, the bar, the trial by jury, or the right to vote.

It has been done for the sake of political power, in order to bring two new slaveholding senators upon this floor and thus to strengthen in the national government the desperate chances of a declining wealthy class in the South.

c

The crisis is here! The slaveholding states must act now, or farewell to Southern rights and independence.

What should we do? We should settle this territory with Southerners. Right now the population is about equal—as many proslavery settlers as abolitionists—but the fanatics have representatives all over the North and are raising money and men to gain power over us. Will Southern men give in without resistance? Never!

Let us, then, form societies to help Southerners settle in the territory. If we permit the North to make it an abolitionist state, the whole South will be controlled by the North.

Southern farmers, come to this territory and bring your slaves. We must not allow this rich and beautiful country to be overrun by our abolitionist enemies. They have spies in almost every town, village, and city in the South, watching our movements and tampering with our slaves. Be careful.

d

Let us admit this territory to the Union, and we shall place the balance of power in the hands of the people in the new state. They, with the Southern states, will control the policy and destiny of this nation. Our tariff will then be held at the will of the supporters of free trade. Are our friends of the North prepared to deliver over this great national policy to the people of this territory? Are the liberty-loving Democrats of Pennsylvania ready to give up our tariff—to strike off all protection from iron and coal, and other productions of that state in order to purchase a slave market for their neighbors, who, in the words of Thomas Jefferson Randolph, "breed men for the market like oxen"?

The map which follows shows the admission of free and slave states into the Union between 1820 and the start of the Civil War.

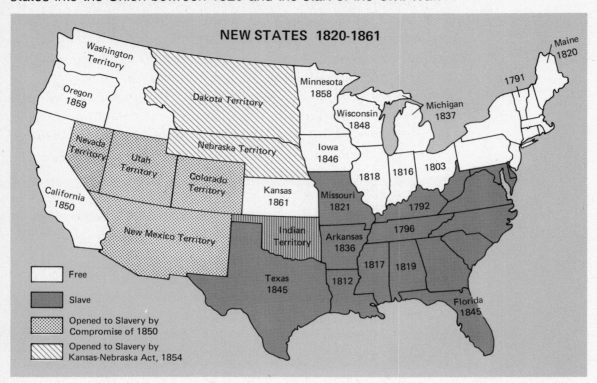

NEW STATES 1820-1861

Washington Territory

Oregon 1859

Nevada Territory

Utah Territory

California 1850

New Mexico Territory

Dakota Territory

Nebraska Territory

Colorado Territory

Indian Territory

Minnesota 1858

Wisconsin 1848

Iowa 1846

Kansas 1861

Missouri 1821

Arkansas 1836

Texas 1845

Michigan 1837

1818

1816

1803

1792

1796

1817

1819

1812

1791

Maine 1820

Florida 1845

Free

Slave

Opened to Slavery by Compromise of 1850

Opened to Slavery by Kansas-Nebraska Act, 1854

Northerners React to Abolition

How did people in the North react to the abolition movement? There was no one "Northern reaction," but the data pieces which follow will give you a general idea of attitudes and feelings.

Identify Northern reactions as shown in these selections.

a One Northern abolitionist, a young minister, described an event in a small Ohio town where previous abolition speakers had been kept from holding meetings. The event, which took place in 1836, is an example of how many Northerners felt at that time.

a

Brother Weld:

After the abolition lecture was announced, many people here in Middlebury began to show their anger.

The arrangements committee came to us and said they were frightened and advised us not to have a meeting. We went down anyway but the church was locked. An audience soon gathered, and we went over to a school to decide what to do. Two church trustees were with us, and after awhile they left with a growl. In a few minutes we heard the church bell ringing like fire and one of the trustees came back to invite us over. We found the door burst in.

A good number soon gathered, and Brother Thome proceeded to lecture. All was quiet until about eight, when in through the church windows came a broadside of eggs. Glass, eggshells, whites and yolks flew everywhere. I have been trying to clean off this morning but can't get rid of the stink. Brother Thome dodged like a stoned gander, then got down behind a desk. This morning he says he thought the stove was exploding!!! Mr. Kent, a local merchant, tried to go out, but got hit in the eye with an egg. I understand that he says this morning he is an abolitionist.

A committee was appointed to try and bring the rioters to justice. None of the committee are abolitionists, but are well on the way. I think this will bring the people here to stand. Abolitionists have always been mobbed out of here before this. We must try to carry the day this time, if possible.

Your Brother Affectionately,
J. W. Alvord

What was the feeling of townspeople toward abolition? Why do you think they felt this way?

Alvord said, "None of the committee are abolitionists, but are well on the way." Alvord was probably right. Why?

b On December 3, 1860, an abolitionist meeting in Boston was broken up by a mob and the police. The engraving below illustrates the scene.

Why do you think Northerners reacted to abolitionists in the ways described?

C Abraham Lincoln expressed his opinions on abolition in a Peoria, Illinois speech on October 16, 1854. His views represented the views of many Northerners at that time.

When Southern people tell us they are no more responsible for the origin of slavery than we are, I agree. When it is said that slavery exists and that it is very difficult to get rid of it in any satisfactory way, I can understand and appreciate the saying. I surely will not blame them for not doing what I should not know how to do myself.

If all earthly power were given to me, I should not know what to do about slavery. My first impulse would be to free all the slaves and send them to Liberia, to their own native land. But a moment's reflection would convince me that this is impossible. If they were all landed there in a day, they would all perish in the next ten days. What then? Free them all and keep them among us as underlings? Is it quite certain that this betters their condition? I think I would not hold one in slavery, at any rate; yet the point is not clear enough for me to denounce people upon.

What next? Free them and make them politically and socially our equals? My own feelings will not agree to this. Even if mine would, we well know that those of the great mass of white peoples will not. A universal feeling, whether well- or ill-founded, cannot be safely disregarded. We cannot then, make them equals. But it does seem to me that systems of gradual emancipation might be adopted.

But all this, in my opinion, is no excuse for permitting slavery to go into our own free territory.

Emancipation refers to freedom from the control or power of another.

Southern Ideology About Slavery

You've already read quite a bit about Northern attitudes toward slavery. What about Southern attitudes? What was Southern ideology regarding slavery?

There wasn't any single "Southern opinion" about slavery, but the following data will give you some understanding of Southern attitudes. It also shows how some of these attitudes changed and became an ideology as polarization grew between North and South.

1. In the materials which follow, find words and short phrases which describe Southern attitudes and ideas about:
   a. The slave system (What was it like? What were its advantages and disadvantages? What should be done about it? Was it good or evil? Why?)
   b. Slaveholders
2. Identify changes in ideas and attitudes between the early and later data, as Southern opinions became more polarized and ideology developed.

a The following letter to the editor of the Milledgeville, Georgia, *Journal* appeared on December 4, 1821.

a Georgia should set an example for the other states. To prevent the growth of a practice everyone agrees is wrong, she should keep new slaves out of the state, while allowing citizens to continue to have them for their own use.

In the long run, Georgia would probably be better off to follow Virginia's plan. That state has closed all its doors to new slaves and is doing everything possible to get rid of slavery itself, a practice they now wish had never been introduced.

b In 1822 Richard Furman, a Baptist minister, presented the following declaration to the governor of South Carolina.

b The Baptist convention considers it their duty to express their opinions on the slave question.

We firmly believe that freedom for the slaves in this country would not, at this time, add to the slaves' happiness. It would also be very damaging to the rest of the community.

Should, however, a time come when the Africans in our country are qualified to enjoy freedom, and can gain it in a way that will not harm the interests or disturb the peace of the rest of the community, we would be happy to see them free, even though there is evidence that much of the human race will always be more or less enslaved.

I come to a part of the subject which this convention feels it has a duty to discuss—the religion of the Negroes. For though they are slaves, they are also men. They have immortal souls and an eternal future just as we. This puts a great responsibility both on the slaves' masters and on the rest of the community.

In the early 1820s, what were Southern attitudes on slavery?

273

c In 1835 Governor George McDuffie delivered this speech to the legislature of South Carolina. His ideology represented the opinions of many in the South.

c No human institution, in my opinion, is more obviously in keeping with the will of God than slavery. No one of His laws is written in plainer letters than the law which says this is the happiest condition for the African.

That the African Negro was meant to be a slave is clear. It is marked on his face, stamped on his skin, and proved by the intellectual inferiority and natural helplessness of this race. They have none of the qualities that fit them to be free men. They are totally unsuited both for freedom and for self-government of any kind. They are, in all respects, physically, morally, and politically inferior.

From an excess of labor, poverty, and trouble our slaves are free. They usually work from two to four hours a day less than workers in other countries. They usually eat as much wholesome food in one day as an English worker or Irish peasant eats in two. And as for the future, slaves are envied even by their masters. Nowhere on earth is there a class of people so perfectly free from care and anxiety.

How are the attitudes on slavery expressed in this 1835 speech different from the attitudes expressed in the two earlier data pieces?

d This illustration presents one view of slavery.

d

e In 1860 William Harper's "Memoirs on Slavery" appeared in a book titled *Cotton Is King and Pro-Slavery Arguments.*

William Harper said that people will not work unless they are forced. Do you agree? Why?

e President Thomas Dew of the College of William and Mary has shown that slavery is a major foundation of civilization. It is, it seems to me, the *only* foundation. If anything can be said for certain about uncivilized man, it is that he will not work any more than just enough to stay alive. Slavery alone forces man into the habit of regular work, and without regular work there can be no accumulation of property, no saving up for the future, and no taste for comfort or the finer things in life. When a man can command the labor of another, civilization can begin. Since the existence of man on earth, with no exception whatever, every society which has become civilized has done it by enslaving others.

Does man have the right to rule the beasts of the field? To make them labor for him? To kill them for food? Of course he does. It is the right of the being of superior intelligence to decide what kind of a relationship he will have with beings of inferior intelligence, and what use he shall make of them.

For the very same reason, civilized man has the right to decide what kind of relationship he will have with the ignorant and the savage. It is a law of nature and of God that the being of superior power should control and use those who are inferior, just as animals prey on each other.

What is William Harper's ideology on slavery? How are his attitudes different from attitudes expressed by others in earlier years?

Identify those events and conditions which caused Southern ideology to develop as it did over the years.

Stereotyped Opinions

As polarization grew between the North and South, each side developed stereotyped opinions of one another. Each side came to view the other in certain fixed, often uncomplimentary, ways. Northerners came to think that Southerners acted in certain stereotyped ways, and vice versa.

Stereotyped opinions can be described in words and in pictures. The materials in this activity consist of statements and drawings by Southerners and Northerners.

Study the materials. Then identify stereotyped opinions.

a The following excerpt is from William Lloyd Garrison's newspaper *The Liberator.* The excerpt is from an issue published on May 31, 1844.

a Three million American people are crushed under the American Union! They are held as slaves—sold as merchandise—registered as goods! The government gives them no protection—the government is their enemy—the government keeps them in chains! There they lie bleeding. The Union which grinds them to the dust rests upon us, and with them we will struggle to overthrow it! The Constitution which subjects them to hopeless bondage, is one that we cannot swear to support! Our motto is, "NO UNION WITH SLAVEHOLDERS," either religious or political. They are the fiercest enemies of mankind, and the bitterest foes of God!

How do you think Northerners and Southerners probably reacted to Garrison's statements? Select certain phrases which you think probably created aroused feelings in the North and in the South.

In 1856 Senator Charles Sumner made a speech in the Senate. In the speech he accused slave interests of evil and corrupt actions in Kansas. Representative Preston Brooks of South Carolina went into the Senate two days after the speech and beat Senator Sumner with a cane until it broke. Sumner was severely injured and did not recover for several years.

b Members of Congress saw Sumner's beating, as shown below.

What does the artist's opinion of this incident seem to be?

▼

b

c An Alabama newspaper commented on the beating. The newspaper's comment contains vivid examples of stereotyping.

This editorial was printed in the South (in Alabama), and reprinted in the North by the abolitionist newspaper The Liberator. *Why would* The Liberator *reprint the editorial? In which section, North or South, would the editorial be likely to have the greater polarizing effect?*

c

This newspaper recommends that other Southern members of Congress adopt the same method of silencing the foul-mouthed abolition agents of the North. Indeed, it is quite apparent, from recent developments, that the club is the best argument to be used with such low-bred mongrels.

More than six years ago, the abolitionists were told that if they intended to carry out their ideas, they must fight. When the northern organizations began to send people to Kansas, they were told that if their object was to establish a colony of thieves under the name of "Free State Men," for the purpose of keeping out Southerners and destroying slavery, they must fight. And let them understand that if they intend to carry their abolitionism into Congress, and pour forth their disgusting obscenity and abuse of the South in the Senate Chamber, and force their doctrines down the throats of Southerners, they must fight.

We repeat, let our Representative in Congress use the cowhide and hickory stick (and, if need be, the bowie knife and revolver) more frequently, and we'll bet our old hat that it will soon come to pass that Southern institutions and Southern men will be respected.

What views of John Brown are expressed in these drawings?
▼

d These drawings show two views of John Brown.

d

Explain how stereotyped opinions affected polarization between the North and South.

BRANCHING OUT

Choose a person who has recently been the subject of controversy. What do supporters say about this person? What are the views of those who oppose or dislike this person? What evidence of stereotyping is there?

Investigate the facts in the controversy and find out whose views come closer to the truth.

The Republican Party and Abraham Lincoln

Opponents of the Fugitive Slave Law and the Kansas-Nebraska Act formed a new political party in 1854. It was called the Republican party. Republicans did not call for the abolition of slavery; most did not want to free the slaves immediately. But they were determined to stop the spread of slavery into the territories.

The Republican party gained support so quickly that within two years a Republican Speaker of the House had been elected. In the presidential election of 1856, the Republican party candidate was John C. Frémont. He was defeated by James Buchanan, but the number of votes he received showed that the Republican party was quickly gaining strength.

Abraham Lincoln was an Illinois lawyer who opposed slavery, although he never became an abolitionist. He was a Republican nominee for the United States Senate in 1858, running against Senator Stephen A. Douglas. Lincoln was deeply aware of the polarization within the nation. He felt that Douglas's popular sovereignty plan was not a good solution to the problem of polarization. Lincoln expressed his views in a speech when he accepted the 1858 Senate nomination. Below is part of that speech.

> "A house divided against itself cannot stand." I believe this government cannot endure permanently half slave and half free. I do not expect the Union to be dissolved; I do not expect the house to fall; but I do expect it will cease to be divided. It will become all one thing, or all the other. Either the opponents of slavery will stop its spread, and begin to eliminate it, or supporters of slavery will push till it becomes lawful in all the states, old as well as new, North as well as South.

The cartoon which follows shows Lincoln and Douglas in the then undecided political prizefight.

Although Lincoln lost the 1858 Senate election, the Republican party nominated him for president in 1860. This election showed the great polarization within the United States. The Democratic party could not agree on one candidate. Northern Democrats nominated Senator Douglas. Southern Democrats nominated John C. Breckinridge from Kentucky, who favored extension of slavery into the territories. The Constitutional Union party was newly formed by people who feared a split in the Union. They nominated John Bell of Tennessee.

As the campaign poster shows, Lincoln's Republican party opposed the extension of slavery and favored protective tariffs and internal improvements. Even though the position of Lincoln and his party was not abolitionist, many Southerners believed that most Republicans wanted to abolish slavery everywhere. Because of this, Southern states threatened to leave the Union if Lincoln were elected.

The map and the table below show the results of this election.

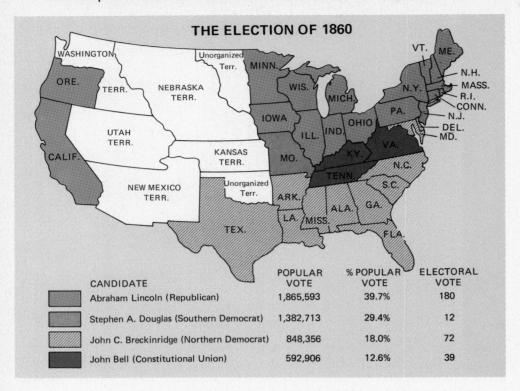

THE ELECTION OF 1860

CANDIDATE	POPULAR VOTE	% POPULAR VOTE	ELECTORAL VOTE
Abraham Lincoln (Republican)	1,865,593	39.7%	180
Stephen A. Douglas (Southern Democrat)	1,382,713	29.4%	12
John C. Breckinridge (Northern Democrat)	848,356	18.0%	72
John Bell (Constitutional Union)	592,906	12.6%	39

Lincoln took the oath of office on March 4, 1861 and became the 16th President of the United States.

Many Southern leaders had threatened to withdraw their states from the Union if Lincoln should win the election. In December 1860 South Carolina, in a special convention, voted unanimously to secede from the United States. (To **secede** is to withdraw from an organization.) Eventually, 11 states left the Union and formed the Confederate States of America. When the Southern states seceded from the Union, the outbreak of war was soon to follow.

Part 3

War and Reconstruction

Polarization doesn't stop when war begins. When violence starts, polarization usually increases even more. Nor does the end of war mean the end of polarization between the groups in conflict. Polarization can continue if bad feelings remain between winner and loser.

The activities in Part 3 will help you answer this question:

What effects did the Civil War and Reconstruction have on polarization within the nation?

Civil War

By the time Lincoln was inaugurated as President, seven states had seceded from the Union and formed the Confederate States of America. In his inaugural address, Lincoln said he thought secession was wrong, but he took no military action.

Lincoln soon faced a major problem. The federal government still controlled Fort Pickens in Florida and Fort Sumter, located on an island in the harbor of Charleston, South Carolina. The problem was that Fort Sumter was running short of supplies. After long discussion with his cabinet, Lincoln decided to attempt to resupply the fort. He notified Confederate authorities that this was what he intended to do.

This created a problem for Jefferson Davis, President of the Confederate States. If he didn't fire on the Union supply ships, he would look weak. If he did, he would be risking war. Davis made his decision. Not waiting for the supply ships, he ordered an attack on the fort on April 12, 1861. Forty hours later, Fort Sumter surrendered.

After the attack at Fort Sumter, war preparations began. North and South each had certain advantages. The North had more people, more money, more industry, and more railroads. The North also kept control of the navy, and with it, the seas.

The South had in its favor the fact that it was fighting on its own territory. This meant that the South could supply its troops more easily. Southern officers were generally superior to Northern officers, and Southern spirit was particularly high. Perhaps the South's greatest advantage was that it did not need to capture Northern territory to win. It needed only to defend itself until the North tired of the war.

Some Northerners thought the war would be short. They learned the truth in July 1861 at Bull Run in Virginia. At this battle, 30,000 Northern troops moved against an equal number of Confederate soldiers. They were driven back in a disorderly retreat.

The war lasted for over four years. The North lost about 360,000 men; the South about 258,000. These are tremendous losses even by today's standards, when weapons are far more powerful. Cities were burned, factories smashed, railroads destroyed, and hundreds of millions of dollars of private property wrecked or burned.

Some of the military action took place on the sea and some fighting occurred in the Mississippi Valley. However, most battles occurred in Virginia and the eastern-seaboard states. For much of the war, especially after 1863, the North maintained a very successful blockade of the South. It prevented the South from shipping cotton to Europe and receiving badly-needed ammunition, clothing, and medical supplies.

The map which follows shows the Union and the Confederacy in 1861.

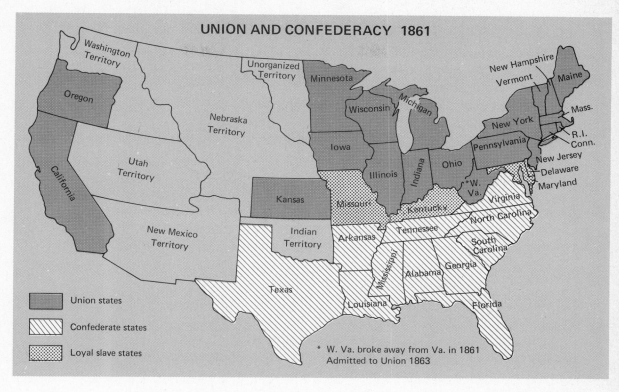

UNION AND CONFEDERACY 1861

Washington Territory
Oregon
California
Utah Territory
New Mexico Territory
Unorganized Territory
Nebraska Territory
Indian Territory
Texas
Kansas
Minnesota
Wisconsin
Michigan
Iowa
Illinois
Indiana
Ohio
Missouri
Kentucky
Arkansas
Tennessee
Mississippi
Louisiana
Alabama
Georgia
Florida
South Carolina
North Carolina
Virginia
*W. Va.
Maryland
Delaware
New Jersey
Pennsylvania
New York
New Hampshire
Vermont
Maine
Mass.
R.I.
Conn.

Union states
Confederate states
Loyal slave states

* W. Va. broke away from Va. in 1861
Admitted to Union 1863

In the Mississippi Valley, Union forces won more battles than they lost. Eventually, they gained control over the whole river and valley, making it almost impossible for supplies from Texas and Arkansas to reach the rest of the South.

The map below shows the main advances of Union and Confederate forces during the Civil War.

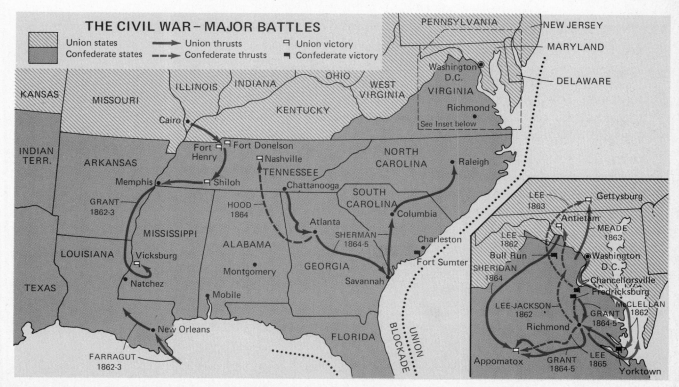

THE CIVIL WAR – MAJOR BATTLES

Union states — Union thrusts — Union victory
Confederate states — Confederate thrusts — Confederate victory

KANSAS
MISSOURI
ILLINOIS
INDIANA
OHIO
WEST VIRGINIA
PENNSYLVANIA
NEW JERSEY
MARYLAND
DELAWARE
Washington D.C.
VIRGINIA
Richmond
See Inset below
INDIAN TERR.
ARKANSAS
KENTUCKY
Cairo
Fort Henry
Fort Donelson
Nashville
TENNESSEE
Shiloh
Memphis
Chattanooga
NORTH CAROLINA
Raleigh
SOUTH CAROLINA
Columbia
GRANT 1862-3
HOOD 1864
MISSISSIPPI
ALABAMA
Atlanta
SHERMAN 1864-5
Charleston
Fort Sumter
LOUISIANA
Vicksburg
Montgomery
GEORGIA
Savannah
TEXAS
Natchez
Mobile
New Orleans
FARRAGUT 1862-3
FLORIDA
UNION BLOCKADE

LEE 1863
Gettysburg
Antietam
MEADE 1863
LEE 1862
Bull Run
Washington D.C.
SHERIDAN 1864
Chancellorsville
Fredericksburg
MCCLELLAN 1862
LEE-JACKSON 1862
GRANT 1864-5
Richmond
Appomatox
GRANT 1864-5
LEE 1865
Yorktown

Northern victory at the battle of Gettysburg in July 1863 marked a turning point in the war. The South's great general, Robert E. Lee, led his troops in that battle. Three days of fighting left Confederate forces permanently crippled. Never again would Lee's forces have the strength to undertake a major offensive.

Early in 1864 when victory already appeared likely for the North, Ulysses S. Grant was made commander of all the Union armies. In battle after battle Union forces defeated Confederate forces. Meanwhile, Union General William Sherman swept down through the South toward Savannah, Georgia, destroying property and laying waste to everything that might help the South continue fighting.

General Lee realized that the South no longer had a chance to win the war. On April 9, 1865 he surrendered his army to General Grant at Appomatox, Virginia.

The Civil War was an important turning point in American history. With the defeat of the Confederacy, the war settled the question of whether a state could secede from the Union. It also freed black people from slavery in this country. On January 1, 1863, while the war was still being fought, President Lincoln issued the Emancipation Proclamation, freeing all slaves in those states in rebellion.

The end of slavery marked the end of the Southern way of life that depended on slave labor. After the Civil War, Southerners had to break up their plantations, because they had no slaves to work them. The land was divided into small farms, which were then owned by some black as well as white families.

After the war there lay ahead the job of rebuilding the nation. The problems in the South were great. Most of the war had been fought in Southern territory, and much of the South was in ruins. Soldiers returned home to fields and homes which had been burned. Railroads had been torn up, and factories had been destroyed. Black people suddenly found themselves free, but without money, jobs, or homes. Reuniting and rebuilding the nation were the major tasks facing the United States after the Civil War.

The Civil War was the first American war to be recorded in photographs. The men in the photographs on page 285 were photographed by men like Mathew B. Brady and his assistants, who traveled with the Union armies.

BRANCHING OUT

Prepare a report on a Civil War leader. Below are the names of some military leaders you may wish to investigate.

Ulysses S. Grant	Robert E. Lee	William T. Sherman
Stonewall Jackson	George B. McClellan	James E. B. (Jeb) Stewart

Reconstruction: Lincoln's Approach

After the Battle of Gettysburg, it began to be clear that victory by the North was just a matter of time. Northern officials began to plan the **reconstruction,** or the rebuilding, of the South. As they discussed these plans, it soon became obvious that there were important differences of opinion about how the South should be treated.

Several important questions had to be considered. By what process should seceded states be readmitted to the Union? How should Confederate officials be treated? What laws were needed to aid and protect newly freed black people?

The following materials describe President Lincoln's approach to Reconstruction. After reading them, summarize Lincoln's opinion about the proper actions to take in rebuilding the South. In the activity which follows this one, you'll compare Lincoln's plans with the program adopted by Congress.

a The following is part of a proclamation issued by Lincoln in 1863.

a

Whereas, the Constitution of the United States provides that a President "shall have power to grant pardons for offenses against the United States;" and

Whereas some persons who have been in rebellion against the United States now wish to resume their allegiance and organize loyal state governments for their states; therefore

I, Abraham Lincoln, President of the United States, do declare that a full pardon is hereby granted to all who take this oath:

I, _____, do solemnly swear, in the presence of Almighty God, that I will faithfully support, protect, and defend the Constitution of the United States; and that I will abide by all acts passed by Congress concerning slaves; and will abide by all proclamations of the President concerning slaves. So help me God.

To **abide by** an act or proclamation is to obey it or follow its instructions.

What conditions did Lincoln set down for granting a full pardon?

b Here is the last paragraph of Lincoln's second inaugural address, presented on March 4, 1865.

b

With malice toward none, with charity for all, with firmness in the right as God gives us to see the right, let us strive on to finish the work we are in, to bind up the nation's wounds, to care

What were Lincoln's attitudes toward reuniting the nation?

for him who shall have borne the battle and for his widow and his orphan, to do all which may achieve and cherish a just and lasting peace among ourselves and with all nations.

C On April 18th, 1865, a surrender agreement was made between General Joseph E. Johnston, Confederate commander, and Major-General William T. Sherman. The agreement reflected Lincoln's views. Part of the agreement is below.

What demands were made by the North upon the South? What guarantees were given? **C**

—The Confederate armies are to disband and return to their state capitals. There they will leave their weapons in the state arsenal. Each officer and soldier will file an agreement to cease from acts of war.

—The Executive of the United States will recognize the state governments when their officers and legislatures take oaths prescribed by the Constitution of the United States.

—The people of all the states are guaranteed, so far as the Executive can, their political rights, as well as their rights of person and property, as defined by the Constitution of the United States and of the states respectively.

—The Executive authority of the Government of the United States will not disturb anyone because of the recent war, so long as they live in peace and quiet and obey the laws.

—A general amnesty is granted on condition that Confederate armies disband, give up their arms, and that peaceful pursuits be followed by the officers and men previously in those armies.

Amnesty is the act of granting pardon to a large group of individuals.

Reconstruction: Congress's Approach

To assassinate is to murder by sudden or secret attack.

President Lincoln was assassinated on April 14, 1865, only five days after Lee surrendered to Grant. Vice President Andrew Johnson took over as President. He began a program of reconstruction similar to that planned by Lincoln. Johnson permitted the rebel states to reorganize their state governments as soon as ten percent of the voters had taken oaths of loyalty to the United States. Several states followed this plan and elected new U.S. congressmen.

These states also approved the 13th Amendment to the Constitution, which abolished slavery throughout the United States.

Republican members of Congress were unhappy with Johnson's plans for dealing with the South. They wanted a different approach to Reconstruction. Also, Republican leaders in Congress felt that Congress, not the President, should decide Reconstruction policy. They rejected Johnson's plan and refused to allow the newly elected Southern congressmen to be a part of Congress. These "Radical" Republicans developed a different program. Their plan, and the reasons for it, are described in the following materials.

Study the materials and then explain how the plans of the Radical Republicans were different from the Lincoln-Johnson Reconstruction approach.

a In June 1866 Congress prepared the 14th Amendment to the Constitution. The purpose of this amendment was to guarantee basic rights to black people. Section 1 of the 14th Amendment is presented below.

Radical means extreme. Radical Republicans were Republicans whose views on Reconstruction were extreme in comparison to Lincoln, Johnson, and the moderate Republicans.

Amendment 14

a

All persons born or naturalized in the United States are citizens of the United States and of the state in which they live. No state shall make any law which shall reduce the privileges of citizens of the United States. No state shall deprive any person of life, liberty, or property, without due process of law; nor deny to any person within its jurisdiction the equal protection of the laws.

Naturalized means admitted to citizenship.

Due process of law refers to the legal proceedings carried out to insure fair protection under the law.

Section 2 declared that any state which did not allow its citizens the right to vote would lose representatives in Congress. Section 3 stated that former officers of the Confederate government could not hold federal or state office.

Of the former Confederate states, only Tennessee ratified the 14th Amendment. The others refused to approve the conditions set down in this newest amendment. In response to the resistance of the former Confederate states, Radical Republicans in Congress passed a reconstruction program in March 1867.

b The first condition of the program is stated here.

b

The rebel states shall be divided into military districts and placed under the military authority of the United States.

It shall be the duty of the President to assign an officer of the army to command each district. Each officer shall be given a military force to enable him to perform his duties and enforce his authority within the district.

Congress set down other conditions as part of its Reconstruction program. To be readmitted to the Union, each Southern state was required to

1. Hold a convention to write a new state constitution giving black people the right to vote.
2. Re-elect a new legislature. No former Confederate soldiers or government officials were allowed to vote or hold office.
3. Approve the 14th Amendment so it could become law.

C The map which follows shows which states were in each of the five military districts.

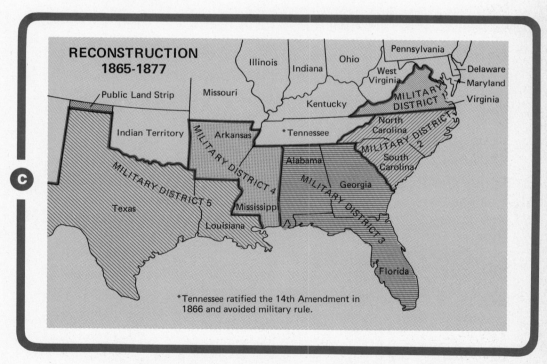

RECONSTRUCTION
1865-1877

*Tennessee ratified the 14th Amendment in 1866 and avoided military rule.

The disagreements between the Radical Rebublicans in Congress and President Andrew Johnson led to Johnson's impeachment. The Senate conducted the impeachment trial and acquitted the President.

President Andrew Johnson vetoed Congress's Reconstruction program. Congress passed the bill over his veto and the Reconstruction program went into effect.

Congress knew that once the ex-Confederate states were readmitted, they could change their constitutions to take the right to vote away from black people. Therefore, Congress passed the 15th Amendment, which was ratified in 1870. Through this amendment, black males were guaranteed the right to vote. The 15th Amendment states that no male American citizen can be denied the right to vote because of race, color, or because of having been a slave.

Based on the data in this activity, answer the following questions.

1. What is your opinion of the Reconstruction program passed by Congress? What were the goals of the Radical Republicans?

2. What effects do you think Lincoln's approach to rebuilding the South would actually have had on polarization? On Southern treatment of black people?

3. In comparing Lincoln's Reconstruction program with the program of the Radical Republicans, which one do you think was better in terms of (a) the polarized situation between North and South; (b) the treatment of Southern black people?

Effects of Reconstruction

After the Reconstruction program was passed by Congress, new state governments were set up. They became known as Reconstruction governments.

Under the new governments, former slaves were allowed to vote and hold office. As a result, many blacks gained political power. Many Northerners who moved South also gained political control in the new governments. These Northerners were called "carpetbaggers" by those who criticized them. (The term **carpetbagger** refers to men who rushed to the South with all their belongings in old-fashioned traveling bags.)

These state governments were all dominated by members of the Republican party, because of black voter support and because many white Democrats were not permitted to vote.

Reconstruction laws prevented former Confederate soldiers and government officials from voting or holding office. Only Southerners who had opposed the Confederacy were allowed a voice in political affairs. These Southerners, together with carpetbaggers and black people, joined to run the new state governments.

Based on the data, make two lists—one describing problems *solved* by Reconstruction governments, the other describing problems *created* by them.

ⓐ The following selection is from an *Address to the Colored People of South Carolina,* adopted by a South Carolina Democratic convention which met in April 1868.

You have been suddenly put in position to use certain powers. It is impossible that your present power can last, whether you use if for good or bad. Let not your pride, nor your pretended friends, flatter you into the belief that you ever can, or ever will, for any length of time, govern the white men of the South. Perhaps you expect to have power by the aid of the radical party at the North. The Almighty, in His wisdom, has placed in every human a sentiment called the prejudice of race. When undue power was given you by the radical party, prejudice of race sprang up.

To repeat, then, as we began: Your present power must surely and soon pass from you. Nothing that it builds will stand, and nothing will remain of it but the prejudices it may create. It is, therefore, a most dangerous tool that you are handling. Your leaders, both white and black, are using your votes for nothing but their individual gain.

b E. L. Godkin, editor of the *Nation* magazine, published in New York, criticized the Reconstruction program in 1871.

The condition of Negroes after they were freed attracted Northerners anxious to take advantage of them, as naturally as a dead ox attracts the buzzard.

And then we passed laws which made the situation worse. We deliberately kept all the leading Southern men from taking active part in the management of their local affairs.

Before the war, it was the custom of the Southern states to put men of the highest social standing and character in office. The result was that it was these men who were most prominent in the steps which led to the rebellion and in the rebellion itself. When the war was over, we singled these men out for punishment by the 14th Amendment and other laws.

The results have been dreadful. Thinking that we were befriending the Negroes, we gave them control of the government. Those with experience were not allowed to help them. Instead of establishing equal rights for all, we set up a government by one class, and this class the least experienced.

Out of this state of things the Ku Klux Klan has grown.

c The scene on the next page pictures the registration of black voters in Richmond, Virginia, in 1870.

d The testimony which follows was given by a black man named Emanuel Fortune.

Question: When did you leave Jackson County?
Answer: In May 1869.
Question: Why did you leave there?
Answer: There got to be such a state of lawlessness that I expected that my life was in danger at all times. I left because of that. In fact I got, indirectly, information very often that I would be missing someday and no one would know where I was, because of my being a leading man in politics, and taking a very active part in it.
Question: Had men in your county been killed before you left?
Answer: Yes, sir; several were killed: Dr. Finlayson was killed, for one, and Major Purman was shot at the same time. Three men were called out of their doors and shot; some were shot through the cracks of the houses, and others as they were going into the houses. I do not remember their names, but there were a great many cases of that kind before I left.
Question: Did you hear any expression in reference to your people having a right to vote?
Answer: Yes, sir: I have had a great many arguments in reference to that. They would argue very strongly against it.
Question: What language would they use?
Answer: "That d....d Republican party has put blacks to rule us and we will not allow it;" "Intelligence shall rule the country instead of the majority;" and all such as that. They always said that this was a "white man's government."

Question: What is the feeling in respect to your people voting?

Answer: They are generally opposed to it; they speak bitterly against it.

Question: How do they regard your people getting land and owning it for themselves?

Answer: Well, they generally do not interfere with them much, not in that line.

Question: Are they ready to sell them land?

Answer: No, sir; they will not sell land. We have to purchase it from the government, or from the state, otherwise we cannot get it. They do not sell our people any land; they have no desire to do so.

e The following picture was drawn by cartoonist Thomas Nast.

f White Southerners organized into secret societies. The Ku Klux Klan was the best known of these groups. The following data piece describes KKK activities.

f

To the Senate and House of Representatives in Congress:

We colored citizens of Frankfort, Kentucky, and vicinity, do this day petition you about the condition of affairs now existing in the state of Kentucky.

We would respectfully state that life, liberty, and property are unprotected among the colored race of this state.

We believe you do not know that Ku Klux Klans are riding nightly over the country, going from county to county, spreading terror wherever they go by robbing, whipping, killing our people without cause, forcing colored people to break the ice and bathe in the water of the Kentucky River.

The state legislature has adjourned. They refused to enact any laws to put down Ku Klux disorder. We regard the Ku Kluxers as now being permitted to continue their dark and bloody deeds under the cover of the dark night. They refuse to allow us to testify in the state courts where a white man is concerned. We find their deeds are done only to colored men and white Republicans. We also find that for our services to the government and our race we have become the special object of hatred and persecution at the hands of the Democratic party. Our people are driven from their homes in great numbers, having no recourse except the United States court, which is in many cases unable to reach them.

We would state that we have been law-abiding citizens and pay our taxes, but in many parts of the state our people have been driven from the polls, refused the right to vote. Many have been murdered while attempting to vote. We ask, how long is this state of things to last?

We appeal to you as law-abiding citizens to pass some laws that will protect us and that will enable us to exercise the rights of citizens.

Why did the Ku Klux Klan attack black people in the ways described?

In the North, where agriculture and industry were both expanding, public opinion gradually turned against the use of military force to support Republican rule in the South. In 1872 Congress passed a law which allowed most ex-Confederates to vote. White Southerners eventually overthrew Republican rule and regained control of their governments. In 1877 federal troops were withdrawn from the South. The last of the Republican state governments collapsed, and Reconstruction officially came to an end.

g In 1907 Senator Benjamin R. Tillman of South Carolina delivered a speech in Congress. In it he described how Southern whites regained control of South Carolina in 1876. Excerpts from the speech are presented below.

Read this data piece, and then review the other data pieces in this activity to answer the following questions:

1. What were the feelings of Southern whites toward the North during Reconstruction?
2. Why did Southerners feel this way?
3. What elements of polarization can you identify in the South's view of the North? Describe them.

g

It was in 1876, 30 years ago, and the people of South Carolina had been living under Negro rule for eight years. Our legislature was composed of a majority of Negroes, most of whom could neither read nor write. They were the easy dupes of as dirty a band of vampires and robbers as ever preyed upon a people. Life ceased to be worth having on the terms under which we were living, and in desperation we determined to take the government away from the Negroes.

We organized the Democratic party of South Carolina with one plank, and only one plank, namely, that "this is a white man's country, and white men must govern it." Under that banner we went to battle.

We knew—who knew better?—that the North then was a unit in its opposition to Southern ideas. We knew it was their purpose to keep Negro governments in whichever states it was possible to do so because of a Negro majority. Having made up our minds, we set about it as practical men.

Clashes came. . . .

It was then that "we shot them"; it was then that "we killed them"; it was then that "we stuffed ballot boxes." After the federal troops came and told us, "You must stop this rioting," we had decided to take the state away. We hesitated at nothing.

Application

Polarization does not always end in violence or other dramatic action. It occurs in many different places on many different levels. Local newspapers show that some polarization exists between different groups in most communities. Liberals and conservatives, labor and management, old and young, apartment builders and homeowners, landlords and tenants, city officials and citizens, one ethnic group and another—these are just a few of many groups which may have differences and make news.

To examine polarization in your community:

1. Collect local newspapers for a week or more.

2. Identify at least one problem or issue that seems to be the basis of local polarization. News articles, letters to the editors, and editorials can serve as data.

3. Based on the data you gather, find evidence of the elements of polarization.

4. Make a list of questions you feel are important which have *not* been answered in your material. If possible, gather from people involved in the conflict additional data to answer these questions. Other sources for your investigation are printed handbills, advertisements, radio or TV statements, and statements made during meetings. Try to get materials that express differing points of view.

5. Make a display or report that shows the data you've collected. Beside or under each data piece, give your analysis of the material. Identify the elements of polarization you find. If possible, present your data in chronological sequence so any changes in degree of polarization can be identified.

6. Describe how the process of polarization developed in the problem or issue you've been investigating. Then answer these questions:

a. Does polarization seem to be decreasing, increasing, or staying the same?

b. What procedures and agencies are available to help solve the disagreement and reduce polarization? Are they effective?

Explain your conclusions as part of the display or in the report.

BRANCHING OUT

Polarization over national and international issues is common. Choose one issue that has been in the news and investigate it. Try to use the procedures that were suggested for investigating polarization in your community.

BIBLIOGRAPHY

Meltzer, Milton. *Underground Man.* Scarsdale, N.Y.: Bradbury Press, 1972. Fiction. Nineteen year old Josh serves as a "slave stealer" and helps runaway slaves cross the Ohio River to freedom in the North.

Hunt, Irene. *Across Five Aprils,* Chicago: Follett, 1964. Fiction. Jethro Creighton, the youngest son, is left to run the family farm in southern Illinois when the Civil War breaks out. He is torn between loyalty to the North and memories of his Southern background.

McPherson, James M. *Marching Toward Freedom.* N.Y.: Alfred A. Knopf, 1965. The story of black soldiers who served in the Civil War is told through letters, diaries, songs and speeches.

Werstein, Irving. *The Many Faces of the Civil War.* N.Y.: Julian Messner, 1961. A compact history of the war which concentrates on the human side of the conflict. This book deals with the people of both North and South who fought and endured these troubled times.

Trelease, Allen W. *Reconstruction: The Great Experiment.* N.Y.: Harper & Row, 1971. The Freedmen's Bureau, the sharecropping system and President Andrew Johnson's impeachment are major topics in this well-balanced account of a much-misunderstood period in American history.

UNIT 5

Growth and Reform

Autonomy

How does the desire for autonomy affect human behavior?

Introduction

Like most people, you probably enjoy directing your own life. There may be some decisions you'd rather share with your parents or other adults, but most of the time you probably want to be independent. It's possible that you've felt this way for quite some time. It's also very likely that you look forward to having more and more to say about how you live your life as you grow older.

The desire for self-direction isn't limited to young people. It seems to be an important idea shared by people in many different societies. Because of this desire, words like "freedom," "independence," and "liberty" are important to people around the world, past and present. When people lack this control over their own lives, their ideas, actions, and feelings are affected in important ways. Your life will probably be affected time after time by your own desire for self-direction.

In this unit you'll study how people are affected when they lack control over their lives. You'll also examine the actions which people take to gain this control.

Your principal has a "mental image" of what your school should be like. Your teachers also have their own ideas about how school should be run. So do your parents and many other citizens in your community.

How about you? Would you change anything about your school if you could? Even if you enjoy school very much, chances are that you can probably think of ways to improve it.

As quickly as you can, make a list of changes you'd like to see in your school.

Autonomy: aw-TAHN-oh-me

As you've just read, many people feel it's important to have at least some control over their own actions. The word for this is **autonomy**. It means "independence," or "freedom from control by others."

Go over the list you just made and identify those suggestions which would directly or indirectly affect your own autonomy in school.

Which suggestions would increase your autonomy? Which suggestions would decrease it? What are your feelings about how these changes could affect your autonomy? Are you interested in more autonomy?

Wanted: More Autonomy

How much autonomy is "right"? How much autonomy is enough? What counts most to people is how much autonomy they have compared to what they think they ought to have. Expectations about the amount of automomy differ greatly from person to person and from society to society.

● In each of the situations on page 302, people believe they don't have enough autonomy.

1. What different kinds of feelings do the individuals or groups seem to have?
2. Why do they have these feelings?

My problem is my parents. They just don't seem to understand people my age, especially me. From where I live, I can walk to my best friend's house, to a show, a shopping center, and several other places where there are things to do. I'm tired of television, and I keep my lessons up, but my parents won't let me go out. They think someone has to be with me every time I get out of sight. I didn't mind it so much when I was in grade school, but I do now.

Our school principal arranged for five of us to spend six weeks last summer learning to operate the school's new closed-circuit TV equipment. When school started, we produced and directed a ten-minute program every day. The school was going to give us credit for this year's work.

But just about the time we started getting ready for the special Thanksgiving program, the school's choral music director got more and more interested in both the operation of the equipment and in the daily programming. By Christmas, he was running everything.

Last week I visited Maplewood School. It was really nice. Kids there work on airplanes, computers, and lots of other things; they have courses in karate, horseback riding, and other kinds of sports that they don't teach here. The students there can choose new Short Courses every few weeks, all year long.

I wish our school was more like Maplewood.

Last night I went to a meeting of the city commission and listened to the members talk about vandalism in city parks. They discussed it for awhile. Then one of the commissioners said that most of the trouble happens at night and is caused by teen-agers. The other commission members agreed with him.

Commissioner Graham said he knew how to solve the problem —by keeping teens home at night. He said if there was a ten o'clock curfew, and the police picked up anyone under eighteen who was out the vandalism would stop. He said he grew up in a town with a curfew, and they never had any trouble. I sure hope they don't approve this curfew idea. If they do, a lot of teen-agers, including me, will have a lot to say about it.

For each situation in this activity, predict two different actions you think could happen next.

● The need for autonomy is so important that some kind of action almost always results when people lose some of their autonomy or feel that it is threatened. Below is a list of ways individuals and groups often react when their autonomy is affected in such ways.

Think of the situations in the last activity and the ways of acting you predicted might result in each case. Match each prediction with one of the reactions in the list below.

Stasis: STAY-sis

> **Group Formation** People who want more autonomy often organize and work together to try to gain it.
>
> **Violence** People who are frustrated by a lack of autonomy sometimes direct their anger at others. They may lose their tempers, attack people, damage property, or take other violent action.
>
> **Over-conformity** Individuals or groups who are dominated by another group may try to increase their autonomy by conforming, or "fitting in," as much as possible with the dominant group.
>
> **Scapegoating** People may blame their difficulties on someone or something that has little or no responsibility for their problem. That person or thing is called a **scapegoat**.
>
> **Opinion Appeal** People may try to influence the opinion of others who can help them.
>
> **Escape** People sometimes try to escape from problems related to their autonomy. They may do this by using drugs, seeking entertainment, putting the situation out of their minds, or through similar means.
>
> **Stasis** Groups or individuals who lack autonomy sometimes take no action at all because they feel helpless or unable to act.

From situations you know about, give at least one example for each of the reactions described in the list.

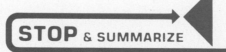

STOP & SUMMARIZE

Make a list of five things you'd like to own. Describe how owning one or more of these items would affect your autonomy.

BRANCHING OUT

What other people or groups can you think of who lack autonomy in some way? Describe the situations.

BRANCHING OUT

If there is a student government organization in your school, report on its powers and responsibilities. (You may need to check its charter or constitution.) What effect does the organization have on the autonomy of the student body?

Do members of student government feel their organization has too much autonomy? Too little autonomy? Explain.

Who can make changes in the organization's autonomy? What would happen if its autonomy were increased? Decreased?

What opinions do teachers, the administration, and the student body have about the autonomy of student government? What might happen if these people felt the organization had too much autonomy? Too little?

Perspective

In 1876 the United States celebrated 100 years of independence. Since its birth in 1776 the nation had changed a great deal. By 1876 the western border of the country was the Pacific Ocean. The population was more than fifteen times what it had been in 1776, and the east and west coasts were linked by telegraph lines and railroad.

In many ways the year 1876 was just as revolutionary as 1776, because great changes were in the process of occurring. This time, however, the changes were not in government, but in how people earned a living. Small family farms were giving way to larger farms, and craftsman's shops were being replaced by factories. Even the neighborhood butcher and baker came to be replaced by meat-packing houses and large bakeries. These changes were part of the new industrialism, which you'll learn about in the following pages.

Parts 1, 2, and 3 of this unit deal with events and conditions in the United States from about 1865, just after the Civil War, until about 1920. Each part focuses on the autonomy of the people who lived during this period.

Part 1   The New Industrialism

How did the changing industrial system affect people's autonomy?

Part 2   Reactions to the New Industrialism

How did people react to limitations upon their autonomy?

Part 3   Women and Black Americans Seek Autonomy

In what ways did women and black Americans lack autonomy during this period?

What actions did they take to increase their autonomy?

1837
Mt. Holyoke—1st women's college

1838
Oberlin College admits woman

1848
Seneca Falls convention

1862
Homestead Act

1867
U.S. buys Alaska

1869
Knights of Labor organizes

1876
Bell invents telephone

1879
Edison invents electric light

1886
A.F. of L. forms

1887
Interstate Commerce Commission

1890
Sherman Antitrust Act

1892
Homestead Steel strike

1894
Pullman strike

1898
Spanish-American War

1909
NAACP organizes

1914
Panama Canal opens

1920
Women gain voting rights

Part 1

The New Industrialism

There were many reasons why life in America began to change rapidly after the Civil War. Most of them were related to technology. New ways had been invented to produce energy and to manufacture goods from raw materials. These goods could be moved from one part of the country to another in large quantities. New machines changed the way workers did their jobs, and new ways of combining people's wealth made larger businesses possible. Inventions such as the telephone and electric light dramatically affected the growth of industry as well as the way people lived.

In the long run, these changes were of benefit to most Americans. At the same time, they caused a number of problems. Many of the benefits and problems were related to personal autonomy.

In Part 1 you'll investigate this question:

How did the changing industrial system affect people's autonomy?

In Unit 3 you read about the textile mills of the Northeast. These mills were a result of the Industrial Revolution, which had begun in Great Britain. In textile mills, cloth was manufactured by power-operated machinery. This machinery replaced the spinning wheel and loom, which had been used by workers in their homes to spin thread. Power-operated machinery soon came to be used in hundreds of different industries.

The invention and use of power-operated machinery led to the development of factories in this country in the first half of the 1800s. Factories, in turn, marked the beginning of a new industrial system—the new industrialism. Before the growth of the factory system, products were made by workers in their homes and shops. The activities in Part 1 will help you investigate some of the important ways people in the late 1800s were affected by the new ways of producing goods.

To find out what the new industrialism was like, copy the following chart. Fill it in as you proceed through Part 1.

*The development of large-scale industry began in Great Britain during the 1700s. It spread to other parts of Europe and to North America in the early 1800s. The term **Industrial Revolution** refers to the changes that resulted from the rapid growth of industry and to the period itself.*

Make sure you leave space for many entries in each block on your chart.

New Industrialism		
1. Way work was organized	2. Effect of new methods on production of goods	3. Job and economic security
4. Attitudes of workers and business owners/managers toward each other	5. Working conditions	
6. Where people lived	7. Feelings and attitudes of workers	

a Charles Litchman was an ex-shoe factory worker. In 1879 he appeared before a committee in Congress which was investigating economic problems. As he answered the committee's questions, he explained some important differences between the old and the new methods of manufacturing.

Read the Litchman piece carefully. In it you'll find information to fill in item 1 on your chart.

Mr. Litchman: In my trade of shoemaking, 20 years ago the work was done almost entirely by hand. A man had to learn how to make an entire shoe. Now with the use of machines, a man is no longer a shoemaker. He is now only the 64th part of a shoemaker, because there are 64 subdivisions in making shoes. A man may work 40 years at our trade and at the end of 40 years he will know no more about making a whole shoe than when he started.

The Chairman: He would only know how to make a peg or a waxed end?

Mr. Litchman: Yes; or he would be a laster, or a beveler, or heeler, or nailer, or he would be running and using a machine, or a peg-measure, or attending to any one of the 64 subdivisions into which the trade is parceled out.

The Chairman: How many of the 48,000 Massachusetts shoemakers can make a shoe?

Mr. Litchman: I have no way to know, but I would guess that not one tenth of them can make a shoe. The shoe that a few could make would be the old kind of turned shoe. I cannot make a machine shoe. My 64th part of making shoes is standing at the bench and cutting the uppers.

The Chairman: Still, because you once were a shoemaker, you might hang out a sign, "Boots and shoes made"; but the man who only makes pegs cannot say to the world, "Here is a shoemaking shop," and go into business for himself.

Mr. Litchman: No, sir. Of course, the man who makes pegs would not be called a shoemaker anyhow.

The Chairman: Does this rule which you have applied to the manufacturing of shoes apply to all other branches of manufacturing industry?

Mr. Litchman: For the most part, yes. I have no hesitation in saying that. It applies to every trade, even stonecutting.

When Charles Litchman learned his trade, he thought of himself as a craftsman. Twenty years later, he was a factory worker. What differences are there between a craftsman and a factory worker?

How were craftsmen such as Mr. Litchman affected by the growth of factories? What course of action did Mr. Litchman take as a result?

Peg *and* ***waxed end*** *refer to items which were used in the shoe manufacturing process.* ***Laster, beveler, heeler,*** *and* ***nailer*** *all refer to people involved in various steps of shoe manufacturing.*

b These men worked under the system described by Mr. Litchman.

Answer: I have not got a cent in the house; didn't have when I came out this morning.

Question: How much money have you had within three months?

Answer: I have had about 16 dollars inside of three months.

Question: Why do you not go west on a farm?

Answer: How could I go, walk it?

Question: Well, I want to know why you do not go out west on a 2,000-dollar farm, or take up a homestead and break it and work it up, and then have it for yourself and family?

Answer: I can't see how I could get out west. I have got nothing to go with.

Question: It would not cost you over 1,500 dollars.

Answer: Well, I never saw over a 20-dollar bill, and that is when I have been getting a month's pay at once. If someone gave me 1,500 dollars I would go.

Question: You do not know anything but mule spinning, I suppose?

Answer: That is what I have been doing, but I sometimes do something with pick and shovel. I am looking for work in a mill. The way they do there is this: There are about 12 or 13 men that go into a mill every morning, and they have to stand their chance, looking for work. The man who has a boy with him stands the best chance. Then, even if it is my turn or a neighbor's turn who has no boy, if another man comes in who has a boy he is taken right in, and we are left out. I said to the boss once, "What am I to do; I have got two little boys at home, one of them three years and a half and the other one year and a half old, and how am I to find something for them to eat; I can't get my turn when I come here?"

He said he could not do anything for me. I says, "Have I got to starve; ain't I to have any work?" They are forcing these young boys into the mills that should not be in mills at all; forcing them in because they are throwing the mules out and putting on ring frames.

What reasons did O'Donnell give for his employment problems? What problems of autonomy did he have?

In what ways did people who were self-employed have better job security than factory workers?

e Children worked in a number of different industries in the 1800s. The right-hand photo on page 312 shows a group of boys who worked in the mines. They were called "breaker boys." Their job was to break large lumps of coal into smaller ones. A child working in a textile factory is shown in the photo on the left.

As you continue in Part 1, remember to fill in your chart.

BRANCHING OUT

The system of work described in the first two data pieces is called division of labor. Imagine you are in charge of making several hundred kites. You have all the supplies you need and 10 people who will work with you. Using the division of labor method, organize the work.

What separate steps are involved in making your product? What is the most efficient way of organizing people? How will you assign the tasks? If these same people were to make their own kites, how would you organize people and supplies?

What advantages and disadvantages are there to division of labor? To having people work on every stage of a product themselves?

c Here is an interview with William H. Vanderbilt, president of the New York Central Railroad.

Vanderbilt: The railroads are not run for the benefit of the "dear public"—that cry is all nonsense—they are built by men who invest their money and expect to get a fair percentage on the same.

Interviewer: Does your Limited Express [railroad] pay?

Vanderbilt: No, not a bit of it. We only run it because we are forced to do so by the action of the Pennsylvania road. It doesn't pay expenses. We would abandon it, if it was not for our competitor keeping its train on.

Interviewer: But don't you run it for the public benefit?

Vanderbilt: The public be d____d. What does the public care for the railroads except to get as much out of them for as small a consideration as possible? I don't take any stock in this silly nonsense about working for anybody's good but our own.

Interviewer: Referring to wages paid your employees, do you consider that they are generally what they should be?

Vanderbilt: Yes, I do. There are always a lot of shiftless fellows who spend their money in drink and riotous living, who are ready to complain of anything.

How did Vanderbilt's views compare with the views of Herbert Spencer?

d The attitudes you've just read weren't directed only at poor workers and their families. In 1889 George Rice, owner of an oil company, testified before the United States Industrial Commission.

*A **trust** is a combination of businesses under the management and control of a single group of people. Because of their power, these people can control competition and prices. The Standard Oil Trust dominated the oil industry in America during the late 1800s.*

Many companies used similar methods of doing business during the last part of the 1800s. How can the autonomy of smaller businesses be affected by larger ones?

My refinery was forced out of business three years ago by the Standard Oil Trust. They did it partly by using their power to force the railroads to give them lower freight rates than I was able to get.

That was only part of the problem. I could sell my oil at two to three cents a gallon cheaper than Standard Oil and still make a nice profit. But because they were so big, they could afford to go to my customers and offer them oil even below the cost of producing it. Of course, after I was driven out of business, my old customers had to pay whatever Standard Oil demanded.

These kinds of savage attacks clearly show both their power to do evil and the uselessness of trying to fight them.

e This cartoon shows the extent of Standard Oil's control.

According to the cartoon, who was affected by Standard Oil? What does the cartoon suggest about Standard Oil's power?

f John D. Rockefeller Jr., son of the founder of Standard Oil, stated the following in 1903.

f The growth of a large business is merely a survival of the fittest. The American Beauty rose can be produced in the splendor and fragrance which brings cheer to its beholder only by sacrificing the early buds which grow up around it. This is not an evil tendency in business. It is merely the working-out of a law of nature and a law of God.

If Rockefeller's Standard Oil Company is the rose, what are the buds?

g The cartoon is an interpretation of Rockefeller's statement.

Based on the materials in this activity, answer the following questions:

1. What kind of autonomy did the industrial leaders seek for themselves?

2. How did the autonomy of Thomas O'Donnell compare with the autonomy of Carnegie, Rockefeller, Vanderbilt, and other leaders of the new industrialism?

3. Were the industrial leaders concerned about worker autonomy?

4. How do you think the autonomy of most workers was affected by the beliefs and actions of these leaders?

5. What relationship is there between wealth and autonomy?

BRANCHING OUT

Many of today's top industrial leaders are involved in the oil industry. As one of the most important sources of energy, oil plays a crucial part in our lives. Report on the many ways in which people and businesses in America depend on oil.

In recent years, the United States has faced difficulties in obtaining enough oil to meet its needs. How is the autonomy of Americans affected by oil shortages? In what ways have Americans attempted to deal with these shortages?

Working Conditions

In the early days of the factory system, when factories were small in size, the owner often knew his workers and had personal concern for their well-being. As industry grew, however, new machines were invented and larger factories were built. This meant in turn that more and more workers were hired to work in the factories. It also meant that workers had to deal with a new set of working conditions.

Based on the following materials, what statements can you make about

1. Factory working conditions during the growth of the new industrialism?
2. The relationship between employee and employer during this time?

Your answers will help you add to item 4 and begin item 5 of your chart.

a Below is a description of work in a steel mill in the 1900s.

a
The nature of the work, with the heat and its dangers, makes much of it exhausting. Yet these men for the most part keep it up 12 hours a day. It is uneconomical to have the plant shut down. In order that the mills may run practically all the time, the 24 hours is divided between two shifts. Most of the men employed in making steel (as distinct from the clerical staff) work half of the time at night. The usual arrangement is for a man to work one week on the day shift and the next week on the night shift. At the request of the men, the night turn is made longer, so that they can have the full evening to themselves the other week. Their hours on the day turn, therefore, are from 7:00 A.M. to 5:30 P.M.: This leaves thirteen and one half hours for the night shift.

b In the selection below a visitor to a Massachusetts factory describes the attitude of its manager.

b
I inquired of the manager of a major factory whether it was the custom of the manufacturers to do anything for the physical, intellectual, and moral welfare of their workpeople. "We never do," he said. "As for myself, I regard my workpeople just as I

318

regard my machinery. So long as they can do my work for what I choose to pay them, I keep them, getting out of them all I can. What they do or how they fare outside my walls I don't know, nor do I consider it my business to know. They must look out for themselves as I do for myself. When my machines get old and useless, I reject them and get new, and these people are part of my machinery."

C These photographs show factory working conditions in several different industries.

d The following rules were adopted by the Cambria Iron Works on April 6, 1874.

d

—Any person known to belong to any secret organization whose aim is to control wages or stop the works, shall be promptly and finally discharged. Persons not satisfied with their work or their wages can leave honorably by giving the required notice.

—Any person going to work intoxicated, or absenting himself from work, without having previously given notice and obtained leave, will be discharged or fined, at the option of the company. Any person failing to do his work in a proper manner, or failing to do a satisfactory amount, may expect to be dismissed whenever it may suit the convenience of the company.

—Quarreling or rioting on the company's premises, shall be punished by a fine of not less than 5 dollars nor more than 10 dollars, or the discharge of the offender, who may also be prosecuted for violation of the law.

—All money collected as fines and penalties will be set apart and reserved for those workers injured by accident.

—Persons found stealing coal will be charged the price of a load of coal for every lump stolen. For a repetition of the offense they will be discharged.

—Persons living in the company's houses will be charged for all damages done to the houses beyond the ordinary wear and tear. They will be forced to leave at once upon ceasing to be employed by the company. In renting the houses, preference will always be given to those whose business requires them to live near the works.

e Below is a contract offered in 1880 to employees of a tobacco manufacturer. In its factory in Jersey City, New Jersey, the company employed about 4,000 men, women, and children.

e

I, the undersigned, in consideration of employment being offered to me and wages agreed to be paid me, by the firm of ——, do hereby agree to allow the said firm to search and examine my person, clothing, or other personal effects and property at any and all times while I am upon the premises of said firm, or while leaving the said premises.

I will also allow the said firm to enter and search my house to determine whether I have taken any of its property.

I do further agree that all injury to life, limb, body, or health, by reason of my employment by said firm shall be at my own risk. I will not prosecute said firm because of any injury that may occur to me, in or upon the premises of the said firm or when about the business of the said firm.

I hereby agree to faithfully observe and keep the rules of said firm, and will promptly obey the orders of my foreman and other superiors. Witness my hand this _____ day of _____ 18__.

f The following information is from a report made by the state of Massachusetts in 1884. The report was the result of an investigation which was made of the living and working conditions of the working girls of Boston.

f

What were the attitudes of company officials toward workers, as shown in the data pieces in this activity? How do you think workers might react to these conditions?

In the manufacture of *Buttons,* the girls say the work is rather dangerous, as they are liable to get their fingers jammed, or caught in the die when it comes down to press the parts of the button together. A man (although not a surgeon) is provided to dress wounds three times for each individual without charge. Afterwards, the person injured must pay all expenses. There are 35 machines in use, and accidents occur often.

In making *Paper boxes,* the girls must stand, a practice they think is very harmful. The coloring matter in materials used in the construction and covering of boxes is considered dangerous to health by some, one girl being at home sick three months from blood poisoning caused by work.

In the *Clothing* business, the general testimony is that the work is very hard, and is the cause of much sickness among the working girls. The tax on the strength is great, and it would seem that unless a girl is strong and robust, the work soon proves too hard for her, and if followed thereafter results disastrously.

Make sure you complete your answers to the questions on page 318. Then see what statements you can make about worker autonomy during the late 1800s.

Income and Autonomy

In the activity *Industrial Leaders,* you thought about the relationship between a person's money and his or her autonomy. In this activity you'll have a chance to think about it again, only this time in terms of worker income.

(a) The table which follows tells something about the autonomy of some Americans in 1884. The statistics are for Illinois, but they are fairly typical of the rest of the United States at that time.

WORKER WAGES 1884

Average annual wages for day laborers	$344.59
Average annual wages for carpenters	$552.44
Average annual wages for locomotive engineers	$1,076.00
Average number of days worked each week	6
Average number of hours worked each day	10

(No vacation or sick pay)

Workers were laid off an average of 8 weeks each year without pay. Figure out how much a worker in one of the categories shown in the table made per hour in 1884. To do this, answer the following questions:

1. How many weeks was a worker employed each year?
2. How much money did a worker make each week?
3. What was the average number of hours worked each week?
4. How much money did a worker make per hour?

(b) The chart which follows shows how much Illinois workers had to pay for certain items in 1884.

Make a shopping list of five items from the list. Find the total cost. How many hours would a worker in the category you chose above have to work to buy these items?

Check the prices of the same five items in your local supermarket. If a person earns $2.30 an hour, how long would he or she have to work to buy these items? What comparison can you make between an average wage earner of today and an average wage earner of 1884?

How do you think that buying power affects a person's autonomy?

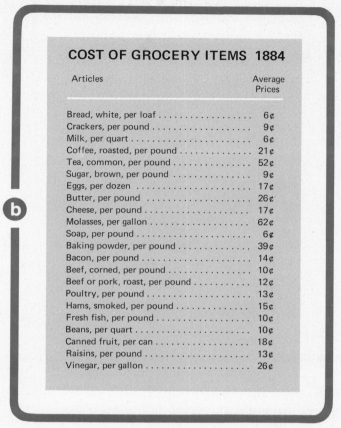

b

COST OF GROCERY ITEMS 1884

Articles	Average Prices
Bread, white, per loaf	6¢
Crackers, per pound	9¢
Milk, per quart	6¢
Coffee, roasted, per pound	21¢
Tea, common, per pound	52¢
Sugar, brown, per pound	9¢
Eggs, per dozen	17¢
Butter, per pound	26¢
Cheese, per pound	17¢
Molasses, per gallon	62¢
Soap, per pound	6¢
Baking powder, per pound	39¢
Bacon, per pound	14¢
Beef, corned, per pound	10¢
Beef or pork, roast, per pound	12¢
Poultry, per pound	13¢
Hams, smoked, per pound	15¢
Fresh fish, per pound	10¢
Beans, per quart	10¢
Canned fruit, per can	18¢
Raisins, per pound	13¢
Vinegar, per gallon	26¢

Business Cycles and Unemployment

Businesses in this country go through periods of prosperity and depression. When business is good, many people are working, and most of the country is prosperous. When business is bad, wages go down, and people lose their jobs.

These conditions often changed rapidly. For example, a decrease in business that began in New England textile plants would soon affect many other businesses. A period of prosperity could change to a national depression in a few months.

The graph on page 324 shows business highs and lows in this country between 1865 and 1895.

Depression is a time marked by declining business activity, widespread unemployment, and falling prices and wages.

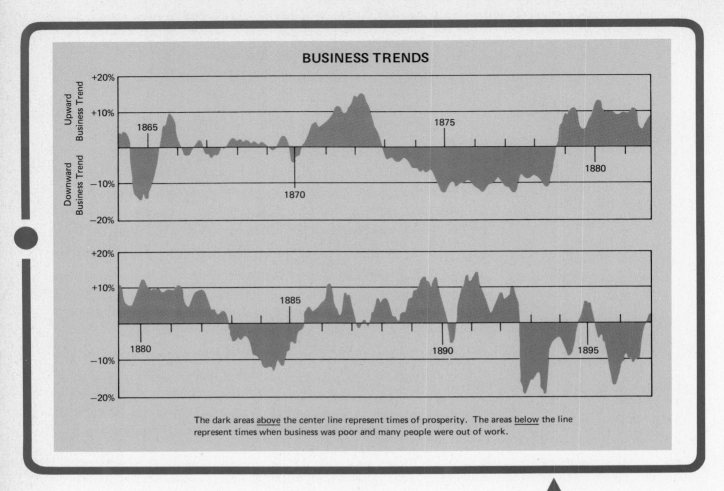

BUSINESS TRENDS

Upward Business Trend
Downward Business Trend

+20%
+10%
−10%
−20%

1865
1870
1875
1880

+20%
+10%
−10%
−20%

1880
1885
1890
1895

The dark areas <u>above</u> the center line represent times of prosperity. The areas <u>below</u> the line represent times when business was poor and many people were out of work.

How do you think worker autonomy is affected in periods of prosperity? In times of economic depression?

The business trends shown on the graph weren't caused by the industrialism of post-Civil War years. There had been ups and downs in the economy in the earlier part of the 1800s too. But the new industrialism did cause a greater number of people to be affected by business lows, because more people had jobs in industry.

What effect do business cycles have on people's economic security? Add comments to item 3 of your chart.

When were the years of prosperity? When were the years of depression?

Railroads and New Opportunities

a One of the most important features of the new industrialism was the growth of railroads. The maps opposite show the growth of railroad networks after 1840.

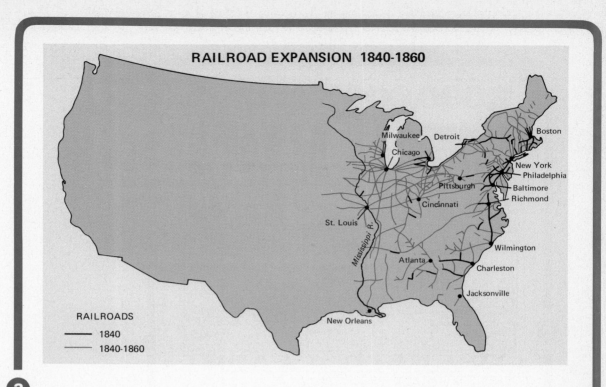

RAILROAD EXPANSION 1840-1860

RAILROADS
— 1840
— 1840-1860

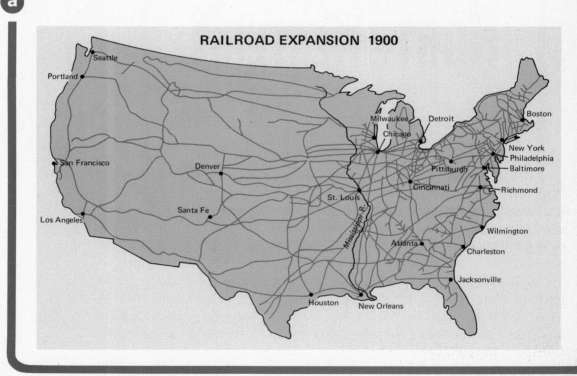

RAILROAD EXPANSION 1900

Based on the materials which follow, answer this question: How did railroads affect people's job opportunities and economic security?

b Many farmers responded to railroad posters like this one.

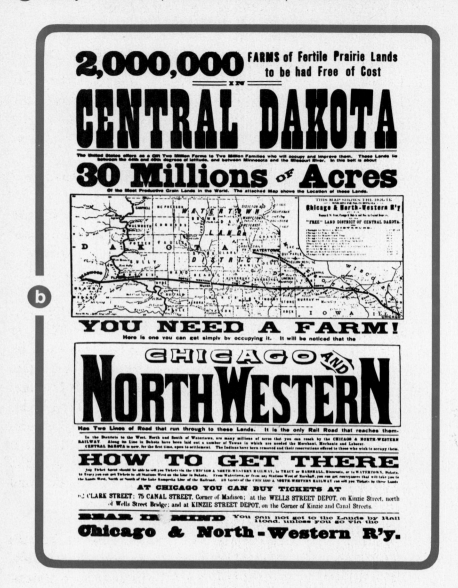

As the poster above suggests, farmers were one group who stood to gain from the extension of railroads into new territories. Before the development of technology, farming had usually been done on a small scale. A farm family would first meet its own needs, then raise whatever could be sold within wagon-hauling distance of the farm. Success or failure depended mainly on the family's hard work and the weather.

Then came the railroads, providing access to millions of acres of farmland, encouraging people to buy new land, and opening up new markets for trade.

Generally, opportunities such as these help increase individual autonomy. Many Americans did benefit from the growth of railroads, but the railroad did not always add to people's prosperity.

Dyke reached the post office in Bonneville toward eleven o'clock; but he did not go at once to Ruggles's office. It was seldom he got into town, and when he did he permitted himself the luxury of enjoying his evident popularity. He held a moment's conversation with each one of his friends that he met.

At the drugstore, his eye was caught by a "transparent slate," a child's toy.

"Now, there's an idea, Jim," he observed to the boy behind the soda-water fountain; "I know a little tad that would just about jump out of her skin for that. Think I'll have to take it with me.

"Smartest little girl in all Tulare County, and more fun! A regular whole show in herself."

"And the hops?" inquired Jim. "Bully," declared Dyke, with the good-natured man's readiness to talk of his private affairs to anyone who would listen. "I'm dead sure of a bonanza crop by now. The rain came *just* right. I actually don't know as I can store the crop in those barns I built, it's going to be so big. That foreman of mine was a daisy. Jim, I'm going to make money in that deal. You know the crop is contracted for already. Sure, the foreman managed that. He's a daisy. Chap in San Francisco will take it all and at the advanced price. I wanted to hang on, to see if it wouldn't go to six cents, but the foreman said, 'No, that's good enough.' So I signed. Ain't it just great?"

"I suppose you'll stay right by hops now?"

"Right you are; I know a good thing when I see it. There's plenty others going into hops next season. I set 'em the example. Wouldn't be surprised if it came to be a regular industry hereabouts. I'm planning ahead for next year already. I can let the foreman go, now that I've learned the game myself. I think I'll buy a piece of land off Quien Sabe; get a bigger crop; build a couple more barns; by George, in about five years' time, I'll have things humming. I'm going to make *money,* Jim."

At Ruggles's office, which was the freight as well as the land office of the P. and S.W. Railroad, Dyke was surprised to see a familiar figure in conference with Ruggles himself.

Dyke recognized the figure as S. Behrman, banker, railroad agent, and political manipulator.

"I'll be wanting some cars of you people before the summer is out," said Dyke to the clerk as he folded up and put away the

Hops *is an herb used to flavor beer.*

327

order that had been handed him. He had arranged the matter of transporting his crop some months before, but he liked to busy himself again and again with the details of his undertaking.

"I suppose," he added, "you'll be able to give 'em to me. There'll be a big wheat crop to move this year, and I don't want to be caught in any car famine."

"Oh, you'll get your cars," murmured the clerk.

"It'll be the means of bringing business your way," Dyke went on; "I've done so well with my hops that there are a lot of others going into the business next season. Suppose we went into some sort of shippers' organization, could you give us special rates, cheaper rates—say a cent and a half?"

The clerk looked up.

"A cent and a half! Say *four* cents and a half and maybe I'll talk business with you."

"Four cents and a half," returned Dyke; "I don't see it. Why, the regular rate is only two cents."

"No, it isn't," answered the clerk, looking him gravely in the eye, "it's five cents."

"Well, there's where you are wrong," Dyke retorted genially. "You look it up. You'll find the freight on hops from Bonneville to 'Frisco is two cents a pound for carload lots. You told me that yourself last fall."

"That was last fall," observed the clerk. There was a silence. Dyke shot a glance of suspicion at the other. Then, reassured, he remarked, "You look it up. You'll see I'm right."

S. Behrman came forward and shook hands politely with Dyke.

"Anything I can do for you, Mr. Dyke?"

"Our regular rate on hops is five cents," explained the clerk.

"Yes," answered S. Behrman, pausing to reflect; "yes, Mr. Dyke, that's right—five cents."

For a moment Dyke was confused. Then the matter became clear in his mind. The railroad had raised the freight on hops from two cents to five.

All his calculations as to a profit on his little investment he had based on a freight rate of two cents a pound. He was under contract to deliver his crop. He could not draw back. The new rate ate up every cent of his gains. He stood there ruined.

He burst out. "You promised me a rate of two cents and I went ahead with my business with that understanding."

S. Behrman and the clerk watched him from the other side of the counter.

"The rate is five cents," declared the clerk doggedly.

"Well, that ruins me!" shouted Dyke. "Do you understand?

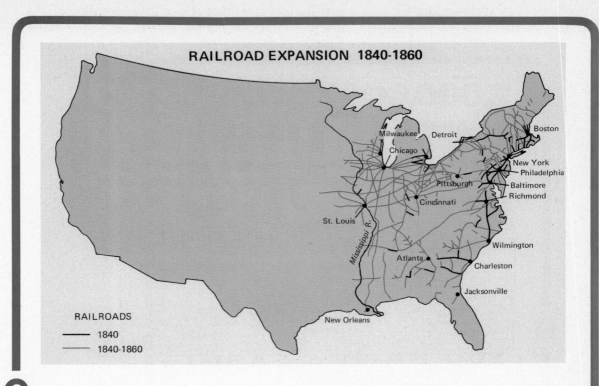

RAILROAD EXPANSION 1840-1860

Milwaukee
Detroit
Boston
Chicago
New York
Philadelphia
Pittsburgh
Baltimore
Cincinnati
Richmond
St. Louis
Wilmington
Atlanta
Charleston
Jacksonville
New Orleans

Mississippi R.

RAILROADS
—— 1840
—— 1840-1860

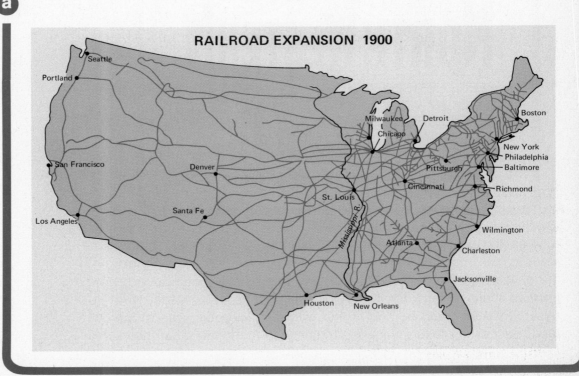

RAILROAD EXPANSION 1900

Seattle
Portland
Milwaukee
Detroit
Boston
Chicago
New York
Philadelphia
San Francisco
Denver
Pittsburgh
Baltimore
Cincinnati
Richmond
St. Louis
Santa Fe
Los Angeles
Wilmington
Atlanta
Charleston
Jacksonville
Houston
New Orleans

Mississippi R.

Based on the materials which follow, answer this question: How did railroads affect people's job opportunities and economic security?

b Many farmers responded to railroad posters like this one.

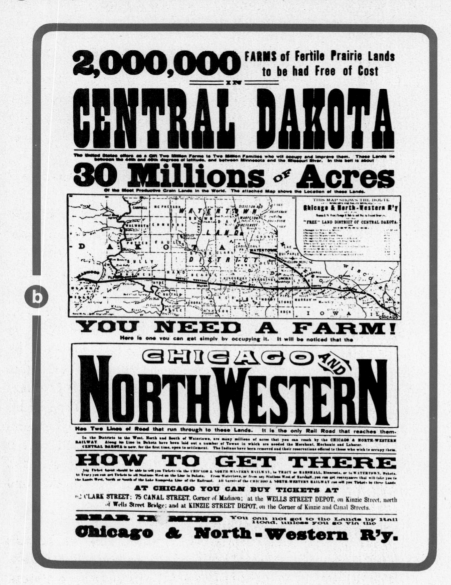

As the poster above suggests, farmers were one group who stood to gain from the extension of railroads into new territories. Before the development of technology, farming had usually been done on a small scale. A farm family would first meet its own needs, then raise whatever could be sold within wagon-hauling distance of the farm. Success or failure depended mainly on the family's hard work and the weather.

Then came the railroads, providing access to millions of acres of farmland, encouraging people to buy new land, and opening up new markets for trade.

Generally, opportunities such as these help increase individual autonomy. Many Americans did benefit from the growth of railroads, but the railroad did not always add to people's prosperity.

c The following excerpt from Frank Norris's novel, *The Octopus,* describes a situation faced by many of the nation's farmers.

Dyke reached the post office in Bonneville toward eleven o'clock; but he did not go at once to Ruggles's office. It was seldom he got into town, and when he did he permitted himself the luxury of enjoying his evident popularity. He held a moment's conversation with each one of his friends that he met.

At the drugstore, his eye was caught by a "transparent slate," a child's toy.

"Now, there's an idea, Jim," he observed to the boy behind the soda-water fountain; "I know a little tad that would just about jump out of her skin for that. Think I'll have to take it with me.

"Smartest little girl in all Tulare County, and more fun! A regular whole show in herself."

"And the hops?" inquired Jim. "Bully," declared Dyke, with the good-natured man's readiness to talk of his private affairs to anyone who would listen. "I'm dead sure of a bonanza crop by now. The rain came *just* right. I actually don't know as I can store the crop in those barns I built, it's going to be so big. That foreman of mine was a daisy. Jim, I'm going to make money in that deal. You know the crop is contracted for already. Sure, the foreman managed that. He's a daisy. Chap in San Francisco will take it all and at the advanced price. I wanted to hang on, to see if it wouldn't go to six cents, but the foreman said, 'No, that's good enough.' So I signed. Ain't it just great?"

"I suppose you'll stay right by hops now?"

"Right you are; I know a good thing when I see it. There's plenty others going into hops next season. I set 'em the example. Wouldn't be surprised if it came to be a regular industry hereabouts. I'm planning ahead for next year already. I can let the foreman go, now that I've learned the game myself. I think I'll buy a piece of land off Quien Sabe; get a bigger crop; build a couple more barns; by George, in about five years' time, I'll have things humming. I'm going to make *money,* Jim."

At Ruggles's office, which was the freight as well as the land office of the P. and S.W. Railroad, Dyke was surprised to see a familiar figure in conference with Ruggles himself.

Dyke recognized the figure as S. Behrman, banker, railroad agent, and political manipulator.

"I'll be wanting some cars of you people before the summer is out," said Dyke to the clerk as he folded up and put away the

Hops *is an herb used to flavor beer.*

order that had been handed him. He had arranged the matter of transporting his crop some months before, but he liked to busy himself again and again with the details of his undertaking.

"I suppose," he added, "you'll be able to give 'em to me. There'll be a big wheat crop to move this year, and I don't want to be caught in any car famine."

"Oh, you'll get your cars," murmured the clerk.

"It'll be the means of bringing business your way," Dyke went on; "I've done so well with my hops that there are a lot of others going into the business next season. Suppose we went into some sort of shippers' organization, could you give us special rates, cheaper rates—say a cent and a half?"

The clerk looked up.

"A cent and a half! Say *four* cents and a half and maybe I'll talk business with you."

"Four cents and a half," returned Dyke; "I don't see it. Why, the regular rate is only two cents."

"No, it isn't," answered the clerk, looking him gravely in the eye, "it's five cents."

"Well, there's where you are wrong," Dyke retorted genially. "You look it up. You'll find the freight on hops from Bonneville to 'Frisco is two cents a pound for carload lots. You told me that yourself last fall."

"That was last fall," observed the clerk. There was a silence. Dyke shot a glance of suspicion at the other. Then, reassured, he remarked, "You look it up. You'll see I'm right."

S. Behrman came forward and shook hands politely with Dyke.

"Anything I can do for you, Mr. Dyke?"

"Our regular rate on hops is five cents," explained the clerk.

"Yes," answered S. Behrman, pausing to reflect; "yes, Mr. Dyke, that's right—five cents."

For a moment Dyke was confused. Then the matter became clear in his mind. The railroad had raised the freight on hops from two cents to five.

All his calculations as to a profit on his little investment he had based on a freight rate of two cents a pound. He was under contract to deliver his crop. He could not draw back. The new rate ate up every cent of his gains. He stood there ruined.

He burst out. "You promised me a rate of two cents and I went ahead with my business with that understanding."

S. Behrman and the clerk watched him from the other side of the counter.

"The rate is five cents," declared the clerk doggedly.

"Well, that ruins me!" shouted Dyke. "Do you understand?

I won't make fifty cents. *Make!* Why, I will *owe!* That ruins me, do you understand?"

The other raised a shoulder.

"We don't force you to ship. You can do as you like. The rate is five cents."

"Well—but—I'm under contract to deliver. What am I going to do? You told me—you promised me a two-cent rate."

"I don't remember it," said the clerk. "I don't know anything about that. But I know this: I know that hops have gone up. I know the German crop was a failure and that the crop in New York wasn't worth the hauling. Hops have gone up to nearly a dollar. You don't suppose we don't know that, do you, Mr. Dyke?"

"What's the price of hops got to do with you?"

"It's got *this* to do with us," returned the clerk with a sudden aggressiveness. "The freight rate has gone up to meet the price. My orders are to raise your rate to five cents."

Dyke stared in blank astonishment.

"Great Scott," he murmured. "Great Scott! What will you people do next? Look here. What's your basis of applying freight rates, anyhow?" he suddenly burst out with furious sarcasm. "What's your rule? What are you guided by?"

S. Behrman, who had kept silent during the heat of the discussion, leaned abruptly forward. For the only time in his knowledge, Dyke saw his face inflamed with anger, and contempt for all this farming element with whom he was contending.

"Yes, what's your rule? What's your basis?" demanded Dyke, turning swiftly to him.

S. Behrman emphasized each word of his reply with a tap of one forefinger on the counter before him:

"All—the traffic—will—bear."

Why did the railroad raise its rates?

Does S. Behrman's action match the ideas of the leaders you investigated in the last activity? Explain.

Which of the reactions to a lack of autonomy do you think Dyke would be most likely to follow?

The same man or men often controlled both the banks and railroads in an area. The banks were the usual source of loans and mortgages to help farmers develop more land and put in crops. How could this situation be used to make money for the men in control?

You've already identified some of the effects of the railroads on farmers. What effects do you think railroads had on businesses and factories? On the size and location of cities?

Growth of Cities

As the new industrialism expanded, many factories were built in cities. As a result, more and more people moved to cities in search of jobs. Many farm people flocked to cities, because new machines had reduced the need for workers on the farm.

a The following graph shows the rural and urban population in the United States from 1860 to 1920.

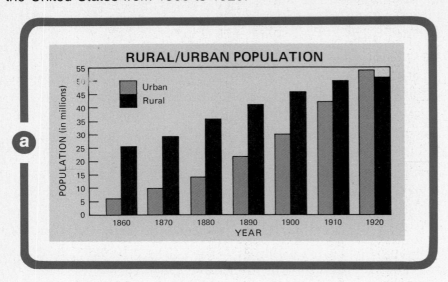

What general statement can be made about this country's population between 1860 and 1920?

Think about a farm family which moved to a city. In what ways would the autonomy of family members change?

b The following chart presents the population of some of the largest cities in the United States in 1860 and in 1920.

CITY POPULATIONS

1860		1920	
New York	1,174,779	New York	5,620,048
Philadelphia	565,529	Chicago	2,701,705
Baltimore	212,418	Philadelphia	1,823,779
Boston	177,840	Baltimore	804,874
New Orleans	168,675	St. Louis	772,897
Cincinnati	161,044	Boston	748,060
St. Louis	160,773	Buffalo	506,775
Chicago	112,172	Newark	414,524
Buffalo	81,129	Cincinnati	401,247
Newark	71,941	New Orleans	387,219

Based on the chart, which cities showed the greatest growth during the period shown? In general, which section of the country grew the fastest during these years?

c   Below are views of what Chicago was like in 1866 and in 1905.

According to these views, in what ways did Chicago change between 1866 and 1905?

The New Industrialism and Human Feelings

Many effects of the new industrialism were easy to identify. The growing population of cities could be counted, the lengthening rail lines could be measured, and the increased production of steel could be weighed.

But some effects of the new industrialism were impossible to measure. As you've learned, the new industrialism changed the kinds of work people did, employer-employee relationships, and the places where people lived. People must certainly have had strong feelings about these changes, yet there is no way to count or measure their feelings. The materials which follow can't provide a method of measurement, but they can suggest some possible feelings of those who were part of the new industrialism.

For each data piece, identify one or more attitudes or feelings which are expressed.

a This poem was written by a factory worker.

A Cry from the Ghetto

THE roaring of the wheels has filled my ears,
    The clashing and the clamor shut me in;
Myself, my soul, in chaos disappears,
    I cannot think or feel amid the din.
Toiling and toiling and toiling—endless toil.
    For whom? For what? Why should the work be done?
I do not ask, or know. I only toil.
    I work until the day and night are one.

The clock above me ticks away the day,
    Its hands are spinning, spinning, like the wheels.
It cannot sleep or for a moment stay,
    It is a thing like me, and does not feel.
It throbs as tho' my heart were beating there—
    A heart? My heart? I know not what it means.
The clock ticks, and below I strive and stare.
    And so we lose the hour. We are machines.

Noon calls a truce, an ending to the sound,
    As if a battle had one moment stayed—
A bloody field! The dead lie all around;
    Their wounds cry out until I grow afraid.

Chaos means confusion or disorder.

It comes—the signal! See, the dead men rise,
    They fight again, amid the roar they fight.
Blindly, and knowing not for whom, or why,
    They fight, they fall, they sink into the night.

b John Henry was a black steel driver who has become a folk hero in American history. According to legend, he took part in a contest during the construction of the Big Bend Tunnel of the Chesapeake and Ohio Railroad in West Virginia, about 1870. As the song below describes, John Henry made a bet with his foreman that he could drive a deeper hole into rock with two hand hammers than the foreman could with a new steam drill.

When John Henry was a little baby,
Sitting on his daddy's knee,
He grabbed a hammer and a little piece of steel,
Said: "This hammer'll be the death of me, oh Lord,
This hammer'll be the death of me.

Well, the captain said to John Henry,
"I'm gonna bring that steam drill around,
I'm gonna take that steam drill out on the job,
I'm gonna whop that steel on down, oh Lord,
Gonna whop that steel on down."

John Henry said to his captain:
"A man ain't nothin' but a man,
But before I'll let your steam drill beat me down,
I'll die with the hammer in my hand, oh Lord,
Die with the hammer in my hand!"

b

John Henry said to his shaker,
"Now, shaker, why don't you sing?
'Cause I'm throwing twelve pounds from my hips on down
Just listen to that cold steel ring, oh Lord,
Just listen to that cold steel ring."

John Henry said to his shaker,
"Shaker, you'd better pray,
If I miss that little piece of steel,
Tomorrow'll be your buryin' day, oh Lord,
Tomorrow'll be your buryin' day."

A **shaker** was an assistant who held the drill in place.

This is one of many versions of the John Henry song which have been passed along over the years.

333

John Henry told his captain,
Hey, captain, Look yonder what I see
Your drill's done broke, and your hole's done choke
And you can't drive steel like me, oh Lord
You can't drive steel like me.

The man that invented the steam drill;
He thought he was mighty fine.
But John Henry he made fourteen feet,
While the steam drill only made nine, oh Lord,
The steam drill only made nine.

John Henry hammered on the mountain,
Till his hammer was striking fire.
And he drove so hard he broke his poor heart,
And he died with his hammer in his hand, oh Lord,
He died with his hammer in his hand.

They carried John Henry to the graveyard,
And they buried him in the sand,
And every locomotive comes rolling by,
Says, "There lies a steel drivin' man, oh Lord,
There lies a steel drivin' man."

Now you've heard big John was born in Texas,
And you've heard he was born in Maine.
Well, I don't care where that poor boy was born,
He was a steel drivin' man, oh Lord,
He was a steel drivin' man.

In the contest between man and machine, who was the victor?

The real John Henry is said to have died when rock fell from a tunnel ceiling and crushed him.

What does the legend of John Henry indicate about worker feelings toward industrialism?

Factories were often built in the central part of the city, and nearby were built the houses and apartments where workers lived. In this way, workers could be within walking distance of their jobs. Many wealthy people built big houses in outer sections of the city.

In some cases, wealthy industrial leaders financed the development of new communities around their factories. This often meant that workers lived in homes and shopped in stores owned by the company they worked for.

C The photographs on page 335 contrast the Vanderbilt mansion with the small, crowded apartments in which many factory workers lived.

What feelings on the part of workers do you think grew out of the differences between their lives and the lives of the rich industrial leaders?

Part 2

Reactions to the New Industrialism

Although many people became rich during the rise of the new industrialism, many others had major cause for complaint. Farmers were taken advantage of by the railroads. Miners and factory workers had problems with wages and working conditions. Many owners of small businesses were forced out of business by their larger competitors. Almost everyone suffered from the uncertainty of the economy.

In Part 1 you examined how people felt about the effects of industrialism on their lives. In Part 2 you'll investigate the ways in which people as well as the government reacted to these effects.

The activities in Part 2 will help you answer this question:

How did people react to limitations in their autonomy?

As you've seen, farmers and factory workers alike faced problems as a result of the changing industrialism. Each group felt it lacked autonomy. The materials in this activity describe actions taken by farmers and workers to improve their situations.

As you read,

1. List the problems faced by farmers and by workers.
2. Identify the actions which were taken and the ideas that were suggested as solutions to their problems.
3. Explain how these ideas and actions would increase individual autonomy.

Farmers faced serious economic difficulties after the Civil War. High railroad rates and a drop in the prices of their crops were two major concerns. One response of farmers to increasing their economic security was the formation of local clubs called **granges.** The grange movement began in 1867 and soon became a national organization.

a The National Grange adopted this declaration in 1874.

The Grange today has about 8,000 local groups in almost 40 states. It works to spread information about modern farming methods and helps promote laws to benefit farmers. It also sponsors recreation programs for its members.

In what ways might cooperation help increase the autonomy of farmers?

*A **middleman** is a go-between—a trader who buys goods from the producer and sells them to the retailer. Why did farmers seek to end their dealings with middlemen?*

a

We propose meeting *together,* talking together, working together, and generally acting together for our mutual protection and advancement.

For our business interests, we desire to bring producers and consumers, farmers and manufacturers into close contact. Hence, we must dispense with middlemen: not that we are unfriendly to them, but we do not need them. Their surplus and their fees reduce our profits.

We hold that transportation companies of every kind are necessary to our success; that their interests are closely connected with our interests, and that cooperation will help us both. We believe that every state should increase all means of transporting goods cheaply to the seaboard, or between producers and consumers.

We are opposed to excessive salaries, high rates of interest, and extremely high profits in trade. They greatly increase our burdens. We desire only self-protection and the protection of every true interest of our land by honest transactions, honest trade, and honest profits.

b Below is an anti-railroad cartoon of the 1870s.

What does this cartoon mean?

During the 1890s, a new political party called the Populist party played an important role in United States politics. The Populist party was formed by farmer and worker groups who united to seek reforms. Many Populist candidates gained seats in state legislatures and in Congress between 1890 and 1896.

c The goals of the Populist party were stated at a convention held in Omaha, Nebraska in 1892. Here is a statement of its objectives.

Preamble

We need to cooperate, for this nation is on the edge of disaster. Most elections are dishonest, and so are many state legislatures, many congressmen, and even some judges. The people are discouraged. Many of the states have even had to put guards at voting booths to prevent threats and bribery. Most newspapers are either

In 1892, when this platform was written, the nation's business cycle was on the downswing. In 1893 the country sank into a serious economic depression. Farm prices dropped, and thousands of workers lost their

338

jobs as factories were forced to close. Why do you think some farmers and workers turned to a new political party instead of to the existing Democratic and Republican parties?

The platform of the Populist party stated that "wealth belongs to those who do the work that creates it; making money from the labor of others is robbery." Do you agree? If a man builds a shoe factory and buys expensive machinery for the factory, how should he divide profits between pay for his workers and himself?

bought off or afraid to tell the truth. People won't say what they believe. Businesses are going bankrupt. Laborers are poor. More and more of the land is in the hands of the rich. Factory workers aren't allowed to form unions to protect themselves, immigrants push wages lower and lower, and paid, private armies shoot laborers down.

Millions of workers are cheated to build a few fortunes greater than any in all history, and those that have those fortunes hate democratic ideas. The system is giving us just two classes—tramps and millionaires.

The government's power to make money is used to make the rich richer. The supply of money is kept low on purpose to make money lenders rich, to bankrupt small business, and turn workers into slaves. The rich of America and Europe have joined together and are rapidly taking over the world. If they are not overthrown at once, either terrible social problems, the destruction of civilization or a dictatorship will result.

We declare:

First—That the laboring people of this country are going to stand together permanently.

Second—That wealth belongs to those who do the work that creates it; that making money from the labor of others is robbery.

Third—That the railroads are either going to own the people, or the people are going to own the railroads. Therefore, the government should take them over.

Finance

1. We want no restrictions on how much silver and gold are mined, coined into money, and put into circulation.
2. We want the amount of money in circulation increased to not less than 50 dollars per person.
3. We want a graduated income tax, so the rich will pay a higher percentage than poor people.
4. To keep money in the hands of the people, we want state and federal governments to operate efficiently and keep taxes low.
5. We want the government to set up safe savings banks.

Transportation

Since transportation is a necessity, the government should own and operate the railroads. And since telegraph systems and telephone systems serve the same purpose as the post office, they should also be owned and operated by the government.

Land

The land and its resources are the heritage of the people. Ownership of land by foreigners should be prohibited. All land now held by railroads and other corporations which is not actually needed by them should be taken back by the government.

Expressions of Sentiments

We submit the following, not as part of the platform, but as expression of how we feel on other matters:

—We want honest elections which use secret ballots.
—We favor restriction of immigration.
—We want shorter hours of work.
—We want the private army known as the Pinkerton system abolished.
—We favor adoption of the referendum.
—We favor limiting the President and Vice President to one term, and electing Senators by a direct vote of the people.
—We oppose government aid to private corporations.
—We sympathize with the Knights of Labor in their struggle with the clothing manufacturers of Rochester, and encourage everyone not to buy goods made by these companies.

Which of the Populist demands would benefit farmers? In what ways? How did these demands compare with the views of the industrial leaders?

*The **Pinkerton system** refers to a private detective agency. Pinkerton detectives were sometimes hired by factory owners to stop strikes by the use of force.*

*A **referendum** is a special election in which people vote on certain issues.*

United States Senators used to be chosen by state legislatures. Today they are elected by the people.

*The **Knights of Labor** was a labor organization founded in 1869.*

d Below is a folksong which was sung by supporters of the Populist party.

A Hayseed Like Me

I was once a tool of oppression
And as green as a sucker could be;
And monopolies banded together
To beat a poor bum like me.

The railroads and party bosses
Together did sweetly agree;
And they thought there would be little trouble
In working a hayseed like me.

But now I've roused up a little
And their greed and corruption I see;
And the ticket we vote next November
Will be made up of hayseeds like me.

Monopoly refers to a large business which controls an entire industry's prices and production.

The strength of the Populist party dropped after 1896. This was partly because the nation's economy improved and partly because the major political parties (Democratic and Republican) came to support much of the Populist program.

Industrial workers and miners also organized to improve their autonomy during this period. The groups they formed were called **unions.** Through their unions, workers banded together to demand better wages and working conditions. Some unions failed, but others were successful in their attempts to gain benefits for the worker.

e Below is part of an 1890 union poster.

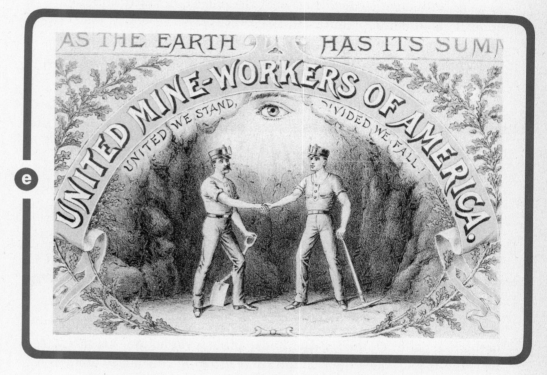

Samuel Gompers was the founder and long-time head of the union group called the American Federation of Labor. Many of the successes—and failures—of organized labor can be traced to his ideas and actions.

f The following piece is from an article written by Gompers in 1894. The article was addressed to a judge who disapproved of labor unions. In it Gompers describes some of the major problems faced by industrial workers in the late 1800s.

You know, or ought to know, that the introduction of machinery is turning into idleness thousands faster than new industries are founded. Yet machinery certainly should not be either destroyed or hampered in its full development.

What shall the workers do? Sit idly by and see the vast resources of nature and the human mind be used for the benefit of a few? No. The laborers must learn to think and act, and soon, too.

You recognize that the industrial forces set in motion by steam and electricity have changed the structure of our society. You also admit that a system has grown up where wages of the individual have passed from his control into that of combinations and trusts, and that the tendency is on the increase. How, then, can you criticize the workingmen for recognizing that as individuals they can have no influence in deciding what the wages, hours of toil, and conditions of employment shall be?

You evidently have observed the growth of business's wealth and influence. You recognize that wealth is concentrated into fewer hands. Yet you sing the old song that the workingman should depend entirely upon his own "individual effort."

What problems faced by workers did Gompers point out? Which of these problems are related to autonomy?

g The following material was written by a man named Josiah Strong in 1893. Strong discusses the economic effects of the new industrialism upon the working class. He also deals with reasons for discontent among workingmen.

First, let us look at the causes of this discontent.

To some it seems without excuse, because workingmen are now better fed, better clothed, better housed than ever before. Yet many working-men believe their condition is growing constantly worse.

No doubt the condition of the workingman has improved, but it by no means follows that he should be any better contented.

We hear it often said and often denied that while the rich are growing richer, the poor are growing poorer. The poor are not growing poorer in the sense that their wages will buy less of the necessaries of life or that they are rated lower on the tax list. It is true in the sense that there is a greater difference now between the workingman's income and his wants than ever before.

The workingman knows, for instance, that a carload of coal can be mined, made ready for market, and loaded in one half the time now that it required ten years ago. But he knows that the miner's wages have not been doubled in ten years. He knows that cotton factories produce nearly four times as much as 50 or 60 years ago, while his wages have been increased only 80 percent.

He knows that in the flouring mill one man now does the work formerly done by four, but he does not receive the wages of four.

The real question is not whether the laborer is receiving larger wages than he used to, nor even whether his increase is proportionate to the general increase of wealth, but whether he is receiving his *just dues.*

What is Strong's explanation for discontent among workers?

h In 1893 John Peter Altgeld, former governor of Illinois, had some advice for the workingpeople of America. In a Labor Day speech in Chicago, Altgeld told them what they ought to do.

h

Let the laborer learn from industry. Faultfinding and idle complaint are useless. Great forces, like great rivers, cannot be stopped. You must be able to fight your own battles. If the laborer stands single-handed before giant corporations, he will be destroyed. The world gives only when it is forced to give, and respects only those who command its respect.

Whenever you prove that you are an active, concentrated power, moving along lawful lines, then you will be felt in government. Until then, you will not.

What was Altgeld's advice?

i One of the most influential and successful labor leaders was John Mitchell, president of the United Mine Workers from 1898 until 1908. He explained the need for labor organizations in a book he wrote in 1903.

i

Under normal conditions the individual workman cannot bargain with his employer about the wages he will receive. The workman usually has not saved much money, and must have work and wages to survive. Each worker has only his own labor to sell. The employer buys the work of hundreds or thousands of men. He can easily do without the work of any one man who asks for more money. Because of this, the individual has little power. The best man is forced to work for the wages of the worst and lowest.

Trade unionism starts with understanding these facts.

What can groups such as labor unions accomplish that people acting alone cannot?

j These figures show the growth of union membership between 1870 and 1920.

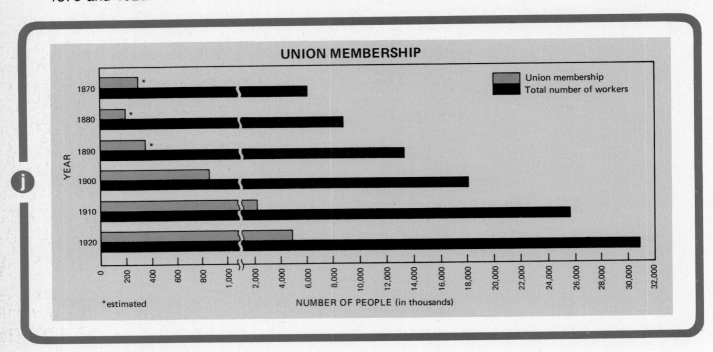

UNION MEMBERSHIP

*estimated

NUMBER OF PEOPLE (in thousands)

BRANCHING OUT

Choose a labor union today and report on its activities. Who are its leaders? What kinds of benefits and protection does the union give its members? Has the union ever gone on strike? If so, what were its demands? How was the strike settled?

Other Reactions

Forming opposition groups was probably the most effective thing that farmers and laborers could have done to increase their autonomy. As you learned in the *Introduction,* group formation is only one of several possible reactions when people feel they don't have enough autonomy.

Lack of autonomy may also lead to

Violence	Opinion Appeal
Over-conformity	Escape
Scapegoating	Stasis

344

Study the following materials. Then decide which of the above reactions each represents.

Look at the chart of business trends on page 324. What relationship can you see between this petition and business conditions of the time? What kinds of problems most likely prompted this petition?

What advantages might there be for business people to employ black men instead of white men?

Who would suffer more from the workingmen's actions—business people or black laborers? Why?

ⓐ In 1875 many workers in Atlanta signed the following petition. As you read it, think about reasons why a petition such as this would have been circulated.

ⓐ

The greed of certain rich business people would force us into hopeless poverty, and thus enslave us and our children forever. Therefore, we, the undersigned mechanics and workingmen, pledge our sacred honor that from and after this date

1. We will not deal in a business way, or support for public office, any man or men (whether grocer, dry goods, provision, or other dealer) who oppresses us by employing Negro instead of skilled white labor.

2. We will not trade with anyone who buys his supplies from those who employ Negro instead of skilled white labor.

3. We will not rent houses owned by persons who employ Negro to the exclusion of skilled white labor in their construction or repairs.

The **temperance movement** of the late 1800s and early 1900s was an effort to ban the production and sale of liquor in this country.

The word **demon** refers to a devil or evil spirit. It is often used to describe a person or thing regarded as cruel or evil.

During the middle and late 1800s, the use of alcoholic beverages increased. A temperance movement developed, supported by many women, churches, and other groups. The National Prohibition party, which favored laws against the production and sale of liquor, and the Women's Christian Temperance Union were two of the many organizations formed to oppose "Demon Rum."

ⓑ Following is an excerpt from a book printed in 1893.

According to this data piece, what was "the most overpowering enemy of the workingclasses"? What kind of reaction to lack of autonomy is this?

ⓑ

Gather up the money that the working classes have spent for rum during the last 30 years, and I will build for every workingman a house, and lay out for him a garden, and clothe his sons in broadcloth and his daughters in silks. I will place at his front door prancing horses, and secure him a policy of life insurance so that the present home may be well maintained after he is dead. The most overpowering enemy of the working classes is intoxicating liquor.

c Below is a poem by Vachel Lindsay.

c

Factory Windows Are Always Broken

Factory windows are always broken.
Somebody's always throwing bricks,
Somebody's always heaving cinders,
Playing ugly Yahoo tricks.

Factory windows are always broken
Other windows are let alone.
No one throws through the chapel window.
The bitter, snarling derisive stone.

Factory windows are always broken.
Something or other is going wrong.
Something is rotten—I think in Denmark.
End of the factory-window song.

A group called the American Protective Association (A.P.A.) was formed in 1887. It soon had a million members, mostly factory workers. The period in which it was most active was one in which millions of immigrants were arriving from Poland, Russia, Czechoslovakia, Italy, and other southern and eastern European countries.

d The goals of the A.P.A. are shown by the secret oath which members took when they joined.

d

I do most solemnly promise and swear that I will always labor, plead, and wage a continuous warfare against ignorance and fanaticism. I will never allow a member of the Roman Catholic Church to become a member of this order. I will use my influence to promote the interest of all Protestants everywhere in the world that I may be. I will not employ a Roman Catholic in any capacity, if I can obtain the services of a Protestant.

I furthermore promise and swear that I will not support the nomination of a Roman Catholic for any political office. I will not vote for, or urge others to vote for, any Roman Catholic. I will vote only for a Protestant, so far as may lie in my power.

To all of which I do most solemnly promise and swear, so help me God. Amen.

Many immigrants from southern and eastern Europe were Roman Catholic. What could members of the American Protective Association gain from their stand against Roman Catholics? Which response to lack of autonomy did this represent? (See page 303.)

Two other methods used in labor disputes were the lockout and the boycott. A **lockout** is when an employer closes his factory to keep employees from working during a labor dispute. A **boycott** is when a labor union tries to persuade (1) people not to buy a product or (2) workers not to deal in any way with an employer involved in a labor dispute.

Not all labor disputes resulted in work stoppage or boycott. Workers also sought to improve their lot through **bargaining** with employers.

Many labor unions fought for better wages and working conditions by going out on strike. A **strike** occurs when employees as a group refuse to work. In the 1870s strikes became the most effective way for workers to protect themselves against big business.

e The following pictures show several of the large worker strikes that occurred in the late 1800s and early 1900s. As one photo shows, federal guards and soldiers were sometimes used to break up worker strikes that were considered illegal. In some instances, companies hired private police forces to put down strikes.

1 Steel strike in Homestead, Pennsylvania, 1892
2 Railway strike in Illinois, 1885
3 Coal strike in Pennsylvania, 1902

347

f One of the most popular fiction writers of the late 1800s was Horatio Alger. Most of his novels described ways in which poor boys became successful. He wrote over 130 of these "rags to riches" stories. An excerpt from one of these stories is below.

f

When Micky had gone out, Mr. Rockwell said, "Well, Richard, I have lost my bookkeeper."

"Yes, sir," said Dick.

"And I can't say I am sorry. I will do Mr. Gilbert the justice to say that he understood his business; but he was personally disagreeable and I never liked him. Now I suppose I must look out for a successor."

"Yes, sir, I suppose so."

"I know a very competent bookkeeper, who is intending to go into business for himself six months from now. Until that time I can hire his services. Now, I have a plan in mind which I think you will approve. You shall at once begin the study of bookkeeping in a commercial school in the evening, and during the day I will direct Mr. Haley to employ you as his assistant. I think in that way you will be able to take over his job when he quits."

Dick was completely taken by surprise. The thought that he, who was so recently working as a shoeshine boy in the streets, could rise in six months to the important job of a bookkeeper in a large wholesale house, seemed almost incredible.

"I should like nothing better," he said, his eyes sparkling with delight, "if you really think I could do the work satisfactorily."

In six months, at the age of 17, Dick took over the bookkeeper's job with a salary, to begin with, of 1,000 dollars a year. To this an annual increase was made, making his income (at 21) 1,400 dollars. Just about that time he had an opportunity to sell his uptown lots, to a gentleman who had taken a fancy to them, for five times the amount he paid, or 5,000 dollars. His savings from his salary was about 2,000 dollars more.

Meanwhile Mr. Rockwell's partner, Mr. Cooper, retired from the business because of bad health. Richard, to his unbounded astonishment and gratification, was admitted to the position of junior partner. He invested the money he had already saved in the business, and received a corresponding share of the profits. These profits were so large that Richard was able to increase his interest yearly by investing his additional savings.

Why do you think people enjoyed this kind of story? Which response to lack of autonomy does it seem to be? (See page 303.)

348

During the late 1800s, labor unions made some progress in improving working conditions for people. But many felt that only the federal government had enough power to regulate big business and protect the interests of working people.

The following data will give you an idea of how some government leaders felt about the situation. Identify the attitudes expressed.

a In 1887 President Grover Cleveland vetoed a bill which would have given seeds to farmers suffering from drought in Texas.

a

To The House Of Representatives:

I do not believe that the power and duty of the government ought to be extended to the relief of individual suffering. Though the people support the government, the government should not support the people.

The friendliness and charity of our countrymen can always be relied upon to relieve their fellow citizens in misfortune. This has been done repeatedly and quite recently. Federal aid in such cases encourages people to expect care from the government and weakens the sturdiness of our national character.

What reasons did Cleveland give for refusing aid to Texas farmers?

b This cartoon suggests one view of why the government didn't do more to help the average American during this period.

What views does the cartoon express?

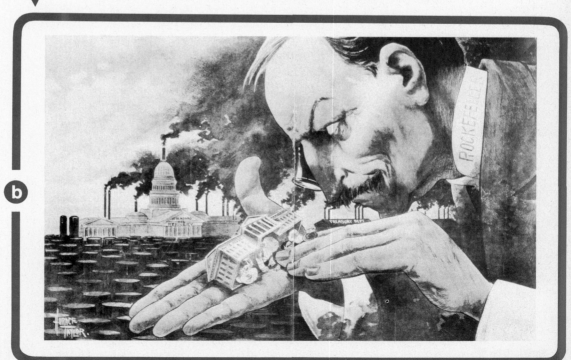

b

c David J. Brewer, Associate Justice of the United States Supreme Court stated the following in an 1893 speech to New York lawyers.

c

It is always true that the wealth of a community will be in the hands of a few. Only a few are willing to make sacrifices to save money. Only a few have business ability and wisdom. For these reasons, only a few are wealthy. The rest live on what they can make from day to day.

One of the main purposes of government is to protect each man's property. Our problem is that the rights of life, liberty, and property are threatened by the masses of people—the majority.

Labor organizations are trying to control property which is not theirs. When they strike, work stops, keeping the employer from using his property. They even stop other workers from taking their places. Irresponsible persons and organizations are trying to control labor in ways that interfere with personal rights and liberties. The many [employees] are trying to control the few [employers]. This is a step toward dictatorship. If it succeeds, the next step is to seize the employer's property.

I am against these trends. The eager cry of the true American is for individual freedom and an absolute protection of all personal and property rights.

What was Brewer's attitude toward labor unions? Toward business people?

How did Brewer's ideas compare with the ideas of the industrial leaders (pages 313–317)?

Eventually the attitude of government leaders toward business and labor began to change. What kind of changes in thinking took place? The following data pieces will help answer this question.

On pages 351–352 you'll read about reasons why changes in government attitudes occurred.

The opinions of Presidents Theodore Roosevelt and Woodrow Wilson regarding big business are in the data below. Compare these opinions with those of President Cleveland and Justice Brewer, and identify the differences.

d President Theodore Roosevelt expressed the following thoughts in 1910.

d

There is no effective state or national control upon unfair money-getting. This has tended to create a small class of enormously wealthy and powerful men, whose chief aim is to hold and increase their power. We need to change the conditions which allow these men to increase their power. We grudge no man a fortune which represents his own power and wisdom when exercised with regard to the welfare of his fellows. We should permit power to be gained only so long as the gaining represents benefit to the community. This, I know, requires far more governmental interference than we have yet had, I think we have got to face the fact that such an increase in governmental control is now necessary.

We are all Americans. Our common interests are as broad as the continent. The national government belongs to the whole American people. Where the whole American people are interested, that interest can be well guarded only by the national government. The improvement which we seek must be brought about, I believe, mainly by the national government.

e Woodrow Wilson, in his successful 1912 campaign for President, gave a speech in which he expressed his attitudes toward the new industrialism.

e

American industry is not free, as once it was free. American enterprise is not free. The man with only a little money is finding it harder to get into a business, more and more impossible to compete with the big fellow. Why? Because the laws of this country do not prevent the strong from crushing the weak. Because the strong have crushed the weak, the strong dominate the industry and economic life of this country.

We used to say that the ideal of government was for every man to be left alone and not interfered with, except when he interfered with someone else. We said that the best government was the government that did as little governing as possible. That was the idea that people believed in during Jefferson's time. But we are coming now to realize that life is so complicated that we are not dealing with the old conditions. Now the law has to step in and create new conditions under which we may live.

Reform

In the late 1800s corporations and trusts grew into giant businesses, controlling the lives of more and more people and limiting their autonomy in ways you have investigated.

Finally so many people became concerned about the power of these trusts and corporations that Congress was forced to act. In 1890 it passed the Sherman Antitrust Act. This law made any combination of businesses illegal if the combination held back free trade in any way. Through this law the principle of government control of excessive business power was established.

A movement for reform began and gathered strength rapidly. "Muckrakers" wrote novels and articles describing the evils of big business. They described political corruption, unfair business practices, uncontrolled sale of dangerous drugs, and filth and disease in food-packing plants. The public became more and more conscious of these problems.

The muckrakers were followed by political reformers—investigators who exposed evil, prosecutors who took legal action against big businesses, and politicians who passed new laws to control business power. New laws gave workers protection on the job, prevented children from doing dangerous or unhealthy work, and controlled working conditions. These and other reforms of the early 1900s were part of what is called the Progressive movement.

Theodore Roosevelt, who became President in 1901, was a leader in the Progressive movement. He was especially determined to enforce the Sherman Antitrust law. Under his strong leadership the power of big businesses and railroads was curbed.

The cartoon below illustrates Roosevelt's first antitrust fight, which was against a railroad combination. Roosevelt was successful, because the Supreme Court ruled that the company had acted to restrain trade illegally.

What does this cartoon tell about the struggle which Roosevelt faced?

▼

Part 3

Women and Black Americans Seek Autonomy

When a group lacks autonomy, it is generally because it is dominated by another group which is more powerful. The dominant group uses its power to take advantage of those less powerful.

In Parts 1 and 2 you investigated the lack of power of American farmers and industrial workers. Their autonomy was limited in large part by the actions of big business and industrial leaders. Farmers and workers were finally able to solve many of their problems by organizing, influencing public opinion, and gaining government support.

The new industrialism limited the autonomy of many Americans, but not all losses of autonomy could be blamed on big business. Groups such as women and black Americans found their autonomy limited for other reasons during the late 1800s and early 1900s. In Part 3 you'll investigate these questions:

In what ways did women and black Americans lack autonomy during this period?

What actions did they take to increase their autonomy?

The Position of Women

During the middle and late 1800s, women grew more and more dissatisfied with restrictions upon what they could and could not do. They realized that there were many ways in which their autonomy was limited.

In 1848 a women's rights convention was held in Seneca Falls, New York. This meeting marks the beginning of the woman's rights movement in this country. At the meeting, a statement of principles based on the Declaration of Independence was prepared: "We hold these truths to be self-evident: that all men and women are created equal; . . ."

The women who organized the Seneca Falls meeting were active in the abolitionist movement. What motivated these women to join together to fight for women's rights? In what ways did they feel their freedom was limited? The materials which follow describe what life was like for many American women during the late 1800s and early 1900s.

Based on the data pieces in this activity, describe ways in which women lacked autonomy.

As you've already read, the new industrialism affected women as well as men. The garment industry, for example, employed thousands of women in the *sweating system* of work. Middlemen (sweaters) took contracts for sewing together cut-out clothing. They then hired women to do the work.

a Leonora Barry, who campaigned to organize women workers, spoke from personal experience when she described the sweating system.

a Men's pants that retail for one to seven dollars a pair are taken by the contractor or middleman. Workers are then employed and huddled together in a stifling back room. The sewing machine operators must furnish their own machines and, usually, the thread. They do all the machine work on the pants for five cents a pair. The pants are then given to the finisher, who puts on the buttons, makes buttonholes, and puts on buckles for five cents a pair. Six pairs is an average day's work.

b The photograph on page 355 shows pants finishers working at home. Women like these worked all day in order to earn about thirty cents. Often, their children helped them.

Factory owners often gave out contracts to middlemen for part of the work. The middlemen hired workers on a piecework basis and put them to work in poorly lighted and ventilated buildings. These makeshift factories came to be called **sweatshops.**

How much money did a sewing machine operator make in an average day? How much did a finisher make in an average day?

Until they organized into unions, many women were reluctant to speak up for higher wages. Why do you think they felt this way?

c Lucy Larcom went to work in the Lowell, Massachusetts textile mills when she was 11 years old. For several years she divided her time between work at the mills and going to school. She eventually became a teacher in the Midwest.

The following is a description of Lucy Larcom's girlhood experiences and thoughts during the time she worked at the mill. It was published in 1889.

When I thought what I should best like to do, my first dream was that it would be a fine thing to be a schoolteacher, like Aunt Hannah.

All my thoughts about my future sent me back to Aunt Hannah and my first childish idea of being a teacher. I foresaw that I should be that before I could be or do anything else. It had been impressed upon me that I must make myself useful in the world, and certainly one could be useful who could "keep school" as Aunt Hannah did. I did not see anything else for a girl to do who wanted to use her brains as well as her hands. So the plan of preparing myself to be a teacher gradually shaped itself in my mind as the only practical one. I could earn my living in that way—an all-important consideration.

My married sisters had families growing up about them, and they liked to have us younger ones come and help take care of their babies. One of them sent for me just when the close air and long days' work [at the mill] were beginning to tell upon my health, and it was decided that I had better go. The salt wind

Lucy said, "I did not see anything else for a girl to do who wanted to use her brains as well as her hands." Why do you think Lucy did not hope to be an engineer, or a lawyer, or to hold public office?

355

soon restored my strength, and those months of quiet family life were very good for me.

My sister had no domestic help besides mine, so I learned a good deal about general housework. A girl's preparation for life was considered incomplete if she had no knowledge of that kind.

A young woman would have been considered a very inefficient being who could not make and mend and wash and iron her own clothing, and get three regular meals and clear them away every day, besides keeping the house tidy, and doing any other neighborly service, such as sitting all night by a sickbed. To be "a good watcher" was considered one of the most important of womanly skills. People who lived side by side exchanged such services without waiting to be asked.

According to Lucy Larcom's experience, what kind of life were women expected to follow?

I found my practical experience of housekeeping and baby-tending very useful to me afterwards. But these were not the things I had most wished to do. The whole world of thought lay unexplored before me—a world of which I had already caught large and tempting glimpses, and I did not like to feel the horizon shutting me in, even to so pleasant corner as this.

When I returned [to the mill] I found that I enjoyed even the familiar, constant clatter of the mill, because it indicated something was going on. I liked to feel the people around me, even those whom I did not know, as a wave may like to feel the surrounding waves urging it forward, with or against its own will. I felt that I belonged to the world, that there was something for me to do in it, though I had not yet found out what. Something to do; it might be very little, but still it would be my own work.

How might Lucy have responded to this question: "Is autonomy important to you? Why?"

d Abigail Scott Duniway was a western pioneer woman who became active in campaigning for women's rights. She described her early married life during the 1850s.

d

It was a friendly neighborhood—mostly bachelors, who found comfort in arriving at meal times at the homes of the few married men in the township. I prepared their meals in the lean-to kitchen, along with washing, scrubbing, churning, and nursing the baby.

I bore two children in two and a half years from my marriage day; I made thousands of pounds of butter every year for market; I sewed and cooked, washed and ironed; I baked and cleaned and stewed and fried. In short, I was a general pioneer drudge, with never a penny of my own. This was unpleasant business for someone who wished to be a schoolteacher.

In what ways did Abigail Scott Duniway feel she lacked autonomy?

e Below is part of a discussion of the black woman as the bread-winner. It is from a report published in 1911 which described the position of black people in New York.

The life of the average New York white woman of the working class is not, however, the life of the average colored woman. With her, work usually begins at 15. It by no means ends with her entrance upon marriage, which only brings new financial burdens.

The contrast in the lives of the colored and white married women is as strongly marked as the contrast in the lives of their unmarried daughters and sisters. Unable to enter any pursuit except housework, the unskilled colored girl goes out to service or helps at home with the laundry or sewing. Factory and store are closed to her, and rarely can she take a place among other working girls. Her hours are the long, irregular hours of domestic service. Far more often than any class of white girls in the city she lives away from home.

Despite her efforts and occasional successes, the colored girl in New York meets with worse race prejudice than the colored man, and is more persistently kept from attractive work. *She gets the job that the white girl does not want.* It may be that the white girls want the wrong thing, and that the jute mill and tobacco and flower factory are more dangerous to health and right living than the mistress's kitchen, but she knows her mind, and follows the business that brings her liberty of action when the six o'clock whistle blows.

According to this woman, what kinds of autonomy did black women lack? How did this compare with the autonomy problems of white women?

f In 1870 Mrs. Myra Blackwell applied to the Illinois State Supreme Court for a license to practice law. The Court refused to give her a license, with this explanation.

God designed the sexes to do different kinds of work. It is man's work to make, apply, and execute the laws—this has always been considered true. The legislature gave the power of granting licenses to practice law to this court. They didn't have the slightest expectation that this privilege would be extended to women.

If we did this, we believe that soon every official job in this state would be filled by women—even those of governor, judges, and sheriffs.

Why do you think the court wanted to guard against women holding political office?

g Until 1920 women did not have the right to vote. During an 1887 debate in Congress over whether to extend the right to vote to women, Senator Brown of Georgia expressed the following attitude. His opinion was held by most men of the time.

> When I go to my home, when I leave the arena where men compete, I don't want to go back to the embrace of some female ward politician. I want to receive the loving look and touch of a true woman. Instead of a lecture on finance or the tariff or the Constitution, I want to hear those blessed loving details of home life and family love.

h This cartoon reflected the response of many American men to the women's rights movement of the late 1800s.

According to the cartoon, what did men expect would happen if women were granted their demands?

BRANCHING OUT

Each of the women below was active in fighting for women's right to vote. Choose one of these women and report on her activities in the suffrage movement.

Susan B. Anthony	Anna Howard Shaw	Lucy Stone
Lucretia Mott	Elizabeth Cady Stanton	

The position of women changed, but very slowly. Through the 1800s and into the 1900s, women won gradual increases in their autonomy. Beginning in the 1830s, colleges for women were founded, and men's schools began opening their doors to women students. With the training and education they needed, women gradually entered professions such as law and medicine. After 1850 more and more women became teachers. Continuing into the 1900s, however, most employed women worked in factories and sweatshops.

The most famous battle of women was over **suffrage,** the right to vote. This struggle took many years, but was finally won in 1920 when the 19th Amendment was added to the Constitution. In their struggle to gain the right to vote, women used a variety of methods to gain support for their cause.

How is autonomy limited by not having the right to vote?

The cartoon was published by the National American Women Suffrage Association in a 1916 newsletter. ▼

● The following data pieces describe several of these methods.

As you study the data pieces, classify the methods according to the reactions to threatened autonomy on page 303.

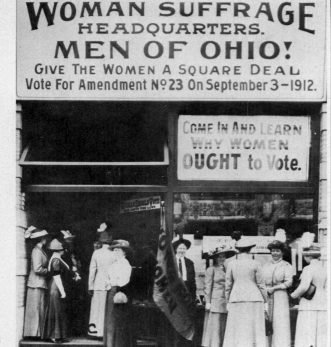

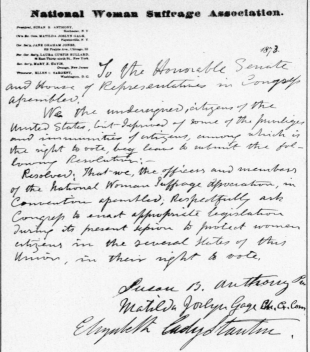

The Position of Black Americans

After the Civil War, slaves in this country were declared free by the 13th Amendment. They were granted citizenship by the 14th Amendment and guaranteed the right to vote by the 15th Amendment. Black Americans reacted to their new freedom in various ways. Many continued to live on plantations. Some, with government help, acquired their own small farms. Some moved to cities in the North, and others migrated west.

The former slaves were free, but many were poverty-stricken. Most had not been taught to read and write. None had owned land, and few had ever worked for wages.

In 1865 Congress created the Freedmen's Bureau to help newly freed black people. The Bureau provided food, clothing, and other assistance. It was the first important example of federal support for needy people. The Freedmen's Bureau also set up schools for black people throughout the South.

In the Polarization unit you learned how black and white Southerners interacted after the Civil War. The Ku Klux Klan and similar groups used terror to control black people and reduce their political power. The autonomy of black people continued to be limited in many ways from that time on. They were free from slavery, but not from many other kinds of problems.

Read the materials which follow. List the ways in which black Americans lacked autonomy.

a Mrs. Selina Wallis, a black woman from Mississippi, testified before a United States Senate committee in 1883.

a

Question: You live in Copiah County, do you?
Answer: Yes, sir.
Question: You are the widow of Thomas Wallis?
Answer: Yes, sir.
Question: Thomas Wallis was killed, was he?
Answer: Yes, sir.
Question: When?
Answer: Friday morning before the election.
Question: Friday morning before the last election?
Answer: Yes, sir.
Question: Who killed him?
Answer: I don't know.
Question: What did you see?
Answer: The men came there to my porch and called.
Question: How many men?
Answer: I don't know, sir, how many there was.
Question: A dozen?
Answer: I think there was more than a dozen.
Question: Twenty?
Answer: I reckon; I couldn't tell how many there was.
Question: Did they come on horseback?
Answer: Yes, sir.
Question: Did they have guns?
Answer: Yes, sir.
Question: What time of the day was it?
Answer: It wasn't in the day; it was in the night.
Question: What time in the night?
Answer: It must have been between one and two o'clock.
Question: You and your husband were in the house?
Answer: Yes, sir.
Question: In bed?
Answer: Yes, sir.
Question: Who else was in the house?
Answer: None but my baby and my other little son in that end of the house I was in.
Question: What did you first hear?
Answer: They called, and I heard them.
Question: What did they do?

Answer: They called and told my husband to get up and open the door and kindle a light. He was trying to kindle a light up and couldn't as quick as they wanted, and they told him to make haste. He told them to give him a little time, and they said "very little time." Then they told him to open the door, and I told them the door wasn't fastened, and they shoved it once, and it didn't shove open because a chair was against it, and they shoved it again, and that time it flew wide open and knocked the chair from behind it. Two come in, and, as well as I could see, there was about five or six on the porch. I couldn't tell how many there was—me in the house and them out-of-doors.

Question: What did they do after they got in?

Answer: They asked Tom who he was and he told them Tom Wallis. Then they told him he was the man that they was after; that they had a writ for him. When they said they had a writ, one of them pulled a line out of his pocket and started to put it over his neck.

Question: A rope, you mean?

Answer: Yes, sir. When he went to put it over, he throwed up his hand and said, "Hold on, gentlemen," and as soon as he said that, one of them shot him. Then they hollered to them that was outside to come in, and they came in from the porch and pulled him out. When the got him to the door, his axe was lying at the door, and he grabbed at the axe, and got hold of the handle.

Question: Who did, Thomas?

Answer: Yes, sir. Then another one shot, sort of up inside of the house and it went through the ceiling. Another one shot right through the door and that went through Tom's neck.

Question: It went through his neck?

Answer: Yes, sir.

Question: And then he was dead?

Answer: Yes, sir; he fell right on my skirt.

Question: How long did they stay there?

Answer: They didn't stay a minute after they shot him.

Question: Did they do anything more?

Answer: They just went and jumped right on their horses and went right off.

Question: Did they visit your house again?

Answer: They came the night before the election. They didn't come in the house that time; just shot all over the house and went right on up the road.

Question: How many times would you say they fired?

Answer: I don't know; I couldn't tell you that.

Question: Was your husband a Republican?

Answer: Yes, sir.

Question: Did he take an interest in politics? Did he generally vote?

Answer: Yes, sir.

Beginning in the late 1800s, southern states passed laws which placed restrictions on black people. Many of these laws segregated black people from white people in public places. Railway cars and waiting stations, streetcars, boarding houses, water fountains, parks, residential areas, schools, and other places were segregated.

b An old minstrel song, "Jump Jim Crow," led to the use of "Jim Crow" as a term of ridicule of black people. Laws which discriminated against blacks came to be called "Jim Crow laws." Two of these laws are below.

In what ways was black autonomy limited by separate facilities?

Section 1. *Be it enacted by the General Assembly of the State of* _____, That all railway companies carrying passengers in this state, shall provide equal but separate accommodations for the white and colored races. This shall be done by providing two or more passenger coaches for each passenger train, or by dividing the passenger coaches by a partition so as to secure separate accommodations. This section shall not apply to street railroads. No one shall be permitted to occupy seats in coaches other than the ones assigned to them on account of the race they belong to.

b

Section 1. *Be it enacted by the General Assembly of the State of* _____, That hereafter it shall be unlawful for any school, academy, college, or other place of learning to allow white and colored persons to attend the same school, academy, college, or other place of learning.

Section 2. *Be it further enacted,* That it shall be unlawful for any teacher, professor, or educator in the state, in any college, academy, or school of learning, to allow the white and colored races to attend the same school or for any teacher or educator, or other person to instruct or teach both the white and colored races in the same class, school, or college building, or in any other place or places of learning, or allow or permit the same to be done with their knowledge, consent, or procurement.

In 1902 a New York newspaper published the following article, written by a black woman from Alabama. Her identity was not revealed, because of possible danger to her life.

I am a colored woman, wife and mother. I have lived all my life in the South. I have often thought what a peculiar fact it is that the less Southern whites know of us, the more they critcize us. They boast that they have little contact with us, never see us in our homes, churches, or places of amusement, but still they know us thoroughly.

The Southerners say we Negroes are a happy, laughing set of people, with no thought of tomorrow. How mistaken they are! The educated, thinking Negro is just the opposite. There is a feeling of unrest, insecurity, almost panic among the best class of Negroes in the South. In our homes, in our churches, wherever two or three are gathered together, there is a discussion of what is best to do. Must we remain in the South or go elsewhere? Where can we go to feel that security which other people feel? Is it best to go in great numbers or only in several families?

I know of houses occupied by poor Negroes in which a respectable farmer would not keep his cattle. It is impossible for them to rent elsewhere. All Southern real estate agents have "white property" and "colored property." In one of the largest Southern cities there is a colored minister, a graduate of Harvard, whose wife is an educated, Christian woman, who lived for weeks in a tumble-down chicken house because he could neither rent nor buy in a respectable locality.

Many colored women who wash, iron, scrub, cook, or sew all the week to help pay the rent for these miserable shacks would deny themselves some of the necessities of life if they could take their little children and teething babies on the streetcars to the parks of a Sunday afternoon and sit under the trees, enjoy the cool breezes, and breathe God's pure air for only two or three hours. But this is denied them. Some of the parks have signs, "No Negroes allowed on these grounds except as servants." Pitiful, pitiful customs and laws that make war on women and babies! There is no wonder that we die. The wonder is that we persist in living.

Fourteen years ago I had just married. My husband had saved enough to buy a small home. On account of our limited money we went to the suburbs, on unpaved streets, to look for a home, only asking for a high, healthy locality. Some real estate agents were "sorry, but had nothing to suit," some had "just the thing," but we discovered on investigation that they had "just the thing" for an unhealthy pigsty. Others had no "colored property." One agent said that he had what we wanted, but we should have to go to see the lot after dark, or walk by and give the place a casual look; for, he said, "all the white people in the neighborhood would be down on me." Finally we bought this lot. When the house was being built we went to see it. Everybody was upset. We had "ruined" this neighborhood of poor people. The people who lived next door received the sympathy of their friends. When we walked on the street (there were no sidewalks) we were embarrassed by the stare of many unfriendly eyes.

Two years passed before a single woman spoke to me, and only then because I helped one of them when a little sudden trouble came to her. Such was the reception I, a happy young woman just married, received from people among whom I wanted to make a home. Fourteen years have now passed, four children have been born to us, and one has died in this same home, among these same neighbors. Although the neighbors speak to us, and occasionally one will send a child to borrow the morning's paper or ask the loan of a pattern, not one woman has been in my house.

The Southerner says the Negro must "keep in his place." That means the particular place the white man says is his. A self-respecting colored man who does not cringe, but walks erect, supports his family, educates his children, and teaches them that God made all men equal, is called a "dangerous Negro"; "he is too smart"; "he wants to be white and acts like white people."

Whenever a crime is committed, the policemen look for the Negro in the case. A white man with face and hands blackened can commit any crime, then wash and join in the hunt to lynch the "big, black burly brute." When a white man in the South does commit a crime, that is simply one white man gone wrong. If his crime is especially brutal he is a freak or temporarily insane. If one low, ignorant black wretch commits a crime, that is different. All of us are condemned. A young white boy's badness is simply the overflowing of young animal spirits; the black boy's badness is badness, pure and simple.

Is it surprising that feeling grows more bitter, when the white mother teaches her boy to hate my boy, not because he is mean, but because his skin is dark? I have seen very small white children hang their black dolls. It is not the child's fault. He is simply a good student.

Sometime, someone will take up our cause and force the world to see that we deserve justice, as other heroes forced it to see that we deserved freedom.

Consider data piece E on page 357 in completing your answers to this activity.

Actions To Gain Autonomy

What were the best ways for black Americans to gain autonomy? Black leaders disagreed over this question. Below are some of their opinions.

Based on the data:
1. Identify the actions and attitudes recommended by black leaders.
2. Classify the actions according to the reactions to threatened autonomy on page 303.

a Booker T. Washington was a black leader and educator. In 1895 he spoke in Atlanta, Georgia. In his speech, Washington presented recommendations for improving conditions for his people.

a

Our greatest danger is that, in the great leap from slavery to freedom, we may overlook the fact that most of us must live by the work of our hands. We shall prosper as we learn to dignify and glorify common labor, and put brains and skill into the common occupations of life. No race can prosper till it learns that there is as much dignity in tilling a field as in writing a poem. It is at the bottom of life we must begin, and not at the top.

To those of the white race who look to the immigrant for the prosperity of the South, consider instead my people. Help and encourage them. With education of head, hand, and heart, you will find that they will buy your surplus land, make blossom the waste places in your fields, and run your factories.

While doing this, you can be sure that in the future, as in the past, you and your families will be surrounded by the most patient, faithful, law-abiding, and unresentful people that the world has seen. We have proved our loyalty to you in the past, in nursing your children, watching by the sickbed of your mothers and fathers, and often following them with tear-dimmed eyes to their graves. In the future, in our humble way, we shall stand by you with a devotion that no foreigner can approach, ready to lay down our lives, if need be, in defense of yours. We shall weave our industrial, commercial, civil, and religious life with yours and make the interests of both races one. In all things that are purely social we can be as separate as the fingers, yet one as the hand in all things necessary to mutual progress.

What course of action did Washington believe black people should follow? Why might some black leaders have objected to Washington's views?

What skills are being taught in the Tuskegee classroom? ▼

b These students worked in the wheelwright shop at Tuskegee Institute.

c Bishop Henry McNeil Turner of the African Methodist Episcopal Church also spoke in Atlanta in 1895. Portions of his speech are presented below.

I believe that the Negro has been free long enough now to begin to think for himself and plan for better conditions than he can find in this country. There is no future in the United States for the Negro. He may manage an existence for generations to come, but he can never be a fully developed man.

A great gap exists between the two races in this country. The white people will not have social contact with any portion of the Negro race. Talk about two races remaining in the same country and working together, with no social contact, is ridiculous.

Senator Morgan of Alabama tells the truth when he says that the Negro will get nowhere without social equality with the whites, and that the whites will never grant it.

The status of the Negro is simply whatever the white man lets him have. The black man can demand nothing. On the railroads, he is the victim of discrimination. He must ride in the Jim Crow car or walk. The Supreme Court of the United States decided, October 15, 1882, that the colored man had no civil rights under the general government. States, from then until now, have been enacting laws which limit and deprive him of civil rights, even the right to vote.

Any oppressed people will not only become cowardly, but will transmit that same quality to their children, and their children's children. As such they will never make a bold and courageous people.

The Negro should, therefore, build up a nation of his own, and create a language in keeping with his color, as the whites have done. Nor will he ever respect himself until he does it.

I believe that two or three million of us should return to the land of our ancestors, and establish our own nation, laws, and customs. We should give the world the benefit of our individuality. We should build up a society of our own, and cease to be grumblers, complainers, and a menace to the white man's country, or the country he claims and is bound to dominate.

How did Bishop Turner's opinions differ from the views of Booker T. Washington?

In the early 1900s, black leader Marcus Garvey led a "Back-to-Africa" movement. Garvey believed that black people would never be given equality in countries where most people were white. He worked to build a homeland for black Americans in Africa. The movement was most popular in 1920 and 1921. It declined in 1925 after the federal government convicted Garvey of illegal actions in connection with his project.

d In 1889 black journalist John Bruce gave these recommendations.

Disturbance is a good thing. Organization is a better thing. The million Negro voters of Georgia, and the millions in other Southern states could, with proper organization and intelligent leadership, meet force with force with most beneficial results.

The man who will not fight for the protection of his wife and children is a *coward* and deserves to be ill-treated. The man who takes his life in his hand and stands up for what he knows to be right will always command the respect of his enemy.

In the present situation, the only hope for the Negro is to be found in a use of force under wise leaders. He must sooner or later set at rest, for all to come, the charge that he is a coward.

To settle this Southern problem, the Negro must not be rash either in action or in words. He must be very determined to bring order out of chaos. He must convince Southern rowdies and cut-throats that more than two can play at the game with which they have amused themselves for nearly a quarter of a century.

Let the Negro require from every white murderer in the South or elsewhere a life for a life. If they burn our houses, burn theirs. If they kill our wives and children, kill theirs. Pursue them, meet force with force everywhere it is offered. If they demand blood, exchange with them until they have had their fill. If we do this, the shedding of human blood by white men will soon become a thing of the past.

Wherever and whenever the Negro shows himself to be a man, he can always command the respect even of a cutthroat. Organized resistance to organized resistance is the best remedy for the solution of the problem. I submit this review of the question, ladies and gentlemen, for your careful consideration.

John Bruce supported the use of force and violence by black people. Under what conditions did he feel they should be used?

e In the early 1900s, the two most important black leaders were Booker T. Washington and W. E. B. DuBois. Their opinions about what black people should do to gain autonomy were quite different. You've already read about Washington's views. Here are the recommendations of DuBois.

e

We must first make American courts build up a set of legal decisions which will protect the plain legal rights of black American citizens.

We must get legislatures and Congress to pass laws to give national aid to public school education, and to remove legal discriminations based simply on race and color.

The human contact between white and black human beings must be increased. It is frightful that ten million black people are coming to believe that all white people are liars and thieves. The whites in turn are coming to believe that the chief industry of Negroes is bothering whites. The publication of the truth repeatedly can help change public opinion and correct these awful lies.

To accomplish all these goals we must organize. Organization among us has already gone far but it must go farther and higher. Organization is sacrifice. It is sacrifice of opinions, of time, of work, and of money. But it is, after all, the cheapest way of buying the most priceless of gifts—freedom and efficiency.

In your opinion, which of the recommendations was the best advice to give black people in this period of history? Is it the best advice for the present? Explain.

Although the policies of Booker T. Washington and W. E. B. DuBois were very different, both men and their ideas had great influence on later advances in black autonomy. Washington worked to provide job skills for black people through industrial training. He believed that through hard work, self-help, and cooperation with whites, black Americans could improve their condition in life.

Washington organized Tuskegee Institute, a school for black people in Tuskegee, Alabama. This and other black colleges improved educational opportunities for black Americans and helped increase their job skills.

DuBois saw the need for industrial training and self-help as preached by Washington. He also felt that blacks should be trained for positions of leadership. DuBois came to believe that his people should work for complete equality and full rights as citizens.

In 1909 DuBois helped form the National Association for the Advancement of Colored People (NAACP). This organization and similar groups formed since then have fought to end discrimination against black people and to obtain their full rights as citizens. They have worked toward these goals by taking legal action and making appeals to public opinion.

World War I played an important part in changing the lives of many black people. After the Civil War most blacks had remained in the South as farmers. Many others had moved to cities in the North, where the only jobs open to them were as servants and unskilled laborers. World War I, which the United States entered in 1917, opened up new job opportunities in industry. In Unit 7 you'll learn more about how black Americans were affected by World War I.

BRANCHING OUT

Report on the autonomy of black Americans today. What gains have been made since the early 1900s? In what ways is autonomy still lacking? What steps are being taken to increase the autonomy of black people?

Application

Several years ago, Douglas McGregor wrote a book called *The Human Side of Enterprise.* In the book he wrote that for at least the last hundred years, the relationship between employers and employees in most factories, shops, and mills has been based on three main beliefs about people.

a McGregor called these beliefs "Theory X."

a

1. The average person has a natural dislike of work and will avoid it if possible.
2. Because most people dislike work, they must be directed, forced, bribed, or threatened with punishment to get a job done. (The worker's paycheck is a kind of bribe.)
3. Most people prefer to be directed, wish to avoid responsibility, have little ambition, and above all, want security.

b Here is an example of management based on Theory X.

b

Frank Clark, foreman: "We have a problem with some of the workers on the loading dock. They're playing cards at lunch time, and they get so involved in their card game that they're late starting back to work after lunch. I suggest we start a new company rule—No card playing allowed."

T. J. Jones, superintendent: "I've got a better suggestion. Have the men punch the time clock before and after lunch. If they take too long, we can dock their pay."

Do you agree with the principles of Theory X? Why? Does Theory X grant workers much autonomy? Explain.

Some people feel that if workers are treated according to Theory X, their reactions will probably fit the theory. Using examples, explain what this means.

c In his book McGregor said he thought that Theory X was at least partly wrong. In its place he suggested a set of ideas he called "Theory Y."

c

1. The average person does *not* have a natural dislike of work.
2. Control, threats, and bribes are not the only way to get people to work. If job objectives are important to them, people will direct their own actions.
3. Job objectives will be important to a worker if the job gives the worker a sense of satisfaction.
4. Under the right conditions, people will accept and seek responsibility.
5. If given the opportunity, almost everyone has the ability to solve problems, make wise decisions, and use imagination.
6. Most present-day jobs do not use the worker's abilities very effectively.

d Here's an example of Theory Y management in action.

d

A foreman to his workers in a machine shop: "Gather around and help me for a minute. We have four projects that *must* be done this week, or our whole plant will fall behind schedule. Now it doesn't matter to me which project is done first, or who works on each one, as long as we meet the deadline and do the jobs well. Why don't you people meet together for a few minutes and decide for yourselves how the jobs will be divided up? Here are the materials and the blueprints.

"If you need more help, I'll be up in the Engineering Department doing work on next week's projects. Don't forget the deadline, or we're all in trouble."

Based on the data describing Theory X and Theory Y, answer these questions.

1. Under which system—Theory X or Theory Y—does the worker have greater autonomy?
2. If you were a Theory Y manager, how would you handle the problem of the men playing cards during working hours? Write a short dialogue to show your solution.
3. Some companies are experimenting with Theory Y. If most companies adopted this approach to management, what do you think the results would be? Why?

BIBLIOGRAPHY

Holland, Ruth. *Mill Child.* N.Y.: Macmillan, 1970. The story of child labor in the United States. Traces the slow development of child labor laws in spite of growing public support for reform. Featured are Jane Addams, Jacob Riis and Margaret Sanger, all pioneers in the battle for change. This book deals also with present-day migrant workers, "the forgotten children."

Weisberger, Bernard A., *Captains of Industry.* N.Y.: American Heritage, 1966. Contemporary drawings, cartoons and photographs illustrate this fast-moving story. Reveals how Vanderbilt, McCormick, Rockefeller, Carnegie and Ford built their huge fortunes and changed the face of the nation.

Drisko, Carol F. and Edgar A. Toppin. *The Unfinished March.* Garden City, N.Y.: Doubleday, 1967. A short history of black Americans from Reconstruction to World War I.

Bolton, Carole. *Never Jam Today.* N.Y.: Atheneum, 1971. Fiction. Seventeen-year old Madeline Franklin is a resourceful career girl. As a suffragette, she pickets the White House in 1917, is jailed, but continues to work for women's suffrage.

Clarke, Mary Stetson. *Bloomers and Ballots.* N.Y.: Viking Press, 1972. A biography of Elizabeth Cady Stanton, one of the first well known defenders of women's rights. She began her life-long fight before the Civil War.

UNIT 6

Native Americans and Newcomers

Cultural Interaction

How does cultural interaction affect ideas and ways of acting?

Introduction

In America, families move more often than they do in most other countries. You've probably moved at least once to a new neighborhood, a new school, a new town or city. If you have, then you know it can be difficult, even when the language, dress, and customs in both places are the same. It takes a while to fit in and become a part of a new place and group of people.

Moving to a new place within the same society can cause problems of adjustment. So, you can imagine how much more difficult the problems are when people move not only to a new place but also into a very different culture. Then, there are often great differences of language, dress, and customs to be overcome.

The society into which newcomers move is affected by their arrival. Sometimes the newcomers change the society. Sometimes the society changes the newcomers.

In this unit you'll examine what happens when people with differing ideas and ways of acting come into contact with one another.

The first contact between two groups which have differing ways of acting may lead only to curious stares. More often, however, contact between unlike groups is more complicated than that.

● Here's the reaction of one member of a group which came in contact with a situation involving differences.

We have what's called an "Exchange Program" here. Thirty students from our high school in Florida spend a week at some school up North or out West. Then 30 students, from wherever we go, come here.

Well, this year we went to a suburb of Philadelphia. We landed late Friday afternoon, and their exchange students were at the airport waiting for us. I was first off the plane and by the time I'd reached the bottom step, I was feeling a little funny. It took me just that long to realize that no boys in their group were wearing shirts like most of us had on.

I'll tell you a fact. Several of us went shopping first thing on Saturday morning.

1. How did this boy feel? Why do you think he felt that way? Do you think his reaction was usual or unusual?
2. What change resulted from contact between the two groups?
3. In this situation which group was most affected, the larger group (the **majority**) or the smaller group (the **minority**)? Why?

New students in your school may be one source of information about what happens when unlike people come in contact with one another. Students who have come from some distance away or from different kinds of communities may be particularly good sources.

Talk to several of the newest students in your school. Interview them on the following subjects:
1. Differences in ways of acting, dressing, talking, dancing, between this and their previous school or community.
2. Feelings about being different.

3. How they were treated by the majority of students in your school.
4. Changes of any kind they have made in their ways of acting, talking, or thinking since they came to your school.
5. Reasons they can give for making these changes.

Think about your own life. Can you remember any situations in which you felt you were part of a minority? Identify your feelings, thoughts, and actions in these situations.

Based on your interviews and your own experiences, make some general statements about the actions and feelings which can result when unlike people come in contact with one another.

The Disappearance of Midland High

At one time there were thousands of very small high schools scattered across the United States. A small town or a country crossroads would be the site of a local school with just a few students. Graduating classes of 20 or less were not unusual.

Most of these small schools are gone now. They have been closed, usually for economic reasons. Students have been transferred to consolidated schools or to the nearest city high school.

The data that follows came from the last yearbook of Midland High School a small high school in a midwestern town.

Use the data to help you understand what it was like to attend Midland High.

Donna Hill, Midland Student Council president

The Junior Prom Committee

Amy Thomas cheers the team.

Peter Hays, Midland's top student

Jim Bradbury and Coach plan the next play.

A few months after this yearbook was published Midland High was closed. The students were transferred to Central High School, a large school in a nearby city.

1. Now, imagine you were one of these people last year: Donna Hill, Amy Thomas, Jim Bradbury, or Peter Hays.
   a. How would your activities be affected by the change?
   b. Describe all the different feelings you or your friends might have in your new situation. Role-play a conversation among several Midland friends at Central.
   c. If you had the feelings you describe, what might you do? Discuss various kinds of actions. What problems would the actions solve?

2. Now, imagine that you have been a student at Central for three years. How will you react to the newcomers from Midland High? How will you feel? What will you do? With several classmates, role-play a conversation about the students from Midland High.

STOP & SUMMARIZE

Make a chart like the one shown below. Fill in the columns, based on your investigation of interaction between majorities and minorities. Each column may have several entries. Keep your chart for use in the future activities in the unit.

Minority feelings about majority	Minority actions	Majority feelings about minority	Majority actions

BRANCHING OUT

If there is a minority group—people from another school, country, or culture—in your school or neighborhood, investigate their treatment by the majority. Interview people in the minority and majority groups. If possible, identify changes in attitudes and actions in both groups. Note whether older people in either group react to the situation differently than young people.

Perspective

Many Americans like to imagine the late 1800s as a happy time when towns were small and quiet, the style of life was simple, neighbors were friendly, and the outside world kept most of its troubles to itself.

This picture is not a very accurate one. In the late 1800s, America's cities were big and were growing bigger. The country seemed to be speeding up. People were moving from place to place more often. Jobs were becoming less permanent and secure.

The main causes of the unsettled conditions of the time are not hard to identify now. Cities were growing faster than the services which made them comfortable places in which to live and work. More and more people were working in factories, then less secure work than farming. Worldwide struggles for raw materials and markets created new political and economic conflicts. Improvements in communication and transportation made the world seem smaller.

In the period from the end of the Civil War to the early 1900s, cultural interaction played an important role in the United States. At this time many Americans moved westward. As they did, they came into increasing conflict with the first Americans—the Indians who lived on land other Americans now wanted. At the same time, immigrants who hoped to become Americans poured into the nation's port cities. In Parts 1 and 2 you will study the cultural interaction that took place as different cultures met.

Part 1   Native Americans

How did interaction with other Americans affect native American cultures?

Part 2   Newcomers to America

How were immigrants to the United States affected by interaction with American culture?

1867
Oklahoma Reservation created for Five Civilized Tribes

1874
Gold discovered on South Dakota Indian reservation
Barbed wire used as fencing

1876
Battle of Little Big Horn

1882
Chinese Exclusion Act

1886
Statue of Liberty completed

1887
Dawes Act

1889
Jane Addams opens Hull House

1890
Battle of Wounded Knee ends 31 year Sioux Wars

1891
Riis publishes his findings on slum life

1907
Gentlemen's Agreement
Record number of immigrants admitted: 1,285,349

1917
Literacy Act

1921
1st National Origins Act limits immigration

1924
National Origins Act further restricts immigration
Indians gain full citizenship

Part 1

Native Americans

Interaction between native Americans—the people Columbus named "Indians"—and other Americans has taken place in every period of American history after Europeans arrived on this continent. Although white people—especially the early colonists—accepted much from the Indian, they hardly ever accepted Indians as people. Every period in American history tells a similar story of interaction between whites and Indians. However, in the period from 1860 to almost 1900, conflict between white and native Americans was at its worst.

In Part 1 you'll investigate the answers to the question:

How did the interaction with other Americans affect native American cultures?

The first English colonists in America could not have survived without the help of the Indians who lived near their settlements. The two selections that follow will tell you something about the early relationships between whites and Indians.

As you read, identify
1. Ways in which Indians helped whites
2. Changes in relationships between Indians and whites

a Pilgrim leader William Bradford described the help Plymouth colonists received from the Algonquin Indian, Squanto.

What was Bradford's attitude toward Squanto? In what ways do you think the Pilgrims needed Squanto?

a Squanto stayed with them and was their interpreter. He was a special instrument sent from God for their good, which was beyond their hopes. He directed them how to set their corn, where to catch fish, and to get other commodities, and was also their guide to take them to unknown places for their profit. He never left them till he died.

b Two hundred years later, in 1830, Speckled Snake, a Cherokee Indian, gave this description of Indian-white relations up to that time.

Hominy is a food made from hulled kernels of corn.

b When the first white man came over the wide waters, he was but a little man, very little. His legs were cramped by sitting long in his big boat, and he begged for a little land. The Indians gave him land, and built fires to make him comfortable.

But when the white man had warmed himself at the Indian's fire and had filled himself with the Indian's hominy, he became very large. He did not stop at the mountain tops, and his foot covered the plains and the valleys. His hands grasped the eastern and western seas. Then he became our Great Father. He loved his red children, but he said "You must move a little farther, so that I don't step on you by accident."

Brothers, I listened to a great many talks from our Great Father. But they have always begun and ended like this: "Go a little farther; you are too near me."

What was Speckled Snake's attitude toward white people?

Whose Land Is This?

In spite of the aid given by Indians like Squanto, the problems of Indian-white relations described by Speckled Snake began soon after colonists arrived in America. The problems were to continue long after Speckled Snake told his story.

The European colonists came and settled on land that Indians had lived and hunted on for thousands of years. Europeans, however, believed that discovery of the land by European explorers gave them the right to claim it and settle it as their own. When there were only a few colonists, there were only a few problems. But more and more Europeans came to the colonies. They pushed Indians further away from the land the Indians believed was theirs to use. For the Indians, the problem was not a simple one of finding new land. They did not want new land; they wanted their traditional hunting grounds. These were often sacred in Indian eyes and could not simply be replaced by other land.

In 1675 bitter wars broke out between Indians and colonists in Virginia (Bacon's Rebellion) and Massachusetts (King Philip's War). In both cases Indians reacted to the loss of land and special hunting grounds by fighting the colonists who had taken them. In both cases the Indians lost both the wars and their land.

As settlers pushed further westward, Indians and their land raised more and more difficult questions for British and colonial governments. Should any settlers be allowed to move into areas still claimed by Indians? Should Indians be paid for their land or should colonials just take it? And what about the trappers and traders who needed Indian help in obtaining valuable furs—should they be regulated in their dealings with the Indians? One answer to these questions came in 1763.

In 1763 the Indians of the Ohio River valley formed a federation. They were led by Pontiac, an Ottawa Indian chief. Desperate for a way to protect their rights, these Indians could see that their land was soon going to become filled with English colonials. The Indians also had been treated very unfairly by traders and trappers. Under Pontiac the Indians captured almost every English fort in the western territory and killed many pioneer families. In the end, however, the rebellion was crushed by British soldiers.

To try to solve the Indian problem, the British issued the Proclamation of 1763. As you have read (pages 88–89), this document stated that all British lands west of the Appalachians were reserved for the Indians (see map, page 89). No colonials were to live in this Indian Territory. The British also worked out a plan for licensing and controlling traders and trappers who worked within the Indian Territory. But these solutions were not to end the problem for long.

In Great Britain and the colonies, there was strong conflict. One side agreed with the Proclamation. They wanted to let the Indian

A **pioneer** is a person who settles in an area in which few —if any—people live. The Americans who moved west to lands occupied only by Indians are called pioneers.

territory be a **reservation**—land reserved, or kept, only for the Indians. The other side thought they should buy land from the Indians and sell it to pioneers who wanted to move west. And of course there were some who wanted simply to take the land.

The Proclamation of 1763 was a British solution to the problem. After the Revolution, the new government of the United States had other ways of dealing with Indians and western land. Even before the Constitution, the Continental Congress passed a law saying that all land that did not belong to any state could be "disposed of for the common benefit of the United States and be settled and formed into states." The lands west of the Appalachians were no longer reserved only for Indians. Land could be bought from Indians and settled by whites. The Constitution and later laws upheld this. The Constitution gave the federal government the right to make treaties with Indians and to control commerce and other business with them.

As you have learned in other units, white Americans continued to move westward. As these white Americans wanted more and more land, Indian chiefs were convinced—often by dishonest means—to lease or sell their rights to land they used. Between 1795 and 1809, just in the Indian Territory, Indians were persuaded to sign away their rights to about 48 million acres of land.

Andrew Jackson, President of the United States from 1829 to 1837, completed the process of gaining Indian lands east of the Mississippi. During his presidency 94 Indian treaties were made, millions of acres of land were transferred from Indian ownership, and thousands of Indians were sent to live west of the Mississippi. Tribes like the Cherokee in Georgia and the Carolinas and the Seminole in Florida were totally removed from their homelands. Many died on the journey west. The picture below shows the Cherokees' journey, sometimes called the "Trail of Tears."

The Indians of the United States were told that the western lands would be theirs forever. Soon this promise too would be broken. As pioneers began to push farther and farther west, they again wanted to own the land on which Indians lived and hunted.

Cultural Conflict

When cultures that differ come in contact with one another, the differences often cause problems. For example, the people of a culture in which it is believed that each tree holds the spirit of an ancestor are likely to take a dim view of a logging crew. Members of a culture who live by exact "clock time" may have problems interacting with another group that uses more relaxed "sun time."

The cultures—the ideas and ways of acting—of the American Indian tribes or groups were not all alike. Many Southwest Indians lived in fixed villages and farmed; others, in the Pacific Northwest, lived by fishing; still others hunted and gathered their food. Their ideas were as varied as their ways of acting.

In spite of overall differences, many tribes did share similar cultures. For example, the tribes who lived in the Great Plains and Rocky Mountain regions had many ideas and ways of acting that were alike. These were the Indian tribes who used the land pioneers moved onto in the second half of the 1800s.

In order to understand the events that happened and the feelings that developed, you must understand the important ideas and ways of acting involved.

Using data pieces A through E, identify Plains Indians' ideas about

1. Ownership of land
2. The "right" way of acting toward nature
3. The role of the individual in a group
4. Farming

a Black Elk, an Oglala Sioux, described his life to John G. Neihardt. Neihardt told Black Elk's story in a book called *Black Elk Speaks.* Born in December 1863, Black Elk saw the move of the whites to the west and the effects of cultural interaction. In the following excerpt from the book, Black Elk tells about a bison, or buffalo, hunt.

The **Oglala Sioux** are a tribe of Indians, one of the Sioux tribes that lived in the Dakota Territory.

Plains Indians ate buffalo meat. They also used parts of the buffalo to make clothes, utensils, and covers for tepees. A **tepee** is a portable cone-shaped frame of wood covered with sewn buffalo hides. Plains Indians lived in camps or villages which consisted of groups of tepees set up near one another. When the camp was moved to another place, tepees and other heavy items were packed on frames and dragged by ponies or horses.

a

One morning the crier came around the circle of the village calling out that we were going to break camp. The advisers were in the council tepee, and he cried to them, "The advisers, come forth to the center and bring your fires along." It was their duty to save fire for the people, because we had no matches then.

"Now take it down, down!" the crier shouted. And all the people began taking down their tepees, and packing them on pony drags.

Then the crier said, "Many bison, I have heard; many bison, I have heard! Your children, you must take care of them!" He meant to keep the children close while traveling, so that they would not scare the bison.

Then we broke camp and started in formation, the four advisers first, a crier behind them, the chiefs next, and then the people with the loaded pony drags in a long line, and the herd of ponies following. Something exciting was going to happen, and even the ponies seemed to know.

When the sun was high, the advisers found a place to camp where there was wood and also water; and while the women were cooking all around the circle, I heard people saying that the scouts were returning, and over the top of a hill I saw three horsebacks coming. They rode to the council tepee in the middle of the village and all the people were going there to hear. I went there too and got up close so that I could look in between the legs of the men. The crier came out of the council tepee and said, speaking to the people for the scouts, "I have protected you; in return you shall give me many gifts." The scouts then sat down before the door of the tepee and one of the advisers filled the sacred pipe with *chacun sha sha,* the bark of the red willow, and set it on a bison chip in front of him, because the bison was sacred and gave us both food and shelter. Then he lit the pipe, offered it to the four quarters, to the Spirit above and to Mother Earth, and passing it to the scouts he said, "The nation has depended upon you. Whatever you have seen, maybe it is for the good of the people you have seen." The scouts smoked, meaning that they would tell the truth. Then the adviser said, "At what place have you stood and seen the good? Report it to me and I will be glad."

One of the scouts answered, "You know where we started from. We went and reached the top of a hill and there we saw a small herd of bison." He pointed as he spoke.

The adviser said, "Maybe on the other side of that you have seen the good. Report it." The scout answered, "On the other side of that we saw a second and larger herd of bison."

Then the adviser said, "I shall be thankful to you. Tell me all that you have seen out there."

The scout replied, "On the other side of that there was nothing but bison all over the country."

And the adviser said, *"Hetchetu aloh!"* ("It is so indeed.")

Then the crier shouted like singing, "Your knives shall be sharpened, your arrows shall be sharpened. Make ready, make haste; your horses make ready! We shall go forth with arrows. Plenty of meat we shall make!"

Everybody began sharpening knives and arrows and getting the best horses ready for the great making of meat.

How did these people feel about the buffalo? About the earth?

In your opinion, who were the most important people in the group of Indians Black Elk described?

Then we started for where the bison were. The soldier band went first, riding 20 abreast, and anybody who dared go ahead of them would get knocked off his horse. They kept order, and everybody had to obey. After them came the hunters, riding five abreast. The people came up in the rear. Then the head man of the advisers went around picking out the best hunters with the fastest horses, and to these he said, "Good young warriors, my relatives, your work I know is good. What you do is good always; so today you shall feed the helpless. Perhaps there are some old and feeble people without sons, or some who have little children and no man. You shall help these, and whatever you kill shall be theirs." This was a great honor for young men.

Then when we had come near to where the bison were, the hunters circled around them, and the cry went up, as in a battle, *"Hoka hey!"* which meant to charge. Then there was a great dust and everybody shouted and all the hunters went in to kill. They were all nearly naked, with their quivers full of arrows hanging on their left sides, and they would ride right up to a bison and shoot him behind the left shoulder. Some of the arrows would go in up to the feathers and sometimes those that struck no bones went right straight through. Everybody was very happy.

What were some ways in which an Oglala Sioux could earn honor and importance?

Indians who depended on buffalo had to follow the movement of the animals. How might this affect ideas about land ownership?

b → c   Wooden Leg was a Cheyenne warrior. In the first selection below, he described some Cheyenne ideas which were shared by other Plains tribes. The second selection contains the words of Chief Smohalla. Although Chief Smohalla was not a Plains Indian, the ideas he stated were believed in by many Indians, including the Plains tribes.

b   All our teachings and beliefs were that land was not made to be owned in separate pieces by persons and that the plowing up and destruction of vegetation placed by the Great Medicine and the planting of other vegetation according to the ideas of men was an interference with the plans of the Above.

Great Medicine and the Above were names for the Cheyenne god.

c   God commanded that the lands and the fisheries should be common to all who lived upon them. God said that they were never to be marked off or divided, but that the people should enjoy the fruits that God planted in the land, and the animals that lived upon it, and the fishes in the water. God said he was the father and the earth was the mother of mankind. He said that nature was the law.

d The following excerpt from *Black Elk Speaks* tells of events that took place in the Dakota Territory in 1874.

Pahuska was a name given to the U.S. Army General George A. Custer. *Wasichus* was a name for white people.

What does Black Elk mean by "yellow metal"?

Pahuska led his soldiers into the Black Hills that summer to see what he could find. He had no right to go in there, because all that country was ours. Also the Wasichus had made a treaty with Red Cloud that said it would be ours as long as grass should grow and water flow. Later I learned too that Pahuska had found there much of the yellow metal that makes the Wasichus crazy; and that is what made the bad trouble, just as it did before, when the hundred were rubbed out.

Our people knew there was yellow metal in little chunks up there; but they did not bother with it, because it was not good for anything.

We stayed all winter at the Soldiers' Town, and all the while the bad trouble was coming fast; for in the fall we heard that some Wasichus had come from the Missouri River to dig in the Black Hills for the yellow metal, because Pahuska had told about it with a voice that went everywhere.

In the Moon When the Calves Grow Hair [September] there was a big council with the Wasichus on the Smoky Earth River at the mouth of White Clay Creek. I can remember the council, but I did not understand much of it then. Many of the Dakotas were there, also Shyelas and Blue Clouds; but Crazy Horse and Sitting Bull stayed away. In the middle of the circle there was a shade made of canvas. Under this the councilors sat and talked, and all around them there was a crowd of people on foot and horseback. They talked and talked for days, but it was just like wind blowing in the end. I asked my father what they were talking about in there, and he told me that the Grandfather at Washington wanted to lease the Black Hills so that the Wasichus could dig yellow metal, and that the chief of the soldiers had said if we did not do this, the Black Hills would be just like melting snow held in our hands, because the Wasichus would take that country anyway.

It made me sad to hear this. It was such a good place to play and the people were always happy in that country.

Dakotas were a group of Sioux Indians. *Shyleas* were Cheyenne Indians, and *Blue Clouds* were Arapahoes.

What does Black Elk mean when he refers to "the Grandfather in Washington"?

What value differences between whites and Indians are shown in this piece?

e Scenes of Plains Indian life.
    1 A Plains Indian encampment
    2 Sioux moving to a new camp
    3 A buffalo hunt

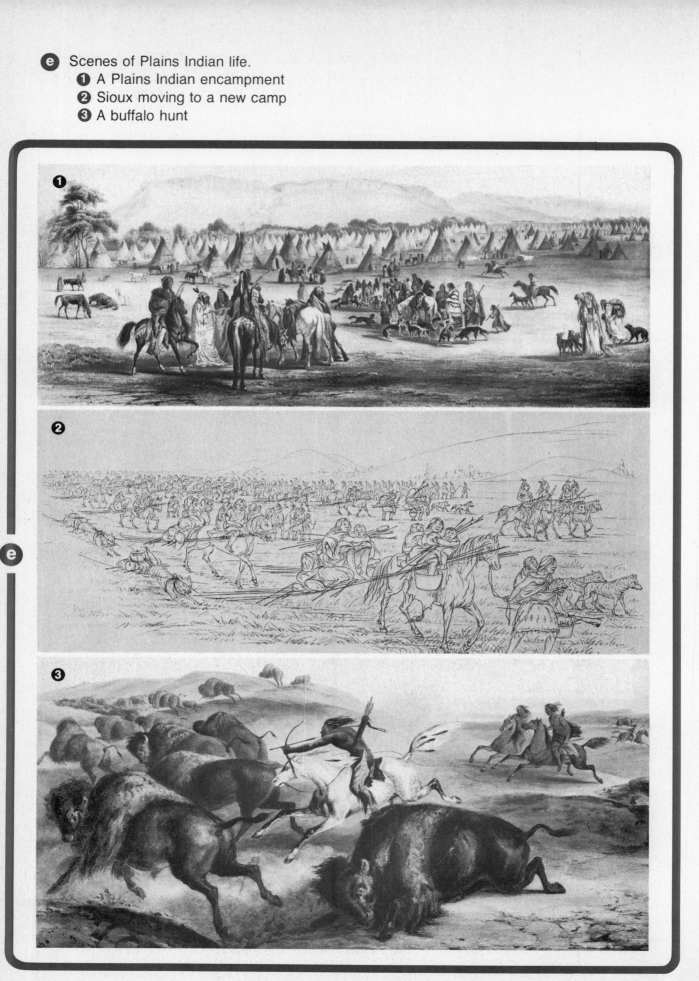

You've identified some important Plains Indian ideas and ways of acting. Whether white Americans shared these ideas and ways of acting would have a powerful effect on the two groups' interaction.

Using data pieces F through J, identify white Americans' attitudes toward

1. Land ownership
2. Land rights
3. Farming

f → g The two selections that follow will tell you something about pioneers' feelings towards the land and their new homes. The first selection is by John Herbert Quick, a pioneer Plains farmer. The second is from *Son of the Middle Border,* a book written by Hamlin Garland. As a child, in about 1870, Garland was taken to the Midwest by his pioneer family.

f   Most of our pioneers were farmers. They were farmers who brought with them the desire only to make homes and to make livings from their farms. Some of the covered-wagon people had the greed of land speculation, but most of them simply desired homes of their own.

g   On the second day, we came to a meadow so wide that its western rim touched the sky without revealing a sign that man lived there except the road in which we travelled.

The plain was covered with grass tall as ripe wheat. When my father stopped his team and came back to us and said, "Well, children, here we are on The Big Prairie," we looked about us with awe, so endless seemed this spread of wild oats and waving flowers.

In the fall Harriet and Frank returned to school but I was too valuable to be spared. The unbroken land of our new farm demanded the plow, and no sooner was the planting on our rented place finished than my father began the work of fencing and breaking the sod of the homestead which lay a mile to the south.

The early 70s were years of swift change in the Middle West. Day by day the settlement thickened. Section by section the prairie was blackened by the plow. Month by month the sweet wild meadows were fenced and pastured. Lanes of barbed wire replaced the winding wagon trails.

h In the middle 1800s, John Louis O'Sullivan, a magazine editor, expressed the idea that appears below. O'Sullivan's idea and his phrase "manifest destiny" were widely accepted.

h No one should limit our greatness or stop the fulfillment of our manifest destiny to spread over the continent given to us by God for the free development of our yearly multiplying millions.

What do you think the phrase "manifest destiny" means? How do you think believers in "manifest destiny" felt about Indians' rights to the land?

i Justice Taylor, a southern judge, gave this opinion on changes in former Indian territories.

i When we think about the change which has been brought about in this once-savage wilderness, by the arts, the industry, and the superior knowledge of the new population; when we visit our busy cities, smiling fields, and happy homes; when we see our numerous bays and harbors, once the home only of the wild fowl and fish; now filled with ships and vessels of all sizes and nations, pouring upon these lands the rich and extensive commerce of a whole world; when, instead of a wandering tribe of hunters, we behold a powerful nation of farmers, as free in every desirable way as the savage Indians; when our happy political institutions and the religion of the Bible, have replaced their ignorant laws and wretched superstitions; can we wish these effects of civilization, religion, and the arts, to disappear, and the dark forests and roaming Indian again to possess the land? Are we not forced to admit that the guiding hand of God who created the earth is to be seen in this mighty change?

How do you think Justice Taylor would have felt about the idea of "manifest destiny"? About pioneers moving west? About Indians' land rights?

j Scenes of pioneer life.
   1 A new town on the plains
   2 Plowing cornfields in Nebraska
   3 Main Street in a western town
   4 A pioneer family in front of their sod house

j

1

Compare these pictures to the pictures of Plains Indian life (page 390). How do the ways of life seem to differ?

You have identified some cultural differences between the pioneers and the Indians they met. Based on these differences, what problems do you think would develop if the two groups shared the same land? Why?

k Historians estimate that about 275,000 Indians lived west of the Mississippi River at the end of the Civil War. The statistics below tell you something about population changes in that area between 1850 and 1900.

Study the statistics. How do you think the changes shown would affect the Indians west of the Mississippi? Why?

What effect would the Home-stead Act have on settlement of the West? ▼

THE GROWTH OF THE WEST

SOME POPULATION CHANGES 1850-1900

State	1850	1860	1870	1880	1890	1900
Minnesota	6,077	172,023	439,706	780,773	1,310,283	1,751,394
Iowa	192,214	674,913	1,194,020	1,624,615	1,912,297	2,231,853
Missouri	682,044	1,182,012	1,721,295	2,168,380	2,679,185	3,106,665
Texas	212,592	604,215	818,579	1,591,749	2,235,527	3,048,710
New Mexico	61,547	93,516	91,874	119,565	160,282	195,310
Colorado		34,277	39,864	194,327	413,249	539,700
North Dakota		4,837	2,405	36,909	190,938	319,146
Kansas		107,206	364,399	996,096	1,428,108	1,470,495
Wyoming			9,118	20,789	62,555	95,531

In 1862 Congress passed a Homestead Act which made free land, in 160 acre parcels, available to farmers in the West. This act provided two methods for acquiring the western farmland. Any head of family (a citizen or an alien intending to become a citizen) who was 21 years or older could become owner of the 160 acre tracts. To do this the person had to pay a small registration fee, and live on and develop the property for five years. An alternate plan simply allowed the person to buy the 160 acres from the government at $1.25 per acre after having lived on the property for six months.

Between 1860 and 1900 more than 1 million new farms were established in the West. In the same period, 400 million acres of land were added to the total amount of farmland in the United States. Most of this new farmland was west of the Mississippi.

Cultural Destruction

When differences in ideas and ways of acting cause conflict between groups, there can be several possible results. One culture may adapt so that it can exist as part of another, more powerful culture. One culture may be peacefully absorbed by another culture. One culture may be forcibly destroyed by another.

Today there are about 800,000 Indian Americans living in the United States. Their ideas and ways of acting are not just the same as those of their ancestors. Much of the Indian cultures that existed before contact with white Americans was destroyed. How did this happen? How did cultural conflict lead to cultural destruction?

Serious problems began in the West in 1862. As thousands of white settlers moved into the Dakota Territory, the Sioux Indians who lived there became desperate. They went "on the warpath" and killed between 500 and 1,000 white settlers before they were stopped by the U.S. Army. For the next 25 years there was constant warfare between whites and Indians in the West.

ⓐ As the Indians lost the land they had lived and hunted on, what would happen to them? A government commission, headed by John Wesley Powell, investigated the problem. Powell—a scientist, explorer, and government official—made these recommendations.

As you study the recommendations, think about
1. How Powell's plan would probably affect Plains Indian culture
2. Powell's attitude toward Indians

ⓐ
All of the Indians who have been visited by the commission know that it is hopeless to fight against the government of the United States and the tide of civilization.

They are broken into many small tribes and their homes are so spread among the settlements of white men that their power is entirely broken and there should be no fear of a general war with them. The time has passed when it was necessary to buy peace. It only remains to decide what should be done with them. To give them a partial supply of clothing and a small amount of food annually, while they live near whites, is to encourage them to be lazy, and tends to make them a class of wandering beggars. If they are not to be collected on reservations, they should no longer receive aid from the General Government, for every dollar given them in their present condition does more harm than good.

The commission does not consider that a reservation should be looked upon as a pen where savages are fed with flour and beef, supplied with blankets from the government, and furnished with paint and trinkets by greedy traders. A reservation should be a place to learn to work and a home for these unfortunate people.

Suggestions in Regard to the Management of these Reservations:

With a view toward finally civilizing these Indians, the commission would like to make some suggestions concerning the management of reservations.

First. All payment given to the Indians should, so far as possible, be used to get them to work. No able-bodied Indian should be either fed or clothed except in payment for labor, even though such labor is to provide for his own future wants.

Second. They should not be given ready-made clothing. Fabrics should be given them from which they can manufacture their own garments.

Third. The Indians should not be furnished with tents; as long as they have tents they move about too easily, and are thus encouraged to continue their wandering way of life. As fast as possible, houses should be built for them.

Fourth. Each Indian family should be supplied with a cow, to enable them to start accumulating property. It is interesting to notice that, as soon as an Indian acquires property, he more thoroughly appreciates the rights of property, and becomes a supporter of law and order.

Fifth. In all this country the soil cannot be cultivated without artificial irrigation. This makes agricultural operations too complicated for the Indian without careful guidance. There will, therefore, be needed on each reservation a number of farmers to give general direction to all such labor.

Sixth. On each reservation there should be a blacksmith, carpenter, and a saddlemaker and harnessmaker, and each of these should employ several Indian apprentices. Each should consider that the most important part of his duty is to teach such apprentices. From time to time a shoemaker and other mechanics should be added to this number.

Seventh. An efficient medical department should be organized on each reservation. A great number of the diseases with which the Indian is plagued cure easily with medical treatment. By such a course many lives can be saved and much suffering prevented. But there is another very important reason for the establishment of a medical department. The magician or "medicine man" has much influence, and such influence is always bad; but in the presence of an intelligent doctor it is soon lost.

Eighth. It is unnecessary to mention the power which schools would have over the rising generation of Indians. Next to teaching them to work, the most important thing is to teach them the English language. Their own language contains so much mythology and sorcery that a new one is needed to help them forget their superstitions. The ideas and thoughts of civilized life cannot be communicated to them in their own tongues.

In your opinion, did Powell believe that his recommendations were for the Indians' benefit? What do you think he thought about Indian culture?

1. Do you think those recommendations were a good solution to the problem?
2. If you disagree with any of these recommendations, what do you think the recommendations should have been?
3. How do you think Indians felt about these ideas? How do you think most whites felt about them?

b In 1887 Congress passed the Dawes Act. Under this act, reservation land was redistributed. Instead of belonging to the entire tribe, land was given to individuals. Indians who accepted land were allowed to become citizens of the United States, a right they had never before had. Here is the oath Indians had to take in the citizenship ceremony.

What does this oath tell you about the government's attitude toward Indian culture? Compare this attitude to that of Powell.

The President of the United States has sent me to speak a solemn and serious word to you, a word that means more to some of you than any other that you have heard. He has been told that there are some among you who should no longer be controlled by the Bureau of Indian Affairs, but should be American citizens. It is his decision that this shall be done, and that those so honored by the people of the United States shall have the meaning of this new and great privilege pointed out by symbol and by word, so that no man or woman shall not know its meaning. The president has sent me papers naming those men and women, and I shall call out their names one by one, and they will come before me.

For men:
————(white name). What was your Indian name? (Gives name.)
————(Indian name). I hand you a bow and an arrow. Take this bow and shoot the arrow. (He shoots.)
————(Indian name). You have shot your last arrow. That means that you are no longer to live the life of an Indian. You are from this day forward to live the life of the white man. But you may keep the arrow; it will be to you a symbol of your noble race and of the pride you feel that you come from the first of all Americans.
————(White name). Take in your hand this plow. (He takes the handles of the plow.)
This act means that you have chosen to live the life of the white man—and the white man lives by work. From the earth we all must get our living, and the earth will not yield unless man

b

pours upon it the sweat of his brow. Only by work do we gain a right to the land or to the enjoyment of life.

————(White name). I give you a purse. This purse will always say to you that the money you gain from your labor must be wisely kept. The wise man saves his money so that when the sun does not smile and the grass does not grow, he will not starve.

For women:

————(White name). Take in your hand this workbag and purse. (She takes the workbag and purse.)

This means that you have chosen the life of the white woman —and the white woman loves her home. The family and the home are the foundation of our civilization. Upon the character and industry of the mother and homemaker largely depends the future of our Nation. The purse will always say to you that the money you gain from your labor must be wisely kept. The wise woman saves her money, so that when the sun does not smile and the grass does not grow, she and her children will not starve.

To men and women:

I give into your hands the flag of your country. This is the only flag you have ever had or ever will have. It is the flag of freedom, the flag of free men, the flag of a hundred million free men and women of whom you are now one. That flag has a request to make of you, (white name); that you take it into your hands and repeat these words:

"For as much as the president has said that I am worthy to be a citizen of the United States, I now promise to this flag that I will give my hands, my head, and my heart to the doing of all that will make me a true American citizen."

And now beneath this flag I place upon your breast the emblem of your citizenship. Wear this badge of honor always; and may the eagle that is on it never see you do anything of which the flag will not be proud.

(The audience rises and shouts, "[white name] is an American citizen.")

What attitude toward Indians' culture is shown in this citizenship ceremony?

C Black Elk explained the effect of reservation life.

c You have noticed that everything an Indian does he does in a circle. That is because the Power of the World always works in circles. Everything tries to be round. In the old days, when we were a strong and happy people, all our power came to us from the sacred hoop of the nation. Our tepees were round like the nests of birds, and they were always set in a circle.

d This photograph was taken on an Indian reservation in the Southwest.

If you felt as Black Elk did, how would living in one of these houses affect you?

e → f Why did Indians living on reservations have to change their way of life? The selections that follow will help you answer that question. The first is from a report on Indian affairs made to Congress in the late 1800s. The second is by Wooden Leg.

e The Great Sioux Reservation was originally much larger, but was reduced by the United States. When precious metals were discovered in 1876, the government took the Black Hills part of the reservation. At the time the 1876 treaty was concluded, and these Indians were on the reservation, they depended largely on hunting for food. This large reservation, in what was then an absolutely unsettled part of the public land, was granted to them for a hunting ground. Since that time this reservation has become the heart of the great Territory of Dakota, fast filling up with population, and being crossed in all directions by railways. The result is that the game has disappeared, and the reservation can be used only for agricultural and grazing purposes. Since the game has disappeared from the reservation, the Indian has become more dependent than ever upon the government for food and will become entirely so unless he is taught, in some way, to support himself by agriculture and grazing.

How can material changes lead to cultural changes?

f My first shoes were given to me at the reservation in Oklahoma. All my life before this, I had worn only the moccasins made by Indians. I still liked moccasins best, but we did not have enough skins to make all of them we needed.

g When people see their culture being destroyed and feel they have little hope for improvement, they sometimes look for help in a new direction. In this selection Black Elk tells about the beginning of the Indian "ghost dance" movement.

g There was hunger among my people because the Wasichus did not give us all the food they promised in the Black Hills treaty. They made that treaty themselves; our people did not want it and did not make it. Yet the Wasichus who made it had given us less than half as much as they promised. So the people were hungry.

It became worse. My people looked pitiful. There was a big drought, and the rivers and creeks seemed to be dying. Nothing would grow that the people had planted, and the Wasichus had been sending less cattle and other food than ever before. The Wasichus had slaughtered all the bison and shut us up in pens.

Three Stars was a name for General Cook who headed the commission that arranged the treaty of 1889. **Rosebud** is a reservation.

It looked as though we might all starve to death. We could not eat lies, and there was nothing we could do.

And now the Wasichus had made another treaty to take away from us about half the land we had left. Our people did not want this treaty either, but Three Stars came and made the treaty just the same, because the Wasichus wanted our land between the Smoky Earth and the Good River. So the flood of Wasichus, dirty with bad deeds, gnawed away half of the island that was left to us. When Three Stars came to kill us on the Rosebud, Crazy Horse whipped him and drove him back. But when he came this time without any soldiers, he whipped us and drove us back. We were penned up and could do nothing.

I went on helping the sick, and there were many, for the measles had come among the people who were already weak because of hunger. There were more sick people that winter when the whooping cough came and killed little children who did not have enough to eat.

So it was. Our people were pitiful and in despair.

But early that summer (1889), strange news had come from the west, and the people had been talking and talking about it. This news came to the Oglalas first of all, and I heard that it came to us from the Shoshones and Blue Clouds. Some believed it and some did not believe. It was hard to believe; and when I first heard of it, I thought it was only foolish talk that somebody had started somewhere. This news said that out yonder in the west at a place near where the great mountains [the Sierras] stand before you come to the big water, there was a holy man among the Paiutes who had talked to the Great Spirit in a vision; and the Great Spirit had told him how to save the Indian peoples and make the Wasichus disappear and bring back all the bison and the people who were dead and how there would be a new earth.

The **Paiutes** are an Indian tribe from the Nevada area.

h These are the words of Wovoka, the Paiute holy man who began the Ghost Dance movement.

h All Indians must dance, everywhere, keep on dancing. Pretty soon in next spring Great Spirit come. He bring back all game of every kind. The game be thick everywhere. All dead Indians come back and live again. They all be strong just like young men, be young again. Old Blind Indian see again and get young and have fine time. When Great Spirit comes this way, then all the Indians go to mountains, high up away from whites. Whites can't hurt Indians then. Then while Indians way up high, big flood comes like water and all white people die, get drowned. After that, water go away and then nobody but Indians everywhere and game all kinds thick. Then medicine man tell Indians to send word to all Indians to keep up dancing and the good time will come. Indians who don't dance, who don't believe in this word, will grow little, just about a foot high, and stay that way. Some of them will be turned into wood and be burned in fire.

By the fall of 1890, many Indians of many different tribes all over the West were performing the ghost dance. The whites thought that the ghost dance was a sign of a new Indian uprising about to take place against the whites, so white soldiers in the West were especially nervous and tense. On December 29, 1890, at Wounded Knee Creek in southern South Dakota, a fight between soldiers and Indians began. The white soldiers quickly killed over 300 Indians, many of them women and children running to reach safety. This was the end of the Indians' dream of a renewal of their old culture, and the Ghost Dance movement died.

In your opinion, why would the Indians be so willing to accept the ideas of the Ghost Dance? Why didn't they try other ways to regain their lost autonomy?

ⓘ The words of Black Elk tell us one way in which Indians viewed the destruction of their culture.

Once we were happy in our own country and we were seldom hungry, for then the two-leggeds and the four-leggeds lived together like relatives, and there was plenty for them and for us. But the Wasichus came, and they have made little islands for us and other little islands for the four-leggeds, and always these islands are becoming smaller, for around them surges the gnawing flood of the Wasichu; and it is dirty with lies and greed.

Why does Black Elk call his reservation an "island"?

A long time ago my father told me what his father told him, that there was once a holy man, called Drinks Water, who dreamed what was to be; and this was long before the coming of the Wasichus. He dreamed that the four-leggeds were going back into the earth and that a strange race had woven a spider's web all around the Dakotas. And he said, "When this happens, you shall live in square gray houses, in a barren land, and beside those square gray houses you shall starve." They say he went back to Mother Earth soon after he saw this vision, and it was sorrow that killed him. You can look about you now and see that he meant these dirt-roofed houses we are living in, and that all the rest was true. Sometimes dreams are wiser than waking.

j The maps that follow show where Indians lived in North America before 1492, the land they **ceded**—that is, signed over—to whites, and the reservations on which Indians lived by 1900.

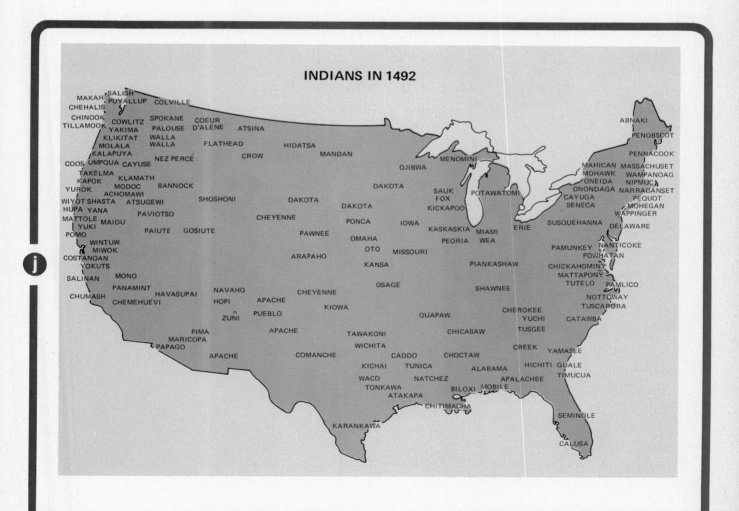

INDIANS IN 1492

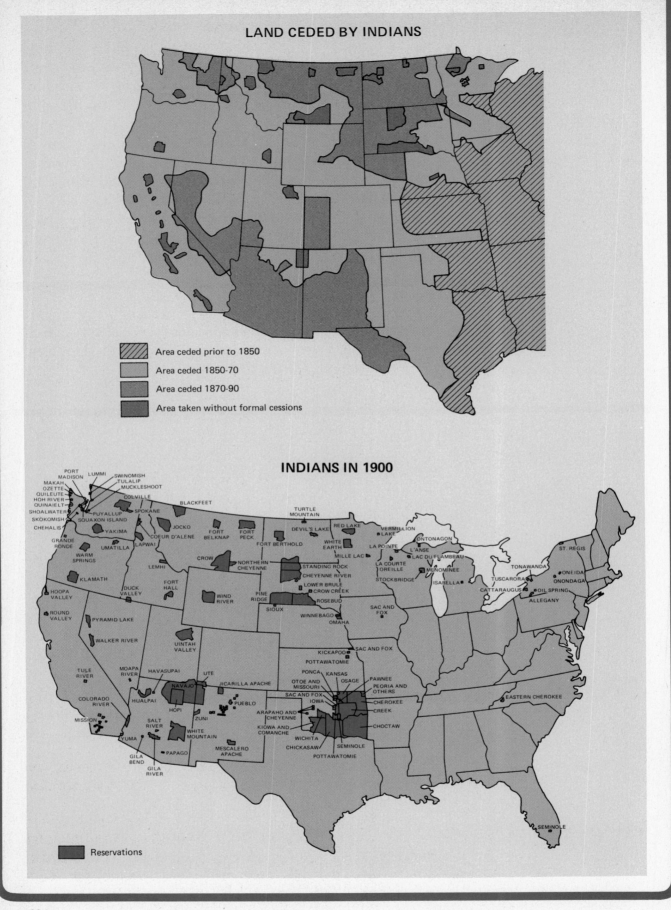

LAND CEDED BY INDIANS

Area ceded prior to 1850

Area ceded 1850-70

Area ceded 1870-90

Area taken without formal cessions

INDIANS IN 1900

PORT MADISON
MAKAH
OZETTE
QUILEUTE
HOH RIVER
QUINAIELT
SHOALWATER
SKOKOMISH
CHEHALIS
LUMMI
SWINOMISH
TULALIP
MUCKLESHOOT
COLVILLE
PUYALLUP
SQUAXON ISLAND
YAKIMA
SPOKANE
JOCKO
COEUR D'ALENE
LAPWAI
GRANDE RONDE
UMATILLA
WARM SPRINGS
KLAMATH
HOOPA VALLEY
ROUND VALLEY
PYRAMID LAKE
WALKER RIVER
DUCK VALLEY
FORT HALL
LEMHI
CROW
NORTHERN CHEYENNE
WIND RIVER
UINTAH VALLEY
BLACKFEET
FORT BELKNAP
FORT PECK
FORT BERTHOLD
TURTLE MOUNTAIN
DEVIL'S LAKE
RED LAKE
WHITE EARTH
MILLE LAC
VERMILLION LAKE
ONTONAGON
L'ANSE
LA POINTE
LA COURTE OREILLE
LAC DU FLAMBEAU
STANDING ROCK
CHEYENNE RIVER
LOWER BRULE
CROW CREEK
PINE RIDGE
ROSEBUD
SIOUX
WINNEBAGO
OMAHA
MENOMINEE
STOCKBRIDGE
ISABELLA
ST. REGIS
TONAWANDA
TUSCARORA
ONEIDA
ONONDAGA
CATTARAUGUS
OIL SPRING
ALLEGANY
SAC AND FOX
KICKAPOO
POTTAWATOMIE
SAC AND FOX
PONCA
KANSAS
OTOE AND MISSOURI
OSAGE
PAWNEE
PEORIA AND OTHERS
CHEROKEE
CREEK
EASTERN CHEROKEE
TULE RIVER
MOAPA RIVER
HAVASUPAI
UTE
JICARILLA APACHE
NAVAJO
HUALPAI
HOPI
ZUNI
PUEBLO
SALT RIVER
WHITE MOUNTAIN
MESCALERO APACHE
MISSION
YUMA
GILA BEND
PAPAGO
GILA RIVER
SAC AND FOX
IOWA
ARAPAHO AND CHEYENNE
KIOWA AND COMANCHE
WICHITA
CHICKASAW
SEMINOLE
POTTAWATOMIE
CHOCTAW
COLORADO RIVER
SEMINOLE

Reservations

Based on what you have studied in this activity,

1. How do you think the conflict between Indians and whites should have been resolved?
2. How do you think all or parts of Indian cultures could have been protected?

Putting the Pieces Together

1. In the Introduction you began a chart of the effects of interaction on majority and minority actions and feelings. Based on Part 2, add to your chart other effects of cultural interaction between majorities and minorities.
2. In Unit 5 you investigated the results blocked autonomy could have on people's actions and reactions. In your opinion, what problems of autonomy were faced by the conquered native American? Which of the results of blocked autonomy did they exhibit when their autonomy was reduced by the white majority?

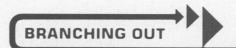

BRANCHING OUT

The problems faced by Indians still continue. Today many Indians are struggling to improve their civil rights and living conditions. Investigate and report on the present-day problems of Indian Americans.

Cultural Borrowing

You've investigated the conflict and destruction that can happen when unlike cultures come in contact. These are not the only possible results, however.

Tools, foods, language, and other parts of one culture are often accepted and used by people of another culture. This is called **cultural borrowing.** Cultural borrowing between Indians and Europeans began almost as soon as the colonization of North America began. Corn and other plants that Squanto introduced to the Pilgrims have become important foods for all Americans.

Borrowing always changes the borrower—sometimes just a little, sometimes a great deal.

● About 1900 a government agency left a wooden wagon with a group of Papago Indians in the southwestern part of the United States. The Indians began using the wagon, which led to a series of changes in their way of life. In the list below are some of the most important changes that occurred in the Papago culture after the wagon was introduced.

1. Copy each change on a slip of paper.
2. The changes are not listed in the sequence in which they happened. Study the changes and look for relationships among them. Which developments might have caused others? For example, what is the relationship between the Indians using money and selling crops to whites?
3. Arrange the changes in correct relationships. As much as you can, arrange them in the sequence in which you think they happened.

- Use of water in households increased.
- Papagos started selling firewood to whites in the nearest town.
- The wagon was used to transport people and equipment between summer and winter camps.
- One Papago man learned to work with iron so that he could shoe horses and repair metal parts.
- Papagos stopped using clay pots to carry water; instead they used wooden barrels which would not break.
- Papago women stopped picking up firewood, which had been one of their jobs; instead, men cut firewood.
- Papago women no longer carried water to the village from a nearby spring; instead, water was brought by wagon.
- Papagos built a road so that the wagon could be taken to the mountains.
- Papagos began growing cash crops to sell to the whites.
- Papagos began using money.

Some of these changes involved more borrowing. Identify the additional borrowing.

Part 2

Newcomers to America

In the years since Europeans first settled in North America, about 50 million immigrants have come to this country. That is the largest migration of people in all human history. Some have come to the United States for religious or political reasons, but most have chosen this country because of its expanding economy. There simply have been more jobs available here than anywhere else.

Immigrants have come to this country in search of a better life, but most have also been pushed by some specific situation or condition in their native lands. For example, many Irish people came because of a potato famine in Ireland beginning in 1846.

The greatest period of immigration—from 1870 to 1920—provides much data for the study of cultural interaction. At that time, immigrants from a wide range of societies settled in the United States. In Part 2 you'll focus on this period of immigration and will investigate this question:

How were immigrants to the United States affected by interaction with American culture?

Where Did the Immigrants Come From?

There were patterns in the flow of immigrants into the United States. During some periods large numbers came from northern Europe. At other times the flow was mostly from different areas.

● The statistics below give you the approximate number of immigrants and the areas from which they came for the period from 1820 to 1970.

Make a graph on immigration using these statistics. Then identify the high and low levels of immigration from each area.

To **migrate** is to move from one place to another. To **emigrate** is to move out of one country to live in another. To **immigrate** is to move into a country from another. What is the difference between an **emigrant** and an **immigrant**?

U.S. IMMIGRATION 1820-1970

	Northern Europe	Eastern Europe	Southern Europe	Asia	The Americas	Africa
1821-30	118,000	40	3000	10	11,000	20
1831-40	700,000	650	5300	45	33,000	50
1841-50	1,600,000	650	4700	80	62,000	55
1851-60	2,400,000	1620	20,000	41,000	74,000	210
1861-70	2,014,000	12,300	21,000	65,000	169,000	310
1871-80	2,038,000	125,000	76,000	124,000	404,000	450
1881-90	2,778,000	625,000	333,000	68,000	427,000	850
1891-1900	1,600,000	1,207,000	808,000	71,000	39,000	370
1901-10	1,800,000	3,834,000	2,390,000	244,000	362,000	7000
1911-20	950,000	1,863,000	1,506,000	193,000	1,143,000	8400
1921-30	1,818,000	575,000	580,000	97,000	1,517,000	6200
1931-40	2,015,000	338,000	84,000	15,000	160,000	1750
1941-50	491,000	107,000	73,000	32,000	355,000	6300
1951-60	931,000	123,000	261,000	153,000	997,000	14,000
1961-70	588,000	106,000	421,000	478,000	1,716,000	29,000

BRANCHING OUT

Unless your ancestors were Indians, you are a descendent of immigrants. Try to find out where some of your ancestors came from, when they came to the United States, where they first settled, and the probable reasons for their move to this country.

When unlike people meet, their first reactions to each other are likely to be based on what can first be seen or heard—differences in physical features, clothing, skin color, or way of speaking. After awhile however, most of these differences are noticed less. In the long run, what determines how unlike people interact depends largely on differences in their ideas, attitudes, and values. This was true of immigrants to America.

It would be impossible to study all the differences between attitudes and values important to Americans and those important to the immigrants. However, we can be aware of the problems such differences can create.

Immigrants, of course, were not all alike. They came from many different societies. Often, even the immigrants from one country had different values and attitudes. A farmer and a professor, for example, might have quite different ideas and ways of acting.

The material that follows shows you just some of the ideas and ways of acting that immigrants brought with them to the United States. By understanding what some immigrants were like, you can begin to understand the cultural interaction that took place between Americans and newcomers.

As you study data pieces A through G, ask yourself how each of these people or groups thought and felt about matters such as

Education	Law	Work
Income	Family	Life goals
Parents	Government	Religion

a → e   The selections that follow express ideas and ways of acting shared by some Europeans. These patterns of thought and behavior were brought to the United States by immigrants.

Do you think people in this Italian town believed that work was the most important part of a person's life? What did they value?

a

In Italy I live in small town—six, seven thousand. It take not much money to live. We pay the rent once a year, only little money. We have fine garden, we live healthy, happy. I obey my mother's word, which is like the God. The people in my town, they are serious, human, good heart. We give everything to the poor. When stranger comes to us, he got always the first chair; we make all we could for him. The stranger can stay a year; he needs no money to pay for anything.

We work little bit, then we take the leisure. We love very much the music, art, poetry. We love the poetical life—poetry today, and tomorrow we take what's coming with the good patience. The way I mean is not only to read the books of the great poets—of Dante that we love more than a father, or Petrarca—but the poetry of the beautiful scenery in the country, the poetry of the music, the poetry of the friendship. Even in the small town we have band and orchestra.

b

November 11, 1902

Dearest Parents,

Please do not be angry with me for what I shall write. I write you that it is hard to live alone, so please find some girl for me. Be sure she is an honest one, for in America there is not even one single honest Polish girl.

December 21, 1902

Dearest Parents,

I thank you kindly for your letter, for it was happy. As to the girl, although I don't know her, a friend of mine who does says that she is stately and pretty. I believe him, as well as you, my parents.

Please tell me which of the sisters is to come, the older or the younger one, Aleksandra or Stanislawa.

Based on these letters, how do you think people from this society chose mates? What was their attitude toward their parents?

c

When I was five years old I began to go to *cheder.* Such was my diligence that I went through the *sidur* and the Pentateuch in one winter. At six and a half, my father brought me into the famous *yeshiva* of Vilna.

The sole source of maintenance for almost all the pupils was the system of "day eating," at the homes of some well-to-do or poorer members of the community—at a different home each day. As a rule, the *bahurim* are not residents of the city where the *yeshiva* is situated. To maintain them, each is assigned to eat one day in the week in certain houses; he thus rotates through seven houses a week.

*In Yiddish, a language spoken by many European Jews, a **cheder** is an elementary school in which children are taught to read important religious books in Hebrew. Among these books are the **sidur** (a prayer book) and the **Pentateuch**. (The Pentateuch is the first five books of the Bible. It is also called the Torah.) In a **yeshiva**, students study the **Talmud,** the important book of Jewish law and tradition. **Bahurim** are young male students.*

The writer of this description was Jewish. Based on his story, how important do you think education and religion were to European Jews? What hardships did students face in order to learn?

d

I am a son of a Polish peasant farmer. Until ten years of age I did not know the alphabet, or, exactly speaking, I knew only the letter B. Father did not send me to school. He was always

What was the father's attitude toward education? What was the son's attitude?

repeating: "We have grown old, and we can't read nor write, and we live; so you, my children, will also live without knowledge."

I said to my father that I wanted to learn from a book. And father scolded me, "And who will peel potatoes in the winter, and pasture the geese in summer?" I cried. Once, while peeling potatoes, I escaped from my father and went to an old man who knew not only how to read, but how to write well. I asked him to show me letters in the printer, and he did not refuse. I went home and thought: "It is bad! Father will probably give me a licking." And so it was. Father showered a few strokes on me and said: "Don't you know that, as old people say, he who knows written stuff casts himself into hell?" But I used to steal out to learn more and more frequently.

Arson *is the crime of purposely setting fire to a building or property. How might this attitude create problems for immigrants?*

e For the peasant, arson is a way of getting even, and does not bring dishonor in the eyes of one's neighbors.

A peasant whom my father scolded for having set fire to his neighbor's buildings said, "I have set fire to his barn, but he could have and still can set fire to mine." I have listened to the stories of many perfectly respectable farmers who tried to set fire to their enemies' farm buildings.

f Chinese agents often recruited workers in China to provide cheap labor in Hawaii and the United States. These agents received a commission on each laborer. The following labor-recruiting poster was circulated in Hong Kong in 1870.

Mandarins *were important public officials in China.*

f All Chinamen make much money in New Orleans, if they work. Chinamen have become richer than mandarins there. The pay, first year, is 300 dollars, but afterwards this more than doubles. One can do as he likes in that country. Nobody else gets more pay than he does. Nice rice, vegetables, and wheat are all very cheap. Three years there will make a poor workman very rich, and he can come home at any time. On the ships that go there, passengers will find nice rooms and very fine food. They can play all sorts of games and have no work. Everything to make man happy. It is nice country. Better than this. No sickness there and no danger of death. Come! Go at once. You cannot afford to wait. Don't heed any wife's counsel or the threats of enemies. Be Chinamen, but go.

g This statement was made at a Russian conference in 1905.

The people believe that it is the Tsar's responsibility to govern them, and that he has no need of advice from the people. They believe that the Tsar thinks about them all the time, not even sleeping at night out of concern for them. They believe the Tsar should govern alone, for that is not only his right, it is his heavy burden to bear.

Occasionally in the past the Tsar has asked the people's advice, but when he has the people have said, "This is what we think, but do what you believe is best."

Many European nations had kings or rulers who had absolute power over the people. The **tsar** was the absolute ruler of Russia. The last Russian tsar was overthrown in 1917. Although, by 1905, many Russians did not believe the tsar should rule Russia, many others agreed with this statement about the tsar's power.

From the previous data choose several ideas, attitudes, or values that you think were different from those of Americans in the period from 1870 to 1920.

1. Describe what you think the differences were.
2. Describe a problem situation which might have been caused by these differences.

h The figures on the chart below come from the immigration records of the year 1870. In that year 387,203 immigrants entered the United States. About half of them gave inspectors some information about the jobs they had done in their homelands.

Based on this information, what general statements could you make about the kinds of work these immigrants were prepared to do?

OCCUPATION OF SOME IMMIGRANTS IN 1870

2,132 professionals, including
   232 doctors
   551 engineers
   285 clergymen
   493 teachers

200 artists

31,964 skilled workmen, including
   2,378 blacksmiths
   4,421 carpenters
    228 cigar makers
   2,190 masons
   4,763 miners
    505 seamstresses
   1,557 shoemakers
   1,703 tailors
   1,178 weavers
   8,061 mechanics

145,782 miscellaneous, including
   1,611 clerks
   35,656 farmers
   84,577 laborers
   7,073 merchants
   1,420 sailors
   14,261 servants

TOTAL	
Professional	2,132
Artist	200
Skilled Workmen	31,964
Miscellaneous	145,782
Without Occupation	16,529
Occupation not stated	190,596
Total immigration	387,203

412

ℹ The pictures that follow tell you more about "what the immigrants were like."

How Did Americans Feel About the Immigrants?

Whenever people who aren't alike come into contact with one another, problems almost always occur. Differences often create misunderstanding and resentment. It isn't surprising then that America had many problems of human relations during periods of heavy immigration. The data in this activity reflects some of the attitudes and feelings toward immigrants which were common about the time your great-grandparents were your age.

Read the data and identify
1. American opinions about the effects of immigration
2. Some American ideas about the immigrants themselves

a As millions of immigrants poured into the United States, Americans began to wonder whether they should restrict the number of newcomers. In 1881 a Bostonian, Hamilton Andrews Hill, gave this opinion at a conference on immigration.

a
> I want to call the attention of the conference to this fact, that the evils which have been pointed out this morning in connection with immigration are but a small part of a great and marvelous movement of population from the Eastern and Western Hemisphere. A large majority of those who come as immigrants are valuable additions to our population and they should be cordially welcomed. They come, many of them, with money and with tools of industry and with honest purposes. They want to be industrious citizens, to take care of themselves and their families, and to add to the national wealth.
>
> It is a mistake to talk as though immigrants were a mass of paupers about to become dependent on us. We must use all the techniques of our Christian civilization in dealing with these people in order to make Christian citizens of them; do not put a stigma upon them by calling them paupers and criminals.

A *pauper* is a person who has no money. A *stigma* is a mark of shame or discredit.

b A Protestant minister, Reverend Josiah Strong, gave this opinion of immigrants in 1885.

b
> The typical immigrant is a European peasant, whose horizon has been narrow, whose moral and religious training has been little or false, and whose ideas of life are low. Many belong to the pauper and criminal classes. Every detective in New York knows that there is scarcely a ship landing immigrants that does not bring English, French, German, or Italian "crooks."
>
> Moreover, immigration not only furnishes most of our criminals, it is also seriously affecting the morals of the native population. It is disease and not health which is contagious. Most foreign-

ers bring with them European ideas of the Sabbath. The result is sadly plain in all our cities, where Sunday is being changed from a holy day into a holiday. But by far the worst threat to morals is the liquor business, and this is mainly carried on by foreigners. In 1880 63 percent of the traders and dealers in liquors and wines were foreign-born. Seventy-five percent of the brewers were foreign-born, while a large part of the remainder were of foreign parentage. Of saloonkeepers, about 60 percent of these corrupters of youth, whose hand is against every man, were of foreign origin.

We can only glance at the political results of immigration. As we have already seen, it is immigration which has fattened the liquor power; and there is a liquor vote. Immigration is the mother and nurse of American socialism; and there will be a socialist vote. Immigrants go to the cities, and give them their political character. And there is no more serious threat to our civilization than our rabble-ruled cities.

Compare the opinions of Mr. Hill and Reverend Strong.

What did the songwriter resent about these Chinese immigrants? ▼

c This song was published in California in 1877.

Twelve Hundred More

O workingmen dear, and did you hear
The news that's goin' round?
Another China steamer
Has been landed here in town.
Today I read the papers,
And it grieved my heart full sore
To see upon the title page,
O, just "Twelve Hundred More!"

O, California's coming down,
As you can plainly see.
They are hiring all the Chinamen
and discharging you and me;
But strife will be in every town
Throughout the Pacific shore,
And the cry of old and young shall be,
"O, damn, 'Twelve Hundred More' "

They run their steamer in at night
Upon our lovely bay;
If 'twas a free and honest trade,

They'd land it in the day.
They come here by the hundreds—
The country is overrun—
And go to work at any price—
By then the labor's done.

Twelve hundred honest laboring men
Thrown out of work today
By the landing of these Chinamen
In San Francisco Bay. . . .

This state of things can never last
In this our golden land,
For soon you'll hear the avenging cry,
"Drive out the China man!"
And then we'll have the stirring times
We had in days of yore,
And the devil take those dirty words
They call 'Twelve Hundred More!"

d These statements were made in 1922 by Kenneth L. Roberts.

Races can not be crossbred without mongrelization, any more than breeds of dogs can be crossbred without mongrelization. The American nation was founded and developed by the Nordic race, but if a few more million members of the Alpine, Mediterranean, and Semitic races are poured among us, the result will be a race of people as worthless as good-for-nothing mongrels.

A mongrelized race of people cannot produce great artists or statesmen or poets or sculptors or explorers or warriors. The government of a mongrelized race becomes corrupt, its art and literature become childish and silly, the courts and judges become unfair, and its public and private morals go bad. All that is left are tricky and cunning traders and people who think they are better than they really are. These facts should be interesting to American citizens. So many millions of non-Nordic aliens have poured into this country since 1880 that several of our largest cities have more foreign-born and children of foreign-born than native Americans.

Unless this is stopped immediately, mongrelization is inevitable. Many of our largest cities are beginning to show the effects of mongrelization. Some Americans think that only snobs believe in racial purity, but race purity is essential for the well-being of our children. Only if our race remains pure can we keep the things that made America great.

*A **mongrel** is an animal of mixed breed.*

What was Mr. Roberts' attitude toward Nordic people? Toward other kinds of people? How could you prove that Mr. Roberts is either right or wrong?

e This cartoon appeared in *Life Magazine* in 1899.

The cartoon's title is "The Last American." What is the attitude of the artist toward immigrants? What kind of person did the artist think was American?

All Americans except Indians are the descendents of immigrants. What do you think most Americans thought about this when they criticized immigrants?

f Both of these cartoons were drawn by the same artist. The upper cartoon was drawn in 1880, the lower in 1893.

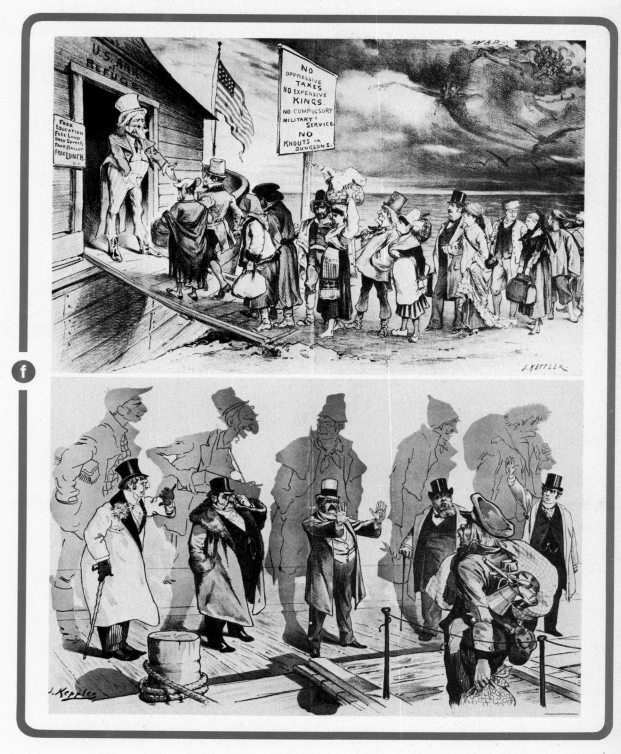

What change in attitude is the artist illustrating? What is the artist's opinion of this change in attitude?

(g) For many years each state made its own laws about admitting newcomers. In 1882, however, Congress began to regulate immigration. Some of the important regulatory laws are described below.

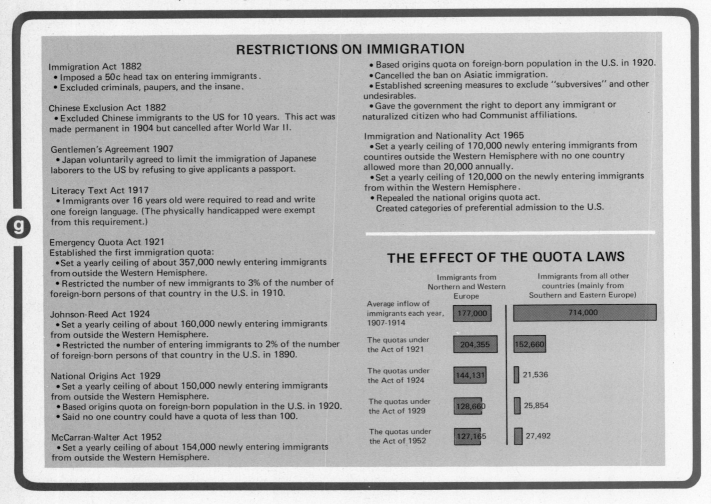

RESTRICTIONS ON IMMIGRATION

Immigration Act 1882
• Imposed a 50c head tax on entering immigrants.
• Excluded criminals, paupers, and the insane.

Chinese Exclusion Act 1882
• Excluded Chinese immigrants to the US for 10 years. This act was made permanent in 1904 but cancelled after World War II.

Gentlemen's Agreement 1907
• Japan voluntarily agreed to limit the immigration of Japanese laborers to the US by refusing to give applicants a passport.

Literacy Text Act 1917
• Immigrants over 16 years old were required to read and write one foreign language. (The physically handicapped were exempt from this requirement.)

Emergency Quota Act 1921
Established the first immigration quota:
• Set a yearly ceiling of about 357,000 newly entering immigrants from outside the Western Hemisphere.
• Restricted the number of new immigrants to 3% of the number of foreign-born persons of that country in the U.S. in 1910.

Johnson-Reed Act 1924
• Set a yearly ceiling of about 160,000 newly entering immigrants from outside the Western Hemisphere.
• Restricted the number of entering immigrants to 2% of the number of foreign-born persons of that country in the U.S. in 1890.

National Origins Act 1929
• Set a yearly ceiling of about 150,000 newly entering immigrants from outside the Western Hemisphere.
• Based origins quota on foreign-born population in the U.S. in 1920.
• Said no one country could have a quota of less than 100.

McCarran-Walter Act 1952
• Set a yearly ceiling of about 154,000 newly entering immigrants from outside the Western Hemisphere.

• Based origins quota on foreign-born population in the U.S. in 1920.
• Cancelled the ban on Asiatic immigration.
• Established screening measures to exclude "subversives" and other undesirables.
• Gave the government the right to deport any immigrant or naturalized citizen who had Communist affiliations.

Immigration and Nationality Act 1965
• Set a yearly ceiling of 170,000 newly entering immigrants from countires outside the Western Hemisphere with no one country allowed more than 20,000 annually.
• Set a yearly ceiling of 120,000 on the newly entering immigrants from within the Western Hemisphere.
• Repealed the national origins quota act.
  Created categories of preferential admission to the U.S.

THE EFFECT OF THE QUOTA LAWS

	Immigrants from Northern and Western Europe	Immigrants from all other countries (mainly from Southern and Eastern Europe)
Average inflow of immigrants each year, 1907-1914	177,000	714,000
The quotas under the Act of 1921	204,355	152,660
The quotas under the Act of 1924	144,131	21,536
The quotas under the Act of 1929	128,660	25,854
The quotas under the Act of 1952	127,165	27,492

The laws passed by Congress usually reflect the attitudes of a majority of the people in the United States. What attitudes toward immigrants are indicated by these immigration laws? What kinds of people are favored by the laws?

What effect do you think each of the following might have had on American attitudes toward immigrants? Explain.

1. More available jobs than workers
2. More available workers than jobs
3. Surplus undeveloped land in the West
4. Most immigrants of Protestant religion
5. Most immigrants Catholic or Jewish

In your opinion, which American objections to immigrants were based on good reasons? Which were based on racism and prejudice?

For most immigrants, coming to America presented major problems. As members of families, they usually had responsibilities at home. Before they could leave the old country, arrangements had to be made for someone else to take over these responsibilities. Separating from friends and family was also difficult, and leaving for an unknown place was surely a little frightening. The trip to a port, the wait for a ship, and the ocean crossing could take weeks or even months. It could also be very expensive.

Unfortunately, the immigrants' problems didn't end with arrival in America. They were simply replaced by different kinds of problems.

Analyze the following data. Identify the many different kinds of problems immigrants faced.

a Once immigrants settled in the United States, most needed to earn money as soon as possible.

After two days of being a guest, I was politely given to understand that it was time for me to enter the race for American dollars. For the rest of that week and all through the next I went out looking for work. Early in the morning I would get one of the children to translate the "Help Wanted" advertisements for me. When I glanced at the length and number of those columns, I saw that I would soon be rich. There were hundreds of shops and factories and offices, it seemed, that wanted my help. They literally begged me to come. They promised me high wages and fine working conditions.

And then I would go and blunder around for hours, trying to find where they were, stand in line with a hundred other applicants, approach timidly when my turn came, and be passed up with a long look at my appearance.

Somehow, I was always refused. Why? At last one morning, a butcher in the upper Eighties in Manhattan gave me the answer. I had got there before anyone else, and when I saw that he was going to pass me up, I got up all my courage and asked him the reason. He looked me over from head to foot, and then, with scornful glance at my shabby foreign shoes he asked me if I thought he wanted a "greenhorn" working in his store.

I thought about that for a long time. Here indeed was a new light on America. Her road to success was a vicious circle. In order to get a job I needed American clothes, and the only way to afford American clothes was to get a job.

b Immigrants often lived in conditions like those shown here.

c The following report was made by a California commission which aided immigrants.

About three years ago a large piece of land was opened for settlement in the Sacramento Valley. The sales agents tried hardest to get immigrants to buy the 20- to 30-acre farms. These agents spoke many languages, and exaggerated and lied about the value of the land. About a 150 families, mostly immigrants, were talked into paying from 100 to 150 dollars an acre. Now, after three years of hard work with no results, about 80 families have left the farms. Their life savings are gone. Much of the soil is hard. Soil experts from the university have said that no one could possibly make a living on these small farms. The families that remain are nearly penniless. Our commission is helping them sue the owners and agents for fraud, and there is some chance they may get some of their money back.

This is only one of about 500 land fraud cases that was handled by the State Immigration Commission.

d A former sailor described his first job in America.

d

One morning Louis and I were standing with some other men on the sidewalk, and a fat man came toward us. "Good morning, *padrone*," said one of the men.

"*Padrone?*" said I to myself. Now the word *padrone* in Italy is used only about a man of some importance. This man not only showed no signs of good breeding, he was unshaven and dirty and his clothes were shabby. I could not understand why he would be called *padrone.* However, I said nothing, because I wanted to be polite when I was in American society.

The *padrone* began to describe in glowing words the advantage of a certain job: "It is not very far, only 12 miles from Boston. For a few cents you can come back any time you wish to see your friends and relatives. The company has a 'shantee' in which you can sleep, and a 'storo' where you can buy your 'grosserie' very cheap. Good pay," he continued, "$1.25 per day, and you only have to pay me 50 cents a week for getting you this good job. I only do it to help you and because you are my countrymen. If you come back here at six o'clock tonight, I will take you out."

The generosity of this man impressed Louis and me very much. We decided we would go, so at six o'clock we returned to the very spot. About 20 men were there and we were led to North Station. We took a train to some suburban place I've never learned the name of.

On reaching our destination we were taken to the shanty and shown two long shelves filled with straw. These were our beds. The store of which we had been told was at one end of the shanty. The next morning we were taken out to work.

It was a warm autumn day. The pick seemed to grow heavier with every stroke and the shovel wider and longer. The second day was no better than the first, and the third was worse than the second. It was especially hard for Louis and me, for we had never been farm workers like the rest. The *padrone,* whose generosity had so impressed us was little better than a brute. We began to do some simple figuring and discovered that when we had paid for our groceries at the store, for the privilege of sleeping in the shanty, and the 50 cents to the *padrone* for having been so kind as to hire us, we would have nothing at the end of the week but sore arms and backs. On the afternoon of the third day, Louis and I had a meeting and decided to part company with picks and shovels forever. We left, without receiving a cent of pay, of course.

e This letter appeared in the *Jewish Daily Forward,* a New York newspaper.

e

Dear Mr. Editor,

I was born in a small town in Russia, and until I was 16 I studied in Hebrew schools, but when I came to America I changed quickly. I was influenced by the progressive newspapers and the literature. I developed spiritually and became a free-thinker. I meet with free-thinking, progressive people, I feel comfortable in their company, and I agree with their convictions.

But the nature of my feelings is remarkable. Listen to me: Every year when the month of *Elul* rolls around, when the time of *Rosh Hashanah* and *Yom Kippur* approaches, my heart grows heavy and sad. A melancholy descends on me, a longing gnaws at my breast. At that time I cannot rest, I wander about through the streets, lost in thought, depressed.

Your reader,
S. R.

Elul is the last month in the Jewish calendar. **Rosh Hashanah** *and* **Yom Kippur** *are Jewish holidays.*

f A young immigrant girl wrote this letter to her aunt in Europe.

f

Dear Auntie:

I received your letter on February 20 and I write you on February 25.

Dear auntie, I inform you that I am in the same place working for an English-speaking master and mistress who don't know a word of Polish, and I don't know English; so we communicate with gestures and I know what to do, that's all. I know the work and therefore I don't mind much about the language. But, dear auntie, I went intentionally into an English household in order that I may learn to speak English, because it is necessary in America. I am in good health, only I am a little ill with my feet. I don't know what it is, whether rheumatism or something else. I walk very much, because from six o'clock in the morning till ten o'clock in the evening I have work and I receive 22 dollars a month, and I have seven persons, and 16 rooms to clean, and I cook. Everything is on my head.

O dear auntie, I write you that I have nothing to write, only I ask you for a quick answer. I wish you a merry holiday of Easter time. O dear God, why cannot I be with my auntie and divide the egg together with parents and brothers and sisters! When I think about all this, I would not be sorry if I had to die right now.

(g) Many years after his arrival in the United States, an immigrant remembered his early days here.

I remember in those days how we used all our resources to keep our parents away from school—particularly our mothers, because they did not speak English and still dressed in the European way, always with a shawl. We didn't want these embarrassing "differences" paraded before our teachers.

At first I was hesitant about taking part in athletics or trying to make one of the school teams. It seemed a strange way to spend one's time and energies—at play! Yet, greater than all else was the desire to excel in the accepted way, to show that you were just as good as the next fellow no matter what the difference socially. Growing up in the rough-and-tumble life of East Harlem had given me certain physical advantages. The test came during a schoolwide chinning contest. I was small but wiry. My arms were strong from pulling dumbwaiter ropes. I placed second in the entire school. This spurred me on to make one of the school teams so that I could proudly display the school emblem, a huge maroon "M" on a white sweater.

The excitement about the chinning contest was more than I could keep to myself. I had to tell the family about it, and it happened to be one of those rare nights when my father was home for supper. To the delights of my younger brothers, I explained the mechanics of chinning. My mother and father listened with interest for a few minutes. They looked at each other. The expression on my father's face changed from mild bewilderment to utter bafflement as I continued. I realized that I had made a tactical blunder but there was nothing I could do about it. Finally I blurted out, "I was second! Second best in the whole school! That's something!"

My father threw down his napkin and pushed away from the table. He paced across the room gripping the back of his head. "There is hardly enough to eat in the house. We kill ourselves. We work so that he can have some future—and he spends his time at school playing!"

Which of the problems you've identified do you think are usually present when unlike cultures come in contact?

Entering America

Anyone who could obtain passage on a boat could come to America, but not all who came were allowed to stay. When immigrants arrived, they were tested for their physical and mental health. They also were asked about their past lives and future plans.

Most immigrants entered the United States through the port of New York City. As the tide of immigrants grew, special facilities were built to handle all of the checking the government required. In 1855 a depot was set up at Castle Garden in lower Manhattan. Later, the entry station was moved to Ellis Island in New York harbor.

Millions of newcomers were questioned and inspected by government officials. Most immigrants were admitted. In 1900, for example, more than 400,000 immigrants came to the United States. Only about 4,000 were **excluded,** or not allowed to enter.

For the newcomers, Ellis Island was often a frightening and difficult experience. Without friends, with little money, and with no understanding of English, many immigrants feared their right to enter the "Promised Land" would be questioned.

The photographs on page 425 were taken at Ellis Island.
❶ Immigrants waiting for inspection
❷ The "pens"
❸ Doctors checking for eye infections
❹ Leaving Ellis Island

424

How Did Immigrants Deal with Problems?

By 1900 state commissions and charities had begun to aid immigrants in some matters. But in general there was little organized effort to help newcomers settle in the United States. Most had to solve the problems of daily life by themselves. The following material provides information about some of the ways immigrants dealt with the problems they faced.

As you study the data, identify actions you think helped immigrants solve some of their problems.

a This is a diagram of a New York City neighborhood in the early 1900's.

Why do you think the people in the neighborhood grouped themselves in that way?

a

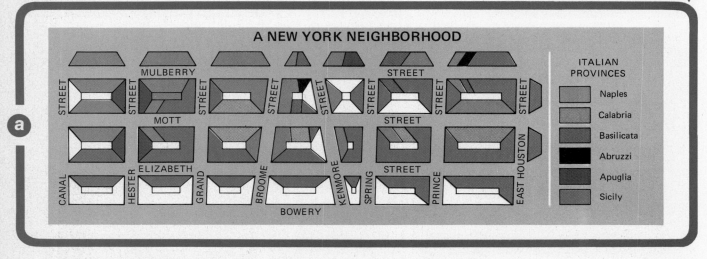

A NEW YORK NEIGHBORHOOD

ITALIAN PROVINCES
- Naples
- Calabria
- Basilicata
- Abruzzi
- Apuglia
- Sicily

b In Chinese neighborhoods, special Chinese foods were sold.

b

426

c Rose Cohen, a member of a Jewish immigrant family, described her father's actions.

At that time most Jewish men in Europe wore beards. Why do you think Rose's father cut his beard?

c

I found that father was already at home. As I came into the room I saw him resting against the wall, clipping his beard. I was so surprised and shocked to see him actually do this thing that I could neither speak nor move for some minutes. And I knew that he, too, felt embarrassed. After the first glance I kept my eyes steadily on the floor in front of me, and began to talk to him quietly, but with great earnestness: "You had been so religious in the old country, father," I said, "more religious than anyone else in our whole neighborhood. And now you are cutting your beard. Grandmother would never have believed it. How she would weep!" The snipping of the scissors still went on. But I knew by the sound that now he was only making a pretense at cutting. At last he laid it down and said in a tone that was bitter yet quiet: "They do not like Jews on Cherry Street."

*A **settlement house** is a community or neighborhood center which offers social and educational activities. How would schools and settlement houses change immigrants? Could this make their lives easier or more difficult?*

d These photographs show immigrant children in school and at a settlement house.

d

e This list shows the 74 organizations connected with one Polish parish of the Roman Catholic Church.

Zuaves of St. Stanislaw Kostka; Society of the Virgins of the Holy Rosary; Brotherhood of the Young Men of St. Joseph; Citizens' Club of Thaddeus Kosciuszko; Theater and Dramatic Club; the Parochial School; the Parish Committee; the Association of Altar Boys; the Marshals of the Upper Church; the Marshals of the Lower Church; the Arch-sorority of the Immaculate Heart of Mary (two groups); the Women of the Holy Rosary (four groups); the Arch-brotherhood of the Saints; the Third Order of St. Francis; the Choirs of the Upper Church; the Choirs of the Lower Church; the Club of Ladies of Queen Labrowska; the Society of the Alumni of the Parish School; the Musical and Literary Society of Leo XIII; the Needlework Club of St. Rose of Lima; the Polish Roman Catholic Union (central office), plus 20 additional affiliates of the Roman Catholic Union; the Polish Alma Mater (central office), plus six additional affiliates of the Alma Mater; the Court of Pulaski (No. 482 of the Union of Catholic Foresters), plus nine additional units of the Catholic Foresters; the Society of the Guardianship of St. Joseph (Group 115 of the Polish Association in America), plus six additional units of the Polish Association; the Society of Young Men of St. Kazimierz (Independent Mutual Help Association); the Society of Ladies of Queen Jadwiga (Mutual Help Association); the Loan and Savings Association of St. Joseph No. 3; the Building Loan and Savings Association of Pulaski; the Building Loan and Savings Association of St. Francis; the Press Committee; the College of St. Stanislaw Kostka; the Novice's Convent of the Resurrectionists; the Convent of the Sisters of St. Francis; the Chicago *Daily News* (Polish).

Why do you think the people of this church had so many organizations?

f This scene is taken from a novel about Norwegian immigrants.

Tonseten straightened up where he sat on the chest, demanding to know what names Hans Olsa and Per Hansa intended to adopt when they took out the title deeds to their land.

"Names?"

"Yes, names! That point would have to be settled clearly beforehand," Tonseten explained. "When the deeds were taken out, their names would then be written into the law of the land, and thereafter would be as unchangeable as the Constitution itself!"

But they all had been baptized! How about Tonseten himself? asked Per Hansa, irritably. He couldn't understand why the name Peder Hansen would not be good enough even for the United States Constitution.

This matter of names brought on a long discussion. Per Hansa found little to say, but his face had a look of quiet excitement. He must speak to his wife about this, alone and right away! He sat there trying the name over in his mind, first on her, then on himself, finally on each of the children. As he ran them over, the radiant light in his face grew stronger. Mrs. Holm, that sounded well; Peder Holm, that has a fine ring! . . .Ole Haldor Holm! . . . Hans Kristian Holm! . . .Peder Holm—no, Peder *Victorious* Holm! . . . *Peder Victorious Holm!* He rolled the name on his tongue, biting it off in three distinct parts, as if to enjoy the sound; then he got up suddenly, grasped the waistband of his trousers, and gave them a hitch.

"That name is both pretty and practical. What do you say, boys—shall we adopt the plan?"

g A young man described his experiences as a worker.

We went one day to Newark and got work on the street. We paid a man five dollars each for getting us the work and we were with that boss for six months. He was Irish, but a good man and he gave us our money every Saturday night. When the work was done we each had nearly 200 dollars saved. Plenty of the men spoke English and they taught us, and we taught them to read and write.

We got up at half-past five o'clock every morning, and had a breakfast of bread and cheese, onions, garlic, and red herrings. We went to work at seven o'clock and in the middle of the day we had soup and bread in a place where we got it for two cents a plate. In the evenings we had a good dinner with meat of some kind and potatoes. We got from the butcher the meat that other people would not buy because they said it was old, but they don't know what is good.

When the Newark boss told us that there was no more work, Francesco and I talked about what we would do and we went back to Brooklyn to a saloon near Hamilton Ferry where we got a job cleaning it out and slept in a little room upstairs. There was a bootblack named Michael on the corner and when I had time I helped him and learned the business. Francesco cooked the lunch in the saloon and he, too, worked for the bootblack and we were soon able to make the best polish.

Then we thought we would go into business and we got a basement on Hamilton avenue, near the Ferry, and put four chairs in it. We paid 75 dollars for the chairs and all the other things. Outside we had a big sign that said:

THE BEST SHINE FOR TEN CENTS

Men that did not want to pay ten cents could get a good shine for five cents, but it was not an oil shine. We had two boys helping us and paid each of them 50 cents a day. The rent of the place was 20 dollars a month, so the expenses were very great, but we made money from the beginning. We slept in the basement, but got our meals in the saloon till we could put a stove in our place, and then Francesco cooked for us all. That would not do, though, because some of our customers said that they did not like to smell garlic and onions and red herrings. I thought that was strange, but we had to do what the customers said.

We had said that when we saved 1,000 dollars each we would go back to Italy and buy a farm, but now that the time is coming we are so busy and making so much more money that we think we will stay. We have opened another parlor near South Ferry.

We have joined a club and have much pleasure in the evenings. We meet many people and are learning new things all the time We were very ignorant when we came here, but now we have learned much.

On Sundays we get a horse and carriage from the grocer and go down to Coney Island. We go to the theaters often, and other evenings we go to the houses of our friends and play cards.

I am now 19 years of age and have 700 dollars saved. Francesco is 21 and has about 900 dollars. We shall open some more parlors soon. I know an Italian who was a bootblack ten years ago and now bosses bootblacks all over the city. He has so much money that if it was turned into gold it would weigh more than himself.

Francesco and I have a room to ourselves and some people call us "swells." Francesco bought a gold watch with a gold chain as thick as his thumb. He is a very handsome fellow and I think he likes a young lady that he met at a picnic out at Ridgewood.

I often think of Ciguciano and Teresa. He is a good man, one in a thousand, and she was very beautiful. Maybe I shall write to them about coming to this country.

What opportunities did this young man take advantage of? What changes did he make? For what reasons?

Which of these responses do you think are likely to be used whenever unlike cultures interact?

h Immigrants worked at many kinds of jobs.
  1 Entire families worked at home.
  2 Some women worked as domestic servants.
  3 In "sweatshops" men and women made clothes.
  4 Many men worked building railroads.

Putting the Pieces Together

America was created by immigrants. It would seem logical then that American culture would be a mixture of all the different cultures of the immigrants. It would be part English, part Spanish, part German, Italian, Hungarian, West African, Swedish. This kind of mixture is sometimes called a "melting pot."

It's logical that America could be a melting pot, but is it true? Think about that idea as you answer these questions:

1. Do you believe that immigrants of the 1800s had a strong effect on *important* American ideas and ways of acting? Why or why not? Base your answer on your own knowledge of present-day America.

2. Study this list of American ways of acting. Do you believe immigrants should be expected to accept or follow any of these? If so, which ones? Why?
   a. Compulsory education for children
   b. Speaking English
   c. Allowing young people to select their own marriage partners
   d. Serving on juries
   e. Wearing American-style clothes while working
   f. Serving in American military forces
   g. Becoming a citizen
   h. Voting
   i. Allowing young people to make most of their own decisions

Now, use your knowledge of cultural interaction between immigrants and Americans to add to your chart on minority and majority actions and feelings.

International Interaction

The actions of people usually reflect the ideas that motivate them. One of the ideas that many Americans shared during the period you've been studying was a belief that America was the best of all countries and that white Anglo-Saxons were superior people. Because of this belief, many immigrants, Indians, and black Americans were treated as "second-class" people.

This same belief in national racial superiority also affected the interaction of Americans with nations and peoples outside the United

States. Americans believed their superiority gave them certain rights and duties when dealing with non-Americans.

Several other ideas also motivated Americans during this era:

—A desire to help those seeking justice or needing "civilization" in other countries

—A desire for military power, including a strong navy and control of ports and bases in many parts of the world

—A desire to limit the power of European countries, especially in Latin America

—A desire for new markets for the products of American industry, and new places suitable for investment of wealth

Partly as a result of these ideas, the United States became involved in international activity. One result was a short war with Spain, fought in Cuba and the Philippine Islands in 1898. In the treaty ending the war, Cuba became independent of Spanish rule, Puerto Rico and Guam became American territories, and the United States gained control of the Philippine Islands. Twenty million dollars was paid to Spain for that country's interests in the Philippines.

During this same period, the Republic of Hawaii was annexed as United States territory. (Alaska had been added in 1867.) The United States also gained control of land in Central America where the Panama Canal was to be built.

American attitudes of the time are reflected in a speech by President McKinley, telling of his decision to continue control of the Philippines.

"I walked the floor of the White House night after night until midnight; and I am not ashamed to tell you, gentlemen, that I went down on my knees and prayed to almighty God for light and guidance more than one night. And one night late it came to me this way (1) that we could not give them [the Phillipines] back to Spain—that would be cowardly and dishonorable; (2) that we could not turn them over to France or Germany, our commercial rivals in the Orient— that would be bad business; (3) that we could not leave them to themselves—they were unfit for self-government and they would soon have anarchy and misrule; and (4) that there was nothing left for us to do but to take them all, and to educate the Filipinos, and uplift and civilize and Christianize them."

BRANCHING OUT

Investigate a recent group of immigrants to the United States—people from Hungary, Mexico, Cuba, or Puerto Rico, for example. Describe why and when they came, where they settled, and how they were treated. Compare their problems and responses to those of earlier groups.

Application

The movement of people across national boundaries to establish new homes has greatly declined. Immigrants still come to the United States, but compared to the total population, the number is not large. Quotas set by Congress determine how many immigrants will be admitted each year.

Fortunately, the decrease in immigration has not ended cultural interaction within the United States. This is fortunate because cultural diversity is very important. Each of us, by looking at ourselves through the eyes of those in other cultures, can discover much about ourselves. Cultural variety also makes it possible for us to learn about (and perhaps borrow) ideas, values, and patterns of action different from, and often better than, our own. This is essential, because no one culture has all the "right" answers.

Your study of cultural interaction should help you better understand the relationships of cultural groups within the United States, and the contributions these groups make to life in America.

For a long time, America was called a "melting pot". This meant that immigrants who came here were expected to lose or give up the varied patterns of their native lands and adopt the ways of acting and thinking they found here in America. They were to "melt together."

In recent years however, a great many Americans have begun to remember and take pride in their native cultures. They are trying to keep alive some of the traditions, values, and customs of their ancestors.

Chicanos are one of the groups in which members are trying to preserve their heritage. Chicanos are Americans of Mexican origin—either descendents of those who lived here when the United States took over the Southwest, or people who have migrated since then. Between five and six million Chicanos now live in the United States, mostly in California and the Southwest.

● The data below points up several characteristics of Chicano culture today.

A Value

Many Chicanos place a very high value on close family relationships. Middle-class Americans will often leave family and friends and move great distances in order to make more money or get a promotion. Strong family ties often make Chicanos less likely to make this kind of choice.

Place Names

Foods

ENTREMESES APPETIZERS

Empanada Chilena Baked turnover filled with beef, onions, olive and spices .80
Quesadilla Mexicana Melted cheese between two flour tortillas .65
Tostada 1 crisp corn tortilla topped with refried beans, rice, shredded cheese and lettuce 1.00
Ceviche a la Peruana White fish marinated in lemon juice with onions 1.00
Tortilla chips with pebre sauce .25

POSTRES – DESSERTS

Flan Custard .75
Pan Dulce Mexican pastry .25
Dulce de Membrillo Quince dessert with cheese slice .75

A Language

More Americans speak Spanish than any other language except English.

A Style of Architecture

A Custom

A Belief

Many Chicanos believe that "life is for living"—that each day should be enjoyed as it comes. Most other Americans, they believe, live too much for the future, spend too much time thinking about how happy they are going to be tomorrow. ("Tomorrow, after I graduate, I will be happy." "Tomorrow, when I get a new car, I will be happy.")

Using the categories in the data above, identify important characteristics of the minority culture most familiar to you.

Most minorities once tried hard to adopt middle-class American values and ways of life. What explanations can you think of for recent attempts by some minorities to hold on to some of their traditional customs and values? Do you think these efforts are likely to increase or decrease?

BIBLIOGRAPHY

Kroeber, Theodora. *Ishi: Last of His Tribe.* Berkeley, Calif.: Parnassus Press, 1964. The Yaha Indians of northern California were driven from their homes at the time of the Gold Rush. Forced into hiding, they slowly died off. The last survivor was Ishi, discovered in 1911. This book recreates Ishi's thoughts and feelings about his former life and his adjustments to the white man's world.

Barnouw, Victor. *Dream of the Blue Heron.* N.Y.: Delacorte, 1966. Fiction. A young Chippewa Indian boy, Wabus or Wallace White Sky, lived in Wisconsin at the turn of the century. He is torn between the traditions of his grandparents and the ways of the modern world.

Gridley, Marion E. *American Indian Tribes.* N.Y.: Dodd, Mead, 1974. A handy, compact reference book of the major tribes of the United States and Canada. Includes information about tribal leaders and about what happened to the tribes in the 20th century.

Perez, Norah A. *The Passage.* Philadelphia: Lippincott, 1975. Fiction. A story of some victims of the 1847 Irish famine and of the hardships they endured in their voyage to the New World. The heroine is Cathleen O'Faoláin, a high spirited girl of 14.

Eiseman, Alberta. *From Many Lands.* N.Y.: Atheneum, 1970. A history of the waves of immigrants who came to this country from Europe and the Orient. Well organized according to different nationality groups.

UNIT **7**

War, Depression, Prosperity

System Change

How do social systems change?

Introduction

Sometime or other, you may have lined dominoes up in a row, knocked the first one against the second, and then watched the whole row fall down.

Human ways of acting can be like dominoes. If one way of acting changes, it can cause changes in other ways of acting. These in turn can create still other new kinds of behavior.

In a very important way, however, human action is different from the domino chain reaction. Each domino directly affects just one other domino. But in human action, one event can trigger many different changes. For example, when a new shopping center is built, it will usually make important changes in local property values, jobs, and shopping habits. Traffic flow, police and fire protection needs, and taxes may also be affected. In this unit you'll explore how changes such as these occur in social systems.

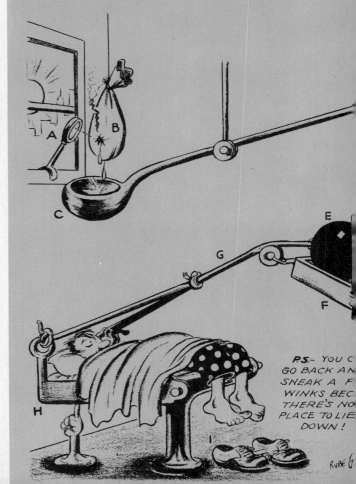

a Changes in people's lives often lead to situations they never expected. A high school student tells about some changes in her life in the account below.

a First, my uncle gave me this old car. But before I could drive it, I had to buy insurance and get the license. I didn't have enough money, so I got a job working in a restaurant. Because of my job, I had to drop out of drama club. After I got the car fixed up, I used it to have fun when I wasn't working or in school.

The job and the car took up a lot of time, and now my grades have gone down. My parents say I have to give up either my car or the job. If I give up the job, I can't afford to buy gas and oil for the car. Problems, problems.

b One way to study changes which are related to each other is to draw a diagram. The changes described in the account above are shown in the following "change diagram." Each arrow in the diagram means "helped cause."

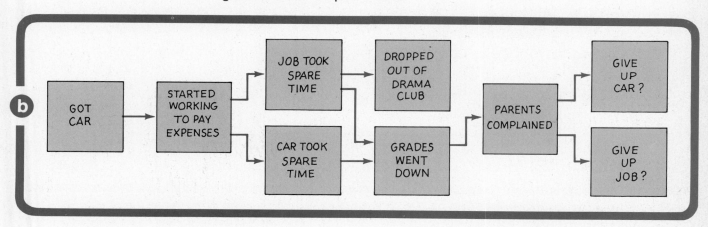

c Changes are especially important when they affect groups of people. A member of a basketball team tells about changes that affected his team.

c We were pretty discouraged when our basketball coach, Mr. Miller, moved away in the middle of the season. We liked Coach Miller and worked hard for him. We had a fairly good team, but our new coach, Mr. Pareto, wanted to change our style of playing.

He had us practicing what he called a "rotating offense." It was really hard to learn.

A couple of players were so unhappy with the coaching change that they quit the team. I guess most of us felt like quitting, especially after we lost the next three games in a row.

In the fourth game, against Central, we started out playing badly. We were ten points behind near the end of the first quarter. All of sudden we started moving around differently. Nobody had said anything, but we had automatically started to use the new "rotating offense." It was working. We were able to move inside Central's defense and score.

Our whole team spirit changed. We pulled ahead and won. We weren't discouraged anymore, and we felt much better about Coach Pareto. He really is an expert. The guys that quit have come back. We have a strong team now.

d The changes just described are shown in the following change diagram.

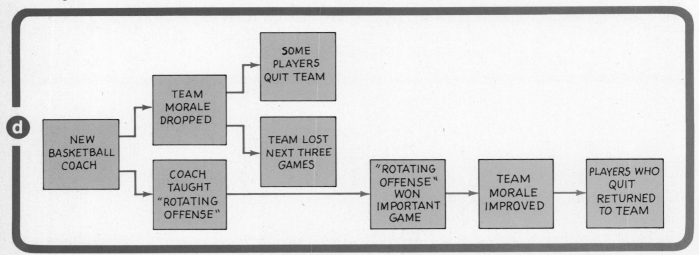

Imagine that one adult in your family or in another family you know had to be in the hospital for several days. What changes would result from this situation? Show your answers in a change diagram like those on page 441 and above.

It may be easier to first make a list of all the changes you can think of. Then arrange these changes in a diagram.

Because the actions of members are related, groups and organizations can be thought of as **social systems.** Families are social systems, as are sports teams. Corporations, schools, work teams, military units, religious groups, and clubs are other examples of social systems.

School buildings are expensive. A high school building, for example, may cost millions of dollars. It may also be located in an area where the demand for property is great and where land values are high.

Taxpayers know this. So when someone suggests a way for school buildings to be operated year-round, taxpayers are interested. Almost everyone agrees that it is bad business to invest millions of dollars in a building and keep it open for only part of the year.

A school is a complex system. This means it is made up of many interacting parts. For example, teachers, students, parents, and taxpayers are all involved in a school system. So are school guards and service workers. The building, classrooms, and equipment in them are also part of the system—as are courses and after-school activities.

ⓐ Since a school system is complex, changing one part of it may affect many other parts. The system change diagram below shows some benefits that could result from keeping a school open during the entire year.

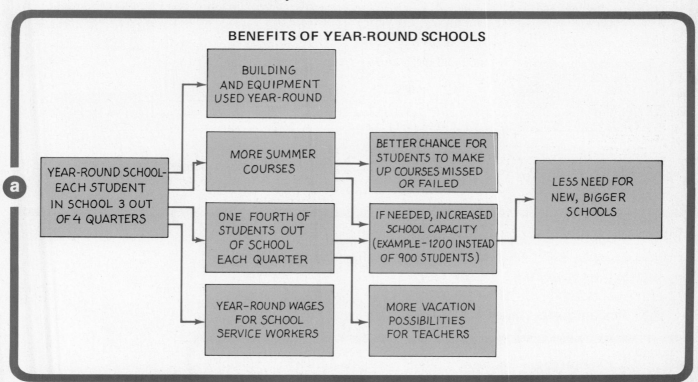

BENEFITS OF YEAR-ROUND SCHOOLS

ⓐ YEAR-ROUND SCHOOL— EACH STUDENT IN SCHOOL 3 OUT OF 4 QUARTERS

- BUILDING AND EQUIPMENT USED YEAR-ROUND
- MORE SUMMER COURSES → BETTER CHANCE FOR STUDENTS TO MAKE UP COURSES MISSED OR FAILED
- ONE FOURTH OF STUDENTS OUT OF SCHOOL EACH QUARTER → IF NEEDED, INCREASED SCHOOL CAPACITY (EXAMPLE-1200 INSTEAD OF 900 STUDENTS) → LESS NEED FOR NEW, BIGGER SCHOOLS
- YEAR-ROUND WAGES FOR SCHOOL SERVICE WORKERS → MORE VACATION POSSIBILITIES FOR TEACHERS

Considering the benefits, it isn't surprising that many cities and towns have thought about having year-round schools. What may be surprising is that many school systems have put year-round programs into effect, only to discontinue them after a one- or two-year trial.

Why has an idea that seems to make sense not caught on? Year-round schools have sometimes been unsuccessful because they created more problems than they solved. Very often new problems did not show up until the experiment was actually tried.

b The system change diagram below shows some of the problems that can occur when a school changes to year-round operations.

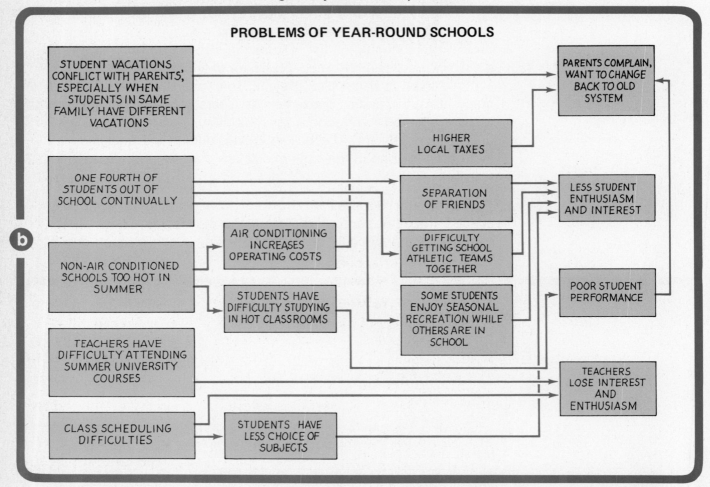

PROBLEMS OF YEAR-ROUND SCHOOLS

Three other possible changes in a school's operation are described in the following data pieces. Read them over, and then do the activity described on page 446.

c This article was taken from a newspaper.

A new program for local schools was presented in a school board meeting Tuesday night. School Board Chairwoman Lucille Wong said the idea had been under consideration for two years.

The superintendent of schools pointed out that new programs and materials were constantly being developed in science, mathematics, social studies, language arts, and other fields. "All these new teaching materials are available," the superintendent said, "but our teachers don't have time to learn how to use them. I'm sure," he said, "that under the new plan our students will be learning more in four-and-a-half days of school than they are now learning in five. The improvement in teaching will more than make up for the shorter school week."

The new program will go into effect when school opens in September. Students will attend classes four complete days per week. On Fridays, school will be dismissed at 12:00 noon. No lunch will be served. In the afternoon, teachers will attend classes conducted by curriculum specialists from the state university.

d The following was taken from a speech to a P.T.A.

d
Some experts have suggested that the quality of education could be improved if school work were organized so that students could move at their own rate. They point out that the "right" speed for learning differs from person to person. They say that school work should be organized to fit students rather than the other way around. Students would accomplish more, and both fast and slow students would be less likely to be bored or discouraged.

With this system, of course, the usual grading system would be abolished. Student reports would probably read, "Course one-third completed," or "Course 80% completed." As soon as students had completed a course, they would move on to a new one.

e Here is an excerpt from an article in a teacher's magazine.

e
The schoolroom is not the best place for many kinds of learning. If you want to study manufacturing, the best place is in a manufacturing plant. If you want to study pollution or life science, you can learn some things outdoors that you can't learn in a classroom. Studying history? How about investigating *local* history by finding signs of the past in your community? Museums, zoos, exhibits, farms, stores, and college campuses all provide chances for learning outside the classroom.

If students spent part of their total course time in each subject studying it "live" outside the classroom, they would learn more, and what they learned would be more realistic. School work would be much more fun. In most classes, at least one fifth of the time should be spent outside the classroom.

Choose one of the changes just described. Identify what might happen if the change were made in your school. Follow the steps below.

1. List all the groups that might be affected by the change. Include groups such as parents, lunchroom workers, store owners near school, bus drivers, the Board of Education, etc. Describe the benefits and problems each group would face as a result of the change.

2. If possible, ask representatives from these groups to help you with your analysis.

3. Show the results of your investigation in a system change diagram. You may wish to prepare two separate diagrams—one for benefits and the other for problems. Keep your diagram(s) for use in the next activity.

Actions That Reinforce Each Other

"What are you worrying about?"
"I'm worried because I'm gaining so much weight."
"Why are you gaining so much weight?"
"Because I eat too much."
"Why do you eat too much?"
"I enjoy eating. Eating helps me forget my worries."
"What are you worrying about?"

As this conversation shows, people's actions very often reinforce each other. (To **reinforce** is to make stronger.) One act leads to another, which in turn leads to still other action changes. In time, the chain of actions may lead to a repeating and reinforcing of the very first action in a kind of "circle of change."

a Below are diagrams of two kinds of actions that reinforce each other.

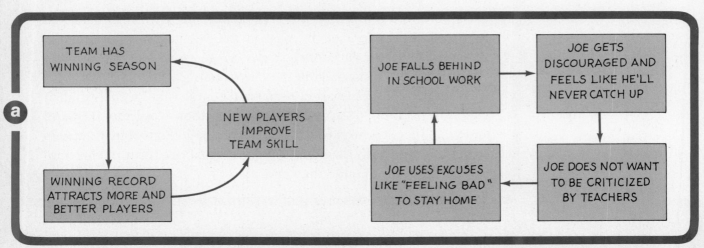

ⓑ Sometimes as few as two actions can reinforce one another. In the system change diagram on page 444, "Poor student performance" and "Teachers lose interest and enthusiasm" are examples of this.

For each list below, make a diagram that shows how the actions can reinforce each other.

ⓑ

People rush to buy tickets to a game.
A rumor (true or false) spreads about a shortage of tickets.
There is an increasing shortage of tickets.
People worry about not having tickets to attend the game.

Students do good work in school.
Teachers maintain high standards.
The school attracts and keeps good teachers.
The school has a good reputation in the community.

Review the diagram you made of how your school could be affected by system changes. Add arrows if you find places where changes reinforce each other. Use a different color for these arrows. (Remember that two actions can reinforce one another, as can a series of actions.)

BRANCHING OUT

Almost every school group or club goes through changes from time to time. Select a group, preferably one to which you belong. Diagram the changes that have taken place since the school year began. Your diagram may include such things as effects of new members, changes in leaders, and results of activities.

STOP & SUMMARIZE

What would happen in your home and neighborhood if water and electricity were not available for a week because of storm damage? Describe some changes that might result and diagram them.

Perspective

As you learned in Unit 5, the years 1865 to 1920 were a time of great change in the United States. Village shoemakers were replaced by city shoe factories. Machinery took over the work of men and horses. Telephone and telegraph lines brought people in the nation in closer contact with one another. Americans were learning to fly airplanes, with the help of wood, wire, and fabric wings.

All these changes led to greater complexity in our national life. People came to depend more and more on the jobs and services of others. A strike of coal miners, in Pennsylvania, for example, could close schools and factories all over the country for lack of heat. A war anywhere in the world could affect business in America. The lives of people everywhere began to be more and more closely joined. In *Perspective* you'll study the effects of this complexity on life in America since the early 1900s.

Part 1   Growing National Complexity

How were people affected by economic and social change after World War I?

Part 2   Depression

What changes occurred in the nation's economic system during the 1930s?

Part 3   World War II

What were some important effects of World War II on the United States?

Part 4   Trends

What trends are affecting American ideas and ways of acting? What trends may continue in the future? How will they affect American ideas and ways of acting?

448

Part 1

Growing National Complexity

In 1914 a war broke out in Europe. There was nothing new about this since there had been many wars in Europe before. When the fighting began, many Americans were convinced that they could ignore the war, because it did not affect the United States.

These people were wrong. Fifty years before, Americans might have been able to ignore the war. But industry and technology had changed all that. New weapons—the submarine, the tank, better guns—soon spread the war until it affected people throughout the world.

Complex systems now tied the lives of people everywhere to each other. Change in one part of the world soon affected people thousands of miles away. Americans were forced to learn this during the period you will study in Part 1.

In this part, you will investigate this question:

How were people affected by economic and social change after World War I?

World War I and System Change

The war that began in Europe soon involved so many nations that it was called "The World War." The United States did not become involved in the fighting until 1917. The effects of the war were felt by most Americans long before that, however. This country began supplying England and France with food and arms in 1915. Producing and shipping these goods across the Atlantic became a major task.

When American troops joined the fighting in 1917, the task became much greater. Men had to be inducted, organized, and transported to areas of conflict. Food, tanks, guns, ammunition, uniforms, fuel, trucks, and hundreds of other items had to be manufactured and shipped overseas.

Factories, especially in the northern cities, expanded. Farm production increased. New rail and ocean transport equipment was built. To do all these jobs, more and more workers were needed.

The materials which follow describe how life in America was affected by World War I. After you complete the reading, describe in your own words (or in a diagram) how World War I helped bring about these changes.

a This account of Bridgeport, Connecticut was written in 1916. It shows how industrial cities were affected by World War I even before America entered the fighting.

a
Until last year Bridgeport was a comfortable manufacturing town of about 115,000 people. Its peacetime industries were various. The boom struck Bridgeport early in 1915. War orders and a stream of European money flowed in. Existing factories were rapidly adapted and new ones were run up. One great concern began to turn out heavy motor wagons; another was making submarines. The population grew by some 50,000 in less than 12 months. Men, especially young men, flocked from all the places round into Bridgeport as a city of unlimited opportunity. In the course of a few months a typical New England town became one of the busiest hives of war industry in America. The greatest single factor in this development has been the Remington Arms Company, which during the summer of last year laid the foundations of an immense factory on the edge of the town. In October it had accommodation for 2,000 workpeople; by the beginning of this year about 15,000 were employed.

The first assumption of the Remington Arms Company appears to have been that, since it was giving Bridgeport the benefit of a fresh industry, the responsibility for housing and ordering the new population rested altogether with the city authorities. The consequences are not difficult to imagine. The problem of house-room became unmanageable. Rents of houses and rooms leapt up. Land values were inflated. The owners and agents of real estate gathered a glorious harvest. It was estimated that at the end of 1914, the number of empty houses in Bridgeport and its suburbs was not far short of 2,000. A few months later there was not a house of any kind vacant nor a room to be obtained. . . . The economic conditions, especially the sharp competition for workmen between the firms and the abundance of money, made a soil favorable to labor disputes. The record of Bridgeport in this regard is quite extraordinary. During a period of two and a half months last summer, fifty-five strikes occurred. They resulted in notable gains to the workers, who were able to secure improved rates of wages and a standard working day. Bridgeport is now an eight-hour town.

In what ways was Bridgeport affected by the industrial boom?

b The wheat farmers of the Middle West found their autonomy affected by World War I, as this 1918 account describes.

b

Six farmers stood near their wheat wagons at a Middle West cooperative elevator waiting to "weigh in" their loads of grain. The scales were out of order and they gathered in a little group discussing the wheat situation, the subject uppermost in their minds. Each wagon held 50 bushels or more—a clean 100 dollars a load at the price paid at that station.

"It's not enough, compared with other things," declared Jim Haywood. Like his neighbors, he was fairly successful, take it one year with another, and a hard worker. "The government took money out of my pocket and hurt nobody else when it fixed the price of wheat, and I can't see that it was right."

"But two dollars a bushel is a good figure," interrupted Sandy McRae, noted for his thriftiness. "I hauled wheat here in the summer of 1914 for 64 cents a bushel. Two dollars is good money."

"Maybe it is," continued Jim "but that don't answer it. You've got money in the bank. Suppose you were like me. Suppose you were in debt 3,000 dollars on a 160-acre farm, had only a fair amount of livestock, barely enough implements, and for two years had only broke even because of crop failure. You raised 100 acres of wheat last season, averaging 18 bushels to the acre and of good grade. Figuring up, it had cost you 300 dollars for the seed, 4 dollars a day for harvest hands, 10 cents a bushel for threshing, and was worth at the elevator $2.75 a bushel—it might even go to 3 dollars a little later. Deducting your expense, you could figure for your labor and use of the land a return of 4,000 dollars—and it would look mighty good to you. Then one morning came news that the government had fixed the price of wheat at 2 dollars a bushel at your market, wiping out 1,350 dollars of your income. How would you feel about it?"

That was what happened to the wheat farmer in the autumn of 1917, and for nine months he has tried to reconcile his financial disappointment with his patriotism.

Were it merely a matter of that one crop, the agitation would already have passed into history, for a new harvest is here. But from that same farmer must come a large part of the foodstuffs for the Allies. Upon him depends the number of wheatless days we shall have in the winter of 1919-20. Never before has the American farmer been held responsible for the season's return. He has sown little or much as conditions favored. Now it is vitally important whether or not he decides to sow an increased acreage.

"Well, what are you going to do about sowing next fall?" put in Miles Minter, whose farm joined Sandy's on the east. "Going to put in more or less?"

"Haven't decided yet," was the reply, "but I suppose I'll do about the same as usual. I'm not kicking on the government and am willing to help the war—but I don't think the wheat farmer should be the only one regulated. There's plenty of others need it."

"Last fall I wanted to be patriotic," added Squire Taylor, who had been quietly listening, "and besides the price looked good—it was $2.80 at one time—and we were guaranteed 2 dollars; so I put in an extra 80 acres. Half of it winter-killed. Don't think I will sow quite so much this year—my boy has gone to the army and it's some job to get a hired man these times. Besides, there's other crops that pay better. Wheat at 2 dollars a bushel here isn't any bonanza, but I'll do all I can, I'll tell you that."

"So will I," agreed Haywood, "but you can't make me believe that it's fair to pick out the wheat farmer and regulate his crop—without helping him to get his implements on a basis of his wheat price—and not touch the cotton grower. Treat us all alike. Why should the wheat raiser be the goat?" The others nodded approvingly. Jim had summarized the attitude of the average producer of the Middle West.

Bonanza refers to any source of wealth or profits.

What did government expect from farmers during World War I? How did this affect the price of wheat? Why do you think the government fixed the price of wheat?

What reasons do you think were behind the mass movement of black people to Northern cities?

c Between 1910 and 1920, hundreds of thousands of black people living in the South moved to the North. Most settled in cities. The table below shows how major urban centers were affected by this mass migration.

c

BLACK POPULATION IN URBAN CENTERS 1910-1920

Region	Cities	1910	1920	Increase	Percentage Increase
NORTH	New York	91,709	152,467	60,758	66.5
	Philadelphia	84,459	134,229	49,770	58.9
	Chicago	44,103	109,458	65,355	148.22
	Detroit	5,471	40,838	35,097	611.3
	Cleveland	8,448	34,451	26,003	307.8
BORDER	Washington, D.C.	94,446	109,966	15,520	16.4
	Baltimore	84,749	108,322	25,573	27.8
	St. Louis	43,960	69,854	25,894	58.9
SOUTH	New Orleans	89,262	100,930	11,668	13.1
	Birmingham	52,305	70,230	17,925	34.3
	Atlanta	51,902	62,796	10,894	21.0
	Memphis	52,441	61,381	8,740	16.7
	Norfolk	25,039	43,392	18,353	73.5
	Nashville	36,523	35,633	−890	−2.4
	Houston	23,929	33,960	10,031	41.9

World War I: An Overview

The rapid industrial growth that took place in the United States in the second half of the 1800s also took place in England, France, Germany, and other European countries. Large businesses were formed, factories were built, and railroads were extended. As manufacturing grew, the industrial nations competed for lands which provided new markets and sources of raw materials. Bad feelings grew among the nations of Europe.

During these same years, the European nations had other kinds of problems. Some wanted to take back lands which they said belonged to them but were now ruled by other countries. In several countries certain groups of people wanted freedom from the government which ruled them. Foreign relations were often carried on in secret, which made for even more bad feelings.

To strengthen themselves against possible attack, some European countries signed military agreements with one another. Through these agreements, or **alliances,** the nations of Europe promised to come to the military aid of one another in case of attack by enemies. They also increased the sizes of their armies and navies as further protection.

Several nations believed they were strong enough to gain from going to war. The assassination of Archduke Francis Ferdinand of Austria-Hungary in June 1914 provided an excuse. One month after the murder, Austria-Hungary declared war on Serbia, the assassin's native country.

In return, Russia, who had promised to support Serbia in case of attack, declared war on Austria-Hungary. Because of the alliance agreements, soon nearly all the major nations of Europe were involved in war—World War I. Austria, Germany, and other countries who fought on their side were called the Central Powers, because of their position in Europe. Russia, France, Great Britain, Belgium, Serbia, and others who fought on their side were called the Allies. (See the map below.)

At the start of World War I, the Central Powers had a number of advantages over the Allies. Germany had the largest and best-

Serbia no longer exists as a separate country. It is now a part of Yugoslavia.

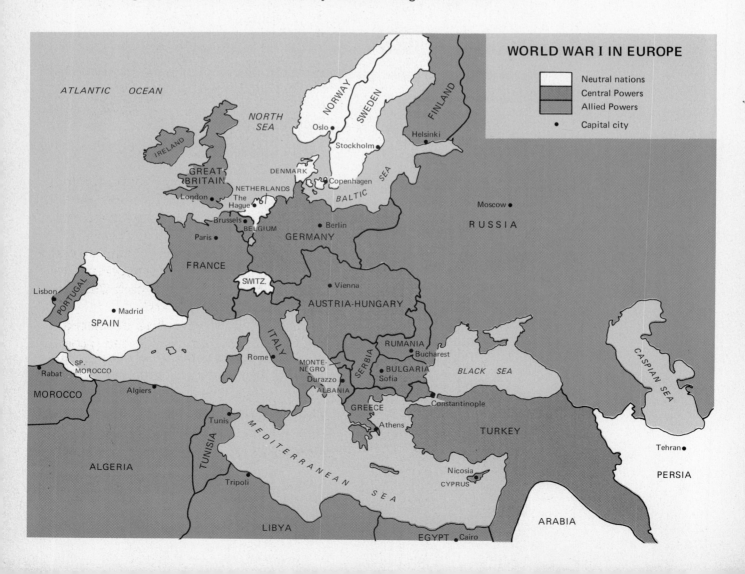

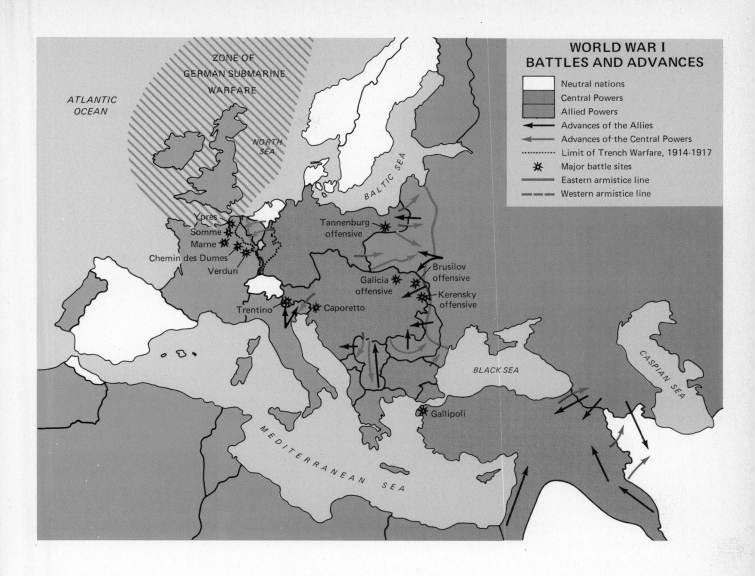

WORLD WAR I
BATTLES AND ADVANCES

	Neutral nations
	Central Powers
	Allied Powers
←	Advances of the Allies
←	Advances of the Central Powers
··········	Limit of Trench Warfare, 1914-1917
✳	Major battle sites
——	Eastern armistice line
– – –	Western armistice line

ZONE OF GERMAN SUBMARINE WARFARE

ATLANTIC OCEAN

NORTH SEA

BALTIC SEA

Ypres
Somme
Marne
Chemin des Dames
Verdun

Tannenburg offensive

Trentino
Caporetto

Galicia offensive

Brusilov offensive

Kerensky offensive

BLACK SEA

CASPIAN SEA

Gallipoli

MEDITERRANEAN SEA

equipped army in Europe. Another advantage was that the Central Powers formed a solid land mass. Their enemies were around them, but not in between them. They were thus able to send troops and supplies to the front lines without having to confront the enemy.

When the war began in the summer of 1914, the Central Powers hoped to overrun France before the Allies could get organized to fight. They almost succeeded, but unexpected resistance in Belgium gave Great Britain time to land troops on the mainland.

By 1916 the Allies and the Central Powers were deadlocked against one another on the western front. Neither side had gained a decisive advantage in the fighting. Both sides built networks of trenches and faced each other along a battle line nearly 600 miles long. It reached from the North Sea to Switzerland.

The Central Powers were successful against Russia and Serbia on the eastern front. Russian troops were neither well-equipped nor well-led, and casualties were very heavy. The Germans steadily pushed them back.

Although much of World War I fighting involved hand-to-hand combat in trenches, new and improved weapons appeared on both sides. For example, motor vehicles—tanks, trucks, and autos—were put to wartime use. For the first time also, submarines were used on a large scale to torpedo ships. Air warfare developed, and airplanes were used on bombing missions, to photograph enemy bases, and in battles against one another. Another first in World War I was the use of poison gas.

The United States was neutral during the early war years. (**Neutral** means not taking part in either side of a dispute). But Germany's policy of sinking unarmed ships suspected of carrying war supplies helped bring the United States into the war. Germany announced early in the war that its submarines would sink ships, including unarmed passenger ships, without warning. Germany did just this, and submarine sinkings of United States ships reached a peak in 1917. These sinkings, plus anti-German news stories in the United States, swayed public opinion in favor of the Allies. In April 1917 President Woodrow Wilson declared war on Germany, in the hope of making the world "safe for democracy."

At almost the same time, revolution in Russia forced her to surrender to Germany in 1917. This allowed the Germans to move their armies to the western front. Here they launched heavy attacks. But with the help of newly arrived American troops, the Allies held their lines and counterattacked. The Allies had greater manpower and resources than the Central Powers. By 1917 they were using them effectively. Very heavy German casualties and widespread hunger resulting from Allied blockades brought German surrender. An agreement to end the fighting was signed in November 1918. Negotiations began and separate peace treaties with each of the Central Powers were signed the next year.

One result of the peace settlements was the formation of the League of Nations. This organization was created in the hope that if nations discussed their disagreements, wars could be avoided. The League was formed in 1919 and lasted until 1946. Although the League of Nations was President Wilson's greatest dream, the United States did not join it. Opposition led the Senate to reject United States membership in the organization.

These photos give some idea of how Americans were affected by World War 1.

❶ Factory work for the war effort.

❷ Recruiting posters.

❸ Leaving home for training camp.

❹ Soldiers in front line trench.

What Were the 20s Like?

When World War I ended in 1918, the switch from a war economy to a peace economy was difficult for the United States. Returning soldiers had trouble finding jobs. Wartime shortages of certain foods and manufactured goods had helped push the prices of these items up. Sales of American goods to other countries were down.

Beginning about 1920, however, conditions changed. A new spirit affected many Americans and their way of living. In this activity you'll see what kind of spirit this was.

The data pieces that follow describe life in the 1920s. Based on the data, identify the attitudes people had toward

1. Money
2. The future
3. The kind of life considered "good"

a   The following is from a 1926 magazine article entitled "Florida Frenzy."

a

The smell of money in Florida, which attracts men as the smell of blood attracts a wild animal, became ripe and strong last spring. The whole United States began to catch whiffs of it. Tales of immense quick wealth carried far.

"Let's drive down this summer when it's quiet," said people to one another in whispers, "and pick up some land cheap."

Concealing their destination from neighbors who might think them crazy, they climbed into the flivver, or big car, or truck, and stole rapidly down to Florida.

Once there, they found themselves in the midst of the mightiest and swiftest popular migration of history—a migration like the pilgrimage of army ants or the seasonal flight of millions of blackbirds. From everywhere came the land-seekers, the profit-seekers. Automobiles moved along the eighteen-foot-wide Dixie Highway, the main artery of East Coast traffic, in a dense, struggling stream. Immense buses bearing subdivision names rumbled down loaded with "prospects" from Mobile, Atlanta, Columbia, or from northern steamers discharging at Jacksonville. A broken-down truck one day stopped a friend of mine in a line. The license plates were from 18 different states, from Massachusetts to Oregon. Most of the cars brimmed over with mother, father, grandmother, several children, and the dog, enticed by three years of publicity about the miracles of Florida land values.

The first stories of the real estate magicians had appeared in small city and country newspapers, particularly in the Middle

West. The propaganda said that Florida was an unappreciated playground. Yet, that was far less effective advertising than the beautiful, costly, free dances given in certain cities. Those who attended shortly afterwards received invitations to go (to Florida) without charge and view lots priced from 1,000 dollars up.

Lured by the free trip, many went. Those who bought at the current prices and promptly resold made money. Whole states got the Florida habit. The big migration began.

Millions—variously estimated from three to ten—visited Florida last year, investing 300 million dollars, and bank deposits swelled till they neared the half-billion mark in July.

The newcomers found themselves in a land where farming was practically at a standstill. Fresh vegetables were almost unobtainable; everybody used canned goods. All food brought top New York prices. Railroads and steamships were inadequate to carry enough food, supplies, and passengers. For more than 30 days at midsummer a food famine (not the first) threatened. . . .

Joining the great migration this summer, I went inclined to scoff. Were the others also confident that they possessed average good sense and were not likely to be fooled much?

Probably. I was lost. I gambled. I won. I remained to turn land salesman. I made in a month about 13,000 dollars. Not much, perhaps, but a lot to a little buyer.

b The cartoon below gives a picture of Palm Beach, Florida, during the real estate boom.

From data pieces A and B, what can you tell about people's expectations toward making money? How do you think this affected confidence in the economy?

b

c This real estate ad appeared in *The New York Times* on May 23, 1926.

d Here are parts of two speeches given by President Calvin Coolidge.

1927

Members of the Congress: It is good to report that for the fourth straight year the state of the United States in general is good. We are at peace. The country as a whole is prosperous. Wages are at their highest, and jobs are plentiful. Some parts of agriculture and industry have slowed, and some places have suffered from storm and flood. These losses, however, have been absorbed without hurting our great economic structure. Interest rates for industry, agriculture, and government have been reduced. Savers and investors are providing money for new construction in industry and public works. The purchasing power of farmers has increased. If the people keep confidence in themselves, in each other, and in America, a comfortable prosperity will continue.

What did President Coolidge report about the general conditions of the nation's economy? What prospects did he see for the future?

How would Americans probably be affected after listening to and reading President Coolidge's speeches?

1928

No Congress of the United States has ever faced a brighter time. Here at home there is peace and contentment. Relations between management and wage earner are good. We enjoy freedom from industrial strife, and the highest record of years of prosperity.

e The following headlines appeared in *The New York Times* on July 1, 1928.

From these headlines, how well in general was business doing? How would these conditions affect employment? Wages? The amount of money people had to spend? The demand for manufactured goods? Prices?

e

MID-YEAR OUTLOOK FOR BUSINESS BRIGHT

Conditions Essentially Sound With Improvement Over Last Year in Many Sections

BUILDING OPERATIONS GAIN

Expected to Make a New High Record This Fall—Automobile Output Expands.

AGRICULTURAL PRICES RISE

Brisk Competition in Most Lines Fosters Mergers, Cutting Production Costs.

f This fashion ad appeared in 1926.

Important Fashions Loom on the Autumn Horizon

Black and white—chiffon—the new transparent velvet—ostrich—vaporous fulness—over-balanced draperies—rhinestone embroidery.

At left, Women's frock of black chiffon with rhinestone embroidery at $150.00. *Center*, Misses' frock of white chiffon with black ostrich and rhinestones at $129.50. *Right*, Women's gown of transparent black velvet with rhinestones and silver-cloth applique at $210.00.

What does this ad tell you about popular fashion of the times? What do these fashion attitudes in turn tell you about economic attitiudes?

g This furniture ad appeared in *The New York Times* on February 3, 1929.

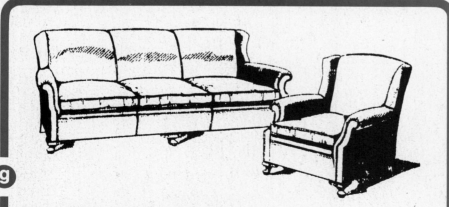

2-Piece Mohair Tuxedo Suite

Combines grace with comfort—important in the scheme of pleasant home life. Choice of fine mohairs in red, green, taupe, mulberry, and walnut. Moss and cotton filled. Webbed construction throughout. An excellent value.

$198.00

Seventh Floor

h The photographs on these pages will help you identify economic conditions and attitudes during the 1920s.

1 Women and black people added to the ranks of workers in the 1920s. They remained in many of the jobs which had opened up to them during World War I.

2 Henry Ford began selling mass-produced Model T automobiles in 1908. Within just a few years, the automobile changed people's habits and recreation. It also created new problems, as this 1920s scene shows.

3 Beginning in the 1920s, listening to the radio became an important part of life at home. News, music, plays, as well as advertising became regular features of radio broadcasting.

What do photographs 1, 2, and 3 indicate about employment during the 1920s? Do you think production of goods rose or declined during these years? What can you infer about spending?

▼

h

4 Short skirts and bobbed hair became popular during this era. Young women who dressed in this fashion were called flappers.

5 In 1927 Charles Lindbergh made the first solo flight across the Atlantic Ocean. He left from Garden City, N.Y. and landed near Paris, France. Upon his return from Europe, Lindbergh was greeted with enthusiasm and excitement, as this New York celebration shows.

6 People developed new interest in sports events, silent film movie stars, and in dance fads. A dance known as the Charleston was one popular dance fad, as seen in this photo.

How do you think Lindbergh's flight affected people's view of the future?

Jazz bands also grew in popularity during this time. Harlem, in New York City, became a center of jazz music. Harlem in the 1920s was also the scene of a "renaissance" in black literature, drama, and dance. **Renaissance** *means rebirth.*

What do the photographs on these two pages tell about the general attitudes toward the "good life"? About how people spent their money?

In 1919 the 18th Amendment to the Constitution was passed. The new law prohibited (forbid) the manufacture and sale of intoxicating liquor. Many people did not support this law and began drinking in illegal clubs called speakeasies. Public disregard for the law increased as gangsters became involved in the illegal distribution of liquor. Because of widespread opposition, the federal government found it almost impossible to enforce prohibition.

ⓘ The photo below was taken inside a speakeasy in the 1920s.

Be sure to complete the activity on page 458.

The Economic Picture

● The graphs and charts which follow show changes in the nation's economy between 1919 and 1929.

Study the data pieces and answer the following questions. Write a short statement in answer to each question.

Between 1919 and 1929, what happened to the
1. Average weekly wages of factory workers?
2. Percent of people unemployed?
3. Gross National Product?
4. Average price of food products?
5. National spending patterns?

Use this data to check your answers to the marginal questions on pages 461 and 463.

In Part 2 you'll investigate these same questions for the 1930s.

Gross National Product *is the total money value of all goods and services produced in a country during one year.*

Times were not especially good for farmers during the 1920s, when farm prices and farm income were at a low level.

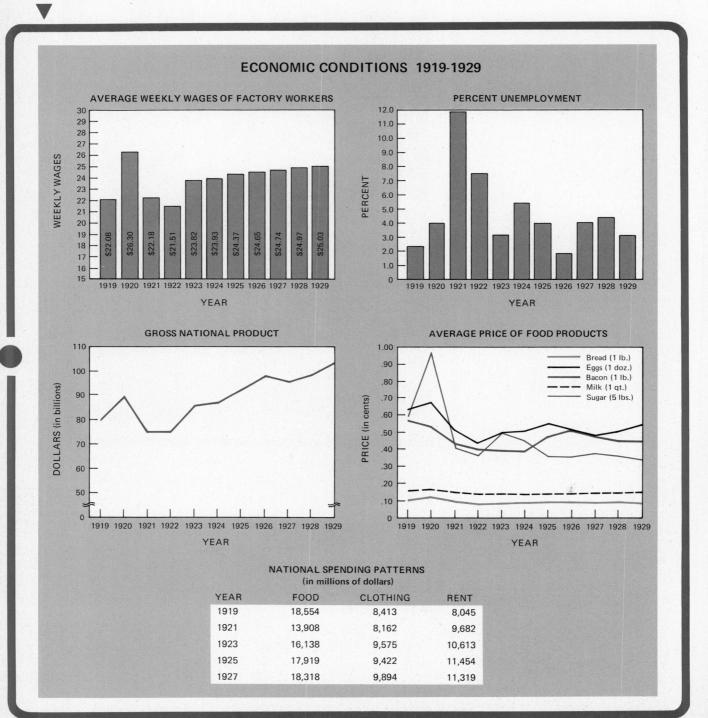

ECONOMIC CONDITIONS 1919-1929

NATIONAL SPENDING PATTERNS
(in millions of dollars)

YEAR	FOOD	CLOTHING	RENT
1919	18,554	8,413	8,045
1921	13,908	8,162	9,682
1923	16,138	9,575	10,613
1925	17,919	9,422	11,454
1927	18,318	9,894	11,319

Part 2

Depression

The hope of making large amounts of money rapidly drove prices higher and higher in the 1920s. Finally, people began to see how much property and products were far over-priced. They became less certain about the future and lacked confidence in the economy. Buying slowed as people decided to save what money they had until the future seemed more secure. Then in October 1929, the prosperity of the 1920s suddenly ended. Prices of stocks plunged downward in the stock market crash. Overnight the country found itself in the middle of the Depression—the most serious economic crisis the nation had ever faced. The materials in Part 2 deal with economic conditions and attitudes during the Depression, which lasted through the late 1930s.

In Part 2 you'll investigate this question:

What changes occurred in the nation's economic system during the 1930s?

What Were the 30s Like?

In Part 1 you identified economic conditions and attitudes during the 1920s. This activity is similar, except that in the following pages you'll be learning about the 1930s. By comparing the 1920s and 1930s, you'll be able to identify the major changes that occurred as one decade led into another.

The data pieces which follow describe life as it was for many people during the 1930s. Based on the data, describe the attitudes people had toward

1. Money
2. Work
3. The future

a The following account is from the book *Union Square,* by Albert Halper.

Union Square is located in New York City.

a He had said good-bye to his wife and kids in the customary manner, as if leaving for work, and by the time he was going down the stairs of the tenement he himself half-believed that he still had a job. . . . Millions were out of work, but he still had a job. He swung along. But by the time he covered a full block he knew he couldn't fool himself any longer, and, his chest growing suddenly heavy, his great legs started dragging, his shoulders sank. People walked by, heading for the square. Some were in a hurry, a lot had plenty of time. The heaviness crept up his limbs like a chill, as if he were wading in some kind of deepening water and pretty soon the cold feeling was in his thighs and climbed on higher. Shoving his hands deep into his pockets, Hank walked along . . .

When he had walked around the square twice, following the wall, Hank saw the bootblacks arriving; they came hurrying into position and by some mutual unspoken law took their posts about ten feet apart; and there was no crowding, either. Some of the "boys" were old and gray, and had shapeless faces, as if hammer blows had been struck them, right between the eyes, on the nose, all over. That's the way they looked. Their knees were ragged from kneeling on the sidewalk while they gave you shines, s'r, shines, s'r, only five cents.

Time and tide. By ten o'clock Hank was sick and tired of walking around the square. There were crowds crossing all the while, and new faces, but he got tired looking at them and also tired of counting sidewalk cracks. In the center of the square a gang of men were standing around a big, empty ashcan because a fire was going there, and the men were chilly and shabby, and Hank saw an old geezer taking off his hat, hold it over the blaze, then clamp it onto his dome quickly. The man was old, was bald, and did this many times, then rubbed his hands with a sort of glee.

Hank struck west. He walked westward on Fourteenth Street, but when he saw the swank of Fifth Avenue, the long cool flanks of gray buildings on each side of the street, he turned back and headed east. . . . Pretty soon Hank reached the Bowery. Here he took his time; he was a man among men here; the heavy flow was still in his chest now, but because it had been there for some time it did not feel so cold.

The bums and unemployed stood on the west side of the street, standing in the sun. The east side was cool and shady, no one walked there at all. The elevated roared overhead. Hank took his time.

By noon he had an unemployed feeling in his bones. He passed a few soup lines and saw men shoving and arguing to keep their places. The line went raggedly around two corners, like a long, disjointed tapeworm. All was meekness, all was humbleness. The sign, JESUS SAVES, was not lit up, it was daylight now. Those who came out of the soup kitchen walked smartly for a half a dozen paces or so, then slouched along, their eyes sniffing at the curbing hungrily for cigarette butts.

Noon arrived over the iron-hooved town, the sun hung brightly brilliant over the rooftops; a wintry day. Hank's legs grew tired from walking. His mind grew tired out from thinking. He turned west again, taking slow, sluggish breaths, and made for home. There was no other place to go; he couldn't run away from it, sooner or later there must be a showdown. Bending his head, staring at sidewalk cracks again, he walked west.

Outside, in the hallway, Hank stood there. His breathing was labored, his broad chest rose and fell unevenly, as if he had just unloaded an extra heavy handtruck piled with pig iron. He stood there, no thoughts at all in his head. At last, placing a heavy fist on the doorknob, he went inside.

His wife gave a little cry, a startled half-scream, as if she had just seen a ghost or something. The kids, their spoons midway to their mouths, turned gapingly, but didn't take it in such a spectacular manner, Hank's dramatic entrance. There he stood, at the threshold, in the center of the Austin stage. He came inside with averted eyes. There was a good, rosy color in his cheeks from walking all morning in the cold air, he looked healthy all right, but oh Christ, how heavy his legs felt, especially up in thighs. He was fagged out, his eyes were dead.

Soup kitchens were places where hot soup or the like was given to people who were jobless and hungry.

469

Hank went slowly to the sink and washed his hands. The hot water felt strange and scalding against the chilled flesh. He wiped each mitt carefully, there was no sense getting his skin chapped this time of the year. His wife, her forehead wrinkled between her brows, grew so nervous she almost dropped the dipper loaded with hot soup over the eldest's head.

Hank pulled up a chair and sat down. He set his elbows on the edge of the kitchen table and stared vacantly ahead. One of the kids kicked his shin playfully under the table, grinned, and waved his spoon, but Hank didn't notice, didn't even feel the blow at all. The kid, disappointed, sniffled, then dug into the bowl again with the shovel of his big tablespoon. The missus put down another plate.

After a few hot gulps of pea soup Hank said, his voice dead, that he had no job. The kids stared pop-eyed. No job? That meant that papa would have something else to do then, that's what it meant.

Little by little, as the soup went down hotly, as the boiled beef was crushed to a dampish, softish mush between his jaws, it all came out. "I was laid off Saturday," Hank told his missus simply. "There were four of us."

b During the Depression, thousands of factories and stores went bankrupt. As a result, millions of people became unemployed. These photographs show how many reacted to being jobless.

c A man describes what it was like to apply for a job in San Francisco, 1931.

c I'd get up at five in the morning and head for the waterfront. Outside the Spreckles Sugar Refinery, outside the gates, there would be a thousand men. You know dang well there's only three or four jobs. The guy would come out with two little Pinkerton cops: "I need two guys for the bull gang. Two guys to go into the hole." A thousand men would fight like a pack of Alaskan dogs to get through there. Only four of us would get through. I was too young a punk.

We were a gentle crowd. These were fathers, 80 percent of them. They had held jobs and didn't want to kick society to pieces. They just wanted to go to work and they just couldn't understand. There was a mysterious thing. You watched the papers, you listened to rumors, you'd get word somebody's gonna build a building.

So the next morning you get up at five o'clock and you dash over there. You got a big tip. There's 3,000 men there, carpenters, cement men, guys who knew machinery and everything else. These fellas always had faith that the job was gonna mature, somehow. More and more men were after fewer and fewer jobs. So San Francisco just ground to a halt. Nothing was moving.

How do you think high unemployment affected the amount of spending in the economy overall? How did this in turn affect the production of goods?

How do you think high unemployment affected wages people were willing to work for?

d Many men with no jobs and little or no money were forced to live in makeshift shacks. Clumps of shacks such as those below were called Hoovervilles, named after President Hoover.

d

e The incidents described below were reported in *The New York Times* in 1931

*A **score** is a set of twenty.*

OKLAHOMA CITY, Jan. 20 (AP).—A crowd of men and women, shouting that they were hungry and jobless, raided a grocery store near the City Hall today. Twenty-six of the men were arrested. Scores loitered near the city jail following the arrests, but kept well out of range of fire hose made ready for use in case of another disturbance.

e

MINNEAPOLIS, Feb. 25 (AP). —Several hundred men and women in an unemployed demonstration late today stormed a grocery and meat market in the Gateway district, smashed plate glass windows and helped themselves to bacon and ham, fruit and canned goods.

One of the storeowners suffered a broken arm when he was attacked as he drew a revolver and attempted to keep out the first to enter.

One hundred policemen were sent to the district and seven persons were arrested as the leaders.

f → **g**   Songs and poems of the Depression are a good indication of how many Americans felt during these years of hardship. The first piece below is a poem by Florence Converse. It was published in the *Atlantic Monthly* in January 1932. The second piece is a song written by a miner from Harlan County, Kentucky, where there were many labor problems during the early 1900s.

Bread Line

*A **queue** is a line.*

f

WHAT's the meaning of this queue,
Tailing down the avenue,
Full of eyes that will not meet
The other eyes that throng the street,—
The questing eyes, the curious eyes,
Scornful, popping with surprise
To see a living line of men
As long as round the block, and then
As long again? The statisticians
Estimate that these conditions
Have not reached their apogee.

***Apogee** means height.*

All lines end eventually;
Except of course in theory.
This one has an end somewhere.
End in what?—Pause, there.
What's the meaning in these faces
Modern industry displaces,
Emptying the factory
To set the men so tidily
Along the pavement in a row?
Now and then they take a slow
Shuffling step, straight ahead,
As if a dead march said:
'Beware! I'm not dead.'

I Don't Want Your Millions, Mister

I don't want your millions, mister;
I don't want your diamond ring.
All I want is the right to live, mister;
Give me back my job again.

I don't want your Rolls-Royce, mister;
I don't want your pleasure yacht;
All I want is food for my babies;
Give to me my old job back.

We worked to build the country, mister,
While you enjoyed a life of ease;
You've stolen all that we built, mister;
Now our children starve and freeze.

Think me dumb if you wish, mister;
Call me green or blue or red;
This one thing I sure know, mister:
My hungry babies must be fed.

I don't want your millions, mister,
I don't want your diamond ring.
All I want is the right to live, mister;
Give me back my job again.

Jim Garland

Who is the "mister" referred to in this poem?

What attitudes toward work and the future do the poem and song reveal?

h This is an example of women's fashion during the 1930s.

h

It's the New Fabrics—It's the New Necklines

It's corduroy. It's for sports. And the colors are deep, dark shades of wine red, brown, or green, the scarf and cuffs of silk to match (first frock, above). See the sailor yoke and corded shoulder; 14 to 40; $4.95. Twin sweaters look hand-knitted, of fine wool; rust, green, or brown; 34 to 40; set, $6.95

It's that touch of velvet. A soft, crinkled velvet in a marvelous shade of coral red or emerald green against black silk (center frock). The velvet forms the sailor collar in back and ends in a bow in front. Perfect for special occasions as well as every day. See the sleeves and low-placed pleats; 14 to 20; $19.95

It's fine rabbit's-hair wool. It's for sports or school or office or the house. It comes in black or brown or green or navy blue, is trimmed with brightly contrasting suède, novel hooks and eyes, cording on the sleeves. The draw-string neckline is young and becoming; and it is semi-made; 14 to 40; $8.95

i This furniture ad appeared in *The New York Times* on February 5, 1933.

Compare these ads with the ads on page 462.

i

FEATURED IN MACY'S FAMOUS FURNITURE SALE!

For One Day Only

200 <u>Down</u> <u>Cushion</u> Mahogany Suites

69.95
USUALLY WOULD BE $119

The value of this suite is apparent from every angle. The way it's built. The way it's tailored. The way it's designed. The fact that it has luxuriously soft down cushions and a gracefully carved mahogany frame. Choice of four covers in attractive shades of rust or green. Better make sure of yours. Get in good and early. NINTH FLOOR

Only One Suite to a Customer

NO MAIL OR TELEPHONE ORDERS

MACY'S the FURNITURE

j These news headings and stories appeared in *The New York Times* on January 1, 1931.

How do you think prices in general were affected by these economic conditions?

THOUSANDS FAIL TO APPLY FOR 1931 AUTO PLATES

Naussau Finds Luxury Cars Were Not Relicensed

MINEOLA, L.I., Dec 31—More than 50,000 residents of Nassau County have been too hard hit by the business depression to license their automobiles for next year, Percy Burrell, Chief Clerk in charge of the bureau, declared here tonight, after the doors of the bureau had been closed.

"We have felt all along," said Mr. Burrell, "that those who used their automobiles as a luxury, rather than a neccessity, would not relicense them. We have found this to be correct. We have only distributed about 75,000 sets of plates. We had received 125,-000. There is no doubt about it, the people are doing without their plates until they have a little more money."

SHARP DROP IN 1930 IN FOREIGN TRADE

Export Total at $3,850,000,000, Off 26%; Imports $3,050,000,000, Down 31%

CONSTRUCTION DROP 30 PERCENT IN 1930

HOUSING DECLINE GREATEST

Slight Gain Registered by Public Works —Costs Are Lower, Being 7 Per Cent Under 1929.

During 1920 construction in this country was valued at $6,525,000,000 which is 30 per cent under the $9,130,000,000 valuation recorded in 1929, Engineering News Record reported yesterday.

The decline for last year is attributed to further recession in residential building activity which fell 42 percent, and a decline of 24 percent in other construction.

k This chart shows total automobile sales in the nation in the years before, during, and just after the Depression.

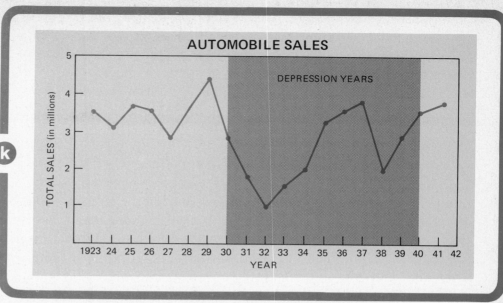

AUTOMOBILE SALES

DEPRESSION YEARS

TOTAL SALES (in millions)

YEAR

How would the drop in auto-mobile sales affect other in-dustries?

k

During a dust storm, high winds carry away large areas of topsoil. Dust storms are likely to occur where there is little rainfall and where grass and farm crops are not deeply rooted in the soil.

l During the 1930s, dust storms in the southwestern United States made bad economic times even worse. Valuable farmland was dam-aged, and thousands of farmers left the land to try their luck else-where. Many migrated westward.

l

m The situation in rural America was just as bad, if not worse, as in the cities. This letter describes how a Kentucky family dealt with its problems.

m

We have been eating wild greens since January this year, such as Polk salad. Violet tops, wild onions, forget-me-not wild lettuce and such weeds as cows eat as cows wont eat a poison weeds. Our family are in bad shape childrens need milk women need nurishments food shoes and dresses—that we cannot get and there at least 10,000 hungry People in Harlan County daily. I know because I am one off them. . . I would leave Harlan County if I only had $6.00 to send my wife and boy to Bristol Va and I could walk away—But I cant clear a dollar per month that Is why I am here, that why houndreds are here they can't ship their family's home. But I am Glad we can find a few wild greens to eat . . . I borrow this postage to send you this informations.

Be sure to complete the activity on page 468.

The Economic Picture

● The graphs and charts on the next page show the state of the nation's economy between 1929 and 1933, the year the economy reached its lowest point.

Study the data pieces and answer the following questions. Write a short statement in answer to each question.

Between 1929 and 1933, what happened to the
1. Average weekly wages of factory workers?
2. Percent of people unemployed?
3. Gross National Product?
4. Average price of food products?
5. National spending patterns?

Check your answers to the marginal questions on pages 472 and 476 against these graphs and charts.

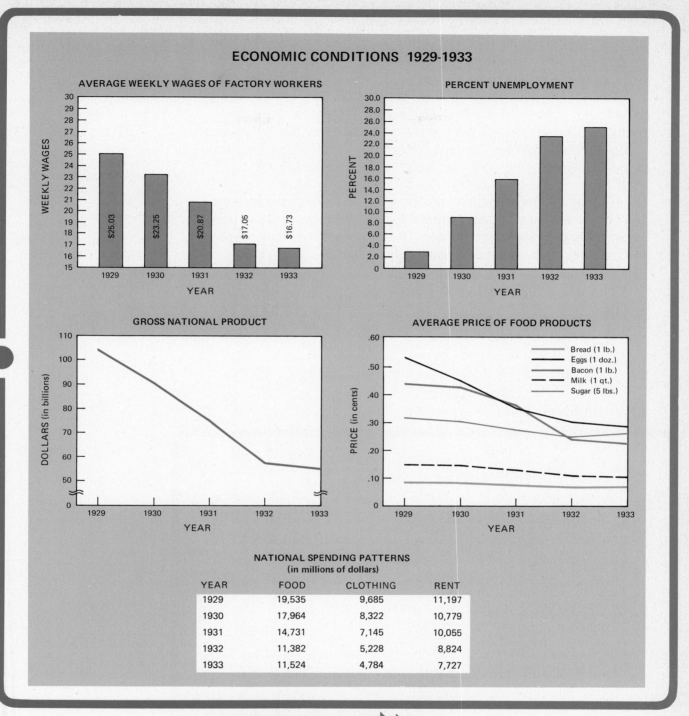

ECONOMIC CONDITIONS 1929-1933

AVERAGE WEEKLY WAGES OF FACTORY WORKERS

WEEKLY WAGES / YEAR

$25.03 (1929), $23.25 (1930), $20.87 (1931), $17.05 (1932), $16.73 (1933)

PERCENT UNEMPLOYMENT

PERCENT / YEAR (1929–1933)

GROSS NATIONAL PRODUCT

DOLLARS (in billions) / YEAR (1929–1933)

AVERAGE PRICE OF FOOD PRODUCTS

PRICE (in cents) / YEAR (1929–1933)

Bread (1 lb.)
Eggs (1 doz.)
Bacon (1 lb.)
Milk (1 qt.)
Sugar (5 lbs.)

NATIONAL SPENDING PATTERNS
(in millions of dollars)

YEAR	FOOD	CLOTHING	RENT
1929	19,535	9,685	11,197
1930	17,964	8,322	10,779
1931	14,731	7,145	10,055
1932	11,382	5,228	8,824
1933	11,524	4,784	7,727

BRANCHING OUT

Interview one or more people who can tell you about the Depression of the 1930s. Find out about

1. Problems people faced
2. How people felt
3. What life was like (how it was different from life today)

Triple-A Plowed Under

During the later years of the Depression, the United States government sponsored the Federal Theater Project for unemployed actors and writers. One of the first plays produced by this group was *Triple-A Plowed Under.* This play described some of the problems of the Depression in an unusual way.

The characters in the play carried signs to show who they were. The characters were usually farmers, factory workers, bankers, businessmen, and government officials. The play used very little scenery and had short scenes and dramatic lighting.

The following scenes are from *Triple-A Plowed Under.* As you read,

1. Identify the problems that individuals and groups faced during the Depression.
2. Find relationships between these problems.

a From Scene Two

Characters:
A Country Banker
A Farmer

(Spotlight comes up on lowest level, left, country BANKER seated at desk, and farmer seated at his side, right.)

BANKER *(As if there had been previous conversation):* I've got to have the money.

FARMER: I can't understand it. Only a little while ago they were preaching and haranguing for us to raise more crops and more crops. I bought more land and cleared all the woods on my place, and planted it to wheat, and now it's rotting in the fields.

BANKER: That was war, Fred.

FARMER: Well, people still need to eat, don't they? And they can't tell me there aren't people who couldn't eat what's lying out in my fields now. My son, Jim, in New York says he can't walk down the street without having hungry men beg him for money.

The term **Triple-A** refers to the Agricultural Adjustment Administration (AAA). The AAA was a United States government agency set up to help farmers during the Depression. One goal of the AAA was to prevent overproduction of farm crops. To do this, it encouraged farmers to plow crops back into the soil. The AAA was disbanded in 1936 when it was declared unconstitutional by the Supreme Court.

Why is the play title an appropriate one?

How do you think farm prices were affected by crop surpluses?

480

BANKER: Well, I don't see what I can do, unless they ease up on me, and they aren't going to do that.

FARMER: Well, if you foreclose on me I'll be in the breadline myself. Then how are any of us going to eat?

BANKER: When that happens the big boys will begin to feel it, and maybe they'll get up another war.

FARMER *(Grimly):* Can't have another war. Every day I get veterans asking for a handout, and not a one of them would go back to war, and I wouldn't raise wheat for another war.

BANKER: At any rate, you see my situation, Fred.

FARMER: I don't see a thing.

b Scene Three

How did the drop in farm incomes affect city workers?

Characters

Voice of Living Newspaper
A Farmer
A Dealer
A Manufacturer
A Worker

b

VOICE OF LIVING NEWSPAPER *(Over loudspeaker)*: In the troubled fifteen years, 1920 to 1935, farm incomes fall five and one-half billion dollars; unemployment rises seven million, five hundred and seventy-eight thousand. *(Four spotlights come up on the four people in this scene. FARMER, stage right, turns head sharply left, speaks to Dealer.)*

FARMER *(To DEALER):* I can't buy that auto. *(Light goes out. DEALER turns head sharply left, speaks to MANUFACTURER.)*

DEALER *(To MANUFACTURER):* I can't take that shipment. *(Count of one, light out. MANUFACTURER turns head sharply left, speaks to WORKER.)*

MANUFACTURER *(To Worker):* I can't use you any more. *(Light goes out. WORKER speaks directly front.)*

WORKER: I can't eat. *(Light goes out.)*

Putting the Pieces Together

1. Based on the data which you have studied, make a list of the important changes that occurred during the Depression of the 1930s.
2. Arrange these changes in a system change diagram. Include the stock market crash. Show how one change led to another by using arrows, and how some changes reinforced each other.
3. Keep your diagram for later use.

The New Deal

After the stock market crash in 1929, things went from bad to worse. In 1930 and 1931, the American economy slid steadily down. Factories shut down, banks closed, and farm prices fell. By 1932 more than 12 million people were out of work. Herbert Hoover, Republican president during these years, was not successful in leading the country out of its economic depression.

As the 1932 presidential election drew near, Herbert Hoover became less and less popular with the American people. Americans wanted a solution to the country's economic problems. In the election, Democratic candidate Franklin D. Roosevelt defeated Hoover in a landslide vote. As soon as he took office, Roosevelt called Congress into special session and presented it with proposals he believed would improve the economy. Roosevelt's programs for economic recovery came to be called the New Deal.

In the 1932 election, the electoral vote count was: Roosevelt, 472 votes; Hoover 59 votes. Roosevelt won 60.8 percent of the popular vote, failing to win only two states—Maine and Vermont.

● Following are descriptions of some New Deal programs.

Study the information about each one. Then, using the diagram you completed for the Depression, explain how each program was intended to affect the economy.

Civilian Conservation Corps (CCC)

The first relief agency set up by the government was the Civilian Conservation Corps (CCC). Unemployed young men were hired to work on conservation projects. Altogether, about three million people were hired by the CCC. Their work consisted of activities such as planting trees, fighting forest fires, building roads and dams, and opening forest trails.

Federal Deposit Insurance Corporation (FDIC)

The FDIC was established by the government to protect bank depositors. As originally set up, it guaranteed that if a bank was unable to return all or part of the money which people had deposited in it, the FDIC would pay whatever money was owed—up to 5,000 dollars.

Today the FDIC insures bank deposits up to 40,000 dollars.

Public Works Administration (PWA)

The PWA was founded to provide work for the unemployed. People were hired to build bridges, schools, courthouses, dams, and similar projects.

Agricultural Adjustment Administration (AAA)

The AAA was set up by the government to help the nation's farmers. In an effort to raise farm prices, the government encouraged farmers to reduce the amount of crops they planted. The AAA paid farmers to do this. The agency also loaned money to farmers who agreed to store their crops for later sale.

Many people disapproved of AAA practices. The agency was declared unconstitutional by the Supreme Court in 1936.

National Recovery Administration (NRA)

Many NRA codes later became law. The Fair Labor Standards Act of 1938 set a minimum wage of 25 cents an hour and a 44-hour work week. It also provided that the minimum wage would gradually be increased to 40 cents an hour and the work week reduced to 40 hours.

The NRA was founded to enforce codes of fair practice for business and industry. These codes set minimum wages and maximum hours for workers. The codes protected the rights of workers to join unions. NRA codes also set standards of quality and prevented excessive competitive price-cutting. The NRA was declared unconstitutional by the Supreme Court in 1935.

Tennessee Valley Authority (TVA)

The Tennessee River Valley includes parts of Virginia, North Carolina, Tennessee, Georgia, Alabama, Kentucky, and Mississippi.

TVA continues to operate today to help prevent the Tennessee River from flooding, provide electricity, and plan the agricultural and industrial growth of the area.

The Tennessee Valley Authority was created by Congress to develop the resources of the Tennessee River Valley. Dams were built to control floods, improve navigation on the Tennessee River, and create electrical power. New forests were planted, and cheap fertilizers were developed to improve farm output.

Works Progress Administration (WPA)

The WPA was created in 1935. It provided jobs building highways, streets, bridges, parks and other projects. It also created work for unemployed artists, writers, actors, and musicians. The WPA provided jobs for about eight and one half million people.

Social Security

The federal social security program was established in 1935. It provided for federal payments to the aged. Under this act employers and employees paid a percentage of the worker's income to the federal government. In return, when the worker reached retirement age, the government furnished monthly income payments. The 1935 law also provided aid to the blind and to dependent children, and set up an unemployment insurance system on a state-by-state basis.

Social security laws today give pensions to the aged, payments to disabled workers, and benefits to the survivors of workers who have died. Unemployment payments, administered by each state, are part of social security laws. Blind people and dependent children also receive assistance. In 1965 Congress set up Medicare, a hospital and voluntary medical insurance plan financed through social security.

How Effective Was the New Deal?

President Roosevelt's New Deal program for Depression relief was not accepted wholeheartedly by everyone. Many people pointed to shortcomings and problems of some of the agencies. Others, business people in particular, objected to the extent of government regulation of industry and farming set up by these programs. They charged that Roosevelt was overregulating the economy and trying to destroy free enterprise. The AAA and NRA were two programs which met with disapproval.

Despite criticism, the New Deal spent billions of dollars to help the suffering economy. Just how effective was the New Deal?

● The materials on the next page provide an overview of some aspects of the economy between 1933 and 1939.

Use the data to judge the New Deal's effectiveness. Did it bring full recovery? Partial recovery? In what areas did it accomplish the most?

Roosevelt's Views

By 1936 President Roosevelt's New Deal programs had taken effect. Although the general attitude of American business toward the New Deal was negative, Roosevelt was voted back into office in that year. He received the largest popular majority ever given a presidential candidate up to that time.

484

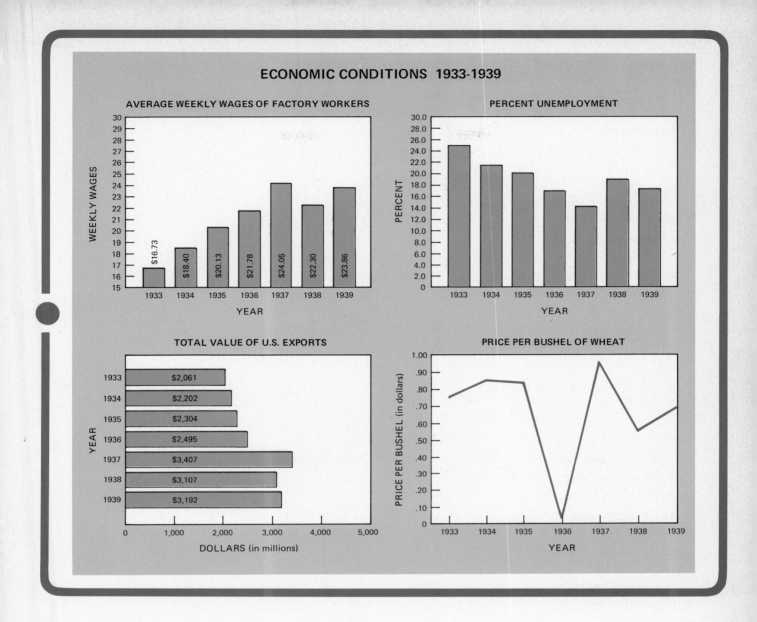

ECONOMIC CONDITIONS 1933-1939

AVERAGE WEEKLY WAGES OF FACTORY WORKERS

WEEKLY WAGES

$16.73 (1933)
$18.40 (1934)
$20.13 (1935)
$21.78 (1936)
$24.05 (1937)
$22.30 (1938)
$23.86 (1939)

YEAR

PERCENT UNEMPLOYMENT

PERCENT

YEAR

TOTAL VALUE OF U.S. EXPORTS

YEAR

1933	$2,061
1934	$2,202
1935	$2,304
1936	$2,495
1937	$3,407
1938	$3,107
1939	$3,192

DOLLARS (in millions)

PRICE PER BUSHEL OF WHEAT

PRICE PER BUSHEL (in dollars)

YEAR

▲
Based on the graphs and charts, what happened to the economy in 1937? What changes took place in the economy after 1937? Do you have any idea why they happened? How would you describe the economy's progress under the New Deal?

During the 1936 campaign, President Roosevelt answered attacks against the New Deal. The following remarks are from a speech delivered by Roosevelt in Chicago on October 14, 1936. In it he presented his views of what the New Deal had accomplished.

Tonight, in this center of business, I give the same message to the businessmen of America—to those who make and sell the processed goods the nation uses and to the men and women who work for them.

To them I say: Do you have a deposit in the bank? It is safer today than it has ever been in our history. It is guaranteed. Last October 1 marked the end of the first full year in 55 years without a single failure of a national bank in the United States. Is that not on the credit side of the government's account with you?

Are you an investor? Your stocks and bonds are up to five- and six-year-high levels.

Are you a merchant? Your markets have the precious lifeblood of purchasing power. Your customers on the farms have better incomes and smaller debts. Your customers in the cities have more jobs, surer jobs, better jobs. Did not your government have something to do with that?

Are you in industry? Industrial earnings, industrial profits are the highest in four, six, or even seven years! Bankruptcies are at a new low. Your government takes some credit for that.

Are you in railroads? Freight loadings are steadily going up. Passenger receipts are steadily going up—have in some cases doubled—because your government made the railroads cut rates and make money.

Are you a middleman in the great stream of farm products? The meat and grain that move through your yards and elevators have a steadier supply, a steadier demand, and steadier prices than you have known for years. And your government is trying to keep it that way.

Some people say that all this recovery has just happened. But in a complicated modern world recoveries from depressions do not just happen. The years from 1929 to 1933, when we waited for recovery just to happen, prove the point.

But in 1933 we did not wait. We acted. Behind the growing recovery of today is a story of deliberate government acceptance of responsibility to save business, to save the American system of private enterprise and economic democracy—a record unequaled by any modern government in history.

Although not everyone agreed with Roosevelt's New Deal policies, he was voted back into office in 1940 and again in 1944. He is the only American President to have been elected to four terms of office.

Part 3

World War II

An important challenge to the world began with the growth of Germany, Italy, and Japan during the 1930s. These countries began to take over lands which did not belong to them. Their actions helped bring on World War II, which lasted from 1939 until 1945. The United States entered World War II in 1941. The war created many important changes in American life, as the activities in Part 3 will show.

In Part 3 you'll investigate this question:

What were some important effects of World War II on the United States?

War and System Change

In 1941 the United States became involved in World War II. You'll learn about this war in the next few activities. First, however, develop some ideas about the probable effects World War II had on the economic system of the United States.

Think about these questions:

1. What is needed to fight a major war? What changes would be needed in industry and farming?
2. How would these changes affect the number of people working? Wages? Production of goods and food for civilian use?
3. What effect would war likely have on the prices of civilian goods and food? What problems could grow out of the price changes? How might these problems be solved?

Use your system change diagram for the Depression to predict some effects World War II had on the economy. Keep records of your predictions to check against the data to follow.

World War II: An Overview

During the 1930s Germany, Italy, and Japan began to increase their military power and use it to gain control of weaker countries. These three nations were determined to increase their wealth and strength by armed force. Germany was under the leadership of Adolf Hitler, Italy was ruled by Benito Mussolini, and Japan was controlled by military leaders. These three nations signed an alliance agreement known as the Rome-Berlin-Tokyo Axis. They later became known as the Axis powers.

In the 1930s Japan invaded China, Italy attacked Ethiopia in North Africa, and Germany moved into the Rhineland, Austria, and Czechoslovakia. (Use the maps on pages 490 and 491 to locate places.) The other nations of the world protested but took no military action to stop these invasions.

Through the 1930s many Americans tried to ignore what was going on elsewhere in the world. Isolationists wanted the United States to take no part in foreign problems. Between 1935 and 1939 Congress passed several neutrality acts that kept the United States from trading with any nation involved in war.

After World War I, national boundaries in Europe changed. Compare the maps on pages 454 and 490 and identify the changes.

*An **isolationist** is one who is against the involvement of one's country in foreign agreements or affairs.*

On September 1, 1939, Germany invaded Poland. This marked the beginning of World War II. Realizing that Germany was not about to stop her invasions, France and Great Britain declared war on Germany two days later. Before they could act, however, Germany had conquered Poland. Norway and Denmark also fell to Germany within a short time. Then Germany turned west. German troops defeated the Netherlands, Belgium, and then France in 1940. It was now clear that Germany, led by Adolf Hitler, intended to conquer all of Europe.

After the defeat of France, Great Britain remained alone in western Europe to fight the Germans. Concerned about the threat of Germany, the United States began sending planes, tanks, and food to Great Britain early in 1941. The United States also cut off trade with Japan to protest that country's growing military action in southeast Asia.

Italy joined the war on Germany's side in June 1940, attacking France in the south. Japan took advantage of the situation to begin to gain control of areas in the western Pacific which had formerly been colonies of the weakened nations of Europe.

Fighting in western Europe eased up temporarily in 1940, but conflict continued in parts of Africa and southeastern Europe. The Germans also kept up an almost continuous air bombardment of Great Britain. During all of 1940, German military forces were generally successful. More and more territory came to be controlled by the Axis nations.

To complete their control of all Europe, the Germans attacked Russia in 1941. At first it appeared that Russia would be another easy victim. But when German troops reached the outskirts of Moscow, Russian troops and winter weather stopped their advance.

On December 7, 1941, the Japanese conducted a surprise attack on the American military base at Pearl Harbor in Hawaii. In less than two hours, most of America's military power in the Pacific was either destroyed or too badly damaged to be of use. This attack was followed by America's declaration of war against the Axis powers.

After Japan attacked Pearl Harbor, she began a rapid conquest of territory in southeast Asia and the southwest Pacific. Japanese forces occupied territory as far east as the Aleutian Islands of Alaska.

After America's entry into the war, it took more than a year to organize American military and industrial strength on a large scale. That power began to be effective in 1943. On the western front, the Allies took control of North Africa, then invaded Sicily and Italy. In Russia, the Germans began to be pushed back. In the Pacific, American forces began to retake islands controlled by the Japanese.

By 1944, Russians had retaken most Russian territory and were pushing into Poland. Italy had been captured, and in June of that year American and British forces invaded the mainland of Europe. Vast amounts of equipment and hundreds of thousands of men poured across the English Channel into France. With some setbacks,

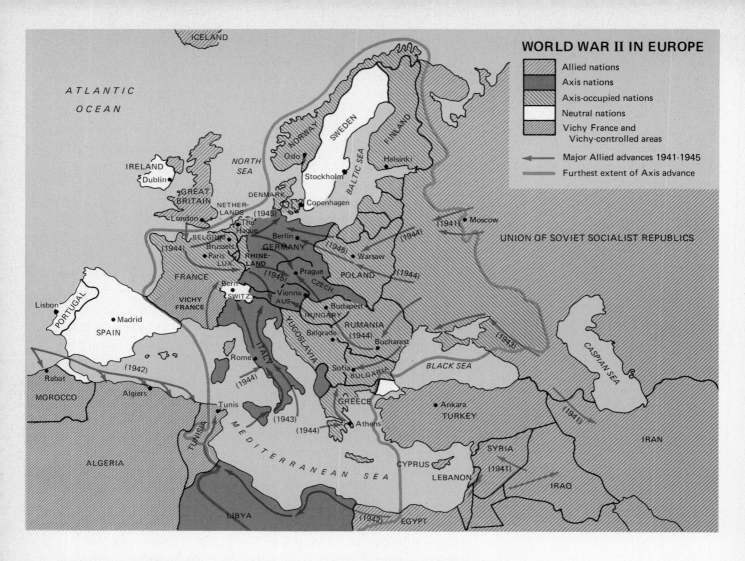

WORLD WAR II IN EUROPE

Allied nations
Axis nations
Axis-occupied nations
Neutral nations
Vichy France and
Vichy-controlled areas
Major Allied advances 1941-1945
Furthest extent of Axis advance

American and British troops continued to move eastward, while the Russians pushed west. In the Pacific, more and more territory was retaken by American and British forces.

Finally, in the spring of 1945, American, British, and Russian troops reached Berlin. On May 7, 1945, Germany surrendered to the Allies.

In the Pacific, the island of Okinawa was captured in preparation for an invasion of the Japanese mainland. The invasion never took place. President Harry S. Truman, who took office after Roosevelt's death in April 1945, ordered the newly developed atomic bomb dropped on Hiroshima, Japan on August 6, 1945. A second one was dropped on Nagasaki three days later. The war in the Pacific ended with Japan's surrender on August 14.

In April 1945, representatives from 50 nations met in San Francisco to organize the United Nations, successor to the League of Nations. The United States became a chief member, and the organization's headquarters was set up in New York City. The main goal of the U.N. is to prevent war through discussion of differences among nations.

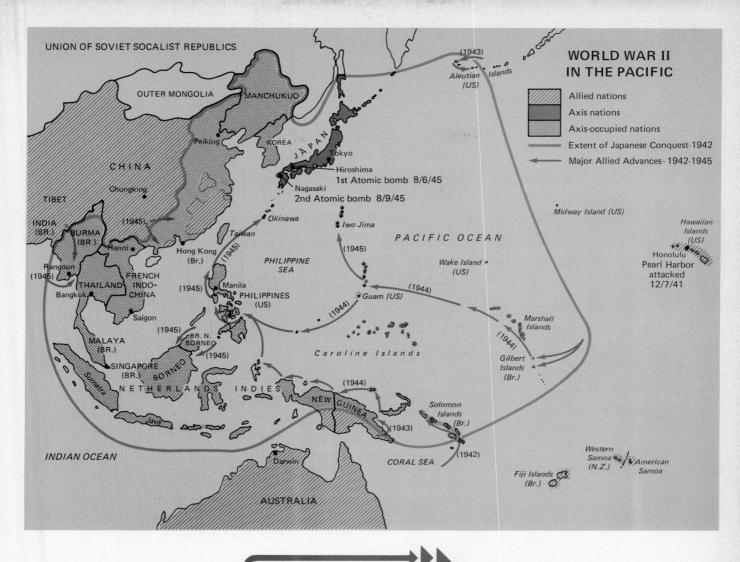

WORLD WAR II IN THE PACIFIC

(hatched)	Allied nations
(dark)	Axis nations
(hatched)	Axis-occupied nations
———	Extent of Japanese Conquest-1942
——→	Major Allied Advances-1942-1945

UNION OF SOVIET SOCIALIST REPUBLICS

OUTER MONGOLIA

MANCHUKUO

Peiking

KOREA

CHINA

Chungking

TIBET

INDIA (BR.)

BURMA (BR.)

Hanoi

Rangoon (1945)

THAILAND

FRENCH INDO-CHINA

Bangkok

Saigon

MALAYA (BR.)

SINGAPORE (BR.)

Sumatra

NETHERLANDS INDIES

Java

INDIAN OCEAN

Darwin

AUSTRALIA

JAPAN

Tokyo

Hiroshima
1st Atomic bomb 8/6/45

Nagasaki
2nd Atomic bomb 8/9/45

Okinawa

Taiwan

Hong Kong (Br.)

Manila

PHILIPPINES (US)

PHILIPPINE SEA

BR. N. BORNEO

BORNEO

NEW GUINEA

CORAL SEA

Iwo Jima
(1945)

PACIFIC OCEAN

(1943)
Aleutian Islands (US)

Midway Island (US)

Hawaiian Islands (US)

Honolulu
Pearl Harbor attacked 12/7/41

Wake Island (US)

Guam (US)

Marshall Islands

Caroline Islands

Gilbert Islands (Br.)

Solomon Islands (Br.)

Western Samoa (N.Z.)

American Samoa

Fiji Islands (Br.)

(1945) (1945) (1945) (1945) (1945) (1944) (1944) (1944) (1944) (1943) (1942)

BRANCHING OUT

During World War II thousands of Japanese-Americans were placed in "relocation camps." Report on how these people were affected.

During the 1920s and 1930s fascist leaders gained control of the governments in Italy and Germany. In Germany the government came to be ruled by a fascist group called Nazis.

Report on the philosophy of fascism and its growth in the years before World War II. You may wish to concentrate on Nazism in particular. Consider this question in your report: In what ways did the growth of fascism (Nazism) create system change?

Another important topic for investigation is the Nazi concentration camps, in which millions of people, including 6 million Jews, were murdered.

Economic Effects of World War II

● The materials on the next page show how the nation's economy was affected by our involvement in World War II.

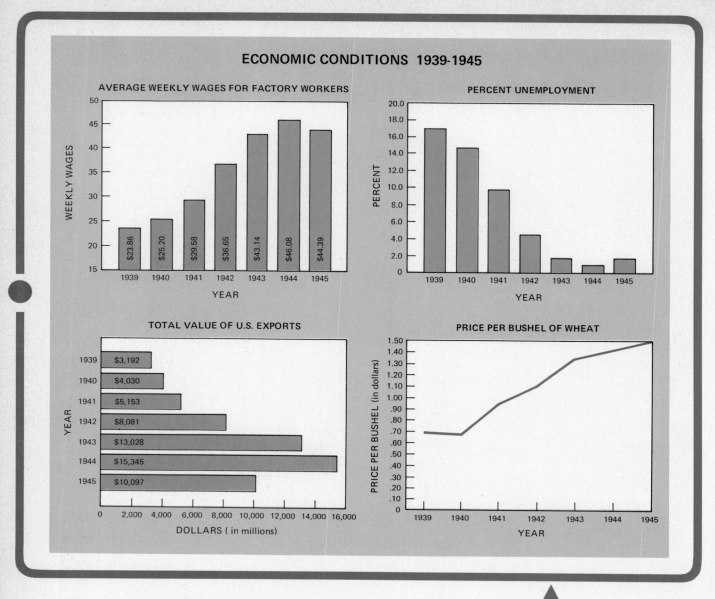

ECONOMIC CONDITIONS 1939-1945

AVERAGE WEEKLY WAGES FOR FACTORY WORKERS

Year	Weekly Wages
1939	$23.86
1940	$25.20
1941	$29.58
1942	$36.65
1943	$43.14
1944	$46.08
1945	$44.39

PERCENT UNEMPLOYMENT

TOTAL VALUE OF U.S. EXPORTS

Year	Dollars (in millions)
1939	$3,192
1940	$4,030
1941	$5,153
1942	$8,081
1943	$13,028
1944	$15,345
1945	$10,097

PRICE PER BUSHEL OF WHEAT

1. How was factory production influenced?
2. How did this in turn affect the number of workers needed in factories?
3. How was farming influenced?

Check these changes against the predictions you made in the *War and System Change* activity.

What major changes in the economy does each graph and chart show?

Culture Change and World War II

On the following pages is a summary of several important events during World War II.

As you study the data, think about ways in which events and conditions at the present time may in part be related to World War II events and conditions. Show your conclusions as a series of statements or in a system change diagram. Some of these items will also help you check the predictions you made in the activity *War and System Change*.

How is penicillin used today?

What effect do you think draft laws had on the growth of families during the war? After the war?

What long-range advantages for women do you think have resulted from the WACS, WAVES, and similar groups?

How could the use of assembly-line methods in manufacturing affect United States military strength?

A **ration** is a fixed portion or amount.

How could rationing and price controls affect the economy?

1941

Sir Howard Florey had been working on the large-scale manufacture of penicillin in England. In 1941 he came to the United States to persuade drug manufacturers of its great value in saving lives. Penicillin was soon turned out in large quantities, though not for unlimited civilian use until after the war.

1942

Draft laws were established to defer married men from military service. Unmarried men with no dependents were to be called for service first. Unmarried men with dependents (such as invalid parents) and then married men with no children were to be called next. Married men with children were drafted last.

On May 14th Congress passed a measure providing for the formation of the Women's Army Auxiliary Corps (WAAC, later WAC). This was soon followed by Women Accepted for Volunteer Emergency Service (WAVES, Navy); Women's Auxiliary Ferrying Squadron (WAFS, Air Force); Women's Reserve of the Coast Guard Reserve (SPARS, from the Coast Guard motto, *Semper Paratus* [Always Ready]); and the Women's Reserve of the United States Marine Corps (WM).

By June 1942 the shipyards of Henry J. Kaiser on the West Coast had been assigned one-third of United States wartime shipbuilding. Assembly-line methods, in which ships are made in parts that are welded together instead of built from the keel up, made it possible for a ship to be completed in less than a week. Kaiser's record was four days from start to finish.

The rationing of foods and materials essential to the war effort began generally in 1942 (although tire rationing had begun almost immediately after Pearl Harbor). Sugar, coffee, fuel oil, gasoline, fats, oils, butter, meats, cheese, canned and processed foods, and finally shoes were rationed.

Congress gave President Roosevelt the power to freeze prices and wages at their levels of September 15th.

On October 1st a test pilot for the Bell Aircraft Corporation flew the first American jet airplane in California.

1943

On May 27th President Roosevelt directed that all war contracts must include clauses prohibiting racial discrimination in war industries. The upgrading of black people resulted in riots. Rioters were controlled by federal troops.

On June 22nd laws setting up the "G.I. Bill of Rights" went into effect for war veterans. This bill gave the following benefits:

Education—One year of college or trade school, including payment for tuition, books, fees, and a monthly income; plus as many more months in school as were served in active duty.

Loans—Guaranteed loans for veterans for purchase or repair of homes, farms, farm equipment, or for setting up a business.

Unemployment Benefits—A weekly allowance (20 dollars) while veteran was unemployed.

1944

On July 16th the first atomic bomb was exploded in the desert at Alamogordo, New Mexico.

From August 21st to October 7th, representatives of the United States, Great Britain, China, and the Soviet Union met in Washington, D.C., to discuss a postwar organization of nations. Proposals agreed on later served as the basis for the United Nations Charter.

What results do you think came from this action once World War II was over?

How might life for war veterans have been different if there hadn't been a G.I. Bill of Rights?

What part do atomic weapons play in foreign policy today?

Post-War Changes

At the end of World War II the United States was the strongest and richest country in the world. After the war a split developed between Russia and the United States. The Russian Communist government took over the goverments of Poland, Czechoslovakia, and other Eastern European countries. Eastern Europe came under Communist control. The United States and its allies in western Europe then united in a "cold war" against Russia and the countries under its influence. No fighting took place, but the United States tried to stop Communist expansion into other countries.

As part of its cold war strategy, the United States made military alliances with countries in different parts of the world. The most successful of these was the North Atlantic Treaty Organization (NATO). Under NATO, the armed forces of several western European nations were combined, and the members agreed to stand united against Russian expansion. An attack on one NATO member would be considered an attack on all.

494

Another United States program was the Marshall Plan. Under this program the United States gave financial help to European countries weakened by World War II. It was felt that strong, stable nations could better resist Communist influence.

War broke out in Korea in June 1950 when North Korean armies invaded South Korea. The North Koreans were armed and trained by Russia. President Truman ordered United States military forces to aid South Korea. The United Nations sent troops to Korea also. The fighting ended in 1953, and North Korea and South Korea remained divided as they had been before the war.

The cold war continued into the 1950s. During these years, fear of communism in the United States ran high. Many believed that people in important positions were Communists trying to overthrow the United States government. Laws were passed by those who felt the country needed to be protected from the "Communist menace." Fear of possible war grew as both Russia and the United States developed new weapons and increased their nuclear power. A race with Russia for superiority in space technology also became an important part of the cold war.

In 1954 much of the attention of the American public turned to events within the United States. In that year the Supreme Court declared that separate schools for black students and white students were unconstitutional. School desegregation was undertaken. The civil rights movement grew and became the most important national issue of the 1960s. Black people and others worked to eliminate unequal treatment of minority groups. Discrimination in housing, transportation, restaurants, hotels, churches, recreation areas, and places of employment were attacked. Many black Americans registered and voted for the first time. One of the leaders who gave inspiration to the civil rights movement was Martin Luther King. In 1968 King was assassinated, but the work he began has continued.

Between 1945 and 1960 great changes occurred in the United States. Business, industry, as well as the population boomed. Advances in science and technology improved the quality and standard of American life. As a result, the United States entered the 1960s richer and stronger than at any other time in her history. There were problems, however.

In 1963 President John F. Kennedy was assassinated. Vice President Lyndon B. Johnson succeeded Kennedy as president. Johnson continued efforts begun by Truman and Kennedy to raise the American standard of living, particularly for the poor. Johnson also succeeded in getting important civil rights legislation passed through Congress. This legislation was aimed at providing equal rights for all citizens.

During Johnson's administration, American involvement in a civil war in Vietnam in southeast Asia grew larger. As the cost in lives and money also grew, Americans became divided over the war. Many supported United States military commitment in southeast Asia. Many others opposed our involvement there and wanted a withdrawal of American troops. Richard Nixon, who took office as president in 1969, promised an "honorable end" to the war in Vietnam. Public dissatisfaction continued until American forces left Vietnam in 1973.

Americans generally approved President Nixon's attempts to open relations with Communist China and to seek peace in the Middle East. He was reelected to the presidency in 1972.

During the 1972 presidential campaign, five men were caught trying to place electronic listening devices in the headquarters of the Democratic party. These headquarters were located in Watergate, an office and apartment complex in Washington, D.C. An investigation of the Watergate break-in was held. Many of President Nixon's highest-ranking advisors were tried and convicted of attempting to cover up the Watergate scandal and other illegal political activities. The scandal forced President Nixon to resign from office in August 1974. Vice President Gerald R. Ford then became president. Soon afterward Ford pardoned Nixon for his role in the Watergate scandal.

President Ford considered inflation and American dependence on foreign oil the country's two most serious problems. In 1975 the rate of unemployment jumped, and the nation was faced with its worst business recession in over 40 years. President Ford assured the nation that better times were ahead as he sought election as president in 1976.

These photos show some important people and events of the 1960s and 1970s.

❶ Civil rights march in 1963 led by Martin Luther King.
❷ President Kennedy, Dean Rusk, and Japanese leaders.
❸ Soldiers in South Vietnam.
❹ Protest against war in Vietnam.
❺ President Nixon's resignation.

Part 4

Trends

Murders, elections, wars, fires, and kidnappings make headlines. In the long run these kinds of events may not directly affect the lives of most people. On the other hand, those events which do change the lives of millions of people are often not announced in the news.

One reason many important changes don't make news headlines is that they don't occur dramatically at one point in time. Instead, they may be spread out over a long period of time. They may be "trends" rather than brief happenings. A **trend** is a change that continues for a period of time. A year-by-year increase in crime and a long-term decrease in population would both be considered trends.

After World War II, and partly as a result of it, several important national trends began. In Part 4 you'll examine these trends and see what effects they have had on the American people.

In Part 4 you'll investigate these questions:

What trends are affecting American ideas and ways of acting? In what ways?

What trends may continue into the future? How will they affect American ideas and ways of acting?

When population changes, other things change too. Hospitals, houses, schools, highways, water supplies, and recreation areas are just some of the thousands of things directly related to population. These things are affected in ways that are often expensive, time-consuming, and troublesome.

For this reason, knowing about population trends is very important. A city government that isn't aware of local population trends is headed for trouble. It may find, for example, that its sewage treatment plants are suddenly overloaded, and that it will take five years to plan, finance, and build new ones. Similarly, business people who don't follow local population trends are not prepared for the future. They may find out too late that the people who buy from them are moving away from the area.

This activity will help you think about some effects of several different population trends.

How Many Americans?

Extrapolation: ex-trap-oh-LAY-shun.

One method used to investigate trends is called **extrapolation.** This term means making a projection about the unknown by extending the information about what is known.

a Below are figures for the enrollment of a school.

Plot these figures on a graph. Then use extrapolation to predict the school enrollment for 1980.

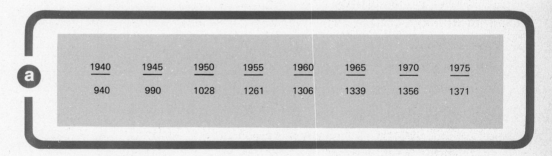

1940	1945	1950	1955	1960	1965	1970	1975
940	990	1028	1261	1306	1339	1356	1371

What could go wrong with your extrapolation? List as many things as you can think of that might make your prediction wrong.

b The following table shows changes in the population of the United States from 1900 to 1970.

**UNITED STATES
POPULATION 1900-1970**

1900	76,212,168
1910	92,228,496
1920	106,021,537
1930	123,202,624
1940	132,164,569
1950	151,325,798
1960	179,323,175
1970	203,212,000

1. Plot these figures on a graph.
2. How would you describe the trend in the size of the United States population? Is the trend continuing steadily at the same rate?
3. Extrapolate the population for 1980, 1990, and 2000.
4. How could trends in family size affect your population projections? What other trends or events could affect your projections?

Increases and decreases in population can each have advantages as well as problems. What are some ways each of the following may be affected in the future if the nation's population continues its present rate of growth? How might these items be affected if the nation's population stayed the same or even decreased?

Education
Local government services
Recreation
Business and industry
Housing
Taxes
Crime

Where Do Americans Live?

Americans move a lot. There have been several important changes in the location of our population in the last 25 years.

c The figures on the next page show how the American population has been distributed since 1950.

POPULATION DISTRIBUTION 1950-1970

	1950	1960	1970
Central cities	48,377,000	57,975,000	63,922,000
Suburban areas	20,872,000	37,873,000	54,525,000
Outside urbanized areas	27,598,000	29,420,000	30,878,000
Rural	54,479,000	54,054,000	53,887,000
Total	151,326,000	179,323,000	203,212,000

Plot these statistics on a graph. You may wish to make four separate graphs, and then combine these into one big graph. Keep your population movement graph for later use.

What trends are shown by the graph? What reasons can you think of for them? What are some possible future effects?

d The following table shows population changes in each of the 50 states between 1920 and 1970. Some of the changes are due to population increase from births and immigrants. Many of the changes are due to population movement from state to state.

Which states are growing the fastest? Which areas of the country are growing the fastest?

STATE OR OTHER AREA	POPULATION (1,000)					
	1920	1930	1940	1950	1960	1970
United States	106,022	123,203	132,165	151,326	179,323	203,212
Regions:						
Northeast	29,662	34,427	35,977	39,478	44,678	49,041
North Central	34,020	38,594	40,143	44,461	51,619	56,572
South	33,126	37,858	41,666	47,197	54,973	62,795
West	9,214	12,324	14,379	20,190	28,053	34,804
New England	7,401	8,166	8,437	9,314	10,509	11,842
Maine	768	797	847	914	969	992
New Hampshire	443	465	492	533	607	738
Vermont	352	360	359	378	390	444
Massachusetts	3,852	4,250	4,317	4,691	5,149	5,689
Rhode Island	604	687	713	792	859	947
Connecticut	1,381	1,607	1,709	2,007	2,535	3,032
Middle Atlantic	22,261	26,261	27,539	30,164	34,168	37,199
New York	10,385	12,588	13,479	14,830	16,782	18,237
New Jersey	3,156	4,041	4,160	4,835	6,067	7,168
Pennsylvania	8,720	9,631	9,900	10,498	11,319	11,794
East North Central	21,476	25,297	26,626	30,399	36,225	40,252
Ohio	5,759	6,647	6,908	7,947	9,706	10,652
Indiana	2,930	3,239	3,428	3,934	4,662	5,194
Illinois	6,485	7,631	7,897	8,712	10,081	11,114
Michigan	3,668	4,842	5,256	6,372	7,823	8,875
Wisconsin	2,632	2,939	3,138	3,435	3,952	4,418
West North Central	12,544	13,297	13,517	14,061	15,394	16,319
Minnesota	2,387	2,564	2,792	2,982	3,414	3,805
Iowa	2,404	2,471	2,538	2,621	2,758	2,824
Missouri	3,404	3,629	3,785	3,955	4,320	4,677
North Dakota	647	681	642	620	632	618
South Dakota	637	693	643	653	681	666
Nebraska	1,296	1,378	1,316	1,326	1,411	1,483
Kansas	1,769	1,881	1,801	1,905	2,179	2,247
South Atlantic	13,990	15,794	17,823	21,182	25,972	30,671
Delaware	223	238	267	318	446	548

STATE OR OTHER AREA	POPULATION (1,000)					
	1920	1930	1940	1950	1960	1970
Maryland	1,450	1,632	1,821	2,343	3,101	3,922
D.C.	438	487	663	802	764	757
Virginia	2,309	2,422	2,678	3,319	3,967	4,648
West Virginia	1,464	1,729	1,902	2,006	1,860	1,744
North Carolina	2,559	3,170	3,572	4,062	4,556	5,082
South Carolina	1,684	1,739	1,900	2,117	2,383	2,591
Georgia	2,896	2,909	3,124	3,445	3,943	4,590
Florida	968	1,468	1,897	2,771	4,952	6,789
East South Central	8,893	9,887	10,778	11,477	12,050	12,803
Kentucky	2,417	2,615	2,846	2,945	3,038	3,219
Tennessee	2,338	2,617	2,916	3,292	3,567	3,924
Alabama	2,348	2,646	2,833	3,062	3,267	3,444
Mississippi	1,791	2,010	2,184	2,179	2,178	2,217
West South Central	10,242	12,177	13,065	14,538	16,951	19,321
Arkansas	1,752	1,854	1,949	1,910	1,786	1,923
Louisiana	1,799	2,102	2,364	2,684	3,257	3,641
Oklahoma	2,028	2,396	2,336	2,233	2,328	2,559
Texas	4,663	5,825	6,415	7,711	9,580	11,197
Mountain	3,336	3,702	4,150	5,075	6,855	8,282
Montana	549	538	559	591	675	694
Idaho	432	445	525	589	667	713
Wyoming	194	226	251	291	330	332
Colorado	940	1,036	1,123	1,325	1,754	2,207
New Mexico	360	423	532	681	951	1,016
Arizona	334	436	499	750	1,302	1,771
Utah	449	508	550	689	891	1,059
Nevada	77	91	110	160	285	489
Pacific	5,878	8,622	10,229	15,115	21,198	26,523
Washington	1,357	1,563	1,736	2,379	2,853	3,409
Oregon	783	954	1,090	1,521	1,769	2,091
California	3,427	5,677	6,907	10,586	15,717	19,953
Alaska	55	²59	²73	129	226	300
Hawaii	256	368	423	500	633	769
Puerto Rico	1,300	1,544	1,869	2,211	2,350	2,712

Age Groups

e Population experts often show the age characteristics of a population in a type of graph called a "population pyramid." A population pyramid below shows the United States population in 1950.

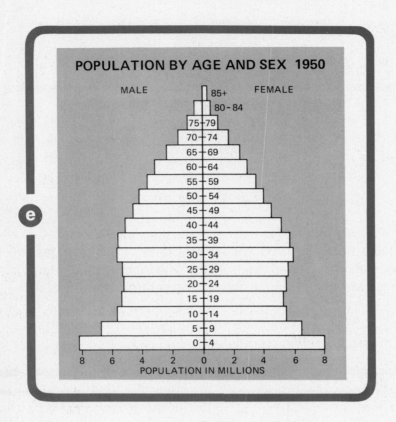

POPULATION BY AGE AND SEX 1950

Each horizontal step of the graph represents one age group. The bottom step shows the percentage of babies and children up through four years old. Percentages to the right of 0 refer to female children; percentages to the left of 0 refer to male children.

f The chart information on the next page will help you construct a population pyramid for 1970.

After you make a population pyramid for 1970, compare it with the 1950 pyramid. Then answer the questions below.

1. What differences do you see between the 1950 and 1970 population graphs? What reasons can you think of for these differences?

2. What might explain the "bulge" in your 1970 pyramid in the 2nd, 3rd, and 4th steps? What might explain the "narrowing" on the 7th and 8th steps?

3. Describe the trends in the size of age groups in this country. What other trends do you see in this data?

502

UNITED STATES POPULATION 1970

Male %	Age	Female %
3.0	75+	4.4
5.5	65-74	6.7
8.9	55-64	9.4
11.3	45-54	11.5
11.4	35-44	11.4
12.4	25-34	12.2
6.3	21-24	6.4
5.3	18-20	5.3
7.8	14-17	7.5
18.0	5-13	17.2
8.4	under 5	8.1

Technology

In the last 100 years, a number of developments in technology have had great impact on the American people. The mass production of automobiles and new machine inventions for farms have probably changed this country the most. New technological ideas and inventions continue to cause changes in the way Americans live.

● Below is a brief summary of some major technological developments since 1950. In several of the following cases, the technology was invented before 1950, but not adopted to any great extent until after that date.

Choose one of the following technological developments. Describe some possible effects this development may have on how we live our lives in the future. For example, consider how things like families, schools, and jobs may be affected.
Show these effects in a system change diagram.

About 99 percent of all households in the United States have television sets. An average of one out of every two households owns a color set.

Most households in this country have access to an automatic washing machine. Much of the clothing now produced does not require ironing or pressing.

Family planning measures have gained increasing acceptance throughout the nation.

503

Before 1950 most new houses being built were single-family dwellings. Since then, the number of multiple-unit dwellings built each year has increased. A majority of new dwellings are now in multiple-unit buildings.

Computers prepare most payroll checks and customer bills. They also store information about individual tax payments, bill-paying habits, and criminal behavior.

New drugs have enormously decreased deaths from infections and diseases.

Increasing numbers of drugs are available to reduce anxiety, emotional distress, worry, and other mental problems, both minor and major.

In 1970 there was 13 times more air travel than in 1950.

Nearly all technology requires some form of energy to create it and make it operate. Use of technology has increased rapidly, and the demand for energy has grown even more rapidly. An energy shortage and higher costs are beginning to affect almost everybody in this country.

The world's major atomic powers have the capability to destroy each other completely, and to make the rest of the earth uninhabitable.

Possible Futures

What's ahead for America—and for you? There's no way to know, of course. Only one thing can be said for certain. Life in the America of the future won't be like life in America today.

Just because we can't predict the future doesn't mean that the future has to be full of unexpected surprises that find us unprepared. Whatever it's like, the future will probably be a result of conditions and trends that are already a part of our lives. For example, we know for certain that the amount of crude oil under the surface of the earth is limited. Very soon the present methods of generating electricity, propelling automobiles, and heating many houses will either have to be changed or we'll have to learn to live without them. Getting ready for the future, then, requires us to consider what the future will be like.

a → c Brief descriptions of possible futures are next. Each is based on trends which some people believe already exist.

Zero Privacy

It was a bright cold day in April, and the clocks were striking 13. Winston Smith, his chin muzzled into his breast in an effort to escape the vile wind, slipped quickly through the glass doors of Victory Mansions, though not quickly enough to prevent a swirl of gritty dust from entering along with him.

The hallway smelt of boiled cabbage and old rag mats. At one end of it a colored poster, too large for indoor display, had been tacked to the wall. It depicted simply an enormous face more than a meter wide; the face of a man of about 45, with a heavy black mustache and ruggedly handsome features. Winston made for the stairs . . . .

The flat was seven flights up, and Winston, who was 39, and had a varicose ulcer above his right ankle, went slowly, resting several times on the way. On each landing, opposite the lift shaft, the poster with the enormous face gazed from the wall. It was one of those pictures which are so contrived that the eyes follow you about when you move. BIG BROTHER IS WATCHING YOU, the caption beneath it ran.

Inside the flat a voice was reading out a list of figures which had something to do with the production of pig iron. The voice came from an oblong metal plaque like a dulled mirror which formed part of the surface of the right-hand wall. Winston turned a switch and the voice sank somewhat, though the words were still distinguishable. The instrument (the telescreen, it was called) could be dimmed, but there was no way of shutting it off completely . . . .

Outside, even through the shut window pane, the world looked cold. Down in the street little eddies of wind were whirling dust and torn paper into spirals, and though the sun was shining and the sky a harsh blue, there seemed to be no color in anything except the posters that were plastered everywhere. The black-mustachio'd face gazed down from every commanding corner. There was one on the house front immediately opposite. BIG BROTHER IS WATCHING YOU, the caption said, while the dark eyes looked deep into Winston's own.

. . . In the far distance a helicopter skimmed down between the roofs, hovered for an instant like a bluebottle, and darted away again with a curving flight. It was the Police Patrol, snooping into people's windows . . . .

Behind Winston's back the voice from the telescreen was still babbling away about pig iron and the overfulfillment of the Ninth

Three-Year Plan. The telescreen received and transmitted simultaneously. Any sound that Winston made, above the level of a very low whisper, would be picked up by it; moreover, so long as he remained within the field of vision which the metal plaque commanded, he could be seen as well as heard. There was of course no way of knowing whether you were being watched at any given moment. How often, or on what system, the Thought Police plugged in on any individual wire was guesswork. It was even conceivable that they watched everybody all the time. But at any rate they could plug in your wire whenever they wanted to. You had to live—did live, from habit that became instinct—in the assumption that every sound you made was overheard, and, except in darkness, every movement scrutinized.

Euphoria

It was only a minor news item. Near the end of the CBS evening news, the announcer briefly summarized several Supreme Court decisions which had been handed down during the week. In one of the cases, he said, the government had that day lost its effort to delay the marketing of a new tranquilizer drug developed by Philathea Pharmaceutical Laboratories.

The newscast ended at 7:28. At 7:28, television screens all over the United States went silent and dark. For 15 long seconds that unfamiliar silence continued, as millions of viewers turned their attention more closely to their television screens.

At the end of 15 seconds, in the far distance, music. Circus music—softer, slower, and somehow richer than most circus music—but circus music nevertheless, echoing inside the Big Top, spilling out to the animal cages and the sideshows, smelling like buttered popcorn and hot candied apples in October.

The music drew closer but no louder. The screen glowed blue, yellow, green, red, then all colors at once. Balloons floating, possibly, but the picture too softly focused to tell for certain. Other sights, the camera floating at child's eye height through bright childhood memories.

An announcer's warm voice grew out of the music. "You can bring it back," he said. "The happiness. Twelve hours of the pure happiness of childhood can now be yours. Anytime, anywhere, under any circumstance. (A pause.) Ecstasil. (Pause) From Philathea Pharmaceutical Laboratories. (Pause) Non habit-forming. Absolutely no side effects. No prescription necessary. At your drugstore on Monday."

Second Independence Day

The February daylight was still hours away when Greer blinked awake. It was 4:30 in the morning. The bedroom was dark, and no clock had alarmed, but Greer knew what time it was. He had awakened at 4:30 every morning for almost 14 years.

Greer also knew that it was useless to try to go back to sleep. He had tried that for the first time four years before on the 4th of July, and he had gone on trying it for months after Second Independence Day.

For the first ten of those fourteen years there was a reason to wake at 4:30. He had depended on a clock then, had rolled out of bed at the alarm's first click, and gone into the kitchen of his small apartment to be certain the automatic coffeemaker was at work on his two cups of coffee. Reassured by the small red light, Greer would complete the morning ritual with a shower, shave, clean clothes, and an instantly-prepared but leisurely-eaten breakfast of the best synthetic meat and eggs. By 5:40 he would have the breakfast dishes in the washer, his door locked, and be seven levels below his apartment in the minisubway waiting room.

Until four years ago, Greer had been a transit controller. His four-hour workday was spent in a soft swivel chair facing a console glowing with hundreds of small green lights moving in ordered patterns. Occasionally, but only occasionally, one of the green lights would change to a rapidly blinking yellow. When that happened, he would note its identification number and push a series of buttons on the panel before him. The light would change to green again, indicating that the pneumatically propelled four-passenger transporter whose performance it monitored was operating normally in its tube 30 feet below the grassy streets of the city.

But Second Independence Day (or SID, as everyone called it) had put an end to his ten year routine. At 12:00 o'clock on the 4th of July nearly four years before, the President of the United States had signed the bill which made it unnecessary for Greer to spend four hours a day at a transit controller's desk—or any other desk. Greer had absolutely *nothing* to do. Since SID, the Volunteer Work Corps did everything.

1. What present trends might lead to each of these futures?
2. What trends might keep these futures from occurring?
3. What are some advantages of these possible futures? Disadvantages?
4. How do you feel about them?

Application

Choose almost any city, travel to its "old downtown" area, and you may see problems. You may find boarded-up stores, abandoned buildings, streets in need of repair, and other signs of downtown decline. Conditions such as these affect thousands of cities and towns across the United States.

Because they are related, the changes which bring about downtown decline form a system. This system often forms a "vicious circle" of decay.

Below is a list of items that are affected when downtown decline begins.

Shopping in downtown stores	Rents for store buildings
Building maintenance	Parking
Crime	Downtown apartment rents
Number of empty buildings	Homes built in suburbs
Jobs	Shopping centers in suburbs

1. Decide how each item is affected by downtown decline, and describe the effects in brief statements.
2. What reasons might a business give for closing its downtown store and opening a store in a suburban shopping center?
3. As downtown decline increases, how is the need for services such as police and fire protection affected? How is the amount of taxes received from downtown property affected? (Taxes pay for city services.) How do these two changes affect one another?
4. Make a system change diagram that summarizes the "vicious circle" of downtown decline.
5. What recommendations would you make to help solve the problems?

BRANCHING OUT

Does your city or town have problems of downtown decline? If so, investigate and report on these problems. Use maps, photographs, and newspaper articles as evidence.

BRANCHING OUT

What would be the system change effects if the largest industry in your community or area closed down? Make a diagram that predicts the effects.

BRANCHING OUT

What would be the effects of *free* bus transportation in your town or city? Would it create some problems? Would it solve some problems? Make a system change diagram to show the effects.

BIBLIOGRAPHY

Werstein, Irving. *Shattered Decade, 1919-1929.* N.Y.: Charles Scribner's, 1970. A fast-moving history of the "Roaring Twenties." The author deals with the glamour of the times but does not neglect the serious problems of this decade.

Hunt, Irene. *No Promises in the Wind.* Chicago: Follett, 1970. Fiction. Fifteen year old Josh has to make his own way in the Chicago of the Depression years.

Meltzer, Milton. *Brother, Can You Spare a Dime?* N.Y.: Alfred A. Knopf, 1969. Eyewitness accounts of the human side of the Great Depression. The title of this book is the title of one of the most popular—and pathetic—songs of the period.

Dodds, John W. *Everyday Life in Twentieth Century America.* N.Y.: G. P. Putnam's, 1965. A social history with information, in the author's words, about "what was read, sung, laughed at, traveled on and lived in." Includes many interesting photographs.

The Best of Life. N.Y.: Time-Life Books, 1973. Nearly 700 of the best photographs from *Life* magazine, taken from 1936 to 1972, the life span of the magazine itself. Chapters include leaders, fashion, soldiers and entertainers. A very interesting mixture of the significant public events and the amusing trivia of the times.

Glossary

Abolition The ending of slavery.

Ambassador The highest ranking representative appointed by one country or government to represent it in another.

Amendment A change or addition in a document.

Amnesty An official pardon, especially for political offenses.

Assassinate To murder by a sudden or secret attack.

Autonomy Independence or freedom from control by others.

Alliance An association of nations for a common purpose.

Balance of power A distribution of power so that no one group is strong enough to overpower other groups.

Bankruptcy The situation in which businesses or people are unable to pay their debts.

Bill A written statement of a proposed law.

Bondage Slavery.

Boycott An organized refusal to buy from, sell, or deal with in order to punish or coerce.

Carpetbaggers Northern men who rushed to the South after the Civil War to gain political power in the new governments.

Checks and balances The three-branch system of the United States government designed to keep any one branch from gaining too much power over another branch.

Colony A body of people living in a new territory governed by their mother country.

Communism A form of totalitarian government, an economic system, or a way of life. Under this system, the government (not individuals or private businesses) owns and manages industry and farming.

Confederation A union of states or nations.

Conquistadores Spanish conquerors in the New World during the sixteenth century.

Constitution A system of laws by which a government or organization is run.

Culture A society's shared ideas and ways of acting.

Democracy A form of government in which the people hold the ruling power, either directly or through elected representatives.

Depression A time marked by declining business activity, widespread unemployment and falling prices.

Despotism A system of government in which the ruler has absolute power.

Division of labor A separation of jobs where each worker does one of many jobs needed to finish a product.

Due process of law The constitutional right guaranteeing citizens they will not be executed, imprisoned or fined without all the required legal procedures.

Electors Persons chosen to cast votes for the President in the Electoral College.

Emigrant A person who leaves one country or region to settle in another.

Empire A collection of nations or territories under the control of one government.

Executive A person whose job it is to manage the affairs of a nation, business or organization to which he or she is responsible and to see that the laws and duties are carried out.

Executive departments Departments or divisions of the President's cabinet such as the State Department or the Defense Department.

Extrapolation A prediction on the basis of certain known information.

Federal Referring to a union of states or other groups in which each member yields major government powers to a central authority and keeps limited powers to itself.

Ideology Ideas or beliefs held by a class or group of people.

Immigrant A person who comes into a new country or region in order to settle there.

Indentured servants People who came to the colonies as servants under contract. They promised to work for a certain amount of time (usually from 4 to 7 years). After this time they were free.

Industrial Revolution A period of rapid growth in industry during the eighteenth and nineteenth centuries, when the system of producing goods changed from making goods at home to manufacturing them in factories.

Isolationist A person who is against the involvement of one's country in foreign agreements or affairs.

Judicial Relating to the administration of judges, courts and their functions.

Legislative Lawmaking.

Lockout The closing of a business or factory by an employer to prevent employees from working during a labor dispute.

Mercantilism An economic policy which required the colonies in America to supply England with raw materials for producing manufactured goods many of which were then sold to the colonies.

Missionaries People who bring their religion to others and try to convert them to their faith.

Monopoly A large business which controls an entire industry's prices and production.

Motivations Reasons for action.

Naturalization The process by which a foreign-born person becomes a citizen.

Neutral Not interfering or taking part in either side in a quarrel or a war.

Nullify To set aside or disobey a law.

Overseer A person who supervised slaves at work.

Pioneer The first person to go into an unsettled land.

Polarization The gradual step-by-step increase in hostility between two groups which moves them further apart.

Popular sovereignty A proposal for letting people in the territories decide for themselves, by voting, whether to permit slavery in their territory.

Preamble An introduction.

Proprietors People to whom the King gave charters to set up colonies in the New World. In return these people gave payment to the King. They were given the right to sell land in their colony and to control the colony's government.

Ratify To give approval.

Reconstruction The period of rebuilding the South after the Civil War.

Referendum A special election in which people vote on certain issues.

Repeal To revoke or cancel.

Republican form of government A government in which power rests in the citizens entitled to vote and is exercised by elected representatives.

Secede To withdraw from an organization.

Sole power of impeachment The power granted to the United States House of Representatives to bring accusations against federal officials who have not properly carried out their duties.

States' rights The powers and rights which the United States Constitution does not grant to the federal government or deny to the state governments.

Stereotyping Fixing a mental image or way of thinking about a person, place or thing, making no allowances for individual differences.

Strike A refusal by laborers to work until their demands are met.

Tariff A tax placed on foreign imported products.

Town meeting A meeting at which local government affairs are discussed and action decided upon. Town meetings were first held in this country in Massachusetts in the 1600s.

Treason Betrayal of one's country to an enemy.

Trend A general course or direction.

Trust A combination of businesses under management and control of a single group of people.

Underground railroad A secret network of black and white Northerners who provided places or 'stations' for slaves escaping to Canada.

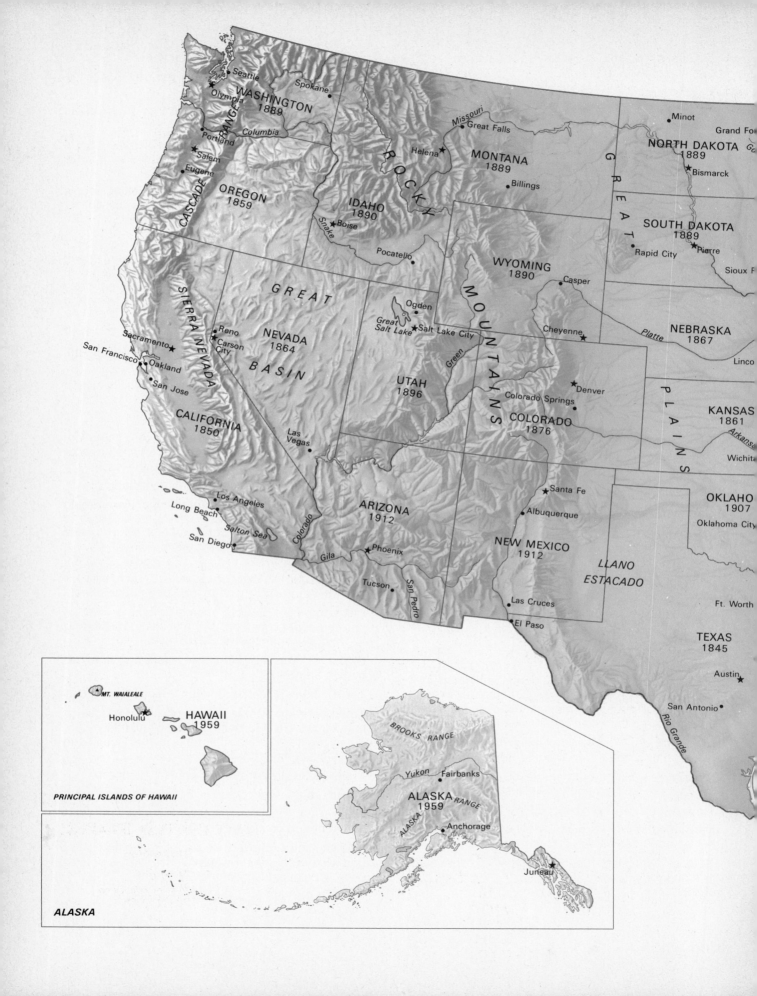

Seattle
Spokane
WASHINGTON
1889
Olympia
Portland
Columbia
Salem
Eugene
CASCADE RANGE
OREGON
1859

Missouri
Great Falls
Helena
MONTANA
1889
Billings

ROCKY

Minot
Grand For
NORTH DAKOTA
1889
Bismarck

IDAHO
1890
Snake
Boise

Pocatello

WYOMING
1890
Casper

SOUTH DAKOTA
1889
Rapid City
Pierre

Sioux F

SIERRA NEVADA

GREAT

NEVADA
1864
Reno
Carson
City

BASIN

Ogden
Great
Salt Lake
Salt Lake City

M O U N T A I N S

Green

Cheyenne

Platte

G R E A T

P L A I N S

NEBRASKA
1867

Linco

Sacramento
San Francisco
Oakland
San Jose

CALIFORNIA
1850

UTAH
1896

Colorado Springs
Denver

COLORADO
1876

KANSAS
1861

Arkansa

Wichita

Las
Vegas

Los Angeles
Long Beach
Salton Sea
San Diego

Colorado

ARIZONA
1912

Gila

Phoenix

Tucson

San Pedro

Santa Fe

Albuquerque

NEW MEXICO
1912

LLANO
ESTACADO

OKLAHO
1907
Oklahoma City

Ft. Worth

Las Cruces
El Paso

TEXAS
1845

Austin

San Antonio

Rio Grande

MT. WAIALEALE
Honolulu
HAWAII
1959

PRINCIPAL ISLANDS OF HAWAII

BROOKS RANGE

Yukon
Fairbanks

ALASKA
1959
ALASKA RANGE
Anchorage

Juneau

ALASKA

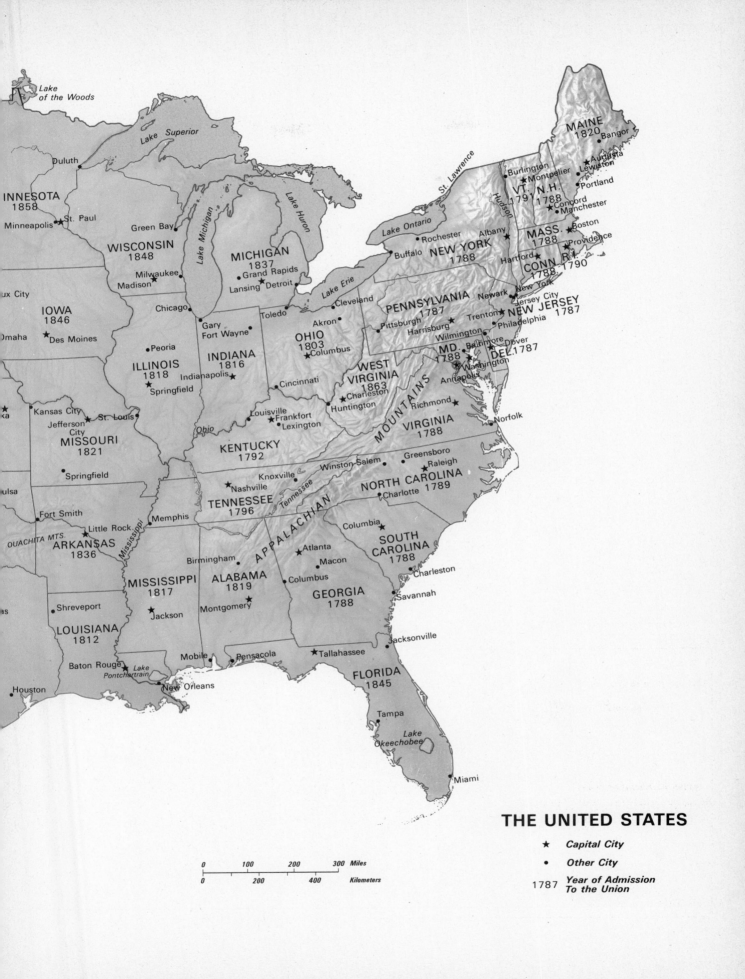

Lake of the Woods

Lake Superior

Duluth

MINNESOTA
1858

Minneapolis • • St. Paul

Sioux City

IOWA
1846

Omaha • Des Moines

Kansas City

Topeka •

Springfield

Tulsa

Fort Smith

ARKANSAS
1836

OUACHITA MTS.

Little Rock

Shreveport

Houston

Baton Rouge

LOUISIANA
1812

New Orleans

Lake Pontchartrain

Mobile

Pensacola

WISCONSIN
1848

Green Bay

Milwaukee
Madison

Chicago

ILLINOIS
1818

Peoria

Springfield

MISSOURI
1821

Jefferson City
St. Louis

Lake Michigan

MICHIGAN
1837

Grand Rapids

Lansing Detroit

Gary
Fort Wayne

INDIANA
1816

Indianapolis

Louisville
Frankfort
Lexington

KENTUCKY
1792

Nashville

TENNESSEE
1796

Memphis

MISSISSIPPI
1817

Jackson

ALABAMA
1819

Montgomery

Birmingham

Columbus

Lake Huron

Toledo

OHIO
1803

Columbus

Cincinnati

Akron

Cleveland

Lake Erie

Knoxville

Tennessee

APPALACHIAN

Atlanta

Macon

GEORGIA
1788

Savannah

Lake Ontario

St. Lawrence

Rochester

Buffalo

NEW YORK
1788

Albany

Hartford

PENNSYLVANIA
1787

Pittsburgh

Harrisburg

WEST VIRGINIA
1863

Charleston

Huntington

MOUNTAINS

Richmond

VIRGINIA
1788

Winston-Salem

Greensboro

Raleigh

NORTH CAROLINA
1789

Charlotte

Columbia

SOUTH CAROLINA
1788

Charleston

Hudson

MAINE
1820

Bangor

Burlington
Montpelier

VT. N.H.
1791 1788

Lewiston
Augusta

Portland

Concord
Manchester

MASS.
1788

Boston

Providence

CONN. R.I.
1788 1790

New York

Newark

Jersey City

NEW JERSEY
1787

Trenton

Philadelphia

Wilmington

MD.
1788

Baltimore

Washington

Annapolis

DEL. 1787

Dover

Norfolk

Jacksonville

Tallahassee

FLORIDA
1845

Tampa

Lake Okeechobee

Miami

THE UNITED STATES

★ Capital City

• Other City

1787 Year of Admission
To the Union

0   100   200   300 Miles

0   200   400 Kilometers

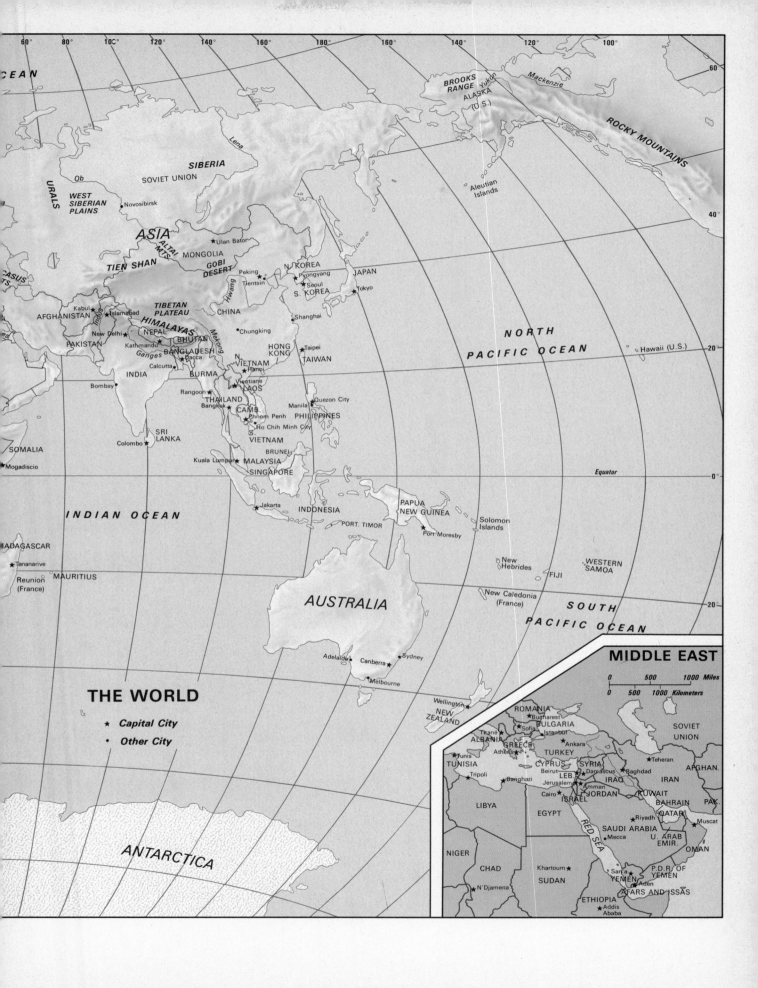

The Declaration of Independence

When in the course of human events it becomes necessary for one people to dissolve the political bands which have connected them with another and to assume, among the powers of the earth, the separate and equal station to which the laws of nature and of nature's God entitle them, a decent respect to the opinions of mankind requires that they should declare the causes which impel them to the separation.

We hold these truths to be self-evident, that all men are created equal; that they are endowed by their Creator with certain unalienable rights; that among these are life, liberty, and the pursuit of happiness. That, to secure these rights, governments are instituted among men, deriving their just powers from the consent of the governed; that, whenever any form of government becomes destructive of these ends, it is the right of the people to alter or to abolish it, and to institute a new government, laying its foundation on such principles, and organizing its powers in such form, as to them shall seem most likely to effect their safety and happiness. Prudence, indeed, will dictate that governments long established should not be changed for light and transient causes; and, accordingly, all experience hath shown that mankind are more disposed to suffer, while evils are sufferable, than to right themselves by abolishing the forms to which they are accustomed. But when a long train of abuses and usurpations, pursuing invariably the same object, evinces a design to reduce them under absolute despotism, it is their right, it is their duty, to throw off such government and to provide new guards for their future security. Such has been the patient sufferance of these colonies, and such is now the necessity which constrains them to alter their former systems of government. The history of the present King of Great Britain is a history of repeated injuries and usurpations, all having, in direct object, the establishment of an absolute tyranny over these States. To prove this, let facts be submitted to a candid world:

He has refused his assent to laws the most wholesome and necessary for the public good.

He has forbidden his governors to pass laws of immediate and pressing importance, unless suspended in their operation till his assent should be obtained; and, when so suspended, he has utterly neglected to attend to them.

He has refused to pass other laws for the accommodation of large districts of people, unless those people would relinquish the right of representation in the legislature; a right inestimable to them and formidable to tyrants only.

He has called together legislative bodies at places unusual, uncomfortable, and distant from the depository of their public records, for the sole purpose of fatiguing them into compliance with his measures.

He has dissolved representative houses, repeatedly for opposing, with manly firmness, his invasions on the rights of the people.

He has refused, for a long time after such dissolutions, to cause others to be elected; whereby the legislative powers, incapable of annihilation, have returned to the people at large for their exercise; the state remaining, in the meantime, exposed to all the danger of invasion from without and convulsions within.

He has endeavored to prevent the population of these States; for that purpose, obstructing the laws for naturalization of foreigners, refusing to pass others to encourage their migration hither, and raising the conditions of new appropriations of lands.

He has obstructed the administration of justice by refusing his assent to laws for establishing judiciary powers.

He has made judges dependent on his will alone for the tenure of their offices and the amount and payment of their salaries.

He has erected a multitude of new offices and sent hither swarms of officers to harass our people and eat out their substance.

He has kept among us, in time of peace, standing armies, without the consent of our legislatures.

He has affected to render the military independent of, and superior to, the civil power.

He has combined with others to subject us to a jurisdiction foreign to our Constitution and unacknowledged by our laws, giving his assent to their acts of pretended legislation—

For quartering large bodies of armed troops among us;

For protecting them by a mock trial from punishment for any murders which they should commit on the inhabitants of these States;

For cutting off our trade with all parts of the world;

For imposing taxes on us without our consent;

For depriving us, in many cases, of the benefit of trial by jury;

For transporting us beyond seas to be tried for pretended offences;

For abolishing the free system of English laws in a neighboring province, establishing therein an arbitrary government, and enlarging its boundaries, so as to render it at once an example and fit instrument for introducing the same absolute rule into these colonies;

For taking away our charters, abolishing our most valuable laws, and altering, fundamentally, the powers of our governments;

For suspending our own legislatures and declaring themselves invested with power to legislate for us in all cases whatsoever.

He has abdicated government here by declaring us out of his protection and waging war against us.

He has plundered our seas, ravaged our coasts, burnt our towns, and destroyed the lives of our people.

He is, at this time, transporting large armies of foreign mercenaries to complete the works of death, desolation, and tyranny already begun with circumstances of cruelty and perfidy scarcely paralleled in the most barbarous ages, and totally unworthy the head of a civilized nation.

He has constrained our fellow citizens, taken captive on the high seas, to bear arms against their country, to become the executioners of their friends and brethren, or to fall themselves by their hands.

He has excited domestic insurrections amongst us and has endeavored to bring on the inhabitants of our frontiers, the merciless Indian savages, whose known rule of warfare is an undistinguished destruction of all ages, sexes, and conditions.

In every stage of these oppressions, we have petitioned for redress in the most humble terms; our repeated petitions have been answered only by repeated injury. A prince whose character is thus marked by every act which may define a tyrant is unfit to be the ruler of a free people.

Nor have we been wanting in attention to our British brethren. We have warned them, from time to time, of attempts made by their legislature to extend an unwarrantable jurisdiction over us. We have reminded them of the circumstances of our emigration and settlement here. We have appealed to their native justice and magnanimity, and we have conjured them, by the ties of our common kindred, to disavow these usurpations, which would inevitably interrupt our connections and correspondence. They, too, have been deaf to the voice of justice and consanguinity. We must, therefore, acquiesce in the necessity which denounces our separation, and hold them, as we hold the rest of mankind, enemies in war, in peace, friends.

We, therefore, the representatives of the United States of America, in general Congress assembled, appealing to the Supreme Judge of the world for the rectitude of our intentions, do, in the name and by the authority of the good people of these colonies, solemnly publish and declare, that these united colonies are, and of right ought to be, free and independent states: that they are absolved from all allegiance to the British Crown, and that all political connection between them and the state of Great Britain is, and ought to be, totally dissolved; and that, as free and independent states, they have full power to levy war, conclude peace, contract alliances, establish commerce, and to do all other acts and things which independent states may of right do. And, for the support of this declaration, with a firm reliance on the protection of Divine Providence, we mutually pledge to each other our lives, our fortunes, and our sacred honor.

The Constitution of the United States

We the people of the United States, in order to form a more perfect union, establish justice, insure domestic tranquility, provide for the common defense, promote the general welfare, and secure the blessings of liberty to ourselves and our posterity, do ordain and establish this Constitution for the United States of America.

Article I

SECTION 1. All legislative powers herein granted shall be vested in a Congress of the United States, which shall consist of a Senate and House of Representatives.

SECTION 2. 1. The House of Representatives shall be composed of members chosen every second year by the people of the several States, and the electors in each State shall have the qualifications requisite for electors of the most numerous branch of the State legislature.

2. No person shall be a representative who shall not have attained to the age of twenty-five years, and been seven years a citizen of the United States, and who shall not, when elected, be an inhabitant of that State in which he shall be chosen.

3. Representatives and direct taxes[1] shall be apportioned among the several States which may be included within this Union, according to their respective numbers, which shall be determined by adding to the whole number of free persons, including those bound to service for a term of

[1]See the Sixteenth Amendment.

years, and excluding Indians not taxed, three fifths of all other persons.[2] The actual enumeration shall be made within three years after the first meeting of the Congress of the United States, and within every subsequent term of ten years, in such manner as they shall by law direct. The number of representatives shall not exceed one for every thirty thousand, but each State shall have at least one representative; and until such enumeration shall be made, the State of New Hampshire shall be entitled to choose three, Massachusetts eight, Rhode Island and Providence Plantations one, Connecticut five, New York six, New Jersey four, Pennsylvania eight, Delaware one, Maryland six, Virginia ten, North Carolina five, South Carolina five, and Georgia three.

4. When vacancies happen in the representation from any State, the executive authority thereof shall issue writs of election to fill such vacancies.

5. The House of Representatives shall choose their speaker and other officers; and shall have the sole power of impeachment.

SECTION 3. 1. The Senate of the United States shall be composed of two senators from each State, chosen by the legislature thereof,[3] for six years; and each senator shall have one vote.

2. Immediately after they shall be assembled in consequence of the first election, they shall be divided as equally as may be into three classes. The seats of the senators of the first class shall be vacated at the expiration of the second year, of the

[2]See the Fourteenth Amendment.
[3]See the Seventeenth Amendment.

second class at the expiration of the fourth year, and of the third class at the expiration of the sixth year, so that one third may be chosen every second year; and if vacancies happen by resignation, or otherwise, during the recess of the legislature of any State, the executive thereof may make temporary appointments until the next meeting of the legislature, which shall then fill such vacancies.[4]

3. No person shall be a senator who shall not have attained to the age of thirty years, and been nine years a citizen of the United States, and who shall not, when elected, be an inhabitant of that State for which he shall be chosen.

4. The Vice President of the United States shall be President of the Senate, but shall have no vote, unless they be equally divided.

5. The Senate shall choose their other officers, and also a president pro tempore, in the absence of the Vice President, or when he shall exercise the office of the President of the United States.

6. The Senate shall have the sole power to try all impeachments. When sitting for that purpose, they shall be on oath or affirmation. When the President of the United States is tried, the chief justice shall preside: and no person shall be convicted without the concurrence of two thirds of the members present.

7. Judgment in cases of impeachment shall not extend further than to removal from office, and disqualifications to hold and enjoy any office of honor, trust or profit under the United States: but the party convicted shall nevertheless be liable and subject ot indictment, trial, judgment and punishment, according to law.

SECTION 4.   1. The times, places, and manner of holding elections for senators and representatives, shall be prescribed in each State by the legislature thereof; but the Congress may at any time by law make or alter such regulations, except as to the places of choosing senators.

2. The Congress shall assemble at least once in every year, and such meeting shall be on the first Monday in December, unless they shall by law appoint a different day.

SECTION 5.   1. Each House shall be the judge of the elections, returns and qualifications of its own members, and a majority of each shall constitute a quorum to do business; but a smaller number may adjourn from day to day, and may be authorized to compel the attendance of absent members, in such manner, and under such penalties as each House may provide.

2. Each House may determine the rules of its proceedings, punish its members for disorderly

behavior, and, with the concurrence of two thirds, expel a member.

3. Each House shall keep a journal of its proceedings, and from time to time publish the same, excepting such parts as may in their judgment require secrecy; and the yeas and nays of the members of either House on any question shall, at the desire of one fifth of those present, be entered on the journal.

4. Neither House, during the session of Congress, shall, without the consent of the other, adjourn for more than three days, nor to any other place than that in which the two Houses shall be sitting.

SECTION 6.   1. The senators and representatives shall receive a compensation for their services, to be ascertained by law, and paid out of the Treasury of the United States. They shall in all cases, except treason, felony, and breach of the peace, be privileged from arrest during their attendance at the session of their respective Houses, and in going to and returning from the same; and for any speech or debate in either House, they shall not be questioned in any other place.

2. No senator or representative shall, during the time for which he was elected, be appointed to any civil office under the authority of the United States, which shall have been created, or the emoluments whereof shall have been increased, during such time; and no person holding any office under the United States shall be a member of either House during his continuance in office.

SECTION 7.   1. All bills for raising revenue shall originate in the House of Representatives; but the Senate may propose or concur with amendments as on other bills.

2. Every bill which shall have passed the House of Representatives and the Senate, shall, before it become a law, be presented to the President of the United States; If he approves he shall sign it, but if not he shall return it, with his objections, to that House in which it shall have originated, who shall enter the objections at large on their journal, and proceed to reconsider it. If after such reconsideration two thirds of that House shall agree to pass the bill, it shall be sent, together with the objections, to the other House, by which it shall likewise be reconsidered, and if approved by two thirds of that House, it shall become a law. But in all such cases the votes of both Houses shall be determined by yeas and nays, and the names of the persons voting for and against the bill shall be entered on the journal of each House respectively. If any bill shall not be returned by the President within ten days (Sundays excepted)

after it shall have been presented to him, the same shall be a law, in like manner as if he had signed it, unless the Congress by their adjournment prevent its return, in which case it shall not be a law.

3. Every order, resolution, or vote to which the concurrence of the Senate and the House of Representatives may be necessary (except on a question of adjournment) shall be presented to the President of the United States; and before the same shall take effect, shall be approved by him, or being disapproved by him, shall be repassed by two thirds of the Senate and House of Representatives, according to the rules and limitations prescribed in the case of a bill.

SECTION 8.   The Congress shall have the power

1. To lay and collect taxes, duties, imposts, and excises, to pay the debts and provide for the common defense and general welfare of the United States; but all duties, imposts, and excises shall be uniform throughout the United States;

2. To borrow money on the credit of the United States;

3. To regulate commerce with foreign nations, and among the several States, and with the Indian tribes;

4. To establish an uniform rule of naturalization, and uniform laws on the subject of bankruptcies throughout the United States;

5. To coin money, regulate the value thereof, and of foreign coin, and fix the standard of weights and measures;

6. To provide for the punishment of counterfeiting the securities and current coin of the United States;

7. To establish post offices and post roads;

8. To promote the progress of science and useful arts, by securing for limited times to authors and inventors the exclusive right to their respective writings and discoveries;

9. To constitute tribunals inferior to the Supreme Court;

10. To define and punish piracies and felonies committed on the high seas, and offenses against the law of nations;

11. To declare war, grant letters of marque and reprisal, and make rules concerning captures on land and water;

12. To raise and support armies, but no appropriation of money to that use shall be for a longer term than two years;

13. To provide and maintain a navy;

14. To make rules for the government and regulation of the land and naval forces;

15. To provide for calling forth the militia to execute the laws of the Union, suppress insurrections and repel invasions;

16. To provide for organizing, arming, and disciplining the militia, and for governing such part of them as may be employed in the service of the United States, reserving to the States respectively, the appointment of the officers, and the authority of training the militia according to the discipline prescribed by Congress;

17. To exercise exclusive legislation in all cases whatsoever, over such district (not exceeding ten miles square) as may, by cession of particular States, and the acceptance of Congress, become the seat of the government of the United States, and to exercise like authority over all places purchased by the consent of the legislature of the State in which the same shall be, for the erection of forts, magazines, arsenals, dockyards, and other needful buildings; and

18. To make all laws which shall be necessary and proper for carrying into execution the foregoing powers, and all other powers vested by this Constitution in the government of the United States, or any department or officer thereof.

SECTION 9.   1. The migration or importation of such persons as any of the States now existing shall think proper to admit, shall not be prohibited by the Congress prior to the year one thousand eight hundred and eight, but a tax or duty may be imposed on such importation, not exceeding ten dollars for each person.

2. The privilege of the writ of habeas corpus shall not be suspended, unless when in cases of rebellion or invasion the public safety may require it.

3. No bill of attainder or ex post facto law shall be passed.

4. No capitation, or other direct, tax shall be laid, unless in proportion to the census or enumeration hereinbefore directed to be taken.[5]

5. No tax or duty shall be laid on articles exported from any State.

6. No preference shall be given by any regulation of commerce or revenue to the ports of one State over those of another; nor shall vessels bound to, or from, one State be obliged to enter, clear, or pay duties in another.

7. No money shall be drawn from the treasury, but in consequence of appropriations made by law; and a regular statement and account of the receipts and expenditures of all public money shall be published from time to time.

[5]See the Sixteenth Amendment.

8. No title of nobility shall be granted by the United States: and no person holding any office of profit or trust under them, shall, without the consent of the Congress, accept of any present, emolument, office, or title, of any kind whatever, from any king, prince, or foreign State.

SECTION 10. 1. No State shall enter into any treaty, alliance, or confederation; grant letters of marque and reprisal; coin money; emit bills of credit; make any thing but gold and silver coin a tender in payment of debts; pass any bill of attainder, ex post facto law, or law impairing the obligation of contracts, or grant any title of nobility.

2. No State shall, without the consent of the Congress, lay any imposts or duties on imports or exports, except what may be absolutely necessary for executing its inspection laws: and the net produce of all duties and imposts laid by any State on imports or exports, shall be for the use of the treasury of the United States; and all such laws shall be subject to the revision and control of the Congress.

3. No State shall, without the consent of the Congress, lay any duty of tonnage, keep troops, or ships of war in time of peace, enter into any agreement or compact with another State, or with a foreign power, or engage in war, unless actually invaded, or in such imminent danger as will not admit of delay.

Article II

SECTION 1. 1. The executive power shall be vested in a President of the United States of America. He shall hold his office during the term of four years, and, together with the Vice President, chosen for the same term, be elected, as follows:

2. Each State shall appoint, in such manner as the legislature thereof may direct, a number of electors, equal to the whole number of senators and representatives to which the State may be entitled in the Congress: but no senator or representative, or person holding an office of trust or profit under the United States, shall be appointed an elector.

The electors shall meet in their respective States, and vote by ballot for two persons, of whom one at least shall not be an inhabitant of the same State with themselves. And they shall make a list of all the persons voted for, and of the number of votes for each; which list they shall sign and certify, and transmit sealed to the seat of the government of the United States, directed to the president of the Senate. The president of the Senate shall, in the presence of the Senate

and House of Representatives, open all the certificates, and the votes shall then be counted. The person having the greatest number of votes shall be the President, if such number be a majority of the whole number of electors appointed; and if there be more than one who have such majority, and have an equal number of votes, then the House of Representatives shall immediately choose by ballot one of them for President; and if no person have a majority, then from the five highest on the list the said House shall in like manner choose the President. But in choosing the President, the votes shall be taken by States, the representation from each State having one vote; a quorum for this purpose shall consist of a member or members from two thirds of the States, and a majority of all the States shall be necessary to a choice. In every case, after the choice of the President, the person having the greatest number of votes of the electors shall be the Vice President. But if there should remain two or more who have equal votes, the Senate shall choose from them by ballot the Vice President.[6]

3. The Congress may determine the time of choosing the electors, and the day on which they shall give their votes; which day shall be the same throughout the United States.

4. No person except a natural born citizen, or a citizen of the United States, at the time of the adoption of this Constitution, shall be eligible to the office of President; neither shall any person be eligible to that office who shall not have attained to the age of thirty-five years, and been fourteen years a resident within the United States.

5. In case of the removal of the President from office, or of his death, resignation, or inability to discharge the powers and duties of the said office, the same shall devolve on the Vice President, and the Congress may by law provide for the case of removal, death, resignation or inability, both of the President and Vice President, declaring what officer shall then act as President, and such officer shall act accordingly, until the disability be removed, or a President shall be elected.

6. The President shall, at stated times, receive for his services a compensation, which shall neither be increased nor diminished during the period for which he shall have been elected, and he shall not receive within that period any other emolument from the United States, or any of them.

7. Before he enter on the execution of his office, he shall take the following oath or affirmation:— "I do solemnly swear (or affirm) that I will faithfully execute the office of President of the United

[6]*Superseded by the Twelfth Amendment.*

States, and will to the best of my ability, preserve, protect and defend the Constitution of the United States."

SECTION 2.   1. The President shall be commander in chief of the army and navy of the United States, and of the militia of the several States, when called into the actual service of the United States; he may require the opinion, in writing, of the principal officer in each of the executive departments, upon any subject relating to the duties of their respective offices, and he shall have power to grant reprieves and pardons for offenses against the United States, except in cases of impeachment.

2. He shall have power, by and with the advice and consent of the Senate, to make treaties, provided two thirds of the senators present concur; and he shall nominate, and by and with the advice and consent of the Senate, shall appoint ambassadors, other public ministers and consuls, judges of the Supreme Court, and all other officers of the United States, whose appointments are not herein otherwise provided for, and which shall be established by law: but the Congress may by law vest the appointment of such inferior officers, as they think proper, in the President alone, in the courts of law, or in the heads of departments.

3. The President shall have power to fill up all vacancies that may happen during the recess of the Senate, by granting commissions which shall expire at the end of their next session.

SECTION 3.   He shall from time to time give to the Congress information of the state of the Union, and recommend to their consideration such measures as he shall judge necessary and expedient; he may, on extraordinary occasions, convene both Houses, or either of them, and in case of disagreement between them with respect to the time of adjournment, he may adjourn them to such time as he shall think proper; he shall receive ambassadors and other public ministers; he shall take care that the laws be faithfully executed, and shall commission all the officers of the United States.

SECTION 4.   The President, Vice President, and all civil officers of the United States, shall be removed from office on impeachment for, and conviction of, treason, bribery, or other high crimes and misdemeanors.

Article III

SECTION 1.   The judicial power of the United States shall be vested in one Supreme Court, and in such inferior courts as the Congress may from time to time ordain and establish. The judges, both of the Supreme and inferior courts, shall hold their offices during good behavior, and shall, at stated times, receive for their services, a compensation, which shall not be diminished during their continuance in office.

SECTION 2.   1. The judicial power shall extend to all cases, in law and equity, arising under this Constitution, the laws of the United States, and treaties made, or which shall be made, under their authority;—to all cases affecting ambassadors, other public ministers and consuls;—to all cases of admiralty and maritime jurisdiction;—to controversies to which the United States shall be a party;[7]—to controversies between two or more States;—between a State and citizens of another State;—between citizens of different States;—between citizens of the same State claiming lands under grants of different States, and between a State, or the citizens thereof, and foreign States, citizens or subjects.

2. In all cases affecting ambassadors, other public ministers and consuls, and those in which a State shall be party, the Supreme Court shall have original jurisdiction. In all the other cases before mentioned, the Supreme Court shall have appellate jurisdiction, both as to law and fact, with such exceptions, and under such regulations as the Congress shall make.

3. The trial of all crimes, except in cases of impeachment, shall be by jury; and such trial shall be held in the State where the said crimes shall have been committed; but when not committed within any State, the trial shall be at such place or places as the Congress may by law have directed.

SECTION 3.   1. Treason against the United States shall consist only in levying war against them, or in adhering to their enemies, giving them aid and comfort. No person shall be convicted of treason unless on the testimony of two witnesses to the same overt act, or on confession in open court.

2. The Congress shall have power to declare the punishment of treason, but no attainder of treason shall work corruption of blood, or forfeiture except during the life of the person attainted.

Article IV

SECTION 1.   Full faith and credit shall be given in each State to the public acts, records, and judicial proceedings of every other State. And the Congress may by general laws prescribe the manner in which such acts, records and proceedings shall be proved, and the effect thereof.

[7]See the Eleventh Amendment.

SECTION 2.   1. The citizens of each State shall be entitled to all privileges and immunities of citizens in the several States.[8]

2. A person charged in any State with treason, felony, or other crime, who shall flee from justice, and be found in another State, shall on demand of the executive authority of the State from which he fled, be delivered up to be removed to the State having jurisdiction of the crime.

3. No person held to service or labor in one State under the laws thereof, escaping into another, shall, in consequence of any law or regulation therein, be discharged from such service or labor, but shall be delivered up on claim of the party to whom such service or labor may be due.[9]

SECTION 3.   1. New States may be admitted by the Congress into this Union; but no new State shall be formed or erected within the jurisdiction of any other State; nor any State be formed by the junction of two or more States, or parts of States, without the consent of the legislatures of the States concerned as well as of the Congress.

2. The Congress shall have power to dispose of and make all needful rules and regulations respecting the territory or other property belonging to the United States; and nothing in this Constitution shall be so construed as to prejudice any claims of the United States, or of any particular State.

SECTION 4.   The United States shall guarantee to every State in this Union a republican form of government, and shall protect each of them against invasion; and on application of the legislature, or of the executive (when the legislature cannot be convened) against domestic violence.

Article V

The Congress, whenever two thirds of both Houses shall deem it necessary, shall propose amendments to this Constitution, or, on the application of the legislatures of two thirds of the several States, shall call a convention for proposing amendments, which in either case, shall be valid to all intents and purposes, as part of this Constitution, when ratified by the legislatures of three fourths of the several States, or by conventions in three fourths thereof, as the one or the other mode of ratification may be proposed by the Congress; Provided that no amendment which may be made prior to the year one thousand eight hundred and eight shall in any manner affect the first and fourth clauses in the ninth section of the

first article; and that no State, without its consent, shall be deprived of its equal suffrage in the Senate.

Article VI

1. All debts contracted and engagements entered into, before the adoption of this Constitution, shall be as valid against the United States under this Constitution, as under the Confederation.[10]

2. This Constitution, and the laws of the United States which shall be made in pursuance thereof; and all treaties made, or which shall be made, under the authority of the United States, shall be the supreme law of the land; and the judges in every State shall be bound thereby, any thing in the Constitution or laws of any State to the contrary notwithstanding.

3. The senators and representatives before mentioned, and the members of the several State legislatures, and all executive and judicial officers, both of the United States and of the several States, shall be bound by oath or affirmation to support this Constitution; but no religious test shall ever be required as a qualification to any office or public trust under the United States.

Article VII

The ratification of the conventions of nine States shall be sufficient for the establishment of this Constitution between the States so ratifying the same.

Done in Convention by the unanimous consent of the States present the seventeenth day of September in the year of our Lord one thousand seven hundred and eighty-seven, and of the independence of the United States of America the twelfth. In witness whereof we have hereunto subscribed our names.

[Names omitted]

*   *   *

Articles in addition to, and amendment of, the Constitution of the United States of America, proposed by Congress, and ratified by the legislatures of the several States, pursuant to the fifth article of the original Constitution.

AMENDMENT I [First ten amendments ratified December 15, 1791]

Congress shall make no law respecting an establishment of religion, or prohibiting the free ex-

---

[8]See the Fourteenth Amendment, Sec. 1.
[9]See the Thirteenth Amendment.

[10]See the Fourteenth Amendment, Sec. 4.

ercise thereof; or abridging the freedom of speech, or of the press; or the right of the people peaceably to assemble, and to petition the government for a redress of grievances.

AMENDMENT II

A well regulated militia, being necessary to the security of a free State, the right of the people to keep and bear arms, shall not be infringed.

AMENDMENT III

No soldier shall, in time of peace be quartered in any house, without the consent of the owner, nor in time of war, but in a manner to be prescribed by law.

AMENDMENT IV

The right of the people to secure in their persons, houses, papers, and effects, against unreasonable searches and seizures, shall not be violated, and no warrants shall issue, but upon probable cause, supported by oath or affirmation, and particularly describing the place to be searched, and the persons or things to be seized.

AMENDMENT V

No person shall be held to answer for a capital, or otherwise infamous crime, unless on a presentment or indictment of a grand jury, except in cases arising in the land or naval forces, or in the militia, when in actual service in time of war or public danger; nor shall any person be subject for the same offense to be twice put in jeopardy of life or limb; nor shall be compelled in any criminal case to be a witness against himself, nor be deprived of life, liberty, or property, without due process of law; nor shall private property be taken for public use, without just compensation.

AMENDMENT VI

In all criminal prosecutions, the accused shall enjoy the right to a speedy and public trial, by an impartial jury of the State and district wherein the crime shall have been committed, which district shall have been previously ascertained by law, and to be informed of the nature and cause of the accusation; to be confronted with the witnesses against him; to have compulsory process for obtaining witnesses in his favor, and to have the assistance of counsel for his defense.

AMENDMENT VII

In suits at common law, where the value in controversy shall exceed twenty dollars, the right of trial by jury shall be preserved, and no fact tried by a jury shall be otherwise reëxamined in any court of the United States, than according to the rules of the common law.

AMENDMENT VIII

Excessive bail shall not be required, nor excessive fines imposed, nor cruel and unusual punishments inflicted.

AMENDMENT IX

The enumeration in the Constitution of certain rights shall not be construed to deny or disparage others retained by the people.

AMENDMENT X

The powers not delegated to the United States by the Constitution, nor prohibited by it to the States, are reserved to the States respectively, or to the people.

AMENDMENT XI [January 8, 1798]

The judicial power of the United States shall not be construed to extend to any suit in law or equity, commenced or prosecuted against one of the United States by citizens of another State, or by citizens or subjects of any foreign State.

AMENDMENT XII [September 25, 1804]

The electors shall meet in their respective States, and vote by ballot for President and Vice President, one of whom, at least, shall not be an inhabitant of the same State with themselves; they shall name in their ballots the person voted for as President, and in distinct ballots, the person voted for as Vice President, and they shall make distinct lists of all persons voted for as President and of all persons voted for as Vice President, and of the number of votes for each, which lists they shall sign and certify, and transmit sealed to the seat of the government of the United States, directed to the President of the Senate;—The President of the Senate shall, in the presence of the Senate and House of Representatives, open all the certificates and the votes shall then be counted;— The person having the greatest number of votes for President, shall be the President, if such number be a majority of the whole number of electors appointed; and if no person have such majority, then from the persons having the highest numbers not exceeding three on the list of those voted for as President, the House of Representatives shall choose immediately, by ballot, the President. But in choosing the President, the votes shall be taken by States, the representation from each State having one vote; a quorum for this purpose shall consist of the member or members from two thirds of the States, and a majority of all the States shall be necessary to a choice. And if the House of Representatives shall not choose a President whenever the right of choice shall devolve upon them, before the fourth day of March next following, then the Vice President shall act as President, as in the case of the death or other constitutional disability of the President. The person having the greatest number of votes as Vice President shall be the Vice President, if such number be a majority of the whole number of electors appointed, and if no person have a majority, then from the two highest numbers on the list, the Senate shall choose the Vice President; a quorum for the purpose shall consist of two thirds of the whole number of Senators, and a majority of the whole number shall be necessary to a choice. But no person constitutionally ineligible to the office of President shall be eligible to that of Vice President of the United States.

AMENDMENT XIII [December 18, 1865]

SECTION 1. Neither slavery nor involuntary servitude, except as a punishment for crime whereof the party shall have been duly convicted, shall exist within the United States, or any place subject to their jurisdiction.

SECTION 2. Congress shall have power to enforce this article by appropriate legislation.

AMENDMENT XIV [July 28, 1868]

SECTION 1. All persons born or naturalized in the United States, and subject to the jurisdiction thereof, are citizens of the United States and of the State wherein they reside. No State shall make or enforce any law which shall abridge the privileges or immunities of citizens of the United States; nor shall any State deprive any person of life, liberty, or property, without due process of law; nor deny to any person within its jurisdiction the equal protection of the laws.

SECTION 2. Representatives shall be apportioned among the several States according to their respective numbers, counting the whole number of persons in each State, excluding Indians not taxed. But when the right to vote at any election

for the choice of electors for President and Vice President of the United States, representatives in Congress, the executive and judicial officers of a State, or the members of the legislature thereof, is denied to any of the male inhabitants of such State, being twenty-one years of age, and citizens of the United States, or in any way abridged, except for participating in rebellion, or other crime, the basis of representation therein shall be reduced in the proportion which the number of such male citizens shall bear to the whole number of male citizens twenty-one years of age in such State.

SECTION 3. No person shall be a senator or representative in Congress, or elector of President and Vice President, or hold any office, civil or military, under the United States, or under any State, who having previously taken an oath, as a member of Congress, or as an officer of the United States, or as a member of any State legislature, or as an executive or judicial officer of any State, to support the Constitution of the United States, shall have engaged in insurrection or rebellion against the same, or given aid or comfort to the enemies thereof. But Congress may by a vote of two thirds of each House, remove such disability.

SECTION 4. The validity of the public debt of the United States, authorized by law, including debts incurred for payment of pensions and bounties for services in suppressing insurrection or rebellion, shall not be questioned. But neither the United States nor any State shall assume or pay any debt or obligation incurred in aid of insurrection or rebellion against the United States, or any claim for the loss or emancipation of any slave; but all such debts, obligations, and claims shall be held illegal and void.

SECTION 5. The Congress shall have power to enforce, by appropriate legislation, the provisions of this article.

AMENDMENT XV [March 30, 1870]

SECTION 1. The right of citizens of the United States to vote shall not be denied or abridged by the United States or by any State on account of race, color, or previous condition of servitude.

SECTION 2. The Congress shall have power to enforce this article by appropriate legislation.

AMENDMENT XVI [February 25, 1913]

The Congress shall have power to lay and collect taxes on incomes, from whatever source derived, without apportionment among the several States, and without regard to any census or enumeration.

AMENDMENT XVII [May 31, 1913]

The Senate of the United States shall be composed of two senators from each State, elected by the people thereof, for six years; and each senator shall have one vote. The electors in each State shall have the qualifications requisite for electors of the most numerous branch of the State legislature.

When vacancies happen in the representation of any State in the Senate, the executive authority of such State shall issue writs of election to fill such vacancies: *Provided*, That the legislature of any State may empower the executive thereof to make temporary appointments until the people fill the vacancies by election as the legislature may direct.

This amendment shall not be so construed as to affect the election or term of any senator chosen before it becomes valid as part of the Constitution.

AMENDMENT XVIII[11] [January 29, 1919]

After one year from the ratification of this article, the manufacture, sale, or transportation of intoxicating liquors within, the importation thereof into, or the exportation thereof from the United States and all territory subject to the jurisdiction thereof for beverage purposes is thereby prohibited.

The Congress and the several States shall have concurrent power to enforce this article by appropriate legislation.

This article shall be inoperative unless it shall have been ratified as an amendment to the Constitution by the legislatures of the several States, as provided in the Constitution, within seven years from the date of the submission hereof to the States by Congress.

AMENDMENT XIX [August 26, 1920]

The right of citizens of the United States to vote shall not be denied or abridged by the United States or by any State on account of sex.

Congress shall have the power to enforce this article by appropriate legislation.

AMENDMENT XX [January 23, 1933]

SECTION 1. The terms of the President and Vice President shall end at noon on the 20th day

[11]Repealed by the Twenty-first Amendment.

of January, and the terms of Senators and Representatives at noon on the 3d day of January, of the years in which such terms would have ended if this article had not been ratified; and the terms of their successors shall then begin.

SECTION 2. The Congress shall assemble at least once in every year, and such meeting shall begin at noon on the 3d day of January, unless they shall by law appoint a different day.

SECTION 3. If, at the time fixed for the beginning of the term of President, the President-elect shall have died, the Vice President-elect shall become President. If a President shall not have been chosen before the time fixed for the beginning of his term, or if the President-elect shall have failed to qualify, then the Vice President-elect shall act as President until a President shall have qualified; and the Congress may by law provide for the case wherein neither a President-elect nor a Vice President-elect shall have qualified, declaring who shall then act as President, or the manner in which one who is to act shall be selected, and such person shall act accordingly until a President or Vice President shall have qualified.

SECTION 4. The Congress may by law provide for the case of the death of any of the persons from whom the House of Representatives may choose a President whenever the right of choice shall have devolved upon them, and for the case of the death of any of the persons from whom the Senate may choose a Vice President whenever the right of choice shall have devolved upon them.

SECTION 5. Sections 1 and 2 shall take effect on the 15th day of October following the ratification of this article.

SECTION 6. This article shall be inoperative unless it shall have been ratified as an amendment to the Constitution by the legislatures of three-fourths of the several States within seven years from the date of its submission.

AMENDMENT XXI [December 5, 1933]

SECTION 1. The Eighteenth Article of amendment to the Constitution of the United States is hereby repealed.

SECTION 2. The transportation or importation into any State, Territory, or possession of the United States for delivery or use therein of intoxicating liquors in violation of the laws thereof, is hereby prohibited.

SECTION 3. This article shall be inoperative unless it shall have been ratified as an amendment to the Constitution by conventions in the several States, as provided in the Constitution, within seven years from the date of the submission thereof to the States by the Congress.

AMENDMENT XXII [March 1, 1951]

No person shall be elected to the office of the President more than twice, and no person who has held the office of President, or acted as President, for more than two years of a term to which some other person was elected President shall be elected to the office of the President more than once.

But this article shall not apply to any person holding the office of President when this article was proposed by the Congress, and shall not prevent any person who may be holding the office of President, or acting as President, during the term within which this article becomes operative from holding the office of President or acting as President during the remainder of such term.

This article shall be inoperative unless it shall have been ratified as an amendment to the Constitution by the legislatures of three-fourths of the several States within seven years from the date of its submission to the States by the Congress.

AMENDMENT XXIII [March 29, 1961]

SECTION 1. The District constituting the seat of Government of the United States shall appoint in such manner as the Congress may direct:

A number of electors of President and Vice President equal to the whole number of Senators and Representatives in Congress to which the District would be entitled if it were a State, but in no event more than the least populous State; they shall be in addition to those appointed by the States, but they shall be considered, for the purposes of the election of President and Vice President, to be electors appointed by a State; and they shall meet in the District and perform such duties as provided by the twelfth article of amendment.

SECTION 2. The Congress shall have power to enforce this article by appropriate legislation.

AMENDMENT XXIV [January 23, 1964]

SECTION 1. The right of citizens of the United States to vote in any primary or other election for President or Vice President, for electors for President or Vice President, or for Senator or Representative in Congress, shall not be denied or abridged by the United States or any State by reason of failure to pay any poll tax or other tax.

SECTION 2. The Congress shall have power to enforce this article by appropriate legislation.

AMENDMENT XXV [February 10, 1967]

SECTION 1. In case of the removal of the President from office or of his death or resignation, the Vice President shall become President.

SECTION 2. Whenever there is a vacancy in the office of the Vice President, the President shall nominate a Vice President who shall take office upon confirmation by a majority vote of both Houses of Congress.

SECTION 3. Whenever the President transmits to the President pro tempore of the Senate and the Speaker of the House of Representatives his written declaration that he is unable to discharge the powers and duties of his office, and until he transmits to them a written declaration to the contrary, such powers and duties shall be discharged by the Vice President as Acting President.

SECTION 4. Whenever the Vice President and a majority of either the principal officers of the executive departments or of such other body as Congress may by law provide, transmit to the President pro tempore of the Senate and the Speaker of the House of Representatives their written declaration that the President is unable to discharge the powers and duties of his office, the Vice President shall immediately assume the powers and duties of the office as Acting President.

Thereafter, when the President transmits to the President pro tempore of the Senate and the Speaker of the House of Representatives his written declaration that no inability exists, he shall resume the powers and duties of his office unless the Vice President and a majority of either the principal officers of the executive departments or of such other body as Congress may by law provide, transmit within four days to the President pro tempore of the Senate and the Speaker of the House of Representatives their written declaration that the President is unable to discharge the powers and duties of his office. Thereupon Congress shall decide the issue, assembling within forty-eight hours for that purpose if not in session. If the Congress, within twenty-one days after receipt of the latter written declaration, or, if Congress is not in session, within twenty-one days after Congress is required to assemble, determines by two-thirds vote of both houses that the President is unable to discharge the powers and duties of his office, the Vice President shall continue to discharge the same as Acting President; otherwise, the President shall resume the powers and duties of his office.

AMENDMENT XXVI [June 30, 1971]

SECTION 1. The right of citizens of the United States who are eighteen years of age or older to vote shall not be denied or abridged by the United States or by any State on account of age.

SECTION 2. The Congress shall have power to enforce this article by appropriate legislation.

Continued from copyright page

Acknowledgments / SOURCES

The authors and editors have made every effort to trace the ownership of all copyrighted selections found in this book and to make full acknowledgment for their use. Many of the text selections have been adapted from original material.

UNIT 1 **Page 14:** R. H. Major, ed., *Select Letters of Christopher Columbus*, 1847. **15:** *Letters of Christopher Columbus and Americus Vespuccius*, 1878. **16t:** Lesley Byrd Simpson, *The Encomienda in New Spain* (Berkeley, Calif.: University of California, 1929), pp. 30–31. Copyright © 1950 by The Regents of the University of California; reprinted by permission of the University of California Press. **16b–17:** F. Tomas de la Torre, "Desde Salamanca . . . hasta . . . Chiapas," *Readings in Latin American Civilization,* Benjamin Keen, trans. and ed. (Boston: Houghton Mifflin Company, 1955), pp. 150–152. Reprinted by permission. **19–22:** "Ordinances Concerning the Laying Out of New Towns," Zelia Nuttall, trans. and ed., *Hispanic-American Historical Review*, v. 4, No. 4, November 1921 (Durham, N.C.: Duke University Press). Reprinted by permission. **25–26:** *A Historical, Political and Natural Description of California by Pedro Fages, Soldier of Spain,* H. I. Priestly, trans. and ed., (Berkeley, Calif.: University of California Press, 1937). Copyright © 1965 by The Regents of the University of California; reprinted by permission of the University of California Press. **32–33:** Richard Hakluyt, *A Discourse Concerning Western Planting*, 1584. **34:** "Sir Thomas Gates, Knight Governor of Virginia (May 1609)," *The Records of the Virginia Company of London,* Susan Myra Kingsbury, ed. (Washington, D.C.: Government Printing Office, 1933), III, pp. 15, 21–22. **35:** John Smith, *The Generall Historie of Virginia, New-England, and the Summer Isles,* 1624 (Rare Book Division, New York Public Library). **38t:** "Winthrop's Conclusions for the Plantation in New England," *Old South Leaflets,* no. 50, pp. 4–6. **38–39:** Captain Edward Johnson, *Wonder Working Providence of Sions Saviour,* 1654. **39b:** John Winthrop, *Christian Charity, A Model Hereof,* from *Collections of the Massachusetts Historical Society,* Series 3, Volume 7, 1838. **40:** Henry Morris, *Early History of Springfield,* 1876. **42:** Sudbury Town Councel. **44t:** *Collections of the Massachusetts Historical Society,* Series 3, Volume 2, 1830. **44–45:** Nathaniel B. Shurtleff, ed., *Records of the Governor and Company of the Massachusetts Bay,* Volume V, 1853–1854. **46:** *New-England Primer,* 1727 (Rare Book Division, New York Public Library). **53–54:** Adapted from "The Autobiography of the Reverend Devereaux Jarratt, 1732–1768," Douglass Adair, ed., *William and Mary Quarterly IX,* July 1952 (Williamsburg, Va.: Institute of Early American History and Culture), pp. 360–371. Adapted by permission. **55 (both):** R. B. Davis, ed., *William Fitzhugh and His Chesapeake World: 1676–1701: The Fitzhugh Letters and Other Documents* (Chapel Hill, N.C.: University of North Carolina Press, 1963). Reprinted by permission of The University Press of Virginia, publishers for The Virginia Historical Society. **56:** Kenneth Silverman, ed., *Literature in America: The Founding of a Nation* (New York: Free Press, 1971), p. 242. **58:** Andrew Burnaby, *Travels Through the Middle Settlements in North America,* 1775. **59:** Reverend Hugh Jones, *The Present State of Virginia,* 1724. **60:** William H. Browne, ed., *Archives of Maryland: Proceedings and Acts of the General Assembly of Maryland,* 1883. **62:** Hector St. Jean de Crèvecoeur, *Letters from an American Farmer,* 1775. **63:** Pehr Kalm, *Travels into North America,* 1770 (Rare Book Division, New York Public Library). **66:** Andrew Burnaby, *Travels Through the Middle Settlements in North America,* 1775. **67:** *American Husbandry,* Volume I, 1775. **72:** National Society Daughters of the American Revolution Manual for Citizenship.

UNIT 2 **Page 84:** Joshua Gee, *The Trade and Navigation of Great Britain Considered,* 1729. **85t:** Danby Pickering, ed. *The Statutes at Large,* Volume XVI, 1762–1807. **85b–86:** Danby Pickering, ed. *The Statutes at Large,* Volume XX, 1762–1807. **86b–87:** *Publications of the Colonial Society of Massachusetts,* Volume VI, 1904. **91:** Thomas Whatley, *Considerations on the Trade and Finances of This Kingdom,* 1766. **92:** Cobbett, ed., *The Parliamentary History of England,* Volume XVI, 1813. **93t:** *American Archives,* 1837–1846. **93c:** Thomas Hutchinson, *The History of the Colony and Province of Massachusetts-Bay,* L. S. Mayo III, ed. (Cambridge, Mass.: Harvard University Press, 1936), pp. 86–87. **93b–94:** *Boston Gazette,* December 13, 1765. **94b:** *Maryland Gazette,* October 10, 1765, reprinted in *Annals of the American Revolution,* Jedidah Morse, 1824. **95t:** Jedidah Morse, *Annals of the American Revolution,* 1824. **95c:** *The Connecticut Courant,* October 29, 1764. **95b:** "Declarations of the Stamp Act Congress," from *Proceedings of the Congress at New York* (Annapolis, 1766), reprinted in Hezekiah Niles, *Principles and Acts of the Revolution,* 1822. **97t:** John Dickinson, *Letter from a Farmer in Pennsylvania to the Inhabitants of the British Colonies,* 1767–1768. **97b:** John P. Kennedy, ed., *Journal of the House of Burgesses of Virginia, 1761–65,* Volume IV,

1907. **98t:** "Declarations of the Stamp Act Congress," from *Proceedings of the Congress at New York,* (Annapolis, 1766), reprinted in Hezekiah Niles, *Principles and Acts of the Revolution,* 1822. **98b:** Boston Town Records, 1765, from *Report of the Record Commissioners, Boston,* 1886. **99–101:** Cobbett, ed., *Parliamentary History of England,* Volume XVI, 1813. **102t:** Jedidah Morse, *Providence Gazette,* 1795, reprinted in *Annals of the American Revolution,* 1824. **102b:** Cobbett, ed., *The Parliamentary History of England,* Volume XVI, 1813. **103:** Boston Selectmen's Minutes, 1764–1768, from *Twentieth Report of the Record Commissioners,* 1886. **104:** Danby Pickering, ed., *The Statutes at Large,* Volume XXVII, 1762–1807. **107t:** *Boston Gazette,* August 8, 1768. **107b:** John Dickinson, *Letters from a Farmer in Pennsylvania to the Inhabitants of the British Colonies,* 1767–1768. **108:** Letter to the Earl of Hillsborough, April 10, 1770. (Carter I). **109t:** Richard B. Morris and James Woodress, eds., *The Times That Tried Mens' Souls* (St. Louis, Mo.: Webster Publishing Co., 1961). **109b–110:** Letter to the Earl of Hillsborough, April 10, 1770 (Carter I). **113:** *Pennsylvania Magazine of History and Biography,* Volume XV, 1891. **114:** *Pennsylvania Magazine of History and Biography,* Volume XV, 1891. **115:** *Massachusetts Gazette and Boston Weekly News-Letter,* December 23, 1773. **117–118:** Danby Pickering, ed., *The Statutes at Large,* Volume XXX, 1762–1807. **119:** *American Archives,* 1837–1846. **120t:** Adapted by permission of the publishers from *Revolutionary Politics in Massachusetts* by Richard D. Brown, Cambridge, Mass.: Harvard University Press, © 1970 by the President and Fellows of Harvard College. **121:** *Journals of the American Congress from 1774 to 1788,* Volume I, 1923. **125t:** John Dickinson, *Letters from a Farmer in Pennsylvania to the Inhabitants of the British Colonies,* 1767–1768. **125b–126:** Thomas Paine, *Common Sense,* 1776. **127:** W. C. Ford, ed., *Journals of the Continental Congress,* Volume V. **130t:** Margery W. Willard, ed., *Letters on the American Revolution, 1774–1776* (Port Washington, N.Y.: Kennikat, 1968) pp. 179–83. **130c:** Daniel Leonard, "Massachusettsensis, or Letters Addressed to the Inhabitants of Massachusetts Bay", *Massachusetts Gazette,* January 9, 1775. **130b:** Found on the back of a certificate of service, signed by Captain David McQueen, April 30, 1782. From *Military Accounts, Militia, 1777–1794,* Pennsylvania State Archives. **135t:** H. C. Lodge, ed., *The Works of Alexander Hamilton,* Volume I, 1904. **135b:** Alexander Hamilton, *Federalist Paper, No. 1.* **136t:** H. C. Lodge, ed., *The Works of Alexander Hamilton,* Volume 1, 1904. **136c:** W. C. Ford, ed., *The Writings of George Washington,* Volume X, 1891. **136b:** *Senate Documents,* Volume 15, 1909. **137t:** Richard Henry Lee, "Letters of the Federal Farmer to the Republican," reprinted in *Essays on the Constitution of the United States,* Paul L. Ford, ed., 1892. **137c:** *Maryland Gazette and Baltimore Advertiser,* March 7, 1788. **137b:** William V. Wells, ed., *The Life and Public Services of Samuel Adams,* Volume 3, 1866. **138t:** Edmund C. Burnett, ed., *Letters of Members of the Continental Congress* (Washington, D.C.: Carnegie Institution of Washington, 1936), vol. III. **139–143:** Max Farrand ed., *The Records of the Federal Convention of 1787,* Volumes I and II, 1911.

UNIT 3 **Pages 162–164:** Published by permission of Outward Bound, Inc. **167–169:** Timothy Dwight *Travels in New England and New York.* **171t:** Charles A. Murray, *Travels in North America,* 1839. **171b:** Frederick Marryat, *A Diary in America,* 1839. **172:** Timothy Dwight, *Travels in New England and New York.* **174t:** James Fenimore Cooper, *Notions of the Americans,* Volume 1, 1828. **174b:** Charles Dickens, *American Notes,* 1842. **175t:** Oscar Handlin, *This Was America* (New York: Harper & Row) pp. 194–195. **175b:** Frederick Marryat, *A Diary in America,* 1839. **177:** *Statistical Abstract,* U.S. Census, 1840, 1850. **180:** *London Times.* **181–182t:** Joseph H. Ingraham, *The South-West,* 1835. **182b–183:** DeBow's *Review,* December 1855. **183b:** Frederick Law Olmstead, *The Cotton Kingdom,* 1861. **185–186:** *Maryland Historical Magazine,* vol. XIII (Baltimore, Md.: Maryland Historical Society, 1918). **186b–187:** Harriet Martineau, *Retrospect of Western Travel,* 1838. **188t:** Frederick Law Olmstead, *The Cotton Kingdom,* 1861. **188b–189:** James D. B. DeBow, *Resources of the South and West.* **192:** *Statistical Abstract,* U.S. Census, 1840, 1850. **193:** Solomon Northrup, *Twelve Years a Slave,* 1853. **196:** Solomon Northrup, *Twelve Years a Slave,* 1853. **200–201:** Oscar Handlin, *This Was America,* (New York: Harper & Row) pp. 138–139. **201b–202:** Mrs. Frances Milton Trollope, *Domestic Manners of the Americans,* 1832. **202b–203:** William Cooper Howells, *Recollections of Life in Ohio from*

1813 to 1840, 1895. **203b:** Elijah Iles, *Sketches of Early Life and Times*, 1883. **206t:** Frederick Marryat, *A Diary in America*, 1839. **206b–209:** *Norwegian-American Studies and Records*, vol. IX (Northfield, Minn.: Norwegian-American Historical Association, 1936). **210t:** Timothy Flint, *Recollections of the Last Ten Years*, 1826. **210c:** Michael Chevalier, *Letters on America*. **210b:** "Prospects of Ohio," *Ohio State Journal*, July 12, 1827. **212:** *Statistical Abstract*, U.S. Census, 1840, 1850. **214–215:** Richard Henry Dana, Jr., *Two Years Before the Mast*, 1840. **226:** Vance Packard, *A Nation of Strangers*, (New York, David McKay Company, Inc., 1972).

UNIT 4 Pages 232–241: Abridged and adapted from Chapters 9 and 10 in *Groups in Harmony and Tension* by Musafer Sherif and Carolyn W. Sherif. Copyright 1953 by Harper & Row, Publishers, Inc. (Further reference, Sherif & Sherif: *Social Psychology*, Harper & Row, 1969) By permission of the publisher. **254t:** W. P. Garrison and F. J. Garrison, *William Lloyd Garrison, 1805–1879*, 1885. **254b–255:** Theodore D. Weld, *Slavery As It Is: Testimony of a Thousand Witnesses*, 1839. **261:** U.S. Statutes at Large, vol. IX, p. 462 ff. **262:** *The Writings of Abraham Lincoln*. **263:** *Dred Scott vs. Sanford*, 1857. **264:** *New York Herald*, 1859. **266:** Joshua R. Giddings, *Speeches in Congress*, 1853. **267:** Joshua R. Giddings, *Congressional Globe*, 31st Congress, 2nd session, Dec. 9, 1850. **268t:** Richmond *Enquirer*, Dec. 23, 1819. **268b–269:** Charles Sumner, *Congressional Globe*, 34th Congress, 1st session, May 19–20, 1856. **269c:** "Kansas Matters—Appeal to the South" *DeBow's Review*, May 1856. **269b:** Joshua Giddings, *Congressional Globe*, 28th Congress, 1st session, May 21, 1844. **270–271:** Gilbert H. Barnes and Dwight L. Dumond, eds., *The Letters of Theodore Dwight Weld, Angelina Grimke Weld, and Sarah Grimke* (Washington, D.C., American Historical Association) vol. I. **272:** *The Writings of Abraham Lincoln*. **273t:** *Milledgeville Journal*, Dec. 4, 1821. **273b:** Rev. Dr. Richard Furman's *Exposition of the Views of the Baptists, Relative to the Coloured Population of the United States, in a Communication to the Governor of South Carolina*, 1823. **274:** Albert B. Hart and Edward Channing, eds., *American History Leaflets, Colonial and Constitutional*, No. 10, July 1893. **275:** E. N. Elliot, ed., *Cotton Is King, and Pro-Slavery Arguments*, 1860. **276:** The *Liberator*, May 31, 1844. **277:** Autauga (Alabama) *Citizen*, in The *Liberator*, July 4, 1856. **278, 286t, 286b–287:** *The Writings of Abraham Lincoln*. **287:** *Memoirs of General W. T. Sherman*, Vol. II. **291t:** Ku-Klux Klan Conspiracy: South Carolina, 42 Cong., 2nd session. **291b:** *Nation*, XIII, Dec. 7, 1871. **292–293:** *The Ku-Klux Klan Conspiracy. Testimony Taken by the Joint Committee to Inquire into the Condition of Affairs in the Late Insurrectionary States: Florida*, 42 Congress, 2d session. **294:** Senate Miscellaneous Documents, 42 Congress, 1st session, No. 49. **295:** *Congressional Record*, 59 Congress, 2nd session, Jan. 21, 1907.

UNIT 5 Page 308: "Testimony of Charles H. Litchman," *Causes of the General Depression in Labor and Business*, Investigation by a Select Committee of the House of Representatives, 46th Congress, 2nd session, Misc. House Doc. No. 5, 1879. **309:** Testimony of John Morrison before *Senate Committee on Labor and Capital, Report of*, vol. 1. **310–311:** *Report upon the Relations between Labor and Capital* 48th Congress, 1885. **313–314:** Herbert Spencer *Social Statics*, 1850. **314b:** Andrew Carnegie, "Wealth," *North American Review*, CXLVIII, 1889. **315t:** *Chicago Daily News*, Oct. 9, 1882. **315b:** U.S. Industrial Commission Report, I, House Document #476, 56th Congress, 1st session, 1899. **316:** William H. Ghent, *Our Benevolent Feudalism*, 1903. **318t:** Byington, *Homestead*. **318b–319:** Massachusetts Senate Document no. 21, 1868. **320t:** "Rules Adopted by the Cambria Iron Works," April 6, 1874. **320b–321:** *Fall River Labor Standard*, June 5, 1880. **321b:** The Working Girls of Boston, from the 15th Annual Report of the Massachusetts Bureau of Statistics of Labor, 1884. **323:** Chart from *Third Annual Report, 1884*, Illinois Bureau of Labor Statistics, 1884. **327–329:** Frank Norris, *The Octopus*, 1901. **332–333:** Upton Sinclair, *The Cry for Justice* (New York: Holt, Rinehart and Winston, Inc., 1915). **333b–334:** James F. Leisy, *The Folk Song Abecedary* (New York: Hawthorn Books, Inc., 1966), p. 189. **337:** *Declaration of Purpose of the National Grange*, 1874. **338–340:** Populist Party Platform, July 4, 1892. **340:** John Greenway, *American Folksongs of Protest* (New York: Octagon Books, 1971) Copyright © 1953 by the University of Pennsylvania Press. **341b–342:** *American Federationist*, September 1894. **342b–343:** *The New Era, or The Coming Kingdom*, 1893. **343c:** "Address to the Laboring Order of Chicago," *Live Questions*, 1899. **343b:** John Mitchell, *Organized Labor*, 1903. **345t:** *Iron Age*, July 22, 1875. **345b:** T. DeWitt Talmage, *Temperance Selections For Readings and Recitations* 1893. **346:** John T. Ellis, ed., *Documents of American Catholic History* (Beverly Hills, Calif.: Bruce Publishing Company, 1956) pp. 500–501. **346b:** Vachel Lindsay, "Factory Windows Are Always Broken," *The Mentor Book of Major American Poets*, Oscar Williams and Edwin Honig, eds. (New York: The New American Library). **348:** *Fame and Fortune*, Horatio Alger, 1868. **349:** Grover Cleveland, Message of February 16,

1887. **350t:** *Proceedings of the New York State Bar Association*, 1893. **350b–351:** Theodore Roosevelt, *The New Nationalism*, 1910. **351b:** Woodrow Wilson, *The New Freedom*, with Introduction and Notes by William E. Leuchtenburg (Englewood Cliffs, N.J.: Prentice-Hall, Inc., 1961), pp. 25–27. **354:** "Report of General Instructor and Director of Woman's Work," *Proceedings of the Knights of Labor*, 1889. **355–356:** Lucy Larcom, *A New England Girlhood*, 1889. **356b:** Abigail Scott Duniway, Pathbreaking, *An Autobiographical History of the Equal Suffrage Movement in Pacific Coast States*, 1914. **357t:** Mary White Ovington, *Half a Man: The Status of the Negro in New York* (New York: Longmans, Green and Co., 1911). **357b:** Stanton, Anthony et al., eds., *The History of Woman Suffrage*, vol II, 1881. **358:** *Congressional Record*, 49th Congress, 2nd session, vol. XVIII, part 1. **361–363:** Senate Report No. 512, 48th Congress, 1st session. **363b:** Louisiana Laws, 1890, No. III. **363b:** Laws of Tennessee, 1901, Ch. 7, House Bill No. 7. **364–365:** *The Independent* (N.Y.), Sept. 18, 1902, LIV. **366:** *The Negro and the Atlanta Exposition*, Trustees of the John F. Slater Fund, Occasional Papers No. 7, 1896. **367–368:** "The American Negro and the Fatherland." *Addresses and Proceedings of the Congress on Africa*, 1896. **368b–369:** Manuscript in John E. Bruce Collection, Folder No. 7, Schomburg Center for Research in Black Culture, The New York Public Library. Astor, Lenox and Tilden Foundations. **369b–370:** W. E. B. DuBois, "The Immediate Program of the American Negro," *The Crisis*, IX, April 1915, pp. 310–312.

UNIT 6 Page 383t: William Bradford, *Of Plymouth Plantation*. **383b:** From the *Portable North American Indian Reader*, edited by Frederick W. Turner III. Reprinted by permission of The Viking Press. Copyright © 1973, 1974 by The Viking Press, Inc. **386–388:** John G. Neihardt, *Black Elk Speaks* (New York: Simon & Schuster, 1972), p. 53–57. Copyright by John G. Neihardt, 1932, 1959, 1961. **388c:** *Wooden Leg, A Warrior Who Fought with Custer*, Interpreted by Thomas B. Marquis (Lincoln, Nebr.: University of Nebraska Press, 1957), p. 155. **389:** John G. Neihardt, *Black Elk Speaks* (New York: Simon & Schuster, 1972), pp. 79–81. Copyright by John G. Neihardt, 1932, 1959, 1961. **391t:** John Herbert Quick, *Excerpt in Land That Our Fathers Plowed*, D. B. Greenberg, ed. (Indianapolis, Ind.: Bobbs Merrill Company, Inc.). **391b:** Hamlin Garland, *A Son of the Middle Border* (New York, Macmillan Publishing Co., Inc., 1917). Copyright © 1917 by Hamlin Garland, renewed 1945 by Mary I. Lord and Constance G. Williams. **392:** Justice Taylor, *Caldwell v The State of Alabama*, 1832. **398t–399:** John G. Neihardt, *Black Elk Speaks* (New York: Simon & Schuster, 1972), p. 198–200. Copyright by J. G. Neihardt 1932, 1959, 1961. **400c:** *Wooden Leg, A Warrior Who Fought with Custer*, Interpreted by Thomas B. Marquis (Lincoln, Nebr.: University of Nebraska Press, 1957), p. 316. **397–398:** Vine Deloria, Jr., *Of Utmost Good Faith* (San Francisco, Calif.: Straight Arrow Books, 1971), p. 93. **400b–401:** John G. Neihardt, *Black Elk Speaks* (New York: Simon & Schuster, 1972), p. 234–236. Copyright by John G. Neihardt 1932, 1959, 1961. **401b–402:** Dee Brown, *Bury My Heart At Wounded Knee* (New York: Holt, Rinehart and Winston, Inc., 1970), p. 416. **402b–403:** John G. Neihardt, *Black Elk Speaks* (New York: Simon & Schuster, 1972) pp. 9–10. Copyright by J. G. Neihardt 1932, 1959, 1961. **406:** Based on a study by John Adair and Edward W. Spicer, in Margaret Mead, ed., *Cultural Patterns and Technical Change*. (New York: Mentor Books, 1955) Copyright 1955 UNESCO, pp. 242–243. **409–410:** Emily F. Robbins, "If One Speak Bad of Your Mother, How You Feel?," *Red Cross Magazine*, September 1919. **410c:** Thomas and Znaniecki, *The Polish Peasant in Europe and America* (New York: Octagon Books, 1971) v. ii, p. 259. **410c:** Eliakum Zunser, *A Jewish Bard*, 1905. **410–411:** Gazeta Swiateczna, Vol. 18, No. 31. **411c:** Thomas and Znaniecki, *The Polish Peasant in Europe and America* (New York: Octagon Books, 1971) v. iv, p. 119. **411b:** "Circulars Recruiting Labor in Hong Kong," Rhoda Hoff, *America's Immigrants* (New York: H. Z. Walck, Inc., 1967). **412:** N. M. Pavlov, *Stenographic Report of the Peterhof Conference*, 1905. **414t:** F. B. Sanborn, ed., *Proceedings of the Eighth Annual Conference of Charities and Correction*, 1881. **414–415:** Josiah Strong, *Our Country*, 1891. **415b:** *The Blue and Grey Songster*, 1877. **416:** Kenneth L. Roberts, *Why Europe Leaves Home* (Indianapolis, Ind.: The Bobbs Merrill Co., Inc., 1949) p. 113–114. **419–420:** Abridged and adapted from pp. 91–92 in *An American In the Making* by M. E. Ravage. Copyright 1917 by Harper & Row, Publishers, Inc. By permission of the publisher. **420–421:** From *Adjusting Immigrant and Industry* by William M. Leiserson. Copyright 1924 by Harper & Row, Publishers, Inc. By permission of the publisher. **421b–422:** Constantine M. Panunzio, *The Soul of an Immigrant* (New York: Macmillan, 1921), pp. 79–80. **422–423:** Thomas and Znaniecki, *The Polish Peasant In Europe and America* (New York: Octagon Books, 1971), v. iv. pp. 254–255. **423b–424:** Leonard Covello with Guido D'Agostino, *The Heart Is a Teacher* (New York: McGraw-Hill Co., Inc., 1958). Reprinted by permission of Lurton Blassingame, the author's agent. Copyright © 1958 by Leonard Covello. **428b–429:** From pp. 284–285 in *Giants in the Earth* by O. E. Rolvaag. Copyright 1927 by Harper & Row,

Publishers, Inc. By permission of the publisher. **429:** Rose Cohen, *Out of the Shadow* (G. H. Doran, 1918), p. 106. **429–430:** "Autobiography of a Bootblack," *Independent Magazine*, Vol. 54.

UNIT 7   Pages 450–451: "The War Boom Town in America," *Living Age* vol. 290, pp. 751–753. **451b–452:** Reprinted by permission of Charles Scribner's Sons from "The Farmer and Three Dollar Wheat," by Charles M. Harger from *Scribner's Magazine*, 1918, 64. **453:** Chart from George Groh, *The Black Migration*. **458–459:** Gertrude Mathews Shelby, "Florida Frenzy," *Harper's Monthly Magazine*, (New York: Harper and Row), January 1926, p. 177. **460t:** *The New York Times*, May 23, 1926. © 1926 by The New York Times Company. Reprinted by permission. **460b–461:** *The State of the Union Messages of the Presidents of the United States*, vol III. **462b:** *The New York Times*, February 3, 1929. © 1929 by The New York Times Company. Reprinted by permission. **468–470:** From *Union Square* by Albert Halper, Copyright 1933 by Albert Halper. Reprinted by permission of The Viking Press. **471b–472:** Studs Terkel, *Hard Times: An Oral History of the Great Depression* (New York: Pantheon Books, Div. of Random House, Inc., 1970). **473t:** *The New York Times*, January 21, 1931. © 1931 by The New York Times Company. Reprinted by permission. **473b–474:** Florence Converse, "Bread Line," *The Atlantic Monthly* (Boston, Mass.: The Atlantic Monthly Co.) January 1932. **474b:** Jim Garland, "I Don't Want Your Million, Mister," *Songs of Work and Freedom*, Edith Fowke and Joe Glazer, eds. (Chicago, Ill.: Roosevelt University, 1960). **475:** *The New York Times*, February 5, 1933. © 1933 by The New York Times Company. Reprinted by permission. *The New York Times*, January 1, 1931. © 1931 by The New York Times Company. Reprinted by permission. **480–481:** "Triple-A Plowed Under," by the Staff of the Living Newspaper, *Federal Theater Plays*, DeRohan, ed. (New York: Random House, Inc., 1938). **485–486:** *The Public Papers and Addresses of Franklin D. Roosevelt*, (New York: Random House, Inc., 1938) vol. 5, pp. 480–489. **493–494:** Excerpt from *The Annals of America*, vol. 16, 1940–1949, pp. xxivff. (Chicago, Ill.: Encyclopaedia Britannica, 1968) By permission. **501:** *Statistical Abstract of the United States: 1972*, U.S. Bureau of the Census. **505–506:** *1984*, Harcourt, Brace Jovanovich, Inc. Copyright © 1949 by Harcourt Brace Jovanovich, Inc. Reprinted by permission of Brandt & Brandt.

PHOTOGRAPHS

UNIT 1   Page 2: *l* New York Public Library (Map Division); *r* Culver. **3:** New York Public Library (I. N. Phelps Stokes Collection, Prints Division). **4:** Monkmeyer (Bijur). **6:** Monkmeyer (Shackman). **9:** *l* Jack LaLanne Health Spas, N.Y.C.; *r* Norcliff Thayer, Inc. **12:** Michael Heron. **13:** New York Public Library (Map Division). **22:** *t* New York Public Library (Rare Book Division); *b* Rotkin, P.F.I. **31:** Culver. **35:** New York Public Library (Rare Book Division). **46:** New York Public Library (Rare Book Division). **52:** New York Public Library (Prints Division). **54:** New York Public Library (Arents Collection). **56:** Metropolitan Museum of Art, Gift of Edgar William and Bernice Chrysler Garbisch, 1963. **57:** *l* Michael Philip Manheim; *r* Culver. **64:** *t* Brown Brothers; *cl* Michael Philip Manheim; *cr* (both) & *b* New York Public Library (I. N. Phelps Stokes Collection, Prints Division). **67:** New York Public Library (I. N. Phelps Stokes Collection, Prints Div.). **69:** American Antiquarian Society. **72:** *tl* Monkmeyer (Conklin); *tr* Wide World; *bl* Rapho/Photo Researchers (Munroe); *br* Rapho/Photo Researchers (Bucher). **73:** *l* Michal Heron; *tr* Rapho/Photo Researchers (Ellis); *br* Combe, Inc.

UNIT 2   Page 74: Granger. **74–75:** Mezzotint of Trumbull, *The Declaration of Independence*, Yale University Art Gallery. **75:** Granger. **77:** *both* Michal Heron. **83:** Granger. **90:** Bettmann Archive. **94:** Sy Seidman. **96:** New York Public Library (Rare Book Division). **103:** New York Public Library (Prints Division). **105:** National Gallery of Art. **111:** New York Public Library (Prints Division). **114:** Granger. **120:** New York Public Library (Prints Division). **124:** detail, Yale University Art Gallery. **126:** New York Public Library (Prints Division). **128:** Historical Society of Pennsylvania. **133:** Culver. **138:** New York Public Library (Rare Book Division). **151:** Connecticut Historical Society. **156:** Black Star (F. Ward). **157:** Wide World.

UNIT 3   Page 158: Granger. **159:** *l* Collection of the J. B. Speed Art Museum, Louisville, Ky.; *r* New York Public Library (Rare Book Division). **160:** *both* Michal Heron. **161:** Steve Satterwhite. **162:** Michal Heron. **166:** New York Public Library (Rare Book Division). **170:** *tl* Courtesy of the Art Institute of Chicago; *tr* Franklin Poole painting, owned by the Wakefield Historical Society; *b* The Harry T. Peters Collection, Museum of the City of New York. **173:** *t* American Antiquarian Society; *b* New York Public Library (I. N. Phelps Stokes Collection, Prints Division). **176:** *t* Smithsonian Institution; *cl* Brown Bros.; *cr* Granger; *b* New York Public Library (Eno Collection, Prints Division). **179:** Bettmann. **184:** *t* The Newberry Library; *b* Brown Bros. **187:** Brown Bros. **188:** Granger. **191:** *t* Mabel Brady Garvan Collection, Yale University Art Gallery

(Szaasztn); *b* New York Public Library (I. N. Phelps Stokes Collection, Prints Division.). **194:** Bettmann. **195:** *both* Granger. **198:** Granger. **204:** *t* Granger; *b* New York Public Library (Rare Book Division). **205:** *tl* New York Public Library (I. N. Phelps Stokes Collection, Prints Division); *tr* Bettmann; *b* New York Public Library (Rare Book Division). **209:** Harry T. Peters Collection, Museum of the City of New York. **211:** *t* New York Public Library (Rare Book Division); *c* (both) Culver; *b* New York Public Library (I. N. Phelps Stokes Collection, Prints Division). **217:** Granger. **225:** Granger.

UNIT 4   Page 228: *l* New York Public Library (Picture Collection). **228–229:** New York Public Library (Picture Collection). **229:** *r* Granger. **230:** Michal Heron. **239:** *both* Sherif, M. and Sherif, C. W., *Groups in Harmony and Tension*, 1953, Harper and Row, Inc. **244:** Bettmann. **249:** New York Public Library (Prints Division). **255:** Culver. **256:** *t* Culver; *bl* American Antiquarian Society; *br* Granger. **258:** *tl* and *tr* Bettmann; *bl* and *br* Granger. **259:** Bettmann. **260:** Culver. **262:** Granger. **265:** Bettmann. **271:** Granger. **274:** Library of Congress. **276:** New York Public Library (Prints Division). **277:** *both* Bettmann. **279:** *t* Granger; *b* Library of Congress. **281:** Bettmann. **285:** *all* Bettmann. **292:** Granger. **293:** Granger.

UNIT 5   Page 298: Bettmann. **299:** *l* Brown Bros; *r* Bettmann. **300:** Michal Heron. **306:** Granger. **309:** Brown Bros. **312:** *l* Bettmann; *r* George Eastman House. **316:** Granger. **317:** Historical Picture Service, Chicago. **319:** *all* Bettmann. **326:** Granger. **331:** *both* Bettmann. **335:** *tl & r* Culver; *bl & r* Museum of the City of New York. **336:** Brown Bros. **337:** Culver. **341:** Bettmann. **347:** *tl & tr* Bettmann; *b* Brown Bros. **349:** *The Verdict*, 1900. **352:** Library of Congress. **353:** Bettmann. **355:** Museum of the City of New York. **358:** Museum of the City of New York. **359:** *t* *Headquarters Newsletter*, 1916; *b* Bettmann. **360:** *l* Bettmann, *r* Granger. **367:** Bettmann.

UNIT 6   Page 374: Pierpont Morgan Library. **375:** *l* Library of Congress; *r* Museum of the City of New York. **376:** Michal Heron. **378–379:** *all* Michal Heron. **382:** New York Public Library (Rare Book Division). **385:** Woolaroc Museum. **390:** *all* New York Public Library (Rare Book Division). **392:** Nebraska State Historical Society (Solomon D. Butcher Collection). **393:** *tl* Nebraska State Historical Society; *tr* Brown Bros.; *b* Bettmann. **399:** Michal Heron. **407:** Brown Bros. **413:** *tl* Bettmann; *tr* Brown Bros; *b* Museum of the City of New York. **416:** New York Public Library (Picture Collection). **417:** *both* New York Public Library (Prints Division). **420:** *tl & tr* Granger; *b* Bettmann. **425:** *t & c* Culver; *bl* Brown Bros.; *br* Bettmann. **426:** Culver. **427:** *l* Brown Bros.; *r* Museum of the City of New York. **431:** *t cr & b* Bettmann; *cl* Brown Bros. **435:** *t & bl* Photolab, Jereboam; *br* Editorial Photocolor Archives (Lisuands). **436:** *tl* Rapho/Photo Researchers (Gerster); *tr* Monkmeyer (Hibbs); *b* Wide World.

UNIT 7   Page 438: *l* National Archives; *r* Culver. **439:** DPI. **440:** *Plan for the Post-War World*, by Rube Goldberg. **449:** Culver. **457:** *tl* Bettmann; *tr* Brown Bros; *cr* Wide World; *b* Culver. **459:** *The New Yorker Magazine*. **460:** *New York Times* (May 23, 1926). **462:** *t* B. Altman & Company; *b* New York Times. **462:** *tl & tr* Brown Bros.; *b* Culver. **464:** *tl* Culver; *tr & b* Brown Bros. **465:** Bettmann. **467:** Culver. **470:** Brown Bros. **471:** *tl* Wide World; *tr* Chicago Historical Society (Korth); *b* Wide World. **472:** Brown Bros. **475:** *t* New York Public Library (Picture Collection); *b* New York Times. **477:** *t* Library of Congress (D. Lange); *b* Culver. **487:** Wide World. **496:** Wide World. **497:** *all* Wide World. **498:** Monkmeyer (Rogers).

UNIT OPENING ILLUSTRATIONS

UNIT 1—pp. 2–3: *l* World map drawn by Juan de la Cosa, 1500; *c* The building of Jamestown; *r* Charleston, South Carolina, 1739.

UNIT 2—pp. 74–75: *l* The battle of Concord; *c* Signing the Declaration of Independence; *r* Drawing in support of the Constitution.

UNIT 3—pp. 158–159: *l* A view of Boston; *c* Oakland Plantation, Louisville, Kentucky; *r* Frontier log cabin, 1826.

UNIT 4—pp. 228–229: *l* Fugitive slaves fleeing Maryland; *c* Battle of Newberne; *r* Surrender at Appomattox.

UNIT 5—pp. 298–299: *l* American railway scene; *c* Eugene Debs addressing workers; *r* Suffragettes speaking before members of the House of Representatives.

UNIT 6—pp. 374–375: *l* Plains Indian tepees; *c* Independence, Missouri; *r* European immigrants traveling to America.

UNIT 7—pp. 438–439: *l* American gun crew during World War I; *c* Roadside camp during the Depression; *r* Fifth Avenue in New York City.